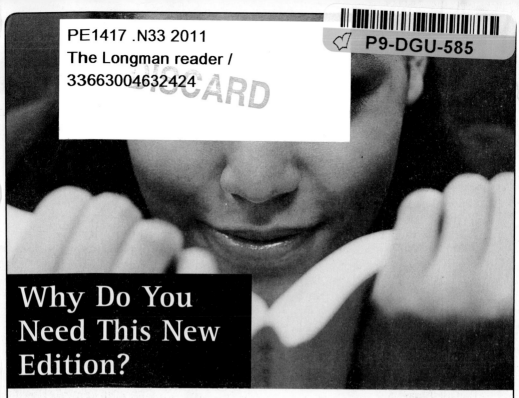

Why Do You Need This New Edition?

If you're wondering why you should by this new edition of *The Longman Reader*, here are a few great reasons!

1 Thirteen new readings have been added in Chapters 3–11 on current topics such as e-mail style, "Gen Nexters," friendship, and teenage driving that are **models for the different patterns of writing** that you'll be learning and practicing.

2 New Development Diagrams illustrate at-a-glance how the distinctive features of different patterns of development are used in essaywriting, **summarizing key concepts in aneasily referenced format** (Chs. 3–11).

3 New Essay Structure Diagrams outline visually the structure of one professional reading for each pattern of development **to help you see how the reading is organized and supported**, a skill that will help you plan your own writing (Chs. 3–11).

4 Concrete guidelines for integrating quotations, summaries, and paraphrases into your papers tell you **what you need to know to avoid unintentional plagiarism** and its consequences (App. A).

5 New material in the revised Appendix A, "A Guide to Using Sources," will **help you with the research tasks of evaluating, analyzing, and synthesizing research sources.**

6 A sample student essay updated to show MLA style for in-text citations and Works Cited lists offers a **model of how to write a research paper for your course** (Ch. 11).

7 Examples for MLA documentation style are completely updated to illustrate the **2008 guidelines published by the Modern Language Association** (App. A).

8 New material on reading illustrations gives insight into how you can **evaluate graphics and photos** you find in your research (Ch. 1).

9 You can use *The Longman Reader*, Brief Edition, alongside Pearson's unique MyCompLab and find a world of resources developed specifically for you!

PEARSON

ABOUT THE AUTHORS

Judith Nadell was until several years ago Associate Professor of Communications at Rowan University (New Jersey). During her eighteen years at Rowan, she coordinated the introductory course in the Freshman Writing Sequence and served as Director of the Writing Lab. More recently, she has developed a special interest in grassroots literacy. Besides designing an adult-literacy project, a children's reading-enrichment program, and a family-literacy initiative, she has volunteered as a tutor and tutor trainer in the programs. A Phi Beta Kappa graduate of Tufts University, she received a doctorate from Columbia University. She is author of *Becoming a Read-Aloud Coach* (Townsend Press) and coauthor of *Doing Well in College* (McGraw-Hill), *Vocabulary Basics* (Townsend Press), and *The Longman Writer*. The recipient of a New Jersey award for excellence in the teaching of writing, Judith Nadell lives with her coauthor husband, John Langan, near Philadelphia.

John Langan taught reading and writing courses at Atlantic Cape Community College in New Jersey for more than twenty years. He earned an advanced degree in reading at Glassboro State College and another in writing at Rutgers University. Active in a mentoring program, he designed a reading-enrichment program for inner-city high school students and wrote a motivational and learning skills guidebook, *Ten Skills You Really Need to Succeed in School*, for urban youngsters. Coauthor of *The Longman Writer* and author of a series of college textbooks on both reading and writing, he has published widely with McGraw-Hill Book Company, Townsend Press, and Longman.

Eliza A. Comodromos taught composition and developmental writing in the English Departments of both Rutgers University and John Jay College of Criminal Justice. After graduating with a B.A. in English and in French from La Salle University, she did graduate work at the City University of New York Graduate School and went on to earn an advanced degree at Rutgers University. A freelance editor and textbook consultant, Eliza Comodromos has delivered numerous papers at language and literature conferences around the country. She lives with her husband, Paul, and daughters, Anna Maria and Sophia Mae, near Philadelphia.

THE LONGMAN READER

BRIEF EDITION

NINTH EDITION

Judith Nadell

John Langan

Eliza A. Comodromos

Longman

Boston   Indianapolis   New York   San Francisco   Upper Saddle River
Amsterdam   Cape Town   Dubai   London   Madrid   Milan   Munich   Paris   Montreal   Toronto
Delhi   Mexico City   Sao Paulo   Sydney   Hong Kong   Seoul   Singapore   Taipei   Tokyo

Acquisitions Editor: Lauren A. Finn
Development Director: Mary Ellen Curley
Development Editor: Linda Stern
Senior Supplements Editor: Donna Campion
Senior Marketing Manager: Sandra McGuire
Production Manager: Eric Jorgensen
Project Coordination, Text Design, and Electronic Page Makeup: Elm Street Publishing
  Services
Cover Design Manager: Nancy Danahy
Cover Design: Nancy Sacks
Cover Image: San Juan National Forest, Colorado, © James Randkley/The Image
  Bank/Getty Images, Inc.
Visual Researcher: Rona Tuccillo
Senior Manufacturing Buyer: Dennis J. Para
Printer and Binder: R R Donnelley & Sons Company/Crawfordsville
Cover Printer: Coral Graphic Services, Inc.

For permission to use copyrighted material, grateful acknowledgment is made to the copyright
  holders on pp. 509–510, which are hereby made part of this copyright page.

Library of Congress Cataloging-in-Publication Data

Nadell, Judith.
  The Longman reader/Judith Nadell, John Langan, Eliza A. Comodromos.—9th ed. , Brief ed.
  p.cm.
  Includes bibliographical references and index.
  ISBN 978-0-205-75226-3
  1. College readers. 2. English language—Rhetoric—Problems, exercises, etc. 3. Report
writing—problems, exercises, etc. I. Langan, John II. Comodromos, Eliza A.   III. Title.

PE1417.N33 2009b
808'.0427—dc22   2009036751

Copyright © 2011, © 2008, © 2005 by Pearson Education, Inc.

1 2 3 4 5 6 7 8 9 10—DOC—12 11 10 09

Longman
is an imprint of

www.pearsonhighered.com

ISBN 13: 978-0-205-75226-3
ISBN 10:   0-205-75226-8

CONTENTS

THEMATIC CONTENTS   xv

PREFACE   xviii

1 THE READING PROCESS   1

Stage 1: Get an Overview of the Selection   1

☑ FIRST READING: A CHECKLIST   2

Stage 2: Deepen Your Sense of the Selection   3

☑ SECOND READING: A CHECKLIST   3

Stage 3: Evaluate the Selection   4

☑ EVALUATING A SELECTION: A CHECKLIST   4

Ellen Goodman   FAMILY COUNTERCULTURE   7

Parents are told to switch the dial if they don't want their kids watching something on TV. But what should parents do when the entire culture warrants being switched off?

2 THE WRITING PROCESS   13

Figure 2.1 Stages of the Writing Process   14

Stage 1: Prewrite   15

☑ ANALYZING YOUR AUDIENCE: A CHECKLIST   19

Activities: Prewrite   27

Stage 2: Identify the Thesis   28

Activities: Identify the Thesis   31

Stage 3: Support the Thesis with Evidence   32

Activities: Support the Thesis with Evidence   38

Stage 4: Organize the Evidence   40

☑ OUTLINING: A CHECKLIST   43

Activities: Organize the Evidence   45

Stage 5: Write the First Draft   46

☑ TURNING OUTLINE INTO FIRST DRAFT: A CHECKLIST   47

Figure 2.2   Structure of an Essay   57

Activities: Write the First Draft   60

Stage 6: Revise the Essay   60

Stage 7: Edit and Proofread   65

Student Essay   66

Commentary   68

Activity: Revise the Essay   70

3   DESCRIPTION   72

What Is Description?   72

How Description Fits Your Purpose and Audience   72

Suggestions for Using Description in an Essay   75

Figure 3.1 Development Diagram: Writing a Description Essay   76

Revision Strategies   79

☑ DESCRIPTION: A REVISION/PEER REVIEW CHECKLIST   79

Student Essay   80

Commentary   82

Activities: Description   85

Maya Angelou   SISTER FLOWERS   87

Hidden deep within herself after the trauma of a rape, young Angelou is escorted back into life by the grand lady of a small town.

Figure 3.2   Essay Structure Diagram: "Sister Flowers" by Maya Angelou   92

Gordon Parks   FLAVIO'S HOME   95

Having battled poverty and prejudice himself, writer-photographer Gordon Parks visits a Brazilian slum and finds, among the wretched thousands forgotten by the outside world, a dying yet smiling boy.

Gary Kamiya   LIFE, DEATH AND SPRING   103

This author muses about cycles of growth and decay as he remembers visits to a family ranch.

Additional Writing Topics   110

4   NARRATION   112

What Is Narration?   112

How Narration Fits Your Purpose and Audience   113

Suggestions for Using Narration in an Essay   113

Figure 4.1   Development Diagram: Writing a
    Narration Essay   114
Revision Strategies   120

☑ NARRATION: A REVISION/PEER REVIEW CHECKLIST   120

Student Essay   121
Commentary   123
Activities: Narration   125

Audre Lorde   THE FOURTH OF JULY   127
On a Fourth of July trip to the nation's capital, a family is
confronted by an ugly truth about American life.
Figure 4.2   Essay Structure Diagram: "The Fourth of July"
    by Audre Lorde   131

George Orwell   SHOOTING AN ELEPHANT   133
The author recounts a dramatic time when, under great pressure, he
acted against his better instincts.

Joan Murray   SOMEONE'S MOTHER   141
A woman gives a ride to a 90-year-old hitchhiker who can't remember
where she lives but doesn't want her son to find out she's lost again.

Additional Writing Topics   145

5   EXEMPLIFICATION   **147**

What Is Exemplification?   147
How Exemplification Fits Your Purpose and Audience   148
Suggestions for Using Exemplification in an Essay   150
Figure 5.1   Development Diagram: Writing an Exemplification
    Essay   151
Revision Strategies   155

☑ EXEMPLIFICATION: A REVISION/PEER REVIEW CHECKLIST   156

Student Essay   156
Commentary   158
Activities: Exemplification   161

Kay S. Hymowitz   TWEENS: TEN GOING ON SIXTEEN   163
Where have all the children gone? According to Hymowitz, they've been
hijacked by a culture that urges them to become teenagers at ten. From
clothes and hairstyles to sex, drugs, and violence, today's "tweens" are
hurled prematurely into the adult world.

Figure 5.2   Essay Structure Diagram: "Tweens: Ten Going On
    Sixteen" by Kay S. Hymowitz   168

Leslie Savan   BLACK TALK AND POP CULTURE   171
Once marginalized, words and phrases from Black English have permeated American English and are now in mainstream use.

Eric G. Wilson   THE MIRACLE OF MELANCHOLIA   180
The author reflects on a number of artists who have found sadness to be a blessing in disguise.

Additional Writing Topics   185

6 DIVISION-CLASSIFICATION   187

What Is Division-Classification?   187
How Division-Classification Fits Your Purpose and Audience   188
Suggestions for Using Division-Classification in an Essay   191
Figure 6.1   Development Diagram: Writing a Division-Classification Essay   192
Revision Strategies   195
☑ DIVISION-CLASSIFICATION: A REVISION/PEER REVIEW CHECKLIST   195
Student Essay   196
Commentary   199
Activities: Division-Classification   202

Ann McClintock   PROPAGANDA TECHNIQUES IN TODAY'S ADVERTISING   204
Propaganda is not just a tool of totalitarian states. American advertisers also use propaganda to get us to buy their products.
Figure 6.2   Essay Structure Diagram: "Propaganda Techniques in Today's Advertising" by Ann McClintock   210

David Brooks   PSST! "HUMAN CAPITAL"   212
Human capital, necessary for a just, prosperous society, is more than skills and knowledge. It includes cultural, social, moral, cognitive, and aspirational capital.

Marion Winik   WHAT ARE FRIENDS FOR?   216
The author takes a good-natured look at the kinds of friendships we all have.

Additional Writing Topics   220

7 PROCESS ANALYSIS   222

What Is Process Analysis?   222
How Process Analysis Fits Your Purpose and Audience   223

Suggestions for Using Process Analysis in an Essay   225

Figure 7.1   Development Diagram: Writing a Process Analysis Essay   226

Revision Strategies   230

☑ PROCESS ANALYSIS: A REVISION/PEER REVIEW CHECKLIST   231

Student Essay   232

Commentary   235

Activities: Process Analysis   237

Clifford Stoll   CYBERSCHOOL   239

Ah, brave new world that relies on computers, cubicles, and e-mails and dispenses with such old-fashioned notions as teachers, classrooms, and human interaction! Skeptical techie Stoll casts a jaundiced eye on the school of the future.

Figure 7.2   Essay Structure Diagram: "Cyberschool" by Clifford Stoll   243

David Shipley   TALK ABOUT EDITING   245

A *New York Times* editor describes the process involved in editing op-ed pieces.

Amy Sutherland   WHAT SHAMU TAUGHT ME ABOUT A HAPPY MARRIAGE   250

The writer rids her husband of some of his annoying habits by using an animal training technique; at the end, he's using the same technique on her.

Additional Writing Topics   256

8 COMPARISON-CONTRAST   258

What Is Comparison-Contrast?   258

How Comparison-Contrast Fits Your Purpose and Audience   259

Suggestions for Using Comparison-Contrast in an Essay   260

Figure 8.1   Development Diagram: Writing a Comparison-Contrast Essay   261

Revision Strategies   266

☑ COMPARISON-CONTRAST: A REVISION/PEER REVIEW CHECKLIST   266

Student Essay   267

Commentary   269

Activities: Comparison-Contrast   272

Eric Weiner   EUROMAIL AND AMERIMAIL   274

The author compares e-mail styles and strategies in America and Europe—and declares a preference for one over the other.

Figure 8.2   Essay Structure Diagram: "Euromail and Amerimail"
    by Eric Weiner   277

Rachel Carson   A FABLE FOR TOMORROW   280
    This renowned ecologist warns us that what seems like a nightmare will
    become all too real if we fail to protect the earth.

Dave Barry   BEAUTY AND THE BEAST   284
    Why do men tend to be unconcerned about their appearance while
    women seem obsessed with how they look? Humorist Dave Barry
    advances an interesting theory.

Additional Writing Topics   288

9 CAUSE-EFFECT   290

    What Is Cause-Effect?   290
    How Cause-Effect Fits Your Purpose and Audience   291
    Suggestions for Using Cause-Effect in an Essay   292
    Figure 9.1   Development Diagram: Writing a Cause-Effect
        Essay   293
    Revision Strategies   299
        ☑ CAUSE-EFFECT: A REVISION/PEER REVIEW CHECKLIST   299
        Student Essay   300
        Commentary   302
        Activities: Cause-Effect   305

Stephen King   WHY WE CRAVE HORROR MOVIES   307
    Who should know more about our appetite for horror than Stephen
    King? This maestro of the macabre shares his thoughts on why movie
    goers eagerly pay to be terrified.

    Figure 9.2   Essay Structure Diagram: "Why We Crave Horror
        Movies" by Stephen King   310

Kurt Kleiner   WHEN MAÑANA IS TOO SOON   312
    Procrastination is irrational, even self-defeating—so why do we do it?

Buzz Bissinger   INNOCENTS AFIELD   317
    The author of a book on high school football claims that the continued
    professionalization of the sport is corrupting athletics for teenagers and
    exploiting teens in the process.

Additional Writing Topics   322

10 DEFINITION   324

What Is Definition?   324
How Definition Fits Your Purpose and Audience   325
Suggestions for Using Definition in an Essay   326
*Figure 10.1   Development Diagram: Writing a Definition
    Essay   327*
Revision Strategies   330
☑ DEFINITION: A REVISION/PEER REVIEW CHECKLIST   331
Student Essay   331
Commentary   333
Activities: Definition   336

K. C. Cole ENTROPY   338
A noted science writer observes that disorder is the natural order of
things—in her life and in the universe at large.
*Figure 10.2   Essay Structure Diagram: "Entropy" by
    K. C. Cole   341*

Natalie Angier THE CUTE FACTOR   343
A science writer explores what people find cute, using a baby panda
bear exhibit as a starting point and citing research on visual signaling
and examples of cuteness.

Ann Hulbert BEYOND THE PLEASURE PRINCIPLE   350
The attitudes and values of "Gen Nexters"—those 18 to 25—seem
contradictory, but perhaps they actually do make sense.

Additional Writing Topics   354

11 ARGUMENTATION-PERSUASION   356

What Is Argumentation-Persuasion?   356
How Argumentation-Persuasion Fits Your Purpose and
    Audience   357
Suggestions for Using Argumentation-Persuasion in an
    Essay   361
*Figure 11.1   Development Diagram: Writing an Argumentation-
    Persuasion Essay   362*
☑ QUESTIONS FOR USING TOULMIN LOGIC: A CHECKLIST   376
Revision Strategies   378
☑ ARGUMENTATION-PERSUASION: A REVISION/PEER REVIEW
    CHECKLIST   378

Student Essay   379

Commentary   386

Activities: Argumentation-Persuasion   390

Stanley Fish   FREE-SPEECH FOLLIES   392

A noted scholar explores the difference between invoking the First Amendment and simply exercising good judgment in academic settings.

Figure 11.2   Essay Structure Diagram: "Free-Speech Follies" by Stanley Fish   396

Anna Quindlen   DRIVING TO THE FUNERAL   399

Every year high school students die in car accidents when other teens are driving. What can be done to stop these tragedies?

Examining an Issue: Gender-Based Education

Gerry Garibaldi   HOW THE SCHOOLS SHORTCHANGE BOYS   403

The author contends that teaching is geared toward the learning style of girls, which leaves boys at a disadvantage.

Michael Kimmel   A WAR AGAINST BOYS?   410

A gender studies researcher believes that if boys seem to perform worse than girls in school, important factors such as race and class may be at work—not a bias against boys in general.

Examining an Issue: Illegal Immigration

Roberto Rodriguez   THE BORDER ON OUR BACKS   418

Illegal immigrants should no longer accept the second-rate status they have been allotted in the United States, argues journalist Rodriguez.

Star Parker   SE HABLA ENTITLEMENT   423

Illegal immigrants have no rights or entitlements in the United States, and they are a strain on U.S. society, according to writer and social advocate Parker.

Additional Writing Topics   428

12 COMBINING THE PATTERNS   430

The Patterns in Action: During the Writing Process   430

The Patterns in Action: In an Essay   431

Student Essay   432

Virginia Woolf   THE DEATH OF THE MOTH   438
Watching the death throes of a moth leads Woolf to wonder at the mystery of life and at the force that opposes it.

Martin Luther King, Jr.   WHERE DO WE GO FROM HERE:
                             COMMUNITY OR CHAOS?   444
America's most influential civil rights leader pleads eloquently for a drastic change in the way that governments pursue world peace.

Joan Didion   MARRYING ABSURD   448
Essayist Didion turns her curious gaze on the wedding industry of Las Vegas, a city created to gratify the illusions of hopeful gamblers, whether at the roulette wheel or in love.

APPENDIX A: A GUIDE TO USING SOURCES   451

Evaluating Source Materials   451

☑ EVALUATING ARTICLES AND BOOKS: A CHECKLIST   453

☑ EVALUATING INTERNET MATERIALS: A CHECKLIST   453

Analyzing and Synthesizing Source Material   454

☑ ANALYZING AND SYNTHESIZING SOURCE MATERIAL: A CHECKLIST   456

Using Quotation, Summary, and Paraphrase Without Plagiarizing   456

☑ USING QUOTATION, SUMMARY, AND PARAPHRASE: A CHECKLIST   462

Integrating Sources into Your Writing   463

☑ INTEGRATING SOURCES INTO YOUR WRITING: A CHECKLIST   469

Documenting Sources: MLA Style   470
How to Document: MLA In-Text References   470

☑ USING MLA PARENTHETICAL REFERENCES: A CHECKLIST   474

How to Document: MLA List of Works Cited   474
Citing Print Sources—Books   475
Citing Print Sources—Periodicals   478
Citing Sources Found on a Website   479
Citing Sources Found Through an Online Database or Scholarly Project   481
Citing Other Common Sources   481

APPENDIX B: AVOIDING TEN COMMON WRITING ERRORS
483

1 Fragments   484
2 Comma Splices and Run-ons   485
3 Faulty Subject-Verb Agreement   485
4 Faulty Pronoun Agreement   487
5 Misplaced and Dangling Modifiers   488
6 Faulty Parallelism   490
7 Comma Misuse   491
8 Apostrophe Misuse   492
9 Confusing Homonyms   493
10 Misuse of Italics and Underlining   495

GLOSSARY   496

ACKNOWLEDGMENTS   509

INDEX   511

THEMATIC CONTENTS

COMMUNICATION AND LANGUAGE

Maya Angelou, Sister Flowers   87   • *Leslie Savan*, Black Talk and Pop Culture   171   • *Ann McClintock*, Propaganda Techniques in Today's Advertising   204   • *Clifford Stoll*, Cyberschool   239   • *David Shipley*, Talk About Editing   245   • *Amy Sutherland*, What Shamu Taught Me About a Happy Marriage   250   • *Eric Weiner*, Euromail and Amerimail   274   • *Dave Barry*, Beauty and the Beast   284   • *Natalie Angier*, The Cute Factor   343   • *Ann Hulbert*, Beyond the Pleasure Principle   350   • *Stanley Fish*, Free-Speech Follies   392   • *Roberto Rodriguez*, The Border on Our Backs   418 • *Star Parker*, Se Habla Entitlement   423

EDUCATION AND WORK

Maya Angelou, Sister Flowers   87   • *George Orwell*, Shooting an Elephant   133 • *Kay S. Hymowitz*, Tweens: Ten Going On Sixteen   163   • *David Brooks*, Psst! "Human Capital"   212   • *Marion Winik*, What Are Friends For?   216 • *Clifford Stoll*, Cyberschool   239   • *Eric Weiner*, Euromail and Amerimail   274 • *Kurt Kleiner*, When Mañana Is Too Soon   312   • *Buzz Bissinger*, Innocents Afield   317   • *Stanley Fish*, Free-Speech Follies   392   • *Anna Quindlen*, Driving to the Funeral   399   • *Gerry Garibaldi*, How the Schools Shortchange Boys   403 • *Michael Kimmel*, A War Against Boys?   410

ETHICS AND MORALITY

Ellen Goodman, Family Counterculture   7   • *Gordon Parks*, Flavio's Home   95 • *George Orwell*, Shooting an Elephant   133   • *Joan Murray*, Someone's Mother   141   • *Kay S. Hymowitz*, Tweens: Ten Going On Sixteen   163   • *Eric G. Wilson*, The Miracle of Melancholia   180   • *Ann McClintock*, Propaganda Techniques in Today's Advertising   204   • *David Brooks*, Psst! "Human Capital"   212   • *Clifford Stoll*, Cyberschool   239   • *Stephen King*, Why We Crave Horror Movies   307   • *Buzz Bissinger*, Innocents Afield   317   • *Ann Hulbert*, Beyond the Pleasure Principle   350   • *Martin Luther King*, Jr., Where Do We Go from Here: Community or Chaos?   444

FAMILY AND CHILDREN

Ellen Goodman, Family Counterculture   7   • *Maya Angelou*, Sister Flowers   87 • *Gordon Parks*, Flavio's Home   95   • *Gary Kamiya*, Life, Death and Spring   103   • *Audre Lorde*, The Fourth of July   127   • *Joan Murray*, Someone's Mother   141   • *Kay S. Hymowitz*, Tweens: Ten Going On Sixteen   163   • *Marion Winik*, What Are Friends For?   216   • *Clifford Stoll*, Cyberschool   239   • *Amy Sutherland*, What Shamu Taught Me About a Happy Marriage   250   • *Stephen King*, Why We Crave Horror Movies   307   • *Buzz Bissinger*, Innocents Afield   317   • *Ann Hulbert*, Beyond the Pleasure Principle   350   • *Anna Quindlen*, Driving to the Funeral   399   • *Gerry Garibaldi*, How the Schools Shortchange Boys   403   • *Michael Kimmel*, A War Against Boys?   410

GOVERNMENT AND LAW

Audre Lorde, The Fourth of July   127   • *George Orwell*, Shooting an Elephant   133   • *David Brooks*, Psst! "Human Capital"   212   • *Stanley Fish*, Free-Speech Follies   392   • *Anna Quindlen*, Driving to the Funeral   399   • *Roberto Rodriguez*, The Border on Our Backs   418   • *Star Parker*, Se Habla Entitlement   423   • *Martin Luther King, Jr.*, Where Do We Go from Here: Community or Chaos?   444

HEALTH AND PSYCHOLOGY

Gordon Parks, Flavio's Home   95   • *Kay S. Hymowitz*, Tweens: Ten Going On Sixteen   163   • *Eric G. Wilson*, The Miracle of Melancholia   180   • *Amy Sutherland*, What Shamu Taught Me About a Happy Marriage   250   • *Kurt Kleiner*, When Mañana Is Too Soon   312   • *Gerry Garibaldi*, How the Schools Shortchange Boys   403   • *Michael Kimmel*, A War Against Boys?   410

HUMAN GROUPS AND SOCIETY

Ellen Goodman, Family Counterculture   7   • *Maya Angelou*, Sister Flowers   87 • *Gordon Parks*, Flavio's Home   95   • *Gary Kamiya*, Life, Death and Spring   103 • *Audre Lorde*, The Fourth of July   127   • *Kay S. Hymowitz*, Tweens: Ten Going On Sixteen   163   • *Leslie Savan*, Black Talk and Pop Culture   171   • *Eric G. Wilson*, The Miracle of Melancholia   180   • *David Brooks*, Psst! "Human Capital"   212   • *Marion Winik*, What Are Friends For?   216   • *Clifford Stoll*, Cyberschool   239   • *Eric Weiner*, Euromail and Amerimail   274   • *Dave Barry*, Beauty and the Beast   284   • *Stephen King*, Why We Crave Horror Movies   307 • *Buzz Bissinger*, Innocents Afield   317   • *Ann Hulbert*, Beyond the Pleasure Principle   350   • *Anna Quindlen*, Driving to the Funeral   399   • *Gerry Garibaldi*, How the Schools Shortchange Boys   403   • *Michael Kimmel*, A War Against Boys?   410   • *Roberto Rodriguez*, The Border on Our Backs   418   • *Star Parker*, Se Habla Entitlement   423   • *Martin Luther King, Jr.*, Where Do We Go from Here: Community or Chaos?   444   • *Joan Didion*, Marrying Absurd   448

HUMOR AND SATIRE

Marion Winik, What Are Friends For?   216   • *Clifford Stoll*, Cyberschool   239
• *Amy Sutherland*, What Shamu Taught Me About a Happy Marriage   250
• *Dave Barry*, Beauty and the Beast   284

MEANING IN LIFE

Maya Angelou, Sister Flowers   87   • *Gordon Parks*, Flavio's Home   95   • *Gary Kamiya*, Life, Death and Spring   103   • *Audre Lorde*, The Fourth of July   127
• *George Orwell*, Shooting an Elephant   133   • *Joan Murray*, Someone's Mother   141   • *Eric G. Wilson*, The Miracle of Melancholia   180   • *Rachel Carson*, A Fable for Tomorrow   280   • *Buzz Bissinger*, Innocents Afield   317
• *Ann Hulbert*, Beyond the Pleasure Principle   350   • *Virginia Woolf*, The Death of the Moth   438   • *Joan Didion*, Marrying Absurd   448

MEDIA AND TECHNOLOGY

Ellen Goodman, Family Counterculture   7   • *Kay S. Hymowitz*, Tweens: Ten Going On Sixteen   163   • *Leslie Savan*, Black Talk and Pop Culture   171
• *Ann McClintock*, Propaganda Techniques in Today's Advertising   204
• *Clifford Stoll*, Cyberschool   239   • *David Shipley*, Talk About Editing   245
• *Eric Weiner*, Euromail and Amerimail   274   • *Dave Barry*, Beauty and the Beast   284   • *Stephen King*, Why We Crave Horror Movies   307   • *Stanley Fish*, Free-Speech Follies   392

MEMORIES AND AUTOBIOGRAPHY

Maya Angelou, Sister Flowers   87   • *Gary Kamiya*, Life, Death and Spring   103
• *Audre Lorde*, The Fourth of July   127   • *George Orwell*, Shooting an Elephant   133   • *Joan Murray*, Someone's Mother   141   • *Amy Sutherland*, What Shamu Taught Me About a Happy Marriage   250   • *Joan Didion*, Marrying Absurd   448

MEN AND WOMEN

Amy Sutherland, What Shamu Taught Me About a Happy Marriage   250   • *Dave Barry*, Beauty and the Beast   284   • *Gerry Garibaldi*, How the Schools Shortchange Boys   403   • *Michael Kimmel*, A War Against Boys?   543

NATURE AND SCIENCE

• *Gary Kamiya*, Life, Death and Spring   103   • *Amy Sutherland*, What Shamu Taught Me About a Happy Marriage   250   • *Rachel Carson*, A Fable for Tomorrow   280   • *Kurt Kleiner*, When Mañana Is Too Soon   312   • *K. C. Cole*, Entropy   338   • *Natalie Angier*, The Cute Factor   343   • *Virginia Woolf*, The Death of the Moth   438

PREFACE

As computers have become firmly established in the lives of students and instructors, the ways in which we acquire information and communicate with one another have been profoundly transformed. Moreover, the ways teachers teach, as well as the ways students learn, have been deeply affected. Perhaps now, more than ever, the need for students to develop sound writing skills has become as essential as it is fundamental. It's to this mission that we continue to be committed.

As in the full version of this text, in this brief edition we have aimed for a different kind of text—one that would offer fresh examples of professional prose, one that would take a more active role in helping students become stronger readers, thinkers, and writers. *The Longman Reader,* Ninth Edition, Brief Edition, continues to include widely read and classic essays, as well as fresh new pieces, such as Gary Kamiya's "Life, Death and Spring" and Amy Sutherland's "What Shamu Taught Me About a Happy Marriage." We've been careful to choose selections that range widely in subject matter and approach, from the humorous to the informative, from personal meditation to polemic. We've also made sure that each selection captures students' interest and clearly illustrates a specific pattern of development or a combination of such patterns.

As before, we have also tried to help students bridge the gap between the product and process approaches to reading and writing. Throughout, we describe possible sequences and structures but emphasize that such steps and formats are not meant to be viewed as rigid prescriptions; rather, they are strategies for helping students discover what works best in a particular situation.

WHAT'S NEW IN *THE LONGMAN READER,* BRIEF EDITION

In preparing this edition, we looked closely at the reviews completed by instructors using the book. Their comments helped us identify new directions the book might take. Here are some of the new features of this brief edition of *The Longman Reader.*

- **Thirteen of the thirty-four selections are new.** Whether written by a journalist such as Anna Quindlen ("Driving to the Funeral"), an academic writer such as Eric G. Wilson ("The Miracle of Melancholia"), or a literary figure such as Joan Murray ("Someone's Mother"), the new selections are bound to stimulate strong writing on a variety of topics—education, technology, interpersonal relationships, gender, and morality, to name a few. When selecting new readings, we took special care to include pieces written from a personal point of view (for example, Marion Winik's "What Are Friends For?") as well as those citing academic research (for example, Kurt Kleiner's "When Mañana Is Too Soon"). Finally, honoring the requests of many instructors, we also made an effort to find compelling pieces on technology and contemporary life, such as Eric Weiner's "Euromail and Amerimail" and Ann Hulbert's "Beyond the Pleasure Principle."

- **Nine new Essay Structure Diagrams**—one for the first professional essay in each pattern-of-development chapter—are unique among rhetorical readers: each diagram outlines the essay's organization, development, and support, paragraph by paragraph, using the visual pedagogy valued by today's students to model an often-taught "outlining" assignment (Chs. 3–11).

- **Nine new Development Diagrams** have been added to the pattern-of-development chapters. Also unique among rhetorical readers, these flowcharts illustrate visually for students how a particular development pattern is expressed at each stage of the writing process, summarizing key chapter content succinctly in innovative and useful at-a-glance pedagogy (Chs. 3–11).

- **Appendix A, "A Guide to Using Sources," has been rewritten** and includes guidelines for students on how to evaluate, analyze, and synthesize printed and Internet source materials. An extensive section that discusses effective uses of summaries, paraphrases, and the incorporation of quotations includes numerous examples. Finally, the appendix gives completely updated information on the most recently published MLA citation guidelines, with examples of major entries in a Works Cited list.

- **A student-authored MLA model paper in the argumentation-persuasion chapter has been redesigned** for ease of use and fast reference as well as revised in accordance with the new MLA documentation standards published in 2009. The paper not only provides students with an easy-to-find, clear, and up-to-date model for documentation, it also serves as a model for formatting an MLA paper.

- **A new pair of pro-con essays** in the argumentation-persuasion chapter further expands coverage of refutation strategies: Gerry Garibaldi's "How the Schools Shortchange Boys" and Michael Kimmel's "A War Against Boys?"—two readings that explore the debate on whether gender discrimination exists in elementary education (Ch. 11).

- **Instruction on reading visuals critically has been added** in Chapter 1 and again in Appendix A so that students have some guidance on how to understand and interpret images they encounter in their research.

ORGANIZATION OF THE TEXT

Buoyed by compliments about the previous editions' teachability, we haven't tinkered with the book's underlying format. Such a structure, we've been told, does indeed help students read more critically, think more logically, and write more skillfully. Here is the book's basic format.

Chapter 1, "The Reading Process"

Designed to reflect current theories about the interaction of reading, thinking, and writing, this chapter provides guided practice in a three-part process for reading with close attention and a high level of interpretive skill. This step-by-step process sharpens students' understanding of the book's selections and promotes the rigorous thinking needed to write effective essays.

An activity at the end of the chapter gives students a chance to use the three-step process. First, they read an essay by the journalist Ellen Goodman. The essay has been annotated both to show students the reading process in action and to illustrate how close critical reading can pave the way to promising writing topics. Then students respond to sample questions and writing assignments, all similar to those accompanying each of the book's selections. The chapter thus does more than just tell students how to sharpen their reading abilities; it guides them through a clearly sequenced plan for developing critical reading skills.

Chapter 2, "The Writing Process"

As an introduction to essay writing and to make the composing process easier for students to grasp, we provide a separate section for each of the following stages: prewriting, identifying a thesis, supporting the thesis with evidence, organizing the evidence, writing the first draft, revising, and editing and proofreading. The stages are also illustrated in a *new diagram*, "Stages of the Writing Process."

From the start, we point out that the stages are fluid. Indeed, the case history of an evolving student paper illustrates just how recursive and individualized the writing process can be. Guided activities at the end of each section give students practice taking their essays through successive stages in the composing process.

To illustrate the link between reading and writing, the writing chapter presents the progressive stages of a student paper written in response to Ellen Goodman's "Family Counterculture," the selection presented in Chapter 1. An easy-to-spot symbol in the margin ![symbol] makes it possible to locate—at a glance—this evolving student essay. Commentary following the student paper highlights the essay's strengths and points out spots that could use additional work. In short, by the end of the second chapter, the entire reading-writing process has been illustrated, from reading a selection to writing about it.

Chapters 3–11: Patterns of Development

The chapters contain selections grouped according to nine patterns of development: description, narration, exemplification, division-classification, process analysis, comparison-contrast, cause-effect, definition, and argumentation-persuasion. The sequence progresses from the more personal and expressive patterns to the more public and analytic. However, because each chapter is self-contained, the patterns may be covered in any order. Instructors preferring a thematic approach will find the Thematic Contents helpful.

The Longman Reader treats the patterns separately because such an approach helps students grasp the distinctive characteristics of each pattern. At the same time, the book continually shows the way writers usually combine patterns in their work. We also encourage students to view the patterns as strategies for generating and organizing ideas. Writers, we explain, rarely set out to compose an essay in a specific pattern. Rather, they choose a pattern or combination of patterns because it suits their purpose, audience, and subject.

Each of the nine pattern-of-development chapters follows the format below.

1. A **striking visual** opens every pattern-of-development chapter. The photo reappears in thumbnail form following the "How [name of pattern] Fits Your Purpose and Audience" section. There, the image prompts a pattern-related writing activity that encourages students to consider issues of purpose and audience in a piece of real-world writing.

2. **A detailed explanation of the pattern** begins the chapter. The explanation includes (a) a definition of the pattern, (b) a description of the way the pattern helps a writer accommodate his or her purpose and audience, and (c) step-by-step guidelines for using the pattern.

3. **A Development Diagram,** *new to this edition,* in each chapter illustrates how the pattern is expressed in each stage of the writing process.

4. **An annotated student essay** using the pattern appears next. Written in response to one of the professional selections in the chapter, each essay illustrates the characteristic features of the pattern discussed in the chapter.

5. **Commentary** after each student essay points out the blend of patterns in the piece, identifies the paper's strengths, and locates areas

needing improvement. "First draft" and "revised" versions of one section of the essay reveal how the student writer went about revising, thus illustrating the relationship between the final draft and the steps taken to produce it.

6. **Prewriting and revising activities** in shaded boxes following the commentary help students understand the unique demands posed by the pattern being studied.

7. **Professional selections** in the pattern-of-development chapters are accompanied by these items:

- **An Essay Structure Diagram,** *new to this edition,* for the first essay in each section shows how the essay makes use of patterns of development.

- **A biographical note** and **Pre-Reading Journal Entry assignment** give students a perspective on the author and creates interest in the piece. The journal assignment encourages students to explore—in a loose, unpressured way—their thoughts about an issue that will be raised in the selection. The journal entry thus motivates students to read the piece with extra care, attention, and personal investment.

- **Questions for Close Reading,** five in all, help students dig into and interpret the selection's content. The first question asks them to identify the selection's thesis; the last provides work on vocabulary development.

- **Questions About the Writer's Craft,** four in all, deal with such matters as purpose, audience, tone, organization, sentence structure, diction, and figures of speech. The first question in the series (labeled "The Pattern") focuses on the distinctive features of the pattern used in the selection. And usually there's another question (labeled "Other Patterns") that asks students to analyze the writer's use of additional patterns in the piece.

- **Writing Assignments,** five in all, follow each selection. Packed with suggestions on how to proceed, the assignments use the selection as a springboard. The first two assignments ask students to write an essay using the same pattern as the one used in the selection; the next two assignments encourage students to experiment with a combination of patterns in their own essay; the last assignment helps students turn the raw material in their pre-reading journal entries into fully considered essays.

  Frequently, the assignments are preceded by the symbol , indicating a cross-reference to at least one other selection in the book. By encouraging students to make connections among readings, such assignments broaden students' perspective and give them additional material to draw on when they write. These "paired assignments" will be especially welcome to instructors stressing recurring ideas and themes. In other cases, assignments are preceded by the symbol ![symbol], indicating that students might benefit from conducting library and/or Internet research.

8. **Two sets of Additional Writing Assignments** close each pattern-of-development chapter: "General Assignments" and "Assignments with a Specific Purpose, Audience, and Point of View." The first set provides open-ended topics that prompt students to discover the best way to use a specific pattern; the second set develops their sensitivity to rhetorical context by asking them to apply the pattern in a real-world situation.

Chapter 12, "Combining the Patterns"

The final chapter offers a sample student essay as well as an essay each by three very different prose stylists. Annotations on the student essay and on one of the professional selections show how writers often blend patterns of development in their work. The chapter also provides guidelines to help students analyze this fusing of patterns.

Appendixes and Glossary

Appendix A, "A Guide to Using Sources," has been extensively rewritten and provides guidelines for evaluating, analyzing, and synthesizing sources; using quotations, summaries, and paraphrases to integrate sources into a paper; and documenting sources following the latest MLA style guidelines. **Appendix B, "Avoiding Ten Common Writing Errors,"** targets common problem areas in student writing and offers quick, accessible solutions for each. The **Glossary** lists and defines all the key terms presented in the text.

SUPPLEMENTS FOR STUDENTS AND INSTRUCTORS

Instructor's Manual

A comprehensive Instructor's Manual contains the following: in-depth answers to the "Questions for Close Reading" and "Questions About the Writer's Craft"; suggested activities; pointers about using the book; a detailed syllabus; and an analysis of the blend of patterns in the selections in the "Combining the Patterns" chapter.

PEARSON
mycomplab

MyCompLab

MyCompLab integrates the market-leading instruction, multimedia tutorials, and exercises for writing grammar and research that users have come to identify with the program with a new online composing space and new assessment tools. The result is a revolutionary application that offers a seamless and flexible teaching and learning environment built specifically for writers. Created after years of extensive research and in partnership with composition faculty and students across the country, MyCompLab provides help for writers in the context of their writing, with instructor and peer commenting functionality, proven tutorials and exercises for writing, grammar and research, an e-portfolio, an assignment-builder, a bibliography tool, tutoring services, and a gradebook and course management organization created specifically for writing classes. Visit www.mycomplab.com for more information.

ACKNOWLEDGMENTS

At Longman, our thanks go to Lauren Finn for her perceptive editorial guidance and enthusiasm for *The Longman Reader*. We're also indebted to Linda Stern, our Development Editor, and to Heather Johnson of Elm Street Publishing Services and Eric Jorgensen of Longman for their skillful handling of the never-ending complexities of the production process.

Over the years, many writing instructors have reviewed *The Longman Reader* and responded to detailed questionnaires about its selections and pedagogy. Their comments have guided our work every step of the way. We are particularly indebted to the following reviewers for the valuable assistance they have provided during the preparation of the ninth edition of *The Longman Reader:* Martha Bachman, Camden County College; Kamala Balasubramanian, Grossmont College; Andrew Ball, Bluegrass Community and Technical College; Samone Polk Brooks, Lane College; Mary Cantrell, Tulsa Community College; Holly Carey, Lamar University; Joseph Couch, Montgomery College; Darren DeFrain, Wichita State University; Jonathan Fegley, Middle Georgia College; Billy Fontenot, Louisiana State University at Eunice; Hank Galmish, Green River Community College; Barbara Goldstein, Hillsborough Community College; Richard Lee, State University of New York College at Oneonta; Dolores MacNaughton, Umpqua Community College; Raphael Okonkwor, Moraine Park Technical College; Dana Resente, Montgomery County Community College; Mary Simpson, Central Texas College; April Van Camp, Indian River Community College; Deborah LeSure Wilbourn, Northwest Mississippi Community College; and Darcy A. Zabel, Friends University.

Some individuals from our at-home office deserve special thanks. During the preparation of the ninth edition, Marion Castellucci provided valuable assistance with the apparatus. Finally, as always, we're thankful to our students. Their reaction to various drafts of material sharpened our thinking and helped focus our work. And we are especially indebted to the eleven students whose essays are included in the book. Their thoughtful, carefully revised papers dramatize the potential of student writing and the power of the composing process.

JUDITH NADELL
JOHN LANGAN
ELIZA A. COMODROMOS

THE READING PROCESS

More than two hundred years ago, essayist Joseph Addison commented, "Of all the diversions of life, there is none so proper to fill up its empty spaces as the reading of useful and entertaining authors." Addison might have added that reading also challenges our beliefs, deepens our awareness, and stimulates our imagination. And the more challenging the material, the more actively involved the reader must be.

The essays in this book, which range from the classic to the contemporary, call for active reading. They contain language that will move you, images that will enlarge your understanding of other people, and ideas that will transform your views on complex issues. They will also help you develop a repertoire of reading skills that will benefit you throughout life.

The novelist Saul Bellow has observed, "A writer is a reader moved to emulation." As you become a better reader, your own writing will become more insightful and polished. Increasingly, you'll be able to employ the techniques that professional writers use to express ideas.

The three-stage approach outlined here will help you get the most out of this book's selections and ultimately improve your own writing too.

STAGE 1: GET AN OVERVIEW OF THE SELECTION

Ideally, you should get settled in a quiet place that encourages concentration. Once you're settled, it's time to read the selection. To ensure a good first reading, try the following hints.

☑ FIRST READING: A CHECKLIST

❑ Start by reading the biographical note that precedes the selection. By providing background information about the author, the biographical note helps you evaluate the writer's credibility as well as his or her slant on the subject. For example, if you know that Leslie Savan has written extensively about advertising for major broadcast and print media, you can better assess whether she is a credible source for the material she presents in her essay "Black Talk and Pop Culture" (page 171).

❑ Do the *Pre-Reading Journal Entry* assignment, which precedes the selection. This assignment "primes" you for the piece by helping you to explore—in an easy, unpressured way—your thoughts about a key point raised in the selection. By preparing the journal entry, you're inspired to read the selection with special care, attention, and personal investment. (For more on pre-reading journal entries, see pages 16–17 and 502.)

❑ Consider the selection's title. A good title often expresses the essay's main idea, giving you insight into the selection even before you read it. For example, the title of Gerry Garibaldi's "How the Schools Shortchange Boys" (page 403) suggests the piece will argue that boys are at a disadvantage in school. A title may also hint at a selection's tone. Amy Sutherland's "What Shamu Taught Me About a Happy Marriage" (page 250) points to an essay that is light in spirit, whereas George Orwell's "Shooting an Elephant" (page 133) suggests a piece with a serious mood.

❑ Read the selection straight through purely for pleasure. Allow yourself to be drawn into the world the author has created. Just as you first see a painting from the doorway of a room and form an overall impression without perceiving the details, you can have a preliminary, subjective feeling about a reading selection. Moreover, because you bring your own experiences and viewpoints to the piece, your reading will be unique. As Ralph Waldo Emerson said, "Take the book, my friend, and read your eyes out; you will never find there what I find."

❑ After this initial reading of the selection, focus your first impressions by asking yourself whether you like the selection. In your own words, briefly describe the piece and your reaction to it.

STAGE 2: DEEPEN YOUR SENSE OF THE SELECTION

At this point, you're ready to move more deeply into the selection. A second reading will help you identify the specific features that triggered your initial reaction.

There are a number of techniques you can use during this second, more focused reading. You may, for example, find it helpful to adapt some of the strategies that Mortimer Adler, a well-known writer and editor, wrote about in his 1940 essay "How to Mark a Book." There, Adler argues passionately for marking up the material we read. The physical act of annotating, he believes, etches the writer's ideas more sharply in the mind, helping readers grasp and remember those ideas more easily. And "best of all," Adler writes, the "marks and notes...stay there forever. You can pick up the...[material] the following week or year, and there are all your points of agreement, doubt, and inquiry. It's like resuming an uninterrupted conversation."

Adler goes on to describe various annotation techniques he uses when reading. Several of these techniques, adapted somewhat, are presented in the checklist below.

☑ SECOND READING: A CHECKLIST

Using a pen (or pencil) and highlighter, you might . . .

❏ Underline or highlight the selection's main idea, or thesis, often found near the beginning or end. If the thesis isn't stated explicitly, write down your own version of the selection's main idea.

❏ Place numbers in the margin to designate the main points that support the thesis.

❏ Circle or put an asterisk next to key ideas that are stated more than once.

❏ Take a minute to write "Yes," "No," or a brief comment beside points with which you strongly agree or disagree. Your reaction to these points often explains your feelings about the aptness of the selection's ideas.

❏ Return to any unclear passages you encountered during the first reading. The feeling you now have for the piece as a whole will probably help you make sense of initially confusing spots. However, this second reading may also reveal that, in places, the writer's thinking isn't as clear as it could be. If that's the case, you might put a question mark in the margin beside the unclear material.

❑ Put brackets around words whose meaning you need to check in a dictionary.

❑ Ask yourself if your initial impression of the selection has changed in any way as a result of this second reading. If your feelings *have* changed, try to determine why you reacted differently on this reading.

STAGE 3: EVALUATE THE SELECTION

Now that you have a good grasp of the selection, you may want to read it a third time, especially if the piece is long or complex. This time, your goal is to make judgments about the essay's effectiveness. Keep in mind, though, that you shouldn't evaluate the selection until after you have a strong hold on it. A negative or even a positive reaction is valid only if it's based on an accurate reading.

At first, you may feel uncomfortable about evaluating the work of a professional writer. But remember: Written material set in type only *seems* perfect; all writing can be fine-tuned. By identifying what does and doesn't work in others' writing, you're taking an important first step toward developing your own power as a writer. You might find it helpful at this point to get together with other students to discuss the selection. Comparing viewpoints often opens up a piece, enabling you to gain a clearer perspective on the selection and the author's approach.

Evaluate the Writing

To evaluate the essay, ask yourself the following questions.

☑ EVALUATING A SELECTION: A CHECKLIST

❑ *Where does support for the selection's thesis seem logical and sufficient? Where does support seem weak?* Which of the author's supporting facts, arguments, and examples seem pertinent and convincing? Which don't?

❑ *Is the selection unified? If not, why not?* Where does something in the selection not seem relevant? Where are there any unnecessary digressions or detours?

❑ *How does the writer make the selection move smoothly from beginning to end?* How does the writer create an easy flow between ideas? Are any parts of the essay abrupt and jarring? Which ones?

❑ *Which stylistic devices are used to good effect in the selection?* Which *pattern of development* or combination of patterns does the writer use to develop the piece? Why do you think those patterns were selected? How do paragraph development, sentence structure, and word choice contribute to the piece's overall effect? What *tone* does the writer adopt? Where does the writer use *figures of speech* effectively? (The next chapter and the glossary explain the terms shown here in italics.)

❑ *How does the selection encourage further thought?* What new perspective on an issue does the writer provide? What ideas has the selection prompted you to explore in an essay of your own?

Evaluate the Images

Some readings use graphics (such as charts, tables, graphs, and diagrams) or illustrations (such as photographs, paintings, and drawings) to support their message. You can read and evaluate these just as you would text.

Preview images.   As you get an overview of a text, ask yourself questions about its images. Who created the image? Is the source reliable? What does the caption say? Is information clearly labeled and presented? What mood, feelings, or other impression does the image convey?

Analyze and interpret images.   Deepen your understanding of images as you read the text. What is the author's purpose? Does the image make assumptions about viewers' beliefs or knowledge? How is the image explained in the text? Are data accurate, up-to-date, and presented without distortion? Do illustrations tell a story? What elements stand out? What mood do the colors and composition (arrangement of elements) convey?

Integrate image evaluations.   Integrate your findings into your evaluation of the reading as a whole. Are the images adequately discussed in the text? Do graphics give relevant, persuasive details? Are illustrations thought-provoking without being sensationalistic? In general, do the images improve the reading and support the writer's main points?

It takes some work to follow the three-step approach just described, but the selections in *The Longman Reader* are worth the effort. Bear in mind that none of the selections sprang full-blown from the pen of its author. Rather, each essay is the result of hours of work—hours of thinking, writing, rethinking, and revising. As a reader, you should show the same willingness to work with the selections, to read them carefully and thoughtfully. Henry David Thoreau, an avid reader and prolific writer, emphasized the importance of this kind of attentive reading when he advised that "books must be read as deliberately and unreservedly as they were written."

To illustrate the multi-stage reading process just described, we've annotated the professional essay that follows: "Family Counterculture" by Ellen Goodman. Note that annotations are provided in the margin of the essay as well as at the end of the essay. As you read Goodman's essay, try applying the three-stage sequence. You can measure your ability to dig into the selection by making your own annotations on Goodman's essay and then comparing them to ours. You can also see how well you evaluated the piece by answering the questions in "Evaluating a Selection: A Checklist" and then comparing your responses to ours on pages 10–11.

Ellen Goodman

The recipient of a Pulitzer Prize, Ellen Goodman (1941–) worked for *Newsweek* and the *Detroit Free Press* before joining the staff of *The Boston Globe* in 1967. A resident of the Boston area, Goodman writes a popular syndicated column that provides insightful commentary on life in the United States. Her pieces have appeared in a number of national publications, including *The Village Voice* and *McCalls*. Collections of her columns have been published in *Close to Home* (1979), *Turning Points* (1979), *At Large* (1981), *Keeping in Touch* (1985), *Making Sense* (1989), and *Value Judgments* (1993). Most recently, she coauthored *I Know Just What You Mean* (1999), a book that examines the complex nature of women's friendships, and *Paper Trail* (2004). The following selection is from *Value Judgments*.

Pre-Reading Journal Entry

Television is often blamed for having a harmful effect on children. Do you think this criticism is merited? In what ways does TV exert a negative influence on children? In what ways does TV exert a positive influence on youngsters? Take a few minutes to respond to these questions in your journal.

Marginal Annotations

Interesting take on the term "counterculture"

Time frame established

Light humor; easy, casual tone

Time frame picked up

Thesis, developed overall by cause-effect pattern

First research-based example to support thesis

Family Counterculture

1   Sooner or later, most Americans become card-carrying members of the counterculture. This is not an underground holdout of hippies. No beads are required. All you need to join is a child.

2   At some point between Lamaze and the PTA, it becomes clear that one of your main jobs as a parent is to counter the culture. What the media delivers to children by the masses, you are expected to rebut one at a time.

3   The latest evidence of this frustrating piece of the parenting job description came from pediatricians. This summer, the American Academy of Pediatrics called for a ban on television food ads. Their plea was hard on the heels of a study showing that one Saturday morning of TV cartoons contained 202 junk-food ads.

4   The kids see, want, and nag. That is, after all, the theory behind advertising to children, since few six-year-olds have their own trust funds. The end result, said the pediatricians, is obesity and high cholesterol.

5   Their call for a ban was predictably attacked by the grocers' association. But it was also attacked by people

assembled under the umbrella marked "parental responsibility." We don't need bans, said these "PR" people; we
need parents who know how to say "no."

*Relevant paragraph?
Identifies Goodman
as a parent, but
interrupts flow*

Well, I bow to no one in my capacity for naysaying.   6
I agree that it's a well-honed skill of child raising. By
the time my daughter was seven, she qualified as a
media critic.

*Transition
doesn't work but
would if ¶6
were cut*

But it occurs to me now that the call for "parental   7
responsibility" is increasing in direct proportion to the
irresponsibility of the marketplace. Parents are expected
to protect their children from an increasingly hostile
environment.

*Series of questions
and brief answers
consistent with
overall casual tone*

Are the kids being sold junk food? Just say no. Is TV   8
bad? Turn it off. Are there messages about sex, drugs,
violence all around? Counter the culture.

*Brief real-life
examples support
thesis*

Fragments

Mothers and fathers are expected to screen virtually   9
every aspect of their children's lives. To check the ratings
on the movies, to read the labels on the CDs, to find out
if there's MTV in the house next door. All the while keeping in touch with school and, in their free time, earning
a living.

More examples

In real life, most parents do a great deal of this moni-   10
toring and just-say-no-ing. Any trip to the supermarket
produces at least one scene of a child grabbing for something only to have it returned to the shelf by a frazzled
parent. An extraordinary number of the family arguments
are over the goodies—sneakers, clothes, games—that the
young know only because of ads.

*Another weak
transition—no
contrast*

But at times it seems that the media have become the   11
mainstream culture in children's lives. Parents have become
the alternative.

*Restatement
of thesis*

*Second research-
based example to
support thesis*

Barbara Dafoe Whitehead, a research associate at the   12
Institute for American Values, found this out in interviews
with middle-class parents. "A common complaint I heard
from parents was their sense of being overwhelmed by the
culture. They felt their voice was a lot weaker. And they
felt relatively more helpless than their parents.

*Citing an expert
reinforces thesis*

*Restatement of
thesis*

"Parents," she notes, "see themselves in a struggle for   13
the hearts and minds of their own children." It isn't that they
can't say no. It's that there's so much more to say no to.

Without wallowing in false nostalgia, there has been   14
a fundamental shift. Americans once expected parents

Comparison-contrast pattern—signaled by "once," "Today," "Once," and "Now"

to raise their children in accordance with the dominant cultural messages. Today they are expected to raise their children in opposition.

Once the chorus of cultural values was full of ministers, teachers, neighbors, leaders. They demanded more conformity, but offered more support. Now the messengers are Ninja Turtles, Madonna, rap groups, and celebrities pushing sneakers. Parents are considered "responsible" only if they are successful in their resistance. 15

Restatement of thesis

It's what makes child raising harder. It's why parents feel more isolated. It's not just that American families have less time with their kids. It's that we have to spend more of this time doing battle with our own culture. 16

Conveys the challenges that parents face

It's rather like trying to get your kids to eat their green beans after they've been told all day about the wonders of Milky Way. Come to think of it, it's exactly like that. 17

Annotations at End of Selection

Thesis: First stated in paragraph 2 (". . . it becomes clear that one of your main jobs as a parent is to counter the culture. What the media delivers to children by the masses, you are expected to rebut one at a time.") and then restated in paragraphs 11 ("the media have become the mainstream culture in children's lives. Parents have become the alternative."); 13 (Parents are frustrated, not because ". . . they can't say no. It's that there's so much more to say no to."); and 16 ("It's not just that American families have less time with their kids. It's that we have to spend more of this time doing battle with our own culture.").

First reading: A quick take on a serious subject. Informal tone and to-the-point style gets to the heart of the media vs. parenting problem. Easy to relate to.

Second and third readings:
1. Uses the findings of the American Academy of Pediatrics, a statement made by Barbara Dafoe Whitehead, and a number of brief examples to illustrate the relentless work parents must do to counter the culture.
2. Uses cause-effect overall to support thesis and comparison-contrast to show how parenting nowadays is more difficult than it used to be.
3. Not everything works (reference to her daughter as a media critic, repetitive and often inappropriate use of "but" as a transition), but overall the essay succeeds.
4. At first, the ending seems weak. But it feels just right after an additional reading. Shows how parents' attempts to counter the culture are as commonplace as their attempts to get kids to eat vegetables. It's an ongoing and constant battle that makes parenting more difficult than it has to be and less enjoyable than it should be.
5. Possible essay topics: A humorous paper about the strategies kids use to get around their parents' saying "no" or a serious paper on the negative effects on kids of another aspect of television culture (cable television, tabloid-style talk shows, and so on).

The following answers to the questions in "Evaluating a Selection: A Checklist" on pages 4–5 will help crystallize your reaction to Goodman's essay.

1. *Where does support for the selection's thesis seem logical and sufficient? Where does support seem weak?*

Goodman begins to provide evidence for her thesis when she cites the American Academy of Pediatrics' call for a "ban on television food ads" (paragraphs 3–5). The ban followed a study showing that kids are exposed to 202 junk-food ads during a single Saturday morning of television cartoons. Goodman further buoys her thesis with a list of brief "countering the culture" examples (8–10) and a slightly more detailed example (10) describing the parent–child conflicts that occur on a typical trip to the supermarket. By citing Barbara Dafoe Whitehead's findings later on (12–13), Goodman further reinforces her point that the need for constant rebuttal makes parenting especially frustrating: Because parents have to say "no" to virtually everything, more and more family time ends up being spent "doing battle" with the culture (16).

2. *Is the selection unified? If not, why not?*

In the first two paragraphs, Goodman identifies the problem and then provides solid evidence of its existence (3–4, 8–10). But Goodman's comments in paragraph 6 about her daughter's skill as a media critic seem distracting. Even so, paragraph 6 serves a purpose because it establishes Goodman's credibility by showing that she, too, is a parent and has been compelled to be a constant naysayer with her child. From paragraph 7 on, the piece stays on course by focusing on the way parents have to compete with the media for control of their children. The concluding paragraphs (16–17) reinforce Goodman's thesis by suggesting that parents' struggle to counteract the media is as common—and as exasperating—as trying to get children to eat their vegetables when all the kids want is to gorge on candy.

3. *How does the writer make the selection move smoothly from beginning to end?*

The first two paragraphs of Goodman's essay are clearly connected: The phrase "sooner or later" at the beginning of the first paragraph establishes a time frame that is then picked up at the beginning of the second paragraph with the phrase "at some point between Lamaze and the PTA." And Goodman's use in paragraph 3 of the word *this* ("The latest evidence of *this* frustrating piece of the parenting job description...") provides a link to the preceding paragraph. Other connecting strategies can be found in the piece. For example, the words *once, Today, Once,* and *Now* in paragraphs 14–15 provide an easy-to-follow contrast between parenting in earlier times and parenting in this era. However, because paragraph 6 contains a distracting aside, the contrast implied by the word *But* at the beginning of paragraph 7 doesn't work. Nor does Goodman's use of the word *But* at the beginning of paragraph 11 work; the point there emphasizes rather than contrasts with the one made in paragraph 10. From this point on, though, the essay is tightly written and moves smoothly along to its conclusion.

4. *Which stylistic devices are used to good effect in the selection?*

Goodman uses several patterns of development in her essay. The selection as a whole shows the *effect* of the mass media on kids and their parents. In paragraphs 3 and 12, Goodman provides *examples in the form of research data* to support her thesis, while paragraphs 8–10 provide a series of *brief real-life examples.* Paragraphs 12–15 use *contrast,* and paragraph 17 makes a *comparison* to punctuate Goodman's concluding point. Throughout, Goodman's *informal, conversational tone* draws readers in, and her *no-holds-barred style* drives her point home forcefully. In paragraph 8, she uses a *question-and-answer format* ("Are the kids being sold junk food? Just say no.") and *short sentences* ("Turn it off" and "Counter the culture") to illustrate how pervasive the situation is. And in paragraph 9, she uses *fragments* ("To check the ratings..." and "All the while keeping in touch with school...") to focus attention on the problem. These varied stylistic devices help make the essay a quick, enjoyable read. Finally, although Goodman is concerned about the corrosive effects of the media, she leavens her essay with dashes of *humor.* For example, the image of parents as counterculturists (1) and the comments about green beans and Milky Ways (17) probably elicit smiles or gentle laughter from most readers.

5. *How does the selection encourage further thought?*

Goodman's essay touches on a problem most parents face at some time or another—having to counter the culture in order to protect their children. Her main concern is how difficult it is for parents to say "no" to virtually every aspect of the culture. Although Goodman offers no immediate solutions, her presentation of the issue urges us to decide for ourselves which aspects of the culture should be countered and which should not.

If, for each essay you read in this book, you consider the preceding questions, you'll be able to respond thoughtfully to the *Questions for Close Reading* and *Questions About the Writer's Craft* presented after each selection. Your responses will, in turn, prepare you for the writing assignments that follow the questions. Interesting and varied, the assignments invite you to examine issues raised by the selections and encourage you to experiment with various writing styles and organizational patterns.

Following are some sample questions and writing assignments based on the Goodman essay; all are similar to the sort that appear later in this book. Note that the final writing assignment paves the way for a student essay, the stages of which are illustrated in Chapter 2.

Questions for Close Reading

1. According to Goodman, what does it mean to "counter the culture"? Why is this harder now than ever before?
2. Which two groups, according to Goodman, protested the American Academy of Pediatrics's ban on television food ads? Which of these two groups does she take more seriously? Why?

Questions About the Writer's Craft

1. What audience do you think Goodman had in mind when she wrote this piece? How do you know? Where does she address this audience directly?
2. What word appears four times in paragraph 16? Why do you think Goodman repeats this word so often? What is the effect of this repetition?

Writing Assignments

1. Goodman believes that parents are forced to say "no" to almost everything the media offer. Write an essay illustrating the idea that not everything the media present is bad for children.
2. Goodman implies that, in some ways, today's world is hostile to children. Do you agree? Drawing upon but not limiting yourself to the material in your pre-reading journal, write an essay in which you support or reject this viewpoint.

The benefits of active reading are many. Books in general and the selections in *The Longman Reader* in particular will bring you face-to-face with issues that concern all of us. If you study the selections and the questions that follow them, you'll be on the way to discovering ideas for your own papers. Chapter 2, "The Writing Process," offers practical suggestions for turning those ideas into well-organized, thoughtful essays.

THE WRITING PROCESS

Not many people retire at age thirty-eight. But Michel Montaigne, a sixteenth-century French attorney, did exactly that. Montaigne retired at a young age because he wanted to read, think, and write about all the subjects that interested him. After spending years getting his ideas down on paper, Montaigne finally published his short prose pieces. He called them *essais*—French for "trials" or "attempts."

In fact, all writing is an attempt to transform ideas into words, thus giving order and meaning to life. By using the term *essais*—or *essays* in English—Montaigne acknowledged that a written piece is never really finished. Of course, writers have to stop at some point, especially if they have deadlines to meet. But, as all experienced writers know, even after they dot the final *i*, cross the final *t*, and say "That's it," there's always something that could have been explored further or expressed a little better.

Because writing is a process, shaky starts and changes in direction aren't uncommon. Although there's no way to eliminate the work needed to write effectively, certain approaches can make the process more manageable and rewarding. This chapter describes a sequence of steps for writing essays. Familiarity with a specific sequence develops your awareness of strategies and choices, making you feel more confident when it comes time to write. You're less likely to look at a blank piece of paper and think, "Help! Now what do I do?" During the sequence, you do the following:

1. Prewrite.
2. Identify the thesis.
3. Support the thesis with evidence.

4. Organize the evidence.
5. Write the first draft.
6. Revise the essay.
7. Edit and proofread.

We present the sequence as a series of stages, but we urge you not to view it as a formula to be followed rigidly. Most people develop personalized approaches to the writing process. Some writers mull over a topic in their heads and then move quickly into a promising first draft; others outline their essays in detail before beginning to write. Between these two extremes are any number of effective approaches. The sequence here—illustrated in Figure 2.1—can be streamlined or otherwise altered to fit individual writing styles as well as the needs of specific assignments.

FIGURE 2.1
Stages of the Writing Process

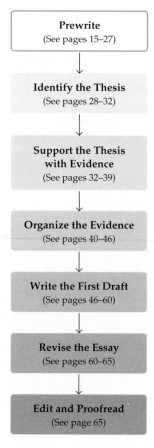

Prewrite
(See pages 15–27)

Identify the Thesis
(See pages 28–32)

Support the Thesis
with Evidence
(See pages 32–39)

Organize the Evidence
(See pages 40–46)

Write the First Draft
(See pages 46–60)

Revise the Essay
(See pages 60–65)

Edit and Proofread
(See page 65)

STAGE 1: PREWRITE

Prewriting refers to strategies you can use to generate ideas *before* starting the first draft of a paper. Prewriting techniques are like the warm-ups you do before going out to jog—they loosen you up, get you moving, and help you to develop a sense of well-being and confidence. Since prewriting techniques encourage imaginative exploration, they also help you discover what interests you most about your subject.

During prewriting, you deliberately ignore your internal critic. Your purpose is simply to get ideas down on paper *without evaluating* their effectiveness. Writing without immediately judging what you produce can be liberating. Once you feel less pressure, you'll probably find that you can generate a good deal of material. And that can make your confidence soar.

Keep a Journal

Of all the prewriting techniques, keeping a journal (daily or almost daily) is most likely to make writing a part of your life. Some entries focus on a single theme; others wander from topic to topic. Your starting point may be a dream, a snippet of overheard conversation, a song, a political cartoon, an issue raised in class or in your reading—anything that surprises, interests, angers, depresses, confuses, or amuses you. You may also use a journal to experiment with your writing style—say, to vary your sentence structure if you tend to use predictable patterns.

Here is a fairly focused excerpt from a student's journal:

Today I had to show Paul around school. He and Mom got here by 9. I didn't let on that this was the earliest I've gotten up all semester! He got out of the car looking kind of nervous. Maybe he thought his big brother would be different after a couple of months of college. I walked him around part of the campus and then he went with me to Am. Civ. and then to lunch. He met Greg and some other guys. Everyone seemed to like him. He's got a nice, quiet sense of humor. When I went to Bio., I told him that he could walk around on his own since he wasn't crazy about sitting in on a science class. But he said "I'd rather stick with you." Was he flattering me or was he just scared? Anyway it made me feel good. Later when he was leaving, he told me he's definitely going to apply. I guess that'd be kind of nice, having him here. Mom thinks it's great and she's pushing it. I don't know. I feel kind of like it would invade my privacy. I found this school and have made a life for myself here. Let him find his own school! But it could be great having my kid brother here. I guess this is a classic case of what my psych teacher calls ambivalence. Part of me wants him to come, and part of me doesn't! (November 10)

Although some instructors collect students' journals, you needn't be overly concerned with spelling, grammar, sentence structure, or organization. While journal writing is typically more structured than freewriting (see page 22), you don't have to strive for entries that read like mini-essays. In fact, sometimes you may find it helpful to use a simple list. The important thing is to let your journal writing prompt reflection and new insights, providing you with material to draw upon in your writing. It is, then, a good idea to reread each week's entries to identify recurring themes and concerns. Keep a list of these issues at the back of your journal, under a heading like "Possible Essay Subjects." Here, for instance, are a few topics suggested by the preceding journal entry: deciding which college to attend, leaving home, sibling rivalry. Each of these topics could be developed in a full-length essay.

The pre-reading journal.   To reinforce the value of journal writing, we've included a journal assignment before every reading selection in the book. This assignment, called *Pre-Reading Journal Entry,* encourages you to explore—in a tentative fashion—your thoughts about an issue that will be raised in the selection. Here, once again, is the *Pre-Reading Journal Entry* assignment that precedes Ellen Goodman's "Family Counterculture" (page 7):

> Television is often blamed for having a harmful effect on children. Do you think this criticism is merited? In what ways does TV exert a negative influence on children? In what ways does TV exert a positive influence on youngsters? Take a few minutes to respond to these questions in your journal.

    The following journal entry shows how one student, Harriet Davids, responded to the journal assignment. A thirty-eight-year-old college student and mother of two young teenagers, Harriet was understandably intrigued by the assignment. As you'll see, Harriet used a listing strategy to prepare her journal entry. She found that lists were perfect for dealing with the essentially "for or against" nature of the journal assignment.

TV's Negative Influence on Kids	TV's Positive Influence on Kids
Teaches negative behaviors (violence, sex, swearing, drugs, alcohol, etc.)	Teaches important educational concepts (*Sesame Street,* shows on The Learning Channel, etc.)
Cuts down on imagination and creativity	Exposes kids to new images and worlds (*Dora the Explorer, Mister Rogers' Neighborhood*)
Cuts down on time spent with parents (talking, reading, playing games together)	Can inspire important discussions (about morals, sexuality, drugs, etc.) between kids and parents

(Continued)

Encourages parents' lack of involvement with kids	Gives parents a needed break from kids
Frightens kids excessively by showing images of real-life violence (terrorist attacks, war, murders, etc.)	Educates kids about the painful realities in the world
Encourages isolation (watching screen rather than interacting with other kids)	Creates common ground among kids, basis of conversations and games
De-emphasizes reading and creates need for constant stimulation	Encourages kids to slow down and read books based on a TV series or show (the *Arthur* and the *Clifford, the Big Red Dog* series, etc.)
Promotes materialism (commercials)	Can be used by parents to teach kids that they can't have everything they see

The journal assignment and subsequent journal entry do more than prepare you to read a selection with extra care and attention; they also pave the way to a full-length essay. Here's how. The final assignment following each selection is called *Writing Assignment Using a Journal Entry as a Starting Point*. This assignment helps you to translate the raw material in your journal entry into a thoughtful, well-considered essay. By the time you get to the assignment, the rough ideas in your journal entry will have been enriched by your reading of the selection. (For an example of a writing assignment that draws upon material in a pre-reading journal entry, turn to page 102.)

As you've just seen, journal writing can stimulate thinking in a loose, unstructured way; it can also prompt the focused thinking required by a specific writing assignment. When you have a specific piece to write, you should approach prewriting in a purposeful, focused manner. You need to:

- Understand the boundaries of the assignment.
- Determine your purpose, audience, and tone.
- Discover your essay's limited subject.
- Generate raw material about your limited subject.
- Organize the raw material.

Understand the Boundaries of the Assignment

Before you start writing a paper, learn what's expected. First, clarify the *kind of paper* the instructor has in mind. Suppose the instructor asks you to discuss the key ideas in an assigned reading. What does the instructor want you to do? Should you include a brief summary of the selection? Should you compare the author's ideas with your own view of the subject? Should you determine if the author's view is supported by valid evidence? If you're not sure about an assignment, ask your instructor to make the requirements clear.

Second, find out *how long* the paper is expected to be. Many instructors will indicate the approximate length of the papers they assign. If no length requirements are provided, discuss with the instructor what you plan to cover and indicate how long you think your paper will be. The instructor will either give you the go-ahead or help you refine the direction and scope of your work.

Determine Your Purpose, Audience, and Tone

Once you understand the requirements for a writing assignment, you're ready to begin thinking about the essay. What is its *purpose?* For what *audience* will it be written? What *tone* will you use? Later on, you may modify your decisions about these issues. That's fine. But you need to understand the way these considerations influence your work in the early phases of the writing process.

Purpose.   The papers you write in college are usually meant to *inform* or *explain,* to *convince* or *persuade,* and sometimes to *entertain.* In practice, writing often combines purposes. You might, for example, write an essay trying to *convince* people to support a new trash recycling program in your community. But before you win readers over, you most likely would have to *explain* something about current waste disposal technology.

When purposes blend this way, the predominant one determines the essay's content, organization, emphasis, and choice of words. Assume you're writing about a political campaign. If your primary goal is to *entertain,* to take a gentle poke at two candidates, you might start with several accounts of one candidate's "foot-in-mouth" disease and then describe the attempts of the other candidate, a multimillionaire, to portray himself as an Average Joe. Your language, full of exaggeration, would reflect your objective. But if your primary purpose is to *persuade* readers that the candidates are incompetent and shouldn't be elected, you might adopt a serious, straightforward style. You would use one candidate's gaffes to illustrate her insensitivity to important issues. Similarly, the other candidate's posturing would be presented not as foolish pretension, but as evidence of his lack of judgment.

Audience.   To write effectively, you need to identify who your readers are and to take their expectations and needs into account. An essay about the artificial preservatives in the food served by the campus cafeteria would take one form if submitted to your chemistry professor and a very different one if written for the college newspaper. The chemistry paper would probably be formal and technical, complete with chemical formulations and scientific data: "Distillation revealed sodium benzoate particles suspended in a gelatinous medium." But such technical material would be inappropriate in a newspaper column intended for general readers. In this case, you might provide specific examples of cafeteria foods containing additives—"Those deliciously smoky cold cuts are loaded with nitrates and nitrites, both known to cause cancer in laboratory animals"—and suggest ways to eat more healthily: "Pass by the deli counter and fill up instead on vegetarian pizza and fruit juices."

When analyzing your audience, ask yourself the following questions.

☑ ANALYZING YOUR AUDIENCE: A CHECKLIST

❑ What are my readers' age, sex, and educational level?

❑ What are their political, religious, and other beliefs?

❑ What interests and needs motivate my audience?

❑ How much do my readers already know about my subject?

❑ Do they have any misconceptions?

❑ What biases do they have about me, my subject, my opinion?

❑ How do my readers expect me to relate to them?

❑ What values do I share with my readers that will help me communicate with them?

Tone.   Just as a voice projects a range of feelings, writing can convey one or more *tones,* or emotional states: enthusiasm, anger, resignation, and so on. Tone is integral to meaning; it permeates writing and reflects your attitude toward yourself, your purpose, your subject, and your readers. How do you project tone? You pay close attention to sentence structure and word choice.

1. Use appropriate sentence structure.   *Sentence structure* refers to the way sentences are shaped. Although the two paragraphs that follow deal with exactly the same subject, note how differences in sentence structure create sharply dissimilar tones:

> During the 1960s, many inner-city minorities considered the police an occupying force and an oppressive agent of control. As a result, violence against police grew in poorer neighborhoods, as did the number of residents killed by police.
>
> An occupying force. An agent of control. An oppressor. That's how many inner-city minorities in the '60s viewed the police. Violence against police soared. Police killings of residents mounted.

Informative in its approach, the first paragraph projects a neutral, almost dispassionate tone. The sentences are fairly long, and clear transitions ("During the 1960s"; "As a result") mark the progression of thought. But the second paragraph, with its dramatic, almost alarmist tone, seems intended to elicit a strong emotional response; its short sentences, fragments, and abrupt transitions reflect the turbulence of those earlier times.

2. Choose effective words.   *Word choice* also plays a role in establishing the tone of an essay. Words have *denotations,* neutral dictionary meanings, as well as *connotations,* emotional associations that go beyond the literal meaning. The word *beach,* for instance, is defined in the dictionary as "a nearly level stretch of pebbles and sand beside a body of water." This definition, however, doesn't capture individual responses to the word. For some, *beach* suggests warmth and relaxation; for others, it calls up images of hospital waste and sewage washed up on a once-clean stretch of shoreline.

Since tone and meaning are tightly bound, you must be sensitive to the emotional nuances of words. In a respectful essay about police officers, you wouldn't refer to *cops, narcs,* or *flatfoots;* such terms convey a contempt inconsistent with the tone intended. Your words must also convey tone clearly. Suppose you're writing a satirical piece criticizing a local beauty pageant. Dubbing the participants "livestock on view" leaves no question about your tone. But if you simply referred to the participants as "attractive young women," readers might be unsure of your attitude. Remember, readers can't read your mind, only your paper.

Discover Your Essay's Limited Subject

Because too broad a subject can result in a diffuse, rambling essay, be sure to restrict your general subject before starting to write. The following examples show the difference between general subjects that are too broad for an essay and limited subjects that are appropriate and workable. The examples, of course, represent only a few among many possibilities.

General Subject	Less General	Limited
Education	Computers in education	Computers in elementary school arithmetic classes
	High school education	High school electives
Transportation	Low-cost travel	Hitchhiking
	Getting around a metropolitan area	The transit system in a nearby city
Work	Planning for a career	College internships
	Women in the work force	Women's success as managers

How do you move from a general to a narrow subject? Imagine that you're asked to prepare a straightforward, informative essay for your writing class. Reprinted below is writing assignment 2 from page 12. The assignment, prompted by Ellen Goodman's essay "Family Counterculture," is an extension of the journal-writing assignment on page 7.

> Goodman implies that, in some ways, today's world is hostile to children. Do you agree? Drawing upon but not limiting yourself to the material in your pre-reading journal, write an essay in which you support or reject this viewpoint.

Two techniques—*questioning* and *brainstorming*—can help you limit such a general assignment. While these techniques encourage you to roam freely over a subject, they also help restrict the discussion by revealing which aspects of the subject interest you most.

1. Question the general subject.   One way to narrow a subject is to ask a series of *who, how, why, where, when,* and *what* questions. The following example shows how Harriet Davids, the mother of two young teenagers, used this technique to limit the Goodman assignment.

You may recall that, before reading Goodman's essay, Harriet had used her journal to explore TV's effect on children (see pages 16–17). After reading "Family Counterculture," Harriet concluded that she essentially agreed with Goodman; like Goodman, she felt that parents nowadays are indeed forced to raise their kids in an "increasingly hostile environment." She was pleased that the writing assignment gave her an opportunity to expand preliminary ideas she had jotted down in her journal.

Harriet soon realized that she had to narrow the Goodman assignment. She started by asking a number of pointed questions about the general topic. As she proceeded, she was aware that the same questions could have led to different limited subjects—just as other questions would have.

General Subject: We live in a world that is difficult, even hostile to children.

Question	Limited Subject
Who is to blame for the difficult conditions under which children grow up?	Parents' casual attitude toward child-rearing
How have schools contributed to the problems children face?	Not enough counseling programs for kids in distress
Why do children feel frightened?	Divorce
Where do kids go to escape?	Television, which makes the world seem even more dangerous

(Continued)

Question	Limited Subject
When are children most vulnerable?	The special problems of adolescents
What dangers or fears should parents discuss with their children?	AIDS, drugs, alcohol, war, terrorism

2. Brainstorm the general subject.   Another way to focus on a limited subject is to list quickly everything about the general topic that pops into your mind. Just jot down brief words, phrases, and abbreviations to capture your free-floating thoughts. Writing in complete sentences will slow you down. Don't try to organize or censor your ideas. Even the most fleeting, random, or seemingly outrageous thoughts can be productive.

Questioning and brainstorming can suggest many possible limited subjects. To identify especially promising ones, reread your material. What arouses your interest, anger, or curiosity? What themes seem to dominate and cut to the heart of the matter? Star or circle ideas with potential.

After marking the material, write several phrases or sentences summarizing the most promising limited subjects. Here are just a few that emerged from Harriet Davids's prewriting for the Goodman assignment:

- TV partly to blame for children having such a hard time
- Relocation stressful to children
- Schools also at fault
- The special problems that parents face raising children today

Harriet decided to write on the last of these limited subjects—the special problems that parents face raising children today.

Generate Raw Material About Your Limited Subject

When a limited subject strikes you as having possibilities, use these techniques to see if you have enough interesting things to say about the subject to write an effective essay.

1. Freewrite on your limited subject.   *Freewriting* means jotting down in rough sentences or phrases everything that comes to mind. To capture this continuous stream of thought, write nonstop for ten minutes or more. Don't censor anything; put down whatever pops into your head. Don't reread, edit, or pay attention to organization, spelling, or grammar. If your mind goes blank, repeat words until another thought emerges.

Here is part of the freewriting that Harriet Davids generated about her limited subject, "The special problems that parents face raising children today":

Parents today have tough problems to face. Lots of dangers. The Internet first and foremost. Also crimes of violence against kids. Parents also have to keep up with cost of living, everything costs more, kids want and expect more. Television? Another thing is *Playboy, Penthouse.* Sexy ads and videos on TV, movies deal with sex. Kids grow up too fast, too fast. Kids grow up too fast, too fast. Drugs and alcohol. Witness real-life violence on TV, like terrorist attacks and school shootings. Little kids can't handle knowing too much at an early age. Both parents at work much of the day. Finding good day care a real problem. Lots of latchkey kids. Another problem is getting kids to do homework, lots of other things to do. Especially like going to the mall or chatting with friends online! When I was young, we did homework after dinner, no excuses accepted by my parents.

2. Brainstorm your limited subject.   Let your mind wander freely, as you did when using brainstorming to narrow your subject. This time, list every idea, fact, and example that occurs to you about your limited subject. Use brief words and phrases. For now, don't worry whether ideas fit together or whether the points listed make sense.

To gather additional material on her limited subject for the Goodman as- signment ("The special problems that parents face raising children today"), Harriet Davids brainstormed the following list:

- Trying to raise kids when both parents work
- Prices of everything outrageous, even when both parents work
- Commercials make everyone want *more* of everything
- Clothes so important
- Day care not always the answer—cases of abuse
- Day care very expensive
- Sex everywhere—TV, movies, magazines, Internet
- Sexy clothes on little kids. Absurd!
- Sexual abuse of kids
- Violence on TV, especially images of real-life terrorist attacks and school shootings—scary for kids!
- Violence against kids when parents abuse drugs
- Meth, "Ecstasy," alcohol, heroin, cocaine, AIDS
- Schools have to teach kids about these things
- Schools doing too much—not as good as they used to be
- Not enough homework assigned—kids unprepared
- Distractions from homework—Internet, TV, cellphones, MP3s, computer games

3. Use group brainstorming.   Brainstorming can also be conducted as a group activity. Thrashing out ideas with other people stretches the imagination, revealing possibilities you may not have considered on your own.

Group brainstorming doesn't have to be conducted in a formal classroom situation. You can bounce ideas around with friends and family anywhere—over lunch, at the student center, and so on.

4. Map out the limited subject.   If you're the kind of person who doodles while thinking, you may want to try *mapping,* sometimes called *diagramming* or *clustering.* Like other prewriting techniques, mapping proceeds rapidly and encourages the free flow of ideas. Begin by expressing your limited subject in a crisp phrase and placing it in the center of a blank sheet of paper. As ideas come to you, put them along lines or in boxes or circles around the limited subject. Draw arrows and lines to show the relationships among ideas. Don't stop there, however. Focus on each idea; as subpoints and details come to you, connect them to their source idea, again using boxes, lines, circles, or arrows to clarify how everything relates.

5. Use the patterns of development.   Throughout this book, we show how writers use various patterns of development (narration, process analysis, definition, and so on), singly or in combination, to develop and organize their ideas. Because each pattern has its own distinctive logic, the patterns encourage you, when you prewrite, to think about a subject in different ways, causing insights to surface that might otherwise remain submerged.

The patterns of development are discussed in detail in Chapters 3–11. The following chart shows the way each pattern can generate raw material for a limited subject.

Limited Subject: The special problems that parents face raising children today.

Pattern	Purpose	Raw Material
Description	To detail what a person, place, or object is like	Detail the sights and sounds of a glitzy mall that attracts kids
Narration	To relate an event	Recount what happened when neighbors tried to forbid their kids from going online
Exemplification	To provide specific instances or examples	Offer examples of family arguments. Will permission be given to go to a party where alcohol will be served? Can parents outlaw certain websites?
Division-classification	To divide something into parts or to group related things in categories	Identify components of a TV commercial that distorts kids' values

(Continued)

		Classify the kinds of commercials that make it difficult to teach kids values
Process analysis	To explain how something happens or how something is done	Explain step by step how family life can disintegrate when parents have to work all the time to make ends meet
Comparison-contrast	To point out similarities and/or dissimilarities	Contrast families today with those of a generation ago
Cause-effect	To analyze reasons and consequences	Explain why parents are not around to be with their kids: Industry's failure to provide day care and its inflexibility about granting time off for parents with sick kids
		Explain the consequences of absentee parents: Kids feel unloved; they spend hours on the Internet, they turn to TV for role models, they're undisciplined; they take on adult responsibility too early
Definition	To explain the meaning of a term or concept	What is meant by "tough love"?
Argumentation-persuasion	To win people over to a point of view	Convince parents that they must work with schools to develop programs that make kids feel safer and more secure

(For more on ways to use the patterns of development in different phases of the writing process, see pages 33, 40–41, and 430–432.)

Conduct research.   Depending on your topic, you may find it helpful to visit the library and/or to go online to identify books and articles about your limited subject. At this point, you don't need to read closely the material you find. Just skim and perhaps take a few brief notes on ideas and points that could be useful.

In researching the Goodman assignment, for instance, Harriet Davids could look under such headings and subheadings as the following:

Day care
Drug abuse
Family

Parent-child relationship
    Child abuse
    Children of divorced parents
    Children of working mothers
School and home

Organize the Raw Material

On pages 43–45, we talk about the more formal outline you may need later on in the writing process. However, a *scratch outline* or *scratch list* can be an effective strategy for imposing order on the tentative ideas generated during prewriting.

Reread your exploratory thoughts about the limited subject. Cross out anything not appropriate for your purpose, audience, and tone; add points that didn't originally occur to you. Star or circle compelling items that warrant further development. Then draw arrows between related items, your goal being to group such material under a common heading. Finally, determine what seems to be the best order for those headings.

By giving you a sense of the way your free-form material might fit together, a scratch outline makes the writing process more manageable. You're less likely to feel overwhelmed once you actually start writing because you'll already have some idea about how to shape your material into a meaningful statement. Remember, though, the scratch outline can, and most likely will, be modified along the way.

The following scratch outline shows how Harriet Davids began to shape her brainstorming (page 23) into a more organized format. Note the way she eliminated some items (for example, the points about outrageous prices and about real-life TV violence), added others (for example, the places to go that distract from homework), and grouped the brainstormed items under four main headings, with the appropriate details listed underneath. (If you'd like to see Harriet's more formal outline and her first draft, turn to pages 43–45 and 58–59.)

Limited Subject: The special problems that parents face raising children today.

1. Day care for two-career families
    • Expensive
    • Before-school problems
    • After-school problems

2. Distractions from homework
    • Internet, television, cellphones, MP3s
    • Places to go—malls, movies, fast-food restaurants

3. Sexually explicit materials
   - Internet
   - Television shows
   - Movies
   - Magazines

4. Life-threatening dangers
   - Drugs
   - Drinking
   - AIDS
   - Violence against children (by sitters, in day care, etc.)

The prewriting strategies just described provide a solid foundation for the next stages of your work. But invention and imaginative exploration don't end when prewriting is completed. As you'll see, remaining open to new ideas is crucial during all phases of the writing process.

Activities: Prewrite

1. Number the items in each set from 1 (*broadest subject*) to 5 (*most limited subject*):

Set A	**Set B**
Abortion	Business majors
Controversial social issue	Students' majors
Cutting state abortion funds	College students
Federal funding of abortions	Kinds of students on campus
Social issues	Why many students major in business

2. Which of the following topics are too broad for an essay of two to five typewritten pages: soap operas' appeal to college students; day care; trying to "kick" the junk-food habit; male and female relationships; international terrorism?

3. Use the techniques indicated in parentheses to limit each general topic listed below. Then, identify a specific purpose, audience, and tone for the one limited subject you consider most interesting. Next, with the help of the patterns of development, generate raw material about that limited subject. (You may find it helpful to work with others when developing this material.) Finally, shape your raw material into a scratch outline—crossing out, combining, and adding ideas as needed. (Save your scratch outline so you can work with it further after reading about the next stage in the writing process.)

   Friendship (*journal writing*)
   Malls (*mapping*)
   Leisure (*freewriting*)
   Television (*brainstorming*)
   Required courses (*group brainstorming*)
   Manners (*questioning*)

STAGE 2: IDENTIFY THE THESIS

The process of prewriting—discovering a limited subject and generating ideas about it—prepares you for the next stage in writing an essay: identifying the paper's *thesis*, or controlling idea. Presenting your opinion on a subject, the thesis should focus on an interesting and significant issue, one that engages your energies and merits your consideration. You may think of the thesis as the essay's hub—the central point around which all the other material revolves. Your thesis determines what does and does not belong in the essay. The thesis, especially when it occurs early in an essay, also helps focus the reader on the piece's central point.

Sometimes the thesis emerges early in the prewriting stage. Often, though, you'll need to do some work to determine your thesis. For some topics, you may need to do some library research. For others, the best way to identify a promising thesis is to look through your prewriting and ask yourself questions such as these: "What statement does all this prewriting support? What aspect of the limited subject is covered in most detail? What is the focus of the most provocative material?"

For a look at the process of finding the thesis within prewriting material, glance back at the scratch outline (page 26–27) that Harriet Davids prepared for the limited subject "The special problems that parents face raising children today." Harriet devised the following thesis to capture the focus of this prewriting: "Being a parent today is much more difficult than it was a generation ago." (The full outline for Harriet's paper appears on pages 43–45; the first draft on pages 58–59; the final draft on pages 66–68.)

Writing an Effective Thesis

Generally expressed in one or two sentences, a thesis statement often has two parts. One part presents the *limited subject;* the other gives your *point of view,* or *attitude,* about that subject. Here are some examples of moving from general subject to limited subject to thesis statement. In each thesis statement, the limited subject is underlined once and the attitude twice.

General Subject	Limited Subject	Thesis
Education	Computers in elementary school arithmetic classes	Computer programs in arithmetic can individualize instruction more effectively than the average elementary school teacher can.

(Continued)

Transportation	A metropolitan transit system	Although the <u>city's transit system</u> still has problems, it <u>has become safer and more efficient in the last two years.</u>
Work	College internships	College internships <u>provide valuable opportunities to students uncertain about what to do after graduation.</u>
Our anti-child world	Special problems that parents face raising children today	Being a parent today <u>is much more difficult than it was a generation ago.</u>

(*Reminder:* The last thesis statement is Harriet Davids's, devised for the essay she planned to write for the assignment on page 12. Harriet's prewriting appears on pages 23 and 26–27, and her first draft on pages 58–59.)

Avoiding Thesis Pitfalls

Because identifying your thesis statement is an important step in writing a sharply focused essay, you need to avoid three common problems that lead to an ineffective thesis.

Don't make an announcement.   Some writers use the thesis statement merely to announce the limited subject of their paper and forget to indicate their attitude toward the subject. Such statements are announcements of intent, not thesis statements.

Compare the following three announcements with the thesis statements beside them.

Announcements	Thesis Statements
My essay will discuss whether a student pub should exist on campus.	This college should not allow a student pub on campus.
Handgun legislation is the subject of this paper.	Banning handguns is the first step toward controlling crime in the United States.
I want to discuss cable television.	Cable television has not delivered on its promise to provide an alternative to network programming.

Don't make a factual statement.   Your thesis and thus your essay should focus on an issue capable of being developed. If a fact is used as a thesis, you have no place to go; a fact generally doesn't invite much discussion. Notice the difference between these factual statements and thesis statements:

Factual Statements	Thesis Statements
Many businesses pollute the environment.	Tax penalties should be levied against businesses that pollute the environment.
Nowadays, many movies are violent.	Movie violence provides a healthy outlet for aggression.
The population of the United States is growing older.	The aging of the U.S. population will eventually create a crisis in the delivery of health-care services.

Don't make a broad statement.   Avoid stating your thesis in vague, general, or sweeping terms. Broad statements make it difficult for readers to grasp your essay's point. Moreover, if you start with a broad thesis, you're saddled with the impossible task of trying to develop a book-length idea in an essay that runs only several pages.

The following examples contrast statements that are too broad with thesis statements that are focused effectively.

Broad Statements	Thesis Statements
Nowadays, high school education is often meaningless.	High school diplomas have been devalued by grade inflation.
Newspapers cater to the taste of the American public.	The success of *USA Today* indicates that people want newspapers that are easy to read and entertaining.
The computer revolution is not all that we have been led to believe it is.	Home computers are still an impractical purchase for many people.

The thesis is often stated near the beginning, but it may be delayed, especially if you need to provide background information before it can be understood. Sometimes the thesis is reiterated—with fresh words—in the essay's conclusion or elsewhere. You may even leave the thesis unstated, relying on strong evidence to convey the essay's central idea.

One final point: Once you start writing your first draft, some feelings, thoughts, and examples may emerge that qualify, even contradict, your initial thesis. Don't resist these new ideas; they frequently move you toward a clearer statement of your main point. Remember, though, your essay must have a thesis. Without this central concept, you have no reason for writing.

Activities: Identify the Thesis

1. For each of the following limited subjects, four possible thesis statements are given. Indicate whether each is an announcement (*A*), a factual statement (*FS*), too broad a statement (*TB*), or an effective thesis (*OK*). Then, for each effective thesis, identify a possible purpose, audience, and tone.

   Limited Subject: The ethics of treating severely handicapped infants

   Some babies born with severe handicaps have been allowed to die.

   There are many serious issues involved in the treatment of handicapped newborns.

   The government should pass legislation requiring medical treatment for handicapped newborns.

   This essay will analyze the controversy surrounding the treatment of severely handicapped babies who would die without medical care.

   Limited Subject: Privacy and computerized records

   Computers raise some significant and crucial questions for all of us.

   Computerized records keep track of consumer spending habits, credit records, travel patterns, and other personal information.

   Computerized records have turned our private lives into public property.

   In this paper, the relationship between computerized records and the right to privacy will be discussed.

2. Each of the following sets lists the key points in an essay. Using the information provided, prepare a possible thesis for each essay.

   Set A
   - One evidence of this growing conservatism is the reemerging popularity of fraternities and sororities.
   - Beauty contests, ROTC training, and corporate recruiting—once rejected by students on many campuses—are again popular.
   - Most important, many students no longer choose risky careers that enable them to contribute to society but select, instead, safe fields with money-making potential.

   Set B
   - We do not know how engineering new forms of life might affect the earth's delicate ecological balance.
   - Another danger of genetic research is its potential for unleashing new forms of disease.
   - Even beneficial attempts to eliminate genetic defects could contribute to the dangerous idea that only perfect individuals are entitled to live.

3. Following are four pairs of general and limited subjects. Generate an appropriate thesis statement for each pair. Select one thesis, and determine which

pattern of development would support it most effectively. Use that pattern to draft a paragraph developing the thesis. (Save the paragraph so you can work with it further after reading about the next stage in the writing process.)

General Subject	Limited Subject
Psychology	The power struggles in a classroom
Health	Doctors' attitudes toward patients
U.S. politics	Television's coverage of presidential campaigns
Work	Minimum-wage jobs for young people

4. Return to the scratch outline you prepared for activity 3 on page 27. After examining the outline, identify a thesis that conveys the central idea behind most of the raw material. Then, ask others to evaluate your thesis in light of the material in the outline. Finally, keeping the thesis—as well as your purpose, audience, and tone—in mind, refine the scratch outline by deleting inappropriate items, adding relevant ones, and indicating where more material is needed. (Save your refined scratch outline and thesis so you can work with them further after reading about the next stage in the writing process.)

STAGE 3: SUPPORT THE THESIS WITH EVIDENCE

Supporting material grounds your essay, showing readers you have good reason for feeling as you do about your subject. Your evidence also adds interest and color to your writing. In college essays of five hundred to fifteen hundred words, you usually need at least three major points of evidence to develop your thesis. These major points—each focusing on related but separate aspects of the thesis—eventually become the supporting paragraphs in the body of the essay.

What Is Evidence?

By *evidence*, we mean a number of different kinds of support. *Examples* are just one option. To develop your thesis, you might also include *reasons, facts, details, statistics, anecdotes,* and *quotations from experts.* Imagine you're writing an essay with the thesis "People normally unconcerned about the environment can be galvanized to constructive action if they feel personally affected by an environmental problem." You could support this thesis with any combination of the following types of evidence:

- *Examples* of successful recycling efforts in several neighborhoods.
- *Reasons* why people got involved in a neighborhood recycling effort.
- *Facts* about other residents' efforts to preserve the quality of their well water.

- *Details* about the steps that people can take to get involved in environmental issues.
- *Statistics* showing the number of Americans concerned about the environment.
- An *anecdote* about your involvement in environmental efforts.
- A *quotation* from a well-known scientist about the impact that citizens can have on environmental legislation.

Where Do You Find Evidence?

Where do you find the examples, anecdotes, details, and other types of evidence needed to support your thesis? As you saw when you followed Harriet Davids's strategies for gathering material for an essay (pages 22–26), a good deal of evidence is generated during the prewriting stage. In this phase of the writing process, you tap into your personal experiences, draw upon other people's observations, perhaps interview a person with special knowledge about your subject. The library, with its abundant material, is another rich source of supporting evidence. In addition, the various patterns of development are a valuable source of evidence.

How the Patterns of Development Help Generate Evidence

On pages 24–25, we discussed the way patterns of development help generate material about a limited subject. The same patterns also help develop support for a thesis. The following chart shows how three patterns can generate evidence for this thesis: "To those who haven't done it, babysitting looks easy. In practice, though, babysitting can be difficult, frightening, even dangerous."

Pattern	Evidence Generated
Division-classification	A typical babysitting evening divided into stages: playing with the kids; putting them to bed; dealing with their nighttime fears once they're in bed
	Kids' nighttime fears classified by type: monsters under their beds; bad dreams; being abandoned by their parents
Process analysis	Step-by-step account of what a babysitter should do if a child becomes ill or injured
Comparison-contrast	Contrast between two babysitters: one well-prepared, the other unprepared

(For more on ways to use the patterns of development in different phases of the writing process, see pages 24–25, 40–41, and 430–432.)

Characteristics of Evidence

No matter how it is generated, all types of supporting evidence share the characteristics described in the following sections. You should keep these characteristics in mind as you review your thesis and scratch outline. That way, you can make the changes needed to strengthen the evidence gathered earlier. As you'll see shortly, Harriet Davids focused on many of these issues as she worked with the evidence she collected during the prewriting phase.

The evidence is relevant and unified.   All the evidence in an essay must clearly support the thesis. It makes no difference how riveting material might be; if it doesn't *relate directly* to the essay's central point, the material should be eliminated. Irrelevant material can weaken your position by implying that no relevant support exists. It also distracts readers from your controlling idea, thus disrupting the paper's overall unity.

The following paragraph, from an essay on changes in Americans' television-viewing habits, focuses on people's reasons for switching from network to cable television. As you'll see, the paragraph lacks unity because it contains points (underlined) unrelated to its main idea. Specifically, the comments about cable's foul language should be deleted. Although these observations bring up interesting points, they shift the paragraph's focus from reasons to objections. If the writer wants to present a balanced view of the pros and cons of cable and network television, these points *should* be covered, but in *another paragraph*.

Nonunified Support

Many people consider cable TV an improvement over network television. For one thing, viewers usually prefer the movies on cable. Unlike network films, cable movies are often only months old, they have not been edited by censors, and they are not interrupted by commercials. Growing numbers of people also feel that cable specials are superior to the ones the networks grind out. Cable viewers may enjoy such pop stars as Billy Joel, Mariah Carey, or Chris Rock in concert, whereas the networks continue to broadcast tired variety shows and boring awards ceremonies. There is, however, one problem with cable comedians. The foul language many of them use makes it hard to watch these cable specials with children. The networks, in contrast, generally present "clean" shows that parents and children can watch together. Then, too, cable TV offers viewers more flexibility since it schedules shows at various times over the month. People working night shifts or attending evening classes can see movies in the afternoon, and viewers missing the first twenty minutes of a show can always catch them later. It's not surprising that cable viewership is growing while network ratings have taken a plunge.

Early in the writing process, Harriet Davids was aware of the importance of relevant evidence. Take a moment to compare Harriet's brainstorming (page 23) and her scratch outline (page 26–27). Even though Harriet hadn't identified her thesis when she prepared the scratch outline, she realized she should delete a number of items from her brainstorming—for example, the second item and third-to-last item ("prices of everything outrageous" and "schools doing too much"). Harriet eliminated these points because they weren't consistent with the focus of her limited subject.

The evidence is specific.   When evidence is vague and general, readers lose interest in what you're saying, become skeptical of your ideas' validity, and feel puzzled about your meaning. In contrast, *specific, concrete evidence* provides sharp *word pictures* that engage your readers, persuade them that your thinking is sound, and clarify meaning.

Consider, for example, the differences between the following two sentences: "The young man had trouble lifting the box out of an old car" and "Joe, only twenty years old but severely weakened by a recent bout with the flu, struggled to lift the heavy wooden crate out of the rusty, dented Chevrolet." The first sentence, filled with generalities, is fuzzy and imprecise while the second sentence, filled with specifics, is crisp and clear.

As the preceding sentences illustrate, three strategies can be used, singly or in combination, to make writing specific. First, you can provide answers to *who, which, what,* and similar *questions.* (The question "How does the car look?" prompts a change in which "an old car" becomes "a rusty, dented Chevrolet.") Second, you can use *vigorous verbs* ("had trouble lifting" becomes "struggled to lift"). Finally, you can replace *vague, abstract* nouns with *vivid, concrete* nouns or phrases ("the young man" becomes "Joe, only twenty years old but severely weakened by a recent bout with the flu").

Following are two versions of a paragraph from an essay about trends in the business community. Although both paragraphs focus on one such trend—flexible working hours—note how the first version's bland language fails to engage the reader and how its vague generalities leave the meaning unclear. What, for example, is meant by the term "flex-time scheduling"? The second paragraph answers this question (as well as several others) with clear specifics; it also uses strong, energetic language. As a result, the second paragraph is more informative and more interesting than the first.

Nonspecific Support

More and more companies have begun to realize that flex-time scheduling offers advantages. Several companies outside Boston have tried flex-time scheduling and are pleased with the way the system reduces the difficulties their employees face getting to work. Studies show that flex-time scheduling also increases productivity, reduces on-the-job conflict, and minimizes work-related accidents.

Specific Support

More and more companies have begun to realize that flex-time scheduling offers advantages over a rigid 9-to-5 routine. Along suburban Boston's Route 128, such companies as Compugraphics and Consolidated Paper now permit employees to schedule their arrival any time between 6 A.M. and 11 A.M. The corporations report that the number of rush-hour jams and accidents has fallen dramatically. As a result, employees no longer arrive at work weighed down by tension induced by choking clouds of exhaust fumes and the blaring horns of gridlocked drivers. Studies sponsored by the journal *Business Quarterly* show that this more mellow state of mind benefits corporations. Traffic-stressed employees begin their workday anxious and exasperated, still grinding their teeth at their fellow commuters, their frustration often spilling over into their performance at work. By contrast, stress-free employees work more productively and take fewer days off. They are more tolerant of coworkers and customers, and less likely to balloon minor irritations into major confrontations. Perhaps most importantly, employees arriving at work relatively free of stress can focus their attention on working safely. They rack up significantly fewer on-the-job accidents, such as falls and injuries resulting from careless handling of dangerous equipment. Flex-time improves employee well-being, and as well-being rises, so do company profits.

 At this point, it will be helpful to compare once again Harriet Davids's brainstorming (page 23) and her scratch outline (page 26–27). Note the way she added new details in the outline to make her evidence more specific. For example, to the item "Distractions from homework," she added the new examples "malls," "movies," and "fast-food restaurants." And, as you'll see when you read Harriet's first and final drafts (pages 58–59 and 66–68), she added many more vigorous specifics during later stages of the writing process.

The evidence is adequate.   Readers won't automatically accept your thesis; you need to provide *enough specific evidence* to support your viewpoint. On occasion, a single extended example will suffice. Generally, though, you'll need various kinds of evidence: facts, examples, reasons, personal observations, expert opinion, and so on.

Following are two versions of a paragraph from a paper showing how difficult it is to get personal, attentive service nowadays at gas stations, supermarkets, and department stores. Both paragraphs focus on the problem at gas stations, but one paragraph is much more effective. As you'll see, the first paragraph starts with good, specific support, yet fails to provide enough of it. The second paragraph offers additional examples, descriptive details, and dialogue—all of which make the writing stronger and more convincing.

Inadequate Support

Gas stations are a good example of this impersonal attitude. At many stations, attendants have even stopped pumping gas. Motorists pull up to a combination convenience store and gas island where an attendant is enclosed in a glass booth with a tray for taking money. The driver must get out of the car, pump the gas, and walk over to the booth to pay. That's a real inconvenience, especially when compared with the way service stations used to be run.

Adequate Support

Gas stations are a good example of this impersonal attitude. At many stations, attendants have even stopped pumping gas. Motorists pull up to a combination convenience store and gas island where an attendant is enclosed in a glass booth with a tray for taking money. The driver must get out of the car, pump the gas, and walk over to the booth to pay. Even at stations that still have "pump jockeys," employees seldom ask, "Check your oil?" or wash windshields, although they may grudgingly point out the location of the bucket and squeegee. And customers with a balky engine or a nonfunctioning heater are usually out of luck. Why? Many gas stations have eliminated on-duty mechanics. The skillful mechanic who could replace a belt or fix a tire in a few minutes has been replaced by a teenager in a jumpsuit who doesn't know a carburetor from a charge card and couldn't care less.

Now take a final look at Harriet Davids's scratch outline (pages 26–27). Harriet realized she needed more than one block of supporting material to develop her limited subject; that's why she identified four separate blocks of evidence (day care, homework distractions, sexual material, and dangers). When Harriet prepared her first and final drafts (pages 58–59 and 66–68), she decided to eliminate the material about day care. But she added so many more specific and dramatic details that her evidence was more than sufficient.

The evidence is accurate.   When you have a strong belief and want readers to see things your way, you may be tempted to overstate or downplay facts, disregard information, misquote, or make up details. Suppose you plan to write an essay making the point that dormitory security is lax. You begin supporting your thesis by narrating the time you were nearly mugged in your dorm hallway. Realizing the essay would be more persuasive if you also mentioned other episodes, you decide to invent some material. Perhaps you describe several supposed burglaries on your dorm floor or exaggerate the amount of time it took campus security to respond to an emergency call from a residence hall. Yes, you've supported your point—but at the expense of truth.

The evidence is representative.   Using representative evidence means that you rely on the typical, the usual, to show that your point is valid. Contrary to the maxim, exceptions don't prove the rule. Perhaps you plan to write an essay contending that the value of seat belts has been exaggerated. To support your position, you mention a friend who survived a head-on collision without wearing a seat belt. Such an example isn't representative because the facts and figures on accidents suggest your friend's survival was a fluke.

Borrowed evidence is documented.   If you include evidence from outside sources (books, articles, interviews), you need to acknowledge where that information comes from. If you don't, readers may consider your evidence nothing more than your point of view, or they may regard as dishonest your failure to cite your indebtedness to others for ideas that obviously aren't your own.

For help in documenting sources in brief, informal papers, turn to page 365. For information on acknowledging sources in longer, more formal papers, refer to Appendix A (pages 451–482).

Strong supporting evidence is at the heart of effective writing. Without it, essays lack energy and fail to convey the writer's perspective. Such lifeless writing is more apt to put readers to sleep than to engage their interest and convince them that the points being made are valid. Taking the time to accumulate solid supporting material is, then, a critical step in the writing process.

Activities: Support the Thesis with Evidence

1. Each of the following sets includes a thesis statement and four points of support. In each set, identify the one point that is off target.

   Set A

   Thesis: Colleges should put less emphasis on sports.

   Encourages grade fixing
   Creates a strong following among former graduates
   Distracts from real goals of education
   Causes extensive and expensive injuries

   Set B

   Thesis: The United States is becoming a homogenized country.
   Regional accents vanishing
   Chain stores blanket country
   Americans proud of their ethnic identities
   Metropolitan areas almost indistinguishable from one another

2. For each of the following thesis statements, develop three points of relevant support. Then use the patterns of development to generate evidence for each point of support.

   Thesis: The trend toward disposable, throwaway products has gone too far.

Thesis: The local (or college) library fails to meet the needs of those it is supposed to serve.

Thesis: Television portrays men as incompetent creatures.

3. Choose one of the following thesis statements. Then identify an appropriate purpose, audience, and tone for an essay with this thesis. Using freewriting, mapping, or the questioning technique, generate at least three supporting points for the thesis. Last, write a paragraph about one of the points, making sure your evidence reflects the characteristics discussed in these pages. Alternatively, you may go ahead and prepare the first draft of an essay having the selected thesis. (If you choose the second option, you may want to turn to page 57 to see a diagram showing how to organize a first draft.) Save whatever you prepare so you can work with it further after reading about the next stage in the writing process.

    • Winning the lottery may not always be a blessing.
    • All of us can take steps to reduce the country's trash crisis.
    • Drug education programs in public schools are (or are not) effective.

4. Select one of the following thesis statements. Then determine your purpose, audience, and tone for an essay with this thesis. Next, use the patterns of development to generate at least three supporting points for the thesis. Finally, write a paragraph about one of the points, making sure that your evidence demonstrates the characteristics discussed in these pages. Alternatively, you may go ahead and prepare a first draft of an essay having the thesis selected. (If you choose the latter option, you may want to turn to page 57 to see a diagram showing how to organize a first draft.) Save whatever you prepare so you can work with it further after reading about the next stage in the writing process.

    • Teenagers should (or should not) be able to obtain birth control devices without their parents' permission.
    • The college's system for awarding student loans needs to be overhauled.
    • E-mail has changed for the worse (or the better) the way Americans communicate with each other.

5. Retrieve the paragraph you wrote in response to activity 3 on pages 31–32. Keeping in mind the characteristics of effective evidence discussed in pages 34–38, make whatever changes are needed to strengthen the paragraph. (Save the paragraph so you can work with it further after reading about the next stage in the writing process.)

6. Look at the thesis and refined scratch outline you prepared in response to activity 4 on page 32. Where do you see gaps in the support for your thesis? By brainstorming with others, generate material to fill these gaps. If some of the new points generated suggest that you should modify your thesis, make the appropriate changes now. (Save this material so you can work with it further after reading about the next stage in the writing process.)

STAGE 4: ORGANIZE THE EVIDENCE

After you've generated supporting evidence, you're ready to *organize* that material. Even highly compelling evidence won't illustrate the validity of your thesis or achieve your purpose if readers have to plow through a maze of chaotic evidence. Some writers can move quickly from generating support to writing a clearly structured first draft. (They usually say they have sequenced their ideas in their heads.) Most, however, need to spend some time sorting out their thoughts on paper before starting the first draft; otherwise, they tend to lose their way in a tangle of ideas.

When moving to the organizing stage, you should have in front of you your scratch outline (see pages 26–27) and thesis plus any supporting material you've accumulated. To find a logical framework for all this material, you'll need to

- Determine which pattern of development is implied in your evidence.
- Select one of four basic approaches for organizing your evidence.
- Outline your evidence.

Use the Patterns of Development

Each pattern of development (see pages 24–25) has its own internal logic that makes it appropriate for some writing purposes but not for others. Once you see which pattern (or combination of patterns) is implied by your purpose, you can block out your paper's general structure. Imagine that you're writing an essay *explaining why* some students drop out of college during the first semester. You might organize the essay around a three-part discussion of the key *causes* contributing to the difficulty that students have adjusting to college: (1) they miss friends and family, (2) they take inappropriate courses, and (3) they experience conflicts with roommates. As you can see, your choice of pattern of development significantly influences your essay's content and organization.

Some essays follow a single pattern, but most blend them with a predominant pattern providing the piece's organizational framework. In our example essay, you might include a brief *description* of an overwhelmed first-year college student; you might *define* the psychological term "separation anxiety"; you might end the paper by briefly explaining a *process* for making students' adjustment to college easier. Still, the essay's overall organizational pattern would be *cause-effect* since the paper's primary purpose is to explain why students drop out of college. (For more information on the way patterns often blend in writing, see Chapter 12, "Combining the Patterns.")

Although writers often combine the patterns of development, writing an essay organized according to a single pattern can help you understand a particular pattern's unique demands. Keep in mind, though, that most writing begins not with a specific pattern but with a specific *purpose*. The pattern or combination of patterns evolves out of that purpose.

Select an Organizational Approach

No matter which pattern(s) of development you select, you need to know four general approaches for organizing supporting evidence—chronological, spatial, emphatic, and simple-to-complex.

Chronological approach. When an essay is organized *chronologically*, supporting material is arranged in a clear time sequence, usually starting with what happened first and ending with what happened last. Occasionally, chronological sequences can be rearranged to create flashback or flashforward effects, two techniques are discussed in Chapter 4 on narration. Essays using narration (for example, an experience with prejudice) or process analysis (for instance, how to deliver an effective speech) are most likely to be organized chronologically. The paper on public speaking might use a time sequence to present its points: how to prepare a few days before the presentation is due; what to do right before the speech; what to concentrate on during the speech itself. (For examples of chronologically arranged student essays, turn to pages 121 and 232.)

Spatial approach. When you arrange supporting evidence *spatially*, you discuss details as they occur in space, or from certain locations. This strategy is particularly appropriate for description. Imagine that you plan to write an essay describing the happy times you spent as a child playing by a towering old oak tree in the neighborhood park. Using spatial organization, you start by describing the rich animal life (the plump earthworms, swarming anthills, and numerous animal tracks) you observed while hunkered down *at the base* of the tree. Next, you re-create the contented feeling you experienced sitting on a branch *in the middle* of the tree. Finally, you end by describing the glorious view of the world you had *from the top* of the tree.

Although spatial arrangement is flexible (you could, for instance, start with a description from the top of the tree), you should always proceed systematically. And once you select a particular spatial order, you should usually maintain that sequence throughout the essay; otherwise, readers may get lost along the way. (A spatially arranged student essay appears on page 80.)

Emphatic approach. In *emphatic* order, the most compelling evidence is saved for last. This arrangement is based on the psychological principle that people remember best what they experience last. Emphatic order has built-in momentum because it starts with the least important point and builds to the most significant. This method is especially effective in argumentation-persuasion essays, in papers developed through examples, and in pieces involving comparison-contrast, division-classification, or causal analysis.

Consider an essay analyzing the negative effect that workaholic parents can have on their children. The paper might start with a brief discussion of relatively minor effects such as the family's eating mostly frozen or takeout foods. Paragraphs on more serious effects might follow: children get no parental help with homework; they try to resolve personal problems without parental advice. Finally, the essay might close with a detailed discussion of the most significant effect—children's lack of self-esteem because they feel unimportant in their parents' lives. (The student essays on pages 156, 267, and 331 all use an emphatic arrangement.)

Simple-to-complex approach.   A final way to organize an essay is to proceed from relatively *simple* concepts to more *complex* ones. By starting with easy-to-grasp, generally accepted evidence, you establish rapport with your readers and assure them that the essay is firmly grounded in shared experience. In contrast, if you open with difficult or highly technical material, you risk confusing and alienating your audience.

Assume you plan to write a paper arguing that your college has endangered students' health by not making an all-out effort to remove asbestos from dormitories and classroom buildings. It probably wouldn't be a good idea to begin with a medically sophisticated explanation of precisely how asbestos damages lung tissue. Instead, you might start with an observation that is likely to be familiar to your readers—one that is part of their everyday experience. You could, for example, open with a description of asbestos—as readers might see it—wrapped around air ducts and furnaces or used as electrical insulation and fireproofing material. Having provided a basic, easy-to-visualize description, you could then go on to explain the complicated process by which asbestos can cause chronic lung inflammation. (See page 300 for an example of a student essay using the simple-to-complex arrangement.)

 Depending on your purpose, any one of these four organizational approaches might be appropriate. For example, assume that you planned to write an essay developing Harriet Davids's thesis: "Being a parent today is much more difficult than it was a generation ago." To emphasize that the various stages in children's lives present parents with different difficulties, you'd probably select a *chronological* sequence. To show that the challenges that parents face vary depending on whether children are at home, at school, or in the world at large, you'd probably choose a *spatial* sequence. To stress the range of problems that parents face (from less to more serious), you'd probably use an *emphatic* sequence. To illustrate today's confusing array of theories for raising children, you might take a *simple-to-complex* approach, moving from the basic to the most sophisticated theories.

Prepare an Outline

Having an outline—a skeletal version of your paper—*before* you begin the first draft makes the writing process much more manageable. The outline helps you organize your thoughts beforehand, and it guides your writing as you work on the draft. Even though ideas continue to evolve during the draft, an outline clarifies how ideas fit together, which points are major, which should come first, and so on. An outline may also reveal places where evidence is weak, underscoring the need, perhaps, for more prewriting.

Some people prepare highly structured outlines; others make only a few informal jottings. Sometimes outlining will go quickly, with points falling easily into place; at other times you'll have to work hard to figure out how points are related. If that happens, be glad you caught the problem while outlining rather than while writing the first draft.

To prepare an effective outline, you should reread and evaluate your scratch outline and thesis as well as any other evidence you've generated since the prewriting stage. Then decide which pattern of development (description, cause-effect, and so on) seems to be suggested by your evidence. Also determine whether your evidence lends itself to a chronological, a spatial, an emphatic, or a simple-to-complex order. Having done all that, you're ready to identify and sequence your main and supporting points.

The amount of detail in an outline will vary according to the paper's length and the instructor's requirements. A scratch outline (like the one on pages 26–27) is often sufficient, but for longer papers, you'll probably need a more detailed and formal outline. In such cases, the suggestions in the accompanying checklist will help you develop a sound plan. Feel free to modify these guidelines to suit your needs.

✔ OUTLINING: A CHECKLIST

❏ Write your purpose, audience, tone, and thesis at the top.

❏ Below the thesis, enter the pattern of development you've chosen.

❏ Record the organizational approach you've selected.

❏ Delete from your supporting material anything that doesn't develop the thesis or that isn't appropriate for your purpose, audience, and tone.

❏ Add any new points or material. Group related items together. Give each group a heading that represents a main topic in support of your thesis.

❏ Label these main topics with roman numerals (I, II, III, and so on). Let the order of the numerals indicate the best sequence.

- ❏ Identify subtopics and group them under the appropriate main topics. Indent and label these subtopics with capital letters (A, B, C, and so on). Let the order of the letters indicate the best sequence.

- ❏ Identify supporting points (often, reasons and examples) and group them under the appropriate subtopics. Indent and label these supporting points with arabic numbers (1, 2, 3, and so on). Let the numbers indicate the best sequence.

- ❏ Identify specific details (secondary examples, facts, statistics, expert opinions, quotations) and group them under the appropriate supporting points. Indent and label these specific details with lowercase letters (a, b, c, and so on). Let the letters indicate the best sequence.

- ❏ Examine your outline, looking for places where evidence is weak. Where appropriate, add new evidence.

- ❏ Double-check that all main topics, subtopics, supporting points, and specific details develop some aspect of the thesis. Also confirm that all items are arranged in the most logical order.

The sample outline that follows develops the thesis "Being a parent today is much more difficult than it was a generation ago"—the thesis that Harriet Davids devised for the essay she planned to write in response to the assignment on page 12. Harriet's scratch list appears on pages 26–27. When you compare Harriet's scratch list and outline, you'll find some differences. On the whole, the outline contains more specifics, but it doesn't include all the material in the scratch list. For example, after reconsidering her purpose, audience, tone, and thesis, Harriet decided to omit from her outline the section on day care and the point about AIDS.

The plan shown below is called a *topic outline* because it uses phrases, or topics, for each entry. For a lengthier or more complex paper, a *sentence outline* would be more appropriate.

Purpose: To inform

Audience: Instructor as well as class members, most of whom are 18–20 years old

Tone: Serious and straightforward

Thesis: Being a parent today is much more difficult than it was a generation ago.

Pattern of development: Exemplification

Organizational approach: Emphatic order

  I. Distractions from homework
    A. At home
      1. MP3 players

      2. Computers—Internet, computer games
      3. Television
   B. Outside home
      1. Malls
      2. Movie theaters
      3. Fast-food restaurants
II. Sexually explicit materials
   A. Internet
      1. Easy-to-access adult chat rooms
      2. Easy-to-access pornographic websites
   B. In print and in movies
      1. Sex magazines
         a. *Playboy*
         b. *Penthouse*
      2. Casual sex
   C. On television
      1. Soap operas
      2. R-rated comedians
      3. R-rated movies on cable
III. Increased dangers
   A. Drugs—peer pressure
   B. Alcohol—peer pressure
   C. Violent crimes against children

(If you'd like to see the first draft that resulted from Harriet's outline, turn to pages 58–59. Hints for moving from an outline to a first draft appear on page 47.)

Before starting to write your first draft, show your outline to several people (your instructor, friends, classmates) for their reactions, especially about areas needing additional work. After making whatever changes are needed, you're in a good position to go ahead and write the first draft of your essay.

Activities: Organize the Evidence

1. The thesis statement below is followed by a scrambled list of supporting points. Prepare an outline for a potential essay, making sure to distinguish between major and secondary points.

   Thesis: Our schools, now in crisis, could be improved in several ways.

   Certification requirements for teachers
   Schedules
   Teachers
   Longer school year
   Merit pay for outstanding teachers
   Curriculum

Better textbooks for classroom use
Longer school days
More challenging content in courses

2. Assume you plan to write an essay based on the following brief outline, which consists of a thesis and several points of support. Determine which pattern of development (page 40) you would probably use for the essay's overall framework. Also identify which organizational approach (pages 41–42) you would most likely adopt to sequence the points of support listed. Then, use one or more patterns of development to generate material to support those points. Having done that, review the material generated, deleting, adding, combining, and arranging ideas in logical order. Finally, make an outline for the body of the essay. (Save your outline so you can work with it further after reading about the next stage in the writing process.)

Thesis: Friends of the opposite sex fall into one of several categories: the pal, the confidant, or the pest.

- Frequently, an opposite-sex friend is simply a "pal."
- Sometimes, though, a pal turns, step by step, into a confidant.
- If a confidant begins to have romantic thoughts, he or she may become a pest, thus disrupting the friendship.

3. Retrieve the writing you prepared in response to activity 3, 4, or 5 on page 39. As needed, reshape that material, applying the organizational principles discussed in these pages. Be sure, for example, that you select the approach (chronological, spatial, emphatic, or simple-to-complex) that would be most appropriate, given your main idea, purpose, audience, and tone. (Save whatever you prepare so you can work with it further after reading about the next stage in the writing process.)

4. Look again at the thesis and scratch outline you refined and elaborated in response to activity 6 on page 39. Reevaluate this material by deleting, adding, combining, and rearranging ideas as needed. Also, keeping your purpose, audience, and tone in mind, consider whether a chronological, a spatial, an emphatic, or a simple-to-complex approach will be most appropriate. Now prepare an outline of your ideas. Finally, ask at least one person to evaluate your organizational plan. (Save your outline. After reading about the next stage in the writing process, you can use it to write the essay's first draft.)

STAGE 5: WRITE THE FIRST DRAFT

Your *first draft*—a rough, provisional version of your essay—may flow quite smoothly. But don't be discouraged if it doesn't. You may find that your thesis has to be reshaped, that a point no longer fits, that you need to return to a prewriting activity to generate additional material. Such stopping and starting is to be expected. Writing the first draft is a process of discovery, involving the continual clarification and refining of ideas.

How to Proceed

There's no single right way to prepare a first draft. Some writers rely heavily on their scratch lists or outlines; others glance at them only occasionally. Some people write in longhand; others use a computer.

However you choose to proceed, consider the suggestions in the following checklist when moving from an outline or scratch list to a first draft.

☑ TURNING OUTLINE INTO FIRST DRAFT: A CHECKLIST

❏ Make the outline's *main topics* (I, II, III) the *topic sentences* of the essay's supporting paragraphs. (Topic sentences are discussed later, on pages 48–49.)

❏ Make the outline's *subtopics* (A, B, C) the *subpoints* in each paragraph.

❏ Make the outline's *supporting points* (1, 2, 3) the key *examples* and *reasons* in each paragraph.

❏ Make the outline's *specific details* (a, b, c) the *secondary examples, facts, statistics, expert opinions,* and *quotations* in each paragraph.

(To see how Harriet Davids moved from outline to first draft, turn to pages 57–59.)
Although outlines and lists are valuable for guiding your work, don't be so dependent on them that you shy away from new ideas that surface during your writing of the first draft. If promising new thoughts pop up, jot them down in the margin. Then, at the appropriate point, go back and evaluate them: Do they support your thesis? Are they appropriate for your essay's purpose, audience, and tone? If so, go ahead and include the material in your draft.

It's easy to get bogged down while preparing the first draft if you try to edit as you write. Remember: A draft isn't intended to be perfect. For the time being, adopt a relaxed, noncritical attitude. Working as quickly as you can, don't stop to check spelling, correct grammar, or refine sentence structure. Save these tasks for later. One good way to help remind you that the first draft is tentative is to write in longhand using scrap paper and pencil. Writing on alternate lines also underscores your intention to revise later on, when the extra space will make it easier to add and delete material. Similarly, writing on only one side of the paper can prove helpful if, during revision, you decide to move a section to another part of the paper.

What should you do if you get stuck while writing your first draft? Stay calm and try to write something—no matter how awkward or imprecise it may seem. Just jot a reminder to yourself in the margin ("Fix this," "Redo," or "Ugh!") to fine-tune the section later. Or leave a blank space to hold a spot for the right words when they finally break loose. It may also help to reread—out loud is best—what you've already written. Regaining a sense of the larger context is often enough to get you moving again. You might also try talking your way through a troublesome section. By speaking aloud, you tap your natural oral fluency and put it to work in your writing.

If a section of the essay is particularly difficult, don't spend time struggling with it. Move on to an easier section, write that, and then return to the challenging part. If you're still getting nowhere, take a break. Watch television, listen to music, talk with friends. While you're relaxing, your thoughts may loosen up and untangle the knotty section.

Because you read essays from beginning to end, you may assume that writers work the same way, starting with the introduction and going straight through to the conclusion. Often, however, this isn't the case. In fact, since an introduction depends so heavily on everything that follows, it's usually best to write the introduction *after* the essay's body.

When preparing your first draft, you may find it helpful to follow this sequence:

1. Write the supporting paragraphs.
2. Connect ideas in the supporting paragraphs.
3. Write the introduction.
4. Write the conclusion.
5. Write the title.

Write the Supporting Paragraphs

Drawn from the main sections in your outline or scratch list (I, II, III, etc.), each *supporting paragraph* should develop an aspect of your essay's thesis. A strong supporting paragraph is (1) often focused by a topic sentence and (2) organized around one or more patterns of development. As you write, keep in mind that you shouldn't expect your draft paragraphs to be perfect; you'll have a chance to revise them later on.

Use topic sentences.   Frequently, a *topic sentence* functions as a kind of mini-thesis for a supporting paragraph. Generally one or two sentences in length, the topic sentence usually appears at or near the beginning of the paragraph. However, it may also appear at the end, in the middle, or—with varied wording—several times within the paragraph.

The topic sentence states the paragraph's main idea while the other sentences in the paragraph provide support for this central point in the form of examples, facts, expert opinion, and so on. Like a thesis statement, the topic sentence *signals the paragraph's subject* and frequently *indicates the writer's attitude* toward that subject. In the topic sentences that follow, the subject of the paragraph is underlined once and the attitude toward that subject is underlined twice:

> Some students select a particular field of study for the wrong reasons.
> The ocean dumping of radioactive waste is a ticking time bomb.
> Several contemporary rock groups show unexpected sensitivity to social issues.
> Political candidates are sold like slickly packaged products.

As you work on the first draft, you may find yourself writing paragraphs without paying too much attention to topic sentences. That's fine, as long as you evaluate the paragraphs later on. When revising, you can provide a topic sentence for a paragraph that needs a sharper focus, recast a topic sentence for a paragraph that ended up taking an unexpected turn, even eliminate a topic sentence altogether if a paragraph's content is sufficiently unified to imply its point.

Use the patterns of development.   As you saw on page 40, an entire essay can be organized around one or more patterns of development (narration, process analysis, definition, and so forth). These patterns can also provide the organizational framework for an essay's supporting paragraphs. Assume you're writing an article for your town newspaper with the thesis "Year-round residents of an ocean community must take an active role in safeguarding the seashore environment." Your supporting paragraphs could develop this thesis through a variety of patterns, with each paragraph's topic sentence suggesting a specific pattern or combination of patterns. For example, one paragraph might start with the topic sentence "In a nearby ocean community, signs of environmental danger are everywhere" and go on to *describe* a seaside town with polluted waters, blighted trees, and diseased marine life. The next paragraph might have the topic sentence "Fortunately, not all seaside towns are plagued by such environmental problems" and continue by *contrasting* the troubled community with another, more ecologically sound shore town. A later paragraph, focused by the topic sentence "Residents can get involved in a variety of pro-environment activities," might use *division-classification* to elaborate on activities at the neighborhood, town, and municipal levels.

Connect Ideas in the Supporting Paragraphs

While writing the supporting paragraphs, you can try to smooth out the progression of ideas within and between paragraphs. In a *coherent* essay, the relationship between points is clear; readers can easily follow the development of your thoughts. (Sometimes, working on coherence causes a first draft to get bogged down; if this happens, move on, and wait until the revision stage to focus on such matters.)

The following paragraph lacks coherence for two main reasons. First, it sequences ideas improperly. (The idea about the toll attendants' being cut off from coworkers is introduced, dropped, then picked up again. References to motorists are similarly scattered throughout the paragraph.) Second, it doesn't indicate how individual ideas are related. (What, for example, is the connection between drivers who pass by without saying anything and attendants who have to work at night?)

Incoherent Support

Collecting tolls on the turnpike must be one of the loneliest jobs in the world. Each toll attendant sits in his or her booth, cut off from other attendants. Many drivers pass by each booth. None stays long enough for a brief "hello." Most don't acknowledge the attendant at all. Many toll attendants work at night, pushing them "out of synch" with the rest of the world. And sometimes the attendants have to deal with rude drivers who treat them like non-people, swearing at them for the long lines at the tollgate. Attendants also dislike how cut off they feel from their coworkers. Except for infrequent breaks, they have little chance to chat with each other and swap horror stories—small pleasures that would make their otherwise routine jobs bearable.

Coherent Support

Collecting tolls on the turnpike must be one of the loneliest jobs in the world. First of all, although many drivers pass by the attendants, none stays long enough for more than a brief "hello." Most drivers, in fact, don't acknowledge the toll collectors at all, with the exception of those rude drivers who treat the attendants like non-people, swearing at them for the long lines at the tollgate. Then, too, many toll attendants work at night, pushing them further "out of synch" with the rest of the world. Worst of all, attendants say, is how isolated they feel from their coworkers. Each attendant sits in his or her booth, cut off from other attendants. Except for infrequent breaks, they have little chance to chat with each other and swap horror stories—small pleasures that would make their otherwise routine jobs bearable.

To avoid the kinds of problems found in the incoherent paragraph, use—as the revised version does—two key strategies: (1) a clearly *chronological, spatial, emphatic* ("*Worst of all,* attendants say..."), or *simple-to-complex* approach and

(2) *signal devices* ("*First of all,* although many drivers pass by...") to show how ideas are connected. To review the four organizational approaches, see pages 41–42. The following paragraphs describe signal devices.

Once you determine a logical approach for presenting your points, you need to make sure readers can follow the progression of those points. Signal devices provide readers with cues, reminding them where they have been and indicating where they are going.

Aim to include some signals—however awkward or temporary—in your first draft. If you find you *can't,* that's probably a warning that your ideas may not be arranged logically. A light touch should be your goal with such signals. Too many call attention to themselves, making the essay mechanical and plodding. In any case, here are some signaling devices to consider.

1. Transitions.   Words and phrases that ease readers from one idea to another are called transitions. The following list gives a variety of such signals.

Time

first, before, earlier, next, then, now, immediately, at the same time, simultaneously, in the meantime, meanwhile, subsequently, afterward, after, finally, later eventually

Addition (or Sequence)

moreover; also; furthermore; in addition; first,... second,... third; one ... another; and; also; too; besides; next; finally; last

Space

above, below, next to, behind

Examples

for instance, for example, to illustrate, specifically, namely

Contrast

but, however, yet, in contrast, on the contrary, although, otherwise, conversely, despite, even though, on the one (other) hand, still, whereas, nevertheless, nonetheless

Comparison

similarly, in the same way, also, likewise, too, in comparison

Cause or Effects

because, as a result, consequently, therefore, then, so, since

Summary or Conclusion

therefore, thus, in short, in conclusion

Here's an earlier paragraph from this chapter. Note how the italicized transitions show readers how ideas fit together.

> *After* you've generated supporting evidence, you're ready to organize that material. Even highly compelling evidence won't illustrate the validity of your thesis or achieve your purpose if the readers have to plow through a maze of chaotic evidence. Some writers can move quickly from generating support to writing a clearly structured first draft. (They usually say they have sequenced their ideas in their heads.) Most, *however,* need to spend some time sorting out their thoughts on paper before starting the first draft; *otherwise,* they tend to lose their way in a tangle of ideas.

2. Bridging sentences.   Although bridging sentences may be used within a paragraph, they are more often used to move readers from one paragraph to the next. Look again at the first sentence in the preceding paragraph. Note that the sentence consists of two parts: The first part reminds readers that the previous discussion focused on techniques for generating evidence; the second part tells readers that the focus will now be the organization of such evidence.

3. Repeated words, synonyms, and pronouns.   The repetition of important words maintains continuity, reassures readers that they are on the right track, and highlights key ideas. Synonyms—words similar in meaning—also provide coherence, but without unimaginative and tedious repetitions. Finally, pronouns (*he, she, it, they, this, that*) enhance coherence by causing readers to think back to the original word the pronoun replaces (antecedent). When using pronouns, however, be sure there is no ambiguity about antecedents.

Reprinted here is another paragraph from this chapter. Repeated words have been underlined once, synonyms underlined twice, and pronouns printed in italic type to illustrate how these techniques were used to integrate the paragraph's ideas.

> The process of prewriting—discovering a limited subject and generating ideas about *it*—prepares you for the next stage in writing an essay: identifying the paper's thesis or controlling idea. Presenting your opinion on a subject, the thesis should focus on an interesting and significant issue, *one* that engages your energies and merits your consideration. You may think of the thesis as the essay's hub—the central point around which all the other material revolves. Your thesis determines what does and does not belong in the essay. The thesis, especially when *it* occurs early in an essay, also helps focus the reader on the piece's central point.

Write the Introduction

Many writers don't prepare an introduction until they have started to revise; others feel more comfortable if their first draft includes in basic form all parts of the final essay. If that's how you feel, you'll probably write the introduction as you complete your first draft. No matter when you prepare it, keep in mind how crucial the introduction is to your essay's success. Specifically, the introduction serves three distinct functions: It arouses readers' interest, introduces your subject, and presents your thesis.

The length of your introduction will vary according to your paper's scope and purpose. Most essays you write, however, will be served best by a one- or two-paragraph beginning. To write an effective introduction, use any of the following methods, singly or in combination. The thesis statement in each sample introduction is underlined.

Broad Statement Narrowing to a Limited Subject

For generations, morality has been molded primarily by parents, religion, and schools. Children traditionally acquired their ideas about what is right and wrong, which goals are important in life, and how other people should be treated from these three sources collectively. But in the past few decades, a single force—television—has undermined the beneficial influence that parents, religion, and school have on children's moral development. Indeed, television often implants in children negative values about sex, work, and family life.

Brief Anecdote

At a local high school recently, students in a psychology course were given a hint of what it is like to be the parents of a newborn. Each "parent" had to carry a raw egg around at all times to symbolize the responsibilities of parenthood. The egg could not be left alone; it limited the "parents'" activities; it placed a full-time emotional burden on "Mom" and "Dad." This class exercise illustrates a common problem facing the majority of new mothers and fathers. Most people receive little preparation for the job of being parents.

Idea That Is the Opposite of the One Developed

We hear a great deal about divorce's disastrous impact on children. We are deluged with advice on ways to make divorce as painless as possible for youngsters; we listen to heartbreaking stories about the confused, grieving children of divorced parents. Little attention has been paid, however, to a different kind of effect that divorce may have on children. Children from divorced families may become skilled manipulators, playing off one parent against the other, worsening an already painful situation.

Series of Short Questions

What happens if a child is caught vandalizing school property? What happens if a child goes for a joyride in a stolen car and accidentally hits a pedestrian? Should parents be liable for their children's mistakes? Should parents have to pay what might be hundreds of thousands of dollars in damages? Adults have begun to think seriously about such questions because the laws concerning the limits of parental responsibility are changing rapidly. With unfortunate frequency, courts have begun to hold parents legally and financially accountable for their children's misdeeds.

Quotation

Educator Neil Postman believes that television has blurred the line between childhood and adulthood. According to Postman, "All the secrets that a print culture kept from children . . . are revealed all at once by media that do not, and cannot, exclude any audience." This media barrage of information, once intended only for adults, has changed childhood for the worse.

Refutation of a Common Belief

Adolescents care only about material things; their lives revolve around brand-name sneakers, designer jeans, the latest fad in electronics. They resist education, don't read, barely know who is president, mainline rock 'n' roll, experiment with drugs, and exist on a steady diet of Ring-Dings, nachos, and beer. This is what many adults, including parents, seem to believe about the young. The reality is, however, that young people today show more maturity and common sense than most adults give them credit for.

Dramatic Fact or Statistic

Seventy percent of the respondents in a poll conducted by columnist Ann Landers stated that if they could live their lives over, they would choose not to have children. This startling statistic makes one wonder what these people believed parenthood would be like. Most parents, it seems, have unrealistic expectations about their children. Parents want their children to accept their values, follow their paths, and succeed where they failed.

Introductory paragraphs sometimes end with a *plan of development:* a quick preview of the essay's major points in the order in which those points will be discussed. The plan of development may be part of the thesis (as in the first sample introduction) or it may immediately follow the thesis (as in the last sample introduction). Because the plan of development outlines the essay's organizational structure, it helps prepare the reader for the essay's progression of ideas. In a brief essay, readers can often keep track of the ideas without this extra help. In a longer paper, though, a plan of development can be an effective unifying device since it highlights the main ideas the essay will develop.

Write the Conclusion

You may have come across essays that ended with jarring abruptness because they had no conclusions at all. Other papers may have had conclusions, but they sputtered to a weak close, a sure sign that the writers had run out of steam and wanted to finish as quickly as possible. Just as satisfying closes are an important part of everyday life (we feel cheated if dinner doesn't end with dessert or if a friend leaves without saying goodbye), a strong conclusion is an important part of an effective essay.

Generally one or two paragraphs, the conclusion should give the reader a feeling of completeness and finality. One way to achieve this sense of "rounding off" is to return to an image, idea, or anecdote from the introduction. Because people tend to remember most clearly the points they read last, the conclusion is also a good place to remind readers of your thesis. You may also use the conclusion to make a final point about your subject. Be careful, though, not to open an entirely new line of thought at the essay's close.

Illustrated briefly here are several strategies for writing sound conclusions. These techniques may be used singly or in combination. The first strategy, the summary conclusion, can be especially helpful in long, complex essays since readers may appreciate a review of your points. Tacked onto a short essay, though, a summary conclusion often seems boring and mechanical.

Summary

Contrary to what many adults think, most adolescents are not only aware of the important issues of the times but also deeply concerned about them. They are sensitive to the plight of the homeless, the destruction of the environment, and the pitfalls of rampant materialism. Indeed, today's young people are not less mature and sensible than their parents were. If anything, they are more so.

Prediction

The growing tendency on the part of the judicial system to hold parents responsible for the actions of their wayward children can have a disturbing impact on all of us. Parents will feel bitter toward their own children and cynical about a system that holds them accountable for the actions of minors. Children, continuing to escape the consequences of their actions, will become even more lawless and destructive. Society cannot afford two such possibilities.

Quotation

The comic W. C. Fields is reputed to have said, "Anyone who hates children and dogs can't be all bad." Most people do not share Fields's cynicism. Viewing childhood as a time of purity, they are alarmed at the way television exposes children to the seamy side of life, stripping youngsters of their innocence and giving them a glib sophistication that is a poor substitute for wisdom.

Statistic

Granted, divorce may, in some cases, be the best thing for families torn apart by parents who battle one another. However, in longitudinal studies of children from divorced families, psychologist Judith Wallerstein found that only 10 percent of the youngsters felt relief at their parents' divorce; the remaining 90 percent felt devastated. Such statistics surely call into question parents' claims that they are divorcing for their children's sake.

Recommendation or Call for Action

It is a mistake to leave parenting to instinct. Instead, we should make parenting skills a required course in schools. In addition, a nationwide hotline should be established to help parents deal with crises. Such training and continuing support would help adults deal more effectively with many of the problems they face as parents.

Write the Title

Some writers say that they began a certain piece with only a title in mind. But for most people, writing a title is a finishing touch. Although creating a title for your paper is usually one of the last steps in writing an essay, it shouldn't be done haphazardly. It may take time to write an effective title—one that hints at the essay's thesis and snares the reader's interest.

Good titles may make use of the following techniques: repetition of sounds ("The Border on Our Backs"); questions ("What Are Friends For?"); and humor ("When Mañana Is Too Soon"). More often, though, titles are straightforward phrases derived from the essay's subject or thesis: "Propaganda Techniques in Today's Advertising" and "The Cute Factor," for example.

Pull It All Together

Now that you know how to prepare a first draft, you might find it helpful to examine Figure 2.2 to see how the different parts of a draft can fit together. Keep in mind that not every essay you write will take this

FIGURE 2.2
Structure of an Essay

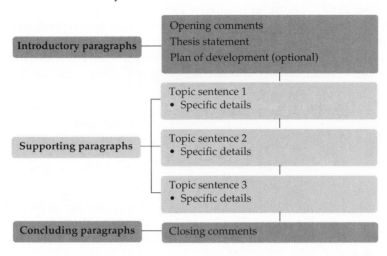

shape. As your purpose, audience, and tone change, so will your essay's structure. An introduction or conclusion, for instance, may be developed in more than one paragraph; the thesis statement may be implied or de-layed until the essay's middle or end; not all paragraphs may have topic sentences; and several supporting paragraphs may be needed to develop a single topic sentence. Even so, the basic format presented here offers a strategy for organizing a variety of writing assignments—from term papers to lab reports. Once you feel comfortable with the structure, you have a foundation on which to base your variations. (This book's student and professional essays illustrate some possibilities.) Even when using a specific format, you always have room to give your spirit and imagination free play. The language you use, the details you select, the perspective you offer are uniquely yours. They are what make your essay different from everyone else's.

Sample First Draft

Here is the first draft of Harriet Davids's essay. (The assignment and prewriting for the essay appear on pages 12, 21–23, and 26–27.) Harriet wrote the draft in one sitting. Working at a computer, she started by typing her thesis at the top of the first page. Then, following the guidelines on page 47, she moved the material in her outline (pages 44–45) to her draft. Harriet worked rapidly; she started with the first body paragraph and wrote straight through to the last supporting paragraph.

By moving quickly, Harriet got down her essay's basic text rather easily. Once she felt she had captured in rough form what she wanted to say, she reread her draft to get a sense of how she might open and close the essay. Then she drafted her introduction and conclusion; both appear here, together with the body of the essay. The commentary following the draft will give you a clearer sense of how Harriet proceeded. (Note that the marginal annotations reflect Harriet's comments to herself about areas she needs to address when revising her first draft.)

Challenges for Today's Parents
by Harriet Davids

Thesis: Being a parent today is much more difficult than it was a generation ago.

Raising children used to be much simpler in the '50s and '60s. I remember TV images from that era showing that parenting involved simply teaching kids to clean their rooms, do their homework, and _____.But being a parent today is much more difficult because nowadays parents have to shield/protect kids from lots of things, like distractions from schoolwork, from sexual material, from dangerous situations.

Add specifics

Parents have to control all the new distractions/ temptations that turn kids away from schoolwork. These days many kids have stereos, computers, and televisions in their rooms. Certainly, my girls can't resist the urge to listen to MTV and go online, especially if it's time to do homework. Unfortunately, though, kids aren't assigned much homework and what is assigned too often is busywork. And there are even more distractions outside the home. Teens no longer hang out/congregate on the corner where Dad and Mom can yell to them to come home and do homework. Instead they hang out at the mall, in movie theaters, and fast-food restaurants. Obviously, parents and school can't compete with all this.

Weak trans.

Also parents have to help kids develop responsible sexual values even though sex is everywhere. Kids see sex magazines and dirty paperbacks in the corner store where they used to get candy and comic books. And instead of the artsy nude shots of the past, kids see ronchey, explicit shots in *Playboy* and *Penthouse*. And movies have sexy stuff in them today. Teachers seduce students and people treat sex casually/as a sport. Not exactly traditional values. TV is no better. Kids see soap-opera characters in bed and cable shows full of nudity by just flipping the dial. Even worse is what's on the Internet. Too easy for kids

Sp?

to access chat rooms and websites dealing with adult, sometimes pornographic material. The situation has gotten so out of hand that maybe the government should establish guidelines on what's permissible.

Worst of all are the life-threatening dangers that parents must help children fend off over the years. With older kids, drugs fall into place as a main concern. Peer pressure to try drugs is bigger to kids than their parents' warnings. Other kinds of warnings are common when children are small. Then parents fear violence since news shows constantly report stories of little children being abused. And when kids aren't much older, they have to resist the pressure to drink. Alcohol has always attracted kids, but nowadays they are drinking more and this can be deadly, especially when drinking is combined with driving.

Most adults love their children and want to be good parents. But it's difficult because the world seems stacked against young people. Even Holden Caufield had trouble dealing with society's confusing pressures. Parents must give their children some freedom but not so much that the kids lose sight of what's important.

Margin notes (left column):
- Awk
- Wrong word
- Add specifics
- Redo
- Sp?

Commentary

As you can see, Harriet's draft is rough. Because she knew she would revise later on (page 60), she "zapped out" the draft in an informal, colloquial style. For example, she occasionally expressed her thoughts in fragments ("Not exactly traditional values"), relied heavily on "and" as a transition, and used slangy expressions such as "kids," "dirty paperbacks," and "lots of things." She also used slashes between alternative word choices and left a blank space when wording just wouldn't come. Then, as Harriet reviewed the printed copy of this rough draft, she made handwritten marginal notes to herself: "Awk" or "Redo" to signal awkward sentences; "Add specifics" to mark overly general statements; "Wrong word" after an imprecise word; "Sp?" to remind herself to check spelling in the dictionary; "Weak trans." to indicate where a stronger signaling device was needed. (Harriet's final draft appears on pages 66–68.)

Writing a first draft may seem like quite a challenge, but the tips offered in these pages should help you proceed with confidence. Indeed, as you work on the draft, you may be surprised how much you enjoy writing. After all, this is your chance to get down on paper something you want to say.

Activities: Write the First Draft

1. Retrieve the writing you prepared in response to activity 3 on page 46. Applying the principles just presented, rework that material. If you wrote a single paragraph earlier, expand the material into a full essay draft. If you prepared an essay, strengthen what you wrote. In both cases, remember to consider your purpose, audience, and tone as you write the body of the essay as well as its introduction and conclusion. (Save your draft so you can rework it even further after reading about the next stage in the writing process.)

2. Referring to the outline you prepared in response to activity 2 or activity 4 on page 46, draft the body of your essay, making your evidence as strong as possible. As you work, keep your purpose, audience, and tone in mind. After reading what you've prepared, go ahead and draft a rough introduction, conclusion, and title. Finally, ask at least one other person to react to your draft by listing its strengths and weaknesses. (Save the draft so you can work with it further after reading about the next stage in the writing process.)

STAGE 6: REVISE THE ESSAY

By now, you've probably abandoned any preconceptions you might have had about good writers sitting down and creating a finished product in one easy step. Alexander Pope's comment that "true ease in writing comes from art, not chance" is as true today as it was more than two hundred years ago. Writing that seems effortlessly clear is often the result of sustained work, not of good luck or even inborn talent. And much of this work takes place during the final stage of the writing process when ideas, paragraphs, sentences, and words are refined and reshaped.

Professional writers—novelists, journalists, textbook authors—seldom submit a piece of writing that hasn't been revised. They recognize that rough, unpolished work doesn't do them justice. What's more, they often look forward to revising. Columnist Ellen Goodman puts it this way: "What makes me happy is rewriting.... It's like cleaning house, getting rid of all the junk, getting things in the right order, tightening up."

In a sense, revision occurs throughout the writing process: At some earlier stage, you may have dropped an idea, overhauled your thesis, or shifted paragraph order. What, then, is different about the rewriting that occurs in the revision stage? The answer has to do with the literal meaning of the word *revision*—to resee, or to see again. Genuine revision involves casting clear eyes on your work, viewing it as though you're a reader rather than the writer. Revision means that you go through your paper looking for trouble, ready to pick a fight with your own writing. And then you must be willing to sit down and make the changes needed for your writing to be as effective as possible.

Revision is not, as some believe, simply touch-up work—changing a sentence here or a word there, eliminating spelling errors, preparing a neat final copy. Revision means cutting deadwood, rearranging paragraphs, substituting new words for old ones, recasting sentences, improving coherence, even generating new material when appropriate. With experience, you'll learn how to streamline the process so you can focus on the most critical issues for a particular piece of writing. (For advice on correcting some common writing errors, see Appendix B on pages 483–495.)

Five Revision Strategies

Because revision is challenging, you may find yourself unsure about how to proceed. Keep in mind that there are no hard-and-fast rules about the revision process. Even so, the following pointers should help get you going if you balk at or feel overwhelmed by revising.

- *Set your draft aside for a while* before revising. When you pick up your paper again, you'll have a fresh, more objective point of view.
- *Work from printed-out material* whenever possible. Having your essay in neutral typed letters instead of in your own familiar writing helps you see the paper impartially, as if someone else had written it. Each time you make major changes, try to print out a copy of that section so that you can see it anew.
- *Read your draft aloud* as often as you can. Hearing how your writing sounds helps you pick up problems that you passed by before: places where sentences are awkward, meaning is ambiguous, words are imprecise. Even better, have another person read aloud to you what you have written. If the reader slows to a crawl over a murky paragraph or trips over a convoluted sentence, you know where you have to do some rewriting.
- *View revision as a series of steps.* Don't try to tackle all of a draft's problems at once; instead, proceed step by step, starting with the most pressing issues. Although there are bound to be occasions when you have time for only one quick pass over a draft, whenever possible, read your draft several times; each time focus on different matters and ask yourself different questions. Move from a broad view of the draft to an up-close look at its mechanics.
- *Evaluate and respond to instructor feedback.* Often, instructors collect and respond to students' first drafts. Like many students, you may be tempted to look only briefly at your instructor's comments. Perhaps you've "had it" with the essay and don't want to think about revising the paper to reflect the instructor's

remarks. But taking your instructor's comments into account when revising is often what's needed to turn a shaky first draft into a strong final draft.

When an instructor returns a final draft graded, you may think that the grade is all that counts. Remember, though: Grades are important, but comments are even more so. They can help you *improve* your writing—if not in this paper, then in the next one. If you don't understand or agree with the instructor's observations, don't hesitate to request a conference. Getting together gives both you and the instructor a chance to clarify your respective points of view.

Peer Review: An Additional Revision Strategy

Many instructors include in-class or at-home peer review as a regular part of a composition course. Peer review—the critical reading of another person's writing with the intention of suggesting changes—accomplishes several important goals. First, peer review helps you gain a more objective perspective on your work. When you write something, you're often too close to what you've prepared to evaluate it fairly; you may have trouble seeing where the writing is strong and where it needs to be strengthened. Peer review supplies the fresh, neutral perspective you need. Second, reviewing your classmates' work broadens your own composing options. You may be inspired to experiment with a technique you admired in a classmate's writing but wouldn't have thought of on your own. Finally, peer review trains you to be a better reader and critic of your *own* writing. When you get into the habit of critically reading other students' writing, you become more adept at critiquing your own.

The Peer Review/Revision Checklist on the inside front cover of this book will help focus your revision—whether you're reworking your own paper or responding to a peer's. Your instructor may have you respond to all questions on the checklist or to several selected items. What follows is a peer review worksheet that Harriet Davids's instructor prepared to help students respond to first drafts based on the assignment on page 12. Wanting students to focus on four areas (thesis statement, support for thesis statement, overall organization, and signal devices), the instructor drew upon relevant sections from the Peer Review/Revision Checklist. With this customized worksheet in hand, Harriet's classmate, Frank Tejada, was able to give Harriet constructive feedback on her first draft (see pages 58–59). (*Note:* Because Harriet didn't want to influence Frank's reaction, the draft she gave him didn't include her marginal notations to herself.)

Peer Review Worksheet

Essay Author's Name: <u>Harriet Davids</u> Reviewer's Name: <u>Frank Tejada</u>

1. What is the essay's thesis? Is it explicit or implied? Does the thesis focus on a limited subject and express the writer's attitude toward that subject?

   Thesis: "Being a parent today is much more difficult [than it used to be]." The thesis is limited and expresses a clear attitude. But the sentence the thesis appears in (last sentence of para. 1) is too long because it also contains the plan of development. Maybe put thesis and plan of development in separate sentences.

2. What are the main points supporting the thesis? List the points. Is each supporting point developed sufficiently? If not, where is more support needed?

   (1) Parents have to control kids' distractions from school.
   (2) Parents have to help kids develop responsible sexual values despite sex being everywhere.
   (3) Parents have to protect kids from life-threatening dangers.
       The supporting points are good and are explained pretty well, except for a few places. The "Unfortunately" sentence in para. 2 is irrelevant. Also, in para. 2, you use the example of your girls, but never again. Either include them throughout or not at all. In para. 3, the final sentence about the government guidelines opens a whole new topic; maybe steer away from this. The items in para. 4 seem vague and need specific examples. In the conclusion, omit Holden Caulfield; since he was from an earlier generation, this example undermines your thesis about parenting today.

3. What overall format (chronological, spatial, emphatic, simple-to-complex) is used to sequence the essay's main points? Does this format work? Why or why not? What organizational format is used in each supporting paragraph? Does the format work? Why or why not?

   The paper's overall emphatic organization seems good. Emphatic order also works in para. 3, and spatial order works well in para. 2. But the sentences in para. 4 need rearranging. Right now, the examples are in mixed-up chronological order, making it hard to follow. Maybe you should reorder the examples from young kids to older kids.

4. What signal devices are used to connect ideas within and between paragraphs? Are there too few signal devices or too many? Where?

> The topic sentence of para. 3 needs to be a stronger bridging sentence. Also, too many "and's" in para. 3. Try "in addition" or "another" in some places. I like the "worst of all" transition to para. 4.

As you can see, Frank flagged several areas that Harriet herself also noted needed work. (Turn to pages 58–59 to see Harriet's marginal comments on her draft.) But he also commented on entirely new areas (for example, the sequence problem in paragraph 4), offering Harriet a fresh perspective on what she needed to do to polish her draft. To see which of Frank's suggestions Harriet followed, take a look at her final draft on pages 66–68 and at the "Commentary" following the essay.

Becoming a skilled peer reviewer.   Even with the help of a checklist, preparing a helpful peer review is a skill that takes time to develop. At first, you, like many students, may be too easy or too critical. Effective peer review calls for rigor and care; you should give classmates the conscientious feedback that you hope for in return. Peer review also requires tact and kindness; feedback should always be constructive and include observations about what works well in a piece of writing. People have difficulty mustering the energy to revise if they feel there's nothing worth revising.

If your instructor doesn't include peer review, you can set up peer review sessions outside of class, with classmates getting together to respond to each other's drafts. Or you may select non-classmates who are objective (not a love-struck admirer or a doting grandparent) and skilled enough to provide useful commentary.

To focus your readers' comments, you may adapt the Peer Review/ Revision Checklist on the inside front cover of this book, or you may develop your own questions. If you prepare the questions yourself, be sure to solicit *specific* observations about what does and doesn't work in your writing. If you simply ask, "How's this?" you may receive a vague comment like "It's not very effective." What you want are concrete observations and suggestions: "I'm confused because what you say in the fifth sentence contradicts what you say in the second." To promote such specific responses, ask your readers targeted (preferably written) questions like "I'm having trouble moving from my second to my third point. How can I make the transition smoother?" Such questions require more than "yes" or "no" responses; they encourage readers to dig into your writing where you sense it needs work. (If it's feasible, encourage readers to *write* their responses to your questions.)

If you and your peer reviewer(s) can't meet in person, e-mail can provide a crucial means of contact. With a couple of clicks, you can simply send each other computer files of your work. You and your reviewer(s) also need to decide exactly how to exchange comments about your drafts. You might conclude, for example, that you'll type your responses, perhaps in bold capitals, into the file itself. Or you might decide to print out the drafts and reply to the comments in writing, later exchanging the annotated drafts in person. No matter what you and your peer(s) decide, you'll probably find e-mail an invaluable tool in the writing process.

Evaluating and responding to peer review.   Accepting criticism isn't easy (even if you asked for it), and not all peer reviewers will be diplomatic. Even so, try to listen with an open mind to those giving you feedback. Take notes on their oral observations and/or have them fill out relevant sections from the Peer Review/Revision Checklist (on the inside front cover). Later, when you're ready to revise your paper, reread your notes. Which reviewer remarks seem valid? Which don't? Rank the problems and solutions that your reviewers identified, designating the most critical as number 1. Using the peer feedback, enter your own notes for revising in the margins of a clean copy of your draft. This way, you'll know exactly what changes need to be made in your draft as you proceed. Then, keeping the problems and remedies in mind, start revising. Type in your changes, or handwrite changes directly on the draft above the appropriate line. (Rework extensive sections on a separate piece of paper.) When revising, always keep in mind that you may not agree with every reviewer suggestion. That's fine. It's *your* paper, and it's *your* decision to implement or reject the suggestions made by your peers.

STAGE 7: EDIT AND PROOFREAD

Your essay is not finished until you have dealt with errors in grammar, punctuation, and spelling.

If you are using a computer,

- Use your computer's spelling check program to identify and correct misspelled words.
- Read the screen slowly, looking for wrong words (such as "there" when "their" is meant), errors in proper names, and errors in grammar.
- Format the essay using your instructor's guidelines, and print a copy.
- Proofread the printed paper slowly to catch typos and other mistakes.

If you find just a few errors in the printed paper, you may correct them by hand in dark ink. But if a page starts to look messy, you will need to print a clean, corrected copy to include in your final paper.

STUDENT ESSAY

In this chapter, we've taken you through the various stages in the writing process. You've seen how Harriet Davids used prewriting (pages 21–23 and 26–27) and outlining (pages 44–45) to arrive at her first draft (pages 58–59). You've also seen how Harriet's peer reviewer, Frank Tejada, critiqued her first draft (pages 63–64). In the following pages, you'll look at Harriet's final draft—the paper she submitted to her instructor.

Harriet, a thirty-eight-year-old college student and mother of two teenagers, wanted to write an informative paper with a straightforward, serious tone. While preparing her essay, she kept in mind that her audience would include her course instructor as well as her classmates, many of them considerably younger than she. This is the assignment that prompted Harriet's essay:

> Goodman implies that, in some ways, today's world is hostile to children. Do you agree? Drawing upon but not limiting yourself to the material in your pre-reading journal, write an essay in which you support or reject this viewpoint.

Harriet's essay is annotated so that you can see how it illustrates the essay format described on page 57. As you read her essay, try to determine how well it reflects the principles of effective writing. The commentary following the paper will help you look at the essay more closely and give you some sense of the way Harriet went about revising her first draft.

Challenges for Today's Parents

By Harriet Davids

Introduction	Reruns of situation comedies from the 1950s and early 1960s dramatize the kinds of problems that parents used to have with their children. On classic television shows such as Leave It to Beaver, the Cleavers scold their son Beaver for not washing his hands before dinner; on Ozzie and Harriet, the Nelsons dock little Ricky's allowance because he keeps forgetting to clean his room. But times have
Thesis	changed dramatically. Being a parent today is much more
Plan of development	difficult than it was a generation ago. Parents nowadays must protect their children from a growing number of distractions, from sexually explicit material, and from life-threatening situations.

1

First
supporting
paragraph

Topic
sentence

Today's parents must try, first of all, to control all the   2
new distractions that tempt children away from schoolwork. At home, a child may have a room furnished with an
MP3 player, television, and computer. Not many young people can resist the urge to listen to music, watch TV, go online, or play computer games and IM their friends—especially if it's time to do schoolwork. Outside the home, the
distractions are even more alluring. Children no longer
"hang out" on a neighborhood corner within earshot of
Mom or Dad's reminder to come in and do homework.
Instead, they congregate in vast shopping malls, movie theaters, and gleaming fast-food restaurants. Parents and
school assignments have obvious difficulty competing with
such enticing alternatives.

Second
supporting
paragraph

Topic
sentence with
link to
previous
paragraph

Besides dealing with these distractions, parents have   3
to shield their children from a flood of sexually explicit materials. Today, children can find pornographic websites and
chat rooms on the Internet with relative ease. With the click
of a mouse, they can be transported, intentionally or unin-
tentionally, to a barrage of explicit images and conversations. Easily obtainable copies of sex magazines can be
found at most convenience stores, many times alongside
the candy. Children will not see the fuzzily photographed
nudes that a previous generation did but will encounter the
hard-core raunchiness of *Playboy* or *Penthouse*. Moreover,
the movies young people view often focus on highly sexual
situations. It is difficult to teach children traditional values
when films show young people treating sex as a casual
sport. Unfortunately, television, with its often heavily sexual
content, is no better. With just a flick of the channel, children can see sexed-up music videos, watch reality-TV stars
cavorting in bed, or watch cable programs where nudity is
common.

Third
supporting
paragraph

Topic
sentence with
emphasis
signal

Most disturbing to parents today, however, is the in-   4
crease in life-threatening dangers that face young people.
When children are small, parents fear that their youngsters
may be victims of violence. Every news program seems to
carry a report about a school shooting or child predator who
has been released from prison, only to repeat an act of violence against a minor. When children are older, parents
begin to worry about their kids' use of drugs. Peer pressure
to experiment with drugs is often stronger than parents'
warnings. This pressure to experiment can be fatal. Finally,
even if young people escape the hazards associated with
drugs, they must still resist the pressure to drink. Although

alcohol has always held an attraction for teenagers, reports indicate that they are drinking more than ever before. As many parents know, the consequences of this attraction can be deadly—especially when drinking is combined with driving.

Conclusion

References to TV shows recall introduction

Within a generation, the world as a place to raise children has changed dramatically. One wonders how yesterday's parents would have dealt with today's problems. Could the Nelsons have shielded little Ricky from sexually explicit material on the Internet? Could the Cleavers have protected Beaver from drugs and alcohol? Parents must be aware of all these distractions and dangers yet be willing to give their children the freedom they need to become responsible adults. This is not an easy task.

5

COMMENTARY

Introduction and thesis.   The opening paragraph attracts readers' interest by recalling several vintage television shows that have almost become part of our cultural heritage. Harriet begins with these examples from the past because they offer such a sharp contrast to the present, thus underscoring the idea expressed in her *thesis:* "Being a parent today is much more difficult than it was a generation ago." Opening in this way, with material that serves as a striking contrast to what follows, is a common and effective strategy. Note, too, that Harriet's thesis states the paper's subject (being a parent) as well as her attitude toward the subject (the job is more demanding than it was years ago).

Plan of development.   Harriet follows her thesis with a *plan of development* that anticipates the three major points to be covered in the essay's supporting paragraphs. When revising her first draft, Harriet followed peer reviewer Frank Tejada's recommendation (page 63–64) to put her thesis and plan of development in separate sentences. Unfortunately, though, her plan of development ends up being somewhat mechanical, with the major points being trotted past the reader in one long, awkward sentence. To deal with the problem, Harriet could have rewritten the sentence or eliminated the plan of development altogether, ending the introduction with her thesis.

Patterns of development.   Although Harriet develops her thesis primarily through *examples,* she also draws on two other patterns of development. The whole paper implies a *contrast* between the way life and parenting are now and the way they used to be. The essay also contains an element of *causal analysis* since all the factors that Harriet cites affect children and the way they are raised.

Purpose, audience, and tone.   Given the essay's *purpose* and *audience,* Harriet adopts a serious *tone,* providing no-nonsense evidence to support her thesis. But assume she had been asked by her daughters' school newspaper to write a humorous column about the trials and tribulations that parents face raising children. Aiming for a different tone, purpose, and audience, Harriet would have taken another approach. Drawing on her personal experience, she might have confessed how she survives her daughters' nearly nonstop use of the computer, as well as the constant thumping sounds that emanate from the ear buds of their MP3s: She cuts off the electricity and hides the ear buds. This material—with its personalized perspective, exaggeration, and light tone—would be appropriate.

Organization.   Structuring the essay around a series of *relevant* and *specific examples,* Harriet uses *emphatic order* to sequence the paper's three main points: that a growing number of distractions, sexually explicit materials, and life-threatening situations make parenting difficult nowadays. The third supporting paragraph begins with the words "Most disturbing to parents today . . . ," signaling that Harriet feels particular concern about the physical dangers children face. Moreover, she uses basic organizational strategies to sequence the supporting examples within each paragraph. The details in the first supporting paragraph are organized *spatially,* starting with distractions at home and moving to those outside the home. The second supporting paragraph arranges examples *emphatically.* Harriet starts with sexually explicit material on the Internet and ends with the "heavily sexual content" on TV. Note that Harriet followed Frank's peer review advice (page 63) about omitting her first-draft observation that kids don't get enough homework—or that they get too much busywork. The third and final supporting paragraph is organized *chronologically;* it begins by discussing dangers to small children and concludes by talking about teenagers. Again, Frank's advice—to use a clearer time sequence in this paragraph (page 63)—was invaluable when Harriet was revising.

The essay also displays Harriet's familiarity with other kinds of organizational strategies. Each supporting paragraph opens with a *topic sentence.* Further, *signal devices* are used throughout the paper to show how ideas are related to one another: *transitions* ("Instead, they congregate in vast shopping malls"; "Moreover, the movies young people attend often focus on highly sexual situations"); *repetition* ("sexual situations" and "sexual content"); *synonyms* ("distractions...enticing alternatives" and "life-threat-ening...fatal"); *pronouns* ("young people...they"); and *bridging sentences* ("Besides dealing with these distractions, parents have to shield their chil-dren from a flood of sexually explicit material").

Two minor problems.   Harriet's efforts to write a well-organized essay re-sult in a somewhat predictable structure. It might have been better had she rewritten one of the paragraphs, perhaps embedding the topic sentence in the middle of the paragraph or saving it for the end. Similarly, Harriet's sig-nal devices are a little heavy-handed. Even so, an essay with a sharp focus and clear signals is preferable to one with a confusing or inaccessible structure. As she gains more experience, Harriet can work on making the structure of her essays more subtle.

Conclusion.   Following Frank's suggestion, Harriet dropped from the final paragraph the first draft's problematic reference to Holden Caulfield (page 63). Having done that, she's able to bring the essay to a satisfying *close* by reminding readers of the paper's central idea and three main points. The final paragraph also extends the essay's scope by introducing a new but related issue: that parents have to strike a balance between their need to provide limitations and their children's need for freedom. Besides eliminating the distracting reference to Holden Caulfield, she deleted the shopworn opening sentence ("Most adults love their children...") and added references to the vintage TV shows mentioned in the introduction: ("Could the Nelsons...? Could the Cleavers...?"). These questions help unify Harriet's paper and bring it to a rounded close.

These are just a few of the changes Harriet made when reworking her essay. Realizing that writing is a process, she left herself enough time to revise—and to carefully consider Frank Tejada's comments. Early in her composition course, Harriet learned that attention to the various stages in the writing process yields satisfying results, for writer and reader alike.

Activity: Revise the Essay

Return to the draft you wrote in response to either activity 1 or activity 2 on page 60. Also look at any written feedback you received on the draft. To identify any further problems in the draft, get together with several people (classmates, friends, or family members) and request that one of them read the draft aloud to you. Then ask your audience focused questions about the areas you sense need work, or use the checklist on the inside front cover to focus the feedback. In either case, summarize and rank the comments on a feedback chart or in marginal annotations. Then, using the comments as a guide, go ahead and revise the draft. Either type a new version or do your revising by hand, perhaps on a photocopy of the draft. Don't forget to proofread closely before submitting the paper to your instructor.

Rudi Von Briel/PhotoEdit, Inc.

DESCRIPTION

WHAT IS DESCRIPTION?

All of us respond in a strong way to sensory stimulation. The sweet perfume of a candy shop takes us back to childhood; the blank white walls of the campus infirmary remind us of long vigils at a hospital where a grandmother lay dying; the screech of a subway car sets our nerves on edge.

Without any sensory stimulation, we sink into a less-than-human state. Neglected babies, left alone with no human touch, no colors, no lullabies, become withdrawn and unresponsive. And prisoners dread solitary confinement, knowing that the sensory deprivation can be unbearable, even to the point of madness.

Because sensory impressions are so potent, descriptive writing has a unique power and appeal. *Description* can be defined as the expression, in vivid language, of what the five senses experience. A richly rendered description freezes a subject in time, evoking sights, smells, sounds, textures, and tastes in such a way that readers become one with the writer's world.

HOW DESCRIPTION FITS YOUR PURPOSE AND AUDIENCE

Description can be a supportive technique that develops part of an essay, or it can be the dominant technique used throughout an essay. Here are some examples of the way description can help you meet the objective of an essay developed chiefly through another pattern of development:

- In a *causal analysis* showing the *consequences* of pet overpopulation, you might describe the desperate appearance of a pack of starving stray dogs.
- In an *argumentation-persuasion* essay urging more rigorous handgun control, you might start with a description of a violent family confrontation that ended in murder.
- In a *process analysis* explaining the pleasure of making ice cream at home, you might describe the beauty of an old-fashioned, hand-cranked ice-cream maker.
- In a *narrative essay* recounting a day in the life of a street musician, you might describe the musician's energy and the joyous appreciation of passersby.

In each case, the essay's overall purpose would affect the amount of description needed.

Your readers also influence how much description to include. As you write, ask yourself, "What do my particular readers need to know to understand and experience keenly what I'm describing? What descriptive details will they enjoy most?" Your answers to these and similar questions will help you tailor your description to specific readers. Consider an article intended for professional horticulturists; its purpose is to explain a new technique for controlling spider mites. Because of readers' expertise, there would be little need for a lengthy description of the insects. Written for a college newspaper, however, the article would probably provide a detailed description of the mites so student gardeners could distinguish between the pesky parasites and flecks of dust.

While your purpose and audience define *how much* to describe, you have great freedom deciding *what* to describe. Description is especially suited to objects (your car or desk, for example), but you can also describe a person, an animal, a place, a time, and a phenomenon or concept. You might write an effective description of a friend who runs marathons (person), a pair of ducks that return each year to a neighbor's pond (animals), the kitchen of a fast-food restaurant (place), a period when you were unemployed (time), the "fight or flight" response to danger (phenomenon or concept).

Description can be divided into two types: *objective* and *subjective*. In an objective description, you describe the subject in a straightforward and literal way, without revealing your attitude or feelings. Reporters, as well as technical and scientific writers, specialize in objective description;

their jobs depend on their ability to detail experiences without emotional bias. For example, a reporter may write an unemotional account of a township meeting that ended in a fistfight. Or a marine biologist may write a factual report describing the way sea mammals are killed by the plastic refuse (sandwich wrappings, straws, fishing lines) that humans throw into the ocean.

In contrast, when writing a subjective description, you convey a highly personal view of your subject and seek to elicit a strong emotional response from your readers. Such subjective descriptions often take the form of reflective pieces or character studies. For example, in an essay describing the rich plant life in an inner-city garden, you might reflect on people's longing to connect with the soil and express admiration for the gardeners' hard work—an admiration you'd like readers to share. Or, in a character study of your grandfather, you might describe his stern appearance and gentle behavior, hoping that the contradiction will move readers as much as it moves you.

The *tone* of a subjective description is determined by your purpose, your attitude toward the subject, and the reader response you wish to evoke. Consider an essay about a dynamic woman who runs a center for disturbed children. If you want readers to admire the woman, your tone will be serious and appreciative. But if you want to criticize her high-pressure tactics and management style, your tone will be disapproving and severe.

The language of a descriptive piece also depends, to a great extent, on whether your purpose is primarily objective or subjective. If the description is objective, the language is straightforward, precise, and factual. Such *denotative* language consists of neutral dictionary meanings. To describe as dispassionately as possible fans' violent behavior at a football game, you might write about the "large crowd" and its "mass movement onto the field." But for a subjective piece that inspires outrage in readers, you might write about the "swelling mob" and its "rowdy stampede onto the field." In the latter case, the language you used would be *connotative* and emotionally charged so that readers would share your feelings.

Subjective and objective descriptions often overlap. Sometimes a single sentence contains both objective and subjective elements: "Although his hands were large and misshapen by arthritis, they were gentle to the touch, inspiring confidence and trust." Other times, part of an essay may provide a factual description (the physical appearance of a summer cabin your family rented), while another part of the essay may be highly subjective (how you felt in the cabin, sitting in front of a fire on a rainy day).

At this point, you have a good sense of the way writers use description to achieve their purpose and to connect with their readers. Now take a moment to look closely at the photograph at the beginning of this chapter. Imagine you're writing a column, accompanied by the photo, for the local newspaper. Your purpose is to encourage businesspeople

to support the city's mural arts program. Jot down some phrases you might use to *describe* the mural and its impact on the community.

SUGGESTIONS FOR USING DESCRIPTION IN AN ESSAY

The suggestions here and in Figure 3.1 on page 76 will be helpful whether you use description as a dominant or a supportive pattern of development.

1. Focus a descriptive essay around a dominant impression.   Like other kinds of writing, a descriptive essay must have a thesis, or main point. In a descriptive essay with a subjective slant, the thesis usually centers on the *dominant impression* you have about your subject. Suppose you decide to write an essay on your ninth-grade history teacher, Ms. Hazzard. You want the paper to convey how unconventional and flamboyant she was. The essay could, of course, focus on a different dominant impression—how insensitive she could be to students, for example. What's important is that you establish—early in the paper—the dominant impression you intend to convey. Although descriptive essays often imply, rather than explicitly state, the dominant impression, that impression should be unmistakable.

2. Select the details to include.   The power of description hinges on your ability to select from all possible details only those that support the dominant impression. All others, no matter how vivid or interesting, must be left out. If you're describing how flamboyant Ms. Hazzard could be, the details in the following paragraph would be appropriate.

A large-boned woman, Ms. Hazzard wore her bright red hair piled on top of her head, where it perched precariously. By the end of class, wayward strands of hair tumbled down and fell into eyes fringed by

FIGURE 3.1
Development Diagram: Writing a Description Essay

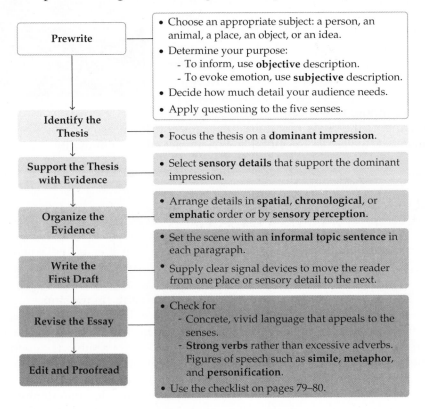

spiky false eyelashes. Ms. Hazzard's nails, filed into crisp points, were painted either bloody burgundy or neon pink. Plastic bangle bracelets, also either burgundy or pink, clattered up and down her ample arms as she scrawled on the board the historical dates that had, she claimed, "changed the world."

Such details—the heavy eye makeup, stiletto nails, gaudy bracelets—contribute to the impression of a flamboyant, unusual person. Even if you remembered times that Ms. Hazzard seemed perfectly conventional and understated, most likely you wouldn't describe those times since they contradict the dominant impression.

You must also be selective in the *number of details* you include. Having a dominant impression helps you eliminate many details gathered during prewriting, but there still will be choices to make. For example, it would be inappropriate to describe in exhaustive detail everything in a messy room:

> The brown desk, made of a grained plastic laminate, is directly under a small window covered by a torn yellow-and-gold plaid curtain. In the left corner of the desk are four crumbled balls of blue-lined yellow paper, three red markers, two fine-point blue pens, an ink eraser, and four letters, two bearing special wildlife stamps. A green down-filled vest and a red cable-knit sweater are thrown over the back of the bright blue metal bridge chair pushed under the desk. Under the chair is an oval braided rug, its once brilliant blues and greens spotted by old coffee stains.

Readers will be reluctant to wade through such undifferentiated specifics. Even more important, such excessive detailing dilutes the focus of the essay. You end up with a seemingly endless list of specifics rather than with a carefully crafted picture in words. In this regard, sculptors and writers are similar—what they take away is as important as what they leave in.

Perhaps you're wondering how to generate the details that support your dominant impression. As you can imagine, you have to develop heightened powers of observation and recall. To sharpen these key faculties, it can be helpful to make up a chart with separate columns for each of the five senses. If you can observe your subject directly, enter in the appropriate columns what you see, hear, taste, and so on. If you're attempting to remember something from the past, try to recollect details under each of these sense headings. Ask yourself questions ("How did it smell? What did I hear?") and list each memory recaptured. You'll be surprised how this simple technique can tune you in to your experiences and help uncover the specific details needed to develop your dominant impression.

3. Organize the descriptive details.   Select the organizational pattern (or combination of patterns) that best supports your dominant impression. The paragraphs in a descriptive essay are usually sequenced *spatially* (from top to bottom, interior to exterior, near to far) or *chronologically* (as the subject is experienced in time). But the paragraphs can also be ordered *emphatically* (ending with your subject's most striking elements) or by *sensory impression* (first smell, then taste, then touch, and so on).

You might, for instance, use a *spatial* pattern to organize a description of a large city as you viewed it from the air, a taxi, and a subway car. A description of your first day on a new job might move *chronologically*, starting with how you felt the first hour on the job and proceeding through the rest of the day. In a paper describing a bout with the flu, you might arrange details *emphatically*, beginning with a description of your low-level aches and pains and concluding with an account of your raging fever. An essay about a neighborhood garbage dump, euphemistically called an "ecology landfill" by its owners, could be organized by *sensory impressions:* the sights of the dump, its smells, its sounds. Regardless of the organizational pattern you use, provide enough *signal devices* (for example, *about, next, worst of all*) so that readers can follow the description easily.

Finally, although descriptive essays don't always have conventional topic sentences, each descriptive paragraph should have a clear focus. Often this focus is indicated by a sentence early in the paragraph that names the scene, object, or individual to be described. Such a sentence functions as a kind of *informal topic sentence;* the paragraph's descriptive details then develop that topic sentence.

4. Use vivid sensory language and varied sentence structure.   The connotative language typical of subjective description should be richly evocative. The words you select must etch in readers' minds the same picture that you have in yours. For this reason, rather than relying on vague generalities, you must use language that involves readers' senses. Consider the difference between the following paired descriptions.

Vague	Vivid
The food was unappetizing.	The stew congealed into an oval pool of milky-brown fat.
The toothpaste was refreshing.	The toothpaste, tasting minty sweet, felt good against slippery teeth, free finally from braces.
Filled with passengers and baggage, the car moved slowly down the road.	Burdened with its load of clamoring children and well-worn suitcases, the car labored down down the interstate on bald tires and worn shocks, emitting puffs of blue exhaust and an occasional backfire.

Unlike the *concrete, sensory-packed* sentences on the right, the sentences on the left fail to create vivid word pictures that engage readers. While all good writing blends abstract and concrete language, descriptive writing demands an abundance of specific sensory language.

Keep in mind, too, that *verbs pack more of a wallop* than adverbs. The following sentence has to rely on adverbs (italicized) because its verbs are so weak: "She walked *casually* into the room and *deliberately* tried not to pay much attention to their stares." Rewritten, so that verbs (italicized), not adverbs, do the bulk of the work, the sentence becomes more powerful: "She *strolled* into the room and *ignored* their stares."

Figures of speech—nonliteral, imaginative comparisons between two basically dissimilar things—are another way to enliven descriptive writing. *Similes* use the words *like* or *as* when comparing; *metaphors* state or imply that two things being compared are alike; and *personification* attributes human characteristics to inanimate things.

The examples that follow show how effective figurative language can be in descriptive writing.

> Moving as jerkily as a marionette on strings, the old man picked himself up off the sidewalk and staggered down the street. (*simile*)
>
> Stalking their prey, the hall monitors remained hidden in the corridors, motionless and ready to spring on any unsuspecting student who dared to sneak into class late. (*metaphor*)
>
> The scoop of vanilla ice cream, plain and unadorned, cried out for hot-fudge sauce and a sprinkling of sliced pecans. (*personification*)

Finally, when writing descriptive passages, you need to *vary sentence structure*. Don't use the same subject-verb pattern in all sentences. The second example above, for instance, could have been written as follows: "The hall monitors stalked their prey. They hid in the corridors. They remained motionless and ready to spring on any unsuspecting student who tried to sneak into class late." But the sentence is richer and more interesting when the descriptive elements are embedded, eliminating what would otherwise have been a clipped and predictable subject-verb pattern.

REVISION STRATEGIES

Once you have a draft of the essay, you're ready to revise. The following checklist will help you and those giving you feedback apply to description some of the revision techniques discussed on pages 60–62.

☑ DESCRIPTION: A REVISION/PEER REVIEW CHECKLIST

Revise Overall Meaning and Structure

❑ What dominant impression does the essay convey? Is the dominant impression stated or implied? Where? Should it be made more obvious or more subtle?

❑ Is the essay primarily objective or subjective? Should the essay be more emotionally charged or less so?

❑ Which descriptive details don't support the dominant impression? Should they be deleted, or should the dominant impression be adjusted to encompass the details?

Revise Paragraph Development

❏ How are the essay's descriptive paragraphs organized—spatially, chronologically, emphatically, or by sensory impression? Would another organizational pattern be more effective? Which one(s)?

❏ Which paragraphs lack a distinctive focus?

❏ Which descriptive paragraphs are mere lists of sensory impressions?

❏ Which descriptive paragraphs fail to engage the reader's senses? How could they be made more concrete?

Revise Sentences and Words

❏ What signal devices guide readers through the description? Are there enough signals? Too many?

❏ Where should sentence structure be varied to make it less predictable?

❏ Which sentences should include more sensory images?

❏ Which flat verbs should be replaced with vigorous verbs?

❏ Where should there be more or fewer adjectives?

❏ Do any figures of speech seem contrived or trite? Which ones?

STUDENT ESSAY

The following student essay was written by Marie Martinez in response to this assignment:

> The essay "Life, Death and Spring" is an evocative piece about a spot that had special meaning for Gary Kamiya. Write an essay about a place that holds rich significance for you, centering the description on a dominant impression.

While reading Marie's paper, try to determine how well it applies the principles of description. The annotations on Marie's paper and the commentary following it will help you look at the essay more closely.

Salt Marsh
by Marie Martinez

Introduction

In one of his journals, Thoreau told of the difficulty he had   1
escaping the obligations and cares of society: "It sometimes happens that I cannot easily shake off the village. The thought of some work will run in my head and I am not where my body is—I am out of my senses. In my walks I . . . return to my senses." All of us feel out of our senses at times. Overwhelmed

Dominant
impression
(thesis)

Informal topic
sentence:
Definition
paragraph

by problems or everyday annoyances, we lose touch with sensory pleasures as we spend our days in noisy cities and stuffy classrooms. Just as Thoreau walked in the woods to return to his senses, I have a special place where I return to mine: the salt marsh behind my grandparents' house.

2   My grandparents live on the East Coast, a mile or so inland from the sea. Between the ocean and the mainland is a wide fringe of salt marsh. A salt marsh is not a swamp, but an expanse of dark, spongy soil threaded with saltwater creeks and clothed in a kind of grass called salt meadow hay. All the water in the marsh rises and falls daily with the ocean tides, an endless cycle that changes the look of the marsh—partly flooded or mostly dry—as the day progresses.

Informal topic
sentence: First
paragraph in a
four-part spatial
sequence

Simile

3   Heading out to the marsh from my grandparents' house, I follow a short path through the woods. As I walk along, a sharp smell of salt mixed with the rich aroma of peaty soil fills my nostrils. I am always amazed by the way the path changes with the seasons. Sometimes I walk in the brilliant green of spring, sometimes in the tawny gold of autumn, sometimes in the grayish tan of winter. No matter the season, the grass flanking the trail is often flattened into swirls, like thick Van Gogh brush strokes that curve and recurve in circular patterns. No people come here. The peacefulness heals me like a soothing drug.

Informal topic
sentence: Second
paragraph in the
spatial sequence

4   After a few minutes, the trail suddenly opens up to a view that calms me no matter how upset or discouraged I might be: a line of tall waving reeds bordering and nearly hiding the salt marsh creek. To get to the creek, I part the reeds.

Informal topic
sentence: Third
paragraph in the
spatial sequence

5   The creek is a narrow body of water no more than fifteen feet wide, and it ebbs and flows as the ocean currents sweep toward the land or rush back toward the sea. The creek winds in a sinuous pattern so that I cannot see its beginning or end, the places where it trickles into the marsh or spills into the open ocean. Little brown birds dip in and out of the reeds on the far shore of the creek, making a special "tweep-tweep" sound peculiar to the marsh. When I stand at low tide on the shore of the creek, I am on a miniature cliff, for the bank of the creek falls abruptly and steeply into the water. Below me, green grasses wave and shimmer under the water while tiny minnows flash their silvery sides as they dart through the underwater tangles.

Informal topic
sentence: Last
paragraph in the
spatial sequence

Simile

6   The creek water is often much warmer than the ocean, so I can swim there in three seasons. Sitting on the edge of the creek, I scoop some water into my hand, rub my face and neck, then ease into the water. Where the creek is shallow, my feet sink into a foot of muck that feels like mashed potatoes mixed with motor oil. But once I become accustomed to it, I enjoy

squishing the slimy mud through my toes. Sometimes I feel brushing past my legs the blue crabs that live in the creek. Other times, I hear the splash of a turtle or an otter as it slips from the shore into the water. Otherwise, it is silent. The salty water is buoyant and lifts my spirits as I stroke through it to reach the middle of the creek. There in the center, I float weightlessly, surrounded by tall reeds that reduce the world to water and sky. I am at peace.

Conclusion

The salt marsh is not the kind of dramatic landscape found on picture postcards. There are no soaring mountains, sandy beaches, or lush valleys. The marsh is a flat world that some consider dull and uninviting. I am glad most people do not respond to the marsh's subtle beauty because that means I can be alone there. Just as the rising tide sweeps over the marsh, floating debris out to the ocean, the marsh washes away my concerns and restores me to my senses.

Echo of idea in introduction

7

COMMENTARY

The dominant impression.   Marie responded to the assignment by writing a moving tribute to a place having special meaning for her—the salt marsh near her grandparents' home. Like most descriptive pieces, Marie's essay is organized around a *dominant impression:* the marsh's peaceful solitude and gentle, natural beauty. The essay's introduction provides a context for the dominant impression by comparing the pleasure Marie experiences in the marsh to the happiness Thoreau felt in his walks around Walden Pond.

Combining patterns of development.   Before developing the essay's dominant impression, Marie uses the second paragraph to *define* a salt marsh. An *objective description,* the definition clarifies that a salt marsh—with its spongy soil, haylike grass, and ebbing tides—is not to be confused with a swamp. Because Marie offers such a factual definition, readers have the background needed to enjoy the personalized view that follows.

Besides the definition paragraph and the comparison in the opening paragraph, the essay contains a strong element of *causal analysis:* Throughout, Marie describes the marsh's effect on her.

Sensory language.   At times, Marie develops the essay's dominant impression explicitly, as when she writes "No people come here" (paragraph 3) and "I am at peace" (6). But Marie generally uses the more subtle techniques characteristic of *subjective description* to convey the dominant impression. First of all, she fills the essay with strong *connotative language,* rich with *sensory images.* The third paragraph describes what she smells (the "sharp smell of salt mixed with the rich aroma of peaty soil") and what she sees ("brilliant green," "tawny gold," and "grayish tan"). In the fifth paragraph, she tells us that she hears the chirping sounds of small birds. And the sixth paragraph includes vigorous descriptions of how the marsh feels to Marie's touch. She splashes water on her face and neck; she digs her toes into the mud at the bottom of the creek; she delights in the delicate brushing of crabs against her legs.

Figurative language, vigorous verbs, and varied sentence structure. You might also have noted that *figurative language, energetic verbs,* and *varied sentence patterns* contribute to the essay's descriptive power. Marie develops a *simile* in the third paragraph when she compares the flattened swirls of swamp grass to the brush strokes in a painting by Van Gogh. Later she uses another simile when she writes that the creek's thick mud feels "like mashed potatoes mixed with motor oil." Moreover, throughout the essay, she uses lively verbs ("shimmer," "flash") to capture the marsh's magical quality. Similarly, Marie enhances descriptive passages by varying the length of her sentences. Long, fairly elaborate sentences are interspersed with short, dramatic statements. In the third paragraph, for example, the long sentence describing the circular swirls of swamp grass is followed by the brief statement "No people come here." And the sixth paragraph uses two short sentences ("Otherwise, it is silent" and "I am at peace") to punctuate the paragraph's longer sentences.

Organization. We can follow Marie's journey through the marsh because she uses an easy-to-follow combination of *spatial, chronological,* and *emphatic* patterns to sequence her experience. The essay relies primarily on a spatial arrangement since the four body paragraphs focus on the different spots that Marie reaches: first, the path behind her grandparents' house (paragraph 3); then the area bordering the creek (4); next, her view of the creek (5); last, the creek itself (6). Each stage of her walk is signaled by an *informal topic sentence* near the start of each paragraph. Furthermore, *signal devices* (marked by italics here) indicate not only her location but also the chronological passage of time: "*As* I walk along, a sharp smell . . . fills my nostrils" (3); "*After* a few minutes, the trail suddenly opens up . . ." (4); "*Below* me, green grasses wave . . ." (5). And to call attention to the creek's serene beauty, Marie saves for last the description of the peace she feels while floating in the creek.

An inappropriate figure of speech. Although the four body paragraphs focus on the distinctive qualities of each location, Marie runs into a minor problem in the third paragraph. Take a moment to reread that paragraph's last sentence. Comparing the peace of the marsh to the effect of a "soothing drug" is jarring. The effectiveness of Marie's essay hinges on her ability to

create a picture of a pure, natural world. A reference to drugs is inappropriate. Now, reread the paragraph aloud, stopping after "No people come
here." Note how much more in keeping with the essay's dominant impression the paragraph is when the reference to drugs is omitted.

Conclusion.   The concluding paragraph brings the essay to a graceful
close. The powerful *simile* found in the last sentence contains an implied reference to Thoreau and to Marie's earlier statement about the joy to be
found in special places having restorative powers. Such an allusion echoes,
with good effect, the paper's opening comments.

Revising the first draft.   When Marie met with some classmates during a
peer review session, the students agreed that Marie's first draft was strong
and moving. But they also said that they had difficulty following her route
through the marsh; they found her third paragraph especially confusing.
Marie kept track of her classmates' comments on a separate piece of paper
and then entered them, numbered in order of importance, in the margin of
her first draft. Following is the first-draft version of Marie's third paragraph.

Original Version of the Third Paragraph

As I head out to the marsh from the house, I follow a short trail through the
woods. A smell of salt mixed with the aroma of soil fills my nostrils. The end of
the trail suddenly opens up to a view that calms me no matter how upset or
discouraged I might be: a line of tall waving reeds bordering the salt marsh
creek. Civilization seems far away as I walk the path of flattened grass and
finally reach my goal, the salt marsh creek hidden behind the tall waving reeds.
The path changes with the seasons; sometimes I walk in the brilliant green of
spring, sometimes in the tawny gold of autumn, sometimes in the quiet grayish
tan of winter. In some areas, the grass is flattened into swirls that make the
marsh resemble one of those paintings by Van Gogh. No people come here. The
peacefulness heals me like a soothing drug. The path stops at the line of tall
waving reeds, standing upright at the border of the creek. I part the reeds to get
to the creek.

When Marie looked more carefully at the paragraph, she agreed it was
confusing. For one thing, the paragraph's third and fourth sentences indicated that she had come to the path's end and had reached the reeds bordering
the creek. In the following sentences, however, she was on the path again.
Then, at the end, she was back at the creek, as if she had just arrived there.
Marie resolved this confusion by breaking the single paragraph into two
separate ones—the first describing the walk along the path, the second
describing her arrival at the creek. This restructuring, especially when combined with clearer transitions, eliminated the confusion.

While revising her essay, Marie also intensified the sensory images in her original paragraph. She changed the "smell of salt and soil" to the "sharp smell of salt mixed with the rich aroma of peaty soil." And when she added the phrase "thick Van Gogh brush strokes that curve and recurve in circular patterns," she made the comparison between the marsh grass and a Van Gogh painting more vivid.

These are just some of the changes Marie made while rewriting her paper. Her skillful revisions provided the polish needed to make an already strong essay even more evocative.

Activities: Description

Prewriting Activities

1. Imagine you're writing two essays: One explains the *process* by which students get "burned out;" the other *argues* that being a spendthrift is better (or worse) than being frugal. Jot down ways you might use description in each essay.

2. Go to a place on campus where students congregate. In preparation for an *objective* description of this place, make notes of various sights, sounds, smells, and textures, as well as the overall "feel" of the place. Then, in preparation for a *subjective* description, observe and take notes on another sheet of paper. Compare the two sets of material. What differences do you see in word choice and selection of details?

Revising Activities

3. Revise each of the following sentence sets twice. The first time, create an unmistakable mood; the second time, create a sharply contrasting mood. To convey atmosphere, vary sentence structure, use vigorous verbs, provide rich sensory details, and pay special attention to words' connotations.

   a. The card players sat around the table. The table was old. The players were, too.
   b. A long line formed outside the movie theater. People didn't want to miss the show. The movie had received a lot of attention recently.
   c. A girl walked down the street in her first pair of high heels. This was a new experience for her.

4. The following descriptive paragraph is from the first draft of an essay showing that personal growth may result when romanticized notions and reality collide. How effective is the paragraph in illustrating the essay's thesis? Which details are powerful? Which could be more concrete? Which should be deleted? Where should sentence structure be more varied? How could the description be made more coherent? Revise the paragraph, correcting any problems you discover and adding whatever sensory details are needed to enliven the description. Feel free to break the paragraph into two or more separate ones.

As a child, I was intrigued by stories about the farm in Harrison County, Maine, where my father spent his teens. Being raised on a farm seemed more interesting than growing up in the suburbs. So about a year ago, I decided to see for myself what the farm was like. I got there by driving on Route 334, a surprisingly easy-to-drive, four-lane highway that had recently been built with matching state and federal funds. I turned into the dirt road leading to the farm and got out of my car. It had been washed and waxed for the occasion. Then I headed for a dirt-colored barn. Its roof was full of huge, rotted holes. As I rounded the bushes, I saw the house. It too was dirt-colored. Its paint must have worn off decades ago. A couple of dead-looking old cars were sprawled in front of the barn. They were dented and windowless. Also by the barn was an ancient refrigerator, crushed like a discarded accordion. The porch steps to the house were slanted and wobbly. Through the open windows came a stale smell and the sound of television. Looking in the front door screen, I could see two chickens jumping around inside. Everything looked dirty both inside and out. Secretly grateful that no one answered my knock, I bolted down the stairs, got into my clean, shiny car, and drove away.

Maya Angelou

Born Marguerite Johnson in 1928, Maya Angelou spent her childhood in Stamps, Arkansas, with her brother, Bailey, and her grandmother, "Momma." Although her youth was difficult—she was raped at age eight and became a mother at sixteen— Angelou somehow managed to thrive. Multi-talented, she later worked as a professional dancer, starred in an off-Broadway play, appeared in the television miniseries *Roots,* served as a coordinator for the Southern Christian Leadership Conference, and wrote several well-received volumes of poetry—among them *Oh Pray My Wings Are Gonna Fit Me Well* (1975) and *And Still I Rise* (1996). She has also written essay collections, such as *Even the Stars Look Lonesome* (1997), and children's books, including *My Painted House, My Friendly Chicken, and Me* (1994), and *Kofi and His Magic* (1996). A professor at Wake Forest University since 1981, Angelou delivered at the 1993 presidential inauguration a stirring poem written for the occasion. The recipient of numerous honorary doctorates, Angelou is best known for her series of six autobiographical books, starting with *I Know Why the Caged Bird Sings* (1970) and concluding with *A Song Flung Up to Heaven* (2002). The following essay is taken from *I Know Why the Caged Bird Sings.*

For ideas about how this description essay is organized, see Figure 3.2 on page 92.

Pre-Reading Journal Entry

Growing up isn't easy. In your journal, list several challenges you've had to face in your life. In each case, was there someone who served as a "lifeline," providing you with crucial guidance and support? Who was that individual? How did this person steer you through the difficulty?

Sister Flowers

For nearly a year [after I was raped], I sopped around the house, the Store, the school and the church, like an old biscuit, dirty and inedible. Then I met, or rather got to know, the lady who threw me my first life line.   1

Mrs. Bertha Flowers was the aristocrat of Black Stamps. She had the grace of control to appear warm in the coldest weather, and on the Arkansas summer days it seemed she had a private breeze which swirled around, cooling her. She was thin without the taut look of wiry people, and her printed voile dresses and flowered hats were as right for her as denim overalls for a farmer. She was our side's answer to the richest white woman in town.   2

Her skin was a rich black that would have peeled like a plum if snagged, but then no one would have thought of getting close enough to Mrs. Flowers to ruffle her dress, let alone snag her skin. She didn't encourage familiarity. She wore gloves too.   3

I don't think I ever saw Mrs. Flowers laugh, but she smiled often. A slow   4
widening of her thin black lips to show even, small white teeth, then the slow
effortless closing. When she chose to smile on me, I always wanted to thank
her. The action was so graceful and inclusively benign.

She was one of the few gentlewomen I have ever known, and has   5
remained throughout my life the measure of what a human being can be.

Momma had a strange relationship with her. Most often when she passed   6
on the road in front of the Store, she spoke to Momma in that soft yet carrying voice, "Good day, Mrs. Henderson." Momma responded with "How
you, Sister Flowers?"

Mrs. Flowers didn't belong to our church, nor was she Momma's famil-   7
iar. Why on earth did she insist on calling her Sister Flowers? Shame made
me want to hide my face. Mrs. Flowers deserved better than to be called
Sister. Then, Momma left out the verb. Why not ask, "How *are* you,
Mrs. Flowers?" With the unbalanced passion of the young, I hated her for
showing her ignorance to Mrs. Flowers. It didn't occur to me for many years
that they were as alike as sisters, separated only by formal education.

Although I was upset, neither of the women was in the least shaken by   8
what I thought an unceremonious greeting. Mrs. Flowers would continue
her easy gait up the hill to her little bungalow, and Momma kept on shelling
peas or doing whatever had brought her to the front porch.

Occasionally, though, Mrs. Flowers would drift off the road and down   9
to the Store and Momma would say to me, "Sister, you go on and play." As
she left I would hear the beginning of an intimate conversation. Momma
persistently using the wrong verb, or none at all.

"Brother and Sister Wilcox is sho'ly the meanest—" "Is," Momma?   10
"Is"? Oh, please, not "is," Momma, for two or more. But they talked, and
from the side of the building where I waited for the ground to open up and
swallow me, I heard the soft-voiced Mrs. Flowers and the textured voice of
my grandmother merging and melting. They were interrupted from time to
time by giggles that must have come from Mrs. Flowers (Momma never gig-
gled in her life). Then she was gone.

She appealed to me because she was like people I had never met per-   11
sonally. Like women in English novels who walked the moors (whatever
they were) with their loyal dogs racing at a respectful distance. Like the
women who sat in front of roaring fireplaces, drinking tea incessantly from
silver trays full of scones and crumpets. Women who walked over the
"heath" and read morocco-bound books and had two last names divided by
a hyphen. It would be safe to say that she made me proud to be Negro, just
by being herself.

She acted just as refined as whitefolks in the movies and books and she   12
was more beautiful, for none of them could have come near that warm color
without looking gray by comparison.

It was fortunate that I never saw her in the company of powhitefolks. 13
For since they tend to think of their whiteness as an evenizer, I'm certain
that I would have had to hear her spoken to commonly as Bertha, and my
image of her would have been shattered like the unmendable Humpty-
Dumpty.

One summer afternoon, sweet-milk fresh in my memory, she stopped 14
at the Store to buy provisions. Another Negro woman of her health and
age would have been expected to carry the paper sacks home in one hand,
but Momma said, "Sister Flowers, I'll send Bailey up to your house with
these things."

She smiled that slow dragging smile, "Thank you, Mrs. Henderson. 15
I'd prefer Marguerite, though." My name was beautiful when she said
it. "I've been meaning to talk to her, anyway." They gave each other age-
group looks.

Momma said, "Well, that's all right then. Sister, go and change your 16
dress. You going to Sister Flowers's."

The chifforobe was a maze. What on earth did one put on to go to 17
Mrs. Flowers's house? I knew I shouldn't put on a Sunday dress. It might be
sacrilegious. Certainly not a house dress, since I was already wearing a fresh
one. I chose a school dress, naturally. It was formal without suggesting that
going to Mrs. Flowers's house was equivalent to attending church.

I trusted myself back into the Store. 18

"Now, don't you look nice." I had chosen the right thing, for once.... 19

There was a little path beside the rocky road, and Mrs. Flowers walked 20
in front swinging her arms and picking her way over the stones.

She said, without turning her head, to me, "I hear you're doing very 21
good school work, Marguerite, but that it's all written. The teachers report
that they have trouble getting you to talk in class." We passed the triangular
farm on our left and the path widened to allow us to walk together. I hung
back in the separate unasked and unanswerable questions.

"Come and walk along with me, Marguerite." I couldn't have refused 22
even if I wanted to. She pronounced my name so nicely. Or more correctly, she
spoke each word with such clarity that I was certain a foreigner who didn't
understand English could have understood her.

"Now no one is going to make you talk—possibly no one can. But bear 23
in mind, language is man's way of communicating with his fellow man and
it is language alone which separates him from the lower animals." That was
a totally new idea to me, and I would need time to think about it.

"Your grandmother says you read a lot. Every chance you get. That's good, 24
but not good enough. Words mean more than what is set down on paper. It
takes the human voice to infuse them with the shades of deeper meaning."

I memorized the part about the human voice infusing words. It seemed 25
so valid and poetic.

She said she was going to give me some books and that I not only must   26
read them, I must read them aloud. She suggested that I try to make a sentence sound in as many different ways as possible.

"I'll accept no excuse if you return a book to me that has been badly   27
handled." My imagination boggled at the punishment I would deserve if
in fact I did abuse a book of Mrs. Flowers's. Death would be too kind
and brief.

The odors in the house surprised me. Somehow I had never connected   28
Mrs. Flowers with food or eating or any other common experience of common people. There must have been an outhouse, too, but my mind never
recorded it.

The sweet scent of vanilla had met us as she opened the door.   29

"I made tea cookies this morning. You see, I had planned to invite you   30
for cookies and lemonade so we could have this little chat. The lemonade is
in the icebox."

It followed that Mrs. Flowers would have ice on an ordinary day, when   31
most families in our town bought ice late on Saturdays only a few times during the summer to be used in the wooden ice-cream freezers.

She took the bags from me and disappeared through the kitchen door.   32
I looked around the room that I had never in my wildest fantasies imagined
I would see. Browned photographs leered or threatened from the walls and
the white, freshly done curtains pushed against themselves and against the
wind. I wanted to gobble up the room entire and take it to Bailey, who
would help me analyze and enjoy it.

"Have a seat, Marguerite. Over there by the table." She carried a platter   33
covered with a tea towel. Although she warned that she hadn't tried her
hand at baking sweets for some time, I was certain that like everything else
about her the cookies would be perfect.

They were flat round wafers, slightly browned on the edges and butter-   34
yellow in the center. With the cold lemonade they were sufficient for childhood's lifelong diet. Remembering my manners, I took nice little lady-like
bites off the edges. She said she had made them expressly for me and that
she had a few in the kitchen that I could take home to my brother. So I
jammed one whole cake in my mouth and the rough crumbs scratched the
insides of my jaws, and if I hadn't had to swallow, it would have been a
dream come true.

As I ate she began the first of what we later called "my lessons in liv-   35
ing." She said that I must always be intolerant of ignorance but understanding of illiteracy. That some people, unable to go to school, were
more educated and even more intelligent than college professors. She
encouraged me to listen carefully to what country people called mother
wit. That in those homely sayings was couched the collective wisdom of
generations.

When I finished the cookies she brushed off the table and brought a thick, small book from the bookcase. I had read *A Tale of Two Cities* and found it up to my standards as a romantic novel. She opened the first page and I heard poetry for the first time in my life. 36

"It was the best of times and the worst of times..." Her voice slid in and curved down through and over the words. She was nearly singing. I wanted to look at the pages. Were they the same that I had read? Or were there notes, music, lined on the pages, as in a hymn book? Her sounds began cascading gently. I knew from listening to a thousand preachers that she was nearing the end of her reading, and I hadn't really heard, heard to understand, a single word. 37

"How do you like that?" 38

It occurred to me that she expected a response. The sweet vanilla flavor was still on my tongue and her reading was a wonder in my ears. I had to speak. 39

I said, "Yes, ma'am." It was the least I could do, but it was the most also. 40

"There's one more thing. Take this book of poems and memorize one for me. Next time you pay me a visit, I want you to recite." 41

I have tried often to search behind the sophistication of years for the enchantment I so easily found in those gifts. The essence escapes but its aura remains. To be allowed, no, invited, into the private lives of strangers, and to share their joys and fears, was a chance to exchange the Southern bitter wormwood for a cup of mead with Beowulf[1] or a hot cup of tea and milk with Oliver Twist.[2] When I said aloud, "It is a far, far better thing that I do, than I have ever done..."[3] tears of love filled my eyes at my selflessness. 42

On that first day, I ran down the hill and into the road (few cars ever came along it) and had the good sense to stop running before I reached the Store. 43

I was liked, and what a difference it made. I was respected not as Mrs. Henderson's grandchild or Bailey's sister but for just being Marguerite Johnson. 44

Childhood's logic never asks to be proved (all conclusions are absolute). I didn't question why Mrs. Flowers had singled me out for attention, nor did it occur to me that Momma might have asked her to give me a little talking to. All I cared about was that she had made tea cookies for *me* and read to *me* from her favorite book. It was enough to prove that she liked me. 45

---

[1]The hero of an Old English epic poem dating from the eighth century (editors' note).
[2]The main character in Charles Dickens's novel *Oliver Twist* (1837) (editors' note).
[3]The last words of Sydney Carton, the selfless hero of Charles Dickens's novel *A Tale of Two Cities* (1859) (editors' note).

FIGURE 3.2
Essay Structure Diagram: "Sister Flowers" by Maya Angelou

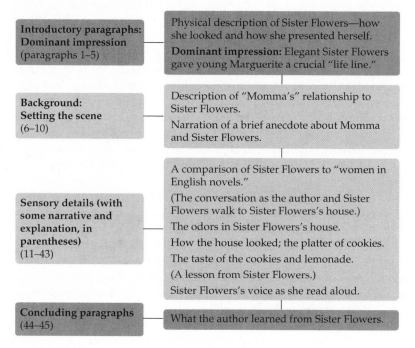

Introductory paragraphs: Dominant impression (paragraphs 1–5)	Physical description of Sister Flowers—how she looked and how she presented herself. **Dominant impression:** Elegant Sister Flowers gave young Marguerite a crucial "life line."
Background: Setting the scene (6–10)	Description of "Momma's" relationship to Sister Flowers. Narration of a brief anecdote about Momma and Sister Flowers.
Sensory details (with some narrative and explanation, in parentheses) (11–43)	A comparison of Sister Flowers to "women in English novels." (The conversation as the author and Sister Flowers walk to Sister Flowers's house.) The odors in Sister Flowers's house. How the house looked; the platter of cookies. The taste of the cookies and lemonade. (A lesson from Sister Flowers.) Sister Flowers's voice as she read aloud.
Concluding paragraphs (44–45)	What the author learned from Sister Flowers.

Questions for Close Reading

1. What is the selection's thesis (or dominant impression)? Locate the sentence(s) in which Angelou states her main idea. If she doesn't state the thesis explicitly, express it in your own words.

2. Angelou states that Mrs. Flowers "has remained throughout my life the measure of what a human being can be" (paragraph 5). What does Angelou admire about Mrs. Flowers?

3. Why is young Angelou so ashamed of Momma when Mrs. Flowers is around? How do Momma and Mrs. Flowers behave with each other?

4. What are the "lessons in living" that Angelou receives from Mrs. Flowers during their first visit? How do you think these lessons might have subsequently influenced Angelou?

5. Refer to your dictionary as needed to define the following words used in the selection: *taut* (paragraph 2), *voile* (2), *benign* (4), *unceremonious* (8), *gait* (8), *moors* (11), *incessantly* (11), *scones* (11), *crumpets* (11), *heath* (11), *chifforobe* (17), *sacrilegious* (17), *infuse* (24), *couched* (35), and *aura* (42).

Questions About the Writer's Craft

1. **The pattern.** Reread the essay, focusing on the descriptive passages first of Mrs. Flowers and then of Angelou's visit to Mrs. Flowers's house. To what senses does Angelou appeal in these passages? What method of organization (see pages 41–42) does she use to order these sensory details?
2. To enrich the description of her eventful encounter with Mrs. Flowers, Angelou draws upon figures of speech (see page 78). Consider, for example, the similes in paragraphs 1 and 11. How do these figures of speech contribute to the essay's dominant impression?
3. **Other patterns.** Because Angelou's description has a strong *narrative* component, it isn't surprising that there's a considerable amount of dialogue in the selection. For example, in paragraphs 7 and 10, Angelou quotes Momma's incorrect grammar. She then provides an imagined conversation in which the young Angelou scolds Momma and corrects her speech. What do these imagined scoldings of Momma reveal about young Angelou? How do they relate to Mrs. Flowers's subsequent "lessons in life"?
4. Although it's not the focus of this selection, the issue of race remains in the background of Angelou's portrait of Mrs. Flowers. Where in the selection does Angelou imply that race was a fact of life in her town? How does this specter of racism help Angelou underscore the significance of her encounter with Mrs. Flowers?

Writing Assignments Using Description as a Pattern of Development

1. At one time or another, just about all of us have met someone who taught us to see ourselves more clearly and helped us understand what we wanted from life. Write an essay describing such a person. Focus on the individual's personal qualities, as a way of depicting the role he or she played in your life. Be sure not to limit yourself to an objective description. Subjective description, filled with lively language and figures of speech, will serve you well as you provide a portrait of this special person.
2. Thrilled by the spectacle of Mrs. Flowers's interesting home, Angelou says she wanted to "gobble up the room entire" and share it with her brother. Write an essay describing in detail a place that vividly survives in your memory. You may describe a setting that you visited only once or a familiar setting that holds a special place in your heart. Before you write, list the qualities and sensory impressions you associate with this special place; then refine the list so that all details support your dominant impression. You may want to read Gary Kamiya's "Life, Death and Spring" (page 103) to see how a professional writer evokes the qualities of a special place in his life.

Writing Assignments Combining Patterns of Development

3. When the young Angelou discovers, thanks to Mrs. Flowers, the thrill of acceptance, she experiences a kind of *epiphany*—a moment of enlightenment. Write an essay about an event in your life that represented a kind of epiphany. You might

write about a positive discovery, such as when you realized you had a special talent for something, or about a negative discovery, such as when you realized that a beloved family member had a serious flaw. To make the point that the moment was a turning point in your life, start by *describing* what kind of person you were before the discovery. Then *narrate* the actual incident, using vivid details and dialogue to make the event come alive. End by discussing the importance of this epiphany in your life. For additional accounts of personal epiphanies, you might read Audre Lorde's "The Fourth of July" (page 127) and Joan Murray's "Someone's Mother" (page 141).

4. Think of an activity that engages you completely, one that provides—as reading does for Angelou—an opportunity for growth and expansion. Possibilities include reading, writing, playing an instrument, doing crafts, dancing, hiking, playing a sport, cooking, or traveling. Write an essay in which you *argue* the merits of your chosen pastime. Assume that some of your readers are highly skeptical. To win them over, you'll need to provide convincing *examples* that demonstrate the pleasure and benefits you have discovered in the activity.

Writing Assignment Using a Journal Entry as a Starting Point

5. Write an essay about a time when someone threw you a much-needed "lifeline" at a challenging time. Review your pre-reading journal entry, selecting *one* time when a person's encouragement and support made a great difference in your life. Be sure to describe the challenge you faced before recounting the specific details of the person's help. Dialogue and descriptive details will help you recreate the power of the experience.

Gordon Parks

The son of deeply religious tenant farmers, Gordon Parks (1912–2006) grew up in Kansas knowing both the comforts of familial love and the torments of poverty and racism. Sent as a teenager to live with his sister in Minnesota after his mother's death, Parks was thrown out on his own in a frigid winter by his brother-in-law. To support himself, Parks worked as a janitor in a flophouse and as a piano player in a bordello. These and other odd jobs gave Parks the means to buy his first camera. Fascinated by photographic images, Parks studied the masters and eventually developed his own powers as a photographer. So evocative were his photographic studies that both *Life* and *Vogue* brought him on staff, the first black photographer to be hired by the two magazines. Parks's prodigious creativity has found expression in filmmaking (*Shaft* in 1971), musical composition (both classical and jazz), fiction, nonfiction, and poetry (titles include *The Learning Tree, A Choice of Weapons, To Smile in Autumn, Arias in Silence, Glimpses Toward Infinity, A Star for Noon,* and *The Sun Stalker,* published, respectively, in 1986, 1987, 1988, 1994, 1996, 2000, and 2003). But it is Parks's photographic essays, covering five decades of American life, that brought him the most acclaim. In the following essay, taken from his 1990 autobiography, *Voices in the Mirror,* Parks tells the story behind one of his most memorable photographic works—that of a twelve-year-old boy and his family, living in the slums of Rio de Janeiro.

Pre-Reading Journal Entry

The problem of poverty has provoked a wide array of proposed solutions. One controversial proposal argues that the government should pay poor women financial incentives to use birth control. What do you think of this proposal? Why is such a policy controversial? Use your journal to explore your thinking on this issue.

Flavio's Home

I've never lost my fierce grudge against poverty. It is the most savage of all human afflictions, claiming victims who can't mobilize their efforts against it, who often lack strength to digest what little food they scrounge up to survive. It keeps growing, multiplying, spreading like a cancer. In my wanderings I attack it wherever I can—in barrios, slums and favelas. 1

Catacumba was the name of the favela[1] where I found Flavio da Silva. It was wickedly hot. The noon sun baked the mud-rot of the wet mountainside. Garbage and human excrement clogged the open sewers snaking down the slopes. José Gallo, a *Life* reporter, and I rested in the shade of a jacaranda tree halfway up Rio de Janeiro's most infamous deathtrap. Below and 2

---

[1]Slums on the outskirts of Rio de Janeiro, Brazil, inhabited by seven hundred thousand people (editors' note).

above us were a maze of shacks, but in the distance alongside the beach stood the gleaming white homes of the rich.

Breathing hard, balancing a tin of water on his head, a small boy climbed   3
toward us. He was miserably thin, naked but for filthy denim shorts. His legs resembled sticks covered with skin and screwed into his feet. Death was all over him, in his sunken eyes, cheeks and jaundiced coloring. He stopped for breath, coughing, his chest heaving as water slopped over his bony shoulders. Then jerking sideways like a mechanical toy, he smiled a smile I will never forget. Turning, he went on up the mountainside.

The detailed *Life* assignment in my back pocket was to find an impover-   4
ished father with a family, to examine his earnings, political leanings, religion, friends, dreams and frustrations. I had been sent to do an essay on poverty. This frail boy bent under his load said more to me about poverty than a dozen poor fathers. I touched Gallo, and we got up and followed the boy to where he entered a shack near the top of the mountainside. It was a leaning crumpled place of old plankings with a rusted tin roof. From inside we heard the babblings of several children. José knocked. The door opened and the boy stood smiling with a bawling naked baby in his arms.

Still smiling, he whacked the baby's rump, invited us in and offered us a   5
box to sit on. The only other recognizable furniture was a sagging bed and a broken baby's crib. Flavio was twelve, and with Gallo acting as interpreter, he introduced his younger brothers and sisters: "Mario, the bad one; Baptista, the good one; Albia, Isabel and the baby Zacarias." Two other girls burst into the shack, screaming and pounding on one another. Flavio jumped in and parted them. "Shut up, you two." He pointed at the older girl. "That's Maria, the nasty one." She spit in his face. He smacked her and pointed to the smaller sister. "That's Luzia. She thinks she's pretty."

Having finished the introductions, he went to build a fire under the   6
stove—a rusted, bent top of an old gas range resting on several bricks. Beneath it was a piece of tin that caught the hot coals. The shack was about six by ten feet. Its grimy walls were a patchwork of misshapen boards with large gaps between them, revealing other shacks below stilted against the slopes. The floor, rotting under layers of grease and dirt, caught shafts of light slanting down through spaces in the roof. A large hole in the far corner served as a toilet. Beneath that hole was the sloping mountainside. Pockets of poverty in New York's Harlem, on Chicago's south side, in Puerto Rico's infamous El Fungito seemed pale by comparison. None of them had prepared me for this one in the favela of Catacumba.

Flavio washed rice in a large dishpan, then washed Zacarias's feet in the   7
same water. But even that dirty water wasn't to be wasted. He tossed in a chunk of lye soap and ordered each child to wash up. When they were finished he splashed the water over the dirty floor, and, dropping to his knees, he scrubbed the planks until the black suds sank in. Just before sundown he

put beans on the stove to warm, then left, saying he would be back shortly. "Don't let them burn," he cautioned Maria. "If they do and Poppa beats me, you'll get it later." Maria, happy to get at the licking spoon, switched over and began to stir the beans. Then slyly she dipped out a spoonful and swallowed them. Luzia eyed her. "I see you. I'm going to tell on you for stealing our supper."

Maria's eyes flashed anger. "You do and I'll beat you, you little bitch." 8 Luzia threw a stick at Maria and fled out the door. Zacarias dropped off to sleep. Mario, the bad one, slouched in a corner and sucked his thumb. Isabel and Albia sat on the floor clinging to each other with a strange tenderness. Isabel held onto Albia's hair and Albia clutched at Isabel's neck. They appeared frozen in an act of quiet violence.

Flavio returned with wood, dumped it beside the stove and sat down to 9 rest for a few minutes, then went down the mountain for more water. It was dark when he finally came back, his body sagging from exhaustion. No longer smiling, he suddenly had the look of an old man and by now we could see that he kept the family going. In the closed torment of that pitiful shack, he was waging a hopeless battle against starvation. The da Silva children were living in a coffin.

When at last the parents came in, Gallo and I seemed to be part of 10 the family. Flavio had already told them we were there. "Gordunn Americano!" Luzia said, pointing at me. José, the father, viewed us with skepticism. Nair, his pregnant wife, seemed tired beyond speaking. Hardly acknowledging our presence, she picked up Zacarias, placed him on her shoulder and gently patted his behind. Flavio scurried about like a frightened rat, his silence plainly expressing the fear he held of his father. Impatiently, José da Silva waited for Flavio to serve dinner. He sat in the center of the bed with his legs crossed beneath him, frowning, waiting. There were only three tin plates. Flavio filled them with black beans and rice, then placed them before his father. José da Silva tasted them, chewed for several moments, then nodded his approval for the others to start. Only he and Nair had spoons; the children ate with their fingers. Flavio ate off the top of a coffee can. Afraid to offer us food, he edged his rice and beans toward us, gesturing for us to take some. We refused. He smiled, knowing we understood.

Later, when we got down to the difficult business of obtaining permis- 11 sion from José da Silva to photograph his family, he hemmed and hawed, wallowing in the pleasant authority of the decision maker. He finally gave in, but his manner told us that he expected something in return. As we were saying good night Flavio began to cough violently. For a few moments his lungs seemed to be tearing apart. I wanted to get away as quickly as possible. It was cowardly of me, but the bluish cast of his skin beneath the sweat, the choking and spitting were suddenly unbearable.

Gallo and I moved cautiously down through the darkness trying not to   12
appear as strangers. The Catacumba was no place for strangers after sundown. Desperate criminals hid out there. To hunt them out, the police came
in packs, but only in daylight. Gallo cautioned me. "If you get caught up
here after dark it's best to stay at the da Silvas' until morning." As we drove
toward the city the large white buildings of the rich loomed up. The world
behind us seemed like a bad dream. I had already decided to get the boy
Flavio to a doctor, and as quickly as possible.

The plush lobby of my hotel on the Copacabana waterfront was crammed   13
with people in formal attire. With the stink of the favela in my clothes, I hur-
ried to the elevator hoping no passengers would be aboard. But as the door
was closing a beautiful girl in a white lace gown stepped in. I moved as far
away as possible. Her escort entered behind her, swept her into his arms and
they indulged in a kiss that lasted until they exited on the next floor. Neither
of them seemed to realize that I was there. The room I returned to seemed
to be oversized; the da Silva shack would have fit into one corner of it. The
steak dinner I had would have fed the da Silvas for three days.

Billowing clouds blanketed Mount Corcovado as we approached the   14
favela the following morning. Suddenly the sun burst through, silhouetting
Cristo Redentor, the towering sculpture of Christ with arms extended, its
back turned against the slopes of Catacumba. The square at the entrance to
the favela bustled with hundreds of favelados. Long lines waited at the sole
water spigot. Others waited at the only toilet on the entire mountainside.
Women, unable to pay for soap, beat dirt from their wash at laundry tubs.
Men, burdened with lumber, picks and shovels and tools important to their
existence threaded their way through the noisy throngs. Dogs snarled,
barked and fought. Woodsmoke mixed with the stench of rotting things. In
the mist curling over the higher paths, columns of favelados climbed like ants
with wood and water cans on their heads.

We came upon Nair bent over her tub of wash. She wiped away sweat   15
with her apron and managed a smile. We asked for her husband and she pointed to a tiny shack off to her right. This was José's store, where he sold
kerosene and bleach. He was sitting on a box, dozing. Sensing our presence,
he awoke and commenced complaining about his back. "It kills me. The
doctors don't help because I have no money. Always talk and a little pink pill
that does no good. Ah, what is to become of me?" A woman came to buy
bleach. He filled her bottle. She dropped a few coins and as she walked away
his eyes stayed on her backside until she was out of sight. Then he was complaining about his back again.

"How much do you earn a day?" Gallo asked.   16

"Seventy-five cents. On a good day maybe a dollar."   17

"Why aren't the kids in school?"   18

"I don't have money for the clothes they need to go to school." 19

"Has Flavio seen a doctor?" 20

He pointed to a one-story wooden building. "That's the clinic right 21
there. They're mad because I built my store in front of their place. I won't
tear it down so they won't help my kids. Talk, talk, talk and pink pills." We
bid him good-bye and started climbing, following mud trails, jutting rock,
slime-filled holes and shack after shack propped against the slopes on shaky
pilings. We sidestepped a dead cat covered with maggots. I held my breath
for an instant, only to inhale the stench of human excrement and garbage.
Bare feet and legs with open sores climbed above us—evils of the terrible soil
they trod every day, and there were seven hundred thousand or more afflict-
ed people in favelas around Rio alone. Touching me, Gallo pointed to Flavio
climbing ahead of us carrying firewood. He stopped to glance at a man
descending with a small coffin on his shoulder. A woman and a small child
followed him. When I lifted my camera, grumbling erupted from a group of
men sharing beer beneath a tree.

"They're threatening," Gallo said. "Keep moving. They fear cameras. 22
Think they're evil eyes bringing bad luck." Turning to watch the funeral
procession, Flavio caught sight of us and waited. When we took the wood
from him he protested, saying he was used to carrying it. He gave in when
I hung my camera around his neck. Then, beaming, he climbed on ahead
of us.

The fog had lifted and in the crisp morning light the shack looked more 23
squalid. Inside the kids seemed even noisier. Flavio smiled and spoke above
their racket. "Someday I want to live in a real house on a real street with
good pots and pans and a bed with sheets." He lit the fire to warm leftovers
from the night before. Stale rice and beans—for breakfast and supper. No
lunch; midday eating was out of the question. Smoke rose and curled up
through the ceiling's cracks. An air current forced it back, filling the place
and Flavio's lungs with fumes. A coughing spasm doubled him up, turned
his skin blue under viscous sweat. I handed him a cup of water, but he waved
it away. His stomach tightened as he dropped to his knees. His veins
throbbed as if they would burst. Frustrated, we could only watch; there was
nothing we could do to help. Strangely, none of his brothers or sisters
appeared to notice. None of them stopped doing whatever they were doing.
Perhaps they had seen it too often. After five interminable minutes it was
over, and he got to his feet, smiling as though it had all been a joke. "Maria,
it's time for Zacarias to be washed!"

"But there's rice in the pan!" 24

"Dump it in another pan—and don't spill water!" 25

Maria picked up Zacarias, who screamed, not wanting to be washed. 26
Irritated, Maria gave him a solid smack on his bare bottom. Flavio stepped over
and gave her the same, then a free-for-all started with Flavio, Maria and

Mario slinging fists at one another. Mario got one in the eye and fled the shack calling Flavio a dirty son-of-a-bitch. Zacarias wound up on the floor sucking his thumb and escaping his washing. The black bean and rice breakfast helped to get things back to normal. Now it was time to get Flavio to the doctor.

The clinic was crowded with patients—mothers and children covered with open sores, a paralytic teenager, a man with an ear in a state of decay, an aged blind couple holding hands in doubled darkness. Throughout the place came wailings of hunger and hurt. Flavio sat nervously between Gallo and me. "What will the doctor do to me?" he kept asking.   27

"We'll see. We'll wait and see."   28

In all, there were over fifty people. Finally, after two hours, it was Flavio's turn and he broke out in a sweat, though he smiled at the nurse as he passed through the door to the doctor's office. The nurse ignored it; in this place of misery, smiles were unexpected.   29

The doctor, a large, beady-eyed man with a crew cut, had an air of impatience. Hardly acknowledging our presence, he began to examine the frightened Flavio. "Open your mouth. Say 'Ah.' Jump up and down. Breathe out. Take off those pants. Bend over. Stand up. Cough. Cough louder. Louder." He did it all with such cold efficiency. Then he spoke to us in English so Flavio wouldn't understand. "This little chap has just about had it." My heart sank. Flavio was smiling, happy to be over with the examination. He was handed a bottle of cough medicine and a small box of pink pills, then asked to step outside and wait.   30

"This the da Silva kid?"   31

"Yes."   32

"What's your interest in him?"   33

"We want to help in some way."   34

"I'm afraid you're too late. He's wasted with bronchial asthma, malnutrition and, I suspect, tuberculosis. His heart, lungs and teeth are all bad." He paused and wearily rubbed his forehead. "All that at the ripe old age of twelve. And these hills are packed with other kids just as bad off. Last year ten thousand died from dysentery alone. But what can we do? You saw what's waiting outside. It's like this every day. There's hardly enough money to buy aspirin. A few wealthy people who care help keep us going." He was quiet for a moment. "Maybe the right climate, the right diet, and constant medical care might..." He stopped and shook his head. "Naw. That poor lad's finished. He might last another year—maybe not." We thanked him and left.   35

"What did he say?" Flavio asked as we scaled the hill.   36

"Everything's going to be all right, Flav. There's nothing to worry about."   37

It had clouded over again by the time we reached the top. The rain swept in, clearing the mountain of Corcovado. The huge Christ figure loomed up   38 again with clouds swirling around it. And to it I said a quick prayer for the boy walking beside us. He smiled as if he had read my thoughts. "Papa says 'El Cristo' has turned his back on the favela."

"You're going to be all right, Flavio." 39

"I'm not scared of death. It's my brothers and sisters I worry about. 40 What would they do?"

"You'll be all right, Flavio."[2] 41

---

[2]Parks's photo-essay on Flavio generated an unprecedented response from *Life* readers. Indeed, they sent so much money to the da Silvas that the family was able to leave the *favela* for better living conditions. Parks brought Flavio to the United States for medical treatment, and the boy's health was restored. However, Flavio's story didn't have an unqualifiedly happy ending. Although he overcame his illness and later married and had a family, Flavio continuously fantasized about returning to the United States, convinced that only by returning to America could he improve his life. His obsession eventually eroded the promise of his life in Brazil (editors' note).

Questions for Close Reading

1. What is the selection's thesis (or dominant impression)? Locate the sentence(s) in which Parks states his main idea. If he doesn't state the thesis explicitly, express it in your own words.
2. What is Flavio's family like? Why does Flavio have so much responsibility in the household?
3. What are some of the distinctive characteristics of Flavio's neighborhood and home?
4. What seems to be the basis of Flavio's fear of giving food to Parks and Gallo? What did Parks and Gallo understand that led them to refuse?
5. Refer to your dictionary as needed to define the following words used in the selection: *barrios* (paragraph 1), *jacaranda* (2), *jaundiced* (3), and *spigot* (14).

Questions About the Writer's Craft

1. **The pattern.** Without stating it explicitly, Parks conveys a dominant impression about Flavio. What is that impression? What details create it?
2. **Other patterns.** When relating how Flavio performs numerous household tasks, Parks describes several *processes*. How do these step-by-step explanations reinforce Parks's dominant impression of Flavio?
3. Parks provides numerous sensory specifics to depict Flavio's home. Look closely, for example, at the description in paragraph 6. Which words and phrases convey strong sensory images? How does Parks use transitions to help the reader move from one sensory image to another?
4. Paragraph 13 includes a scene that occurs in Parks's hotel. What's the effect of this scene? What does it contribute to the essay that the most detailed description of the *favela* could not?

Writing Assignments Using Description as a Pattern of Development

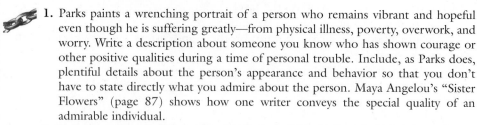

1. Parks paints a wrenching portrait of a person who remains vibrant and hopeful even though he is suffering greatly—from physical illness, poverty, overwork, and worry. Write a description about someone you know who has shown courage or other positive qualities during a time of personal trouble. Include, as Parks does, plentiful details about the person's appearance and behavior so that you don't have to state directly what you admire about the person. Maya Angelou's "Sister Flowers" (page 87) shows how one writer conveys the special quality of an admirable individual.

2. Parks presents an unforgettable description of the *favela* and the living conditions there. Write an essay about a region, city, neighborhood, or building that also projects an overwhelming negative feeling. Include only those details that convey your dominant impression, and provide—as Parks does—vivid sensory language to convey your attitude toward your subject.

Writing Assignments Combining Patterns of Development

3. The doctor reports that a few wealthy people contribute to the clinic, but the reader can tell from the scene in Parks's hotel that most people are insensitive to those less fortunate. Write an essay *describing* a specific situation that you feel reflects people's tendency to ignore the difficulties of others. Analyze why people distance themselves from the problem; then present specific *steps* that could be taken to sensitize them to the situation. Joan Murray's "Someone's Mother" (page 141) will provide some perspective on the way people deal with others in need.

4. Although Parks celebrates Flavio's generosity of spirit, the writer also *illustrates* the brutalizing effect of an impoverished environment. Prepare an essay in which you also show that setting, architecture, even furnishings can influence mood and behavior. You may, as Parks does, focus on the corrosive effect of a negative environment, or you may write about the nurturing effect of a positive environment. Either way, provide vivid *descriptive* details of the environment you're considering. Possible subjects include a park in the middle of a city, a bus terminal, and a college library.

Writing Assignment Using a Journal Entry as a Starting Point

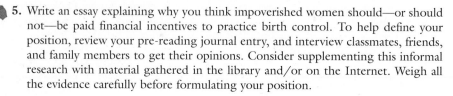

5. Write an essay explaining why you think impoverished women should—or should not—be paid financial incentives to practice birth control. To help define your position, review your pre-reading journal entry, and interview classmates, friends, and family members to get their opinions. Consider supplementing this informal research with material gathered in the library and/or on the Internet. Weigh all the evidence carefully before formulating your position.

Gary Kamiya was born in Oakland, California, in 1953. He was educated at Yale University and the University of California at Berkeley, where he was awarded the Mark Schorer Citation as the outstanding undergraduate in English literature. After receiving a master's degree from Berkeley, he worked as a freelance writer for publications including *ArtForum* and *Sports Illustrated* before becoming an editor and culture writer at *The San Francisco Examiner*. Kamiya cofounded the website *Salon.com*, where he was executive editor for many years and is now a columnist. His essays have appeared in Harvard University Press's *A New Literary History of America*, the essay and photography collection *What Matters*, and other books. He lives in San Francisco with his wife—the novelist Kate Moses—and their two children. This essay was published on *Salon.com* on April 22, 2008.

Pre-Reading Journal Entry

All of us have places that we cherish, perhaps because they are beautiful, or perhaps because they play a big role in our lives. Think about the special places in your life, whether they are rooms, landscapes, buildings, or childhood hiding spots. What are some of these places? What are they like? Why are they important to you? Use your journal to answer these questions.

Life, Death and Spring

The stench hit us right after we climbed up the dug-out steps in the bank, by the bend in the stream where the mountain lion and I surprised each other four years ago. It had to be something pretty big. I walked through the little meadow toward the lake, gingerly following my nose. After 30 yards or so I saw it. A small, delicate white skull, like an overgrown rodent's, with a surprisingly thick spine, 2 or 3 feet long. Nothing else—no body or legs. A deer. Almost all the flesh was gone, but there was still enough left to raise a powerful stink. We walked on through the young grass, where in a few weeks the lupine and sweet pea would cover the ground with their exuberant bluish-purple and pink and white blossoms.

I'd driven with my mother up to our family ranch in the Sierra foothills to join my brother, uncle, cousin and some other clan members for a work weekend. We were going to clear brush along the edge of the big meadow, hauling out fallen wood, clearing pine needles and debris and cutting down the cedars and yellow pines that were crowding a magnificent avenue of oaks. If weather permitted, we were going to ignite the piles of brush that were evenly spaced out in the meadow. We were looking forward to this atavistic ritual, heaping branches onto the pyres, consuming last year's dead matter, leaning on our McLeods[1] and watching the orange tongues twisting and leaping upward in the cool April air.

But mostly I was looking for spring.   3

San Francisco, where I live, doesn't really have seasons. Yes, we have   4
an Indian summer in September and October, a week or two of 80 degree days that overheats our delicate constitutions and causes all the fans in the hardware stores to immediately disappear. It rains a lot in the winter months. And around the time school gets out in June, the summer fog starts rolling in, a giant cotton-candy wave breaking in slow motion over Twin Peaks at 4 p.m. But aside from those minor markers, the seasons are pretty indistinguishable. Most Februaries I can sunbathe on my deck, and I frequently shiver in July. The temperature rarely goes below 50 in the day, or above 70. This city belongs to the sea, not the land, and the sea's seasons are inscrutable.

And I don't really see the signs of spring that are there. When you live   5
in a city, the world is blocked from view. Too many buildings, too many people, too many street lights changing mechanically, too many thoughts changing just as mechanically. Even the moon, that harbinger of mystery, feels like an impostor.

You can exist without spring, but it cramps your soul. It's good to have   6
a place where you can go to watch the world get old and young, live and die. Mine is the ranch.

It lies a shade under 4,000 feet in Calaveras County, which means   7
"skulls" and which an unknown journalist, writing under the peculiar, Mississippi-redolent pseudonym "Mark Twain," made famous when he penned a story[2] about a celebrated jumping frog that some wag stuffed full of birdshot. Calaveras is gold country, but the ranch is too high for prospecting. The property was a double homestead spread, 320 acres, first worked in 1882 by a driven German-American pioneer and his wife who together cleared 25 forested acres for a meadow, using a mule team to pull the stumps out of the ground. He then erected an astonishingly grandiloquent structure at the edge of the meadow, a 55-foot-high asymmetrical barn that may still be the tallest building in the county. The hay from the meadow wouldn't even fill a fifth of this vast structure. He must have built it so high just because he could. The German is long gone but his barn still stands, a great gray monument to his sublime orneriness.

One infamous day, we almost lost the whole place. On Sept. 10, 2001,   8
a devastating forest fire roared up out of the Stanislaus River canyon to the east. When the flames crowned the trees on the other side of the ridge and

[1]A firefighting tool with a hoe-like blade on one side and a rake-like blade on the other (editors' note).
[2]"The Celebrated Jumping Frog of Calaveras County" (editors' note).

were visible from the meadow, my mother and my uncles simultaneously decided to tell the firemen, "Save the barn before the houses." Hundreds of firemen from all over the state made their stand, fighting tree to tree on the steep ridge. The meadow looked like a war zone, filled with dozens of fire trucks. We were the last line of defense for the town of Arnold. The battle wasn't won until bombers swept in low and dumped borate[3] on the inferno. It was the last day the big planes could have saved us: The next day all civil aviation in the United States was grounded. My uncle's partner called from New York the next day early in the morning. First she asked, "Is the ranch still there?" Then she said, "Turn on your television."

My grandparents bought the ranch in 1943 for next to nothing. Land in   9 the middle of nowhere wasn't worth anything then. It comprises a long, narrow valley watered by a creek and most of the two ridges on each side. It lies in what naturalists call the Yellow Pine Forest, also known as the Mixed Coniferous Forest or the Transition Zone, located between the oak woodland of the lower foothills and the higher lodgepole-red fir forest. Yellow pine (also known as Ponderosa) is the dominant tree. Incense cedar, white fir and John Muir's[4] favorite conifer, the sugar pine, the tallest pine in the world, share the woods with slender-trunked maples and stands of dogwoods, which in May dress up in dazzling white. The royalty of our trees, though, are the black oaks. They are greatly outnumbered by conifers at this elevation, but if the world keeps getting hotter and drier, they will become the dominant species. And if there are any human beings left on the earth then, they will probably enjoy them.

The German also planted 20 or so acres of apple trees in three orchards.   10 The old trees still bear fruit, rare and delicious varietals—King Davids and Spitzenbergs and Winter Bananas and Black Johns—but they are rapidly dying off. My grandfather, a truck driver who later opened the first gas station in Angel's Camp, maintained the ranch as a gentleman farmer, pruning and irrigating and harvesting. But he died 24 years ago, none of the rest of us have time or inclination, and anyway the trees are nearing the end. Every year, snow in the winter and ravenous climbing bears in the fall crack a few more big branches off the old trees. Their gnarled remaining limbs look like twisted gray hands outstretched to the sky, waving a very long goodbye.

The day we left San Francisco for the ranch was scorching hot for April,   11 and the unseasonable heat carried through the Central Valley and all the way through the oak foothills to the ranch. But the winter rains and snows were not long past, and everything was still green, that deep, fragile green that you wish could last forever, but that fades almost as you look at it.

[3]Fire retardant and suppressant (editors' note).
[4]John Muir (1838–1914), a preservationist who helped save Western wilderness areas and influenced the modern environmental movement (editors' note).

April is unpredictable, edgy—the turning month. The apple trees had   12
barely begun to leaf out, the ferns had not yet started their scarily fast
growth, and only a few modest wildflowers had begun to appear—five-spots
and red-flowered gooseberries and tiny exquisite white stars that none of us
knew the names of. We plunged into the creek-side trail that my cousin, my
uncle Bob and I hacked out of the woods a dozen years ago. Winter had
been here and left chaos and destruction, and no one had cleaned up after
it. Black-tongued trilliums and crimson snow plants, eerie post-winter
arrivals, had pushed through the pine needles. A big yellow pine had fallen
across the trail and an even larger cedar had fallen below the spillway of the
big lake. Chain-saw work. All of the big trees on this steep bank were in danger, more of them falling every year as erosion exposed their roots.

Years ago Bob had put up a wooden bench by a gentle bend downstream   13
on the creek, a place where he could sit and take in the Sierra summer before
heading back to Manhattan and his life as a college professor. Then he found
out he had pancreatic cancer and died a few weeks later. The winter after his
death, a cedar by the stream came down and smashed right through the center of the bench. Bob's ashes and my aunt Wendy's are buried on the ranch,
along with their parents'. When my time comes, mine will join them.

The ranch exists on the boundary of wilderness and the familiar, and you   14
make your negotiations between them. Walking down to the big lake, I saw
a familiar form slowly rouse itself on the bank and creak arthritically into the
air, at first barely able to get moving, but with each ponderous flap of its
heavy wings gaining disconcerting chunks of altitude and speed. We rushed
down to the water and got there just in time to see it in full flight, our great
blue heron, now soaring high above the far end of the lake. Two herons used
to live on the lake. Years ago one of them vanished and never returned, and
for a couple of years the remaining heron was rarely seen. When he began to
return regularly, it felt like a benediction.

Not for the frogs, though. For them, he's Heron the Impaler. He stands   15
motionless in the shallow water, waiting for a frog to come within reach, and
then strikes with incredible speed, driving his heavy pointed beak right
through the frog's body. He then leaves the indigestible bits on the raft for
us to clean up.

It's the Great Chain of Killing. We love the fat bullfrogs that the heron   16
kills. They're musical croakers, an indicator species[5] and a link with the
romance of Mark Twain. But these old friends are the implacable destroyers
of our equally beloved orange and blue dragonflies. And the dragonflies are
like mini Apache gunships, swerving with insane precision to devour the tiny

[5]A species that defines a trait or characteristic of an environment, such as climate, pollution,
disease, and so on. Changes in an indicator species often warn biologists that the environment
is changing (editors' note).

insects that dance above the surface of the lake. In the Sierra foothills, you begin to see that beauty is just a surface effect—below it, jaws are always about to snap shut.

One animal stands at the top of the killing chain: the mountain lion. 17 One afternoon in August I was walking along the creek-side trail when I heard a crunching noise. I looked up to see an enormous male mountain lion staring right at me, about 20 yards away on the other side of the stream. These supreme predators are normally soundless, but I was coming from upwind and walking quietly, and he was thirsty and had to make his way through a maze of fallen branches to drink, and even he couldn't avoid breaking some branches. We stared at each other for a second or two. For the first time in my life I was put emphatically and finally in my species place. If this 250-pound predator, so muscular, lethal and coiled that he might as well have weighed 400, decided he wanted to take me, there would be nothing I could do about it.

The experience was so alien, so unfathomable, that it was hard to believe 18 it even while it was happening. We stared at each other. Then he turned and bounded with massive hydraulic power up the bank, knocking aside little trees and disappearing in seconds. With shaking hands, I went looking for the biggest stick I could find. It was not a relaxing walk back to the cabin.

The heron settled into one of his favorite perches, a large cedar tree. If 19 the trees at the ranch seem exceptionally tall, it's probably because their cousins next door are the biggest ones on earth. If you climb up to the top of the valley where it narrows and bear off to the left, in a mile or so you come to the rarely used back gate of Big Trees State Park, one of 75 groves, all on the gentle western face of the Sierra, where the Sequoia gigantea, the world's largest living things, are found. A hunter stumbled upon the Calaveras Grove in 1852 while chasing a wounded bear. News of the stupendous trees spread, and entrepreneurs soon arrived, eager to make money off the "vegetable monsters."

They decided to cut one of the largest sequoias down, strip off its bark, 20 and ship it to the east for exhibition. A 19th century writer described how five men attacked the tree for 22 days, "until at last, the noble monarch of the forest was forced to tremble, and then to fall, after braving 'the battle and the breeze,' for nearly three thousand years." He then cheerfully reported that the resulting stump "easily accommodates 32 dancers." An appalled John Muir remarked that removing the bark of the big trees to spread their fame was "as sensible a scheme as skinning our great men would be to prove their greatness."

We didn't skin any big trees, but we killed a lot of fledgling ones. We 21 spent our days clearing brush and small trees away from the oaks, snipping the little ones off with compound shears, cutting the big ones down with a chain saw and pulling the tiny ones right out of the ground.

One day we tried to burn, but the wind was too strong. The flames   22
jumped the perimeter and started making for the next brush pile. My uncle
and I had to attack the outlying flames with our McLeods, smashing the
burning grass down hard with the flat, heavy heads of our tools in the instant
we had before the superheated gusts of wind forced us to back off. We would
no sooner kill one hot spot than another would spring up. I got my eyebrows
singed. For a minute there was a whiff of panic in the air.

The day we left, the snow still lay in patches on the far side of the mead-   23
ow, but it would soon be gone. My cousin had cut through the fallen trees
blocking the trail with the chain saw. The stream was running, but we needed one more good rain. The velvety grass was getting longer. In a few weeks
the cold knife edge of spring, having only just come, would be gone.

The night before we left, we heard Canadian geese at dusk, barking and   24
snuffling like dogs, and saw them circling the lake before flying away.

On the last day, I walked through the little meadow where we'd seen the   25
deer. The smell was gone. I went over to look at the spot where it had been
lying and there was nothing. Something had taken it away.

Questions for Close Reading

1. What is the selection's thesis (or dominant impression)? Locate the sentence(s) in
   which Kamiya states his main idea. If he doesn't state his thesis explicitly, express
   it in your own words.
2. According to Kamiya, why is it difficult to experience spring in a city, particularly
   in San Francisco?
3. What role does the ranch play in Kamiya's family?
4. How have people helped shape the landscape of the ranch?
5. Refer to your dictionary as needed to define the following words used in the selection: *atavistic* (paragraph 2), *pyres* (2), *constitutions* (4), *harbinger* (5), *redolent* (7),
   grandiloquent (7), *infamous* (8), *ponderous* (14), *disconcerting* (14), *implacable*
   (16), *unfathomable* (18), *appalled* (20), and *singed* (22).

Questions About the Writer's Craft

1. **The pattern.** Through vivid language, descriptive writing evokes sensory experiences and emotions. In this essay, Kamiya overlays several sets of sensory details,
   from different times in the ranch's history. Which times seem most vivid? How do
   these glimpses of the ranch at different points in time relate to the essay's themes?
2. **Other patterns.** Narrative plays a big role in this essay. Identify passages in which
   Kamiya tells stories about events that happened on the ranch.
3. Kamiya's descriptive language and figures of speech powerfully evoke the ranch as
   a setting for the "Great Chain of Killing" (paragraph 16). Choose a passage about
   the ranch today or one of its animals, and analyze the sensory details and figures
   of speech, explaining how the language contributes to the main idea of the essay.
4. What does the title "Life, Death and Spring" suggest? Does the essay live up to its
   title? Do you think a more specific title would have been better? Why or why not?

Writing Assignments Using Description as a Pattern of Development

1. Several readers of this essay commented on *Salon.com* that Kamiya had evoked their memories of the Sierra by vividly describing the scent of pine trees and burning brush. Scents often trigger memories or associations. A perfume or the smell of cigarettes can evoke a particular person; the odor of crayons or paste can bring back childhood memories. Write an essay describing a place, thing, or person you associate with a particular scent. You need not limit your description to the sense of smell; use other sensory language as well. Enliven your writing with figures of speech, as Kamiya does.

2. Kamiya was fortunate that his family's ranch was not destroyed by wildfire. But many other special spots have been destroyed or are threatened by destruction, whether by natural disaster or the slow encroachment of human development. Write an essay describing a place (for example, a park, a school, an old-fashioned ice cream parlor) that doesn't exist any more. For your dominant theme, show which aspects of your subject made it worthy of being preserved for future generations. Before writing your essay, you might want to read Rachel Carson's "A Fable for Tomorrow" (page 280), an essay that laments the loss of a special place.

Writing Assignments Combining Patterns of Development

3. Sometimes we, like Kamiya, are suddenly reminded of the nearness of death: a crushed animal lies in the road, a political leader is assassinated, a classmate is killed in a car crash. Write an essay about a time you were forced to think about mortality. *Narrate* what happened and *describe* your thoughts and feelings afterward.

4. Have your older relatives attempted to share with you some special experiences of their own? These experiences may center on a special family place, like Kamiya's family ranch, or they may have involved sharing photographs, stories, or heirlooms. Write an essay in which you *recount* how an older relative shared some experience with you. Explain the motivations of the older generation and the *effects* on the younger one.

Writing Assignment Using a Journal Entry as a Starting Point

5. Review your pre-reading journal entry in which you described several places that are special for you. Select one of these places, and write an essay describing it. The place need not be a natural setting like Kamiya's ranch; it could be a city or building that has meant a great deal to you. Use sensory details and figurative language, as Kamiya does, to enliven your description and convey the place's significance for you. Before writing, read Maya Angelou's "Sister Flowers" (page 87) to see how another professional writer conveys the special qualities of a memorable childhood place.

Additional Writing Topics

DESCRIPTION

General Assignments

Write an essay using description to develop any of the following topics. Remember that an effective description focuses on a dominant impression and arranges details in a way that best supports that impression. Your details—vivid and appealing to the senses—should be carefully chosen so that the essay isn't overburdened with material of secondary importance. When writing, keep in mind that varied sentence structure and imaginative figures of speech are ways to make a descriptive piece compelling.

1. A favorite item of clothing
2. A school as a young child might see it
3. A hospital room you visited or stayed in
4. An individualist's appearance
5. A coffee shop, a bus shelter, a newsstand, or some other small place
6. A parade or victory celebration
7. A banana, a squash, or another fruit or vegetable
8. A particular drawer in a desk or bureau
9. A houseplant
10. A "media event"
11. A dorm room
12. An elderly person
13. An attractive man or woman
14. A prosthetic device or wheelchair
15. A TV, film, or music celebrity
16. A student lounge
17. A once-in-a-lifetime event
18. The inside of something, such as a cave, boat, car, shed, or machine
19. A friend, a roommate, or another person you know well
20. An essential gadget or a useless gadget

Assignments with a Specific Purpose, Audience, and Point of View

On Campus

1. For an audience of incoming first-year students, prepare a speech describing registration day at your college. Use specific details to help prepare students for the actual event. Choose an adjective that represents your dominant impression of the experience, and keep that word in mind as you write.
2. Your college has decided to replace an old campus structure (for example, a dorm or dining hall) with a new version. Write the administration a letter of

protest describing the place so vividly and appealingly that its value and need for preservation are unquestionable.

3. As a staff member of the campus newspaper, you have been asked to write a weekly column of social news and gossip. For your first column, you plan to describe a recent campus event—a dance, party, or concert, or other social activity. With a straightforward or tongue-in-cheek tone, describe where the event was held, the appearance of the people who attended, and so on.

At Home or in the Community

4. As a subscriber to a community-wide dating service, you've been asked to submit a description of the kind of person you'd like to meet. Describe your ideal date. Focus on specifics about physical appearance, personal habits, character traits, and interests.

5. As a resident of a particular town, you're angered by the appearance of a certain spot and by the activities that take place there. Write the town council a letter describing in detail the undesirable nature of this place (a video arcade, an adult bookstore, a bar, a bus station, a neglected park or beach). End with some suggestions about ways to improve the situation.

On the Job

6. You've noticed a recurring problem in your workplace, and you want to bring it to the attention of your boss, who is typically inattentive. Write a letter to your boss describing the problem. Your goal is not to provide solutions, but rather, to provide vivid description—complete with sensory details—so that your boss can no longer deny the problem.

NARRATION

WHAT IS NARRATION?

Human beings are instinctively storytellers. In prehistoric times, our ancestors huddled around campfires to hear tales of hunting and magic. In ancient times, warriors gathered in halls to listen to bards praise in song the exploits of epic heroes. Things are no different today. Boisterous children invariably settle down to listen when their parents read to them; millions of people tune in day after day to the ongoing drama of their favorite soap operas; vacationers sit motionless on the beach, caught up in the latest best-sellers; and all of us enjoy saying, "Just listen to what happened to me today." Our hunger for story-telling is a basic part of us.

Narration means telling a single story or several related stories. The story can be a way to support a main idea or thesis. For instance, to demonstrate that television has become the constant companion of many children, you might narrate a typical child's day in front of the television—from frantic cartoons in the morning to dizzy situation come-dies at night.

Narration is powerful. Every public speaker, from politician to classroom teacher, knows that stories capture the attention of listeners as nothing else can. Narration speaks to us strongly because it is about us; we want to know what happened to others, not simply because we're curious, but because their experiences shed light on the nature of our own lives. Narration lends force to opinions, triggers the flow of memory, and evokes places and times in ways that are compelling and affecting.

HOW NARRATION FITS YOUR PURPOSE AND AUDIENCE

Narration can appear in essays as a supplemental pattern of development. For example, if your purpose in a paper is to *persuade* apathetic readers that airport security regulations must be followed strictly, you might lead off with a brief account of a friend who inadvertently boarded a plane with a pocket knife in his backpack. In a paper *defining* good teaching, you might keep readers engaged by including satirical anecdotes about one hapless instructor, the antithesis of an effective teacher. An essay on the *effects* of an overburdened judicial system might provide a dramatic account of the way one clearly guilty murderer plea-bargained his way to freedom.

Narration can also serve as an essay's dominant pattern of development. You might choose to narrate the events of a day spent with your three-year-old nephew as a way of revealing how you rediscovered the importance of family life. Or you might relate the story of your roommate's mugging, evoking the powerlessness and terror of being a victim. Any story can form the basis for a narrative essay as long as you convey the essence of the experience and evoke its meaning.

At this point, you have a good sense of the way writers use narration to achieve their purpose and to connect with their readers. Now take a moment to look closely at the photograph at the beginning of this chapter. Imagine you're writing a "Recent Events" update, accompanied by the photo, for the website of an organization that supports (*or* opposes) the wars in Iraq and Afghanistan. Your purpose is to recount what happened at the protest in a way 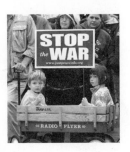 that supports the website's position. Jot down some phrases you might use when *narrating* the events of the day.

SUGGESTIONS FOR USING NARRATION IN AN ESSAY

The suggestions here and in Figure 4.1 on page 114 will help you use narration as a dominant or a supportive pattern of development.

1. Identify the conflict in the event. The power of many narratives is rooted in a special kind of tension that "hooks" readers and makes them want to follow

FIGURE 4.1
Development Diagram: Writing a Narration Essay

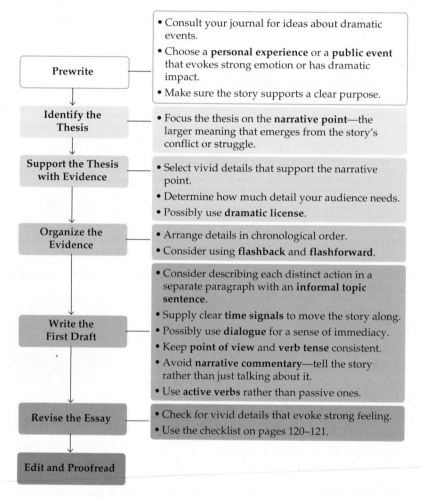

Prewrite	• Consult your journal for ideas about dramatic events. • Choose a **personal experience** or a **public event** that evokes strong emotion or has dramatic impact. • Make sure the story supports a clear purpose.
Identify the Thesis	• Focus the thesis on the **narrative point**—the larger meaning that emerges from the story's conflict or struggle.
Support the Thesis with Evidence	• Select vivid details that support the narrative point. • Determine how much detail your audience needs. • Possibly use **dramatic license**.
Organize the Evidence	• Arrange details in chronological order. • Consider using **flashback** and **flashforward**.
Write the First Draft	• Consider describing each distinct action in a separate paragraph with an **informal topic sentence**. • Supply clear **time signals** to move the story along. • Possibly use **dialogue** for a sense of immediacy. • Keep **point of view** and **verb tense** consistent. • Avoid **narrative commentary**—tell the story rather than just talking about it. • Use **active verbs** rather than passive ones.
Revise the Essay	• Check for vivid details that evoke strong feeling. • Use the checklist on pages 120–121.
Edit and Proofread	

the story to its end. This narrative tension is often a by-product of some form of *conflict* within the story. Many narratives revolve around an internal conflict experienced by a key person in the story. Or the conflict may be between people in the story or between a pivotal character and some social institution or natural phenomenon.

2. Identify the point of the narrative. In *The Adventures of Huckleberry Finn*, Mark Twain warned: "Persons attempting to find a motive in this narrative will be prosecuted; persons attempting to find a moral in it will be banished; persons attempting to find a plot in it will be shot." Twain was, of course, being ironic; his novel's richness lies in its "motives" and "morals." Similarly, when you recount a narrative, it's your responsibility to convey the event's *significance* or *meaning*. In other words, be sure readers are clear about your *narrative point,* or thesis.

Suppose you decide to write about the time you got locked in a mall late at night. Your narrative might focus on the way the mall looked after hours and the way you struggled with mounting terror. But you would also use the narrative to make a point. Perhaps you want to emphasize that fear can be instructive. Or your point might be that malls have a disturbing, surreal underside. You could state this thesis explicitly. ("After hours, the mall shed its cheerful daytime demeanor and took on a more sinister quality.") Or you could rely on your details and language to convey the point of the narrative: "The mannequins stared at me with glazed eyes and frozen smiles" and "The steel grates pulled over each store's entrance glinted in the cold light, making each shop look like a prison cell."

3. Develop only those details that advance the narrative point. You know from experience that nothing is more boring than a storyteller who gets sidetracked and drags out a story with nonessential details. If a friend started to tell about the time his car broke down in the middle of an expressway—but interrupted his story to complain at length about the slipshod work done by his auto repair shop—you might become annoyed, wishing your friend would get back to the interesting part of the story.

Brainstorming ("What happened? When? Where? Who was involved? Why did it happen?") can be valuable for helping you amass narrative details. Then, after generating the specifics, you cull out the nonessential and devote your energies to the key specifics needed to advance your narrative point. When telling a story, you maintain an effective narrative pace by focusing on that point and eliminating details that don't support it. A good narrative depends not only on what is included, but also on what has been left out.

But how do you determine which specifics to omit, which to treat briefly, and which to emphasize? Having a clear sense of your narrative point and knowing your audience are crucial. Assume you're writing a narrative about a disastrous get-acquainted dance sponsored by your college the first week of the academic year. In addition to telling what happened, you want to make a point; perhaps you want to emphasize that, despite the college's good intentions, such official events actually make it difficult to meet people. So you might write about how stiff and unnatural students seemed, all dressed up in their best clothes; you might narrate snatches of strained conversation; you might describe the way males gathered on one side of the room, females on the other—reverting to behaviors supposedly abandoned in fifth grade. All these details would support your narrative point.

Because you don't want to get away from that point, you would leave out details about the topnotch band and the appetizing refreshments. The music and food may have been surprisingly good, but since these details don't advance the point you want to make, they should be omitted.

You also need to keep your audience in mind when selecting narrative details. If the audience consists of your instructor and other students—all of them familiar with the new student center where the dance was held—specific details about the center probably wouldn't have to be provided. But imagine that the essay is going to appear in the quarterly magazine published by the college's community relations office. Many of the magazine's readers are former graduates who haven't been on campus for several years. They may need some additional specifics about the student center: its location, how many people it holds, how it is furnished.

As you write, keep asking yourself, "Is this detail or character or snippet of conversation essential? Does my audience need this detail to understand the conflict in the situation? Does this detail advance or intensify the narrative action?" Summarize details that have some importance but do not deserve lengthy treatment ("Two hours went by..."). And try to limit *narrative commentary*—statements that tell rather than show what happened—since such remarks interrupt the narrative flow. Focus instead on the specifics that propel action forward in a vigorous way.

Sometimes, especially if the narrative re-creates an event from the past, you won't be able to remember what happened detail for detail. In such a case, you should take advantage of what is called *dramatic license*. Using as a guide your powers of recall as well as the perspective you now have of that particular time, feel free to reshape events to suit your narrative point.

4. Organize the narrative sequence.   Every narrative begins somewhere, presents a span of time, and ends at a certain point. Frequently, you'll want to use a straightforward time order, following the event *chronologically* from beginning to end: first this happened, next this happened, finally this happened.

But sometimes a strict chronological recounting may not be effective—especially if the high point of the narrative gets lost somewhere in the middle of the time sequence. To avoid that possibility, you may want to disrupt chronology, plunge the reader into the middle of the story, and then return in a *flashback* to the beginning of the tale. You're probably familiar with the way flashback is used on television and in film. You see someone appealing to the main character for financial help, then return to an earlier time when both were students in the same class, before learning how the rest of the story unfolds. Narratives can also use *flashforward*. You give readers a glimpse of the future (the main character being jailed) before the story continues in the present (the events leading to the arrest). These techniques shift the story onto several planes and keep it from becoming a step-by-step, predictable account. Reserve flashforwards and flashbacks, however, for crucial incidents only, since breaking out of chronological order acts as emphasis. Here are examples of how flashback and flashforward can be used:

Flashback

Standing behind the wooden counter, Greg wielded his knife expertly as he shucked clams—one every ten seconds—with practiced ease. The scene contrasted sharply with his first day on the job, when his hands broke out in blisters and when splitting each shell was like prying open a safe.

Flashforward

Rushing to move my car from the no-parking zone, I waved a quick goodbye to Karen as she climbed the steps to the bus. I didn't know then that by the time I picked her up at the bus station later that day, she had made a decision that would affect both our lives.

Whether or not you choose to include flashbacks or flashforwards in an essay, remember to limit the time span covered by the narrative. Otherwise, you will have trouble generating the details needed to give the story depth and meaning. Also, regardless of the time sequence you select, organize the tale so that it drives toward a strong finish. Be careful that your story doesn't trail off into minor, anticlimactic details.

5. Make the narrative easy to follow. Describing each distinct action in a separate paragraph helps readers grasp the flow of events. Although narrative essays don't always have conventional topic sentences, each narrative paragraph should have a clear focus. Often this focus is indicated by a sentence early in the paragraph that directs attention to the action taking place. Such a sentence functions as a kind of *informal topic sentence;* the rest of the paragraph then develops that topic sentence. You should also be sure to use time signals when narrating a story. Words like *now, then, next, after,* and *later* ensure that your reader won't get lost as the story progresses.

6. Make the narrative vigorous and immediate.   A compelling narrative provides an abundance of specific details, making readers feel as if they're experiencing the story being told. Readers must be able to see, hear, touch, smell, and taste the event you're narrating. *Vivid sensory description* is, therefore, an essential part of an effective narrative. Not only do specific sensory details make writing a pleasure to read—we all enjoy learning the particulars about people, places, and things—but they also give the narrative the stamp of reality. The specifics convince the reader that the event actually did, or could, occur.

Compare the following excerpts from a narrative essay. The first version is lifeless and dull; the revised version, packed with sensory images, grabs readers with its sense of foreboding:

> That eventful day started out like every other summer day. My sister Tricia and I made several elaborate mud pies, which we decorated with care. A little later on, as we were spraying each other with the garden hose, we heard my father walk up the path.

> That sad summer day started out uneventfully enough. My sister Tricia and I spent a few hours mixing and decorating mud pies. Our hands caked with dry mud, we sprinkled each lopsided pie with alternating rows of dandelion and clover petals. Later when the sun got hotter, we tossed our white T-shirts over the red picket fence–forgetting my grandmother's frequent warnings to be more ladylike. Our sweaty backs bared to the sun, we doused each other with icy sprays from the garden hose. Caught up in the primitive pleasure of it all, we barely heard my father as he walked up the garden path, the gravel crunching under his heavy work boots.

A caution: Sensory language enlivens narration, but it also slows the pace. Be sure that the slower pace suits your purpose. For example, a lengthy description fits an account of a leisurely summer vacation but is inappropriate in a tale about a frantic search for a misplaced wallet.

Another way to create an aura of narrative immediacy is to use *dialogue*. Our sense of other people comes, in part, from what they say and how they sound. Dialogue allows the reader to experience characters directly. Compare the following fragments of a narrative, one with dialogue and one without, noting how much more energetic the second version is.

> When I finally found my way back to the campsite, the trail guide commented on my disheveled appearance.

> When I finally found my way back to the campsite, the trail guide took one look at me and drawled, "What on earth happened to you, Daniel Boone? You look as though you've been dragged through a haystack backwards."
> "I'd look a lot worse if I hadn't run back here. When a bullet whizzes by me, I don't stick around to see who's doing the shooting."

When using dialogue, begin a new paragraph to indicate a shift from one person's speech to another's (as in the second example above).

Using *varied sentence structure* is another strategy for making narratives lively and vigorous. Sentences that plod along predictably (subject-verb, subject-verb) put readers to sleep. Experiment with your sentences by juggling length and sentence type; mix long and short sentences, simple and complex. Compare the following original and revised versions to get an idea of how effective varied sentence rhythm can be in narrative writing.

Original

The store manager went to the walk-in refrigerator every day. The heavy metal door clanged shut behind her. I had visions of her freezing to death among the hanging carcasses. The shiny door finally swung open. She waddled out.

Revised

Each time the store manager went to the walk-in refrigerator, the heavy metal door clanged shut behind her. Visions of her freezing to death among the hanging carcasses crept into my mind until the shiny door finally swung open and she waddled out.

Original

The yellow-and-blue-striped fish struggled on the line. Its scales shimmered in the sunlight. Its tail waved frantically. I saw its desire to live. I decided to let it go.

Revised

Scales shimmering in the sunlight, tail waving frantically, the yellow-and-blue-striped fish struggled on the line. Seeing its desire to live, I let it go.

Finally, *vigorous verbs* lend energy to narratives. Use active verb forms ("The boss *yelled at* him") rather than passive ones ("He *was yelled at* by the boss"), and try to replace anemic *to be* verbs ("She *was* a good basketball player") with more dynamic constructions ("She *played* basketball well").

7. Keep your point of view and verb tense consistent.   All stories have a *narrator,* the person who tells the story. If you, as narrator, tell a story as you experienced it, the story is written in the *first-person point of view* ("*I* saw the dog pull loose"). But if you observed the event (or heard about it from others) and want to tell how someone else experienced the incident, you would use the *third-person point of view* ("*Anne* saw the dog pull loose"). Each point of view has advantages and limitations. First person allows you to express ordinarily private thoughts and to re-create an event as you actually experienced it. This point of view is limited, though, in its ability to depict the inner thoughts of other people involved in the event. By way of contrast, third person makes it easier to provide insight into the thoughts of all the participants. However, its objective, broad perspective may undercut some of the subjective immediacy of the "I was there" point of view. No matter which you select, stay with that vantage point throughout the narrative.

Knowing whether to use the *past* or *present tense* ("I *strolled* into the room" as opposed to "I *stroll* into the room") is important. In most narrations, the past tense predominates, enabling the writer to span a considerable period of time. Although more rarely used, the present tense can be powerful for events of short duration—a wrestling match or a medical emergency, for instance. A narrative in the present tense prolongs each moment, intensifying the reader's sense of participation. Be careful, though; unless the event is intense and fast-paced, the present tense can seem contrived. Whichever tense you choose, avoid shifting midstream—starting, let's say, in the past tense ("she skated") and switching to the present ("she runs").

REVISION STRATEGIES

Once you have a draft of the essay, you're ready to revise. The following checklist will help you and those giving you feedback apply to narration some of the revision techniques discussed on pages 60–62.

☑ NARRATION: A REVISION/PEER REVIEW CHECKLIST

Revise Overall Meaning and Structure

❑ What is the essay's main point? Is it stated explicitly or is it implied? Where? Could the point be conveyed more clearly? How?

❑ What is the narrative's conflict? Is it stated explicitly or is it implied? Where? Could the conflict be made more dramatic? How?

❑ From what point of view is the narrative told? Is it the most effective point of view for this essay? Why or why not?

Revise Paragraph Development

❑ Which paragraphs fail to advance the action, reveal character, or contribute to the story's mood? Should these sections be condensed or eliminated?

❑ Where should the narrative pace be slowed down or quickened?

❑ Where is it difficult to follow the chronology of events? Should the order of paragraphs be changed? How? Where would additional time signals help?

❑ How could flashback or flashforward paragraphs be used to highlight key events?

❏ Would dramatic dialogue or mood-setting description help make the essay's opening paragraph more compelling?

❏ What could be done to make the essay's closing paragraph more effective? Should the essay end earlier? Should it close by echoing an idea or image from the opening?

Revise Sentences and Words

❏ Where is sentence structure monotonous? Where would combining sentences, mixing sentence types, and alternating sentence length help?

❏ Where could dialogue replace commentary to convey character and propel the story forward?

❏ Which sentences and words are inconsistent with the essay's tone?

❏ Where do vigorous verbs convey action? Where could active verbs replace passive ones? Where could dull *to be* verbs be converted to more dynamic forms?

❏ Where are there inappropriate shifts in point of view or verb tense?

STUDENT ESSAY

The following student essay was written by Paul Monahan in response to this assignment:

> In "Shooting an Elephant," George Orwell tells about an incident that forced him to act in a manner that ran counter to his better instincts. Write a narrative about a time when you faced a disturbing conflict and ended up doing something you later regretted.

While reading Paul's paper, try to determine how well it applies the principles of narration. The annotations on Paul's paper and the commentary following it will help you look at the essay more closely.

If Only

by Paul Monahan

Introduction

        Having worked at a 7-Eleven store for two years, I thought I had become successful at what our manager calls "customer relations." I firmly believed that a friendly smile and an automatic "sir," "ma'am," and "thank you" would see me through any situation that might arise, from soothing impatient or unpleasant people to apologizing for giving out the wrong change. But the other night an old woman shattered

Narrative point
(thesis)

1

my belief that a glib response could smooth over the rough spots of dealing with other human beings.

Informal topic sentence → The moment she entered, the woman presented a sharp contrast to our shiny store with its bright lighting and neatly arranged shelves. Walking as if each step were painful, she slowly pushed open the glass door and hobbled down the nearest aisle. Sensory details → She coughed dryly, wheezing with each breath. On a forty-degree night, she was wearing only a faded print dress, a thin, light beige sweater too small to button, and black vinyl slippers with the backs cut out to expose calloused heels. There were no stockings or socks on her splotchy, blue-veined legs.   2

After strolling around the store for several minutes, the old woman stopped in front of the rows of canned vegetables. She picked up some corn niblets and stared with a strange intensity at the label. At that point, I decided to be a good, courteous Informal topic sentence → employee and asked her if she needed help. As I stood close to her, my smile became harder to maintain; Sensory details → her red-rimmed eyes were partially closed by yellowish crusts; her hands were covered with layer upon layer of grime; and the stale smell of sweat rose in a thick vaporous cloud from her clothes.   3

Start of dialogue → "I need some food," she muttered in reply to my bright "Can I help you?"   4

"Are you looking for corn, ma'am?"   5

"I need some food," she repeated. "Any kind."   6

"Well, the corn is ninety-five cents," I said in my most helpful voice. "Or, if you like, we have a special on bologna today."   7

"I can't pay," she said.   8

Conflict established → For a second, I was tempted to say, "Take the corn." But the employee rules flooded into my mind: Remain polite, but do not let customers get the best of you. Let them know that you are in control. For a moment, I even entertained the idea that this was some sort of test, and that this woman was someone from the head office, testing my loyalty. I responded dutifully, "I'm sorry, ma'am, but I can't give away anything free."   9

Informal topic sentence → The old woman's face collapsed a bit more, if that were possible, and her hands trembled as she put the can back on the shelf. She shuffled past me toward the door, her torn and dirty clothing barely covering her bent back.   10

Conclusion   Moments after she left, I rushed out the door with the can of corn, but she was nowhere in sight. For the rest of my shift, the image of the woman haunted me. I had been Echoing of narrative point in the introduction → young, healthy, and smug. She had been old, sick, and desperate. Wishing with all my heart that I had acted like a human being rather than a robot, I was saddened to realize how fragile a hold we have on our better instincts.   11

COMMENTARY

Point of view, tense, and conflict.   Paul chose to write "If Only" from the *first-person point of view,* a logical choice because he appears as a main character in his own story. Using the *past tense,* Paul recounts an incident filled with *conflicts*—between him and the woman and between his fear of breaking the rules and his human instinct to help someone in need.

Narrative point.   It isn't always necessary to state the *narrative point* of an essay; it can be implied. But Paul decided to express the controlling idea of his narrative in two places—in the introduction ("But the other night an old woman shattered my belief that a glib response could smooth over the rough spots of dealing with other human beings") and again in the conclusion, where he expands his idea about rote responses overriding impulses of independent judgment and compassion. All of the essay's *narrative details* contribute to the point of the piece; Paul does not include any extraneous information that would detract from the central idea he wants to convey.

Organization.   The narrative is *organized chronologically,* from the moment the woman enters the store to Paul's reaction after she leaves. Paul limits the narrative's time span. The entire incident probably occurs in under ten minutes, yet the introduction serves as a kind of *flashback* by providing some necessary background about Paul's past experiences. To help the reader follow the course of the narrative, Paul uses *time signals:* "*The moment* she entered, the woman presented a sharp contrast" (paragraph 2); "*At that point,* I decided to be a good, courteous employee" (3); "*For the rest of my shift,* the image of the woman haunted me" (11).

   The paragraphs (except for those consisting solely of dialogue) also contain *informal topic sentences* that direct attention to the specific stage of action being narrated. Indeed, each paragraph focuses on a distinct event: the elderly woman's actions when she first enters the store, the encounter between Paul and the woman, Paul's resulting inner conflict, the woman's subsequent response, and Paul's delayed reaction.

Combining patterns of development.   This chronological chain of events, with one action leading to another, illustrates that the *cause-effect* pattern underlies the basic structure of Paul's essay. And by means of another pattern—*description*—Paul gives dramatic immediacy to the events being recounted. Throughout, he provides rich sensory details to engage the reader's interest. For instance, the sentence "her red-rimmed eyes were partially closed by yellowish crusts" (3) vividly re-creates the woman's appearance while also suggesting Paul's inner reaction to the woman.

Dialogue and sentence structure.   Paul dramatizes the conflict through *dialogue* that crackles with tension. And he achieves a vigorous narrative pace by *varying the length and structure of his sentences.* In the second paragraph, a short sentence ("There were no stockings or socks on her splotchy, blue-veined legs") alternates with a longer one ("On a forty-degree night, she was wearing only a faded print dress, a thin, light beige sweater too small to button, and black vinyl slippers with the backs cut out to expose calloused heels"). Some sentences open with a subject and verb ("She coughed dryly"), while others start with dependent clauses or participial phrases ("As I stood close to her, my smile became harder to maintain"; "Walking as if each step were painful, she slowly pushed open the glass door") or with a prepositional phrase ("For a second, I was tempted").

Revising the first draft.   Comparing the final version of the essay's third paragraph with the following preliminary version reveals some of the changes Paul made while revising the essay.

Original Version of the Third Paragraph

After sneezing and hacking her way around the store, the old woman stopped in front of the vegetable shelves. She picked up a can of corn and stared at the label. She stayed like this for several minutes. Then I walked over to her and asked if I could be of help.

After putting the original draft aside for a while, Paul reread his paper aloud and realized the third paragraph especially lacked power. So he decided to add compelling descriptive details about the woman ("the stale smell of sweat," for example). Also, by expanding and combining sentences, he gave the paragraph an easier, more graceful rhythm. Much of the time, revision involves paring down excess material. In this case, though, Paul made the right decision to elaborate his sentences. Furthermore, he added the following comment to the third paragraph: "I decided to be a good, courteous employee." These few words introduce an appropriate note of irony and serve to echo the essay's controlling idea.

Finally, Paul decided to omit the words "sneezing and hacking" because he realized they were too comic or light for his subject. Still, the first sentence in the revised paragraph is somewhat jarring. The word *strolling* isn't quite appropriate since it implies a leisurely grace inconsistent with the impression he wants to convey. Replacing *strolling* with, say, *shuffling* would bring the image more into line with the essay's overall mood.

Despite this slight problem, Paul's revisions are right on the mark. The changes he made strengthened his essay, turning it into a more evocative, more polished piece of narrative writing.

Activities: Narration

Prewriting Activities

1. Imagine you're writing two essays: One analyzes the *effect* of insensitive teachers on young children; the other *argues* the importance of family traditions. With the help of your journal or freewriting, identify different narratives you could use to open each essay.

2. For each of the situations below, identify two different conflicts that would make a story worth relating. Then prepare six to ten lines of natural-sounding dialogue for each potential conflict in *one* of the situations.
   a. Going to the supermarket with a friend
   b. Telling your parents which college you've decided to attend
   c. Participating in a demonstration
   d. Preparing for an exam in a difficult course

Revising Activities

3. Revise each of the following narrative sentence groups twice: once with words that carry negative connotations, and again with words that carry positive connotations. Use varied sentence structure, sensory details, and vigorous verbs to convey mood.

   a. The bell rang. It rang loudly. Students knew the last day of class was over.
   b. Last weekend, our neighbors burned leaves in their yard. We went over to speak with them.
   c. The sun shone in through my bedroom window. It made me sit up in bed. Daylight was finally here, I told myself.

4. The following paragraph is the introduction from the first draft of an essay proposing harsher penalties for drunk drivers. Revise this narrative paragraph to make it more effective. How can you make sentence structure less predictable? Which details should you delete? As you revise, provide

language that conveys the event's sights, smells, and sounds. Also, clarify
the chronological sequence.

As I drove down the street in my bright blue sports car, I saw a car
coming rapidly around the curve. The car didn't slow down as it headed
toward the traffic light. The light turned yellow and then red. A young
couple, dressed like models, started crossing the street. When the woman
saw the car, she called out to her husband. He jumped onto the shoulder.
The man wasn't hurt but, seconds later, it was clear the woman was. I ran
to a nearby emergency phone and called the police. The ambulance
arrived, but the woman was already dead. The driver, who looked terrible,
failed the sobriety test, and the police found out that he had two previous
offenses. It's apparent that better ways have to be found for getting drunk
drivers off the road.

Audre Lorde

Named poet laureate of the state of New York in 1991, Audre Lorde (1934–92) was a New Yorker born of African-Caribbean parents. After earning degrees at Hunter College and Columbia University, Lorde held numerous teaching positions throughout the New York City area. She later toured the world as a lecturer, forming women's rights coalitions in the Caribbean, Africa, and Europe. Best known as a feminist theorist, Lorde combined social criticism and personal revelation in her writing on such topics as race, gender relations, and sexuality. Her numerous poems and nonfiction pieces were published in a variety of magazines and literary journals. Her books include *The Black Unicorn: Poems* (1978), *Sister Outsider: Essays and Speeches* (1984), and *A Burst of Light* (1988). The following selection is an excerpt from her autobiography, *Zami: A New Spelling of My Name* (1982).

For ideas about how this narration essay is organized, see Figure 4.2 on page 131.

Pre-Reading Journal Entry

When you were a child, what beliefs about the United States did you have? List these beliefs. For each, indicate whether subsequent experience maintained or shattered your childhood understanding of these beliefs. Take a little time to explore these issues in your journal.

The Fourth of July

The first time I went to Washington, D.C., was on the edge of the summer when I was supposed to stop being a child. At least that's what they said to us all at graduation from the eighth grade. My sister Phyllis graduated at the same time from high school. I don't know what she was supposed to stop being. But as graduation presents for us both, the whole family took a Fourth of July trip to Washington, D.C., the fabled and famous capital of our country.

It was the first time I'd ever been on a railroad train during the day. When I was little, and we used to go to the Connecticut shore, we always went at night on the milk train, because it was cheaper.

Preparations were in the air around our house before school was even over. We packed for a week. There were two very large suitcases that my father carried, and a box filled with food. In fact, my first trip to Washington was a mobile feast; I started eating as soon as we were comfortably ensconced in our seats, and did not stop until somewhere after Philadelphia. I remember it was Philadelphia because I was disappointed not to have passed by the Liberty Bell.

My mother had roasted two chickens and cut them up into dainty bite-size pieces. She packed slices of brown bread and butter and green pepper

1

2

3

4

and carrot sticks. There were little violently yellow iced cakes with scalloped edges called "marigolds," that came from Cushman's Bakery. There was a spice bun and rock-cakes from Newton's, the West Indian bakery across Lenox Avenue from St. Mark's School, and iced tea in a wrapped mayonnaise jar. There were sweet pickles for us and dill pickles for my father, and peaches with the fuzz still on them, individually wrapped to keep them from bruising. And, for neatness, there were piles of napkins and a little tin box with a washcloth dampened with rosewater and glycerine for wiping sticky mouths.

I wanted to eat in the dining car because I had read all about them, but   5
my mother reminded me for the umpteenth time that dining car food always costs too much money and besides, you never could tell whose hands had been playing all over that food, nor where those same hands had been just before. My mother never mentioned that Black people were not allowed into railroad dining cars headed south in 1947. As usual, whatever my mother did not like and could not change, she ignored. Perhaps it would go away, deprived of her attention.

I learned later that Phyllis's high school senior class trip had been   6
to Washington, but the nuns had given her back her deposit in private, explaining to her that the class, all of whom were white, except Phyllis, would be staying in a hotel where Phyllis "would not be happy," meaning, Daddy explained to her, also in private, that they did not rent rooms to Negroes. "We will take you to Washington, ourselves," my father had avowed, "and not just for an overnight in some measly fleabag hotel."

American racism was a new and crushing reality that my parents had   7
to deal with every day of their lives once they came to this country. They handled it as a private woe. My mother and father believed that they could best protect their children from the realities of race in america and the fact of american racism by never giving them name, much less discussing their nature. We were told we must never trust white people, but *why* was never explained, nor the nature of their ill will. Like so many other vital pieces of information in my childhood, I was supposed to know without being told. It always seemed like a very strange injunction coming from my mother, who looked so much like one of those people we were never supposed to trust. But something always warned me not to ask my mother why she wasn't white, and why Auntie Lillah and Auntie Etta weren't, even though they were all that same problematic color so different from my father and me, even from my sisters, who were somewhere in-between.

In Washington, D.C., we had one large room with two double beds and   8
an extra cot for me. It was a back-street hotel that belonged to a friend of my father's who was in real estate, and I spent the whole next day after Mass

squinting up at the Lincoln Memorial where Marian Anderson[1] had sung after the D.A.R.[2] refused to allow her to sing in their auditorium because she was Black. Or because she was "Colored," my father said as he told us the story. Except that what he probably said was "Negro," because for his time, my father was quite progressive.

I was squinting because I was in that silent agony that characterized all   9
of my childhood summers, from the time school let out in June to the end of July, brought about by my dilated and vulnerable eyes exposed to the summer brightness.

I viewed Julys through an agonizing corolla of dazzling whiteness and I   10
always hated the Fourth of July, even before I came to realize the travesty such a celebration was for Black people in this country.

My parents did not approve of sunglasses, nor of their expense.   11

I spent the afternoon squinting up at monuments to freedom and past   12
presidencies and democracy, and wondering why the light and heat were both so much stronger in Washington, D.C., than back home in New York City. Even the pavement on the streets was a shade lighter in color than back home.

Late that Washington afternoon my family and I walked back down   13
Pennsylvania Avenue. We were a proper caravan, mother bright and father brown, the three of us girls step-standards in-between. Moved by our historical surroundings and the heat of the early evening, my father decreed yet another treat. He had a great sense of history, a flair for the quietly dramatic and the sense of specialness of an occasion and a trip.

"Shall we stop and have a little something to cool off, Lin?"   14

Two blocks away from our hotel, the family stopped for a dish of vanil-   15
la ice cream at a Breyer's ice cream and soda fountain. Indoors, the soda fountain was dim and fan-cooled, deliciously relieving to my scorched eyes.

Corded and crisp and pinafored, the five of us seated ourselves one by   16
one at the counter. There was I between my mother and father, and my two sisters on the other side of my mother. We settled ourselves along the white mottled marble counter, and when the waitress spoke at first no one understood what she was saying, and so the five of us just sat there.

The waitress moved along the line of us closer to my father and spoke   17
again. "I said I kin give you to take out, but you can't eat here. Sorry." Then she dropped her eyes looking very embarrassed, and suddenly we heard what it was she was saying all at the same time, loud and clear.

---

[1]Acclaimed African-American opera singer (1902–93), famed for her renderings of Black spirituals (editors' note).
[2]Daughters of the American Revolution. A society, founded in 1890, for women who can prove direct lineage to soldiers or others who aided in winning American independence from Great Britain during the Revolutionary War (1775–83) (editors' note).

Straight-backed and indignant, one by one, my family and I got down   18
from the counter stools and turned around and marched out of the store,
quiet and outraged, as if we had never been Black before. No one would
answer my emphatic questions with anything other than a guilty silence.
"But we hadn't done anything!" This wasn't right or fair! Hadn't I written
poems about Bataan and freedom and democracy for all?

My parents wouldn't speak of this injustice, not because they had con-   19
tributed to it, but because they felt they should have anticipated it and avoided it. This made me even angrier. My fury was not going to be acknowledged
by a like fury. Even my two sisters copied my parents' pretense that nothing
unusual and anti-american had occurred. I was left to write my angry letter
to the president of the united states all by myself, although my father did
promise I could type it out on the office typewriter next week, after I showed
it to him in my copybook diary.

The waitress was white, and the counter was white, and the ice cream I   20
never ate in Washington, D.C., that summer I left childhood was white, and
the white heat and the white pavement and the white stone monuments of
my first Washington summer made me sick to my stomach for the whole
rest of that trip and it wasn't much of a graduation present after all.

Questions for Close Reading

1. What is the selection's thesis (or narrative point)? Locate the sentence(s) in which
   Lorde states her main idea. If she doesn't state the thesis explicitly, express it in
   your own words.
2. In paragraph 4, Lorde describes the elaborate picnic her mother prepared for the
   trip to Washington, D.C. Why did Lorde's mother make such elaborate preparations? What do these preparations tell us about Lorde's mother?
3. Why does Lorde have trouble understanding her parents' dictate that she "never
   trust white people" (paragraph 7)?
4. In general, how do Lorde's parents handle racism? How does the family as a whole
   deal with the racism they encounter in the ice-cream parlor? How does the family's
   reaction to the ice-cream parlor incident make Lorde feel?
5. Refer to your dictionary as needed to define the following words used in the selection: *fabled* (paragraph 1), *injunction* (7), *progressive* (8), *dilated* (9), *vulnerable*
   (9), *travesty* (10), *decreed* (13), and *pretense* (19).

Questions About the Writer's Craft

1. **The pattern.** What techniques does Lorde use to help readers follow the unfold-
   ing of the story as it occurs in both time and space?
2. When telling a story, skilled writers limit narrative commentary—statements that
   tell rather than show what happened—because it tends to interrupt the narrative
   flow. Lorde, however, provides narrative commentary in several spots. Find these
   instances. How is the information she provides essential to her narrative?

FIGURE 4.2

Essay Structure Diagram: "The Fourth of July" by Audre Lorde

Introductory paragraph: **Narrative point** (paragraph 1)	Going on a trip to Washington, D.C., as a graduation present. **Narrative point:** This experience marked the end of the narrator's childhood.
Narrative details (2–19) Also, descriptive and explanatory material (in parentheses at right)	Preparing for the train trip. (The food packed for the trip.) *Flashback:* Not allowed in the dining car. *Flashforward:* Learning later that her sister had been denied a trip to Washington because of racist hotel policies. (How the author's parents and relatives dealt with the "crushing reality" of racism.) (The hotel room and its location.) Spending the day "squinting up at monuments." Deciding to stop for ice cream at a soda fountain and waiting to be served. Waitress's refusing to serve the family. Leaving the soda fountain. (The parents' response and the author's anger.)
Concluding paragraph (20)	The incident at the soda fountain marked an end to the narrator's childhood.

3. In paragraphs 7 and 19, Lorde uses all lowercase letters for *America, American,* and *President of the United States.* Why do you suppose she doesn't follow the rules of capitalization? In what ways does her rejection of these rules reinforce what she is trying to convey through the essay's title?

4. What key word does Lorde repeat in paragraph 20? What effect do you think she hopes the repetition will have on readers?

Writing Assignments Using Narration as a Pattern of Development

1. Lorde recounts an incident during which she was treated unfairly. Write a narrative about a time when either you were treated unjustly or you treated someone else in an unfair manner. Like Lorde, use vivid details to make the incident come alive and to convey how it affected you. George Orwell's "Shooting an Elephant" (page 133) will prompt some ideas worth exploring.

2. Write a narrative about an experience that dramatically changed your view of the world. The experience might have been jarring and painful, or it may have been

positive and uplifting. In either case, recount the incident with compelling narrative details. To illustrate the shift in your perspective, begin with a brief statement of the way you viewed the world before the experience. Maya Angelou's "Sister Flowers" (page 87) provides insight into the way a single experience can alter one's understanding of the world.

Writing Assignments Combining Patterns of Development

3. Lorde suggests that her parents use the coping mechanism of denial to deal with life's harsh realities, writing that whatever her mother "did not like and could not change, she ignored." Refer to a psychology textbook to learn more about denial. When is it productive? Counterproductive? Drawing upon your own experiences as well as those of friends, family, and classmates, write an essay *contrasting* effective and ineffective uses of denial. Near the end of the paper, present brief *guidelines* that will help readers identify when denial may be detrimental.

4. In her essay, Lorde decries and by implication takes a strong stance against racial discrimination. Brainstorm with friends, family members, and classmates to identify other injustices in American society. You might begin by considering attitudes toward the elderly, the overweight, the physically disabled; the funding of schools in poor and affluent neighborhoods; the portrayal of a specific ethnic group on television; and so on. Focusing on *one* such injustice, write an essay *arguing* that such an injustice indeed exists. To document the nature and extent of the injustice, use the library and/or Internet research. You should also consider *recounting* your own and other people's experiences. Acknowledge and, when you can, dismantle the views of those who think there isn't a problem.

Writing Assignment Using a Journal Entry as a Starting Point

5. Write an essay comparing and/or contrasting the beliefs you had about the United States as a child with those you have as an adult. Review your pre-reading journal entry, and select *one* American belief to focus on. Provide strong, dramatic examples that show why your childhood belief in this concept has been strengthened or weakened. Before writing, you should consider reading Stanley Fish's "Free-Speech Follies" (page 392), a strongly argued examination of rights covered by the First Amendment of the Constitution. Roberto Rodriguez's "The Border on Our Backs" (page 418) and Star Parker's "*Se Habla* Entitlement" (page 423) also address conflicting attitudes toward immigration, long held to be a significant aspect of the American dream.

George Orwell

Born Eric Blair in the former British colony of India, George Orwell (1903–50) is probably best known for his two novels, *Animal Farm* (1946) and *1984* (1949), both searing depictions of totalitarian societies. Orwell was also the author of numerous books and essays, many based on his diverse life experiences. He served with the Indian imperial police in Burma, worked at various jobs in London and Paris, and fought in the Spanish Civil War. His experiences in Burma provide the basis for the following essay, which is taken from his collection, *Shooting an Elephant and Other Essays* (1950).

Pre-Reading Journal Entry

Think of times when you were keenly aware of institutional injustice—an action, law, or regulation that was legally in the right but that you felt was wrong. In your journal, record several such examples. Why do you consider them wrong? Have you always felt that way? If not, what changed your opinion?

Shooting an Elephant

In Moulmein, in Lower Burma, I was hated by large numbers of people—the only time in my life that I have been important enough for this to happen to me. I was sub-divisional police officer of the town, and in an aimless, petty kind of way anti-European feeling was very bitter. No one had the guts to raise a riot, but if a European woman went through the bazaars alone somebody would probably spit betel juice over her dress. As a police officer I was an obvious target and was baited whenever it seemed safe to do so. When a nimble Burman tripped me up on the football field and the referee (another Burman) looked the other way, the crowd yelled with hideous laughter. This happened more than once. In the end the sneering yellow faces of young men that met me everywhere, the insults hooted after me when I was at a safe distance, got badly on my nerves. The young Buddhist priests were the worst of all. There were several thousand of them in the town and none of them seemed to have anything to do except stand on street corners and jeer at Europeans.

All this was perplexing and upsetting. For at that time I had already made up my mind that imperialism was an evil thing and the sooner I chucked up my job and got out of it the better. Theoretically—and secretly, of course—I was all for the Burmese and all against their oppressors, the British. As for the job I was doing, I hated it more bitterly than I can perhaps make clear. In a job like that you see the dirty work of Empire at close quarters. The wretched prisoners huddling in the stinking cages of the lock-ups, the grey, cowed faces of the long-term convicts, the scarred buttocks of the men who had been flogged with bamboos—all these oppressed me with

1

2

133

an intolerable sense of guilt. But I could get nothing into perspective. I was young and ill-educated and I had had to think out my problems in the utter silence that is imposed on every Englishman in the East. I did not even know that the British Empire is dying, still less did I know that it is a great deal better than the younger empires that are going to supplant it. All I knew was that I was stuck between my hatred of the empire I served and my rage against the evil-spirited little beasts who tried to make my job impossible. With one part of my mind I thought of the British Raj as an unbreakable tyranny, as something clamped down, in *saecula saeculorum*,[1] upon the will of prostrate peoples; with another part I thought that the greatest joy in the world would be to drive a bayonet into a Buddhist priest's guts. Feelings like these are the normal by-products of imperialism; ask any Anglo-Indian official, if you can catch him off duty.

One day something happened which in a roundabout way was enlight-   3
ening. It was a tiny incident in itself, but it gave me a better glimpse than I had had before of the real nature of imperialism—the real motives for which despotic governments act. Early one morning the sub-inspector at a police station at the other end of the town rang me up on the 'phone and said that an elephant was ravaging the bazaar. Would I please come and do something about it? I did not know what I could do, but I wanted to see what was happening and I got onto a pony and started out. I took my rifle, an old .44 Winchester and much too small to kill an elephant, but I thought the noise might be useful *in terrorem*.[2] Various Burmans stopped me on the way and told me about the elephant's doings. It was not, of course, a wild elephant, but a tame one which had gone "must." It had been chained up, as tame elephants always are when their attack of "must" is due, but on the previous night it had broken its chain and escaped. Its mahout, the only person who could manage it when it was in that state, had set out in pursuit, but had taken the wrong direction and was now twelve hours' journey away, and in the morning the elephant had suddenly reappeared in the town. The Burmese population had no weapons and were quite helpless against it. It had already destroyed somebody's bamboo hut, killed a cow and raided some fruit-stalls and devoured the stock; also it had met the municipal rubbish van and, when the driver jumped out and took to his heels, had turned the van over and inflicted violence upon it.

The Burmese sub-inspector and some Indian constables were waiting   4
for me in the quarter where the elephant had been seen. It was a very poor quarter, a labyrinth of squalid bamboo huts, thatched with palm-leaf, winding all over a steep hillside. I remember that it was a cloudy, stuffy morning at the beginning of the rains. We began questioning the people as to where

---

[1]For ever and ever (editors' note).
[2]As a warning (editors' note).

the elephant had gone and, as usual, failed to get any definite information. That is invariably the case in the East; a story always sounds clear enough at a distance, but the nearer you get to the scene of events the vaguer it becomes. Some of the people said that the elephant had gone in one direction, some said that he had gone in another, some professed not even to have heard of any elephant. I had almost made up my mind that the whole story was a pack of lies, when we heard yells a little distance away. There was a loud, scandalized cry of "Go away, child! Go away this instant!" and an old woman with a switch in her hand came round the corner of a hut, violently shooing away a crowd of naked children. Some more women followed, clicking their tongues and exclaiming; evidently there was something that the children ought not to have seen. I rounded the hut and saw a man's dead body sprawling in the mud. He was an Indian, a black Dravidian coolie, almost naked, and he could not have been dead many minutes. The people said that the elephant had come suddenly upon him round the corner of the hut, caught him with its trunk, put its foot on his back and ground him into the earth. This was the rainy season and the ground was soft, and his face had scored a trench a foot deep and a couple of yards long. He was lying on his belly with arms crucified and head sharply twisted to one side. His face was coated with mud, the eyes wide open, the teeth bared and grinning with an expression of unendurable agony. (Never tell me, by the way, that the dead look peaceful. Most of the corpses I have seen looked devilish.) The friction of the great beast's foot had stripped the skin from his back as neatly as one skins a rabbit. As soon as I saw the dead man I sent an orderly to a friend's house nearby to borrow an elephant rifle. I had already sent back the pony, not wanting it to go mad with fright and throw me if it smelt the elephant.

The orderly came back in a few minutes with a rifle and five cartridges, and meanwhile some Burmans had arrived and told us that the elephant was in the paddy fields below, only a few hundred yards away. As I started forward practically the whole population of the quarter flocked out of the houses and followed me. They had seen the rifle and were all shouting excitedly that I was going to shoot the elephant. They had not shown much interest in the elephant when he was merely ravaging their homes, but it was different now that he was going to be shot. It was a bit of fun to them, as it would be to an English crowd; besides they wanted the meat. It made me vaguely uneasy. I had no intention of shooting the elephant—I had merely sent for the rifle to defend myself if necessary—and it is always unnerving to have a crowd following you. I marched down the hill, looking and feeling a fool, with the rifle over my shoulder and an ever-growing army of people jostling at my heels. At the bottom, when you got away from the huts, there was a metalled road and beyond that a miry waste of paddy fields a thousand yards across, not yet ploughed but soggy from the first rains and dotted with

5

coarse grass. The elephant was standing eight yards from the road, his left side towards us. He took not the slightest notice of the crowd's approach. He was tearing up bunches of grass, beating them against his knees to clean them and stuffing them into his mouth.

I had halted on the road. As soon as I saw the elephant I knew with per-   6 fect certainty that I ought not to shoot him. It is a serious matter to shoot a working elephant—it is comparable to destroying a huge and costly piece of machinery—and obviously one ought not to do it if it can possibly be avoided. And at that distance, peacefully eating, the elephant looked no more dangerous than a cow. I thought then and I think now that his attack of "must" was already passing off; in which case he would merely wander harmlessly about until the mahout came back and caught him. Moreover, I did not in the least want to shoot him. I decided that I would watch him for a little while to make sure that he did not turn savage again, and then go home.

But at that moment I glanced round at the crowd that had followed me.   7 It was an immense crowd, two thousand at the least and growing every minute. It blocked the road for a long distance on either side. I looked at the sea of yellow faces above the garish clothes—faces all happy and excited over this bit of fun, all certain that the elephant was going to be shot. They were watching me as they would watch a conjurer about to perform a trick. They did not like me, but with the magical rifle in my hands I was momentarily worth watching. And suddenly I realized that I should have to shoot the elephant after all. The people expected it of me and I had got to do it; I could feel their two thousand wills pressing me forward, irresistibly. And it was at this moment, as I stood there with the rifle in my hands, that I first grasped the hollowness, the futility of the white man's dominion in the East. Here was I, the white man with his gun, standing in front of the unarmed native crowd—seemingly the leading actor of the piece; but in reality I was only an absurd puppet pushed to and fro by the will of those yellow faces behind. I perceived in this moment that when the white man turns tyrant it is his own freedom that he destroys. He becomes a sort of hollow, posing dummy, the conventionalized figure of a sahib. For it is the condition of his rule that he shall spend his life in trying to impress the "natives," and so in every crisis he has got to do what the "natives" expect of him. He wears a mask, and his face grows to fit it. I had got to shoot the elephant. I had committed myself to doing it when I sent for the rifle. A sahib has got to act like a sahib; he has got to appear resolute, to know his own mind and do definite things. To come all that way, rifle in hand, with two thousand people marching at my heels, and then to trail feebly away, having done nothing—no, that was impossible. The crowd would laugh at me. And my whole life, every white man's life in the East, was one long struggle not to be laughed at.

But I did not want to shoot the elephant. I watched him beating his   8 bunch of grass against his knees, with that preoccupied grandmotherly air that elephants have. It seemed to me that it would be murder to shoot him. At that age I was not squeamish about killing animals, but I had never shot an elephant and never wanted to. (Somehow it always seems worse to kill a *large* animal.) Besides, there was the beast's owner to be considered. Alive, the elephant was worth at least a hundred pounds; dead, he would only be worth the value of his tusks, five pounds, possibly. But I had got to act quickly. I turned to some experienced-looking Burmans who had been there when we arrived, and asked them how the elephant had been behaving. They all said the same thing: he took no notice of you if you left him alone, but he might charge if you went too close to him.

It was perfectly clear to me what I ought to do. I ought to walk up to within, say, twenty-five yards of the elephant and test his behavior. If he charged, I could shoot; if he took no notice of me, it would be safe to leave him until the mahout came back. But also I knew that I was going to do no such thing. I was a poor shot with a rifle and the ground was soft mud into which one would sink at every step. If the elephant charged and I missed him, I should have about as much chance as a toad under a steam-roller. But even then I was not thinking particularly of my own skin, only of the watchful yellow faces behind. For at that moment, with the crowd watching me, I was not afraid in the ordinary sense, as I would have been if I had been alone. A white man mustn't be frightened in front of "natives"; and so, in general, he isn't frightened. The sole thought in my mind was that if anything went wrong those two thousand Burmans would see me pursued, caught, trampled on and reduced to a grinning corpse like that Indian up the hill. And if that happened it was quite probable that some of them would laugh. That would never do. There was only one alternative. I shoved the cartridges into the magazine and lay down on the road to get a better aim. 9

The crowd grew very still, and a deep, low, happy sigh, as of people who see the theatre curtain go up at last, breathed from innumerable throats. They were going to have their bit of fun after all. The rifle was a beautiful German thing with cross-hair sights. I did not then know that in shooting an elephant one would shoot to cut an imaginary bar running from ear-hole to ear-hole. I ought, therefore, as the elephant was sideway on, to have aimed straight at his ear-hole; actually I aimed several inches in front of this, thinking the brain would be further forward. 10

When I pulled the trigger I did not hear the bang or feel the kick—one never does when a shot goes home—but I heard the devilish roar of glee that went up from the crowd. In that instant, in too short a time, one would have thought, even for the bullet to get there, a mysterious, terrible change had come over the elephant. He neither stirred nor fell, but every line of his body had altered. He looked suddenly stricken, shrunken, immensely old, as though the frightful impact of the bullet had paralyzed him without knocking him down. At last, after what seemed a long time—it might have been 11 five seconds, I dare say—he sagged flabbily to his knees. His mouth slob-bered. An enormous senility seemed to have settled upon him. One could have imagined him thousands of years old. I fired again into the same spot. At the second shot he did not collapse but climbed with desperate slowness to his feet and stood weakly upright, with legs sagging and head drooping. I fired a third time. That was the shot that did for him. You could see the agony of it jolt his whole body and knock the last remnant of strength from his legs. But in falling he seemed for a moment to rise, for as his hind legs collapsed beneath him he seemed to tower upward like a huge rock toppling, his trunk reaching skywards like a tree. He trumpeted, for the first and only time. And then down he came, his belly towards me, with a crash that seemed to shake the ground even where I lay.

I got up. The Burmans were already racing past me across the mud. It   12
was obvious that the elephant would never rise again, but he was not dead. He was breathing very rhythmically with long rattling gasps, his great mound of a side painfully rising and falling. His mouth was wide open—I could see far down into caverns of pale pink throat. I waited a long time for him to die, but his breathing did not weaken. Finally I fired my two remain-ing shots into the spot where I thought his heart must be. The thick blood welled out of him like red velvet, but still he did not die. His body did not even jerk when the shots hit him, the tortured breathing continued without a pause. He was dying, very slowly and in great agony, but in some world remote from me where not even a bullet could damage him further. I felt that I had got to put an end to that dreadful noise. It seemed dreadful to see the great beast lying there, powerless to move and yet powerless to die, and not even to be able to finish him. I sent back for my small rifle and poured shot after shot into his heart and down his throat. They seemed to make no impression. The tortured gasps continued as steadily as the ticking of a clock.

In the end I could not stand it any longer and went away. I heard later   13
that it took him half an hour to die. Burmans were bringing dahs and bas-kets even before I left, and I was told they had stripped the body almost to the bones by the afternoon.

Afterwards, of course, there were endless discussions about the shooting   14
of the elephant. The owner was furious, but he was only an Indian and could do nothing. Besides, legally I had done the right thing, for a mad elephant has to be killed, like a mad dog, if its owner fails to control it. Among the Europeans opinion was divided. The older men said I was right, the younger men said it was a damn shame to shoot an elephant for killing a coolie, because an elephant was worth more than any damn Coringhee coolie. And afterwards I was very glad that the coolie had been killed; it put me legally in the right and it gave me a sufficient pretext for shooting the elephant. I often wondered whether any of the others grasped that I had done it solely to avoid looking a fool.

Questions for Close Reading

1. What is the selection's thesis (or narrative point)? Locate the sentence(s) in which Orwell states his main idea. If he doesn't state the thesis explicitly, express it in your own words.
2. How does Orwell feel about the Burmans? What words does he use to describe them?
3. What reasons does Orwell give for shooting the elephant?
4. In paragraph 3, Orwell says that the elephant incident gave him a better understanding of "the real motives for which despotic governments act." What do you think he means? Before you answer, reread paragraph 7 carefully.
5. Refer to your dictionary as needed to define the following words used in the selection: *imperialism* (paragraph 2), *prostrate* (2), *despotic* (3), *mahout* (3), *miry* (5), *conjurer* (7), *futility* (7), and *sahib* (7).

Questions About the Writer's Craft

1. **The pattern.** Most effective narratives encompass a restricted time span. How much time elapses from the moment Orwell gets his gun to the death of the elephant? What time signals does Orwell provide to help the reader follow the sequence of events in this limited time span?
2. Orwell doesn't actually begin his narrative until the third paragraph. What purposes do the first two paragraphs serve?
3. **Other patterns.** In paragraph 6, Orwell says that shooting a working elephant "is comparable to destroying a huge and costly piece of machinery." This kind of *comparison* is called an *analogy*—describing something unfamiliar, often abstract, in terms of something more familiar and concrete. Find at least three additional analogies in Orwell's essay. What effect do they have?
4. **Other patterns.** Much of the power of Orwell's narrative comes from his ability to convey sensory impressions—what he saw, heard, smelled. Orwell's *description* becomes most vivid when he writes about the death of the elephant in paragraphs 11 and 12. Find some evocative words and phrases that give the description its power.

Writing Assignments Using Narration as a Pattern of Development

1. Orwell recounts a time he acted under great pressure. Write a narrative about an action you once took simply because you felt pressured. Perhaps you were attempting to avoid ridicule or to fulfill someone else's expectations. Like Orwell, use vivid details to bring the incident to life and to convey its effect on you. Anna Quindlen's "Driving to the Funeral" (page 399) may lead you to some insights about the ways different pressures influence behavior.
2. Write a narrative essay about an experience that gave you, like Orwell, a deeper insight into your own nature. You may have discovered, for instance, that you can be surprisingly naive, compassionate, petty, brave, rebellious, or good at something. Consider first reading Joan Murray's "Someone's Mother" (page 141), an essay showing how a person's response to a challenge can reveal much about his or her character.

Writing Assignments Combining Patterns of Development

3. Was Orwell justified in shooting the elephant? Write an essay *arguing* that Orwell was either justified *or* not justified. To develop your thesis, cite several specific reasons, each supported by *examples* drawn from the essay. Here are some points you might consider: the legality of Orwell's act, the elephant's temperament, the crowd's presence, the aftermath of the elephant's death, the death itself.

4. Orwell's essay concerns, in part, the tendency to conceal indecision and confusion behind a facade of authority. Focusing on one or two groups of people (parents, teachers, doctors, politicians, and so on), write an essay *arguing* that people in authority sometimes *pretend* to know what they're doing so that subordinates won't suspect their insecurity or incompetence. Part of your essay should focus on the *consequences* of such behaviors.

Writing Assignment Using a Journal Entry as a Starting Point

5. Review your pre-reading journal entry, and select *one* action, law, or regulation that you consider indefensible. Interview friends, family, and classmates in an effort to gather views on all sides of the issue. Also consider supplementing this informal research with information gathered in the library and/or on the Internet. After weighing all your material, formulate a thesis; then write an essay convincing readers of the validity of your position.

Joan Murray

Joan Murray—a poet, writer, editor, and playwright—was born in New York City in 1945. She attended Hunter College and New York University, and published her first volume of poetry, which she also illustrated, in 1975. Three of her poetry books—*Queen of the Mist, Looking for the Parade*, and *The Same Water*—have won prizes. Her most recent volume of poetry is *Dancing on the Edge*, published in 2002. This essay appeared in the "Lives" section of the weekly *New York Times Magazine* on May 13, 2007.

Pre-Reading Journal Entry

We are used to having our mothers care for us, but sometimes we have to care for our mothers. Reflect on an occasion when you had to do something important for your mother or other caregiver. What was the situation? How did you help? How did you feel about helping someone who normally helped you? Use your journal to respond to these questions.

Someone's Mother

Hitchhiking is generally illegal where I live in upstate New York, but it's not unusual to see someone along Route 20 with an outstretched thumb or a handmade sign saying "Boston." This hitchhiker, though, was waving both arms in the air and grinning like a president boarding Air Force One. 1

I was doing 60—eager to get home after a dental appointment in Albany—and I was a mile past the hitchhiker before something made me turn back. I couldn't say if the hitchhiker was a man or a woman. All I knew was that the hitchhiker was old. 2

As I drove back up the hill, I eyed the hitchhiker in the distance: dark blue raincoat, jaunty black beret. Thin arms waving, spine a little bent. Wisps of white hair lilting as the trucks whizzed by. I made a U-turn and pulled up on the gravel, face to face with an eager old woman who kept waving till I stopped. I saw no broken-down vehicle. There was no vehicle at all. She wore the same broad grin I noticed when I passed her. 3

I rolled my window down. "Can I call someone for you?" 4

"No, I'm fine—I just need a ride." 5

"Where are you going?" 6

"Nassau." 7

That was three miles away. "Are you going there to shop?" 8

"No. I live there." 9

"What are you doing here?" I asked with a tone I hadn't used since my son was a teenager. 10

"I was out for a walk." 11

I glanced down the road: Jet's Autobody. Copeland Coating. Thoma Tire Company. And the half-mile hill outside Nassau—so steep that there's 12 a second lane for trucks. She must have climbed the shoulder of that hill. And the next one. And the next. Until something made her stop and throw her hands in the air.

"Did you get lost?" I asked, trying to conceal my alarm.   13

"It was a nice day," she said with a little cry. "Can't an old lady go for a   14
walk on a nice day and get lost?"

It wasn't a question meant to be answered. She came around to the pas-   15
senger side, opened the door and sat down. On our way to Nassau, she admitted to being 92. Though she ducked my questions about her name, her address and her family. "Just leave me at the drugstore," she said.

"I'll take you home," I said. "Then you can call someone."   16

"Please," she said, "just leave me at the drugstore."   17

"I can't leave you there," I replied just as firmly. "I'm going to take you   18
to your house. Or else to the police station."

"No, no," she begged. She was agitated now. "If my son finds out, he'll   19
put me in a home."

Already I was seeing my own mother, who's 90. A few years ago, she was   20
living in her house on Long Island, surrounded by her neighbors, her bird feeders, her azaleas. Then one morning she phoned my brother to say she didn't remember how to get dressed anymore. A few weeks later, with sorrow and worry, we arranged her move to a nursing home.

I noticed that the hitchhiker had a white dove pinned to her collar. "Do   21
you belong to a church?" I tried. "Yes," she said. She was grinning. "I'd like to take you there," I said. "No, please," she said again. "My son will find out."

Things were getting clearer. "You've gotten lost before?"   22

"A few times," she shrugged. "But I always find my way home. Just take   23
me to the drugstore."

As we drove, I kept thinking about my mother, watched over and cared   24
for in a bright, clean place. I also thought about her empty bird feeders, her azaleas blooming for no one, the way she whispers on the phone, "I don't know anyone here."

When I pulled into the parking strip beside the drugstore, the hitchhik-   25
er let herself out. "I just need to sit on the step for a while," she said before closing the door. I stepped out after her. "Can't I take you home?" I asked as gently as I could.

She looked into my eyes for a moment. "I don't know where I live," she   26
said in the tiniest voice. "But someone will come along who knows me. They always do."

I watched as she sat herself down on the step. Already she had dismissed   27
me from her service. She was staring ahead with her grin intact, waiting for the next person who would aid her.

I should call the police, I thought. But then surely her son would be told.   28
I should speak with the pharmacists. Surely they might know her—though

they might know her son as well. Yet who was I to keep this incident from him? And yet how could I help him put the hitchhiker in a home?

"Promise me you'll tell the druggist if no one comes soon," I said to her   29
with great seriousness.

"I promise," she said with a cheerful little wave.   30

Questions for Close Reading

1. What is the selection's thesis? Locate the sentence(s) in which Murray states her main idea. If she doesn't state her thesis explicitly, express it in your own words.
2. What is the external conflict Murray experiences in this essay? What is the internal conflict?
3. In paragraph 22, the author says "Things were getting clearer." What does she mean by this?
4. Why does Murray finally go along with the hitchhiker's wishes?
5. Refer to your dictionary as needed to define the following words used in the selection: *jaunty* (paragraph 3), *beret* (3), *lilting* (3), *shoulder* (12), *agitated* (19), and *azaleas* (20).

Questions About the Writer's Craft

1. **The pattern.** How does Murray organize the events in this essay? How does she keep the reader oriented as her story progresses?
2. **Other patterns.** In some passages, Murray *describes* the hitchhiker's appearance. What do these descriptions contribute to the narrative?
3. In paragraphs 12, 20, 24 and 28, Murray tells us her thoughts. What effect do these sections have on the pace of the narrative? How do they affect our understanding of what is happening?
4. Murray uses a lot of dialogue in this essay. Explain why the use of dialogue is (or is not) effective. What function does the dialogue have?

Writing Assignments Using Narration as a Pattern of Development

1. Murray's encounter with the hitchhiker happens as she is driving home. Recall a time when you were traveling in a car, bus, or other vehicle and something surprising occurred. Were you frightened, puzzled, amused? Did you learn something about people or about yourself? Tell the story using first-person narration, being sure to include your thoughts as well as your actions and the actions of others.
2. Write a narrative about an incident in your life in which a stranger helped you, and explain how this made you feel. The experience might have made you grateful, resentful, or anxious like the hitchhiker. Use either flashback or flashforward to emphasize an event in your narrative. To read an essay that uses flashback, see Gary Kamiya's "Life, Death and Spring" (page 103) and Audre Lorde's "The Fourth of July" (page 127).

Writing Assignments Combining
Patterns of Development

3. Did Murray do the right thing when she left the elderly woman sitting in front of the drugstore? Write an essay in which you *argue* that Murray did or did not act properly. You can support your argument using *examples* from the essay showing the hitchhiker's state of mental and physical health. You can also support your argument by presenting the possible positive or negative effects of Murray's action, depending on your point of view.

4. Murray is concerned that the hitchhiker, like Murray's own mother, may not able to take care of herself sufficiently. Do some research on the Internet or in the library about options available for elderly people who can no longer live alone. Write an essay in which you give *examples* of these options and *compare* them in terms of price, services, and quality of life.

Writing Assignment Using a Journal
Entry as a Starting Point

5. Review your pre-reading journal entry in which you described a time when you had to help your mother or other caregiver. Compare your experience to those of Joan Murray, who helped her own mother as well as the hitchhiker, who was "someone's mother." How did your experience differ from hers? How was it similar? If you were to do it again, would you do so the same way, or would you do it differently? Why?

Additional Writing Topics

NARRATION

General Assignments

Prepare an essay on any of the following topics, using narration as the paper's dominant method of development. Be sure to select details that advance the essay's narrative purpose; you may even want to experiment with flashback or flashforward. In any case, keep the sequence of events clear by using transitional cues. Within the limited time span covered, use vigorous details and varied sentence structure to enliven the narrative. Tell the story from a consistent point of view.

1. An emergency that brought out the best or worst in you
2. The hazards of taking children out to eat
3. An incident that made you believe in fate
4. Your best or worst day at school or work
5. A major decision
6. An encounter with a machine
7. An important learning experience
8. A narrow escape
9. Your first date, first day on the job, or first anything
10. A memorable childhood experience
11. A fairy tale the way you would like to hear it told
12. A painful moment
13. An incredible but true story
14. A significant family event
15. An experience in which a certain emotion (pride, anger, regret, or some other) was dominant
16. A surprising coincidence
17. An act of heroism
18. An unpleasant confrontation
19. A cherished family story
20. An imagined meeting with an admired celebrity or historical figure

Assignments with a Specific Purpose, Audience, and Point of View

On Campus

1. Write an article for your old high school newspaper. The article will be read primarily by seniors who are planning to go away to college next year. In the article, narrate a story that points to some truth about the "breaking away" stage of life.
2. A friend of yours has seen someone cheat on a test, plagiarize an entire paper, or seriously violate some other academic policy. In a letter, convince this friend to

inform the instructor or a campus administrator by narrating an incident in which a witness did (or did not) speak up in such a situation. Tell what happened as a result.

At Home or in the Community

3. You have had a disturbing encounter with one of the people who seems to have "fallen through the cracks" of society—a homeless person, an unwanted child, or anyone else who is alone and abandoned. Write a letter to the local newspaper describing this encounter. Your purpose is to arouse people's indignation and compassion and to get help for such unfortunates.
4. Your younger brother, sister, relative, or neighborhood friend can't wait to be your age. Write a letter in which you narrate a dramatic story that shows the young person that your age isn't as wonderful as he or she thinks. Be sure to select a story that the person can understand and appreciate.

On the Job

5. As fund-raiser for a particular organization (for example, the Red Cross, the SPCA, Big Brothers/Big Sisters), you're sending a newsletter to contributors. Support your cause by telling the story of a time when your organization made all the difference—the blood donation that saved a life, the animal that was rescued from abuse, and so on.
6. A customer has written a letter to you (or your boss) telling about a bad experience that he or she had with someone in your workplace. On the basis of that single experience, the customer now regards your company and its employees with great suspicion. It's your responsibility to respond to this complaint. Write a letter to the customer balancing his or her negative picture by narrating a story that shows the "flip side" of your company and its employees.

Bill Arnon/PhotoEdit, Inc.

EXEMPLIFICATION

WHAT IS EXEMPLIFICATION?

If someone asked you, "Have you been to any good restaurants lately?" you probably wouldn't answer "Yes" and then immediately change the subject. Most likely, you would go on to illustrate with *examples*. Perhaps you'd give the names of restaurants you've enjoyed and talk briefly about the specific things you liked: the attractive prices, the tasty main courses, the pleasant service, the tempting desserts. Such examples and details are needed to convince others that your opinion—in this or any matter—is valid. Similarly, when you talk about larger and more important issues, people won't pay much attention to your opinion if all you do is string together vague generalizations: "We have to do something about acid rain. It's had disastrous consequences for the environment. Its negative effects increase every year. Action must be taken to control the problem." To be taken seriously and to convince others that your point is well-founded, you must provide specific supporting examples: "The forests in the Adirondacks are dying"; "Yesterday's rainfall was fifty times more acidic than normal"; "Pine Lake, in the northern part of the state, was once a great fishing spot but now has no fish population."

Examples are equally important when you write an essay. It's not fuzzy generalities and highfalutin abstractions that make writing impressive. Just the opposite is true. Facts, anecdotes, statistics, details, opinions, and observations are at the heart of effective writing, giving your work substance and solidity.

HOW EXEMPLIFICATION FITS YOUR PURPOSE AND AUDIENCE

The wording of assignments and essay exam questions may signal the need for specific examples:

> Soap operas, whether shown during the day or in the evening, are among the most popular television programs. Why do you think this is so? Provide specific examples to support your position.

> Some observers claim that college students are less interested in learning than in getting ahead in their careers. Cite evidence to support or refute this claim.

> A growing number of people feel that parents should not allow young children to participate in highly competitive team sports. Basing your conclusion on your own experiences and observations, indicate whether you think this point of view is reasonable.

Such phrases as "Provide specific examples," "Cite evidence," and "Basing your conclusion on your own experiences and observations" signal that each essay should be developed through examples.

Usually, though, you won't be told so explicitly to provide examples. Instead, as you think about the best way to achieve your essay's purpose, you'll see the need for illustrative details—no matter which patterns of development you use. For instance, to *persuade* skeptical readers that the country needs a national health system, you might mention specific cases to dramatize the inadequacy of our current health-care system: a family bankrupted by medical bills; an uninsured accident victim turned away by a hospital; a chronically ill person rapidly deteriorating because he didn't have enough money to visit a doctor. Or imagine a lightly satiric piece that pokes fun at cat lovers. Insisting that "cat people" are pretty strange creatures, you might make your point—and make readers chuckle—with a series of examples *contrasting* cat lovers and dog lovers: the qualities admired by each group (loyalty in dogs versus independence in cats) and the different expectations each group has for its pets (dog lovers want Fido to be obedient and lovable, whereas cat lovers are satisfied with Felix's occasional spurts of docility and affection). Similarly, you would supply examples in a *causal analysis* speculating on the likely impact of a proposed tuition hike at your college. To convince the college administration of the probable negative effects of such a hike, you might cite the following examples: articles reporting a nationwide upswing in student transfers to less expensive schools; statistics indicating a significant drop in grades among already employed students forced to work more hours to pay increased tuition costs; interviews with students too financially strapped to continue their college education.

Whether you use examples as the primary or a supplemental method of development, they serve a number of important purposes. For one thing, examples make writing *interesting*. Assume you're writing an essay showing that television commercials are biased against women. Your essay would be lifeless and boring if all it did was repeat, in a general way, that commercials present stereotyped views of women.

> An anti-female bias is rampant in television commercials. It is very much alive, yet most viewers seem to take it all in stride. Few people protest the obviously sexist characters and statements in such commercials. Surely, these commercials misrepresent the way most of us live.

Without interesting particulars, readers may respond, "Who cares?" But if you provide specific examples, you'll attract your readers' attention:

> Sexism is rampant in television commercials. Although millions of women hold responsible jobs outside the home, commercials continue to portray women as simple creatures who spend most of their time thinking about wax buildup, cottony-soft bathroom tissue, and static-free clothes. Men, apparently, have better things to do than fret over such mundane household matters. How many commercials can you recall that depict men proclaiming the virtues of squeaky-clean dishes or sparkling bathrooms? Not many.

Examples also make writing *persuasive*. Most writing conveys a point, but many readers are reluctant to accept someone else's point of view unless evidence demonstrates its validity. Imagine you're writing an essay showing that latchkey children are more self-sufficient and emotionally secure than children who return from school to a home where a parent awaits them. Your thesis is obviously controversial. Without specific examples—from your own experience, personal observations, or research studies—your readers would undoubtedly question your position's validity.

Further, examples *help explain* difficult, abstract, or unusual ideas. Suppose you're assigned an essay on a complex subject such as inflation, zero population growth, or radiation exposure. As a writer, you have a responsibility to your readers to make these difficult concepts concrete and understandable. If writing an essay on radiation exposure in everyday life, you might start by providing specific examples of home appliances that emit radiation—color televisions, computers, and microwave ovens—and tell exactly how much radiation we absorb in a typical day from such equipment. To illustrate further the extent of our radiation exposure, you could also provide specifics about unavoidable sources of natural radiation (the sun, for instance) and details about the widespread use of radiation in medicine (X rays, radiation therapy). These examples would ground your discussion, making it immediate and concrete, preventing it from flying off into the vague and theoretical.

Finally, examples *help prevent unintended ambiguity.* All of us have experienced the frustration of having someone misinterpret what we say. In face-to-face communication, we can provide on-the-spot clarification. In writing, however, instantaneous feedback isn't available, so it's crucial that meaning be as unambiguous as possible. Examples will help.

Assume you're writing an essay asserting that ineffective teaching is on the rise in today's high schools. To clarify what you mean by "ineffective," you provide examples: the instructor who spends so much time disciplining unruly students that he never gets around to teaching; the moonlighting teacher who is so tired in class that she regularly takes naps during tests; and the teacher who accepts obviously plagiarized reports because he's grateful that students hand in something. Without such concrete examples, your readers will supply their own ideas—and these may not be what you had in mind. Readers might imagine "ineffective" to mean harsh and punitive, whereas your concrete examples would show that you intend it to mean out of control and irresponsible. Such specifics help prevent misunderstanding.

At this point, you have a good sense of the way writers use exemplification to achieve their purposes and to connect with their readers. Now take a moment to look closely at the advertisement at the beginning of this chapter. Imagine you're taking part in a "focus group" assembled by the advertiser of this product. Your task is to rate the ad on a  scale of 1 (negative) to 10 (positive) on the basis of the images it promotes. To support your rating, jot down some phrases that express the values that you believe are *illustrated* by the ad.

SUGGESTIONS FOR USING EXEMPLIFICATION IN AN ESSAY

The suggestions here and in Figure 5.1 will be helpful whether you use examples as a dominant or a supportive pattern of development.

1. Generate examples.   Where do you get the examples to develop your essay? The first batch of examples is generated during the prewriting stage.

FIGURE 5.1
Development Diagram: Writing an Exemplification Essay

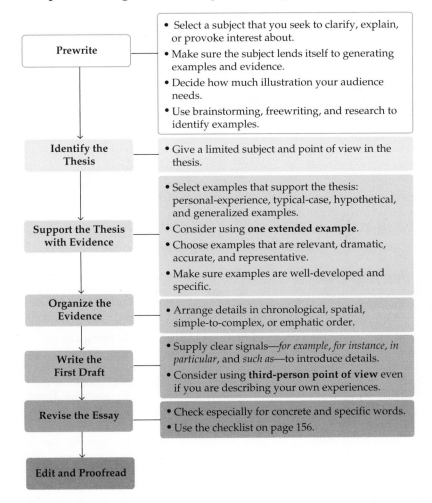

Prewrite
- Select a subject that you seek to clarify, explain, or provoke interest about.
- Make sure the subject lends itself to generating examples and evidence.
- Decide how much illustration your audience needs.
- Use brainstorming, freewriting, and research to identify examples.

Identify the Thesis
- Give a limited subject and point of view in the thesis.

Support the Thesis with Evidence
- Select examples that support the thesis: personal-experience, typical-case, hypothetical, and generalized examples.
- Consider using **one extended example**.
- Choose examples that are relevant, dramatic, accurate, and representative.
- Make sure examples are well-developed and specific.

Organize the Evidence
- Arrange details in chronological, spatial, simple-to-complex, or emphatic order.

Write the First Draft
- Supply clear signals—*for example, for instance, in particular,* and *such as*—to introduce details.
- Consider using **third-person point of view** even if you are describing your own experiences.

Revise the Essay
- Check especially for concrete and specific words.
- Use the checklist on page 156.

Edit and Proofread

With your purpose and thesis in mind, you make a broad sweep for examples, using brainstorming, freewriting, the mapping technique—whichever prewriting technique you prefer. During this preliminary search for examples, you may also read through your journal for relevant specifics, interview other people, or conduct library research.

Examples can take several forms, including specific names (of people, places, products, and so on), anecdotes, personal observations, expert opinion, as well as facts, statistics, and case studies gathered through research. While prewriting, try to generate more examples than you think you'll need. Starting with abundance—and then picking out the strongest examples—will give you a firm base on which to build the essay. If you have a great deal of trouble finding examples to support your thesis, you may need to revise the thesis; you may be trying to support an idea that has little validity. On the other hand, while prewriting, you may unearth numerous examples but find that many of them contradict the point you started out to support. If that happens, don't hesitate to recast your central point, always remembering that your thesis and examples must fit.

2. Select the examples to include.   Once you've used prewriting to generate as many examples as possible, you're ready to limit your examples to the strongest ones. Keeping your purpose, thesis, and audience in mind, ask yourself several key questions: "Which examples support my thesis? Which do not? Which are most convincing? Which are most likely to interest readers and clarify meaning?"

You may include several brief examples within a single sentence:

The French people's fascination with some American literary figures, such as Poe and Hawthorne, is understandable, but their great respect for "artists" like comedian Jerry Lewis is a mystery.

Or you may develop a paragraph with a number of "for instances":

A uniquely American style of movie-acting reached its peak in the 1950s. Certain charismatic actors completely abandoned the stage techniques and tradition that had been the foundation of acting up to that time. Instead of articulating their lines clearly, the actors mumbled; instead of making firm eye contact with their colleagues, they hung their heads, shifted their eyes, even talked with their eyes closed. Marlon Brando, Montgomery Clift, and James Dean were three actors who exemplified this new trend.

As the preceding paragraph shows, *several examples* are usually needed to make a point. An essay with the thesis "Rock videos are dangerously violent" wouldn't be convincing if you gave only one example of a violent rock video. Several strong examples would be needed for readers to feel you had illustrated your point sufficiently.

As a general rule, you should strive for variety in the kinds of examples you include. For instance, you might choose a *personal-experience example* drawn from your own life or from the life of someone you know. Such examples pack the wallop of personal authority and lend drama to writing. Or you might include a *typical-case example,* an actual event or situation that did occur—but not to you or to anyone you know. (Perhaps you learned about the event through a magazine article, newspaper account, or television report.) The objective nature of such cases makes them especially convincing. You might also include a speculative or *hypothetical example* ("Imagine how difficult it must be for an elderly person to carry bags of groceries from the market to a bus stop several blocks away"). You'll find that hypothetical cases are effective for clarifying and dramatizing key points, but be sure to acknowledge that the example is indeed invented ("*Suppose* that..." or "Let's for a moment *assume* that..."). Make certain, too, that the invented situation is easily imagined and could conceivably happen. Finally, you might create a *generalized example*—one that is a composite of the typical or usual. Such generalized examples are often signaled by words that involve the reader ("*All of us,* at one time or another, have been driven to distraction by a trivial annoyance like the buzzing of a fly or the sting of a paper cut"), or they may refer to humanity in general ("When *most people* get a compliment, they perk up, preen, and think the praise-giver is blessed with astute powers of observation").

Occasionally, *one extended example,* fully developed with many details, can support an essay. It might be possible, for instance, to support the thesis "States should raise the legal driving age to eighteen" with a single compelling, highly detailed example of the effects of one sixteen-year-old's high-speed driving spree.

The examples you choose must also be *relevant;* that is, they must have direct bearing on the point you want to make. You would have a hard time convincing readers that Americans have callous attitudes toward the elderly if you described the wide range of new programs, all staffed by volunteers, at a well-financed center for senior citizens. Because these examples *contradict,* rather than support, your thesis, readers are apt to dismiss what you have to say.

Make certain, too, that your examples are *accurate.* Exercise special caution when using statistics. An old saying warns that there are lies, damned lies, and statistics—meaning that statistics can be misleading. A commercial may claim, "In a taste test, 80 percent of those questioned indicated that they preferred Fizzy Cola." Impressed? Don't be—at least, not until you find out how the test was conducted. Perhaps the subjects had to choose between Fizzy Cola and battery acid, or perhaps there were only five subjects, all Fizzy Cola vice presidents.

Finally, select *representative* examples. Picking the oddball, one-in-a-million example to support a point—and passing it off as typical—is dishonest. Consider an essay with the thesis "Part-time jobs contribute to academic success." Citing only one example of a student who works at a job twenty-five hours a week while earning straight A's isn't playing fair. Why not? You've made a *hasty generalization* based on only one case. To be convincing, you need to show how holding down a job affects *most* students' academic performance. (For more on hasty generalizations, see pages 370–371.)

3. Develop your examples sufficiently.   To ensure that you get your ideas across, your examples must be *specific*. An essay on the types of heroes in American movies wouldn't succeed if you simply strung together a series of undeveloped examples in paragraphs like this one:

> Heroes in American movies usually fall into types. One kind of hero is the tight-lipped loner, men like Clint Eastwood and Humphrey Bogart. Another movie hero is the quiet, shy, or fumbling type who has appeared in movies since the beginning. The main characteristic of this hero is lovableness, as seen in actors like Jimmy Stewart. Perhaps the most one-dimensional and predictable hero is the superman who battles tough odds. This kind of hero is best illustrated by Sylvester Stallone as Rocky and Rambo.

If you developed the essay in this way—if you moved from one undeveloped example to another—you would be doing little more than making a list. To be effective, key examples must be expanded in sufficient detail. The examples in the preceding paragraph could be developed in paragraphs of their own. You could, for instance, develop the first example this way:

> Heroes can be tight-lipped loners who appear out of nowhere, form no permanent attachments, and walk, drive, or ride off into the sunset. In many of his westerns, from the low-budget "spaghetti westerns" of the 1960s to *Unforgiven* in 1992, Clint Eastwood personifies this kind of hero. He is remote, mysterious, and not talkative. Yet he guns down an evil sheriff, runs other villains out of town, and helps a handicapped girl—acts that cement his heroic status. The loner might also be Sam Spade as played by Humphrey Bogart. Spade solves the crime and sends the guilty off to jail, yet he holds his emotions in check and has no permanent ties beyond his faithful secretary and shabby office. One gets the feeling that he could walk away from these, too, if necessary. Even in *The Right Stuff*, an account of the United States' early astronauts, the scriptwriters mold Chuck Yeager, the man who broke the sound barrier, into a classic loner. Yeager, portrayed by the aloof Sam Shepard, has a wife, but he is nevertheless insular. Taking mute pride in his ability to distance himself from politicians, bureaucrats, even colleagues, he soars into space, dignified and detached.

(For hints on ways to make writing specific, see pages 35–36.)

4. Organize the examples.   If, as is usually the case, several examples support your point, be sure that you present the examples in an *organized* manner. Often you'll find that other patterns of development (cause-effect, comparison-contrast, definition, and so on) suggest ways to sequence examples. Let's say you're writing an essay showing that stay-at-home vacations offer numerous opportunities to relax. You might begin the essay with examples that *contrast* stay-at-home and get-away vacations. Then you might move to a *process analysis* that illustrates different techniques for unwinding at home. The essay might end with examples showing the *effect* of such leisurely at-home breaks.

Finally, you need to select an *organizational approach consistent* with your *purpose* and *thesis*. Imagine you're writing an essay about students' adjustment during the first months of college. The supporting examples could be arranged *chronologically*. You might start by illustrating the ambivalence many students feel the first day of college when their parents leave for home; you might then offer an anecdote or two about students' frequent calls to Mom and Dad during the opening weeks of the semester; the essay might close with an account of students' reluctance to leave campus at the midyear break.

Similarly, an essay demonstrating that a room often reflects the character of its occupant might be organized *spatially:* from the empty soda cans on the floor to the spitballs on the ceiling. In an essay illustrating the kinds of skills taught in a composition course, you might move from *simple* to *complex* examples: starting with relatively matter-of-fact skills such as spelling and punctuation and ending with more conceptually difficult skills such as formulating a thesis and organizing an essay. Last, the *emphatic sequence*—in which you lead from your first example to your final, most significant one—is another effective way to organize an essay with many examples. A paper about Americans' characteristic impatience might progress from minor examples (dependence on fast food, obsession with ever faster mail delivery) to more disturbing manifestations of impatience (using drugs as quick solutions to problems, advocating simple answers to complex international problems: "Bomb them!").

5. Choose a point of view.   Many essays developed by illustration place the subject in the foreground and the writer in the background. Such an approach calls for the *third-person point of view.* For example, even if you draw examples from your own personal experience, you can present them without using the *first-person* "I." You might convert such personal material into generalized examples (see page 153), or you might describe the personal experience as if it happened to someone else. Of course, you may use the first person if the use of "I" will make the example more believable and dramatic. But remember: Just because an event happened to you personally doesn't mean you have to use the first-person point of view.

REVISION STRATEGIES

Once you have a draft of the essay, you're ready to revise. The following checklist will help you and those giving you feedback apply to exemplification some of the revision techniques discussed on pages 60–62.

☑ EXEMPLIFICATION: A REVISION/PEER REVIEW CHECKLIST

Revise Overall Meaning and Structure

- ❏ What thesis is being advanced? Which examples don't support the thesis? Should these examples be deleted, or should the thesis be reshaped to fit the examples? Why?
- ❏ Which patterns of development and methods of organization (chronological, spatial, simple-to-complex, emphatic) provide the essay's framework? Would other ordering principles be more effective? If so, which ones?

Revise Paragraph Development

- ❏ Which paragraphs contain too many or too few examples? Which contain examples that are too brief or too extended? Which include insufficiently or overly detailed examples?
- ❏ Which paragraphs contain examples that could be made more compelling?
- ❏ Which paragraphs include examples that are atypical or incorrect?

Revise Sentences and Words

- ❏ What signal devices introduce examples and clarify the line of thought? Where are there too many or too few of these devices?
- ❏ Where would more varied sentence structure heighten the essay's illustrations?
- ❏ Where would more concrete and specific words make the examples more effective?

STUDENT ESSAY

The following student essay was written by Michael Pagano in response to this assignment:

> In "Tweens: Ten Going On Sixteen," Kay S. Hymowitz contends that a "media-driven marketplace" has prompted her daughter and other children to grow up too fast. Observe how your behavior and the behavior of others is shaped by pressures from the surrounding culture. Choose one area to explore, and write an essay that shows how your behavior is affected by cultural expectations.

While reading Michael's paper, try to determine how effectively it applies the principles of exemplification. The annotations on Michael's paper and the commentary following it will help you look at the essay more closely.

Pursuit of Possessions
by Michael Pagano

Introduction   In the essay "Tweens: Ten Going On Sixteen," Kay   1
S. Hymowitz suggests that commerce and the media are responsible for pressuring children to grow up too fast and, in effect, lose out on childhood. Our commercially dominated culture, which encourages a frenzied acquisitiveness, affects us in other ways too.
Thesis —— Very often we lose sight of what truly matters in life. Instead, many of us choose to spend our lives distracted by the trivial pursuit of material possessions. Much of our time goes into buying
Plan of development — new things, dealing with the complications they create, and working madly to buy more things or pay for the things we already have.

     We devote a great deal of our lives to acquiring the materi-   2
al goods we imagine are essential to our well-being. Hours are
The first of three paragraphs in a chronological sequence   spent planning and thinking about our future purchases. We window-shop for designer jogging shoes; we leaf through magazines looking at ads for new sound equipment; we research back issues of *Consumer Reports* to find out about recent developments in exercise equipment. Moreover, once we find what we are looking for, more time is taken up when we decide to actually buy the items. How do we find this time? That's easy. We turn evenings, weekends, and holidays–time that used to be set aside for family and friends–into shopping expeditions. No wonder family life is deteriorating and children spend so much time in front of television sets. Their parents are seldom around.

Topic sentence ———• As soon as we take our new purchases home, they begin to   3
complicate our lives. A sleek new sports car has to be washed,
The second paragraph in the chronological sequence   waxed, and vacuumed. A fashionable pair of overpriced dress pants can't be thrown in the washing machine but must be taken to the dry cleaner. New sound equipment has to be con-
A paragraph with many specific examples   nected with a tangled network of cables to the TV, computer, and speakers. Eventually, of course, the inevitable happens. Our indispensable possessions break down and need to be repaired. The home computer starts to lose data, the microwave has to have its temperature controls adjusted, and the DVD player has to be serviced when a disc becomes jammed in the machine.

Topic sentence ———• After more time has gone by, we sometimes discover that   4
our purchases don't suit us anymore, and so we decide to

The third paragraph in the chronological sequence

replace them. Before making our replacement purchases, though, we have to find ways to get rid of the old items. If we want to replace our "small" 19-inch television set with a 35-inch flat-screen, we have to find time to put an ad in the classified section of the paper. Then we have to handle phone calls and set up times people can come to look at the TV. We could store the set in the basement–if we are lucky enough to find a spot that isn't already filled with other discarded purchases.

Topic sentence with emphasis signal

Worst of all, this mania for possessions often influences our approach to work. It is not unusual for people to take a second or even a third job to pay off the debt they fall into because they have overbought. After paying for food, clothing, and shelter, many people see the rest of their paycheck go to Visa, MasterCard, department store charge accounts, and time payments. Panic sets in when they realize there simply is not enough money to cover all their expenses. Just to stay afloat, people may have to work overtime or take on additional jobs.   5

Conclusion

It is clear that many of us have allowed the pursuit of possessions to dominate our lives. We are so busy buying, maintaining, and paying for our worldly goods that we do not have much time to think about what is really important. We should try to step back from our compulsive need for more of everything and get in touch with the basic values that are the real point of our lives.   6

COMMENTARY

Thesis, combining patterns of development, and plan of development. In "Pursuit of Possessions," Michael analyzes the mania for acquiring material goods that permeates our society. He begins by addressing a main idea conveyed in Kay S. Hymowitz's "Tweens: Ten Going On Sixteen"—that commercialism in our culture pressures children to grow up too fast. This reference to Hymowitz gives Michael a chance to suggest another way in which commercialism negatively affects us; he *contrasts* "frenzied acquisitiveness" with a focus on "what truly matters in life." Michael is then able to state the essay's *thesis*: "[M]any of us choose to spend our lives in pursuit of material possessions."

Besides introducing the basic contrast at the heart of the essay, Michael's opening paragraph helps readers see that the essay contains an element of *causal analysis*. The final sentence of the introductory paragraph lays out the effects of our possession obsession. This sentence also serves as the essay's *plan of development* and reveals that Michael feels the pursuit of possessions negatively affects our lives in three key ways.

Essays of this length often don't need a plan of development. But since Michael's paper is filled with many *examples*, the plan of development helps readers see how all the details relate to the essay's central point.

Evidence.   Support for the thesis consists of numerous examples presented in the *first-person-plural point of view* ("*[W]e* lose sight of . . .," "*We* devote a great deal of our lives . . .," and so on). Many of these examples seem drawn from Michael's, his friends', or his family's experiences; however, to emphasize the events' universality, Michael converts these essentially personal examples into generalized ones that "we" all experience.

These examples, in turn, are organized around the three major points signaled by the plan of development. Michael uses one paragraph to develop his first and third points and two paragraphs to develop his second point. Each of the four supporting paragraphs is focused by a *topic sentence* that appears at the start of the paragraph. The transitional phrase "Worst of all" (paragraph 5) signals that Michael has sequenced his major points *emphatically*, saving for last the issue he considers most significant: how the "mania for possessions . . . influences our approach to work."

Organizational strategies.   Emphatic order isn't Michael's only organizational technique. When reading the paper, you probably felt that there was an easy flow from one supporting paragraph to the next. How does Michael achieve such *coherence between paragraphs*? For one thing, he sequences paragraphs 2–4 *chronologically:* what happens before a purchase is made; what happens afterward. Secondly, topic sentences in paragraphs 3 and 4 include *signal devices* that indicate this passage of time. The topic sentences also strengthen coherence by *linking back* to the preceding paragraph: "*As soon as we take our new purchases home,* they . . . complicate our lives" and "*After more time has gone by,* we . . . discover that our purchases don't suit us anymore."

The same organizing strategies are used *within paragraphs* to make the essay coherent. Details in paragraphs 2 through 4 are sequenced chronologically, and to help readers follow the chronology, Michael uses *signal devices:* "*Moreover, once* we find what we are looking for, more time is taken up . . ." (2); "*Eventually,* of course, the inevitable happens" (3); "*Then* we have to handle phone calls . . ." (4).

Problems with paragraph development.   You probably recall that an essay developed primarily through exemplification must include examples that are *relevant, interesting, convincing, representative, accurate,* and *specific.* On the whole, Michael's examples meet these requirements. The third and fourth paragraphs, especially, include vigorous details that show how our mania for buying things can govern our lives. We may even laugh with self-recognition when reading about "overpriced dress pants [that] can't be thrown in the washing machine" or a basement "filled with other discarded purchases."

The fifth paragraph, however, is underdeveloped. We know that this paragraph presents what Michael considers his most significant point, but the paragraph's examples are rather *flat* and *unconvincing*. To make this final section more compelling, Michael could mention specific people who overspend, revealing how much they are in debt and how much they have to work to become solvent again. Or he could cite a television documentary or magazine article dealing with the issue of consumer debt. Such specifics would give the paragraph the solidity it now lacks.

Shift in tone.   The fifth paragraph has a second, more subtle problem: *a shift in tone.* Although Michael has, up to this point, been critical of our possession-mad culture, he has poked fun at our obsession and kept his tone conversational and gently satiric. In this paragraph, though, he adopts a serious tone and, in the next paragraph, his tone becomes even weightier, almost preachy. It is, of course, legitimate to have a serious message in a lightly satiric piece. In fact, most satiric writing has such an additional layer of meaning. But because Michael has trouble blending these two moods, there's a jarring shift in the essay.

Shift in focus.   The second paragraph shows another kind of shift—in *focus.* The paragraph's controlling idea is that too much time is spent acquiring possessions. However, starting with "No wonder family life is deteriorating," Michael includes two sentences that introduce a complex issue beyond the scope of the essay. Since these last two sentences disrupt the paragraph's unity, they should be deleted.

Revising the first draft.   Although the final version of the essay needs work in spots, it's much stronger than Michael's first draft. To see how Michael went about revising the draft, compare his paper's second and third supporting paragraphs with his draft version reprinted here.

Original Version of the Second Paragraph

Our lives are spent not only buying things but in dealing with the inevitable complications that are created by our newly acquired possessions. First, we have to find places to put all the objects we bring home. More clothes demand more closets; a second car demands more garage space; a home entertainment center requires elaborate shelving. We shouldn't be surprised that the average American family moves once every three years. A good many families move simply because they need more space to store all the things they buy. In addition, our possessions demand maintenance time. A person who gets a new car will spend hours washing it, waxing it, and vacuuming it. A new pair of pants has to go to the dry cleaners. New sound systems have to be connected to already existing equipment. Eventually, of course, the inevitable happens. Our new items need to be repaired. Or we get sick of them and decide to replace them. Before making our replacement purchases, though, we have to get rid of the old items. That can be a real inconvenience.

When Michael looked more closely at this paragraph, he realized it rambled and lacked energy. He started to revise the paragraph by tightening the first sentence, making it more focused and less awkward. Certainly, the revised sentence ("As soon as we take our new purchases home, they begin to complicate our lives") is crisper than the original. Next, he decided to omit the discussion about finding places to put new possessions; these sentences about inadequate closet, garage, and shelf space were so exaggerated that they undercut the valid point he wanted to make. He also chose to eliminate the sentences about the mobility of American families. This was, he felt, an interesting point, but it introduced an issue too complex to be included in the paragraph.

Michael strengthened the rest of the paragraph by making his examples more specific. A "new car" became a "sleek new sports car," and a "pair of pants" became a "fashionable pair of overpriced dress pants." Michael also realized he had to do more than merely write, "Eventually, . . .our new items need to be repaired." This point had to be dramatized by sharp, convincing details. Therefore, Michael added lively examples to describe how high-tech possessions—microwaves, home computers, DVD players—break down. Similarly, Michael realized it wasn't enough simply to say, as he had in the original, that we run into problems when we try to replace out-of-favor purchases. Vigorous details were again needed to illustrate the point. Michael thus used a typical "replaceable" (a "small" 19-inch TV set) as his key example and showed the annoyance involved in handling phone calls and setting up appointments so people could see the TV.

After adding these specifics, Michael realized he had enough material to devote a separate paragraph to the problems associated with replacing old purchases. By dividing his original paragraph, Michael ended up with two well-focused paragraphs, neither of which has the rambling quality found in the original.

In short, Michael strengthened his essay through substantial revision. Another round of rewriting would have made the essay stronger still. Even without this additional work, Michael's essay provides an interesting perspective on an American preoccupation.

Activities: Exemplification

Prewriting Activities

1. Imagine you're writing two essays: One is a serious paper analyzing the factors that *cause* large numbers of public school teachers to leave the profession each year; the other is a light essay *defining* "preppie," "head banger," or some other slang term used to describe a kind of person. Jot down ways you might use examples in each essay.

2. Use mapping or another prewriting technique to gather examples illustrating the truth of *one* of the following familiar sayings. Then, using the same or a different

prewriting technique, accumulate examples that counter the saying. Weigh both sets of examples to determine the saying's validity. After developing an appropriate thesis, decide which examples you would elaborate in an essay.

a. Haste makes waste.

b. There's no use crying over spilled milk.

c. A bird in the hand is worth two in the bush.

Revising Activities

3. The following paragraph is from the first draft of an essay about the decline of small-town shopping districts. The paragraph is meant to show what small towns can do to revitalize business. Revise the paragraph, strengthening it with specific and convincing examples.

> A small town can compete with a large new mall for shoppers. But merchants must work together, modernizing the stores and making the town's main street pleasant, even fun to walk. They should also copy the malls' example by including attention-getting events as often as possible.

4. Reprinted here is a paragraph from the first draft of a light-spirited essay showing that Americans' pursuit of change for change's sake has drawbacks. The paragraph is meant to illustrate that infatuation with newness costs consumers money yet leads to no improvement in product quality. How effective is the paragraph? Which examples are specific and convincing? Which are not? Do any seem non-representative, offensive, or sexist? How could the paragraph's organization be improved? Consider these questions as you rewrite the paragraph. Add specific examples where needed. Depending on the way you revise, you may want to break this one paragraph into several.

> We end up paying for our passion for the new and improved. Trendy clothing styles convince us that last year's outfits are outdated, even though our old clothes are fine. Women are especially vulnerable in this regard. What, though, about items that have to be replaced periodically, like shampoo? Even slight changes lead to new formulations requiring retooling of the production process. That means increased manufacturing costs per item—all of which get passed on to us, the consumer. Then there are those items that tout new, trendsetting features that make earlier versions supposedly obsolete. Some manufacturers, for example, boast that their sound systems transmit an expanded-frequency range. The problem is that humans can't even hear such frequencies. But the high-tech feature dazzles men who are too naive to realize they're being hoodwinked.

Kay S. Hymowitz

A senior fellow at the Manhattan Institute and a contributing editor of the urban-policy magazine *City Journal*, Kay S. Hymowitz (1948–) writes on education and childhood in America. A native of Philadelphia, Hymowitz received graduate degrees from Tufts University and Columbia University. She has taught English literature and composition at Brooklyn College and at Parsons School of Design. Hymowitz is the author of *Liberation's Children: Parents and Kids in a Postmodern Age* (2003) and *Ready or Not: Why Treating Our Children as Small Adults Endangers Their Future and Ours* (1999) and is a principal contributor to *Modern Sex: Liberation and Its Discontents* (2001). In 2006, she published *Marriage and Caste in America: Separate and Unequal Families in a Post-Marital Age,* a collection of her *City Journal* essays. Her work has appeared in publications including *The New York Times, The Washington Post,* and *The New Republic.* Hymowitz lives in Brooklyn with her husband and three children. The following essay appeared in the Autumn 1998 issue of *City Journal.*

For ideas about how this exemplification essay is organized, see Figure 5.2 page 168.

Pre-Reading Journal Entry

Think back on your childhood. What were some possessions and activities that you cherished and enjoyed? Freewrite for a few moments in your pre-reading journal about these beloved objects and/or pastimes. What exactly were they? Why did you enjoy them so much? Did your feelings about them change as you matured into adolescence?

Tweens: Ten Going On Sixteen

During the past year my youngest morphed from child to teenager. Down came the posters of adorable puppies and the drawings from art class; up went the airbrushed faces of Leonardo di Caprio and Kate Winslet. CDs of Le Ann Rimes and Paula Cole appeared mysteriously, along with teen fan magazines featuring glowering movie and rock-and-roll hunks.... She started reading the newspaper—or at least the movie ads—with all the intensity of a Talmudic scholar, scanning for glimpses of her beloved Leo or, failing that, Matt Damon. As spring approached and younger children skipped past our house on their way to the park, she swigged from a designer water bottle, wearing the obligatory tank top and denim shorts as she whispered on the phone to friends about games of Truth or Dare. The last rites for her childhood came when, embarrassed at reminders of her foolish past, she pulled a sheet over her years-in-the-making American Girl doll collection, now dead to the world.

So what's new in this dog-bites-man story? Well, as all this was going on, my daughter was ten years old and in the fourth grade.

Those who remember their own teenybopper infatuation with Elvis or the Beatles might be inclined to shrug their shoulders as if to say, "It was ever thus." But this is different. Across class lines and throughout the country, elementary and middle-school principals and teachers, child psychologists and psychiatrists, marketing and demographic researchers all confirm the pronouncement of Henry Trevor, middle-school director of the Berkeley Carroll School in Brooklyn, New York: "There is no such thing as preadolescence anymore. Kids are teenagers at ten."

Marketers have a term for this new social animal, kids between eight and   4
12: they call them "tweens." The name captures the ambiguous reality: though chronologically midway between early childhood and adolescence, this group is leaning more and more toward teen styles, teen attitudes, and, sadly, teen behavior at its most troubling.

The tween phenomenon grows out of a complicated mixture of biology,   5
demography, and the predictable assortment of Bad Ideas. But putting aside its causes for a moment, the emergence of tweendom carries risks for both young people and society. Eight- to 12-year-olds have an even more wobbly sense of themselves than adolescents; they rely more heavily on others to tell them how to understand the world and how to place themselves in it. Now, for both pragmatic and ideological reasons, they are being increasingly "empowered" to do this on their own, which leaves them highly vulnerable both to a vulgar and sensation-driven marketplace and to the crass authority of their immature peers. In tweens, we can see the future of our society taking shape, and it's not at all clear how it's going to work.

Perhaps the most striking evidence for the tweening of children comes   6
from market researchers. "There's no question there's a deep trend, not a passing fad, toward kids getting older younger," says research psychologist Michael Cohen of Arc Consulting, a public policy, education, and marketing research firm in New York. "This is not just on the coasts. There are no real differences geographically." It seems my daughter's last rites for her American Girl dolls were a perfect symbol not just for her own childhood but for childhood, period. The Toy Manufacturers of America Factbook states that, where once the industry could count on kids between birth and 14 as their target market, today it is only birth to ten. "In the last ten years we've seen a rapid development of upper-age children," says Bruce Friend, vice president of worldwide research and planning for Nickelodeon, a cable channel aimed at kids. "The 12- to 14-year-olds of yesterday are the ten to 12s of today." The rise of the preteen teen is "the biggest trend we've seen."

Scorning any symbols of their immaturity, tweens now cultivate a self-image   7
that emphasizes sophistication. The Nickelodeon-Yankelovich Youth Monitor found that by the time they are 12, children describe themselves as "flirtatious, sexy, trendy, athletic, cool." Nickelodeon's Bruce Friend reports that by 11, children in focus groups say they no longer even think of themselves as children.

They're very concerned with their "look," Friend says, even more so   8
than older teens. Sprouting up everywhere are clothing stores like the chain

Limited Too and the catalog company Delia, geared toward tween girls who scorn old-fashioned, little-girl flowers, ruffles, white socks, and Mary Janes[1] in favor of the cool—black mini-dresses and platform shoes.... Teachers complain of ten- or 11-year-old girls arriving at school looking like madams, in full cosmetic regalia, with streaked hair, platform shoes, and midriff-revealing shirts. Barbara Kapetanakes, a psychologist at a conservative Jewish day school in New York, describes her students' skirts as being about "the size of a belt." Kapetanakes says she was told to dress respectfully on Fridays, the eve of the Jewish Sabbath, which she did by donning a long skirt and a modest blouse. Her students, on the other hand, showed their respect by looking "like they should be hanging around the West Side Highway," where prostitutes ply their trade.

Lottie Sims, a computer teacher in a Miami middle school, says that the 9 hooker look for tweens is fanning strong support for uniforms in her district. But uniforms and tank-top bans won't solve the problem of painted young ladies. "You can count on one hand the girls not wearing makeup," Sims says. "Their parents don't even know. They arrive at school with huge bags of lipstick and hair spray, and head straight to the girls' room."

Though the tweening of youth affects girls more visibly than boys, espe- 10 cially since boys mature more slowly, boys are by no means immune to these obsessions. Once upon a time, about ten years ago, fifth- and sixth-grade boys were about as fashion-conscious as their pet hamsters. But a growing minority have begun trading in their baseball cards for hair mousse and baggy jeans. In some places, $200 jackets, emblazoned with sports logos like the warm-up gear of professional athletes, are *de rigueur;* in others, the preppy look is popular among the majority, while the more daring go for the hipper style of pierced ears, fade haircuts, or ponytails. Often these tween peacocks strut through their middle-school hallways taunting those who have yet to catch on to the cool look....

Those who seek comfort in the idea that the tweening of childhood is 11 merely a matter of fashion—who maybe even find their lip-synching, hip-swaying little boy or girl kind of cute—might want to think twice. There are disturbing signs that tweens are not only eschewing the goody-goody childhood image but its substance as well....

The clearest evidence of tweendom's darker side concerns crime. 12 Although children under 15 still represent a minority of juvenile arrests, their numbers grew disproportionately in the past 20 years. According to a report by the Office of Juvenile Justice and Delinquency Prevention, "offenders under age 15 represent the leading edge of the juvenile crime problem, and their numbers are growing." Moreover, the crimes committed by younger

---

[1]Trademark name of patent-leather shoes for girls, usually having a low heel and a strap that fastens at the side (editors' note).

teens and preteens are growing in severity. "Person offenses,[2] which once constituted 16 percent of the total court cases for this age group," continues the report, "now constitute 25 percent." Headline grabbers—like Nathaniel Abraham of Pontiac, Michigan, an 11-year-old who stole a rifle from a neighbor's garage and went on a shooting spree in October 1997, randomly killing a teenager coming out of a store; and 11-year-old Andrew Golden, who, with his 13-year-old partner, killed four children and one teacher at his middle school in Jonesboro, Arkansas—are extreme, exceptional cases, but alas, they are part of a growing trend toward preteen violent crime. . . .

The evidence on tween sex presents a troubling picture, too. Despite a 13 decrease among older teens for the first time since records have been kept, sexual activity among tweens increased during that period. It seems that kids who are having sex are doing so at earlier ages. Between 1988 and 1995, the proportion of girls saying they began sex before 15 rose from 11 percent to 19 percent. (For boys, the number remained stable, at 21 percent.) This means that approximately one in five middle-school kids is sexually active. Christie Hogan, a middle-school counselor for 20 years in Louisville, Kentucky, says: "We're beginning to see a few pregnant sixth-graders." Many of the principals and counselors I spoke with reported a small but striking minority of sexually active seventh-graders. . . .

Certainly the days of the tentative and giggly preadolescent seem to 14 be passing. Middle-school principals report having to deal with miniskirted 12-year-olds "draping themselves over boys" or patting their behinds in the hallways, while 11-year-old boys taunt girls about their breasts and rumors about their own and even their parents' sexual proclivities. Tweens have even given new connotations to the word "playground": one fifth-grade teacher from southwestern Ohio told me of two youngsters discovered in the bushes during recess.

Drugs and alcohol are also seeping into tween culture. The past six 15 years have seen more than a doubling of the number of eighth-graders who smoke marijuana (10 percent today) and those who no longer see it as dangerous. "The stigma isn't there the way it was ten years ago," says Dan Kindlon, assistant professor of psychiatry at Harvard Medical School and co-author with Michael Thompson of *Raising Cain*. "Then it was the fringe group smoking pot. You were looked at strangely. Now the fringe group is using LSD."

Aside from sex, drugs, and rock and roll, another teen problem—eating 16 disorders—is also beginning to affect younger kids. This behavior grows out of premature fashion-consciousness, which has an even more pernicious effect on tweens than on teens, because, by definition, younger kids have a more

[2]Crimes against a person. They include assault, robbery, rape, and homicide (editors' note).

vulnerable and insecure self-image. Therapists say they are seeing a growing number of anorexics and obsessive dieters even among late-elementary-school girls. "You go on Internet chat rooms and find ten- and 11-year-olds who know every [fashion] model and every statistic about them," says Nancy Kolodny, a Connecticut-based therapist and author of *When Food's a Foe: How You Can Confront and Conquer Your Eating Disorder.* "Kate Moss is their god. They can tell if she's lost a few pounds or gained a few. If a powerful kid is talking about this stuff at school, it has a big effect."

What change in our social ecology has led to the emergence of tweens?   17
Many note that kids are reaching puberty at earlier ages, but while earlier physical maturation may play a small role in defining adolescence down, its importance tends to be overstated. True, the average age at which girls begin to menstruate has fallen from 13 to between 11 and $12^{1}/_{2}$ today, but the very gradualness of this change means that 12-year-olds have been living inside near-adult bodies for many decades without feeling impelled to build up a cosmetics arsenal or head for the bushes at recess. In fact, some experts believe that the very years that have witnessed the rise of the tween have also seen the age of first menstruation stabilize. Further, teachers and principals on the front lines see no clear correlation between physical and social maturation. Plenty of budding girls and bulking boys have not put away childish things, while an abundance of girls with flat chests and boys with squeaky voices ape the body language and fashions of their older siblings....

Of course, the causes are complex, and most people working with tweens   18
know it. In my conversations with educators and child psychologists who work primarily with middle-class kids nationwide, two major and fairly predictable themes emerged: a sexualized and glitzy media-driven marketplace and absentee parents. What has been less commonly recognized is that at this age, the two causes combine to augment the authority of the peer group, which in turn both weakens the influence of parents and reinforces the power of the media. Taken together, parental absence, the market, and the peer group form a vicious circle that works to distort the development of youngsters....

Questions for Close Reading

1. What is the selection's thesis? Locate the sentence(s) in which Hymowitz states her main idea. If she doesn't state the thesis explicitly, express it in your own words.
2. According to Hymowitz, what self-image do tweens cultivate? How do they project this image to others?
3. What physically dangerous behavioral trends does Hymowitz link to the tween phenomenon?
4. According to Hymowitz, what are the primary causes of the tween phenomenon?
5. Refer to your dictionary as needed to define the following words used in the selection: *glowering* (paragraph 1), *Talmudic* (1), *rites* (1), *demographic* (3), *pragmatic* (5), *ideological* (5), *regalia* (8), *donning* (8), *ply* (8), *emblazoned* (10), *de rigueur* (10),

eschewing (11), *tentative* (14), *proclivities* (14), *connotations* (14), *stigma* (15), *pernicious* (16), *correlation* (17), and *augment* (18).

Questions About the Writer's Craft

1. **The pattern.** Hymowitz opens her essay with an anecdotal example of tweenhood—her daughter's. What does this example add to her essay?
2. **The pattern.** What types of examples does Hymowitz provide in her essay? (See pages 150–152 for a discussion of the various forms that examples can take.) Cite at least one example of each type. How does each type of example contribute to her thesis?
3. How would you characterize Hymowitz's tone in the selection? Cite vocabulary that conveys this tone.
4. **Other patterns.** In paragraph 8, Hymowitz uses clothing as a means of presenting an important *contrast*. What does she contrast in these paragraphs? How does this contribute to her thesis?

FIGURE 5.2
Essay Structure Diagram: "Tweens: Ten Going On Sixteen" by Kay S. Hymowitz

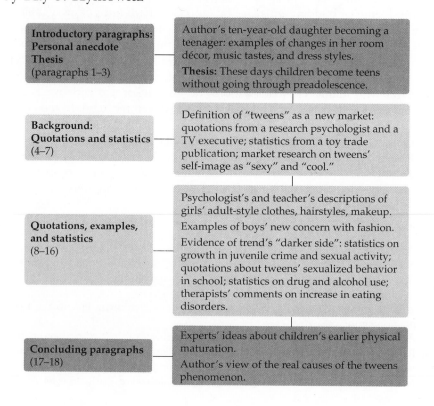

Introductory paragraphs:
Personal anecdote
Thesis
(paragraphs 1–3)

Author's ten-year-old daughter becoming a teenager: examples of changes in her room décor, music tastes, and dress styles.
Thesis: These days children become teens without going through preadolescence.

Background:
Quotations and statistics
(4–7)

Definition of "tweens" as a new market: quotations from a research psychologist and a TV executive; statistics from a toy trade publication; market research on tweens' self-image as "sexy" and "cool."

Quotations, examples,
and statistics
(8–16)

Psychologist's and teacher's descriptions of girls' adult-style clothes, hairstyles, makeup.
Examples of boys' new concern with fashion.
Evidence of trend's "darker side": statistics on growth in juvenile crime and sexual activity; quotations about tweens' sexualized behavior in school; statistics on drug and alcohol use; therapists' comments on increase in eating disorders.

Concluding paragraphs
(17–18)

Experts' ideas about children's earlier physical maturation.
Author's view of the real causes of the tweens phenomenon.

Writing Assignments Using Exemplification as a Pattern of Development

1. Hymowitz is troubled and perplexed by her daughter's behavior. Think about an older person, such as a parent or another relative, who finds *your* behavior troubling and perplexing. Write an essay in which you illustrate why your behavior distresses this person. (Or, conversely, think of an elder whose behavior *you* find problematic, and write an essay illustrating why that person evokes this response in you.) You might structure your essay by picking the two or three most irksome characteristics or habits and developing supporting paragraphs around each of them. However you choose to organize your essay, be sure to provide abundant examples throughout.

2. The cultivation of a sophisticated self-image is, according to Hymowitz, a hallmark of tweenhood. Think back to when you were around that age. What was your self-image at that time? Did you think of yourself as worldly or inexperienced? Cool or awkward? Attractive or unappealing? In your journal, freewrite about the traits that you would have identified in yourself as either a tween or an adolescent. Write an essay in which you illustrate your self-image at that age, focusing on two to three dominant characteristics you associated with yourself. It's important that you illustrate each trait with examples of when and how you displayed it. For example, if you saw yourself as "dorky," you might recall an embarrassing time when you tripped and fell in the middle of your school lunchroom. Conclude your essay by reflecting on whether the way you saw yourself at the time was accurate, and whether your feelings about yourself have changed since then. You'd also benefit from reading either of the following authors' musings on their childhood self-perceptions: Maya Angelou's "Sister Flowers" (page 87) and Audre Lorde's "The Fourth of July" (page 127).

Writing Assignments Combining Patterns of Development

3. Hymowitz advances a powerful argument about the alarming contemporary trend of tweenhood. But many would disagree with her entirely pessimistic analysis. Write an essay in which you *argue*, contrary to Hymowitz, that tweens today actually exhibit several *positive* characteristics. You might say, for example, that tweens today are more independent or more socially conscious than kids in the past. In order to develop your argument, you'll need to show how each characteristic you're discussing *contrasts* favorably with that characteristic in a previous generation of kids. Be sure, too, to acknowledge opposing arguments as you proceed. Research conducted in the library and/or on the Internet might help you develop your pro-tween argument.

4. Though she doesn't use the term explicitly, Hymowitz points to peer pressure as a significant factor in tweens' premature maturity. In your journal, take a few moments to reflect on your own experiences with peer pressure, whether as a pre-teen or teen, or even into adulthood. What are some incidents that stand out in your memory? Write an essay *narrating* a particularly memorable incident of peer pressure in which you were involved. You may have been the object of the pressure,

or even perhaps the source. What were the circumstances? Who was involved? How did you respond at the time? How did the episode *affect* you? In retrospect, how do you feel about the incident today? Be sure to use dialogue as well as *descriptive* language in order to make the episode come alive.

Writing Assignment Using a Journal Entry as a Starting Point

5. As a way of illustrating her daughter's evolving tween tastes, Hymowitz cites the "years-in-the-making American Girl doll collection" over which her disaffected daughter has now drawn a sheet. Reviewing what you wrote in your pre-reading journal entry, identify some once-loved childhood items or activities that you distanced yourself from as you got older. Write an essay in which you exemplify your growth into adolescence by identifying two or three childhood possessions or activities that you cast off. You might, for example, discuss building up a beloved rock collection or playing with action figures. As you introduce these items, be sure to describe them and to explain the significance they once held for you, as well as your reasons for leaving them behind. Conclude your essay by offering some reflections on whether you currently regard the childhood items with the same distaste or disinterest you felt as a teen.

Leslie Savan

Leslie Savan is a critic and writer whose work has appeared in *The Village Voice, Time, The New Yorker, The New York Times,* and *Salon.* Born in 1951, she has been a finalist for the Pulitzer Prize and a commentator on National Public Radio. In 1994 she published her first book, *The Sponsored Life: Ads, TV, and American Culture.* For several years, Savan wrote a column on advertising for *The Village Voice,* and she began to notice that certain popular words and phrases kept reoccurring in ads. She paid attention to the "pop" language of advertising and other media and eventually wrote a book about it. This essay is excerpted from *Slam Dunks and No-Brainers: Language in Your Life, the Media, Business, Politics, and Like, Whatever,* which was published in 2005.

Pre-Reading Journal Entry

Different groups of people have special words and phrases—often slang—that they frequently use among themselves. Think about the slang words and phrases that are in common use among your friends. In your journal, list some of these words and phrases. What do they mean?

Black Talk and Pop Culture

African-American vernacular, black English, black talk, Ebonics, hip-hop slang—whatever you want to call it, black-inspired language is all over mainstream pop talk like white on rice.   1

The talk may be everywhere, but, oddly enough, even during the rabid debate over Ebonics in the late 1990s rarely was there any mention of black English's deep imprint on American English. Yet linguists and other language experts know that America's language wouldn't be what it is—and certainly wouldn't pop as much—without black English.   2

"In the past, White society has resisted the idea," wrote Robert McCrum, William Cran, and Robert MacNeil in *The Story of English,* "but there is now no escaping the fact that [Blacks' influence] has been one of the most profound contributions to the English language."   3

"First, one cannot help but be struck by the powerful influence of African-American vernacular on the slang of all 20th-century American youth," Tom Dalzell wrote in *Flappers 2 Rappers.* "There were other influences, to be sure, on the slang of America's young, but none as powerful as that of the streets of Harlem and Chicago."   4

The linguist Connie Eble, author of *Slang and Sociability* and a college and youth slang expert at the University of North Carolina, Chapel Hill, calls the black influence on the American language "overwhelming."   5

White people (and not just the young) draw from a black lexicon every day, sometimes unaware of the words' origins, sometimes using them   6 because of their origins. Here are just some of the words and phrases—born in different decades and now residing at various levels of popdom—that African Americans either coined or popularized, and, in either case, that they created the catchiest meaning of: *all that, back in the day, bling bling, blues, bogus, boogie, bootie, bro, chick, chill, come again, cook, cool, dawg, dig, dis, do your own thing, don't go there, freak, funky, get-go, get it on, get over, gig, give it up, groovy, heavy, hip, homeboy, hot, in your face, kick back, lame, living large, man, my bad, Micky D's, old school, nitty gritty, player, riff, righteous, rip off, rock 'n' roll, soul, tell it like it is, 24/7, uptight, wannabe, whack, Whassup?/sup?, Whassup with that?, when the shit hits the fan, you know what I'm saying?*

You know what I'm saying. Most of us talk, and all of us hear in the media, some of that talk every day. Some phrases are said with an implicit nod to their source (*street cred, chill, You the man,* as well as a fist pound or high five), while others have been so widely adopted that they're beginning to feel sourceless (*24/7, lame, in your face*). *It's a black thang* has become everybody's thing, from *It's a dick thing* to (most offensively, considering who pushed it) "Virginia Slims: It's a Woman Thing."   7

But black vernacular didn't just add more lively, "colorful" words to the pop vocabulary. Much as marketing has influenced pop language, so black English has changed the American language in more fundamental ways. And that's what we're talking here—not about black talk per se, but about what happens when black talk meets, and transforms, the wider, whiter pop.   8

First and foremost, this language of outsiders has given us *cool:* the word itself—the preeminent pop word of all time—and quite a sizable chunk of the cool stance that underlies pop culture itself. Pop culture's desire for cool is second only to its desire for money—the two, in fact, are inextricably linked. (Cool may be first and foremost, but more on why it rules later.)   9

A second way African-American vernacular has affected the broader pop is that black talk has operated as a template for what it means to talk pop in the first place. As an often playful, ironic alternative to the official tongue, black slang has prefigured pop language in much the same way that black music has prefigured, and has often become, pop music. While there are important differences, some of the dynamics underlying black talk and pop talk are similar: Like black English, pop language sparks with wordplays and code games; it assumes that certain, often previously unacknowledged experiences deserve their own verbal expression; and it broadcasts the sense that only those who share the experiences can really get the words. For instance, black talk's running commentary on social exclusion is a model for pop talk's running commentary on media experiences.   10

Why do I say that pop is modeled on black and not the other way around? It's not just because black talk did these things earlier and still does them more intensely than pop, but as the original flipside to the voice of the   11

Man, as the official unofficial speech of America, black talk is the object of pop talk's crush on everything "alternative" and "outsider."

There's an attitude in pop language that it is somehow undermining the   12
stale old ways and sending a wake-up call to anyone who just doesn't get it. You can feel the attitude in everything from advertising's furious but phony rebelliousness to the faintly up-yours, tough-talking phrases like *Get a life* and *Don't even* think *about it.* It's not that these particular phrases are black or black-inspired, or that white people aren't perfectly capable of rebelliousness, anger at authority, and clever put-downs on their own. But the black experience, publicized more widely than ever now through hip-hop and its celebrities, has encouraged everyone else to more vigorously adopt the style of fighting the power—at least with the occasional catchphrase.

It may seem twisted, given American history, that general pop language   13
draws from the experience of black exclusion at all. But white attempts to *yo* here and *dis* there are an important piece of identity-and-image building for individuals and corporations alike. Today, the language of an excluded people is repeated by the nonexcluded in order to make themselves sound more included. As the mainstream plays the titillating notes of marginalization, we are collectively creating that ideal mass personality mentioned earlier: We can be part black (the part presumed to be cool and soulful, real and down, jazzy or hip-hop, choose your sound) and be part white (the privileged part, the part that has the luxury to easily reference other parts).

Related to all this imitation and referencing is the most noticeable way   14
that pop talk is affected by black talk: Black talk has openly joined the sales force. At white society's major intersection with black language—that is, in entertainment—white society has gone from mocking black talk, as in minstrel shows, to marketing it, as in hip-hop. In the more than a hundred years between these two forms of entertainment, black language has by and large entered white usage as if it were a sourceless slang or perhaps the latest lingo of some particularly hep white cats, like the fast-talking disc jockeys of the 1950s and 1960s who purveyed black jive to white teenagers. Black language may have been the single most important factor in shaping generations of American slang, primarily through blues, jazz, and rock 'n' roll. But only relatively recently has black talk been used openly, knowingly, and not mockingly to sell products.

This would have been unthinkable once. Even fifteen or twenty years   15
ago, car makers were loath to show black people in commercials for fear that their product would be tainted as inferior or, worse, as "a black car." Although many car companies are still skittish, by 2001 Buick was actually ending its commercials with the rap-popularized phrase "It's all good." (And by 2004, a BMW ad was featuring an interracial couple.) The phrase went from M. C. Hammer's 1994 song "It's All Good" to replacing "I love this game" as the official slogan of the National Basketball Association in 2001.

Both Buick and the NBA have since dropped *It's all good,* but with their help the phrase massified, at least for a while. "It's huge" among white "sorority sisters and stoners alike," a twenty-seven-year-old white friend in Chicago told me in 2003.

So it's not all bad, this commercialization of black talk, especially if it can   16
get the auto industry to move from shunning to quoting African Americans. But it comes laden with price tags. To read them, look at MTV, which has to be *the* major force in the sea change from whites-only to black's-da-bomb.

It may be difficult to believe now, but for years MTV wouldn't touch   17
black music videos. The channel relented only under pressure, with videos by Prince and Michael Jackson. Black just wouldn't appeal to its white suburban teen audience, MTV explained. In 1989 with the appearance of the successful *Yo! MTV Raps,* that rationale was turned inside out, and— ka-ching!—black videos began to appear regularly. Since so much of MTV is advertising posing as entertainment (the videos are record company promo- tions, the parties and other bashes that appear are often visibly sponsored events), MTV has contributed significantly to two marketing trends: To the young, advertising has become an acceptable—nay, desirable—part of the cool life they aspire to; and a black, hip-hop-ish vernacular has become a cru- cial cog in the youth market machinery.

The outsider style is not solely black or hip-hop, but, at least in the mar-   18
keting mind, a black package can be the most efficient buy to achieve that style. For corporate purposes, hip-hop in particular is a lucrative formula. Not only does the hip-hop black man represent the ultimate outsider who simultaneously stands at the nexus of cool, but much of hip-hop, creat- ed by the kind of people gated communities were meant to exclude, sings the praises of acquiring capitalism's toys. These paradoxes of racism are commercial-ready. . . .

When Sprite realized that teenagers no longer believed its TV   19
commercials telling them that "Image Is Nothing" and that they should- n't trust commercials or celebrity endorsements (said only half tongue-in- cheek by celebrities like NBA star Grant Hill), the soft drink's marketing department decided to up the ante. So, when you need outsider verisimil- itude, who ya gonna call? Why, black rappers, of course, preferably on the hardcore side. Get *them* to testify to the soft drink's beyond-the-bounds, can't-be-bought spirit at Sprite.com launch parties (to be run later on MTV). Or get real kids, looking and sounding ghetto, to rap their own lyrics in TV spots about, say, "a situation that is not too sweet, which is an attribute of Sprite," as a Sprite publicist said. How else to get kids, usual- ly white kids, to understand that you understand that they're sick of commercials telling them what's cool?

And so, while Sprite had long used rappers in its overall "Obey Your   20
Thirst" campaign, now it pumped up the volume. Only by obeying the first

commandment that image is everything can you become, as Sprite did by the late nineties, the fastest-growing soft-drink brand in the world. . . .

When whites talk black—or, just as commonly, when major corporations   21
do it for them—it makes you wanna shout, *Whassup with that?!*

Terms and Props

Before I address wannabe black talk and other points where black lan-   22
guage crosses over into pop, a few words about what "black language" and "black words" are.

I've been using the terms "black English," "black slang," "black talk,"   23
and "African-American vernacular" rather interchangeably, which, in plain English, seems OK. Yet, at the same time, each term is a bit off the mark.

No one phrase is the perfect vehicle to explain how a people speak,   24
because "a people" don't all speak (or do anything) one way. That's one of the problems with the terms "black English" and "black dialect." "Black English" was more or less booted out of formal linguistic circles, because, as linguist Peter Trudgill wrote in the 1995 revised edition of his book *Sociolinguistics,* "it suggested that all Blacks speak this one variety of English—which is not the case." The newer scholarly term, African American Vernacular English (AAVE), has pros and cons: It "distinguishes those Blacks who do not speak standard American English from those who do," wrote Trudgill, "although it still suggests that only one nonstandard variety, homogeneous through the whole of the USA, is involved, which is hardly likely." The word *Ebonics* was created in 1973 by African-American scholars to "define black language from a black perspective," writes Geneva Smitherman, director of the African American Language and Literacy Program at Michigan State University. But the 1997 Ebonics controversy loaded the word with so much baggage . . . that, outside of some hip-hop use, it has become nearly immobile.

"Black slang" can't describe black language, because clearly most black   25
language is composed of standard English. However, when referring to actual slang that blacks created (*my bad, dis*), "black slang" is the right term. Personally, I like "black talk" (which is also the title of one of Smitherman's books). Although, like any phrase starting with the adjective "black," it might suggest that all black people talk this way all the time, "black talk" (like "pop talk") is colloquial and flexible, encompassing vocabulary and then some. . . .

Origins tend to get lost in the roaring mainstream. Some words that seem   26
white are black, and vice versa. For instance, until I looked into *24/7,* I would have guessed its roots were cyber or maybe something out of the convenience-store industry. But *24/7* arose from a hip-hop fondness for number phrases. Rapdict.org lists some sixty number phrases, many of which are too obscure

or gangsta to cross over; *411* is one of the few others that has gone pop. (A recent Mercedes-Benz magazine ad advised, "Get the 411.")

Bogus, which sounds so surfer, dude, dates back at least as far as 1798, when a glossary defined it as a "spurious coin," write David Barnhart and Allan Metcalf in *America in So Many Words.* "Its origins are obscure, but one guess that is as good as any is that it is from *boko,* meaning 'deceit' or 'fake' in the Hausa language of west central Africa. The word then would have been brought over by Africans sold into slavery here." In addition, some nuances that no one doubts are African-American may run deeper in black history than most people, black or white, imagine. When *bad* is used to mean good, the meaning (though obviously not the word itself) is derived, Smitherman writes,[1] from a phrase in the Mandinka language in West Africa, "*a ka nyi ko-jugu,* which means, literally, 'it is good badly,' that is, it is very good, or it is so good that it's bad!" 27

Meanwhile, some words that most people would identify as black, and that black people did indeed popularize, originated among others. Southern phrases in particular jumped races, "from black to white in the case of *bubba* and *big daddy,* from white to black in the case of *grits* and *chitlins,*" write the Rickfords.[2] *Cat,* meaning a hip guy, is a dated piece of slang (though often on the verge of a comeback) that most people attribute to black jazz musicians; Ken Burns's television series *Jazz* states that Louis Armstrong was the first person to have said it. But, as Tom Dalzell writes, in "the late 19th century and early 20th century, *cat* in the slang and jargon of hobos meant an itinerant worker . . . possibly because the migratory worker slunk about like a 'homeless cat.' " However, it did take Armstrong, and then other jazz musicians in the 1920s, to introduce the word into broader usage. That old rap word *fly* (stylish, good-looking, smooth) was flying long before rap. "The most well-established slang meaning of *fly* was in the argot of thieves, where *fly* meant sly, cunning, wide-awake, knowing, or smart," writes Dalzell, who notes those uses of *fly* as early as 1724 and in *Bleak House* by Dickens in 1853. But again, *fly* didn't really buzz until black musicians picked up on it, beginning around 1900, well before *Superfly* in the 1970s and rap in the 1980s. 28

Wannabe Nation

Whether black-born or black-raised, black words are the ones that many white people are wearing like backwards baseball caps. That brings us to a particularly telling term that went from black to pop. *Wannabe* originally 29

---

[1] In her book, *Black Talk: Words and Phrases from the Hood to the Amen Corner* (editors' note).
[2] In *Spoken Soul: The Story of Black English,* by John R. Rickford and Russell J. Rickford (editors' note).

referred to people who wanted to be something they weren't; it was often said of a black person who wanted to be white. In Spike Lee's 1988 film *School Daze,* the conflict was between the dark-skinned, activist "Jigaboos" and the light-skinned sorority sister "Wannabes." Beginning around the time of that movie, *wannabe* was used by just about everybody to mean anybody who wanted to be somebody he or she wasn't—there have been surfer wannabes, Madonna wannabes, and dot.com start-up wannabes. But *wannabe* is not just a blast from decades past. More recently, "podcaster wannabes" have developed, and in just one week on TV and radio in late 2004, I heard of "artist wannabes," "geek wannabes," and "wannabe home-land security chief" Bernard Kerik.

Racially speaking, *wannabe* has reversed field. Since at least the early 30 nineties, with hip-hop an entrenched, virtually mainstream hit, *wannabe* has been far more likely to refer to whites, especially teenagers, who want to be black or do the style. Sometimes called *wiggers* or *wiggas* (*white* plus *nigger/nigga*), black wannabes try to dance the dance and talk the talk. Even whites who would hate to be black will maintain the right to add the occasional black flourish. Some whites flash a black word or gesture like an honorary badge of cool, to show they're down with black people on certain occasions, usually involving sports or entertainment. Or maybe they do it because some of their best friends and some of the best commercials are flashing it, too. Or maybe they just need to know that black people like them. Take "Johnny and Sally," the fictitious white couple on the very funny Web site BlackPeople LoveUs.com, which is full of "testimonials" to their racial bigheartedness. As one unnamed black man attested, "Johnny always alters his given name and refers to himself in the third person—for example, 'J-Dog don't play that' or 'J-Dog wants to know wusssaappp.' It comforts me to know that my parl-ance has such broad appeal."

African-Americans aren't the only people whose parlance has broad 31 appeal. Non-Latino blacks dabble in Spanish, Catholics in Yiddish, adults in teenage talk. Cultural skin is always permeable, absorbing any word that has reached a critical mass of usefulness or fun. The human species can't help but borrow—after all, that's how languages develop.

But whether we call it wannabe talk or the less derogatory crossover talk, 32 something about white society's sampling of black speech is more loaded than the usual borrowing. Black vernacular's contributions to English are larger in number and run deeper linguistically and psychologically than do any other ethnic group's. And black English, born in slavery, resounds with our society's senses of guilt, fear, identity, and style.

Black-to-white crossover talk, which also began during slavery, is hardly 33 new. But, like most pop talk today, it radiates a new gloss, a veneer in which you can catch the reflection of its increased market value. Black talk comes from something real—"serious as a heart attack," Smitherman says—but, whoop, there it is, sparking out of TV commercials, out of white politicians, out of anyone who has something to promote, spin, or get over.

Questions for Close Reading

1. What is the selection's thesis? Locate the sentence(s) in which Savan states her main idea. If she doesn't state her thesis explicitly, express it in your own words.
2. What does Savan mean by "pop language" and "pop talk"? What are some examples of these?
3. Why does Savan characterize the word *cool* as the most important pop word of all time?
4. In the section "Wannabe Nation," Savan describes the appeal of being Black to white Americans. According to Savan, what is troubling about the white mainstream culture's appropriation of Black words and phrases?
5. Refer to your dictionary as needed to define the following words used in the selection: *vernacular* (paragraph 1), *lexicon* (6), *per se* (8), *preeminent* (9), *template* (10), *catchphrase* (12), *minstrel shows* (14), *loath* (15), *lucrative* (18), *nexus* (18), *verisimilitude* (19), *colloquial* (25), *spurious* (27), and *argot* (28).

Questions About the Writer's Craft

1. **The pattern.** Why does Savan use so many examples of Black talk to illustrate its role in modern American English? Why does she use several lengthy examples as well? What are some of these extended examples?
2. **The pattern.** In paragraphs 16 through 21, Savan discusses the use of Black talk in marketing products. How does she organize the examples in this section of the essay? What is the purpose of this organization?
3. **Other patterns.** In the section entitled "Terms and Props," Savan discusses the *definitions* of the terms she has been using for Black talk. Why does she stop the flow of the essay to delve deeper into these terms? Why does she prefer the term "black talk" over the terms "black English," "black dialect," and "African American Vernacular English"? How effective is this section of the essay?
4. To support her thesis, Savan uses evidence from advertising, MTV, and the Internet. Find one example of a use of Black talk in each of these media. Why do you think Savan chose each example? How does each example support the essay's thesis? Would the essay have been as effective without these examples?

Writing Assignments Using Exemplification as a Pattern of Development

1. Savan discusses the role hip-hop artists play in modern marketing. Select a current hip-hop artist who markets products and do research on him or her. Write an essay about the role of marketing and advertising in this artist's career, providing examples to support your thesis.
2. Savan's essay focuses on Black talk, but there are many other subgroups of American English. For example, there is "Spanglish," a blend of Spanish and English occasionally spoken by Hispanic Americans; jargon, which includes words

such as *debug* associated with a specific field like computer science; place names that have their origin in Native American languages; and regional dialects that have their own special words and phrases. Select one type of specialized American English words with which you are familiar and write an essay that *exemplifies* it. Include specific examples of words and phrases and their use to make your essay interesting.

Writing Assignments Combining Patterns of Development

3. Savan discusses how marketers use Black language and culture to sell products. Select two TV commercials or print ads for the same type of product and *describe* them using vivid, sensory language. Then analyze each commercial or ad, *dividing* your analysis into the various techniques it uses to persuade you, the consumer, to buy the product. *Compare* and *contrast* the effectiveness of the two ads. For another perspective on advertising, you may want to read Ann McClintock's "Propaganda Techniques in Today's Advertising" (page 204).

4. Most of the examples in Savan's essay are of the use of Black talk in spoken popular language. In contrast, written language is usually more formal. Write an essay in which you *compare* and *contrast* the language you use when speaking with the language you use when writing. Give examples of both spoken and written language to support your thesis. You might find it useful to read David Shipley's "Talk About Editing" (page 245).

Writing Assignment Using a Journal Entry as a Starting Point

5. Review your pre-reading journal entry, and select two or three of the words and phrases that you and your friends use among yourselves. Then write an essay giving examples of situations in which these words are used. Explain why you choose to use them rather than using conventional phrases from standard English. What function do these words and phrases have in the psychology of the group?

Eric G. Wilson

Eric G. Wilson is a professor of English at Wake Forest University, where he teaches courses on British and American Romanticism. Born in 1967, Wilson attended Appalachian State University and Wake Forest University, and he earned a Ph.D. from the City University of New York. He has written several books, including *Secret Cinema: Gnostic Vision in Film* (2006), *The Melancholy Android* (2006), and *Against Happiness: In Praise of Melancholy* (2008). This essay was published in the *Los Angeles Times* on February 17, 2008.

Pre-Reading Journal Entry

Recall a period of sadness, grief, or suffering in your own life. What was your mood like? How did it affect your normal activities? In your journal, describe what your life was like during such a time, and also explain how you dealt with feeling low.

The Miracle of Melancholia

In April of 1819, right around the time that he began to suffer the first symptoms of tuberculosis—the disease that had already killed his mother and his beloved brother, Tom—the poet John Keats sat down and wrote, in a letter to his brother, George, the following question: "Do you not see how necessary a World of Pains and troubles is to school an Intelligence and make it a Soul?" 1

Implied in this inquiry is an idea that is not very popular these days— at least not in the United States, which is characterized by an almost collective yearning for complete happiness. That idea is this: A person can only become a fully formed human being, as opposed to a mere mind, through suffering and sorrow. This notion would seem quite strange, possibly even deranged, in a country in which almost 85% of the population claims, according to the Pew Research Center, to be "very happy" or at least "happy." 2

Indeed, in light of our recent craze for positive psychology—a brand of psychotherapy designed not so much to heal mental illness as to increase happiness—as well as in light of our increasing reliance on pills that reduce sadness, anxiety and fear, we are likely to challenge Keats' meditation outright, to condemn it as a dangerous and dated affront to the modern American dream. 3

But does the American addiction to happiness make any sense, especially in light of the poverty, ecological disaster and war that now haunt the globe, daily annihilating hundreds if not thousands? Isn't it, in fact, a recipe for delusion? 4

And aren't we merely trying to slice away what is most probably an essential part of our hearts, that part that can reconcile us to facts, no 5 matter how harsh, and that also can inspire us to imagine new and more creative ways to engage with the world? Bereft of this integral element of our selves, we settle for a status quo. We yearn for comfort at any cost. We covet a good night's sleep. We trade fortitude for blandness.

When Keats invoked the fertility of pain, he knew what he was talking about. Though he was young when he composed his question—only 24— he had already experienced a lifetime of pain. His father had died after falling from a horse when the future poet was only 9. A few years later, Keats nursed his mother assiduously through tuberculosis, but she died in 1810, when he was 15. Soon after, he was taken from a boarding school he loved and required to apprentice as an apothecary; he then underwent a gruesome course in surgery in one of London's hospitals (in the days before anesthesia). 6

Orphaned and mournful, Keats spent his days brooding. But after much contemplation, he decided that sorrow was not a state to be avoided, not a weakness of the will or a disease requiring cure. On the contrary, Keats discovered that his ongoing gloom was in fact the inspiration for his greatest ideas and his most enduring creations. 7

What makes us melancholy, Keats concluded, is our awareness of things inevitably passing—of brothers dying before they reach 20; of nightingales that cease their songs; of peonies drooping at noon. But it is precisely when we sense impending death that we grasp the world's beauty. 8

Keats was of course not the only great artist to translate melancholia into exuberance. This metamorphosis of sadness to joy has been a perennial if frequently unacknowledged current in Western art. 9

Consider George Frideric Handel, the 18th century composer. By 1741, when he was in his mid-50s, Handel found himself a fallen man. Once a ruler of the musical world, he had suffered several failed operas as well as poor health. He was left in a state of poverty, sickness and heartsickness. Living in a run-down house in a poor part of London, he expected any day to be thrown into debtor's prison or to die. 10

But then, out of nowhere, as if by some divine agency, Handel received a libretto based on the life of Jesus and an invitation to compose a work for a charity benefit performance. On Aug. 22, 1741, in his squalid rooms on Brook Street, Handel saw potentialities no one had before seen. Immediately, he felt a creative vitality course through his veins. During a 24-day period, he barely slept or ate. He only composed, and then composed more. At the close of this brief period, he had completed "Messiah," his greatest work, a gift from the depths of melancholia. 11

We could also recall Georgia O'Keeffe, the 20th century painter. In the late 1920s and early 1930s, O'Keeffe left the East Coast for Taos, N.M. She fell profoundly in love with the lonely vistas of this world denuded of human corruption. However, even though she was enlivened by this part of the 12 world, in 1932, her lifelong battle with melancholia caught up with her. She was hospitalized for psychoneurosis.

Rather than quelling her creative spirit, this breakdown did the oppo- 13
site. Upon being discharged, she returned to the Southwest. There, in 1935, she painted some of her bleakest and most beautiful landscapes: "Purple Hills near Abiquiu" and "Ram's Head, White Hollyhock Hills." Both feature dark things amid the desert's glare—gloomy shadows and stormy clouds. Into these haunting shades—hovering amid hard-scrabble rock and a sinister skull—one stares. One senses something there as silent and sacred as bones.

Joni Mitchell[1] confessed in an interview that she has frequently 14
endured long periods of gloom. But she has not shied away from the darkness. Instead, she sees her sorrow as the "sand that makes the pearl"—as the terrible friction that produces the lustrous sphere. Given her fruitful struggles with sadness, Mitchell has understandably feared its absence. "Chase away the demons," she has said, "and they will take the angels with them."

Melancholia, far from error or defect, is an almost miraculous invitation 15
to rise above the contented status quo and imagine untapped possibilities. We need sorrow, constant and robust, to make us human, alive, sensitive to the sweet rhythms of growth and decay, death and life.

This of course does not mean that we should simply wallow in gloom, 16
that we should wantonly cultivate depression. I'm not out to romanticize mental illnesses that can end in madness or suicide.

On the contrary, following Keats and those like him, I'm valorizing a 17
fundamental emotion too frequently avoided in the American scene. I'm offering hope to those millions who feel guilty for being downhearted. I'm saying that it's more than all right to descend into introspective gloom. In fact, it is crucial, a call to what might be the best portion of ourselves, those depths where the most lasting truths lie.

---

[1]Joni Mitchell (1943–) is a Canadian singer, guitarist, and songwriter who has won nine Grammy awards for her albums (editors' note).

Questions for Close Reading

1. What is the selection's thesis? Locate the sentence(s) in which Wilson states his main idea. If he doesn't state his thesis explicitly, express it in your own words.
2. According to Wilson, what does the "American addiction to happiness" lead to?
3. In paragraph 16, Wilson attempts to distinguish between melancholia and depression. What is the difference, according to Wilson?

4. What does Wilson mean by the title of this essay, "The Miracle of Melancholia"? How do the examples in the essay reflect the title?
5. Refer to your dictionary as needed to define the following words used in the selection: *affront* (paragraph 3), *delusion* (4), *bereft* (5), *assiduously* (6), *melancholia* (9), *exuberance* (9), *libretto* (11), *squalid* (11), *quelling* (13), *status quo* (15), *wantonly* (16), and *valorizing* (17).

Questions About the Writer's Craft

1. **The pattern.** What kind of examples does Wilson use in this essay? List the examples he provides to support his thesis. Is Wilson's use of examples effective?
2. Why does Wilson give the example of John Keats first? What purposes does this one example serve?
3. **Other patterns.** *Cause* and *effect* play a big role in this essay. Identify passages in which Wilson explains the possible effects of melancholia.
4. The audience for this essay was readers of the *Los Angeles Times*. Do you think that Wilson did a good job addressing this audience? Explain.

Writing Assignments Using Exemplification as a Pattern of Development

1. Choose a common human emotion or behavior other than melancholia (for example, happiness, anger, anxiety, laziness, selfishness, generosity), and write an essay in which you explain how a positive emotion or behavior can have negative effects or a negative emotion or behavior can have positive effects. For example, if you choose happiness, a positive emotion, you might write about lack of awareness of the problems of others as a possible negative effect. Use examples from your own experience to support your thesis. To get another perspective on a common human behavior, read "When Mañana Is Too Soon" by Kurt Kleiner (page 312).
2. Choose one of the people mentioned in the Wilson essay and do some Internet or library research on his or her life and work. Write an essay describing the artist's achievements in which you give specific examples of his or her works.

Writing Assignments Combining Patterns of Development

3. Do you agree with Wilson's view that experiencing suffering and melancholia is necessary "to make us human, alive, sensitive to the sweet rhythms of growth and decay, death and life"? Write an essay in which you *argue* that suffering and melancholia are—or are not—necessary for spiritual growth. Brainstorm with others to come up with ideas and *examples* from the lives of ordinary people—not great artists—that support your position.
4. The word *melancholia* has a long and interesting medical and literary history, going back to Hippocrates (about 460–370 B.C.E.), an ancient Greek physician who thought that good health resulted when the four humors, or bodily fluids—blood, black bile, yellow bile, and phlegm—were in balance. According to Hippocrates, when

black bile increased, the result was melancholia. Do some research on the history of the word *melancholia,* and write an essay in which you discuss various *definitions* of the term and *compare and contrast* historical and modern uses of the word.

Writing Assignment Using a Journal Entry as a Starting Point

5. Review your pre-reading journal entry in which you described a time when you experienced sadness, grief, or suffering. Has reading Wilson's essay caused you to re-evaluate this experience? Was there anything positive about it? Did you learn anything about life or about yourself? Write an essay in which you describe the effects, whether negative and positive, of your experience.

Additional Writing Topics

EXEMPLIFICATION

General Assignments

Use examples to develop any one of the following topics into a well-organized essay. When writing the paper, choose enough relevant examples to support your thesis. Organize the material into a sequence that most effectively illustrates the thesis, keeping in mind that emphatic order is often the most compelling way to present specifics.

1. Many of today's drivers have dangerous habits.
2. Drug and alcohol abuse is (or is not) a serious problem among many young people.
3. One rule of restaurant dining is "Management often seems oblivious to problems that are perfectly obvious to customers."
4. Children today are not encouraged to use their imaginations.
5. The worst kind of hypocrite is a religious hypocrite.
6. The best things in life are definitely not free.
7. A part-time job is an important experience that every college student should have.
8. The Internet has resulted in a generation of lazy young people.
9. _____(name someone you know well) is a _____ (use a quality: open-minded, dishonest, compulsive, reliable, gentle, and so on) person.
10. Television commercials stereotype the elderly (or another minority group).
11. Today, salespeople act as if they're doing you a favor by taking your money.
12. Most people behave decently in their daily interactions with each other.
13. Pettiness, jealousy, and selfishness abound in our daily interactions with each other.
14. You can tell a lot about people by observing what they wear and eat.
15. Too many Americans are overly concerned/completely unconcerned with being physically fit.
16. There are several study techniques that will help a student learn more efficiently.
17. Some teachers seem to enjoy turning tests into ordeals.
18. "How to avoid bad eating habits" is one course all college students should take.
19. More needs to be done to eliminate obstacles faced by the physically disabled.
20. Some of the best presents are those that cost the least.

Assignments with a Specific Purpose, Audience, and Point of View

On Campus

1. Lately, many people at your college have been experiencing stress. As a member of the Student Life Committee, you've been asked to prepare a pamphlet illustrating strategies for reducing different kinds of stress. Decide which stresses to discuss, and explain coping strategies for each, providing helpful examples as you go.

2. A friend of yours will be going away to college in an unfamiliar environment—in a bustling urban setting or in a quiet rural one. To help your friend prepare for this new environment, write a letter giving examples of what life on an urban or a rural campus is like. You might focus on the benefits and dangers with which your friend is unlikely to be familiar.

At Home or in the Community

3. Shopping for a new car, you become annoyed at how many safety features are available only as expensive options. Write a letter of complaint to the auto manufacturer, citing at least three examples of such options. Avoid sounding hostile.
4. A pet food company is having an annual contest to choose a new animal to feature in its advertising. To win the contest, you must convince the company that your pet is personable, playful, and unique. Write an essay giving examples of your pet's special qualities.

On the Job

5. Assume that you're an elementary school principal planning to give a speech in which you'll try to convince parents that television distorts children's perceptions of reality. Write the speech, illustrating your point with vivid examples.
6. The online publication you work for has asked you to write an article on what you consider to be the "three best consumer products of the past twenty-five years." Support your opinion with lively, engaging specifics that are consistent with the website's offbeat and slightly ironic tone.

6

DIVISION-CLASSIFICATION

WHAT IS DIVISION-CLASSIFICATION?

Imagine what life would be like if this is how an average day unfolded:

> You go to the supermarket for only five items, but your marketing takes over an hour because all the items in the store are jumbled together. Clerks put new shipments anywhere they please; the milk might be with the vegetables on Monday but with hair products on Thursday. Next, you go to the drugstore to pick up photos you left to be developed. You don't have time, though, to wait while the cashier roots through the large carton into which all the pickup envelopes have been thrown. You leave to go visit a friend in the hospital with the flu. There you find your friend in a room with three other patients: a middle-aged man with a heart problem, a young boy ready to have his tonsils removed, and a woman in labor.

Such a muddled world, lacking the most basic forms of organization, would make daily life chaotic. All of us instinctively look for ways to order our environment. Without sorting mechanisms, we'd be overwhelmed by life's complexity. An organization such as a university, for example, is made manageable by being divided into various schools (Liberal Arts, Performing Arts, Engineering, and so on). The schools are then separated into departments (English, History, Political Science), and each department's offerings are grouped into categories—English, for instance, into Literature and Composition—before being further divided into specific courses.

The kind of ordering system we've been discussing is called *division-classification*, a logical way of thinking that allows us to make sense of a complex world. Division and classification, though separate processes, are often used together as complementary techniques. *Division* involves taking a single unit or concept, breaking the unit down into its parts, and then analyzing the connections among the parts and between the parts and the whole. For instance, if we wanted to organize the chaotic hospital described at the start of the chapter, we might think about how the single concept "a hospital" could be broken down into its components. We might come up with the following breakdown: pediatric wing, cardiac wing, maternity wing, and so on.

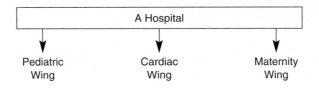

What we have just done involves division: We've taken a single entity (a hospital) and divided it into some of its component parts (wings), each with its own facilities and patients.

In contrast, *classification* brings two or more related items together and categorizes them according to type or kind. If the disorganized supermarket described earlier were to be restructured, the clerks would have to classify the separate items arriving at the loading dock. Cartons of lettuce, tomatoes, cucumbers, butter, yogurt, milk, shampoo, conditioner, and styling gel would be assigned to the appropriate categories:

HOW DIVISION-CLASSIFICATION FITS YOUR PURPOSE AND AUDIENCE

The reorganized hospital and supermarket show the way division and classification work in everyday life. But division and classification also come into play during the writing process. Because division involves breaking a subject into parts, it can be a helpful strategy during prewriting, especially if you're analyzing a broad, complex subject: the structure of a film; the motivation of a character in a novel; the problem your community has with vandalism; the controversy surrounding school prayer. An editorial examining a recent hostage crisis, for example, might divide the crisis into three areas: how the hostages were treated by (1) their captors, (2) the governments negotiating their release, and (3) the media. The purpose of the editorial might be to show readers that the governments' treatment of the hostages was particularly exploitative.

Classification can be useful for imposing order on ideas generated during prewriting. You examine that material to see which of your rough ideas are alike, so that you can cluster related items in the same category. Classification would, then, be a helpful strategy for topics like these: techniques for impressing teachers; comic styles of talk-show hosts; views on abortion; reasons for the current rise in volunteerism. You might, for instance, use classification in a paper showing that Americans are undermining their health through their obsessive pursuit of various diets. Perhaps you begin by brainstorming all the diets that have gained popularity in recent years (Atkins, South Beach, Zone, whatever). Then you categorize the diets according to type: high-fiber, low-protein, high-carbohydrate, and so on. Once the diets are grouped, you can discuss the problems within each category, demonstrating to readers why some of the diets may not be safe or effective.

Division-classification can be crucial when responding to college assignments like the following:

> From your observations, what kinds of appeals do television advertisers use when selling automobiles? In your view, are any of these appeals morally irresponsible?

> Analyze the components of effective parenting. Indicate those you consider most vital for raising confident, well-adjusted children.

> Describe the hierarchy of the typical high school clique, identifying the various parts of the hierarchy. Use your analysis to support or refute the view that adolescence is a period of rigid conformity.

> Many social commentators have observed that discourtesy is on the rise. Indicate whether you think this is a valid observation by characterizing the types of everyday encounters you have with people.

These assignments suggest division-classification through the use of such words as *kinds, components, parts,* and *types.* Generally, though, you won't receive such clear signals to use division-classification. Instead, the broad purpose of the essay—and the point you want to make—will lead you to the analytical thinking characteristic of division-classification.

Sometimes division-classification will be the dominant technique for structuring an essay; other times it will be used as a supplemental pattern in an essay organized primarily according to another pattern of development. Say you want to write a paper *explaining a process* (surviving divorce; creating a hit record; shepherding a bill through Congress; using the Heimlich maneuver on people who are choking). You could *divide* the process into parts or stages, showing, for instance, that the Heimlich maneuver is an easily mastered skill that readers should acquire. Or perhaps you plan to write a light-spirited essay analyzing the *effect* that increased awareness of sexual stereotypes has had on college students' social lives. In such a case, you might use *classification*. To show readers that shifting gender roles make young men and women comically self-conscious, you could categorize the places where students scout each other out: in class, at the library, at parties, in dorms. You could then show how students—not wishing to be macho or coyly feminine—approach each other with laughable tentativeness in these four environments.

Now imagine that you're writing an *argumentation-persuasion* essay urging that the federal government prohibit the use of growth-inducing antibiotics in livestock feed. The paper could begin by *dividing* the antibiotics cycle into stages: the effects of antibiotics on livestock; the short-term effects on humans who consume the animals; the possible long-term effects of consuming antibiotic-tainted meat. To increase readers' understanding of the problem, you might also discuss the antibiotics controversy in terms of an even larger issue: the dangerous ways food is treated before being consumed. In this case, you would consider the various procedures (use of additives, preservatives, artificial colors, and so on), *classifying* these treatments into several types—from least harmful (some additives or artificial colors, perhaps) to most harmful (you might slot the antibiotics here). Such an essay would be developed using both division *and* classification: first, the division of the antibiotics cycle and then the classification of the various food treatments. Frequently, this interdependence will be reversed, and classification will precede rather than follow division.

At this point, you have a good sense of the way writers use division-classification to achieve their purpose and to connect with their readers. Now take a moment to look closely at the photograph at the beginning of this chapter. Imagine you're writing an article, accompanied by the photo, for a parenting magazine. Your purpose is twofold: to alert parents to the danger of pushing young children to achieve, and to help parents foster in children healthy attitudes toward achievement.  Jot down some ideas you might include when *dividing* and/or *classifying* things parents should and shouldn't do to foster a balanced view of accomplishment and success in youngsters.

SUGGESTIONS FOR USING DIVISION-CLASSIFICATION IN AN ESSAY

The suggestions here and in Figure 6.1 on page 192 will help you use division-classification as a dominant or a supportive pattern of development.

1. Select a principle of division-classification consistent with your purpose.   Most subjects can be divided or classified according to a *number of different principles*. For example, when writing about an ideal vacation, you could divide your subject according to any of these principles: location, cost, recreation available. Similarly, when analyzing students at your college, you could base your classification on a variety of principles: students' majors, their racial or ethnic background, whether they belong to a fraternity or sorority. In all cases, though, the principle of division-classification must help you meet your overall purpose and reinforce your central point.

Sometimes a principle of division-classification seems so attractive that you use it without asking whether it supports your purpose. Suppose you want to write a paper asserting that several episodes of a new television comedy are destined to become classics. Here's how you might go wrong.

You begin by doing some brainstorming about the episodes. Then, as you start to organize the prewriting material, you hit on a possible principle of classification: grouping the characters in the show according to the frequency with which they appear (main characters appearing in every show, supporting characters appearing in most shows, and guest characters appearing once or twice). You name the characters and explain which characters fit where. But is this principle of classification significant? Has it anything to do with why the shows will become classics? No, it hasn't. Such an essay would be little more than a meaningless exercise in classifying things just to classify them.

In contrast, a significant principle of classification might involve categorizing a number of shows according to the easily recognized human types portrayed: the Pompous Know-It-All, the Boss Who's Out of Control, the Lovable Grouch, the Surprisingly Savvy Innocent. You might illustrate the way certain episodes offer delightful twists on these stock figures, making such shows models of comic plotting and humor.

When you write an essay that uses division-classification as its primary method of development, a *single principle* of division-classification provides the foundation for each major section of the paper. Imagine you're writing an essay showing that the success of contemporary music groups has less to do with talent than with the groups' ability to market themselves to distinct audiences. To develop your point, you might categorize several performers according to the age ranges they appeal to (preteens, adolescents, people in their late twenties) and then analyze the marketing strategies the musicians use to gain their fans' support. The essay's logic would be undermined if

FIGURE 6.1
Development Diagram: Writing a Division-Classification Essay

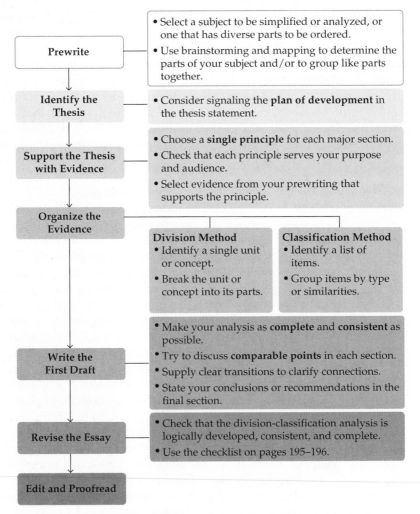

you switched, in the middle of your analysis, to another principle of classification—say, the influence of earlier groups on today's music scene.

Don't, however, take this caution to mean that essays can never use more than one principle of division-classification. They can—as long as the *shift from one principle to another* occurs in *different parts* of the paper. Imagine you want to write about widespread disillusionment with student government leaders at your college. You could develop this point by breaking down the dissatisfaction into the following: disappointment with the students' qualifications for office; disenchantment with their campaign tactics; frustration with their performance once elected. That section of the essay completed, you might move to a second principle of division—how students can get involved in campus government. Perhaps you give the following possibilities: serving on nominating committees; helping to run candidates' campaigns; attending open sessions of the student government.

2. Apply the principle of division-classification logically.   You need to demonstrate to readers that your analysis is the result of careful thought. First of all, your division-classification should be as *complete* as possible. Your analysis should include—within reason—all the parts into which you can divide your subject, or all the types into which you can categorize your subjects. Let's say you're writing an essay showing that where college students live is an important factor in determining how satisfied they are with college life. You classify students according to where they live: with parents, in dorms, in fraternity and sorority houses. But what about all the students who live in rented apartments, houses, or rooms off campus? If these places of residence are ignored, your classification won't be complete; you will lose credibility with your readers because they'll probably realize that you have overlooked several important considerations.

Your division-classification should also be *consistent:* The parts into which you break your subject or the groups into which you place your subjects should be as mutually exclusive as possible. The parts or categories should not be mixed, nor should they overlap. Assume you're writing an essay describing the animals at the zoo in a nearby city. You decide to describe the zoo's mammals, reptiles, birds, and endangered species. But such a classification is inconsistent. You begin by categorizing the animals according to scientific class (mammals, birds, reptiles), then switch to another principle when you classify some animals according to whether they are endangered. Because you drift over to a different principle of classification, your categories are no longer mutually exclusive: Endangered species could overlap with any of the other categories. In which section of the paper, for instance, would you describe an exotic parrot that is obviously a bird but is also nearly extinct? And how would you categorize the zoo's rare mountain gorilla? This impressive creature is a mammal, but it is also an endangered species. Such overlapping categories undercut the logic that gives an essay its integrity.

A helpful tip: A solid outline is invaluable when you use division-classification. The outline encourages you to do the rigorous thinking needed to arrive at divisions and classifications that are logical, complete, and consistent.

3. Prepare an effective thesis.   If your essay uses division-classification as its dominant method of development, it might be helpful to prepare a thesis that does more than signal the paper's subject and suggest your attitude toward that general subject. You might also want the thesis to state the principle of division-classification at the heart of the essay. Furthermore, you might want the thesis to reveal which part or category you regard as most important.

Consider the two thesis statements that follow:

> As the observant beachcomber moves from the tidal area to the upper beach to the sandy dunes, rich variations in marine life become apparent.

> Although most people focus on the dangers associated with the disposal of toxic waste in the land and ocean, the incineration of toxic matter may pose an even more serious threat to human life.

The first thesis statement makes clear that the writer will organize the paper by classifying forms of marine life according to location. Because the purpose of the essay is to inform as objectively as possible, the thesis doesn't suggest the writer's opinion about which category is most significant.

The second thesis signals that the essay will divide the issue of toxic waste by methods of disposal. Moreover, because the paper takes a stance on a controversial subject, the thesis is worded to reveal which aspect of the topic the writer considers most important. Such a clear statement of the writer's position is an effective strategy in an essay of this kind.

You may have noted that each thesis statement also signals the paper's plan of development. The first essay, for example, will use specific facts, examples, and details to describe the kinds of marine life found in the tidal area, upper beach, and dunes. However, thesis statements in papers developed primarily through division-classification don't have to be so structured. If a paper is well written, your principle of division-classification, your opinion about which part or category is most important, and the essay's plan of development will become apparent as the essay unfolds.

4. Organize the paper logically.   Whether your paper is developed wholly or in part by division-classification, it should have a logical structure. As much as possible, try to discuss *comparable points* in each section of the paper. In the essay on seashore life, for example, you might describe life in the tidal area by discussing the mollusks, crustaceans, birds, and amphibians that live or feed there. You would then follow through, as much as you could, with this arrangement in the paper's other sections (upper beach and dune). Not describing the bird life thriving in the dunes, especially when you had discussed bird life in the tidal and upper-beach areas, would compromise the paper's structure. Of course, perfect parallelism is not always possible— there are no mollusks in the dunes, for instance. You should also use *signal devices* to connect various parts of the paper: "*Another* characteristic of marine life battered by the tides"; "A *final* important trait of both tidal and upper-beach crustaceans"; "*Unlike* the creatures of the tidal area and the upper beach." Such signals clarify the connections among the essay's ideas.

5. State any conclusions or recommendations in the paper's final section. The analytic thinking that occurs during division-classification often leads to surprising insights. Such insights may be introduced early on, or they may be reserved for the end, where they are stated as conclusions or recommendations. A paper might categorize different kinds of coaches—from inspiring to incompetent—and make the point that athletes learn a great deal about human relations simply by having to get along with their coaches, regardless of the coaches' skills. Such a paper might conclude that participation in a team sport teaches more about human nature than several courses in psychology. Or the essay might end with a proposal: Rookies and seasoned team members should be paired so that novice players can get advice on dealing with coaching eccentricities.

REVISION STRATEGIES

Once you have a draft of the essay, you're ready to revise. The following checklist will help you and those giving you feedback apply to division-classification some of the revision techniques discussed on pages 60–62.

☑ DIVISION-CLASSIFICATION: A REVISION/PEER REVIEW
CHECKLIST

Revise Overall Meaning and Structure

❏ What is the principle of division-classification at the heart of the essay? How does this principle contribute to the essay's overall purpose and thesis?

❏ Does the thesis state the essay's principle of division-classification? Should it? Does the thesis signal which part or category is most important? Should it? Does the thesis reveal the essay's plan of development? Should it?

❏ Is the essay organized primarily through division, classification, or a blend of both?

❏ If the essay is organized mainly through division, is the subject sufficiently complex to be broken down into parts? What are the parts?

❏ If the essay is organized mainly through classification, what are the categories? How does this categorizing reveal similarities and/or differences that would otherwise not be apparent?

Revise Paragraph Development

❏ Are comparable points discussed in each of the paper's sections? What are these points?

❏ In which paragraphs does the division-classification seem illogical, incomplete, or inconsistent? In which paragraphs are parts or categories not clearly explained?

❏ Are the subject's different parts or categories discussed in separate paragraphs? Is there any overlap among categories?

Revise Sentences and Words

❏ What signal devices help integrate the paper? Are there enough signals? Too many?

❏ Where should sentences and words be made more specific in order to clarify the parts and categories being discussed?

STUDENT ESSAY

The following student essay was written by Gail Oremland in response to this assignment:

> In "Propaganda Techniques in Today's Advertising," Ann McClintock describes the flaws in many of the persuasive strategies used by advertisers. Choose another group of people whose job is also to communicate—for example, parents, bosses, teachers. Then, in an essay of your own, divide the group into types according to the flaws they make when communicating.

While reading Gail's paper, try to determine how effectively it applies the principles of division-classification. The annotations on Gail's paper and the commentary following it will help you look at the essay more closely.

The Truth About College Teachers
by Gail Oremland

Introduction

A recent TV news story told about a group of college   1
professors from a nearby university who were hired by a local school system to help upgrade the teaching in the community's public schools. The professors were to visit classrooms, analyze teachers' skills, and then conduct workshops to help the teachers become more effective at their jobs. But after the first round of workshops, the superintendent of schools decided to cancel the whole project. He fired the

learned professors and sent them back to their ivory tower. Why did the project fall apart? There was a simple reason. The college professors, who were supposedly going to show the public school teachers how to be more effective, were themselves poor teachers. Many college students could have predicted such a disastrous outcome. They know, first-hand, that college teachers are strange. They know that professors often exhibit bizarre behaviors, relating to students in ways that make it difficult for students to stay awake, or—if awake—to learn.

Thesis

One type of professor assumes, legitimately enough, that her function is to pass on to students the vast store of knowledge she has acquired. But because the "Knowledgeable One" regards herself as an expert and her students as the ignorant masses, she adopts an elitist approach that sabotages learning. The Knowledgeable One enters a lecture hall with a self-important air, walks to the podium, places her yellowed-with-age notes on the stand, and begins her lecture at the exact second the class is officially scheduled to begin. There can be a blizzard or hurricane raging outside the lecture hall; students can be running through freezing sleet and howling winds to get to class on time. Will the Knowledgeable One wait for them to arrive before beginning her lecture? Probably not. The Knowledgeable One's time is precious. She's there, set to begin, and that's what matters.

Topic sentence

The first of three paragraphs on the first category of teacher

The first paragraph in a three-part chronological sequence: What happens before *class*

2

Once the monologue begins, the Knowledgeable One drones on and on. The Knowledgeable One is a fact person. She may be the history prof who knows the death toll of every Civil War battle, the biology prof who can diagram all the common biological molecules, the accounting prof who enumerates every clause of the federal tax form. Oblivious to students' glazed eyes and stifled yawns, the Knowledgeable One delivers her monologue, dispensing one dry fact after another. The only advantage to being on the receiving end of this boring monologue is that students do not have to worry about being called on to question a point or provide an opinion; the Knowledgeable One is not willing to relinquish one minute of her time by giving students a voice. Assume for one improbable moment that a student actually manages to stay awake during the monologue and is brave enough to ask a question. In such a case, the Knowledgeable One will address the questioning student as "Mr." or "Miss." This formality does not, as some students mistakenly suppose, indicate respect for the student as a fledgling member of the academic community. Not at all. This impersonality represents the Knowledgeable One's desire to keep as wide a distance as possible between her and her students.

Topic sentence

The second paragraph on the first category of teacher

The second paragraph in the chronological sequence: What happens during *class*

3

Topic sentence ————•

The third paragraph on the first category of teacher

The final paragraph in the chronological sequence: What happens *after* class

The Knowledgeable One's monologue always comes to a   4
close at the precise second the class is scheduled to end. No sooner has she delivered her last forgettable word than the Knowledgeable One packs up her notes and shoots out the door, heading back to the privacy of her office, where she can pursue her specialized academic interests—free of any possible interruption from students. The Knowledgeable One's hasty departure from the lecture hall makes it clear she has no desire to talk with students. In her eyes, she has met her obligations; she has taken time away from her research to transmit to students what she knows. Any closer contact might mean she would risk contagion from students, that great unwashed mass. Such a danger is to be avoided at all costs.

Unlike the Knowledgeable One, the "Leader of Intellectual   5
Discussion" seems to respect students. Emphasizing class discussion, the Leader encourages students to confront ideas ("What is Twain's view of morality?" "Was our intervention in Iraq

Topic sentence ————•

Paragraph on the second category of teacher

justified?" "Should big business be given tax breaks?") and discover their own truths. Then, about three weeks into the semester, it becomes clear that the Leader wants students to discover *his* version of the truth. Behind the Leader's democratic guise lurks a dictator. When a student voices an opinion that the Leader accepts, the student is rewarded by hearty nods of approval and "Good point, good point." But if a student is rash enough to advance a conflicting viewpoint, the Leader responds with killing politeness: "Well, yes, that's an interesting perspective. But don't you think that...?" Grade-conscious students soon learn not to chime in with their viewpoint. They know that when the Leader, with seeming honesty, says, "I'd be interested in hearing what you think. Let's open this up for discussion," they had better figure out what the Leader wants to hear before advancing their own theories. "Me-tooism" rather than independent thinking, they discover, guarantees good grades in the Leader's class.

Topic sentence ————•

Paragraph on the third category of teacher

Then there is the professor who comes across as the   6
students' "Buddy." This kind of professor does not see himself as an imparter of knowledge or a leader of discussion but as a pal, just one in a community of equals. The Buddy may start his course this way. "All of us know that this college stuff—grades, degrees, exams, required reading—is a game. So let's not play it, okay?" Dressed in jeans, sweatshirt, and scuffed sneakers, the Buddy projects a relaxed, casual attitude. He arranges the class seats in a circle (he would never take a position in front of the room) and insists that students call him by his first name. He uses no syllabus and gives few tests, believing that such constraints keep students from directing their own learning. A free spirit, the Buddy often teaches courses like "The Psychology of Interpersonal Relations" or "The Social

Dynamics of the Family." If students choose to use class time to discuss the course material, that's fine. If they want to discuss something else, that's fine, too. It's the self-expression, the honest dialogue, that counts. In fact, the Buddy seems especially fond of digressions from academic subjects. By talking about his political views, his marital problems, his tendency to drink one too many beers, the Buddy lets students see that he is a regular guy—just like them. At first, students look forward to classes with the Buddy. They enjoy the informality, the chitchat, the lack of pressure. But after a while, they wonder why they are paying for a course where they learn nothing. They might as well stay home and watch the soaps.

Conclusion

Echoes opening anecdote

Obviously, some college professors are excellent. They   7
are learned, hardworking, and imaginative; they enjoy their work and like being with students. On the whole, though, college professors are a strange lot. Despite their advanced degrees and their own exposure to many different kinds of teachers, they do not seem to understand how to relate to students. Rather than being hired as consultants to help others upgrade their teaching skills, college professors should themselves hire consultants to tell them what they are doing wrong and how they can improve. Who should these consultants be? That's easy: the people who know them best—their students.

COMMENTARY

Introduction and thesis.   After years of being graded by teachers, Gail took special pleasure in writing an essay that gave her a chance to evaluate her teachers—in this case, her college professors. Even the essay's title, "The Truth About College Teachers," implies that Gail is going to have fun knocking profs down from their ivory towers. To introduce her subject, she uses a timely news story. This brief anecdote leads directly to the essay's *thesis:* "[P]rofessors often exhibit bizarre behaviors, relating to students in ways that make it difficult for students to stay awake, or—if awake—to learn." Note that Gail's thesis isn't highly structured; it doesn't, for example, name the specific categories to be discussed. Still, her thesis suggests that the essay is going to *categorize* a range of teaching behaviors, using as a *principle of classification* the strange ways that college profs relate to students.

Purpose.   As with all good papers developed through division-classification, Gail's essay doesn't use classification as an end in itself. Gail uses classification because it helps her achieve a broader *purpose*. She wants to *convince* readers—without moralizing or abandoning her humorous tone—that such teaching styles inhibit learning. In other words, there's a serious underside to her essay. This additional layer of meaning is characteristic of satiric writing.

Categories and topic sentences.   The essay's body, consisting of five paragraphs, presents the three categories that make up Gail's analysis. According to Gail, college teachers can be categorized as the Knowledgeable One (paragraphs 2–4), the Leader of Intellectual Discussion (5), or the Buddy (6). Obviously, there are other ways professors might be classified. But given Gail's purpose, audience, tone, and point of view, her categories are appropriate; they are reasonably *complete, consistent,* and *mutually exclusive.* Note, too, that Gail uses *topic sentences* near the beginning of each category to help readers see which professorial type she's discussing.

Overall organization and paragraph structure.   Gail is able to shift smoothly and easily from one category to the next. How does she achieve such graceful transitions? Take a moment to reread the sentences that introduce her second and third categories (paragraphs 5 and 6). Look at the way each sentence's beginning (in italics here) links back to the preceding category or categories: "*Unlike the Knowledgeable One,* the 'Leader of Intellectual Discussion' seems to respect students"; and "[the Buddy]... *does not see himself as an imparter of knowledge or a leader of discussion* but as a pal...."

Gail is equally careful about providing an easy-to-follow structure within each section. She uses a *chronological sequence* to organize her three-paragraph discussion of the Knowledgeable One. The first paragraph deals with the beginning of the Knowledgeable One's lecture; the second, with the lecture itself; the third, with the end of the lecture. And the paragraphs' *topic sentences* clearly indicate this passage of time. Similarly, *transitions* are used in the paragraphs on the Leader of Intellectual Discussion and the Buddy to ensure a logical progression of points: "*Then,* about three weeks into the semester, it becomes clear that the Leader wants students to discover *his* version of the truth" (5) and "*At first,* students look forward to classes with the Buddy....But *after a while,* they wonder why they are paying for a course where they learn nothing" (6).

Tone.   The essay's unity can also be traced to Gail's skill in sustaining her satiric tone. Throughout the essay, Gail selects details that fit her gently mocking attitude. She depicts the Knowledgeable One lecturing from "yellowed-with-age notes..., oblivious to students' glazed eyes and stifled yawns," unwilling to wait for students who "run...through freezing sleet and howling winds to get to class on time." Then she presents another tongue-in-cheek description, this one focusing on the way the Leader of Intellectual Discussion conducts class: "Good point, good point....Well, yes, that's an interesting perspective. But don't you think that...?" Finally, with similar killing accuracy, Gail portrays the Buddy, democratically garbed in "jeans, sweatshirt, and scuffed sneakers."

Combining patterns of development.   Gail's satiric depiction of her three professorial types employs a number of techniques associated with *narrative* and *descriptive writing*: vigorous images, highly connotative language, and dialogue. *Definition, exemplification, causal analysis,* and *comparison-contrast* also come into play. Gail defines the characteristics of each type of professor; she provides numerous examples to support her categories; she explains the effects of the different teaching styles on students; and, in her description of the Leader of Intellectual Discussion, she contrasts the appearance of democracy with the dictatorial reality.

Unequal development of categories.   Although Gail's essay is unified, organized, and well-developed, you may have felt that the first category outweighs the other two. There is, of course, no need to balance the categories exactly. But Gail's extended treatment of the first category sets up an expectation that the others will be treated as fully. One way to remedy this problem would be to delete some material from the discussion of the Knowledgeable One. Gail might, for instance, omit the last five sentences in the third paragraph (about the professor's habit of addressing students as "Mr." or "Miss"). Such a change could be made without taking the bite out of her portrayal. Even better, Gail could simply switch the order of her sections, putting the portrait of the Knowledgeable One at the essay's end. Here, the extended discussion wouldn't seem out of proportion. Instead, the sections would appear in *emphatic order*, with the most detailed category saved for last.

Revising the first draft.   It's apparent that an essay as engaging as Gail's must have undergone a good deal of revising. That was in fact the case. Gail made many changes in the body of the essay, but it's particularly interesting to review what happened to the introduction as she revised the paper. Printed here is Gail's original introduction.

Original Version of the Introduction

Despite their high IQs, advanced degrees, and published papers, some college professors just don't know how to teach. Found in almost any department, in tenured and untenured positions, they prompt student apathy. They fail to convey ideas effectively and to challenge or inspire students. Students thus finish their courses having learned very little. Contrary to popular opinion, these professors' ineptitude is not simply a matter of delivering boring lectures or not caring about students. Many of them care a great deal. Their failure actually stems from their unrealistic perceptions of what a teacher should be. Specifically, they adopt teaching styles or roles that alienate students and undermine learning. Three of the most common ones are "The Knowledgeable One," "The Leader of Intellectual Discussion," and "The Buddy."

When Gail showed the first draft of the essay to her composition instructor, he laughed—and occasionally squirmed—as he read what she had prepared. He was enthusiastic about the paper but felt that there was a problem with the introduction's tone; it was too serious when compared to the playful, lightly satiric mood of the rest of the essay. When Gail reread the paragraph, she agreed, but she was uncertain about the best way to remedy the problem. After revising other sections of the essay, she decided to let the paper sit for a while before going back to rewrite the introduction.

In the meantime, Gail switched on the TV. The timing couldn't have been better: She tuned into a news story about several supposedly learned professors who had been fired from a consulting job because they had turned out to know so little about teaching. This was exactly the kind of item Gail needed to start her essay. Now she was able to prepare a completely new introduction, making it consistent in spirit with the rest of the paper.

With this stronger introduction and the rest of the essay well in hand, Gail was ready to write a conclusion. Now, as she worked on the concluding paragraph, she deliberately shaped it to recall the story about the fired consultants. By echoing the opening anecdote in her conclusion, Gail was able to end the paper with another poke at professors—a perfect way to close her clever and insightful essay.

Activities: Division-Classification

Prewriting Activities

1. Imagine you're writing two essays: One is a humorous paper outlining a *process* for impressing college instructors; the other is a serious essay examining the *causes* of the recent rise in volunteerism. What about the topics might you divide and/or classify?

2. Use group brainstorming to identify three principles of division for *one* of the topics in Set A below. Focusing on one of the principles, decide what your thesis might be if you were writing an essay. That done, use group brainstorming to identify three principles of classification that might provide the structure for *one* of the topics in Set B. Focusing on one of the principles, decide what your thesis might be if you were writing an essay.

Set A
- Rock music
- A shopping mall
- A good horror movie

Set B
- Why people get addicted to computers
- How fast-food restaurants affect family life
- Why long-term relationships break up

Revising Activities

3. Following is a scratch outline for an essay developed through division-classification. On what principle of division-classification is the essay based? What problem do you see in the way the principle is applied? How could the problem be remedied?

Thesis: The same experience often teaches opposite things to different people.

- What working as a fast-food cook teaches: Some learn responsibility; others learn to take a "quick and dirty" approach.
- What a negative experience teaches optimists: Some learn from their mistakes; others continue to maintain a positive outlook.
- What a difficult course teaches: Some learn to study hard; others learn to avoid demanding courses.
- What the breakup of a close relationship teaches: Some learn how to negotiate differences; others learn to avoid intimacy.

4. Following is a paragraph from the first draft of an essay urging that day care centers adopt play programs tailored to children's developmental needs. What principle of division-classification focuses the paragraph? Is the principle applied consistently and logically? Are parts/categories developed sufficiently? Revise the paragraph, eliminating any problems you discover and adding specific details where needed.

Within a few years, preschool children move from self-absorbed to interactive play. Babies and toddlers engage in solitary play. Although they sometimes prefer being near other children, they focus primarily on their own actions. This is very different from the highly interactive play of the elementary school years. Sometime in children's second year, solitary play is replaced by parallel play, during which children engage in similar activities near one another. However, they interact only occasionally. By age three, most children show at least some cooperative play, a form that involves interaction and cooperative role-taking. Such role-taking can be found in the "pretend" games that children play to explore adult relationships (games of "Mommy and Daddy") and anatomy (games of "Doctor"). Additional signs of youngsters' growing awareness of peers can be seen at about age four. At this age, many children begin showing a special devotion to one other child and may want to play only with that child. During this time, children also begin to take special delight in physical activities such as running and jumping, often going off by themselves to expend their abundant physical energy.

Ann McClintock

Ann McClintock (1946–) was educated at Temple University in Philadelphia and later earned an advanced degree from the University of Pennsylvania. Formerly director of occupational therapy at Ancora State Hospital in New Jersey, she has also worked as a freelance editor and writer. A frequent speaker before community groups, McClintock is especially interested in the effects of advertising on American life. The following selection, revised for this text, is part of a work in progress on the way propaganda techniques are used to sell products and political candidates.

For ideas on how this division-classification essay is organized, see Figure 6.2 on page 210.

Pre-Reading Journal Entry

How susceptible are you to ads and commercials? Do you consider yourself an easy target, or are you a "hard sell"? Have you purchased any products simply because you were won over by effective advertising strategies? What products have you not purchased because you deliberately didn't let yourself be swayed by advertisers' tactics? In your journal, reflect on these questions.

Propaganda Techniques in Today's Advertising

Americans, adults and children alike, are being seduced. They are being brainwashed. And few of us protest. Why? Because the seducers and the brainwashers are the advertisers we willingly invite into our homes. We are victims, content—even eager—to be victimized. We read advertisers' propaganda messages in newspapers and magazines; we watch their alluring images on television. We absorb their messages and images into our subconscious. We all do it—even those of us who claim to see through advertisers' tricks and therefore feel immune to advertising's charm. Advertisers lean heavily on propaganda to sell products, whether the "products" are a brand of toothpaste, a candidate for office, or a particular political viewpoint.

1

Propaganda is a systematic effort to influence people's opinions, to win them over to a certain view or side. Propaganda is not necessarily concerned with what is true or false, good or bad. Propagandists simply want people to believe the messages being sent. Often, propagandists will use outright lies or more subtle deceptions to sway people's opinions. In a propaganda war, any tactic is considered fair.

2

When we hear the word "propaganda," we usually think of a foreign menace: anti-American radio programs broadcast by a totalitarian regime or brainwashing tactics practiced on hostages. Although propaganda may seem

3

relevant only in the political arena, the concept can be applied fruitfully to the way products and ideas are sold in advertising. Indeed, the vast majority of us are targets in advertisers' propaganda war. Every day, we are bombarded with slogans, print and Internet pop-up ads, commercials, packaging claims, billboards, trademarks, logos, and designer brands—all forms of propaganda. One study reports that each of us, during an average day, is exposed to over *five hundred* advertising claims of various types. This saturation may even increase in the future since current trends include ads on movie screens, shopping carts, videocassettes, even public television.

What kind of propaganda techniques do advertisers use? There are seven basic types: 4

1. *Name Calling*   Name calling is a propaganda tactic in which negatively charged names are hurled against the opposing side or competitor. By using such names, propagandists try to arouse feelings of mistrust, fear, and hate in their audiences. For example, a political advertisement may label an opposing candidate a "loser," "fence-sitter," or "warmonger." Depending on the advertiser's target market, labels such as "a friend of big business" or "a dues-paying member of the party in power" can be the epithets that damage an opponent. Ads for products may also use name calling. An American manufacturer may refer, for instance, to a "foreign car" in its commercial— not an "imported" one. The label of foreignness will have unpleasant connotations in many people's minds. A childhood rhyme claims that "names can never hurt me," but name calling is an effective way to damage the opposition, whether it is another car maker or a congressional candidate.   5

2. *Glittering Generalities*   Using glittering generalities is the opposite of name calling. In this case, advertisers surround their products with attractive—and slippery—words and phrases. They use vague terms that are difficult to define and that may have different meanings to different people: *freedom, democratic, all-American, progressive, Christian,* and *justice.* Many such words have strong, affirmative overtones. This kind of language stirs positive feelings in people, feelings that may spill over to the product or idea being pitched. As with name calling, the emotional response may overwhelm logic. Target audiences accept the product without thinking very much about what the glittering generalities mean—or whether they even apply to the product. After all, how can anyone oppose "truth, justice, and the American way"?   6

The ads for politicians and political causes often use glittering generalities because such "buzz words" can influence votes. Election slogans include high-sounding but basically empty phrases like the following: 7

> "He cares about people." (That's nice, but is he a better candidate than his opponent?)

"Vote for progress." (Progress by *whose* standards?)
"They'll make this country great again." (What does "great" mean?
    Does "great" mean the same thing to others as it does to me?)
"Vote for the future." (What kind of future?)
"If you love America, vote for Phyllis Smith." (If I don't vote for Smith,
    does that mean I don't love America?)

Ads for consumer goods are also sprinkled with glittering generalities.   8
Product names, for instance, are supposed to evoke good feelings: *Luvs*
diapers, *Stayfree* feminine hygiene products, *Joy* liquid detergent, *Loving
Care* hair color, *Almost Home* cookies, *Yankee Doodle* pastries. Product slo-
gans lean heavily on vague but comforting phrases: Sears is "Good life.
Great price," General Electric "brings good things to life," and Dow
Chemical "lets you do great things." Chevrolet, we are told, is the "heart-
beat of America," and Chrysler boasts cars that are "built by Americans for
Americans."

3. *Transfer*   In transfer, advertisers try to improve the image of a prod-   9
uct by associating it with a symbol most people respect, like the American
flag or Uncle Sam. The advertisers hope that the prestige attached to the
symbol will carry over to the product. Many companies use transfer devices
to identify their products: Lincoln Insurance shows a profile of the president; Continental Insurance portrays a Revolutionary War minuteman;
Amtrak's logo is red, white, and blue; Liberty Mutual's corporate symbol is
the Statue of Liberty; Allstate's name is cradled by a pair of protective,
fatherly hands.

Corporations also use the transfer technique when they sponsor presti-   10
gious shows on radio and television. These shows function as symbols of dignity and class. Kraft Corporation, for instance, sponsored a "Leonard
Bernstein Conducts Beethoven" concert, while Gulf Oil is the sponsor of
National Geographic specials and Mobil supports public television's
Masterpiece Theater. In this way, corporations can reach an educated, influential audience and, perhaps, improve their public image by associating
themselves with quality programming.

Political ads, of course, practically wrap themselves in the flag. Ads for a   11
political candidate often show either the Washington Monument, a Fourth
of July parade, the Stars and Stripes, a bald eagle soaring over the mountains,
or a white-steepled church on the village green. The national anthem or
"America the Beautiful" may play softly in the background. Such appeals to
Americans' love of country can surround the candidate with an aura of patri-
otism and integrity.

4. *Testimonial*   The testimonial is one of advertisers' most-loved and most-   12
used propaganda techniques. Similar to the transfer device, the testimonial

capitalizes on the admiration people have for a celebrity to make the product shine more brightly—even though the celebrity is not an expert on the product being sold.

Print and television ads offer a nonstop parade of testimonials: here's William Shatner for Priceline.com; here's basketball star Michael Jordan eating Wheaties; a slew of well-known people (including pop star Madonna) advertise clothing from the Gap; and Jerry Seinfeld assures us he never goes anywhere without his American Express card. Testimonials can sell movies, too; newspaper ads for films often feature favorable comments by well-known reviewers. And, in recent years, testimonials have played an important role in pitching books; the backs of paperbacks frequently list complimentary blurbs by celebrities.

Political candidates, as well as their ad agencies, know the value of testimonials. Barbra Streisand lent her star appeal to the presidential campaign of Bill Clinton, while Arnold Schwarzenegger endorsed George H. W. Bush. Even controversial social issues are debated by celebrities. The nuclear-freeze debate, for instance, starred Paul Newman for the pro side and Charlton Heston for the con.

As illogical as testimonials sometimes are (Pepsi's Michael Jackson, for instance, is a health-food adherent who does not drink soft drinks), they are effective propaganda. We like the *person* so much that we like the *product* too.

5. *Plain Folks*   The plain folks approach says, in effect, "Buy me or vote for me. I'm just like you." Regular folks will surely like Bob Evans's Down on the Farm Country Sausage or good old-fashioned Countrytime Lemonade. Some ads emphasize the idea that "we're all in the same boat." We see people making long-distance calls for just the reasons we do—to put the baby on the phone to Grandma or to tell Mom we love her. And how do these folksy, warmhearted (usually saccharine) scenes affect us? They're supposed to make us feel that AT&T—the multinational corporate giant—has the same values we do. Similarly, we are introduced to the little people at Ford, the ordinary folks who work on the assembly line, not to bigwigs in their executive offices. What's the purpose of such an approach? To encourage us to buy a car built by these honest, hardworking "everyday Joes" who care about quality as much as we do.

Political advertisements make almost as much use of the "plain folks" appeal as they do of transfer devices. Candidates wear hard hats, farmers' caps, and assembly-line coveralls. They jog around the block and carry their own luggage through the airport. The idea is to convince voters that the candidates are average people, not the elite—not wealthy lawyers or executives but common citizens.

6. *Card Stacking* When people say that "the cards were stacked against   18
me," they mean that they were never given a fair chance. Applied to propaganda, card stacking means that one side may suppress or distort
evidence, tell half-truths, oversimplify the facts, or set up a "straw man"—
a false target—to divert attention from the issue at hand. Card stacking is
a difficult form of propaganda both to detect and to combat. When a candidate claims that an opponent has "changed his mind five times on this
important issue," we tend to accept the claim without investigating
whether the candidate had good reasons for changing his mind. Many people are simply swayed by the distorted claim that the candidate is "waf-
fling" on the issue.

Advertisers often stack the cards in favor of the products they are pushing.   19
They may, for instance, use what are called "weasel words." These are small
words that usually slip right past us, but that make the difference between reality and illusion. The weasel words are underlined in the following claims:

> "Helps control dandruff symptoms." (The audience usually interprets
> this as *stops* dandruff.)
> "Most dentists surveyed recommend sugarless gum for their patients who
> chew gum." (We hear the "most dentists" and "for their patients,"
> but we don't think about how many were surveyed or whether
> the dentists first recommended that the patients not chew gum
> at all.)
> "Sticker price $1,000 lower than most comparable cars." (How many is
> "most"? What car does the advertiser consider "comparable"?)

Advertisers also use a card stacking trick when they make an unfin-   20
ished claim. For example, they will say that their product has "twice as
much pain reliever." We are left with a favorable impression. We don't
usually ask, "Twice as much pain reliever as what?" Or advertisers may
make extremely vague claims that sound alluring but have no substance:
Toyota's "Oh, what a feeling!"; Vantage cigarettes' "The taste of success"; "The spirit of Marlboro"; Coke's "the real thing." Another way to
stack the cards in favor of a certain product is to use scientific-sounding
claims that are not supported by sound research. When Ford claimed that
its LTD model was "400% quieter," many people assumed that the LTD
must be quieter than all other cars. When taken to court, however, Ford
admitted that the phrase referred to the difference between the noise level
inside and outside the LTD. Other scientific-sounding claims use mysterious ingredients that are never explained as selling points: "Retsyn,"
"special whitening agents," "the ingredient doctors recommend."

7. *Bandwagon* In the bandwagon technique, advertisers pressure,   21
"Everyone's doing it. Why don't you?" This kind of propaganda often

succeeds because many people have a deep desire not to be different. Political ads tell us to vote for the "winning candidate." Advertisers know we tend to feel comfortable doing what others do; we want to be on the winning team. Or ads show a series of people proclaiming, "I'm voting for the Senator. I don't know why anyone wouldn't." Again, the audience feels under pressure to conform.

In the marketplace, the bandwagon approach lures buyers. Ads tell us   22
that "nobody doesn't like Sara Lee" (the message is that you must be weird if you don't). They tell us that "most people prefer Brand X two to one over other leading brands" (to be like the majority, we should buy Brand X). If we don't drink Pepsi, we're left out of "the Pepsi generation." To take part in "America's favorite health kick," the National Dairy Council asks us, "Got Milk?" And Honda motorcycle ads, praising the virtues of being a follower, tell us, "Follow the leader. He's on a Honda."

Why do these propaganda techniques work? Why do so many of us   23
buy the products, viewpoints, and candidates urged on us by propaganda messages? They work because they appeal to our emotions, not to our minds. Often, in fact, they capitalize on our prejudices and biases. For example, if we are convinced that environmentalists are radicals who want to destroy America's record of industrial growth and progress, then we will applaud the candidate who refers to them as "treehuggers." Clear thinking requires hard work: analyzing a claim, researching the facts, examining both sides of an issue, using logic to see the flaws in an argument. Many of us would rather let the propagandists do our thinking for us.

Because propaganda is so effective, it is important to detect it and under-   24
stand how it is used. We may conclude, after close examination, that some propaganda sends a truthful, worthwhile message. Some advertising, for instance, urges us not to drive drunk, to become volunteers, to contribute to charity. Even so, we must be aware that propaganda is being used. Otherwise, we have consented to handing over to others our independence of thought and action.

Questions for Close Reading

1. What is the selection's thesis? Locate the sentence(s) in which McClintock states her main idea. If she doesn't state the thesis explicitly, express it in your own words.
2. What is *propaganda*? What mistaken associations do we have with this term?
3. What are "weasel words"? How do they trick listeners?
4. Why does McClintock believe we should know about propaganda techniques?
5. Refer to your dictionary as needed to define the following words used in the selection: *seduced* (paragraph 1), *warmonger* (5), and *elite* (17).

FIGURE 6.2

Essay Structure Diagram: "Propaganda Techniques in Today's Advertising" by Ann McClintock

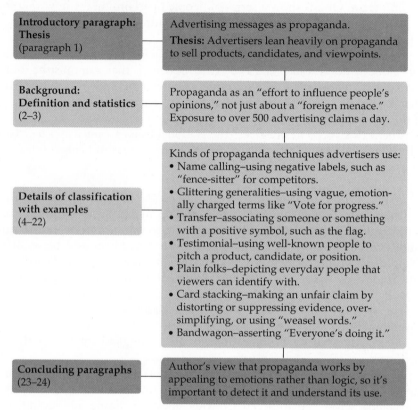

Introductory paragraph: Thesis (paragraph 1)	Advertising messages as propaganda. **Thesis:** Advertisers lean heavily on propaganda to sell products, candidates, and viewpoints.
Background: Definition and statistics (2–3)	Propaganda as an "effort to influence people's opinions," not just about a "foreign menace." Exposure to over 500 advertising claims a day.
Details of classification with examples (4–22)	Kinds of propaganda techniques advertisers use: • Name calling–using negative labels, such as "fence-sitter" for competitors. • Glittering generalities–using vague, emotionally charged terms like "Vote for progress." • Transfer–associating someone or something with a positive symbol, such as the flag. • Testimonial–using well-known people to pitch a product, candidate, or position. • Plain folks–depicting everyday people that viewers can identify with. • Card stacking–making an unfair claim by distorting or suppressing evidence, over-simplifying, or using "weasel words." • Bandwagon–asserting "Everyone's doing it."
Concluding paragraphs (23–24)	Author's view that propaganda works by appealing to emotions rather than logic, so it's important to detect it and understand its use.

Questions About the Writer's Craft

1. **The pattern and other patterns.** Before explaining the categories into which propaganda techniques can be grouped, McClintock provides a *definition* of propaganda. Is the definition purely informative, or does it have a larger objective? If you think the latter, what is the definition's broader purpose?

2. In her introduction, McClintock uses loaded words such as *seduced* and *brainwashed*. What effect do these words have on the reader?

3. Locate places in the essay where McClintock uses questions. Which are rhetorical and which are genuine queries?

4. What kind of conclusion does McClintock provide for the essay?

Writing Assignments Using Division-Classification as a Pattern of Development

1. McClintock cautions us to be sensitive to propaganda in advertising. Young children, however, aren't capable of this kind of awareness. With pen or pencil in hand, watch some commercials aimed at children, such as those for toys, cereals, and fast food. Then analyze the use of propaganda techniques in these commercials. Using division-classification, write an essay describing the main propaganda techniques you observed. Support your analysis with examples drawn from the commercials. Remember to provide a thesis that indicates your opinion of the advertising techniques. For additional insight into this issue, read Ellen Goodman's "Family Counterculture" (page 7) and Kay S. Hymowitz's "Tweens: Ten Going On Sixteen" (page 163).

2. Like advertising techniques, television shows can be classified. Avoiding the obvious system of classifying according to game shows, detective shows, and situation comedies, come up with your own original division-classification principle. Possibilities include how family life is depicted, the way work is presented, how male-female relationships are portrayed. Using one such principle, write an essay in which you categorize popular TV shows into three types. Refer to specific shows to support your classification system. Your attitude toward the shows being discussed should be made clear.

Writing Assignments Combining Patterns of Development

3. McClintock says that card stacking "distort[s] evidence, tell[s] half-truths, oversimpli[fies] the facts" (paragraph 18). Focusing on an extended *example* such as an editorial, a political campaign, a print ad, or a television commercial, analyze the extent to which card stacking is used as a *persuasive* strategy. Reading David Shipley's "Talk About Editing" (page 245) will deepen your understanding of the difficulty of expressing the "truth" in writing.

4. To increase further your sensitivity to the moral dimensions of propaganda, write a proposal outlining an ad campaign for a real or imaginary product or elected official. The introduction to your proposal should identify who or what is to be promoted, and the thesis or plan of development should indicate the specific propaganda techniques you suggest. In the paper's supporting paragraphs, explain the *process* by which these techniques would be used to promote your product or candidate and what their desired *effects* would be.

Writing Assignment Using a Journal Entry as a Starting Point

5. Write an essay showing that, on the whole, you are fairly susceptible to *or* are fairly immune to advertising ploys. Drawing upon your pre-reading journal entry, illustrate your position with lively details of advertising campaigns that won you over— or that failed to sway you. Use some of McClintock's terminology when describing advertisers' techniques. Your essay may be serious or playful.

David Brooks

David Brooks is a syndicated columnist whose work appears in newspapers through-out the nation. Born in 1961, Brooks began his journalism career as a police reporter for the City News Bureau in Chicago and then spent nine years at *The Wall Street Journal* as a critic, foreign correspondent, and op-ed page editor. In 1995 he joined *The Weekly Standard* at its inception, and in 2003 he began to write a regular column for *The New York Times*. Brooks is interested in cultural as well as political issues. He often is on National Public Radio, including *The Diane Rehm Show,* as an analyst and is a commentator on *The NewsHour with Jim Lehrer* (Public Broadcasting Service). He has written two books, *Bobos in Paradise: The New Upper Class and How They Got There* (2000) and *On Paradise Drive: How We Live Now (and Always Have) in the Future Tense* (2004). He is editor of the anthology *Backward and Upward: The New Conservative Writing.* This column was published in *The New York Times* on November 13, 2005.

Pre-Reading Journal Entry

When you are a student, it's natural to think of success and failure simply in terms of grades. However, academic accomplishment is not the only measure of success in one's life. What are your own strengths and successes in life, beyond what you may have achieved in school? Who or what has inspired you to undertake each of these pursuits? Take a few minutes to respond to these questions in your journal.

Psst! "Human Capital"

Help! I'm turning into the "plastics" guy from *The Graduate.*[1] I'm pulling people aside at parties and whispering that if they want to understand the future, it's just two words: "Human Capital." 1

If we want to keep up with the Chinese and the Indians, we've got to develop our Human Capital. If we want to remain a just, fluid society: Human Capital. If we want to head off underclass riots: Human Capital. 2

As people drift away from me at these parties by pretending to recognize long-lost friends across the room, I'm convinced that they don't really understand what human capital is. 3

Most people think of human capital the way economists and policy mak-ers do—as the skills and knowledge people need to get jobs and thrive in a modern economy. When President [George W.] Bush proposed his big 4

[1]Refers to an oft-cited scene in the 1967 film, *The Graduate.* The main character, Benjamin Braddock, has just graduated college and feels adrift about the future. At a family party, the character of Mr. McGuire cryptically "tips off" Benjamin about the plastics industry. He says, "There's a great future in plastics. Think about it. Will you think about it?...Shh! Enough said." (editors' note).

education reform, he insisted on tests to measure skills and knowledge. When commissions issue reports, they call for longer school years, revamped curriculums and more funds so teachers can transmit skills and knowledge.

But skills and knowledge—the stuff you can measure with tests—is only the most superficial component of human capital. U.S. education reforms have generally failed because they try to improve the skills of students without addressing the underlying components of human capital. 5

These underlying components are hard to measure and uncomfortable to talk about, but they are the foundation of everything that follows. 6

There's cultural capital: the habits, assumptions, emotional dispositions and linguistic capacities we unconsciously pick up from families, neighbors and ethnic groups—usually by age 3. In a classic study, James S. Coleman found that what happens in the family shapes a child's educational achievement more than what happens in school. In more recent research, James Heckman and Pedro Carneiro found that "most of the gaps in college attendance and delay are determined by early family factors." 7

There's social capital: the knowledge of how to behave in groups and within institutions. This can mean, for example, knowing what to do if your community college loses your transcript. Or it can mean knowing the basic rules of politeness. The University of North Carolina now offers seminars to poorer students so they'll know how to behave in restaurants. 8

There's moral capital: the ability to be trustworthy. Students who drop out of high school, but take the G.E.D. exam, tend to be smarter than high school dropouts. But their lifetime wages tend to be no higher than they are for those with no high school diplomas. That's because many people who pass the G.E.D. are less organized and less dependable than their less educated peers—as employers soon discover. Brains and skills don't matter if you don't show up on time. 9

There's cognitive capital. This can mean pure, inherited brainpower. But important cognitive skills are not measured by IQ tests and are not fixed. Some people know how to evaluate themselves and their abilities, while others with higher IQ's are clueless. Some low-IQ people can sense what others are feeling, while brainier peers cannot. Such skills can be improved over a lifetime. 10

Then there's aspirational capital: the fire-in-the-belly ambition to achieve. In his book *The Millionaire Mind,* Thomas J. Stanley reports that the average millionaire had a B-minus collegiate G.P.A.—not very good. But millionaires often had this experience: People told them they were too stupid to achieve something, so they set out to prove the naysayers wrong. 11

Over the past quarter-century, researchers have done a lot of work trying to understand the different parts of human capital. Their work has been almost completely ignored by policy makers, who continue to treat human capital as just skills and knowledge. The result? A series of expensive policy failures. 12

We now spend more per capita on education than just about any other 13
country on earth, and the results are mediocre. No Child Left Behind treats
students as skill-acquiring cogs in an economic wheel, and the results have
been disappointing. We pour money into Title 1 and Head Start, but the
long-term gains are insignificant.

These programs are not designed for the way people really are. The only 14
things that work are local, human-to-human immersions that transform the
students down to their very beings. Extraordinary schools, which create
intense cultures of achievement, work. Extraordinary teachers, who inspire
students to transform their lives, work. The programs that work touch all the
components of human capital.

There's a great future in Human Capital, buddy. Enough said. 15

Questions for Close Reading

1. What is the selection's thesis? Locate the sentence(s) in which Brooks states
   his main idea. If he doesn't state his thesis explicitly, express it in your own
   words.
2. According to Brooks, why do policies that focus on teaching children skills and
   knowledge ultimately fail to develop human capital? What policies does he use as
   examples of such failure?
3. In Brooks's view, what role does the family play in the development of human
   capital?
4. What type of human capital do many millionaires possess, and how did they
   acquire it?
5. Refer to your dictionary as needed to define the following words used in the selection: *capital* (paragraph 1), *revamped* (4), *cognitive* (10), *aspirational* (11),
   naysayers (11), *per capita* (13), and *immersions* (14).

Questions About the Writer's Craft

1. Brooks opens this essay by comparing himself to a character in the 1967 movie
   The Graduate. What are the benefits and risks of using such a reference to frame
   the contents of an essay? In your opinion, is this a successful opening? Why or
   why not?
2. **The pattern.** How does Brooks organize his explanation of what human capital
   really consists of? What cues guide the reader in following Brooks's discussion?
3. **Other patterns.** In paragraphs 7 through 11, Brooks develops his ideas about
   the components of human capital. What patterns does he use in each of these
   paragraphs?
4. This essay was published as a newspaper op-ed column, a type of writing that is
   relatively short—about 750 words. How does the limited length of the piece
   affect the development of Brooks's ideas and evidence? If the piece were longer,
   how could Brooks strengthen its argument?

Writing Assignments Using Division-Classification as a Pattern of Development

1. Choose one of the elements of human capital that Brooks describes, and write an essay in which you analyze it further into its component parts. For example, if you choose cognitive capital, you can write about specific cognitive skills such as memorizing, learning, problem solving, and creativity.
2. According to economists, capital is any human-made resource used to produce goods and services. For example, capital includes buildings, factories, machinery, equipment, parts, tools, roads, and railroads. Do some research on the concept of capital as used by economists, and write an essay explaining how economists categorize various types of capital, including the human capital Brooks discusses in his essay.

Writing Assignments Combining Patterns of Development

3. Brooks indicates that the results of the government programs No Child Left Behind, Title I, and Head Start fail to improve human capital. Select one of these programs, and do some research on it at the library or on the Internet. Write an essay that *explains* how aspects of the program are designed to solve specific problems. *Compare* and *contrast* the goals of the program with its actual *effects*.
4. Brooks's concept of moral capital is closely tied to the moral values that society holds important and that children learn from their families and others with whom they interact. Write an essay in which you *narrate* the story of a moral issue you have faced, *comparing* and *contrasting* the choices you had. Explain the *process* you went through to resolve the problem.

Writing Assignment Using a Journal Entry as a Starting Point

5. Review your pre-reading journal entry about your successes and strengths beyond what you may have achieved in school. Select the two or three most significant ones, and write an essay in which you divide and classify these achievements. Are these achievements athletic, artistic, or service- or family-oriented—or do they belong to some other category? As you write about each achievement, consider who or what has *caused* or inspired you to strive for that accomplishment. To see how two writers address the issue of how children's character can be influenced, read Ellen Goodman's "Family Counterculture" (page 7) and Gordon Parks's "Flavio's Home" (page 95).

Marion Winik

Marion Winik was born in New York City in 1958 and grew up in New Jersey. She attended Brown University as an undergraduate and received a master of fine arts degree from Brooklyn College. Winik has written many essays that have appeared in popular magazines like *Parenting, Redbook, Glamour,* and the *Utne Reader.* She has published several memoirs, essay collections, and advice books, including *Telling* (1994), in which this essay appeared; *First Comes Love* (1996); *Rules for the Unruly: Living an Unconventional Life* (2001); and the *Glen Rock Book of the Dead* (2008).

Pre-Reading Journal Entry

As you grow older, your relationships with your friends change. Think back on friends from each stage of your life, from before you entered kindergarten until now. In your journal, list one friend from each stage of your life, and describe a key element of your friendship with that person.

What Are Friends For?

I was thinking about how everybody can't be everything to each other, but some people can be something to each other, thank God, from the ones whose shoulder you cry on to the ones whose half-slips you borrow to the nameless ones you chat with in the grocery line. 1

Buddies, for example, are the workhorses of the friendship world, the people out there on the front lines, defending you from loneliness and boredom. They call you up, they listen to your complaints, they celebrate your successes and curse your misfortunes, and you do the same for them in return. They hold out through innumerable crises before concluding that the person you're dating is no good, and even then understand if you ignore their good counsel. They accompany you to a movie with subtitles or to see the diving pig at Aquarena Springs. They feed your cat when you are out of town and pick you up from the airport when you get back. They come over to help you decide what to wear on a date. Even if it is with that creep. 2

What about family members? Most of them are people you just got stuck with, and though you love them, you may not have very much in common. But there is that rare exception, the Relative Friend. It is your cousin, your brother, maybe even your aunt. The two of you share the same views of the other family members. Meg never should have divorced Martin. He was the best thing that ever happened to her. You can confirm each other's memories of things that happened a long time ago. Don't you remember when Uncle Hank and Daddy had that awful fight in the middle of Thanksgiving dinner? Grandma always hated Grandpa's stamp collection; she probably left the window open during the hurricane on purpose. 3

While so many family relationships are tinged with guilt and obligation,   4
a relationship with a Relative Friend is relatively worry-free. You don't even
have to hide your vices from this delightful person. When you slip out Aunt
Joan's back door for a cigarette, she is already there.

Then there is that special guy at work. Like all the other people at the   5
job site, at first he's just part of the scenery. But gradually he starts to stand
out from the crowd. Your friendship is cemented by jokes about co-workers
and thoughtful favors around the office. Did you see Ryan's hair? Want half
my bagel? Soon you know the names of his turtles, what he did last Friday
night, exactly which model CD player he wants for his birthday. His handwriting is as familiar to you as your own.

Though you invite each other to parties, you somehow don't quite fit   6
into each other's outside lives. For this reason, the friendship may not survive a job change. Company gossip, once an infallible source of entertainment, soon awkwardly accentuates the distance between you. But wait. Like
School Friends, Work Friends share certain memories which acquire a nos-
talgic glow after about a decade.

A Faraway Friend is someone you grew up with or went to school with   7
or lived in the same town as until one of you moved away. Without a Faraway
Friend, you would never get any mail addressed in handwriting. A Faraway
Friend calls late at night, invites you to her wedding, always says she is coming to visit but rarely shows up. An actual visit from a Faraway Friend is a
cause for celebration and binges of all kinds. Cigarettes, Chips Ahoy, bottles
of tequila.

Faraway Friends go through phases of intense communication, then   8
may be out of touch for many months. Either way, the connection is
always there. A conversation with your Faraway Friend always helps to put
your life in perspective: when you feel you've hit a dead end, come to a
confusing fork in the road, or gotten lost in some crackerbox subdivision
of your life, the advice of the Faraway Friend—who has the big picture,
who is so well acquainted with the route that brought you to this place—
is indispensable.

Another useful function of the Faraway Friend is to help you remember   9
things from a long time ago, like the name of your seventh-grade history
teacher, what was in that really good stir-fry, or exactly what happened that
night on the boat with the guys from Florida.

Ah, the Former Friend. A sad thing. At best a wistful memory, at worst   10
a dangerous enemy who is in possession of many of your deepest secrets.
But what was it that drove you apart? A misunderstanding, a betrayed confidence, an unrepaid loan, an ill-conceived flirtation. A poor choice of
spouse can do in a friendship just like that. Going into business together can
be a serious mistake. Time, money, distance, cult religions: all noted friendship killers. . . .

And lest we forget, there are the Friends You Love to Hate. They call at   11
inopportune times. They say stupid things. They butt in, they boss you
around, they embarrass you in public. They invite themselves over. They take
advantage. You've done the best you can, but they need professional help.
On top of all this, they love you to death and are convinced they're your best
friend on the planet.

So why do you continue to be involved with these people? Why do you   12
tolerate them? On the contrary, the real question is, What would you do
without them? Without Friends You Love to Hate, there would be nothing
to talk about with your other friends. Their problems and their irritating
stunts provide a reliable source of conversation for everyone they know.
What's more, Friends You Love to Hate make you feel good about yourself,
since you are obviously in so much better shape than they are. No matter
what these people do, you will never get rid of them. As much as they need
you, you need them too.

At the other end of the spectrum are Hero Friends. These people are bet-   13
ter than the rest of us, that's all there is to it. Their career is something you
wanted to be when you grew up—painter, forest ranger, tireless doer of good.
They have beautiful homes filled with special handmade things presented to
them by villagers in the remote areas they have visited in their extensive travels.
Yet they are modest. They never gossip. They are always helping others, especially those who have suffered a death in the family or an illness. You would
think people like this would just make you sick, but somehow they don't.

A New Friend is a tonic unlike any other. Say you meet her at a party.   14
In your bowling league. At a Japanese conversation class, perhaps. Wherever,
whenever, there's that spark of recognition. The first time you talk, you can't
believe how much you have in common. Suddenly, your life story is interesting again, your insights fresh, your opinion valued. Your various short-comings
are as yet completely invisible.

It's almost like falling in love.   15

Questions for Close Reading

1. What is the selection's thesis? Locate the sentence(s) in which Winik states her
   main idea. If she doesn't state her thesis explicitly, express it in your own words.
2. Into how many types does Winik classify her friends? List each of them. Which
   types does Winik seem to value the most?
3. According to Winik, what makes a "Relative Friend" different from most family
   members?
4. Which of Winik's types of friends are characterized more by negative than positive
   qualities?
5. Refer to your dictionary as needed to define the following words used in the selection: *innumerable* (paragraph 2), *tinged* (4), *infallible* (6), *accentuates* (6), *wistful*
   (10), *inopportune* (11), and *tonic* (14).

Questions About the Writer's Craft

1. **The pattern.** What principle does Winik use to classify friends? How does she make her categories of friends stand out sharply?
2. **Other patterns.** What other patterns, besides division-classification, does Winik use in this essay? Cite examples of at least two other patterns.
3. What is the tone of this essay? What contributes to the tone?
4. Is Winik's title effective? Does the essay fulfill the expectations raised by the title?

Writing Assignments Using Division-Classification as a Pattern of Development

1. Choose two types of friends mentioned in the Winik essay and add a third category based on your own experiences. Then write an essay in which you explain the three categories. Use examples from your own life and those of people you know to support your points.
2. Winik chose to classify her friends, but there are many other types of people that can be classified. For example, you can classify types of coworkers, bosses, relatives, neighbors, students, or teachers. Choose one of these categories, or another such subject, and write an essay in which you further classify the members of this group. Decide whether your primary purpose is to inform or to entertain, and then choose a principle of classification that will fit your purpose. To get another perspective on a group of people, read Ann Hulbert's "Beyond the Pleasure Principle" (page 350).

Writing Assignments Combining Patterns of Development

3. Since this essay was published in 1994, a new type of friend has emerged—the Facebook or MySpace friend. Write an essay in which you *define* what it means to be a friend in an online social network. Take a position on whether online "friendship" is a positive or negative social development, and *argue* your case.
4. In her essay, Winik develops many categories for her *actual* friends. Think of qualities you might want in an *ideal* friend. *Describe* these qualities, and give *examples* of how an ideal friend would act in various situations. *Compare and contrast* how the ideal of friendship might differ from the reality.

Writing Assignment Using a Journal Entry as a Starting Point

5. Review your pre-reading journal entry in which you listed the friends you had at each stage of your life. Instead of focusing on the friends themselves, think about how they functioned at each stage of your life. For example, before you entered school, a friend might simply have been a playmate, and as you got older, a friend might have shared some of your interests. Write an essay in which you describe the different functions your friends have played at different times in your life.

Additional Writing Topics

DIVISION-CLASSIFICATION

General Assignments

Choose one of the following subjects and write an essay developed wholly or in part through division-classification. Start by determining the purpose of the essay. Do you want to inform, compare and contrast, or persuade? Apply a single, significant principle of division or classification to your subject. Don't switch the principle midway through your analysis. Also, be sure that the types or categories you create are as complete and mutually exclusive as possible.

Division

1. A shopping mall
2. A video and/or sound system
3. A fruit, such as a pineapple, an orange, or a banana
4. A tax dollar
5. A particular kind of team
6. A word-processing system
7. A human hand
8. A meal
9. A meeting
10. A favorite poem, story, or play
11. A favorite restaurant
12. A school library
13. A basement
14. A playground, gym, or other recreational area
15. A church service
16. A wedding or funeral
17. An eventful week in your life
18. A college campus
19. A television show or movie
20. A homecoming or other special weekend

Classification

1. People in a waiting room
2. Holidays
3. Closets
4. Roommates
5. Salad bars
6. Divorces
7. Beds
8. Students in a class
9. Shoes

10. Summer movies
11. Teachers
12. Neighbors
13. College courses
14. Bosses
15. Computer/Internet users
16. Mothers or fathers
17. Commercials
18. Vacations
19. Trash
20. Relatives

Assignments with a Specific Purpose, Audience, and Point of View

On Campus

1. You're a dorm counselor. During orientation week, you'll be talking to students on your floor about the different kinds of problems they may have with roommates. Write your talk, describing each kind of problem and explaining how to cope with it.
2. As your college newspaper's TV critic, you plan to write a review of the fall shows, most of which—in your opinion—lack originality. To show how stereotypical the programs are, select one type (for example, situation comedies or crime dramas). Then use a specific division-classification principle to illustrate that the same stale formulas are trotted out from show to show.
3. Asked to write an editorial for the campus paper, you decide to do a half-serious piece on taking "mental health" days off from classes. Structure your essay around three kinds of occasions when "playing hooky" is essential for maintaining sanity.

At Home or in the Community

4. Your favorite magazine runs an editorial asking readers to send in what they think are the main challenges facing their particular gender group. Write a letter to the editor in which you identify at least three categories of problems that your sex faces. Be sure to provide lively, specific examples to illustrate each category. In your letter, you may adopt a serious or lighthearted tone, depending on your overall subject matter.

On the Job

5. As a driving instructor, you decide to prepare a lecture on the types of drivers that your students are likely to encounter on the road. In your lecture, categorize drivers according to a specific principle and show the behaviors of each type.
6. A seasoned camp counselor, you've been asked to prepare, for new counselors, an informational sheet on children's emotional needs. Categorizing those needs into types, explain what counselors can do to nurture youngsters emotionally.

PROCESS ANALYSIS

WHAT IS PROCESS ANALYSIS?

Perhaps you've noticed the dogged determination of small children when they learn how to do something new. Whether trying to tie their shoelaces or tell time, little children struggle along, creating knotted tangles, confusing the hour with the minute hand. But they don't give up. Mastering such basic skills makes them feel less dependent on the adults of the world—all of whom seem to know how to do everything. Actually, none of us is born knowing how to do very much. We spend a good deal of our lives learning—everything from speaking our first word to balancing our first bank statement. Indeed, the milestones in our lives are often linked to the processes we have mastered: how to cross the street alone; how to drive a car; how to make a speech without being paralyzed by fear.

Process analysis, a technique that explains the steps or sequence involved in doing something, satisfies our need to learn as well as our curiosity about how the world works. All the self-help books continually flooding the market (*Managing Stress, How to Make a Million in Real Estate, Ten Days to a Perfect Body*) are examples of process analysis. The instructions on the federal tax form and the recipes in a cookbook are also process analyses. Several television shows also capitalize on our desire to learn how things happen: *Nature* shows how animals and ecosystems survive, and *CSI: Crime Scene Investigation* details how investigators gather evidence and use crime lab techniques to catch criminals. Process analysis can be more than merely interesting or entertaining, though; it can be of critical importance. Consider a waiter hurriedly skimming the "Choking Aid" instructions posted on a restaurant wall or an air-traffic

222

controller following emergency procedures in an effort to prevent a midair collision. In these last examples, the consequences could be fatal if the process analyses were slipshod, inaccurate, or confusing.

Undoubtedly, all of us have experienced less dramatic effects of poorly written process analyses. Perhaps you've tried to assemble a bicycle and spent hours sorting through a stack of parts, only to end up with one or two extra pieces never mentioned in the instructions. Or maybe you were baffled when putting up a set of wall shelves because the instructions used unfamiliar terms such as *mitered cleat, wing nut,* and *dowel pin.* No wonder many people stay clear of anything that actually admits "assembly required."

HOW PROCESS ANALYSIS FITS YOUR PURPOSE AND AUDIENCE

You will use process analysis in two types of writing situations: (1) when you want to give step-by-step instructions to readers showing how they can do something, or (2) when you want readers to understand how something happens even though they won't actually follow the steps outlined. The first kind of process analysis is *directional;* the second is *informational.*

When you look at the cooking instructions on a package of frozen vegetables or follow guidelines for completing a job application, you're reading directional process analysis. A serious essay explaining how to select a college and a humorous essay telling readers how to get on the good side of a professor are also examples of directional process analysis. Using a variety of tones, informational process analyses can range over equally diverse subjects; they can describe mechanical, scientific, historical, sociological, artistic, or psychological processes: for example, how the core of a nuclear reactor melts down; how television became so important in political campaigns; how abstract painters use color; how to survive a blind date.

Process analysis, both directional and informational, is often appropriate in *problem-solving situations.* In such cases, you say, "Here's the problem and here's what should be done to solve the problem." Indeed, college assignments frequently take the form of problem-solving process analyses. Consider these examples:

> Community officials have been accused of mismanaging recent unrest over the public housing ordinance. Describe the steps the officials took, indicating why you think their strategy was unwise. Then explain how you think the situation should have been handled.

> Over the years, there have been many reports citing the abuse of small children in day-care centers. What can parents do to guard against the mistreatment of their children?

Because many colleges have changed the eligibility requirements for financial aid, fewer students can depend on loans or scholarships. How can students cope with the rising costs of higher education?

Note that the first assignment asks students to explain what's wrong with the current approach before they present their own step-by-step solution. Problem-solving process analyses are often organized in this way. You may also have noted that none of the assignments explicitly requires an essay response using process analysis. However, the wording of the assignments—"*Describe* the *steps*," "*What* can parents *do*," "*How* can students *cope*,"—suggests that process analysis would be an appropriate strategy for developing the responses.

Assignments don't always signal the use of process analysis so clearly. But during the prewriting stage, you'll often realize that you can best achieve your purpose by developing the essay using process analysis. Sometimes process analysis will be the primary strategy for organizing an essay; other times it will help make a point in an essay organized according to another pattern of development. Let's look at process analysis as a supporting strategy.

Assume that you're writing a *causal analysis* examining the impact of television commercials on people's buying behavior. To help readers see that commercials create a need where none existed before, you might describe the various stages of an advertising campaign to pitch a new, completely frivolous product. In an essay *defining* a good boss, you could convey the point that effective managers must be skilled at settling disputes by explaining the steps your boss took to resolve a heated disagreement between two employees. If you write an *argumentation-persuasion* paper urging the funding of programs to ease the plight of the homeless, to dramatize the tragedy of these people's lives, you could explain how the typical street person goes about the desperate jobs of finding a place to sleep and getting food to eat.

At this point, you have a good sense of the way writers use process analysis to achieve their purpose and to connect with their readers. Now take a moment to look closely at the photograph of the brand-new mall at the beginning of this chapter. Imagine you're writing an article, accompanied by the photo, for a local newspaper. Your purpose is to suggest to local store owners, who are losing business to the new mall, ways they might attract more customers to the area's downtown shopping district. Jot down some ideas you might include in a *process analysis* explaining the steps the business owners should take.

SUGGESTIONS FOR USING PROCESS ANALYSIS IN AN ESSAY

The suggestions here and in Figure 7.1 (page 226) will be helpful whether you use process analysis as a dominant or a supportive pattern of development.

1. Identify the desired outcome of the process analysis.   Many papers developed primarily through process analysis have a clear-cut purpose—simply to *inform* readers as objectively as possible about a process: "Here's a way of making french fries at home that will surpass the best served in your favorite fast-food restaurant." But a process analysis essay may also have a *persuasive* edge, with the writer advocating a point of view about the process, perhaps even urging a course of action: "If you don't want your arguments to deteriorate into ugly battles, you should follow a series of foolproof steps for having disagreements that leave friendships intact." Before starting to write, you need to decide if the essay is to be purely factual or if it will include this kind of persuasive dimension.

2. Formulate a thesis that clarifies your attitude toward the process.   Like the thesis in any other paper, the thesis in a process analysis should do more than announce your subject. ("Here's how the college's work-study program operates.") It should also state or imply your attitude toward the process: "Enrolling in the college's work-study program has become unnecessarily complicated. The procedure could be simplified if the college adopted the helpful guidelines prepared by the Student Senate."

3. Keep your audience in mind.   Only when you gauge how much your readers already know (or don't know) about the process can you determine how much explanation you'll have to provide. Suppose you've been asked to write an article informing students of the best way to use the university computer center. The article will be published in a newsletter for computer science majors. You would seriously misjudge your audience—and probably put them to sleep—if you explained in detail how to transfer material from disk to disk or how to delete information from a file. However, an article on the same topic prepared for a general audience—your composition class, for instance—might require such detailed instructions.

To determine how much explanation is needed, put yourself in your readers' shoes. Don't assume readers will know something just because you do. Ask questions such as these about your audience: "Will my readers need some background about the process before I describe it in depth?" "Are there technical terms I should define?" "If my essay is directional, should I specify near the beginning the ingredients, materials, and equipment needed to perform the process?" (For more help in analyzing your audience, see the checklist on page 19.)

FIGURE 7.1

Development Diagram: Writing a Process Analysis Essay

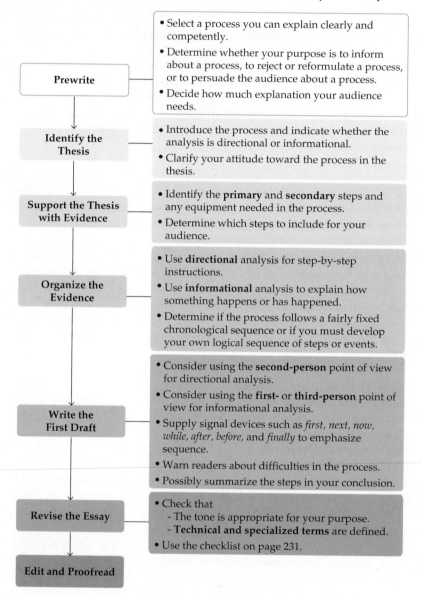

Prewrite
- Select a process you can explain clearly and competently.
- Determine whether your purpose is to inform about a process, to reject or reformulate a process, or to persuade the audience about a process.
- Decide how much explanation your audience needs.

Identify the Thesis
- Introduce the process and indicate whether the analysis is directional or informational.
- Clarify your attitude toward the process in the thesis.

Support the Thesis with Evidence
- Identify the **primary** and **secondary** steps and any equipment needed in the process.
- Determine which steps to include for your audience.

Organize the Evidence
- Use **directional** analysis for step-by-step instructions.
- Use **informational** analysis to explain how something happens or has happened.
- Determine if the process follows a fairly fixed chronological sequence or if you must develop your own logical sequence of steps or events.

Write the First Draft
- Consider using the **second-person** point of view for directional analysis.
- Consider using the **first-** or **third-person** point of view for informational analysis.
- Supply signal devices such as *first, next, now, while, after, before,* and *finally* to emphasize sequence.
- Warn readers about difficulties in the process.
- Possibly summarize the steps in your conclusion.

Revise the Essay
- Check that
  - The tone is appropriate for your purpose.
  - **Technical and specialized terms** are defined.
- Use the checklist on page 231.

Edit and Proofread

4. Use prewriting to identify the steps in the process.   To explain a sequence to your readers, you need to think through the process thoroughly, identifying its major parts and subparts, locating possible missteps or trouble spots. With your purpose, thesis, and audience in mind, use the appropriate prewriting techniques (brainstorming and mapping should be especially helpful) to break down the process into its component parts. In prewriting, it's a good idea to start by generating more material than you expect to use. Then the raw material can be shaped and pruned to fit your purpose and the needs of your audience. The amount of work done during the prewriting stage will have a direct bearing on the clarity of your presentation.

5. Identify the directional and informational aspects of the process analysis.   Directional and informational process analyses are not always distinct. In fact, they may be complementary. Your prewriting may reveal that you'll need to provide background information about a process before outlining its steps. For example, in a paper describing a step-by-step approach for losing weight, you might first need to explain how the body burns calories. Or, in a paper on gardening, you could provide some theory about the way organic fertilizers work before detailing a plan for growing vegetables. Although both approaches may be appropriate in a paper, one generally predominates.

The kind of process analysis chosen has implications for the way you will relate to your reader. When the process analysis is *directional,* the reader is addressed in the *second person:* "You should first rinse the residue from the radiator by . . . ," or "Wrap the injured person in a blanket and then. . . ." (In the second example, the pronoun *you* is implied.)

If the process analysis has an *informational* purpose, you won't address the reader directly but will choose from a number of other options. For example, you might use the *first-person* point of view. In a humorous essay explaining how not to prepare for finals, you could cite your own disastrous study habits: "Filled with good intentions, I sit on my bed, pick up a pencil, open my notebook, and promptly fall asleep." The *third-person singular or plural* can also be used in informational process essays: "The door-to-door salesperson walks up the front walk, heart pounding, more than a bit nervous, but also challenged by the prospect of striking a deal," or "The new recruits next underwent a series of important balance tests in what was called the 'horror chamber.'" Whether you use the first, second, or third person, avoid shifting point of view midstream.

You might have noticed that in the third-person examples, the present tense ("walks up") is used in one sentence, the past tense ("underwent") in the other. The past tense is appropriate for events already completed, whereas the present tense is used for habitual or ongoing actions. ("A dominant male goose usually flies at the head of the V-wedge during migration.") The present tense is also effective when you want to lend a sense of dramatic immediacy to a process, even if the steps were performed in the past. ("The surgeon gently separates the facial skin and muscle from the underlying bony skull.") As with point of view, be on guard against changing tenses in the middle of your explanation.

6. Explain the process, one step at a time.   Prewriting helped you identify key stages and sort out the directional and informational aspects of the process. Now you're ready to organize your raw material into an easy-to-follow sequence. At times your purpose will be to explain a process with a *fairly fixed chronological sequence:* how to make pizza, how to pot a plant, how to change a tire. In such cases, you should include all necessary steps, in the correct chronological order. However, if a strict chronological ordering of steps means that a particularly important part of the sequence gets buried in the middle, the sequence probably should be juggled so that the crucial step receives the attention it deserves.

Other times your goal will be to describe a process having *no commonly accepted sequence.* For example, in an essay explaining how to discipline a child or how to pull yourself out of a blue mood, you will have to come up with your own definition of the key steps and then arrange those steps in some logical order. You may also use process analyses to *reject* or *reformulate* a traditional sequence. In this case, you would propose a more logical series of steps: "Our system for electing congressional representatives is inefficient and undemocratic; it should be reformed in the following ways."

Whether the essay describes a generally agreed-on process or one that is not commonly accepted, you must provide all the details needed to explain the process. Your readers should be able to understand, even visualize, the process. There should be no fuzzy patches or confusing cuts from one step to another. Don't, however, go into obsessive detail about minor stages or steps. If you dwell for several hundred words on how to butter the pan, your readers will never stay with you long enough to learn how to make the omelet.

It's not unusual, especially in less defined sequences, for some steps in a process to occur simultaneously and overlap. When this happens, you should present the steps in the most logical order, being sure to tell your readers that several steps are not perfectly distinct and may merge. For example, in an essay explaining how a species becomes extinct, you would have to indicate that overpopulation of hardy strains and destruction of endangered breeds are often simultaneous events. You would also need to clarify that the depletion of food sources both precedes and follows the demise of a species.

7. Provide readers with the help they need to follow the sequence.   As you move through the steps of a process analysis, don't forget to *warn readers about difficulties* they might encounter. For example, when writing a paper on the artistry involved in butterflying a shrimp, you might say something like this:

> Next, make a shallow cut with your sharpened knife along the convex curve of the shrimp's intestinal tract. The tract, usually a thin black line along the outside curve of the shrimp, is faintly visible beneath the translucent flesh. But some shrimp have a thick orange, blue, or gray line instead of a thin black one. In all cases, be careful not to slice too deeply, or you will end up with two shrimp halves instead of one butterflied shrimp.

You have told readers what to look for, citing the exceptions, and have warned them against making too deep a cut. Anticipating spots where communication might break down is a key part of writing an effective process analysis.

Transitional words and phrases are also critical in helping readers understand the order of the steps being described. Time signals such as *first, next, now, while, after, before,* and *finally* provide readers with a clear sense of the sequence. Entire sentences can also be used to link parts of the process, reminding your audience of what has already been discussed and indicating what will now be explained: "Once the panel of experts finishes its evaluation of the exam questions, randomly selected items are field-tested in schools throughout the country."

8. Maintain an appropriate tone.   When writing a process analysis essay, be sure your tone is consistent with your purpose, your attitude toward your subject, and the effect you want to have on the reader. When explaining how fraternities and sororities recruit new members, do you want to use an objective, nonjudgmental tone? To decide, take into account readers' attitudes toward your subject. Does your audience have a financial or emotional investment in the process being described? Does your own interest in the process coincide or conflict with that of your audience? Awareness of your readers' stance can be crucial. Consider another example: Assume you're writing a letter to the director of the student health center proposing a new system to replace the currently chaotic one. You'd do well to be tactful in your criticisms. Offend your reader, and your cause is lost. If, however, the letter is slated for the college newspaper and directed primarily to other students, you could adopt a more pointed, even sarcastic tone. Readers, you would assume, will probably share your view and favor change.

Once you settle on the essay's tone, maintain it throughout. If you're writing a light piece on the way computers are taking over our lives, you wouldn't include a grim step-by-step analysis of the way confidential computerized medical records may become public.

9. Open and close the process analysis effectively.   A paper developed primarily through process analysis should have a strong beginning. The introduction should state the process to be described and imply whether the essay has an informational or directional intent.

If you suspect readers are indifferent to your subject, use the introduction to motivate them, telling them how important the subject is:

> Do you enjoy the salad bars found in many restaurants? If you do, you probably have noticed that the vegetables are always crisp and fresh—no matter how many hours they have been exposed to the air. What are the restaurants doing to make the vegetables look so inviting? There's a simple answer. Many restaurants spray the vegetables with, or dip them into, potent chemicals to make them appetizing.

If you think your audience may be intimidated by your subject (perhaps because it's complex or relatively obscure), the introduction is the perfect spot to reassure them that the process being described is not beyond their grasp:

> Studies show that many people willingly accept a defective product just so they won't have to deal with the uncomfortable process of making a complaint. But once a few easy-to-learn basics are mastered, anyone can register a complaint that gets results.

Most process analysis essays don't end as soon as the last step in the sequence is explained. Instead, they usually include some brief final comments that round out the piece and bring it to a satisfying close. This final section of the essay may summarize the main steps in the process—not by repeating the steps verbatim but by rephrasing and condensing them in several concise sentences. The conclusion can also be an effective spot to underscore the significance of the process, recalling what may have been said in the introduction about the subject's importance. Or the essay can end by echoing the note of reassurance that may have been included at the start.

REVISION STRATEGIES

Once you have a draft of the essay, you're ready to revise. The following checklist will help you and those giving you feedback apply to process analysis some of the revision techniques discussed on pages 60–62.

☑ PROCESS ANALYSIS: A REVISION/PEER REVIEW CHECKLIST

Revise Overall Meaning and Structure

❏ What purpose does the process analysis serve—to inform, to persuade, or to do both?

❏ Is the process analysis primarily *directional* or *informational*? How can you tell?

❏ Where does the process seem confusing? Where have steps been left out? Which steps need simplifying?

❏ What is the essay's tone? Is the tone appropriate for the essay's purpose and readers? Where are there distracting shifts in tone?

Revise Paragraph Development

❏ Does the introduction specify the process to be described? Does it provide an overview? Should it?

❏ Which paragraphs are difficult to follow? Have any steps or materials been omitted or explained in too much or too little detail? Which paragraphs should warn readers about potential trouble spots or overlapping steps?

❏ Where are additional time signals needed to clarify the sequence within and between paragraphs? Where does overreliance on time signals make the sequence awkward and mechanical?

❏ Which paragraph describes the most crucial step in the sequence? How has the step been highlighted?

❏ How could the conclusion be more effective?

Revise Sentences and Words

❏ What technical or specialized terms appear in the essay? Have they been sufficiently explained? Where could simpler, less technical language be used?

❏ Are there any places where the essay's point of view awkwardly shifts? How could this problem be corrected?

❏ Does the essay use correct verb tenses—the past tense for completed events, the present tense for habitual or ongoing actions?

❏ Where does the essay use the passive voice ("The hole is dug")? Would the active voice ("You dig the hole") be more effective?

STUDENT ESSAY

The following student essay was written by Robert Barry in response to this assignment:

> In "What Shamu Taught Me About a Happy Marriage," Amy Sutherland takes a light-hearted look at ways to change human behavior. Identify a relatively harmless habit or behavior that a person might want to change; for example, drinking too much high-priced coffee or spending too much time on the Internet. Then write a light-spirited essay explaining how the habit developed and the steps that could be taken to change the behavior.

While reading Robert's paper, try to determine how effectively it applies the principles of process analysis. The annotations on Robert's paper and the commentary following it will help you look at the essay more closely.

Becoming a Recordoholic
by Robert Barry

Introduction

As a technological breakthrough, the DVR (digital video recorder) has been an enormous success—almost as popular as television itself. Not only can you watch TV while you record other programs, but you can pause and rewind live TV. Better yet, you can program the DVR to record a roster of programs—even entire seasons—with a simple push of a button. No consumer warning labels are attached to this ingenious invention, DVRs, but there should be. DVRs can be dangerous.

Start of two-sentence thesis

Barely aware of what is happening, a person can turn into a compulsive recorder. The descent from innocent hobby to full-blown addiction takes place in several stages.

Topic sentence

First stage in process (DVR addiction)

In the first innocent stage, the unsuspecting person buys a DVR for occasional use. I was at this stage when I asked my parents if they would buy me a DVR as a birthday gift. With the DVR, I could record reruns of *Seinfeld* and new episodes of *The Simpsons* while watching *Grey's Anatomy.* The DVR was perfect. I hooked it up to the TV in my bedroom and recorded the antics of Jerry, Elaine, George, and Kramer and the adventures of my favorite cartoon family, while watching the residents of Seattle Grace save lives and make utter fools of themselves. Occasionally, I'd DVR a movie, which my friends and I watched over the weekend. I recorded only a few shows, and after I watched those shows, I'd delete them from the

Beginning of analogy to alcoholism

DVR. In these early days, my use of the DVR was the equivalent of light social drinking.

1

2

Topic sentence

Second stage in process

In the second phase on the road to recordoholism, an **3** individual uses the DVR more frequently and begins to stock-pile recordings rather than watch them. My troubles began in July when my family and I went to the shore for two weeks of vacation. I set my DVR to record all five episodes of *Seinfeld* and *The Sopranos,* and two episodes each of *Heroes, The Simpsons,* and *Grey's Anatomy,* while I was at the beach working on my tan. Even I, an avid TV viewer, didn't have time to sit and watch all those shows. The DVR continued to record these programs, but there weren't enough hours in the day to watch everything and do my schoolwork, so the programs piled up in my DVR queue. How did I resolve this problem? Very easily. I set my DVR to record episodes of *Seinfeld* three days a week, rather than five. However, with this notion that I had such control with my DVR, I began to realize that there were probably other shows out there that I could record and watch whenever I desired. I could DVR classics like *Law & Order* and *Buffy the Vampire Slayer.* Very quickly, I accumulated six *Seinfeld*s, four *Law & Order*s, and three *Buffy*s. Then a friend—who shall go nameless—told me that only 144 episodes of *Buffy* were ever made. Excited by the thought that I could acquire as impressive a collection of episodes as a Hollywood executive, I continued recording *Buffy,* even recording shows while I watched them. Clearly, my once innocent hobby was getting out of control. I was now

Continuation of analogy

using the DVR on a regular basis—the equivalent of several stiff drinks a day.

Topic sentence

Third stage in process

In the third stage of recordoholism, the amount of record- **4** ing increases significantly, leading to an even more irrational stockpiling of programs in the DVR queue. The catalyst that propelled me into this third stage was my parents' decision to get a premium movie package added to their cable. Selfless guy that I am, I volunteered to move my DVR into the living room, where the connection was located. Now I could record

Continuation of analogy

all the most recent movies and specials. I began to record a couple of other shows every day. I also went movie-crazy and taped *Gangs of New York, Barbershop 2,* and *The Godfather I, II,* and *III.* I recorded an HBO comedy special with Chris Rock and an MTV concert featuring Radiohead. Where did I get time to watch all these shows? I didn't. Using the DVR was more satisfying than watching. Reason and common sense were abandoned. Getting things on the DVR had become an obsession, and I was setting the DVR to record programs all the time.

Topic sentence

Fourth stage in process

In the fourth stage, recordoholism creeps into other parts **5** of the addict's life, influencing behavior in strange ways. Secrecy becomes commonplace. One day, my mother came into my room and asked about a recent test I had taken. What she didn't know was that the night before the exam, I had checked my DVR recording list and found that I had run out of storage space. For three hours after everyone went to bed, I watched episodes of *The Sopranos* so I could delete them and record a movie on Showtime. I was so tired the next morning that I wound up getting a bad grade on my biology exam. "Robert," my mother exclaimed, "isn't this getting a bit out of

Continuation of analogy ——⌐ hand?" I assured her it was just a hobby, but I continued to sneak downstairs in the middle of the night to watch recorded shows, removing any trace of my presence from the living room when I was finished. Also, denial is not unusual during this stage of DVR addiction. At the dinner table, when my younger sister commented, "Robert records all the time," I laughingly told everyone—including myself—that the recording was no big deal. I was getting bored with it and was going to stop any day, I assured my family. Obsessive behavior also characterizes the fourth stage of recordoholism. Each week, I pulled out the TV magazine from the Sunday paper and went through it carefully, circling in red all the shows I wanted to record. Another sign of addiction was the secret calender I kept in my desk drawer. With more diligence than I ever had for any term paper, I would log in each program I recorded and plan for the coming week's recording schedule.

Topic sentence ——⌐   In the final stage of an addiction, the individual either   6
succumbs completely to the addiction or is able to break away
Continuation of analogy ——⌐ from the habit. I broke my addiction, and I broke it cold turkey. This total withdrawal occurred when I went off to college. There was no point in taking my DVR to school because TVs were not allowed in the freshman dorms. Even though there were many things to occupy my time during the school week, cold sweats overcame me whenever I thought about everything on TV I was not recording. I even considered calling

Final stage in process home and asking members of my family to record things for me, but I knew they would think I was crazy. At the beginning of the semester, I also had to resist the overwhelming desire to travel the three hours home every weekend so I could get my fix. But after a while, the urgent need to record subsided. Now, months later, as I write this, I feel detached and sober.

Conclusion   I have no illusions, though. I know that once a recordo-   7
holic, always a recordoholic. Soon I will return home for the holidays, which, as everyone knows, can be a time for excess
Final references to analogy ——⌐ eating—and recording. But I will cope with the pressure. I will take each day one at a time. I plan to watch what I'm able to, and no more. And if I feel myself succumbing to the temptations of recording, I will pick up the telephone and dial the recordoholics' hot line: 1-800-DVR-STOP. I will win the battle.

COMMENTARY

Purpose, thesis, and tone.   Robert's essay is an example of *informational process analysis;* his purpose is to describe—rather than teach—the process of becoming a "recordoholic." The title, with its coined term *recordoholic,* tips us off that the essay is going to be entertaining. And the introductory paragraph clearly establishes the essay's playful, mock-serious tone. The tone established, Robert briefly defines the term *recordoholic* as a "compulsive recorder" and then moves to the essay's *thesis:* "Barely aware of what is happening, a person can turn into a compulsive recorder. The descent from innocent hobby to full-blown addiction takes place in several stages."

Throughout the essay, Robert sustains the introduction's humor by mocking his own motivations and poking fun at his quirks: "Selfless guy that I am, I volunteered to move my DVR" (paragraph 4), and "With more diligence than I ever had for any term paper, I would log in each program I recorded and plan for the coming week's recording schedule" (5). Robert probably uses a bit of *dramatic license* when reporting some of his obsessive behavior, and we, as readers, understand that he's exaggerating for comic effect. Most likely, he didn't break out in a cold sweat at the thought of the TV shows he was unable to record. Nevertheless, this tinkering with the truth is legitimate because it allows Robert to create material that fits the essay's lightly satiric tone.

Organization and topic sentences.   To meet the requirements of the assignment, Robert needed to provide a *step-by-step* explanation of a process. And because he invented the term *recordoholism,* Robert also needed to invent the stages in the progression of his addiction. During his prewriting, Robert discovered five stages in his recordoholism. Presented *chronologically,* these stages provide the organizing focus for his paper. Specifically, each supporting paragraph is devoted to one stage, with the *topic sentence* for each paragraph indicating the stage's distinctive characteristics.

Transitions.   Although Robert's essay is playful, it is nonetheless a process analysis and so must have an easy-to-follow structure. Keeping this in mind, Robert wisely includes *transitions* to signal what happened at each stage of his recordoholism: "*However* with this notion that I had such control" (paragraph 3); "*Now,* I could record all the most recent movies and specials." (4); "*One day,* my mother came into my room" (5); and "*But after a while,* the urgent need to record subsided" (6). In addition to such transitions, Robert uses crisp questions to move from idea to idea within a paragraph: "How did I resolve this problem? Very easily. I set my DVR to record episodes of *Seinfeld* three days a week, rather than five" (3), and "Where did I get time to watch all these shows? I didn't" (4).

Combining patterns of development.   Even though Robert's essay is a process analysis, it contains elements of other patterns of development. For example, his paper is unified by an *analogy*—a sustained *comparison* between Robert's recording addiction and the obviously more serious addiction to alcohol. Handled incorrectly, the analogy could have been offensive, but Robert makes the comparison work to his advantage. The analogy is stated specifically in several spots: "In these early days, my use of the DVR was the equivalent of light social drinking" (2); "I was now using the DVR on a regular basis—the equivalent of several stiff drinks a day" (3). Finally, he generates numerous lively details or *examples* to illustrate the different stages in his addiction.

Two unnecessary sentences.   Perhaps you noticed that Robert runs into a minor problem at the end of the fourth paragraph. Starting with the sentence, "Reason and common sense were abandoned," he begins to ramble and repeat himself. The paragraph's last two sentences fail to add anything substantial. Take a moment to read paragraph 4 aloud, omitting the last two sentences. Note how much sharper the new conclusion is: "Where did I get time to watch all these tapes? I didn't. Using the DVR was more satisfying than watching." This new ending says all that needs to be said.

Revising the first draft.   When it was time to revise, Robert—in spite of his apprehension—showed his paper to his roommate and asked him to read it out loud. Robert knew this strategy would provide a more objective point of view on his work. His roommate, at first an unwilling recruit, nonetheless laughed as he read the essay aloud. That was just the response Robert wanted. But when his roommate got to the conclusion, Robert heard that the closing paragraph was flat and anticlimactic. His roommate agreed, so the two of them brainstormed ways to make the conclusion livelier and more in spirit with the rest of the essay. Printed here is Robert's original conclusion.

Original Version of the Conclusion

I have no illusions, though, that I am over my recordoholism. Soon I will be returning home for the holidays, which can be a time for excess recording. All I can do is watch what I'm able to and not use the DVR. After that, I will hope for the best.

Robert and his roommate brainstormed ways to make the conclusion livelier and more in spirit with the rest of the essay. They decided that the best approach would be to reinforce the playful, mock-serious tone that characterized earlier parts of the essay. Robert thus made three major changes to his conclusion. First, he tightened the first sentence of the paragraph ("I have no illusions, though, that I am over my recordoholism"), making it crisper and more dramatic: "I have no illusions, though." Second, he added a few sentences to sustain the light, self-deprecating tone he had used earlier: "I know that once a recordoholic, always a recordoholic"; "But I will cope with the pressure"; "I will win the battle." Third, and perhaps most important, he returned to the alcoholism analogy: "I will take each day one at a time....And if I feel myself succumbing to the temptations of recording, I will pick up the telephone and dial the recordoholics' hotline..."

These weren't the only changes Robert made while reworking his paper, but they help illustrate how sensitive he was to the effect he wanted to achieve. Certainly, the recasting of the conclusion was critical to the overall success of this amusing essay.

Activities: Process Analysis

Prewriting Activities

1. Imagine you're writing two essays: One *defines* the term "comparison shopping"; the other *contrasts* two different teaching styles. Jot down ways you might use process analysis in each essay.

2. Select *one* of the essay topics that follow and determine what your purpose, tone, and point of view would be for each audience indicated in parentheses. Then use brainstorming, questioning, mapping, or another prewriting technique to identify the points you'd cover for each audience. Finally, organize the raw material, noting the differences in emphasis and sequence for each group of readers.

   a. How to buy a car (*young people who have just gotten a driver's license; established professionals*)
   b. How children acquire their values (*first-time parents; elementary school teachers*)
   c. How to manage money (*grade school children; college students*)
   d. How loans or scholarships are awarded to incoming students on your campus (*high school graduates applying for financial aid; high school guidance counselors*)
   e. How arguments can strengthen relationships (*preteen children; young adults*)
   f. How to relax (*college students; parents with young children*)

Revising Activities

3. Below is the brainstorming for a brief essay that describes the steps involved in making a telephone sales call. The paper has the following thesis: "Establishing rapport with customers is the most challenging and the most important part of phone sales." Revise the brainstormed material by deleting anything that undermines the paper's unity and organizing the steps in a logical sequence.

   • Keep customers on the phone as long as possible to learn what they need
   • The more you know about customers' needs, the better
   • The tone of the opening comments is very important

- Gently introduce the product
- Use a friendly tone in opening comments
- End on a friendly tone, too
- Don't introduce the product right away
- Growing rudeness in society. Some people hang up right away. Very upsetting.
- Try in a friendly way to keep the person on the phone
- Many people are so lonely they don't mind staying on the phone so they can talk to someone—anyone
- How sad that there's so much loneliness in the world
- Describe the product's advantages—price, convenience, installment plan
- If person is not interested, try in a friendly way to find out why
- Don't tell people that their reasons for not being interested are silly
- Don't push people if they're not interested
- Encourage credit card payment—the product will arrive earlier
- Explain payment—check, money order, or credit card payment

4. Reprinted here is a paragraph from the first draft of a humorous essay advising shy college students how to get through a typical day. Written as a process analysis, the paragraph outlines techniques for surviving class. Revise the paragraph, deleting digressions that disrupt the paragraph's unity, eliminating unnecessary repetition, and sequencing the steps in the proper order. Also correct inappropriate shifts in person and add transitions where needed. Feel free to add any telling details.

Simply attending class can be stressful for shy people. Several strategies, though, can lessen the trauma. Shy students should time their arrival to coincide with that of most other class members—about two minutes before the class is scheduled to begin. If you arrive too early, you may be seen sitting alone, or, even worse, may actually be forced to talk with another early arrival. If you arrive late, all eyes will be upon you. Before heading to class, the shy student should dress in the least conspicuous manner possible—say, in the blue jeans, sweatshirt, and sneakers that 99.9 percent of your classmates wear. That way you won't stand out from everyone else. Take a seat near the back of the room. Don't, however, sit at the very back since professors often take sadistic pleasure in calling on students back there, assuming they chose those seats because they didn't want to be called on. A friend of mine who is far from shy uses just the opposite ploy. In an attempt to get in good with her professors, she sits in the front row and, incredibly enough, volunteers to participate. However, since shy people don't want to call attention to themselves, they should stifle any urge to sneeze or cough. You run the risk of having people look at you or offer you a tissue or cough drop. And of course, never, ever volunteer to answer. Such a display of intelligence is sure to focus all eyes on you. In other words, make yourself as inconspicuous as possible. How, you might wonder, can you be inconspicuous if you're blessed (or cursed) with great looks? Well,...have you ever considered earning your degree through the mail?

Clifford Stoll

Clifford Stoll, born in 1950, is an astronomer, lecturer, commentator on MSNBC, and occasional visiting teacher of astronomy in elementary, middle, and high schools. He is the best-selling author of *The Cuckoo's Egg: Tracking a Spy Through the Maze of Computer Espionage* (1990) and *Silicon Snake Oil: Second Thoughts on the Information Superhighway* (1995), both of which address the complications of the computer age. As he reveals in the preface of *High-Tech Heretic: Reflections of a Computer Contrarian* (1999), despite having programmed and used computers since the mid-sixties, Stoll seeks to inject "a few notes of skepticism into the utopian dreams of a digital wonderland." The following essay appears as a chapter in *High-Tech Heretic*.

For ideas about how this process analysis essay is organized, see Figure 7.2 on page 243.

Pre-Reading Journal Entry

The Internet has become increasingly popular as an educational resource. What do you think are the merits and drawbacks of including the Internet as part of school assignments? Is your response affected by the age of the students in question? Record in your journal the pros and cons of requiring students—at the elementary, high school, and college levels, respectively—to access the Net as part of their studies.

Cyberschool

Welcome to the classroom of the future! Complete with electronic links to the world, it'll revolutionize education. Students will interact with information infrastructures and knowledge processors to learn group work and telework, whatever that means. You'll be enriched, empowered, and enabled by the digital classroom; immersed in an optimal learning environment. Yee-ha!   1

Worried that things rarely turn out as promised? Well, let me present a pessimal[1] view of the schoolroom of the future.   2

Suppose you're a harried school board member. Voters complain about high taxes. Teachers' unions strike for higher wages and smaller classes. Parents worry about plummeting scores on standardized tests. Newspapers criticize backward teaching methods, outdated textbooks, and security problems. Unruly students cut classes and rarely pay attention. Instructors teach topics which aren't in the curriculum or, worse, inject their own opinions into subject matter.   3

Sound like a tough call? Naw—it's easy to solve all these problems, placate the taxpayers, and get re-elected. High technology!   4

---

[1]The opposite of optimal?

First, the school district buys a computer for every student. Sure, this'll   5
set back the budget—maybe a few hundred dollars per student. Quantity dis-
counts and corporate support should keep the price down, and classroom
savings will more than offset the cost of the equipment.

Next buy a pile of CD-ROMs for the students, each preprogrammed   6
with fun edutainment[2] programs. The educational games will exactly cover
the curriculum . . . for every paragraph in the syllabus, the game will have an
interactive aspect. As students climb to more advanced levels, the game naturally becomes more challenging and rewarding. But always fun.

Every student will work at her own pace. The youngest will watch happy   7
cartoon characters and exciting animations. The kid that likes horses will listen to messages from a chatty pony; the child that dreams of fire engines will
hear from Fred the Firefighter. High schoolers get multimedia images of film
stars and rock and roll celebrities. With access to interactive video sessions,
chat rooms, and e-mail, students can collaborate with each other. It's the
ultimate in individualized, child-centered instruction.

Naturally, the edu-games will be programmed so that students become   8
adept at standardized tests. No reason to teach anything that's not on the
ACT, PSAT, or SAT exams. And the students will have fun because all this
information will be built into games like Myst, Dungeon, or Doom. They'll
master the games, and automatically learn the material.

Meanwhile, the computers will keep score, like pinball machines.   9
They'll send e-mail to parents and administrators . . . scores that will
become part of each kid's permanent record. No more subjectivity in
grading: The principal will know instantly how each child's doing. And if
a student gets confused or falls behind, automated help will be just a
mouse click away.   10

We'll update crowded classrooms, too. Replace desks with individual
cubicles, comfortable chairs, and multimedia monitors. With no outside
interruptions, kids' attention will be directed into the approved creative
learning experiences, built into the software. Well compartmentalized,
students will hardly ever see other . . . neatly ending classroom discipline
problems.

Naturally, teachers are an unnecessary appendix at this cyberschool.   11
No need for 'em when there's a fun, multimedia system at each student's
fingertips. Should students have a question, they can turn to the latest online encyclopedia, enter an electronic chat room, or send e-mail to a
professional educator. Those laid-off teachers can be retrained as data
entry clerks.

As librarians and teachers become irrelevant, they'll be replaced by a   12
cadre of instructional specialists, consultants, and professional hall monitors.

---

[2]A term, coined by Stoll, combining the words *education* and *entertainment* (editors' note).

Any discipline problems could be handled by trained security guards, who'd monitor the cubicles via remote video links.

Effect? With no more wasted time on student-teacher interactions or off-topic discussions, education will become more efficient. Since the computers' content would be directed at maximizing test performance, standardized test scores will zoom. 13

Eliminating teachers and luxuries such as art lessons and field trips will save enough to recoup the cost of those fancy computers. With little effort, this electronic education could even become a profit center. Merely sell advertising space in the edutainment programs. Corporate sponsors, eager to market their messages to impressionable minds, would pay school systems to plug their products within the coursework. 14

Concerned that such a system might be dehumanizing? Not to worry. Interactive chat sessions will encourage a sense of community and enhance kids' social skills. Should a student have questions, the Internet will put her in instant touch with a trained support mentor. When necessary, real-time instructors will appear on the distance learning displays, available to interact via two-way video. 15

The Cyberschool will showcase technology and train students for the upcoming electronic workplace. As local employment prospects change, the school board will issue updates to the curriculum over its interactive website. And the school board will monitor what each student learns—without idiosyncratic teachers to raise unpopular topics or challenge accepted beliefs. 16

Advanced students can sign up for on-line extracurricular activities—perhaps joining the Virtual Compassion Corps. There, students will be paired up across racial, gender, and class lines. Our children would offer foreigners advice and even arrange interviews with prospective employers. In this way, students will perform community service and mentor others, while displaying their cultural awareness over the network. All without ever having to shake hands with a real person, travel to a distant country, or (gasp!) face the real problems of another culture.[3] Simple, safe, and sterile. 17

Should parents worry about Johnny's progress, they need only log in over the Internet to see their son's latest test scores. In addition, they'll receive e-mailed reports summarizing their child's work. And at any time, they can click on an icon to see live images of their young scholar, automatically uploaded by a school video camera. 18

Yep, just sign up for the future: the parent-pleasin', tax-savin', teacher-firin', interactive-educatin', child-centerin' Cyberschool. No 19

[3]An actual proposal from the director of MIT's Laboratory for Computer Science, Michael Dertouzos.

stuffy classrooms. No more teacher strikes. No outdated textbooks. No expensive clarinet lessons. No boring homework. No learning. Coming soon to a school district near you.[4]

---

[4]Idea for a computer game: Cyberschool Superintendent. Players score by saving money. They could eliminate teachers, close libraries, or blow up music studios. Competitors advance by wiring schools, adding computers, and plugging in multimedia systems. Evil monsters might appear in the form of teachers, scholars, and librarians who insist that you read a book. Bonus points, labeled Pilot Project Grants, would be awarded for writing vapid press releases.

Questions for Close Reading

1. What is the selection's thesis? Locate the sentence(s) in which Stoll states his main idea. If he doesn't state the thesis explicitly, express it in your own words.
2. What process does Stoll describe in the essay? What are the basic steps of this process? What is Stoll's underlying attitude toward these measures?
3. What specific group of people does Stoll imagine as being especially in favor of the "cyberschool"? According to Stoll, how do these individuals justify using computers to teach children?
4. What role does Stoll indicate teachers will play in the "cyberschool"? What attitude does he convey about this role? Explain.
5. Refer to your dictionary as needed to define the following words used in the selection: *infrastructures* (paragraph 1), *optimal* (1), *harried* (3), *placate* (4), *adept* (8), *standardized* (8), *cubicles* (10), *compartmentalized* (10), *cadre* (12), *recoup* (14), and *idiosyncratic* (16).

Questions About the Writer's Craft

1. **The pattern.** Is Stoll's process analysis primarily directional or primarily informational? Explain. To what extent does Stoll try to persuade readers that the process he describes should be followed?
2. Focusing on his word choices, how would you characterize Stoll's tone in his essay? In your opinion, does his tone enhance or detract from the point he's trying to make? Explain.
3. **Other patterns.** Underlying Stoll's process analysis is an *argument* against a particular form of education. To write an effective argument, writers need to establish their own credibility. Based on what you learned about Stoll in his biography (page 239), what makes him appear qualified to write about his subject?
4. **Other patterns.** In his persona of pro-cyberschool spokesman, Stoll addresses opposition to idea of the cyberschool in paragraph 15. How does Stoll represent and rebut the *arguments* against the cyberschool? Are his arguments effective, in your opinion?

FIGURE 7.2
Essay Structure Diagram: "Cyberschool" by Clifford Stoll

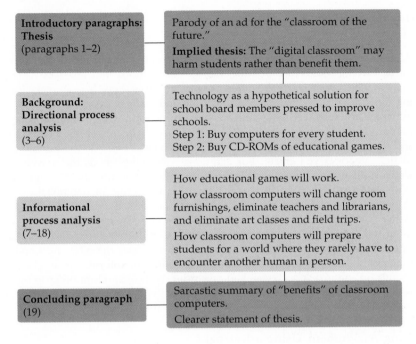

Introductory paragraphs: Thesis (paragraphs 1–2)	Parody of an ad for the "classroom of the future." **Implied thesis:** The "digital classroom" may harm students rather than benefit them.
Background: Directional process analysis (3–6)	Technology as a hypothetical solution for school board members pressed to improve schools. Step 1: Buy computers for every student. Step 2: Buy CD-ROMs of educational games.
Informational process analysis (7–18)	How educational games will work. How classroom computers will change room furnishings, eliminate teachers and librarians, and eliminate art classes and field trips. How classroom computers will prepare students for a world where they rarely have to encounter another human in person.
Concluding paragraph (19)	Sarcastic summary of "benefits" of classroom computers. Clearer statement of thesis.

Writing Assignments Using Process Analysis as a Pattern of Development

1. In his essay, Stoll offers a cynical recipe for creating an "optimal learning environment." Write an essay in which you present a process analysis of concrete ways the school you currently attend or one you have attended in the past could realistically be improved. You might, for instance, discuss physical improvements such as updating the equipment in the computer lab, or less tangible measures such as cultivating a more interactive classroom environment. Brainstorm on your own or with others to generate specific ideas to include in your process.

2. In his essay, Stoll ironically suggests a course of action that he implies should not be taken in order to improve children's education. Taking a similarly ironic stance, write an essay *mis*guiding readers on how to "improve" some other significant institution or serious condition. For instance, you might discuss ways to increase the efficiency of a particular government agency, how to even out inequities between classes or races of people, how to protect the environment, and so on—all the while presenting steps that would work to the contrary. Like Stoll, you should ultimately reveal your true position in the concluding paragraph, preferably in a subtle way. You should consider reading

Dave Barry's "Beauty and the Beast" (page 284) to see how another writer recommends a course of action in a humorous or ironical way.

Writing Assignments Combining Patterns of Development

3. According to Stoll, computers serve as a distraction to students rather than a legitimate learning tool. What are other kinds of distractions students face? Write an essay in which you *classify* the different types of distractions that can make learning difficult. You may adopt a serious tone and address categories such as, for example, problems at home and pressure from peers. Or you might adopt a humorous tone and discuss distractions that include interest in the opposite sex and the temptation of computer games. Provide vivid *examples* to illustrate each of the categories you create. For additional viewpoints about the pressures to which students are subject, read Buzz Bissinger's "Innocents Afield" (page 317).

4. With the increasing popularity of the Internet, the future of traditional printed materials—such as books, magazines, and newspapers—has come into question. Write an essay in which you *compare* and *contrast* using printed materials with using the Internet in order to perform research. Be sure to provide at least one extended example or a few briefer examples to *illustrate* the differences and/or similarities you're pointing out. Your best source of information might be a "hands-on" approach: to research a topic using both methods in order to see for yourself what the differences are. By the end of your essay, make clear to your reader which of the two methods you find preferable, and why.

Writing Assignment Using a Journal Entry as a Starting Point

5. In an indirect way, Stoll argues against the wholesale computerization of the classroom. Write an essay in which you argue that the Internet specifically should *or* should not play a significant role in the education of *one* particular age group of students (elementary, high school, or college). In formulating your argument, refer to the material you generated in your pre-reading journal entry. For additional perspectives on this issue, you might consider doing some research on this topic in the library and/or on the Internet. In writing your essay, you should acknowledge and rebut opposing points of view.

David Shipley is the editor of *The New York Times*'s op-ed page, on which opinion pieces by *Times* columnists and others are published. He was born in Portland, Oregon, in 1963 and graduated with a degree in English from Williams College in 1985. Shipley won a Thomas J. Watson Fellowship for 1985–1986, which allowed him to spend a year traveling to do independent study. From 1993 to 1995 he was executive editor of *The New Republic,* and from 1995 to 1997 he was a special assistant and senior speechwriter for President Bill Clinton. Shipley joined *The New York Times* in 1998 and was deputy editor of the Sunday *New York Times Magazine*'s millennium issues, senior editor of the magazine, and enterprise editor of the national desk before moving to his present position as op-ed editor. With coauthor Will Schwalbe, Shipley wrote a book about e-mail entitled *Send.* It was published in 2007 and revised in 2008. This essay, originally entitled "What We Talk About When We Talk About Editing," appeared in *The New York Times* on July 31, 2005.

Pre-Reading Journal Entry

People often seek advice and help from others to help them do a job or improve their performance. For example, if you were writing your résumé, you might ask a friend to edit and proofread it. Or if you were trying out for a sports team, you might ask a coach for feedback and advice. Think of some occasions in the past when you asked others for help with your work or gave help to someone else when asked. What was the task? What was your goal in helping or being helped? Did the assistance actually improve the end product, or was it useless? Use your journal to answer these questions.

Talk About Editing

... Not surprisingly, readers have lots of questions about the editing that goes on [on the *New York Times* op-ed page]. What kind of changes do we suggest—and why? What kind of changes do we insist on—and why? When do we stay out of the way? And the hardy perennial: do we edit articles to make them adhere to a particular point of view? I thought I'd try to provide a few answers.   1

Just like Times news articles and editorials, Op-Ed essays are edited. Before something appears in our pages, you can bet that questions have been asked, arguments have been clarified, cuts have been suggested—as have additions—and factual, typographical and grammatical errors have been caught. (We hope.)   2

Our most important rule, however, is that nothing is published on the Op-Ed page unless it has been approved by its author. Articles go to press only after the person under whose name the article appears has explicitly O.K.'d the editing.   3

While it's important to know that we edit, it's also important to know how   4
we edit. The best way to explain this is to take a walk through the process.

Say you send us an article by regular mail, e-mail, fax or, this summer at   5
least, owl post[1]—and it's accepted. You'll be told that we'll contact you once
your article is scheduled for publication. That could be days, weeks or even
months away.

When your article does move into the on-deck circle, you'll be sent a   6
contract, and one of the several editors here will get to work.

Here are the clear-cut things the editor will do: 7

- Correct grammatical and typographical errors.   8
- Make sure that the article conforms to *The New York Times Manual*   9
  of Style and Usage. Courtesy titles, for example, will miraculously
  appear if they weren't there before; expletives will be deleted; some
  words will be capitalized, others lowercased.
- See to it that the article fits our allotted space. With staff columnists,   10
  advertisements and illustrations, there's a limit to the number of
  words we can squeeze onto the page.
- Fact-check the article. While it is the author's responsibility to ensure   11
  that everything written for us is accurate, we still check facts—names,
  dates, places, quotations.

We also check assertions. If news articles—from The Times and other   12
publications—are at odds with a point or an example in an essay, we need to
resolve whatever discrepancy exists.

For instance, an Op-Ed article critical of newly aggressive police tactics in   13
Town X can't flatly say the police have no reason to change their strategy if
there have been news reports that violence in the town is rising. This doesn't
mean the writer can't still argue that there are other ways to deal with Town
X's crime problem—he just can't say that the force's decision to change came
out of the blue.

How would we resolve the Town X issue? Well, we'd discuss it with the   14
writer—generally by telephone or e-mail—and we'd try to find a solution
that preserves the writer's argument while also adhering to the facts.

Now to some people, this may sound surprising, as if we're putting   15
words in people's mouths. But there's a crucial distinction to be made
between changing a writer's argument—and suggesting language that will
help a writer make his point more effectively.

Besides grammar and accuracy, we're also concerned about readability.   16
Our editors try to approach articles as average readers who know nothing

---

[1]In J. K. Rowling's Harry Potter books, mail is delivered each morning to Hogwarts, Harry's
school, by owls (editors' note).

about the subject. They may ask if a point is clear, if a writer needs transitional language to bridge the gap between two seemingly separate points, if a leap of logic has been made without sufficient explanation.

To make a piece as clear and accessible as possible, the editor may add 17
a transition, cut a section that goes off point or move a paragraph. If a description is highly technical, the editor may suggest language that lay readers will understand. If it isn't clear what a writer is trying to say, the editor may take a guess, based on what he knows from the author, and suggest more precise language. (There are also times when we do precious little.)

The editor will then send the edited version of the article to the writer. 18
The changes will often be highlighted to make it easy for the author to see what's been done. (I tend to mark edits I've made with an //ok?//.) If a proposed revision is significant, the editor will often write a few sentences to describe the reasoning behind the suggestion.

Every change is a suggestion, not a demand. If a solution offered by an 19
editor doesn't work for a writer, the two work together to find an answer to the problem. Editing is not bullying.

Of course, it's not always warm and cuddly, either. The people who write 20
for Op-Ed have a responsibility to be forthright and specific in their arguments. There's no room on the page for articles that are opaque or written in code.

What our editors expressly do not do is change a point of view. If you've 21
written an article on why New York's street fairs should be abolished, we will not ask you to change your mind and endorse them. We're going to help you make the best case you can. If you followed this page carefully in the run-up to the Iraq war, for example, you saw arguments both for and against the invasion—all made with equal force.

Editing is a human enterprise. Like writing, it is by nature subjective. 22
Sometimes an editor will think a writer is saying something that she isn't. But our editing process gives writer and editor plenty of time to sort out any misunderstandings before the article goes to press. And if a mistake gets through, we do our best to correct it as quickly as possible.

The Op-Ed page is a venue for people with a wide range of perspectives, 23
experiences and talents. Some of the people who appear in this space have written a lot; others haven't. If we published only people who needed no editing, we'd wind up relying on only a very narrow range of professional writers, and the page would be much the worse for it.

So what's the agenda? A lively page of clashing opinions, one where as 24
many people as possible have the opportunity to make the best arguments they can.

And just so you know, this article has been edited. Changes have been 25
suggested—and gratefully accepted. Well, most of them.

Questions for Close Reading

1. What is the selection's thesis? Locate the sentence(s) in which Shipley states his main idea. If he doesn't state his thesis explicitly, express it in your own words.
2. What tasks are involved in editing an op-ed piece for *The New York Times*? Of these, which does Shipley seem to think need the most explanation?
3. In paragraphs 18 through 22, Shipley describes the relationship between the editor and writer of an op-ed piece. What is the nature of this relationship?
4. In paragraph 22, Shipley says that "Editing is a human enterprise." What does he mean by this?
5. Refer to your dictionary as needed to define the following words used in the selection: *hardy* (paragraph 1), *perennial* (1), *on-deck circle* (6), *expletives* (9), *assertions* (12), *adhering* (14), *readability* (16), and *venue* (23).

Questions About the Writer's Craft

1. **The pattern.** Who is the audience for Shipley's essay? Why would this audience be interested in this topic? What type of process analysis does Shipley use?
2. **Other patterns.** Shipley *divides* the editing process into three main types of tasks and covers each type in its own section. Identify the main editing tasks and the paragraph(s) that introduce each type. Why does he break down the process this way rather than deal with the editing process as a whole?
3. In paragraphs 13 and 14, Shipley uses an example to clarify what he means by checking "assertions." Why does he provide an example here? Is the example effective?
4. Shipley concludes this essay with some mild humor. What is the joke? What does this use of humor contribute to the point he has been making in his essay?

Writing Assignments Using Process Analysis as a Pattern of Development

1. Shipley describes the process involved in editing opinion pieces, or arguments, that appear in a newspaper with national circulation. However, many other types of works are edited. For example, news articles, news broadcasts, documentaries, movies, commercials, advertisements, novels, and comic strips are all edited. Select one of these media and do research on the tasks involved in editing it. Write an essay in which you analyze the editing process and explain why it is important.
2. Before a piece can be edited, it must be written. Examine the process involved in producing an essay from the writer's rather than the editor's point of view. What process do you use when you write an essay in your English course? Write an essay in which you analyze your own writing process. For inspiration, you might want to read "Euromail and Amerimail" by Eric Weiner (page 274).

Writing Assignments Combining Patterns of Development

3. Op-ed pieces are usually arguments about current issues; in contrast, news articles are more objective, describing or narrating events. From *The New York Times* or your local newspaper, select one op-ed page essay and one news article on a related topic, if possible. *Compare* and *contrast* the two pieces, analyzing their purpose and content. What patterns of development are used in each piece? Give *examples* to support your analysis.

4. A process analysis essay describes a general procedure, such as how to make chili, whereas a narrative presents a specific story, for example, a story about the time you dropped a pot of chili right before your guests arrived for dinner. Write an essay in which you blend a *process analysis* with a *specific narrative*. You can emphasize either the process analysis or the narrative, whichever seems more effective. Your essay can be humorous, serious, fantastical, or ironic.

Writing Assignment Using a Journal Entry as a Starting Point

5. Review your pre-reading journal entry and select one of the occasions on which you helped someone or were helped to perform a task. First, identify the steps in the process and any missteps or problems. Second, decide whether the process lends itself to an informative or a directional process analysis, or some combination of the two. Finally, write an essay in which you describe the process. To add interest to your essay, you might want to use humor, describe interpersonal conflicts, give examples, or focus on problem areas. Be sure—perhaps in your conclusion—to indicate whether the assistance you gave or received was effective in getting the task done.

Amy Sutherland

Amy Sutherland was born in 1959 and grew up in suburban Cincinnati, Ohio. She has a B.A. in art history from the University of Cincinnati, and an M.S.J. from the Medill School of Journalism at Northwestern University. After thirteen years as an arts and features reporter for newspapers in Vermont and Maine, Sutherland accompanied a Maine resident to the 2000 Pillsbury Bake-off in San Francisco, an assignment that turned into a book, *Cookoff: Recipe Fever in America* (2003). Her next book, *Kicked, Bitten, and Scratched: Life and Lessons at the Premier School for Exotic Animal Trainers,* was published in 2006 and inspired the essay that follows, which appeared in *The New York Times.* In turn, the essay led to another book, *What Shamu Taught Me About Life, Love, and Marriage* (2008) as well as a movie. In addition to writing, Sutherland teaches journalism at Boston University.

Pre-Reading Journal Entry

All of us have habits—patterns of behavior that we repeat, sometimes even without being aware that we are performing them. Reflect on your own habits, good and bad, past and present. In your journal, list some of your habits, and describe the situations in which they arise and the patterns of behavior that characterize them.

What Shamu Taught Me About a Happy Marriage

As I wash dishes at the kitchen sink, my husband paces behind me, irritated. "Have you seen my keys?" he snarls, then huffs out a loud sigh and stomps from the room with our dog, Dixie, at his heels, anxious over her favorite human's upset.   1

In the past I would have been right behind Dixie. I would have turned off the faucet and joined the hunt while trying to soothe my husband with bromides like, "Don't worry, they'll turn up." But that only made him angrier, and a simple case of missing keys soon would become a full-blown angst-ridden drama starring the two of us and our poor nervous dog.   2

Now, I focus on the wet dish in my hands. I don't turn around. I don't say a word. I'm using a technique I learned from a dolphin trainer.   3

I love my husband. He's well read, adventurous and does a hysterical rendition of a northern Vermont accent that still cracks me up after 12 years of marriage.   4

But he also tends to be forgetful, and is often tardy and mercurial. He hovers around me in the kitchen asking if I read this or that piece in *The New Yorker* when I'm trying to concentrate on the simmering pans. He leaves wadded tissues in his wake. He suffers from serious bouts of spousal deafness   5 but never fails to hear me when I mutter to myself on the other side of the house. "What did you say?" he'll shout.

These minor annoyances are not the stuff of separation and divorce, but in sum they began to dull my love for Scott. I wanted—needed—to nudge him a little closer to perfect, to make him into a mate who might annoy me a little less, who wouldn't keep me waiting at restaurants, a mate who would be easier to love. 6

So, like many wives before me, I ignored a library of advice books and set about improving him. By nagging, of course, which only made his behavior worse: he'd drive faster instead of slower; shave less frequently, not more; and leave his reeking bike garb on the bedroom floor longer than ever. 7

We went to a counselor to smooth the edges off our marriage. She didn't understand what we were doing there and complimented us repeatedly on how well we communicated. I gave up. I guessed she was right—our union was better than most—and resigned myself to stretches of slow-boil resentment and occasional sarcasm. 8

Then something magical happened. For a book I was writing about a school for exotic animal trainers, I started commuting from Maine to California, where I spent my days watching students do the seemingly impossible: teaching hyenas to pirouette on command, cougars to offer their paws for a nail clipping, and baboons to skateboard. 9

I listened, rapt, as professional trainers explained how they taught dolphins to flip and elephants to paint. Eventually it hit me that the same techniques might work on that stubborn but lovable species, the American husband. 10

The central lesson I learned from exotic animal trainers is that I should reward behavior I like and ignore behavior I don't. After all, you don't get a sea lion to balance a ball on the end of its nose by nagging. The same goes for the American husband. 11

Back in Maine, I began thanking Scott if he threw one dirty shirt into the hamper. If he threw in two, I'd kiss him. Meanwhile, I would step over any soiled clothes on the floor without one sharp word, though I did sometimes kick them under the bed. But as he basked in my appreciation, the piles became smaller. 12

I was using what trainers call "approximations," rewarding the small steps toward learning a whole new behavior. You can't expect a baboon to learn to flip on command in one session, just as you can't expect an American husband to begin regularly picking up his dirty socks by praising him once for picking up a single sock. With the baboon you first reward a hop, then a bigger hop, then an even bigger hop. With Scott the husband, I began to praise every small act every time: if he drove just a mile an hour slower, tossed one pair of shorts into the hamper, or was on time for anything. 13

I also began to analyze my husband the way a trainer considers an exotic animal. Enlightened trainers learn all they can about a species, from anatomy to social structure, to understand how it thinks, what it likes and dislikes, what comes easily to it and what doesn't. For example, an elephant is a herd animal, so it responds to hierarchy. It cannot jump, but can stand on its head. It is a vegetarian.   14

The exotic animal known as Scott is a loner, but an alpha male. So hierarchy matters, but being in a group doesn't so much. He has the balance of a gymnast, but moves slowly, especially when getting dressed. Skiing comes naturally, but being on time does not. He's an omnivore, and what a trainer would call food-driven.   15

Once I started thinking this way, I couldn't stop. At the school in California, I'd be scribbling notes on how to walk an emu or have a wolf accept you as a pack member, but I'd be thinking, "I can't wait to try this on Scott."   16

On a field trip with the students, I listened to a professional trainer describe how he had taught African crested cranes to stop landing on his head and shoulders. He did this by training the leggy birds to land on mats on the ground. This, he explained, is what is called an "incompatible behavior," a simple but brilliant concept.   17

Rather than teach the cranes to stop landing on him, the trainer taught the birds something else, a behavior that would make the undesirable behavior impossible. The birds couldn't alight on the mats and his head simultaneously.   18

At home, I came up with incompatible behaviors for Scott to keep him from crowding me while I cooked. To lure him away from the stove, I piled up parsley for him to chop or cheese for him to grate at the other end of the kitchen island. Or I'd set out a bowl of chips and salsa across the room. Soon I'd done it: no more Scott hovering around me while I cooked.   19

I followed the students to SeaWorld San Diego, where a dolphin trainer introduced me to least reinforcing syndrome (L. R. S.). When a dolphin does something wrong, the trainer doesn't respond in any way. He stands still for a few beats, careful not to look at the dolphin, and then returns to work. The idea is that any response, positive or negative, fuels a behavior. If a behavior provokes no response, it typically dies away.   20

In the margins of my notes I wrote, "Try on Scott!"   21

It was only a matter of time before he was again tearing around the house searching for his keys, at which point I said nothing and kept at what I was doing. It took a lot of discipline to maintain my calm, but results were immediate and stunning. His temper fell far shy of its usual pitch and then waned like a fast-moving storm. I felt as if I should throw him a mackerel.   22

Now he's at it again; I hear him banging a closet door shut, rustling through papers on a chest in the front hall and thumping upstairs. At the sink, I hold steady. Then, sure enough, all goes quiet. A moment later, he walks into the kitchen, keys in hand, and says calmly, "Found them."   23

Without turning, I call out, "Great, see you later."   24

Off he goes with our much-calmed pup.   25

After two years of exotic animal training, my marriage is far smoother, 26
my husband much easier to love. I used to take his faults personally; his dirty
clothes on the floor were an affront, a symbol of how he didn't care enough
about me. But thinking of my husband as an exotic species gave me the distance I needed to consider our differences more objectively.

I adopted the trainers' motto: "It's never the animal's fault." When my 27
training attempts failed, I didn't blame Scott. Rather, I brainstormed new
strategies, thought up more incompatible behaviors and used smaller
approximations. I dissected my own behavior, considered how my actions
might inadvertently fuel his. I also accepted that some behaviors were too
entrenched, too instinctive to train away. You can't stop a badger from dig-
ging, and you can't stop my husband from losing his wallet and keys.

Professionals talk of animals that understand training so well they even- 28
tually use it back on the trainer. My animal did the same. When the training
techniques worked so beautifully, I couldn't resist telling my husband what
I was up to. He wasn't offended, just amused. As I explained the techniques
and terminology, he soaked it up. Far more than I realized.

Last fall, firmly in middle age, I learned that I needed braces. They were 29
not only humiliating, but also excruciating. For weeks my gums, teeth, jaw
and sinuses throbbed. I complained frequently and loudly. Scott assured me
that I would become used to all the metal in my mouth. I did not.

One morning, as I launched into yet another tirade about how uncom-   30
fortable I was, Scott just looked at me blankly. He didn't say a word or
acknowledge my rant in any way, not even with a nod.

I quickly ran out of steam and started to walk away. Then I realized what 31
was happening, and I turned and asked, "Are you giving me an L.R.S.?"
Silence. "You are, aren't you?"

He finally smiled, but his L.R.S. has already done the trick. He'd begun 32
to train me, the American wife.

Questions for Close Reading

1. What is the selection's thesis? Locate the sentence(s) in which Sutherland states her
   main idea. If she doesn't state her thesis explicitly, express it in your own words.
2. Sutherland tries a couple of solutions to her problems with her husband before she
   starts using the behavioral techniques that are the main focus of the essay. What
   were these initial solutions, and why did they fail to improve her relationship with
   her husband?
3. What techniques for changing behavior did Sutherland learn from the animal
   trainers? How did she apply each of these techniques to her husband Scott's
   behavior?
4. Why did changing her husband's behavior improve Sutherland's marriage?

5. Refer to your dictionary as needed to define the following words used in the selection: *bromides* (paragraph 2), *angst* (2), *mercurial* (5), *reeking* (7), *pirouette* (9), *basked* (12), *hierarchy* (14), *alpha male* (15), *omnivore* (15), *emu* (16), *incompatible* (17), *provokes* (20), *affront* (26), *inadvertently* (27), and *tirade* (30).

Questions About the Writer's Craft

1. The pattern. What type of process analysis does Sutherland use in this essay? How does the first-person point of view support the pattern of development?
2. What is the tone of Sutherland's essay? What contributes to the tone?
3. Other patterns. What pattern of development, besides process analysis, helps organize this essay? What does the other pattern contribute to the essay?
4. Is Sutherland's conclusion effective? How does her conclusion change your response to the essay?

Writing Assignments Using Process Analysis as a Pattern of Development

1. In this essay, Sutherland describes how animal trainers teach cranes, dolphins, and other animals to behave in certain ways. Imagine turning this scenario around, and thinking of animals teaching their human masters how to behave. For example, a cat might train its owner to feed it at 5:00 a.m. by ceasing to howl the second her bowl of food is set on the floor. Write an essay from an animal's point of view in which you explain how the animal trains its human "master" to meet its needs.
2. The animal-training techniques Sutherland describes in this essay are similar to behavioral therapies used by psychologists and other mental health professionals to treat people for phobias, anxiety, and other disorders, and to change specific behaviors, like smoking and other undesirable habits. Do some research in the library and on the Internet about behavioral therapies. Select one type of behavioral therapy and write an essay explaining how it works. Give examples of its use in your essay.

Writing Assignments Combining Patterns of Development

3. Recent television shows have been devoted to showing viewers how to train animals—and even children. *Dog Whisperer,* starring Cesar Millan, and *Supernanny,* starring Jo Frost, are two examples of shows that feature an "expert" working with ordinary people who have agreed to be filmed. The point of these shows is to (entertainingly) train the adults as well as their pets and children. Watch one of these shows or video clips (you can do so on their websites), or another similar show of your choosing, and write an essay in which you explain the *processes* used to train the animals and their owners or the children and their parents. Then evaluate the show's techniques, and *argue* that the show does (or does not) present effective and humane methods of changing behaviors.
4. Sutherland's essay shows how irritating even the people we love can sometimes be. Select one of your own close relationships, and write an essay in which you *describe*

what you find annoying about the other person. Give *examples* of the person's behavior to illustrate your points. What *effects* do this person's annoying traits have on the relationship as a whole? How would you change this person if you could? If you choose to write about a friend, read Marion Winik's "What Are Friends For?" (page 216) for some perspectives on friendship.

Writing Assignment Using a Journal Entry as a Starting Point

5. Review your pre-reading journal entry in which you listed and described some of your own habits. Choose one habit that you tried to break, successfully or not, and write an essay describing the habit and the steps you took to change your behavior. Before you write, decide on your purpose. For example, is your main purpose to inform others about a useful technique to change behavior or to entertain readers with a humorous narrative of your attempts to break a habit?

Additional Writing Topics

PROCESS ANALYSIS

General Assignments

Develop one of the following topics through process analysis. Explain the process one step at a time, organizing the steps chronologically. If there's no agreed-on sequence, design your own series of steps. Use transitions to ease the audience through the steps in the process. You may use any tone you wish, from serious to light.

Directional: How to Do Something

1. How to improve a course you have taken
2. How to drive defensively
3. How to get away with _____
4. How to succeed at a job interview
5. How to relax
6. How to show appreciation to others
7. How to get through school despite personal problems
8. How to be a responsible pet owner
9. How to conduct a garage or yard sale
10. How to look fashionable on a limited budget
11. How to protect a home from burglars
12. How to meet more people
13. How to improve the place where you work
14. How to gain or lose weight
15. How to get over a disappointment

Informational: How Something Happens

1. How a student becomes burned out
2. How a library's computerized catalog organizes books
3. How a dead thing decays (or how some other natural process works)
4. How the college registration process works
5. How *Homo sapiens* choose a mate
6. How a DVD player (or some other machine) works
7. How a bad habit develops
8. How people fall into debt
9. How someone becomes an Internet addict/junkie
10. How a child develops a love of reading

Assignments with a Specific Purpose, Audience, and Point of View

On Campus

1. As an experienced campus tour guide for prospective students, you've been asked by your school's Admissions Office to write a pamphlet explaining to

new tour guides how to conduct a tour of your school's campus. When explaining the process, keep in mind that tour guides need to portray the school in its best light.

2. You write an "advice to the lovelorn" column for the campus newspaper. A correspondent writes saying that he or she wants to break up with a steady girl-friend/boyfriend but doesn't know how to do this without hurting the person. Give the writer guidance on how to end a meaningful relationship with a minimal amount of pain.

At Home or in the Community

3. To help a sixteen-year-old friend learn how to drive, explain a specific driving maneuver one step at a time. You might, for example, describe how to make a three-point turn, parallel park, or handle a skid. Remember, your friend lacks self-confidence and experience.

4. Your best friend plans to move into his or her own apartment but doesn't know the first thing about how to choose one. Explain the process of selecting an apartment—where to look, what to investigate, what questions to ask before signing a lease.

On the Job

5. As a staff writer for a consumer magazine, you've been asked to write an article on how to shop for a certain product. Give specific steps explaining how to save money, buy a quality product, and the like.

6. As an author of books for elementary school children, you want to show children how to do something—take care of a pet, get along with siblings, keep a room clean. Explain the process in terms a child would understand yet not find condescending.

The Advertising Archive Ltd.

COMPARISON-CONTRAST

WHAT IS COMPARISON-CONTRAST?

Seeing how things are alike (comparing) and how they are different (contrasting) helps us impose meaning on experiences that otherwise might remain fragmented and disconnected. Barely aware that we're comparing and contrasting, we may think, "I woke up in a great mood this morning, but now I feel uneasy and anxious. I wonder why I feel so different." This inner questioning, which may occur in a flash, is just one example of how we use comparison and contrast to understand ourselves and our world.

Comparing and contrasting also help us make choices. We compare and contrast everything—from two brands of soap we might buy to two colleges we might attend. We listen to a favorite radio station, watch a preferred nightly news show, select a particular dessert from a menu—all because we have done some degree of comparing and contrasting. We often weigh these alternatives in an unstudied, casual manner, as when we flip from one radio station to another. But when we have to make important decisions, we tend to think rigorously about how things are alike or different: Should I live in a dorm or rent an apartment? Should I accept the higher-paying job or the lower-paying one that offers more challenges? Such a deliberate approach to comparison-contrast may also provide us with needed insight into complex contemporary issues: Is television's coverage of political campaigns more or less objective than it used to be? What are the merits of the various positions on abortion?

HOW COMPARISON-CONTRAST FITS
YOUR PURPOSE AND AUDIENCE

Comparison-contrast works well if you want to demonstrate any of the following: (1) that one thing is better than another (the first example below); (2) that things which seem different are actually alike (the second example below); (3) that things which seem alike are actually different (the third example below).

> Compare and contrast the way male and female relationships are depicted in *Cosmopolitan, Ms., Playboy,* and *Esquire.* Which publication has the most limited view of men and women? Which has the broadest perspective?

> Football, basketball, and baseball differ in how they appeal to fans. Describe the unique drawing power of each sport, but also reach some conclusions about the appeals the three sports have in common.

> Studies show that both college students and their parents feel that post-secondary education should equip young people to succeed in the marketplace. Yet the same studies report that the two groups have a very different understanding of what it means to succeed. What differences do you think the studies identify?

Other assignments will, in less obvious ways, lend themselves to comparison-contrast. For instance, although terms like *compare, contrast, differ,* and *have in common* don't appear in the following assignments, essay responses could be organized around the comparison-contrast format:

> The emergence of the two-career family is one of the major phenomena of our culture. Discuss the advantages and disadvantages of having both parents work, showing how you feel about such two-career households.

> Some people believe that the 1950s, often called the golden age of television, produced several never-to-be-equaled comedy classics. Do you agree that such shows as *I Love Lucy* and *The Honeymooners* are superior to the situation comedies aired on television today?

> There has been considerable criticism recently of the news coverage by the city's two leading newspapers, *The Herald* and *The Beacon.* Indicate whether you think the criticism is valid by discussing the similarities and differences in the two papers' news coverage.

Note: The last assignment shows that a comparison-contrast essay may cover similarities *and* differences, not just one or the other.

As you have seen, comparison-contrast can be the key strategy for achieving an essay's purpose. But comparison-contrast can also be a supplemental method used to help make a point in an essay organized chiefly around another pattern of development. A serious, informative essay intended for laypeople might *define* clinical depression by contrasting that state of mind with ordinary run-of-the-mill blues. Writing humorously about the exhausting *effects* of trying to get in shape, you might dramatize your plight for readers by contrasting the leisurely way you used to spend your day with your current rigidly compulsive exercise regimen. Or, in an urgent *argumentation-persuasion* essay on the need for stricter controls over drug abuse in the workplace, you might provide readers with background by comparing several companies' approaches to the problem.

At this point, you have a good sense of the way writers use comparison-contrast to achieve their purpose and to connect with their readers. Now take a moment to look closely at the photograph at the beginning of this chapter. Imagine you're writing a blog entry for a consumer advocacy web-  site. Jot down some phrases you might use when *comparing* and/or *contrasting* the vehicles in this picture, with the end of recommending one over the other.

SUGGESTIONS FOR USING COMPARISON-CONTRAST IN AN ESSAY

The suggestions here and in Figure 8.1 (page 261) will be helpful whether you use comparison-contrast as a dominant or a supportive pattern of development.

1. Be sure your subjects are at least somewhat alike.   Unless you plan to develop an *analogy* (see below), the subjects you choose to compare or contrast should share some obvious characteristics or qualities. It makes sense to compare different parts of the country, two comedians, or several college teachers. But a reasonable paper wouldn't result from, let's say, a comparison of a television game show with a soap opera. Your subjects must belong to

FIGURE 8.1

Development Diagram: Writing a Comparison-Contrast Essay

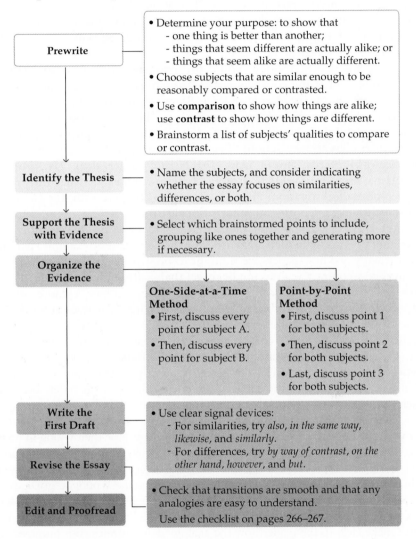

| Prewrite | • Determine your purpose: to show that
  - one thing is better than another;
  - things that seem different are actually alike; or
  - things that seem alike are actually different.
• Choose subjects that are similar enough to be reasonably compared or contrasted.
• Use **comparison** to show how things are alike; use **contrast** to show how things are different.
• Brainstorm a list of subjects' qualities to compare or contrast. |

| Identify the Thesis | • Name the subjects, and consider indicating whether the essay focuses on similarities, differences, or both. |

| Support the Thesis with Evidence | • Select which brainstormed points to include, grouping like ones together and generating more if necessary. |

Organize the Evidence

One-Side-at-a-Time Method	Point-by-Point Method
• First, discuss every point for subject A. • Then, discuss every point for subject B.	• First, discuss point 1 for both subjects. • Then, discuss point 2 for both subjects. • Last, discuss point 3 for both subjects.

| Write the First Draft | • Use clear signal devices:
  - For similarities, try *also, in the same way, likewise,* and *similarly.*
  - For differences, try *by way of contrast, on the other hand, however,* and *but.* |

| Revise the Essay | |

| Edit and Proofread | • Check that transitions are smooth and that any analogies are easy to understand.
Use the checklist on pages 266–267. |

the same general group so that your comparison-contrast stays within good logical bounds and doesn't veer off into pointlessness.

2. Stay focused on your purpose. When writing, remember that comparison-contrast isn't an end in itself. That is, your objective isn't to turn an essay into a mechanical list of "how A differs from B" or "how A is like B." Like the other patterns of development discussed in this book, comparison-contrast is a strategy for making a point or meeting a larger purpose.

Consider the assignment on page 259 about the two newspapers. Your purpose here might be simply to *inform,* to present information as objectively as possible: "This is what *The Herald*'s news coverage is like. This is what *The Beacon*'s news coverage is like."

More frequently, though, you'll use comparison-contrast to *evaluate* your subjects' pros and cons, your goal being to reach a conclusion or make a judgment: "Both *The Herald* and *The Beacon* spend too much time reporting local news," or "*The Herald*'s analysis of the recent hostage crisis was more insightful than *The Beacon*'s." Comparison-contrast can also be used to *persuade* readers to take action: "People interested in thorough coverage of international events should read *The Herald* rather than *The Beacon*." Persuasive essays may also propose a change, contrasting what now exists with a more ideal situation: "For *The Beacon* to compete with *The Herald*, it must assign more reporters to international stories."

Yet another purpose you might have is to *clear up misconceptions* by revealing previously hidden similarities or differences. For example, perhaps your town's two newspapers are thought to be sharply different. However, a comparison-contrast analysis might reveal that—although one paper specializes in sensationalized stories while the other adopts a more muted approach—both resort to biased, emotionally charged analyses of local politics. Or the essay might illustrate that the tabloid's treatment of the local arts scene is surprisingly more comprehensive than that of its competitor.

Comparing and contrasting also make it possible to *draw an analogy* between two seemingly unrelated subjects. An analogy is an imaginative comparison that delves beneath the surface differences of subjects in order to expose their significant and often unsuspected similarities or differences. Your purpose may be to show that singles bars and zoos share a number of striking similarities. Or you may want to illustrate that wolves and humans raise their young in much the same way, but that wolves go about the process in a more civilized manner. The analogical approach can make a complex subject easier to understand—as when the national deficit is compared to a household budget gone awry. Analogies are often dramatic and instructive, challenging you and your audience to consider subjects in a new light. But analogies don't speak for themselves. You must make clear to the reader how the analogy demonstrates your purpose.

3. Formulate a strong thesis.   Your essay should be focused by a solid thesis. Besides revealing your attitude, the thesis may do the following:

- Name the subjects being compared and contrasted.
- Indicate whether the essay focuses on the subjects' similarities, differences, or both.
- State the essay's main point of comparison or contrast.

Not all comparison-contrast essays need thesis statements as structured as those that follow. Even so, these examples can serve as models of clarity. Note that the first thesis statement signals similarities, the second differences, and the last both similarities and differences:

Middle-aged parents are often in a good position to empathize with adolescent children because the emotional upheavals experienced by the two age groups are much the same.

The priorities of most retired people are more conducive to health and happiness than the priorities of most young professionals.

College students in their thirties and forties face many of the same pressures as younger students, but they are better equipped to withstand these pressures.

4. Select the points to be discussed.   Once you have identified the essay's subjects, purpose, and thesis, you need to decide which aspects of the subjects to compare or contrast. College professors, for instance, could be compared and contrasted on the basis of their testing methods, ability to motivate students, confidence in front of a classroom, personalities, level of enthusiasm, and so forth.

Brainstorming, freewriting, and mapping are valuable for gathering possible points to cover. Whichever prewriting technique you use, try to produce more raw material than you'll need, so that you have the luxury of narrowing the material down to the most significant points.

When selecting points to cover, be sure to consider your audience. Ask yourself: "Will my readers be familiar with this item? Will I need it to get my message across? Will my audience find this item interesting or convincing?" What your readers know, what they don't know, and what you can predict about their reactions should influence your choices. And, of course, you need to select points that support your thesis. If your essay explains the differences between healthy, sensible diets and dangerous crash diets, it wouldn't be appropriate to talk about aerobic exercise. Similarly, imagine you want to write an essay making the point that, despite their differences, hard rock of the 1960s and punk rock of the 1970s both reflected young people's disillusionment with society. It wouldn't make much sense to contrast the long, uncombed hairstyle of the 1960s with the short, spikey cuts of the 1970s. But contrasting song lyrics (protest versus nihilistic messages) would help support your thesis and lead to interesting insights.

5. Organize the points to be discussed.   There are two common ways to organize an essay developed wholly or in part by comparison-contrast: the one-side-at-a-time method and the point-by-point method. Although both strategies may be used in a paper, one method usually predominates.

In the *one-side-at-a-time method* of organization, you discuss everything relevant about one subject before moving to another subject. For example, responding to the earlier assignment that asked you to analyze the news coverage in two local papers, you might first talk about *The Herald's* coverage of international, national, and local news; then you would discuss *The Beacon's* coverage of the same categories. Note that the areas discussed should be the same for both newspapers. It wouldn't be logical to review *The Herald's* coverage of international, national, and local news and then to detail *The Beacon's* magazine supplements, modern living section, and comics page. Moreover, the areas compared and contrasted should be presented in the same order.

This is how you would organize the essay using the one-side-at-a-time method.

Everything about A   *The Herald's* news coverage

- International
- National
- Local

Everything about B   *The Beacon's* news coverage

- International
- National
- Local

In the *point-by-point method* of organization, you alternate from one aspect of the first subject to the same aspect of your other subject(s). For example, you would first discuss *The Herald's* international coverage, then *The Beacon's* international coverage; next *The Herald's* national coverage, then *The Beacon's*; and finally, *The Herald's* local coverage, then *The Beacon's*.

Using the point-by-point method, this is how the essay would be organized.

First aspect of A and B   *The Herald:* International coverage
                            The Beacon: International coverage

Second aspect of A and B   *The Herald:* National coverage
                            The Beacon: National coverage

Third aspect of A and B   *The Herald:* Local coverage
                            The Beacon: Local coverage

Deciding which of these two methods of organization to use is largely a personal choice, though there are several factors to consider. The one-side-at-a-time method tends to convey a more unified feeling because it highlights broad similarities and differences. It is, therefore, an effective approach for subjects that are fairly uncomplicated. This strategy also works well when essays are brief; the reader won't find it difficult to remember what has been said about subject A when reading about subject B.

Because the point-by-point method permits more extensive coverage of similarities and differences, it is often a wise choice when subjects are complex. This pattern is also useful for lengthy essays since readers would probably find it difficult to remember, let's say, ten pages of information about subject A while reading the next ten pages about subject B. The point-by-point approach, however, may cause readers to lose sight of the broader picture, so remember to keep them focused on your central point.

6. Supply the reader with clear transitions. Although a well-organized comparison-contrast format is important, it doesn't guarantee that readers will be able to follow your line of thought easily. *Transitions*—especially those signaling similarities or differences—are needed to show readers where they have been and where they are going. Such cues are essential in all writing, but they're especially crucial in a paper using comparison-contrast. By indicating clearly when subjects are being compared or contrasted, the transitions help weave the discussion into a coherent whole.

The transitions (in boldface) in the following examples would *signal similarities* in an essay on the news coverage in *The Herald* and *The Beacon*:

- *The Beacon* **also** allots only a small portion of the front page to global news.
- **In the same way,** *The Herald* tries to include at least three local stories on the first page.
- **Likewise,** *The Beacon* emphasizes the importance of up-to-date reporting of town meetings.
- *The Herald* is **similarly** committed to extensive coverage of high school and college sports.

The transitions (in boldface) in the following examples would *signal differences:*

- **By way of contrast,** *The Herald's* editorial page deals with national matters on the average of three times a week.
- **On the other hand,** *The Beacon* does not share *The Herald's* enthusiasm for interviews with national figures.

- *The Beacon,* **however,** does not encourage its reporters to tackle national stories the way *The Herald* does.
- **But** *The Herald's* coverage of the Washington scene is much more comprehensive than its competitor's.

REVISION STRATEGIES

Once you have a draft of the essay, you're ready to revise. The following check-list will help you and those giving you feedback apply to comparison-contrast some of the revision techniques discussed on pages 60–62.

✔️ COMPARISON-CONTRAST: A REVISION/PEER REVIEW CHECKLIST

Revise Overall Meaning and Structure

❑ Are the subjects sufficiently alike for the comparison-contrast to be logical and meaningful?

❑ What purpose does the essay serve—to inform, to evaluate, to persuade readers to accept a viewpoint, to eliminate misconceptions, or to draw a surprising analogy?

❑ What is the essay's thesis? How could the thesis be stated more effectively?

❑ Is the overall essay organized primarily by the one-side-at-a-time method or by the point-by-point method? Why is that the best strategy for this essay?

❑ Are the same features discussed for each subject? Are they discussed in the same order?

❑ Which points of comparison and/or contrast need further development? Which points should be deleted? Where do significant points seem to be missing? How has the most important similarity or difference been emphasized?

Revise Paragraph Development

❑ If the essay uses the one-side-at-a-time method, which paragraph marks the switch from one subject to another?

❑ If the essay uses the point-by-point method, do paragraphs consistently alternate between subjects? If this alternation becomes too elaborate or predictable, what could be done to eliminate the problem?

❑ If the essay uses both methods, which paragraph marks the switch from one method to the other? If the switch is confusing, how could it be made less so?

❑ Where would signal devices make it easier to see similarities and differences between the subjects being discussed?

Revise Sentences and Words

❑ Where do too many signal devices make sentences awkward and mechanical?

❑ Which sentences and words fail to convey the intended tone?

STUDENT ESSAY

The following student essay was written by Carol Siskin in response to this assignment:

> In "Beauty and the Beast," Dave Barry humorously contrasts two attitudes toward personal appearance, finding merit in the one normally considered less praiseworthy. In an essay of your own, contrast two personality types, lifestyles, or stages of life, showing that the one most people consider inferior is actually superior.

While reading Carol's paper, try to determine how well it applies the principles of comparison-contrast. The annotations on Carol's paper and the commentary following it will help you look at the essay more closely.

The Virtues of Growing Older
by Carol Siskin

The first of a two-paragraph introduction ⟶ Our society worships youth. Advertisements convince us to buy Grecian Formula and Oil of Olay so we can hide the gray in our hair and smooth the lines on our face. Television shows feature attractive young stars with firm bodies, perfect complexions, and thick manes of hair. Middle-aged folks work out in gyms and jog down the street, trying to delay the effects of age.   1

The second introductory paragraph ⟶ Wouldn't any person over thirty gladly sign with the devil just to be young again? Isn't aging an experience to be dreaded? Perhaps it is un-American to say so, but I believe the Thesis ⟶ answer is "No." Being young is often pleasant, but being older has distinct advantages.   2

First half of topic
sentence for point
1: Appearance

Start of what
it's like being
young

Second half of
topic sentence for
point 1

Start of what
it's like being
older

First half of
topic sentence
for point 2:
Life choices

Start of what
it's like being
older

Second half of
topic sentence
for point 2

Start of what
it's like being
younger

Topic sentence
for point 3:
Self-concept

Start of what
it's like being
younger

3   When young, you are apt to be obsessed with your appearance. When my brother Dave and I were teens, we worked feverishly to perfect the bodies we had. Dave lifted weights, took megadoses of vitamins, and drank a half-dozen milkshakes a day in order to turn his wiry adolescent frame into some muscular ideal. And as a teenager, I dieted constantly. No matter what I weighed, though, I was never satisfied with the way I looked. My legs were too heavy, my shoulders too broad, my waist too big. When Dave and I were young, we begged and pleaded for the "right" clothes. If our parents didn't get them for us, we felt our world would fall apart. How could we go to school wearing loose-fitting overcoats when everyone else would be wearing fitted leather jackets? We would be considered freaks. I often wonder how my parents, and parents in general, manage to tolerate their children during the adolescent years. Now, however, Dave and I are beyond such adolescent agonies. My rounded figure seems fine, and I don't deny myself a slice of pecan pie if I feel in the mood. Dave still works out, but he has actually become fond of his tall, lanky frame. The two of us enjoy wearing fashionable clothes, but we are no longer slaves to style. And women, I'm embarrassed to admit, even more than men, have always seemed to be at the mercy of fashion. Now my clothes—and my brother's—are attractive yet easy to wear. We no longer feel anxious about what others will think. As long as we feel good about how we look, we are happy.

4   Being older is preferable to being younger in another way. Obviously, I still have important choices to make about my life, but I have already made many of the critical decisions that confront those just starting out. I chose the man I wanted to marry. I decided to have children. I elected to return to college to complete my education. But when you are young, major decisions await you at every turn. "What college should I attend? What career should I pursue? Should I get married? Should I have children?" These are just a few of the issues facing young people. It's no wonder that, despite their carefree facade, they are often confused, uncertain, and troubled by all the unknowns in their future.

5   But the greatest benefit of being forty is knowing who I am. The most unsettling aspect of youth is the uncertainty you feel about your values, goals, and dreams. Being young means wondering what is worth working for. Being young means feeling happy with yourself one day and wishing you were never born the next. It means trying on new selves by taking up with different crowds. It means resenting your parents and their way of life one minute and then feeling you will never be as good or as accomplished as they

Start of what
it's like being
older

are. By way of contrast, forty is sanity. I have a surer self-concept now. I don't laugh at jokes I don't think are funny. I can make a speech in front of a town meeting or complain in a store because I am no longer terrified that people will laugh at me; I am no longer anxious that everyone must like me. I no longer blame my parents for my every personality quirk or keep a running score of everything they did wrong raising me. Life has taught me that I, not they, am responsible for who I am. We are all human beings—neither saints nor devils.

Conclusion

Most Americans blindly accept the idea that newer is automatically better. But a human life contradicts this premise. There is a great deal of happiness to be found as we grow older. My own parents, now in their sixties, recently told me that they are happier now than they have ever been. They would not want to be my age. Did this surprise me? At first, yes. Then it gladdened me. Their contentment holds out great promise for me as I move into the next—perhaps even better—phase of my life.

6

COMMENTARY

Purpose and thesis.   In her essay, Carol disproves the widespread belief that being young is preferable to being old. The *comparison-contrast* pattern allows her to analyze the drawbacks of one and the merits of the other, thus providing the essay with an *evaluative purpose*. Using the title to indicate her point of view, Carol places the *thesis* at the end of her two-paragraph introduction: "Being young is often pleasant, but being older has distinct advantages." Note that the thesis accomplishes several things. It names the two subjects to be discussed and clarifies Carol's point of view about her subjects. The thesis also implies that the essay will focus on the contrasts between these two periods of life.

Points of support and overall organization.   To support her assertion that older is better, Carol supplies examples from her own life and organizes the examples around three main points: attitudes about appearance, decisions about life choices, and questions of self-concept. Using the *point-by-point method* to organize the overall essay, she explores each of these key ideas in a separate paragraph. Each paragraph is further focused by one or two sentences that serve as a topic sentence.

Sequence of points, organizational cues, and paragraph development.   Let's look more closely at the way Carol presents her three central points in the essay. She obviously considers appearance the least important of a person's worries, life choices more important, and self-concept the most critical. So she uses *emphatic order* to sequence the supporting paragraphs, with the phrase "But the greatest benefit" signaling the special significance of the last issue. Carol is also careful to use *transitions* to help readers follow her line of thinking: "*Now, however,* Dave and I are beyond such adolescent agonies" (paragraph 3); "*But* when you are young, major decisions await you at every turn" (4); and "*By way of contrast,* forty is sanity" (5).

Although Carol has worked hard to write a well-organized paper—and has on the whole been successful—she doesn't feel compelled to make the paper fit a rigid format. As you've seen, the essay as a whole uses the point-by-point method, but each supporting paragraph uses the *one-side-at-a-time* method—that is, everything about one age group is discussed before there is a shift to the other age group. Notice too that the third and fifth paragraphs start with young people and then move to adults, whereas the fourth paragraph reverses the sequence by starting with older people.

Combining patterns of development.   To illustrate her points, Carol makes extensive use of *exemplification,* and her discussion also has elements typical of *causal analysis.* Throughout the essay, for instance, she traces the effect of being a certain age on her brother, herself, and her parents.

A problem with unity.   As you read the third paragraph, you might have noted that Carol's essay runs into a problem. Two sentences in the paragraph disrupt the *unity* of Carol's discussion: "I often wonder how my parents, and parents in general, manage to tolerate their children during the adolescent years," and "women, I'm embarrassed to admit...have always seemed to be at the mercy of fashion." These sentences should be deleted because they don't develop the idea that adolescents are overly concerned with appearance.

Conclusion.   Carol's final paragraph brings the essay to a pleasing and interesting close. The conclusion recalls the point made in the introduction: Americans overvalue youth. Carol also uses the conclusion to broaden the scope of her discussion. Rather than continuing to focus on herself, she briefly mentions her parents and the pleasure they take in life. By bringing her parents into the essay, Carol is able to make a gently philosophical observation about the promise that awaits her as she grows older. The implication is that a similarly positive future awaits us, too.

Revising the first draft.   To help guide her revision, Carol asked her husband to read her first draft aloud. As he did, Carol took notes on what she sensed were the paper's strengths and weaknesses. She then jotted down her observations, as well as her husband's, on the draft. Keeping these comments in mind, Carol made a number of changes in her paper. You'll get a good sense of how she proceeded if you compare the original introduction printed here with the final version in the full essay.

Original Version of the Introduction

America is a land filled with people who worship youth. We admire dynamic young achievers; our middle-aged citizens work out in gyms; all of us wear tight tops and colorful sneakers—clothes that look fine on the young but ridiculous on aging bodies. Television shows revolve around perfect-looking young stars, while commercials entice us with products that will keep us young.

Wouldn't every older person want to be young again? Isn't aging to be avoided? It may be slightly unpatriotic to say so, but I believe the answer is "No." Being young may be pleasant at times, but I would rather be my forty-year-old self. I no longer have to agonize about my physical appearance, I have already made many of my crucial life decisions, and I am much less confused about who I am.

After hearing her original two-paragraph introduction read aloud, Carol was dissatisfied with what she had written. Although she wasn't quite sure how to proceed, she knew that the paragraphs were flat and that they failed to open the essay on a strong note. She decided to start by whittling down the opening sentence, making it crisper and more powerful: "Our society worships youth." That done, she eliminated two bland statements ("We admire dynamic young achievers" and "all of us wear tight tops and colorful sneakers") and made several vague references more concrete and interesting. For example, "Commercials entice us with products that will keep us young" became "Grecian Formula and Oil of Olay...hide the gray in our hair and smooth the lines on our face"; "perfect-looking young stars" became "attractive young stars with firm bodies, perfect complexions, and thick manes of hair." With the addition of these specifics, the first paragraph became more vigorous and interesting.

Carol next made some subtle changes in the two questions that opened the second paragraph of the original introduction. She replaced "Wouldn't every older person want to be young again?" and "Isn't aging to be avoided?" with two more emphatic questions: "Wouldn't any person over thirty gladly sign with the devil just to be young again?" and "Isn't aging an experience to be dreaded?" Carol also made some changes at the end of the original second paragraph. Because the paper is relatively short and the subject matter easy to understand, she decided to omit her somewhat awkward *plan of development* ("I no longer have to agonize about my physical appearance, I have already made many of my crucial life decisions, and I am much less confused about who I am"). This deletion made it possible to end the introduction with a clear statement of the essay's thesis.

Once these revisions were made, Carol was confident that her essay got off to a stronger start. Feeling reassured, she moved ahead and made changes in other sections of her paper. Such work enabled her to prepare a solid piece of writing that offers food for thought.

Activities: Comparison-Contrast

Prewriting Activities

1. Imagine you're writing two essays: One explores the *effects* of holding a job while in college; the other explains a *process* for budgeting money wisely. Jot down ways you might use comparison-contrast in each essay.

2. Using your journal or freewriting, jot down the advantages and disadvantages of two ways of doing something (for example, watching movies in the theater versus watching them on a DVD player at home; following trends versus ignoring them; dating one person versus playing the field; and so on). Reread your prewriting and determine what your thesis, purpose, audience, tone, and point of view might be if you were to write an essay. Make a scratch list of the main ideas you would cover. Would a point-by-point or a one-side-at-a-time method of organization work more effectively?

Revising Activities

3. Of the statements that follow, which would *not* make effective thesis statements for comparison-contrast essays? Identify the problem(s) in the faulty statements and revise them accordingly.

   a. Although their classroom duties often overlap, teacher aides are not as equipped as teachers to handle disciplinary problems.
   b. This college provides more assistance to its students than most schools.
   c. During the state's last congressional election, both candidates relied heavily on television to communicate their messages.
   d. There are many differences between American and foreign cars.

4. The following paragraph is from the draft of an essay detailing the qualities of a skillful manager. How effective is this comparison-contrast paragraph? What revisions would help focus the paragraph on the point made in the topic sentence? Where should details be added or deleted? Rewrite the paragraph, providing necessary transitions and details.

   A manager encourages creativity and treats employees courteously, while a boss discourages staff resourcefulness and views it as a threat. At the hardware store where I work, I got my boss's approval to develop a system for organizing excess stock in the storeroom. I shelved items in roughly the same order as they were displayed in the store. The system was helpful to all the salespeople, not just to me, since everyone was stymied by the boss's helter-skelter system. What he did was store overstocked items according to each wholesaler, even though most of us weren't there long enough to know which items came from which wholesaler. His supposed system created chaos. When he saw what I had done, he was furious and insisted that we continue to follow the old slapdash system. I had assumed he would welcome my ideas the way my manager did last summer when I worked in a drugstore. But he didn't and I had to scrap my work and go back to his eccentric system. He certainly could learn something about employee relations from the drugstore manager.

Eric Weiner

Eric Weiner (1963–) is a national correspondent for NPR.org, part of National Public Radio. He began his journalism career by reporting on business issues for *The New York Times* and NPR's Washington, D.C., bureau and then spent most of the 1990s reporting on wars and world events from South Asia and the Middle East. A licensed pilot who loves to eat sushi, Weiner occasionally writes lighter pieces drawing on his experience with other cultures. He is the author of *The Geography of Bliss: One Grump's Search for the Happiest Places in the World* (2008). A short version of this piece about e-mail was broadcast on *Day to Day,* a National Public Radio magazine show, on March 24, 2005; the full version, which appears here, was posted on Slate.com the next day.

For ideas about how this comparison–contrast essay is organized, see Figure 8.2 on page 277.

Pre-Reading Journal Entry

Just one hundred years ago, people communicated only by speaking face to face or by writing a letter—with an occasional brief telegram in emergencies. Today, technology has given us many ways to communicate. Think over all the different ways you communicate with your family, friends, classmates, instructors, coworkers, and others. What methods of communication do you use with each of these groups? Which forms do you prefer, and why? Use your journal to answer these questions.

Euromail and Amerimail

North America and Europe are two continents divided by a common technology: e-mail. Techno-optimists assure us that e-mail—along with the Internet and satellite TV—make the world smaller. That may be true in a technical sense. I can send a message from my home in Miami to a German friend in Berlin and it will arrive almost instantly. But somewhere over the Atlantic, the messages get garbled. In fact, two distinct forms of e-mail have emerged: Euromail and Amerimail. 1

Amerimail is informal and chatty. It's likely to begin with a breezy "Hi" and end with a "Bye." The chances of Amerimail containing a smiley face or an "xoxo" are disturbingly high. We Americans are reluctant to dive into the meat of an e-mail; we feel compelled to first inform hapless recipients about our vacation on the Cape which was really excellent except the jellyfish were biting and the kids caught this nasty bug so we had to skip the whale watching trip but about that investors' meeting in New York…Amerimail is a bundle of contradictions: rambling and yet direct; deferential, yet arrogant. In other words, Amerimail *is* America. 2

Euromail is stiff and cold, often beginning with a formal "Dear Mr. X" and ending with a brusque "Sincerely." You won't find any mention of kids or the weather or jellyfish in Euromail. It's also business. It's also slow. 3

Your correspondent might take days, even weeks, to answer a message. Euromail is also less confrontational in tone, rarely filled with the overt nastiness that characterizes American e-mail disagreements. In other words, Euromail is exactly like the Europeans themselves. (I am, of course, generalizing. German e-mail style is not exactly the same as Italian or Greek, but they have more in common with each other than they do with American mail.)

These are more than mere stylistic differences. Communication matters. Which model should the rest of the world adopt: Euromail or Amerimail? 4

A California-based e-mail consulting firm called People-onthego sheds some light on the e-mail divide. It recently asked about 100 executives on both sides of the Atlantic whether they noticed differences in e-mail styles. Most said yes. Here are a few of their observations: 5

"Americans tend to write (e-mails) exactly as they speak."

"Europeans are less obsessive about checking e-mail."

"In general, Americans are much more responsive to email—they respond faster and provide more information."

One respondent noted that Europeans tend to segregate their e-mail accounts. Rarely do they send personal messages on their business accounts, or vice versa. These differences can't be explained merely by differing comfort levels with technology. Other forms of electronic communication, such as SMS text messaging, are more popular in Europe than in the United States.

The fact is, Europeans and Americans approach e-mail in a fundamentally different way. Here is the key point: For Europeans, e-mail has replaced the business letter. For Americans, it has replaced the telephone. That's why we tend to unleash what e-mail consultant Tim Burress calls a "brain dump": unloading the content of our cerebral cortex onto the screen and hitting the send button. "It makes Europeans go ballistic," he says. 6

Susanne Khawand, a German high-tech executive, has been on the receiving end of American brain dumps, and she says it's not pretty. "I feel like saying, 'Why don't you just call me instead of writing five e-mails back and forth,'" she says. Americans are so overwhelmed by their bulging inboxes that "you can't rely on getting an answer. You don't even know if they read it." In Germany, she says, it might take a few days, or even weeks, for an answer, but one always arrives. 7

Maybe that's because, on average, Europeans receive fewer e-mails and spend less time tending their inboxes. An international survey of business owners in 24 countries (conducted by the accounting firm Grant Thornton) found that people in Greece and Russia spend the least amount of time dealing with e-mail every day: 48 minutes on average. Americans, 8 by comparison, spend two hours per day, among the highest in the world. (Only Filipinos spend more time on e-mail, 2.1 hours.) The survey also found that European executives are skeptical of e-mail's ability to boost their bottom line.

It's not clear why European and American e-mail styles have evolved   9 separately, but I suspect the reasons lie within deep cultural differences. Americans tend to be impulsive and crave instant gratification. So we send e-mails rapid-fire and get antsy if we don't receive a reply quickly. Europeans tend to be more methodical and plodding. They send (and reply to) e-mails only after great deliberation.

For all their Continental fastidiousness, Europeans can be remarkably lax   10 about e-mail security, says Bill Young, and executive vice president with the Strickland Group. Europeans are more likely to include trade secrets and business strategies in e-mails, he says, much to the frustration of their American colleagues. This is probably because identity theft—and other types of backing—are much less of a problem in Europe than in the United States. Privacy laws are much stricter in Europe.

So, which is better: Euromail or Amerimail? Personally, I'm a convert—   11 or a defector, if you prefer—to the former. I realize it's not popular these days to suggest we have anything to learn from Europeans, but I'm fed up with an inbox cluttered with rambling, barely cogent missives from friends and colleagues. If the alternative is a few stiffly written, politely worded bits of Euromail, then I say...bring it on.

Questions for Close Reading

1. What is the selection's thesis? Locate the sentence(s) in which Weiner states his main idea. If he doesn't state his thesis explicitly, express it in your own words.
2. According to Weiner, what are the main characteristics of American e-mail? What are the main characteristics of European e-mail?
3. When Americans and Europeans e-mail one another for business reasons, frustration often ensues. Why, according to Weiner, is this so? What are some examples of e-mail differences that cause frustration?
4. Which type of e-mail does Weiner favor? Why?
5. Refer to your dictionary as needed to define the following words used in the selection: *hapless* (paragraph 2), *deferential* (2), *brusque* (3), *confrontational* (3), *overt* (3), *bottom line* (8), *fastidiousness* (10), *lax* (10), *cogent* (11), and *missives* (11).

Questions About the Writer's Craft

1. The opening paragraph of this essay is full of technology-related words: *technology, e-mail, techno-optimists, Internet, Satellite TV, technical sense, Euromail,* and *Amerimail.* What is the effect of using all these "techno-terms"? How does the remainder of the essay contrast with the dominant impression of the first paragraph?

FIGURE 8.2
Essay Structure Diagram: "Euromail and Amerimail" by Eric Weiner

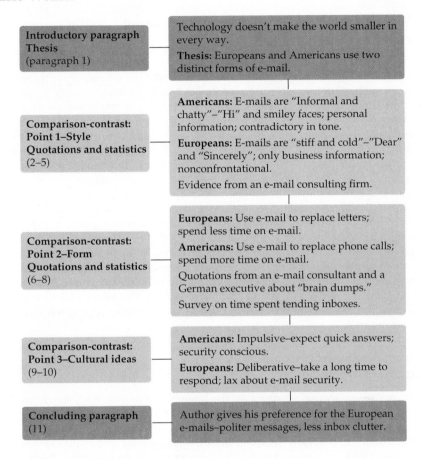

Introductory paragraph Thesis (paragraph 1)

Technology doesn't make the world smaller in every way.

Thesis: Europeans and Americans use two distinct forms of e-mail.

Comparison-contrast: Point 1–Style Quotations and statistics (2–5)

Americans: E-mails are "Informal and chatty"–"Hi" and smiley faces; personal information; contradictory in tone.

Europeans: E-mails are "stiff and cold"–"Dear" and "Sincerely"; only business information; nonconfrontational.

Evidence from an e-mail consulting firm.

Comparison-contrast: Point 2–Form Quotations and statistics (6–8)

Europeans: Use e-mail to replace letters; spend less time on e-mail.

Americans: Use e-mail to replace phone calls; spend more time on e-mail.

Quotations from an e-mail consultant and a German executive about "brain dumps."

Survey on time spent tending inboxes.

Comparison-contrast: Point 3–Cultural ideas (9–10)

Americans: Impulsive–expect quick answers; security conscious.

Europeans: Deliberative–take a long time to respond; lax about e-mail security.

Concluding paragraph (11)

Author gives his preference for the European e-mails–politer messages, less inbox clutter.

2. **The Pattern.** What type of organization does Weiner use for the essay? How else could he have organized the points he makes? Which method of organization do you think is more effective for this essay?

3. **The Pattern.** Identify the transitional expressions that Weiner uses to signal similarities and differences. Why do you think there are so few of these expressions? How might the fact that this essay was meant to be read aloud affect Weiner's transitions between Amerimail and Euromail? (You can listen to the short version of the essay at www.npr.org; search using the key term "Euromail.") Do you think the essay would be better if Weiner had used more transitional expressions? Explain.

4. What type of conclusion does Weiner use? (To review strategies for conclusions, see pages 55–56). What is his concluding point? Were you surprised by this conclusion? Why or why not?

Writing Assignments Using Comparison-Contrast as a Pattern of Development

1. Weiner attributes differences between Americans and Europeans in the use of e-mail to underlying cultural differences. Consider the differences in the use of e-mail among specific sub-groups of Americans, for example, among Americans of different generations, different genders, or different ethnic groups. Drawing on your own personal experience and that of people you know, write an essay comparing and contrasting some of the ways these two different groups of Americans use e-mail. For another take on differences in communication—of the racial variety—read Leslie Savan's "Black Talk and Pop Culture" (page 171).

2. The etiquette of e-mail correspondence certainly is not the only way in which Americans differ from Europeans. Consider some additional ways that Americans as a whole differ from another specific nationality or ethnic group, European or otherwise. Write an essay in which you *contrast* the way Americans and the other group approach at least three cultural practices. You might look at attitudes toward gender roles, child-rearing, personal fitness, treatment of the ill or the elderly, leisure to work ratios, the environment, and so on. Before you begin to write, consider what sort of tone might best suit your essay. You might adopt a straight-forward tone (like Weiner's), or you might find a humorous approach better suits your material.

Writing Assignments Combining Patterns of Development

3. Weiner's essay focuses primarily on the business use of e-mail among Americans and Europeans. Do some research on the Internet about the various uses of e-mail that have developed. Write an essay identifying how e-mail has *affected* our personal lives, our academic lives, and our business lives. Be sure to provide specific examples and data, where possible, to support the claims you make about these areas of change. Consider concluding your essay by summarizing whether e-mail has been beneficial, harmful, or both.

4. Weiner's preference for Euromail indicates that he longs for a more formal approach to communication. Over time, several other types of behaviors have evolved to be less formal than they once were. Select another aspect of behavior that has acquired a more casual mode; examples include dining etiquette, forms of address, dress codes, classroom protocol or student-teacher dynamics, and so on. Write an essay in which you explore at least two to three *causes* for the shift from more formal to more casual expressions of this behavior. As you examine the causes, you'll probably find yourself *contrasting* former and current practices. And your conclusion should *argue* for the superiority of either the casual or the formal approach.

Writing Assignment Using a Journal
Entry as a Starting Point

5. Review your pre-reading journal entry about the different communication methods you use. Select three of your favorite methods, and write an essay dividing and classifying each of these methods, analyzing how you use it to communicate, and with whom. What are each method's advantages and disadvantages? Be sure to provide specific examples along the way. For additional perspectives on modern communication, read Leslie Savan's "Black Talk and Pop Culture" (page 171) and David Shipley's "Talk About Editing" (page 245).

Once accused of being a fearmonger, biologist Rachel Carson (1907–64) is now recognized as one of the country's first environmentalists. She was the author of three popular books about the marine world: *The Sea Around Us* (1951), *Under the Sea Wind* (1952), and *The Edge of the Sea* (1955). But it was the publication of *Silent Spring* (1962), Carson's alarming study of the use of pesticides and herbicides, that brought her special attention and established her reputation as a passionate advocate for a clean environment. The following selection is taken from *Silent Spring*.

Pre-Reading Journal Entry

Take a few minutes to record in your journal your impressions of a place that has special meaning for you—but that is being threatened in one way or another. Jot down sensory details about the place, focusing on those specifics that capture its unique qualities.

A Fable for Tomorrow

There was once a town in the heart of America where all life seemed 1 to live in harmony with its surroundings. The town lay in the midst of a checkerboard of prosperous farms, with fields of grain and hillsides of orchards where, in spring, white clouds of bloom drifted above the green fields. In autumn, oak and maple and birch set up a blaze of color that flamed and flickered across a backdrop of pines. Then foxes barked in the hills and deer silently crossed the fields, half hidden in the mists of the fall mornings.

Along the roads, laurel, viburnum and alder, great ferns and wildflowers 2 delighted the traveler's eye through much of the year. Even in winter the roadsides were places of beauty, where countless birds came to feed on the berries and on the seed heads of the dried weeds rising above the snow. The countryside was, in fact, famous for the abundance and variety of its bird life, and when the flood of migrants was pouring through in spring and fall people traveled from great distances to observe them. Others came to fish the streams, which flowed clear and cold out of the hills and contained shady pools where trout lay. So it had been from the days many years ago when the first settlers raised their houses, sank their wells, and built their barns.

Then a strange blight crept over the area and everything began to 3 change. Some evil spell had settled on the community: mysterious maladies swept the flocks of chickens; the cattle and sheep sickened and died. Everywhere was a shadow of death. The farmers spoke of much illness among their families. In the town the doctors had become more and more puzzled by new kinds of sickness appearing among their patients. There had been several sudden and unexplained deaths, not only among adults but even among children, who would be stricken suddenly while at play and die within a few hours.

There was a strange stillness. The birds, for example—where had they 4 gone? Many people spoke of them, puzzled and disturbed. The feeding stations in the backyards were deserted. The few birds seen anywhere were moribund; they trembled violently and could not fly. It was a spring without voices. On the mornings that had once throbbed with the dawn chorus of robins, catbirds, doves, jays, wrens, and scores of other bird voices there was now no sound; only silence lay over the fields and woods and marsh.

On the farms the hens brooded, but no chicks hatched. The farmers 5 complained that they were unable to raise any pigs—the litters were small and the young survived only a few days. The apple trees were coming into bloom but no bees droned among the blossoms, so there was no pollination and there would be no fruit.

The roadsides, once so attractive, were now lined with browned and 6 withered vegetation as though swept by fire. These, too, were silent, deserted by all living things. Even the streams were now lifeless. Anglers no longer visited them, for all the fish had died.

In the gutters under the eaves and between the shingles of the roofs, a 7 white granular powder still showed a few patches; some weeks before it had fallen like snow upon the roofs and the lawns, the fields and streams.

No witchcraft, no enemy action had silenced the rebirth of new life in 8 this stricken world. The people had done it themselves.

This town does not actually exist, but it might easily have a thousand 9 counterparts in America or elsewhere in the world. I know of no community that has experienced all the misfortunes I describe. Yet every one of these disasters has actually happened somewhere, and many real communities have already suffered a substantial number of them. A grim specter has crept upon us almost unnoticed, and this imagined tragedy may easily become a stark reality we all shall know.

Questions for Close Reading

1. What is the selection's thesis? Locate the sentence(s) in which Carson states her main idea. If she doesn't state the thesis explicitly, express it in your own words.
2. What are some of the delights of Carson's beautiful, healthy countryside?
3. When Carson writes of "a strange blight," an "evil spell" (paragraph 3), whose point of view is she adopting?
4. What are the effects of the blight?
5. Refer to your dictionary as needed to define the following words used in the selection: *viburnum* (paragraph 2), *alder* (2), *moribund* (4), and *specter* (9).

Questions About the Writer's Craft

1. **The pattern.** To develop her essay, Carson uses the one-side-at-a-time method of comparison-contrast. What does this method enable her to do that the point-by-point approach would not?
2. **Other patterns.** Throughout the essay, Carson appeals to the reader's senses of sight and hearing. Which paragraphs are developed primarily through visual or auditory *description?* How do the sensory images in these paragraphs reinforce Carson's thesis?
3. Carson's diction (word choice) and sentence rhythm often resemble those of the Bible. For example, we read, "So it had been from the days many years ago" (paragraph 2), "a strange blight crept over the area" (3), and "Everywhere was a shadow of death" (3). Why do you suppose Carson chose to echo the Bible in this way?
4. How does Carson's approach to her subject change in the last paragraph? What is the effect of this change?

Writing Assignments Using Comparison-Contrast as a Pattern of Development

1. Carson imagines a fictional town that has changed for the worse. Consider a place you know well that has changed for the *better.* You might focus on a renovated school, a rehabilitated neighborhood, a newly preserved park. Write an essay contrasting the place before and after the change. At the end of your essay, describe briefly the effects of the change.
2. In her essay, Carson provides descriptive details unique to particular seasons. For example, she writes that "in autumn, oak and maple and birch set up a blaze of color that flamed and flickered across a backdrop of pines" (paragraph 1). Choosing a place you know well, contrast its sights, sounds, and smells during one season with those you've noticed during another time of year. Use rich sensory details to convey the differences between the two seasons. Consider first reading Gary Kamiya's "Life, Death and Spring" (page 103), which recounts, in vivid detail, specific natural places and phenomena.

Writing Assignments Combining Patterns of Development

3. Carson cites "white granular powder" (paragraph 7) as the cause of the blight. Write an essay about a time you noticed a visible environmental problem—say, smog blurring a city skyline, soot coating a window, or medical syringes discarded on the beach. Use vivid *narrative details* to capture the effect of the experience on you.
4. Carson graphically shows the effects of herbicides and pesticides on the environment. Focus on some other less global environmental problem: graffiti on a public building; vandalized trees and shrubs; beer cans thrown in a neighborhood park, for example. Discuss the *effects* of this situation on the physical environment

and on people's attitudes and actions. Conclude with suggestions about possible *strategies* for remedying the problem. Gordon Parks's "Flavio's Home" (page 95) will help you appreciate the interaction between the environment and human behavior.

Writing Assignment Using a Journal Entry as a Starting Point

5. Write an essay describing an endangered place that is very important to you. Describe the potential threat either at the beginning or at the end of the essay, and paint such a vivid picture of the place in the rest of the essay that readers understand why the potential threat is so unfortunate. Select from your pre-reading journal entry only those details that convey the special qualities of the place, adding more texture and specifics where needed.

Dave Barry

Pulitzer Prize–winning humorist Dave Barry (1947–) began his writing career covering—as he puts it—"incredibly dull municipal meetings" for the *Daily Local News* of West Chester, Pennsylvania. Next came an eight-year stint trying to teach businesspeople not to write sentences like "Enclosed please find the enclosed enclosures." In 1983, Barry joined the staff of the *The Miami Herald,* where his rib-tickling commentary on the absurdities of everyday life quickly brought him a legion of devoted fans. Barry's column is now syndicated in more than 150 newspapers. A popular guest on television and radio, Barry has written dozens of books, including *Dave Barry's Complete Guide to Guys* (1995), *Dave Barry in Cyberspace* (1996), *Dave Barry Hits Below the Beltway* (2001), *Boogers Are My Beat* (2003), and most recently *Dave Barry's Money Secrets* (2006). He has also written the the comic mystery novels *Big Trouble* (1999) and *Tricky Business* (2002). The father of two, Barry lives in Miami with his wife. The following essay, published also under the title "The Ugly Truth About Beauty," first appeared in *The Miami Herald* in 1998.

Pre-Reading Journal Entry

To what extent would you say our images of personal attractiveness are influenced by TV commercials and magazine advertisements? Think of commercials and ads you've seen recently. What physical traits are typically identified as attractive in women? In men? List as many as you can. What assumptions does each trait suggest? Use your journal to respond to these questions.

Beauty and the Beast

If you're a man, at some point a woman will ask you how she looks.   1

"How do I look?" she'll ask.   2

You must be careful how you answer this question. The best technique   3
is to form an honest yet sensitive opinion, then collapse on the floor with
some kind of fatal seizure. Trust me, this is the easiest way out. Because you
will never come up with the right answer.

The problem is that women generally do not think of their looks in the   4
same way that men do. Most men form an opinion of how they look in the
seventh grade, and they stick to it for the rest of their lives. Some men form
the opinion that they are irresistible stud muffins, and they do not change
this opinion even when their faces sag and their noses bloat to the size of
eggplants and their eyebrows grow together to form what appears to be a
giant forehead-dwelling tropical caterpillar.

Most men, I believe, think of themselves as average-looking. Men will   5
think this even if their faces cause heart failure in cattle at a range of 300 yards.
Being average does not bother them; average is fine, for men. This is why men
never ask anybody how they look. Their primary form of beauty care is to

shave themselves, which is essentially the same form of beauty care that they give to their lawns. If, at the end of his four-minute daily beauty regimen, a man has managed to wipe most of the shaving cream out of his hair and is not bleeding too badly, he feels that he has done all he can, so he stops thinking about his appearance and devotes his mind to more critical issues, such as the Super Bowl.

Women do not look at themselves this way. If I had to express, in three words, what I believe most women think about their appearance, those words would be: "not good enough." No matter how attractive a woman may appear to be to others, when she looks at herself in the mirror, she thinks: woof. She thinks that at any moment a municipal animal-control officer is going to throw a net over her and haul her off to the shelter.   6

Why do women have such low self-esteem? There are many complex psychological and societal reasons, by which I mean Barbie. Girls grow up playing with a doll proportioned such that, if it were human, it would be seven feet tall and weigh 81 pounds, of which 53 pounds would be bosoms. This is a difficult appearance standard to live up to, especially when you contrast it with the standard set for little boys by their dolls...excuse me, by their action figures. Most of the action figures that my son played with when he was little were hideous-looking. For example, he was very fond of an action figure (part of the He-Man series) called "Buzz-Off," who was part human, part flying insect. Buzz-Off was not a looker. But he was extremely self-confident. You could not imagine Buzz-Off saying to the other action figures: "Do you think these wings make my hips look big?"   7

But women grow up thinking they need to look like Barbie, which for most women is impossible, although there is a multibillion-dollar beauty industry devoted to convincing women that they must try. I once saw an Oprah show wherein supermodel Cindy Crawford dispensed makeup tips to the studio audience. Cindy had all these middle-aged women applying beauty products to their faces; she stressed how important it was to apply them in a certain way, using the tips of their fingers. All the women dutifully did this, even though it was obvious to any sane observer that, no matter how carefully they applied these products, they would never look remotely like Cindy Crawford, who is some kind of genetic mutation.   8

I'm not saying that men are superior. I'm just saying that you're not going to get a group of middle-aged men to sit in a room and apply cosmetics to themselves under the instruction of Brad Pitt, in hopes of looking more like him. Men would realize that this task was pointless and demeaning. They would find some way to bolster their self-esteem that did not require looking like Brad Pitt. They would say to Brad: "Oh YEAH? Well what do you know about LAWN CARE, pretty boy?"   9

Of course many women will argue that the reason they become obsessed with trying to look like Cindy Crawford is that men, being as   10 shallow as a drop of spit, WANT women to look that way. To which I have two responses:

1. Hey, just because WE'RE idiots, that does not mean YOU have to be; and   11

2. Men don't even notice 97 percent of the beauty efforts you make any-   12
way. Take fingernails. The average woman spends 5,000 hours per year worrying about her fingernails; I have never once, in more than 40 years of listening to men talk about women, heard a man say, "She has a nice set of fingernails!" Many men would not notice if a woman had upward of four hands.

Anyway, to get back to my original point: If you're a man, and a woman   13
asks you how she looks, you're in big trouble. Obviously, you can't say she looks bad. But you also can't say that she looks great, because she'll think you're lying, because she has spent countless hours, with the help of the multibillion-dollar beauty industry, obsessing about the differences between herself and Cindy Crawford. Also, she suspects that you're not qualified to judge anybody's appearance. This is because you have shaving cream in your hair.

Questions for Close Reading

1. What is the selection's thesis? Locate the sentence(s) in which Barry states his main idea. If he doesn't state the thesis explicitly, express it in your own words.
2. Barry tells us that most men consider themselves to be "average-looking" (paragraph 5). Why, according to Barry, do men feel this way?
3. When Barry writes that most women think of themselves as "not good enough" (6), what does he mean? What, according to Barry, causes women to develop low opinions of themselves?
4. Barry implies that women could have a more rational response to the "difficult appearance standard" that pervades society (7). What would that response be?
5. Refer to your dictionary as needed to define the following words used in the selection: *regimen* (paragraph 5), *municipal* (6), *societal* (7), *dispensed* (8), *genetic* (8), *mutation* (8), *demeaning* (9), and *bolster* (9).

Questions About the Writer's Craft

1. **The pattern.** Which comparison-contrast method of organization (point-by-point or one-side-at-a-time) does Barry use to develop his essay? Why might he have chosen this pattern?
2. Barry uses exaggeration, a strategy typically associated with humorous writing. Locate instances of exaggeration in the selection. Why do you think he uses this strategy?
3. **Other patterns.** Barry demonstrates a series of *cause-effect* chains in his essay. Locate some of the cause-effect series. How do they help Barry reinforce his thesis?
4. How does the essay's title foreshadow the essay's ideas?

Writing Assignments Using Comparison-Contrast as a Pattern of Development

1. Examine the pitches made in magazines and on TV for the male and female versions of *one* kind of grooming product. Possibilities include deodorant, hair

dye, soap, and so on. Then write an essay contrasting the persuasive appeals that the product makes to men with those it makes to women. (Don't forget to examine the assumptions behind the appeals.) To gain insight into advertising techniques, you'll find it helpful to read Ann McClintock's "Propaganda Techniques in Today's Advertising" (page 204). For useful perspectives on gender issues, consider reading Amy Sutherland's "What Shamu Taught Me About a Happy Marriage" (page 250). For more insight into how we judge beauty, read Natalie Angier's "The Cute Factor" (page 343).

2. Barry contrasts women's preoccupation with looking good to men's lack of concern about their appearance. Now consider the flip side—something men care about deeply that women virtually ignore. Write an essay contrasting men's stereotypical fascination with *one* area to women's indifference. You might, for example, examine male and female attitudes toward sports, cars, tools, even lawn care. Following Barry's example, adopt a playful tone in your essay, illustrating the absurdity of the obsession you discuss.

Writing Assignments Combining Patterns of Development

3. Barry implies that most men, unaffected by the "multibillion-dollar beauty industry," are content to "think of themselves as average looking." Do you agree? Conduct your own research into whether or not Barry's assertions about men are true. Begin by interviewing several male friends, family members, and classmates to see how these men feel about their physical appearance. In addition, in the library or online, research magazines such as *People, GQ,* or *Men's Health* for articles describing how everyday men as well as male celebrities view their looks. Then write an essay *refuting* or *defending* the view that being average-looking doesn't bother most men. Start by acknowledging the opposing view; then support your assertion with convincing *examples* and other evidence drawn from your research.

4. Barry blames Barbie dolls for setting up "a difficult appearance standard" for girls to emulate. Many would *argue* that the toys that *boys* play with also teach negative, ultimately damaging values. Write an essay exploring the values that are conveyed to boys through their toys. Brainstorm with others, especially males, about the toys of their youth or the toys that boys have today. Identify two to three key negative values to write about, *illustrating* each with several examples of toys.

Writing Assignment Using a Journal Entry as a Starting Point

5. Review your pre-reading journal entry. Focusing on the characteristics of male *or* female attractiveness conveyed by the mass media, identify two to three assumptions suggested by these standards. Illustrate each assumption with examples from TV commercials and/or magazine advertisements. Be sure to make clear how you feel about these assumptions.

Additional Writing Topics

COMPARISON-CONTRAST

General Assignments

Using comparison-contrast, write an essay on one of the following topics. Your thesis should indicate whether the two subjects are being compared, contrasted, or both. Organize the paper by arranging the details in a one-side-at-a-time or point-by-point pattern. Remember to use organizational cues to help the audience follow your analysis.

1. Living at home versus living in an apartment or dorm
2. Two-career family versus one-career family
3. Two approaches for dealing with problems
4. Children's pastimes today and yesterday
5. Life before the Internet versus after the Internet
6. Neighborhood stores versus shopping malls
7. Two characters in a novel or other literary work
8. Two attitudes toward money
9. A sports team then and now
10. Watching a movie on television versus viewing it in a theater
11. Two attitudes about a controversial subject
12. Two approaches to parenting
13. A typical fan of one type of music versus another
14. Marriage versus living together
15. The atmosphere in two classes
16. Two approaches to studying
17. The place where you live and the place where you would like to live
18. Two comedians
19. The coverage of an event on television versus the coverage in a newspaper
20. Significant trend versus passing fad
21. Two horror or adventure movies
22. Handwriting a letter versus sending an e-mail message
23. Two candidates for an office
24. Your attitude before and after getting to know someone
25. Two friends with different lifestyles

Assignments with a Specific Purpose, Audience, and Point of View

On Campus

1. You would like to change your campus living arrangements. Perhaps you want to move from a dormitory to an off-campus apartment or from home to a dorm. Before you do, though, you'll have to convince your parents (who are paying most of your college costs) that the move will be beneficial. Write out what you

would say to your parents. Contrast your current situation with your proposed one, explaining why the new arrangement would be better.

2. Write a guide on "Passing Exams" for first-year college students, contrasting the right and wrong ways to prepare for and take exams. Although your purpose is basically serious, write the section on how not to approach exams with some humor.

At Home or in the Community

3. As president of your local Neighbors' Association, you're concerned about the way your local government is dealing with a particular situation (for example, an increase in robberies, muggings, graffiti, and so on). Write a letter to your mayor contrasting the way your local government handles the situation with another city or town's approach. In your conclusion, point out the advantages of adopting the other neighborhood's strategy.

4. Your old high school has invited you back to make a speech before an audience of seniors. The topic will be "how to choose the college that is right for you." Write your speech in the form of a comparison-contrast analysis. Focus on the choices available (two-year versus four-year schools, large versus small, local versus faraway, and so on), showing the advantages and/or disadvantages of each.

On the Job

5. As store manager, you decide to write a memo to all sales personnel explaining how to keep customers happy. Compare and/or contrast the needs and shopping habits of several different consumer groups (by age, spending ability, or sex), and show how to make each group comfortable in your store.

6. You work as a volunteer for a mental health hot line. Many people call simply because they feel "stressed out." Do some research on the subject of stress management, and prepare a brochure for these people, recommending a "Type B" approach to stressful situations. Focus the brochure on the contrast between "Type A" and "Type B" personalities: the former is nervous, hard-driving, competitive; the latter is relaxed and noncompetitive. Give specific examples of how each type tends to act in stressful situations.

CAUSE-EFFECT

WHAT IS CAUSE-EFFECT?

Superstition has it that curiosity killed the cat. Maybe so. Yet our science, technology, storytelling, and fascination with the past and future all spring from our determination to know "Why" and "What if." Seeking explanations, young children barrage adults with endless questions: "Why do trees grow tall?" "What would happen if the sun didn't shine?" But children aren't the only ones who wonder in this way. All of us think in terms of cause and effect, sometimes consciously, sometimes unconsciously: "Why did they give me such an odd look?" we wonder, or "How would I do at another college?" we speculate. This exploration of reasons and results is also at the heart of most professions: "What led to our involvement in Vietnam?" historians question; "What will happen if we administer this experimental drug?" scientists ask.

Cause-effect writing, often called *causal analysis,* is rooted in this elemental need to make connections. Because the drive to understand reasons and results is so fundamental, causal analysis is a common kind of writing. An article analyzing the unexpected outcome of an election, a report linking poor nutrition to low academic achievement, an editorial analyzing the impact of a proposed tax cut—all are examples of cause-effect writing.

Done well, cause-effect pieces can uncover the subtle and often surprising connections between events or phenomena. By rooting out causes and projecting effects, causal analysis enables us to make sense of our experiences, revealing a universe that is somewhat less arbitrary and chaotic.

HOW CAUSE-EFFECT FITS YOUR PURPOSE AND AUDIENCE

Many assignments and exam questions in college involve writing essays that analyze causes, effects, or both. Sometimes, as in the following examples, you'll be asked to write an essay developed primarily through the cause-effect pattern:

> Although divorces have leveled off in the last few years, the number of marriages ending in divorce is still greater than it was a generation ago. What do you think are the causes of this phenomenon?

> Political commentators were surprised that so few people voted in the last election. Discuss the probable causes of this weak voter turnout.

> Americans never seem to tire of gossip about the rich and famous. What effect has this fascination with celebrities had on U.S. culture?

> The federal government is expected to pass legislation that will significantly reduce the funding of student loans. Analyze the possible effects of such a cutback.

Other assignments and exam questions may not explicitly ask you to address causes and effects, but they may use words that suggest causal analysis would be appropriate. Consider these examples, paying special attention to the words in boldface:

> In contrast to the socially involved youth of the 1960s, many young people today tend to remove themselves from political issues. What do you think are the **sources** of the political apathy found among 18- to 25-year-olds? (*cause*)

> A number of experts forecast that drug abuse will be the most significant factor affecting U.S. productivity in the coming decade. Evaluate the validity of this observation by discussing the **impact** of drugs in the workplace. (*effect*)

> According to school officials, a predictable percentage of entering students drop out of college at some point during their first year. What **motivates** students to drop out? What **happens** to them once they leave? (*cause and effect*)

In addition to serving as the primary strategy for achieving an essay's purpose, causal analysis can also be a supplemental method used to help make a point in an essay developed chiefly through another pattern of development. Assume, for example, that you want to write an essay *defining* the term *the homeless*. To help readers see that unfavorable circumstances can result in nearly anyone becoming homeless, you might discuss some of the unavoidable, everyday factors causing people to live on streets and in subway stations. Similarly, in a *persuasive* proposal urging your college administration to institute an honors program, you would probably spend some time analyzing the positive effect of such a program on students and faculty.

At this point, you have a good sense of the way writers use cause-effect to achieve their purpose and to connect with their readers. Now take a moment to look closely at the photograph at the beginning of this chapter. Imagine you're writing a column, accompanied by the photo, for the website of a local environmental organization. Your purpose is to prevent further development of nearby wilderness areas. Jot down ideas you might include when discussing the *effects* of such development.

SUGGESTIONS FOR USING CAUSE-EFFECT IN AN ESSAY

The suggestions here and in Figure 9.1 (page 293) will be helpful whether you use causal analysis as a dominant or a supportive pattern of development.

1. Stay focused on the purpose of your analysis.   When writing a causal analysis, don't lose sight of your overall purpose. Consider, for example, an essay on the causes of widespread child abuse. If you're concerned primarily with explaining the problem of child abuse to your readers, you might take a purely *informative* approach:

> Although parental stress is the immediate cause of child abuse, the more compelling reason for such behavior lies in the way parents were themselves mistreated in their own families.

Or you might want to *persuade* the audience about some point or idea concerning child abuse:

> The tragic consequences of child abuse provide strong support for more aggressive handling of such cases by social workers and judges.

FIGURE 9.1
Development Diagram: Writing a Cause-Effect Essay

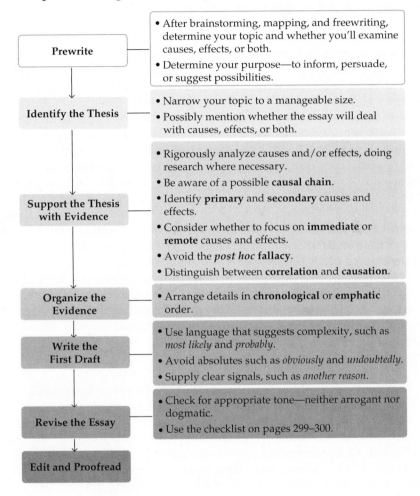

Then again, you could choose a *speculative* approach, your main purpose being to suggest possibilities:

> Psychologists disagree about the potential effect on youngsters of all the media attention to child abuse. Will children exposed to this media coverage grow up assertive, self-confident, and able to protect themselves? Or will they become fearful and distrustful?

These examples illustrate that an essay's causal analysis may have more than one purpose. For instance, although the last example points to a paper with a primarily speculative purpose, the essay would probably start by informing readers of experts' conflicting views. The paper would also have a persuasive slant if it ended by urging readers to complain to the media about their sensationalized treatment of the child-abuse issue.

2. Adapt content and tone to your purpose and readers.   Your purpose and audience determine what supporting material and what tone will be most effective in a cause-effect essay. Assume you want to direct your essay on child abuse to general readers who know little about the subject. To *inform* readers, you might use facts, statistics, and expert opinion to provide an objective discussion of the causes of child abuse. Your analysis might show the following: (1) adults who were themselves mistreated as children tend to abuse their own offspring; (2) marital stress contributes to the mistreatment of children; and (3) certain personality disorders increase the likelihood of child abuse. Sensitive to what your readers would and wouldn't understand, you would stay away from a technical or formal tone. Rather than writing "Pathological preabuse symptomatology predicts adult transference of high aggressivity," you would say "Psychologists can often predict, on the basis of family histories, who will abuse children."

Now imagine that your purpose is to *convince* future social workers that the failure of social service agencies to act authoritatively in child-abuse cases often has tragic consequences. Hoping to encourage more responsible behavior in the prospective social workers, you would adopt a more emotional tone in the essay, perhaps citing wrenching case histories that dramatize what happens when child abuse isn't taken seriously.

3. Think rigorously about causes and effects.   To write a meaningful causal analysis, you should do some careful thinking about the often complex relationship between causes and effects. Children tend to oversimplify causes and effects ("Mommy and Daddy are getting divorced because I was bad the other day"), and adults' arguments can be characterized by hasty, often slipshod thinking ("All these immigrants willing to work cheaply have made us lose our jobs"). But imprecise thinking has no place in essay writing. You should be willing to dig for causes, to think creatively about effects. You should examine your subject in depth, looking beyond the obvious and superficial.

Brainstorming, freewriting, and mapping will help you explore causes and effects thoroughly. No matter which prewriting technique you use, generate as many explanations as possible by asking yourself questions like these:

> *Causes:* What happened? What are the possible reasons? Which are
>   most likely? Who was involved? Why?
> *Effects:* What happened? Who was involved? What were the observable results? What are some possible future consequences?
>   Which consequences are negative? Which are positive?

If you remain open and look beyond the obvious, you'll discover that a cause may have many effects. Imagine that you're writing a paper on the effects of cigarette smoking. Prewriting would probably generate a number of consequences that could be discussed, some less obvious but perhaps more interesting than others: increased risk of lung cancer and heart disease, harm traced to secondhand smoke, legal battles regarding the rights of smokers and nonsmokers, lower birth weights in babies of mothers who smoke, and developmental problems experienced by such underweight infants.

In the same way, prewriting will help you see that an effect may have multiple causes. An essay analyzing the reasons for world hunger could discuss many causes, again some less evident but perhaps more thought-provoking than others: climatic changes, inefficient use of land, cultural predispositions for large families, and poor management of international relief funds.

Your analysis may also uncover a *causal chain* in which one cause (or effect) brings about another, which, in turn, brings about another, and so on. Here's an example of a causal chain: The Prohibition Amendment to the U.S. Constitution went into effect on January 29, 1920; bootleggers and organized crime stepped in to supply public demand for alcoholic beverages; ordinary citizens began breaking the law by buying illegal alcohol and patronizing speakeasies; disrespect for legal authority became widespread and acceptable. As you can see, a causal chain often leads to interesting points. In this case, the subject of Prohibition leads not just to the obvious (illegal consumption of alcohol) but also to the more complex issue of society's decreasing respect for legal authority.

Don't grapple with so complex a chain, however, that you become hopelessly entangled. If your subject involves multiple causes and effects, limit what you'll discuss. Identify which causes and effects are *primary* and which are *secondary*. How extensively you cover secondary factors will depend on your purpose and audience. In an essay intended to inform a general audience about the harmful effects of pesticides, you would most likely focus on everyday dangers—polluted drinking water, residues in food, and the like. You probably wouldn't include a discussion of more long-range consequences (evolution of resistant insects, disruption of the soil's acid-alkaline balance).

Similarly, decide whether to focus on *immediate,* more obvious causes and effects, or on less obvious, more *remote* ones. Or perhaps you need to focus on both. In an essay about a faculty strike at your college, should you attribute the strike simply to the faculty's failure to receive a salary increase? Or should you also examine other factors: the union's failure to accept a salary package that satisfied most professors; the administration's inability to coordinate its negotiating efforts? It may be more difficult to explore more remote causes and effects, but it can also lead to more original and revealing essays. Thoughtful analyses take these less obvious considerations into account.

When developing a causal analysis, be careful to avoid the *post hoc fallacy*. Named after the Latin phrase *post hoc, ergo propter hoc,* meaning "after this, therefore because of this," this kind of faulty thinking occurs when you assume that simply because one event *followed* another, the first event *caused* the second. For example, if the Republicans win a majority of seats in Congress and, several months later, the economy collapses, can you conclude that the Republicans caused the collapse? A quick assumption of "Yes" fails the test of logic, for the timing of events could be coincidental and not indicative of any cause-effect relationship. The collapse may have been triggered by uncontrolled inflation that began well before the congressional elections. (For more information on the *post hoc* fallacy, see page 376.)

Also, be careful not to mistake *correlation* for *causation*. Two events correlate when they occur at about the same time. Such co-occurrence, however, doesn't guarantee a cause-effect relationship. For instance, while the number of ice cream cones eaten and the instances of heat prostration both increase during the summer months, this doesn't mean that eating ice-cream causes heat prostration! A third factor—in this case, summer heat—is the actual cause. When writing causal analyses, then, use with caution words that imply a causal link (such as *therefore* and *because*). Words that express simply time of occurrence (like *following* and *previously*) are safer and more objective.

Finally, keep in mind that a rigorous causal analysis involves more than loose generalizations about causes and effects. Creating plausible connections may require library research, interviewing, or both. Often you'll need to provide facts, statistics, details, personal observations, or other corroborative material if readers are going to accept the reasoning behind your analysis.

4. Write a thesis that focuses the paper on causes, effects, or both. The thesis in an essay developed through causal analysis often indicates whether the essay will deal with mostly causes, effects, or both causes and effects. Here, for example, are three thesis statements for causal analyses dealing with the public school system. You'll see that each thesis signals that essay's particular emphasis:

> Our school system has been weakened by an overemphasis on trendy electives. (*causes*)
>
> An ineffectual school system has led to crippling teachers' strikes and widespread disrespect for the teaching profession. (*effects*)
>
> Bureaucratic inefficiency has created a school system unresponsive to children's emotional, physical, and intellectual needs. (*causes and effects*)

Note that the thesis statement—in addition to signaling whether the paper will discuss causes or effects or both—may also point to the essay's plan of development. Consider the last thesis statement; it makes clear that the paper will discuss children's emotional needs first, their physical needs second, and their intellectual needs last.

The thesis statement in a causal analysis doesn't have to specify whether the essay will discuss causes, effects, or both. Nor does the thesis have to be worded in such a way that the essay's plan of development is apparent. But when first writing cause-effect essays, you may find that a highly focused thesis will keep your analysis on track.

5. Choose an organizational pattern.   There are two basic ways to organize the points in a cause-effect essay: You may use a chronological or an emphatic sequence. If you select a *chronological order*, you discuss causes and effects in the order in which they occur or will occur. Suppose you're writing an essay on the causes for the popularity of imported cars. These causes might be discussed in chronological sequence: American plant workers became frustrated and dissatisfied on the job; some workers got careless while others deliberately sabotaged the production of sound cars; a growing number of defective cars hit the market; consumers grew dissatisfied with American cars and switched to imports.

Chronology might also be used to organize a discussion about effects. Imagine you want to write an essay about the need to guard against disrupting delicate balances in the country's wildlife. You might start the essay by discussing what happened when the starling, a non-native bird, was introduced into the American environment. Because the starling had few natural predators, the starling population soared out of control; starlings took over the food sources and habitats of native species; the bluebird, a native species, declined and is now threatened with extinction.

Although a chronological pattern can be an effective way to organize material, a strict time sequence can present a problem if your primary cause or effect ends up buried in the middle of the sequence. In such a case, you might use *emphatic order*, reserving the most significant cause or effect for the end. For example, time order could be used to present the reasons behind a candidate's unexpected victory: Less than a month after the candidate's earlier defeat, a full-scale fund-raising campaign for the next election was started; the candidate spoke to many crucial power groups early in the campaign; the candidate did exceptionally well in the pre-election debates; good weather and large voter turnout on election day favored the candidate. However, if you believe that the candidate's appearance before influential groups was the key factor in the victory, it would be more effective to emphasize that point by saving it for the end. This is what is meant by emphatic order—saving the most important point for last.

Emphatic order is an especially effective way to sequence cause-effect points when readers hold what, in your opinion, are mistaken or narrow views about a subject. To encourage readers to look more closely at the issues, you present what you consider the erroneous or obvious views first, show why they are unsound or limited, and then present what you feel to be the actual causes and effects. Such a sequence nudges the audience into giving further thought to the causes and effects you have discovered. Here are informal outlines for two causal analyses using this approach.

Subject: The causes of the riot at the rock concert

1. Some commentators blame the excessively hot weather.
2. Others cite drug use among the concertgoers.
3. Still others blame the beer sold at the concessions.
4. But the real cause of the disaster was poor planning by the concert promoters.

Subject: The effects of campus crime

1. Immediate problems
   a. Students feel insecure and fearful.
   b. Many nighttime campus activities have been curtailed.
2. More significant long-term problems
   a. Unfavorable publicity about campus crime will affect future student enrollments.
   b. Hiring faculty will become more difficult.

When using emphatic order in a causal analysis, you might want to word the thesis in such a way that it signals which point your essay will stress. Look at the following thesis statements:

Although many immigrants arrive in this country without marketable skills, their most pressing problem is learning how to make their way in a society whose language they don't know.

The space program led to dramatic advances in computer technology and medical science. Even more important, though, the program helped change many people's attitudes toward the planet we live on.

These thesis statements reflect an awareness of the complex nature of cause-effect relationships. While not dismissing secondary issues, the statements establish which points the writer considers most noteworthy. The second thesis, for instance, indicates that the paper will touch on the technological and medical advances made possible by the space program but will emphasize the way the program changed people's attitudes toward the earth.

Whether you use a chronological or emphatic pattern to organize your essay, you'll need to provide clear *signals* to identify when you're discussing causes and when you're discussing effects. Expressions such as "Another reason" and "A final outcome" help readers follow your line of thought.

6. Use language that hints at the complexity of cause-effect relationships. Because it's difficult—if not impossible—to identify causes and effects with certainty, you should avoid such absolutes as "It must be obvious" and "There is no doubt." Instead, try phrases like "Most likely" or "It's probable that." Using such language is not indecisive; rather, it reflects your understanding of the often tangled nature of causes and effects. Be careful, though, of going to the other extreme and being reluctant to take a stand on the issues. If you've thought carefully about causes and effects, you have a right to state your analysis with conviction. Don't undercut the hard work you've done by writing as if your ideas were unworthy of your reader's attention.

REVISION STRATEGIES

Once you have a draft of the essay, you're ready to revise. The following checklist will help you and those giving you feedback apply to cause-effect some of the revision techniques discussed on pages 60–62.

☑ CAUSE-EFFECT: A REVISION/PEER REVIEW CHECKLIST

Revise Overall Meaning and Structure

❑ Is the essay's purpose informative, persuasive, speculative, or a combination of these?

❑ What is the essay's thesis? Is it stated specifically or implied? Where? Could it be made any clearer? How?

❑ Does the essay focus on causes, effects, or both? How do you know?

❑ Where has correlation been mistaken for causation? Where is the essay weakened by *post hoc* thinking?

❑ Where does the essay distinguish between primary and secondary causes and effects? Do the most critical causes and effects receive special attention?

❑ Where does the essay dwell on the obvious?

Revise Paragraph Development

❑ Are the essay's paragraphs sequenced chronologically or emphatically? Could they be sequenced more effectively? How?

❑ Where would signal devices make it easier to follow the progression of thought within and between paragraphs?

❏ Which paragraphs would be strengthened by vivid examples (such as statistics, facts, anecdotes, or personal observations) that support the causal analysis?

Revise Sentences and Words

❏ Where do expressions like *as a result, because,* and *therefore* mislead the reader by implying a cause-effect relationship? Would words such as *following* and *previously* eliminate the problem?

❏ Do any words or phrases convey an arrogant or dogmatic tone (*there is no question, undoubtedly, always, never*)? What other expressions (*most likely, probably*) would improve credibility?

STUDENT ESSAY

The following student essay was written by Carl Novack in response to this assignment:

> In "Innocents Afield," Buzz Bissinger explores the way high school sports have changed in the last few years. Think of another aspect of everyday life that has changed recently, and discuss those factors that you believe are responsible for the change.

While reading Carl's paper, try to determine how well it applies the principles of causal analysis. The annotations on Carl's paper and the commentary following it will help you look at the essay more closely.

Americans and Food
by Carl Novack

Introduction   An offbeat but timely cartoon recently appeared in the   1
local newspaper. The single panel showed a gravel-pit opera-
tion with piles of raw earth and large cranes. Next to one of the
cranes stood the owner of the gravel pit—a grizzled, tough-
looking character, hammer in hand, pointing proudly to the
new sign he had just tacked up. The sign read, "Fred's Fill Dirt
and Croissants." The cartoon illustrates an interesting phenomenon: the changing food habits of Americans. Our meals
used to consist of something like home-cooked pot roast,
mashed potatoes laced with butter and salt, a thick slice of
apple pie topped with a healthy scoop of vanilla ice cream—
plain, heavy meals, cooked from scratch, and eaten leisurely at
Thesis ⌐   home. But America has changed, and as it has, so have what
we Americans eat and how we eat it.

We used to have simple, unsophisticated tastes and 2
looked with suspicion at anything more exotic than hamburg-

Topic sentence: Background paragraph — er. Admittedly, we did adopt some foods from the various immigrant groups who flocked to our shores. We learned to eat Chinese food, pizza, and bagels. But in the last few years, the international character of our diet has grown tremendously. We can walk into any mall in Middle America and buy pita sandwiches, quiche, and tacos. Such foods are often changed

Topic sentence: Three causes answer the question — on their journey from exotic imports to ordinary "American" meals (no Pakistani, for example, eats frozen-on-a-stick boysenberry-flavored yogurt), but the imports are still a long way from hamburger on a bun.

First cause — Why have we become more worldly in our tastes? For one 3
thing, television blankets the country with information about new food products and trends. Viewers in rural Montana know that the latest craving in Washington, D.C., is Cajun cooking or that something called tofu is now available in the local

Second cause — supermarket. Another reason for the growing international flavor of our food is that many young Americans have traveled abroad and gotten hooked on new tastes and flavors. Backpacking students and young professionals vacationing in Europe come home with cravings for authentic French bread

Third cause — or German beer. Finally, continuing waves of immigrants settle in the cities where many of us live, causing significant changes in what we eat. Vietnamese, Haitians, and Thais, for instance, bring their native foods and cooking styles with them and eventually open small markets or restaurants. In time, the new food will become Americanized enough to take

Topic sentence: Another cause — its place in our national diet.

Our growing concern with health has also affected the 4
way we eat. For the last few years, the media have warned us about the dangers of our traditional diet, high in salt and fat, low in fiber. The media also began to educate us about the

Start of a causal chain — dangers of processed foods pumped full of chemical additives. As a result, consumers began to demand healthier foods, and manufacturers started to change some of their products. Many foods, such as lunch meat, canned vegetables, and soups, were made available in low-fat, low-sodium versions. Whole-grain cereals and higher-fiber breads also began to appear on the grocery shelves. Moreover, the food industry started to produce all-natural products—everything from potato chips to ice cream—without additives and preservatives. Not surprisingly, the restaurant industry responded to this switch to healthier foods, luring customers with salad bars, broiled fish, and

Topic sentence: Another cause — steamed vegetables.

Our food habits are being affected, too, by the rapid 5
increase in the number of women working outside the home.

Sociologists and other experts believe that two important factors triggered this phenomenon: the women's movement and a changing economic climate. Women were assured that it was acceptable, even rewarding, to work outside the home; many women also discovered that they had to work just to keep up with the cost of living. As the traditional role of home-maker changed, so did the way families ate. With Mom work-ing, there wasn't time for her to prepare the traditional three square meals a day. Instead, families began looking for alterna-tives to provide quick meals. What was the result? For one thing, there was a boom in fast-food restaurants. The subur-ban or downtown strip that once contained a lone McDonald's now features Wendy's, Roy Rogers, Taco Bell, Burger King, and Pizza Hut. Families also began to depend on frozen foods as another time-saving alternative. Once again, though, demand changed the kind of frozen food available. Frozen foods no longer consist of foil trays divided into greasy fried chicken, watery corn niblets, and lumpy mashed potatoes. Supermarkets now stock a range of supposedly gourmet frozen dinners—from fettucini in cream sauce to braised beef en brochette.

Start of a causal chain

Conclusion

It may not be possible to pick up a ton of fill dirt and a half-dozen croissants at the same place, but America's food habits are definitely changing. If it is true that "you are what you eat," then America's identity is evolving along with its diet.

6

COMMENTARY

Title and introduction.   Asked to prepare a paper analyzing the reasons behind a change in our lives, Carl decided to write about a shift he had no-ticed in Americans' eating habits. The title of the essay, "Americans and Food," identifies Carl's subject but could be livelier and more interesting.

Despite his rather uninspired title, Carl starts his *causal analysis* in an engaging way—with the vivid description of a cartoon. He then connects the cartoon to his subject with the following sentence: "The cartoon illustrates an interesting phenomenon: the changing food habits of Americans." To back up his belief that there has been a revolution in our eating habits, Carl uses the first paragraph to summarize the kind of meal that people used to eat. He then moves into his *thesis:* "But America has changed, and as it has, so have what Americans eat and how we eat it." The thesis implies that Carl's paper will focus on both causes and effects.

Purpose.   Carl's *purpose* was to write an *informative* causal analysis. But before he could present the causes of the change in eating habits, he needed to show that such a change had, in fact, taken place. He therefore uses the second paragraph to document one aspect of this change—the internationalization of our eating habits.

Topic sentences.   At the beginning of the third paragraph, Carl uses a question—"Why have we become more worldly in our tastes?"—to signal that his discussion of causes is about to begin. This question also serves as the paragraph's *topic sentence*, indicating that the paragraph will focus on reasons for the increasingly international flavor of our food. The next two paragraphs, also focused by topic sentences, identify two other major reasons for the change in eating habits: "Our growing concern with health has also affected the way we eat" (paragraph 4), and "Our food habits are being affected, too, by the rapid increase in the number of women working outside the home" (5).

Combining patterns of development.   Carl draws on two patterns—comparison-contrast and exemplification—to develop his causal analysis. At the heart of the essay is a basic *contrast* between the way we used to eat and the way we eat now. And throughout his essay, Carl provides convincing *examples* to demonstrate the validity of his points. Consider for a moment the third paragraph. Here Carl asserts that one reason for our new eating habits is our growing exposure to international foods. He then presents concrete evidence to show that we have indeed become more familiar with international cuisine: Television exposes rural Montana to Cajun cooking; students traveling abroad take a liking to French bread; urban dwellers enjoy the exotic fare served by numerous immigrant groups. The fourth and fifth paragraphs use similarly specific evidence (for example, "low-fat, low-sodium versions" of "lunch meat, canned vegetables, and soups") to illustrate the soundness of key ideas.

Causal chains.   Let's look more closely at the evidence in the essay. Not satisfied with obvious explanations, Carl thought through his ideas carefully and even brainstormed with friends to arrive at as comprehensive an analysis as possible. Not surprisingly, much of the evidence Carl uncovered took the form of *causal chains*. In the fourth paragraph, Carl writes, "The media also began to educate us about the dangers of processed foods pumped full of chemical additives. As a result, consumers began to demand healthier foods, and manufacturers started to change some of their products." And the next paragraph shows how the changing role of American women caused families to search for alternative ways of eating. This shift, in turn, caused the restaurant and food industries to respond with a wide range of food alternatives.

Making the paper easy to follow.   Although Carl's analysis digs beneath the surface and reveals complex cause-effect relationships, he wisely limits his pursuit of causal chains to *primary causes and effects*. He doesn't let the complexities distract him from his main purpose: to show why and how the

American diet is changing. Carl is also careful to provide his essay with abundant *connecting devices,* making it easy for readers to see the links between points. Consider the use of *transitions* (signaled by italics) in the following sentences: "*Another* reason for the growing international flavor of our food is that many young Americans have traveled abroad" (paragraph 3); "*As a result,* consumers began to demand healthier foods" (4); and "*As* the traditional role of homemaker changed, so did the way families ate" (5).

A problem with the essay's close.   When reading the essay, you probably noticed that Carl's conclusion is a bit weak. Although his reference to the cartoon works well, the rest of the paragraph limps to a tired close. Ending an otherwise vigorous essay with such a slight conclusion undercuts the effectiveness of the whole paper. Carl spent so much energy developing the body of his essay that he ran out of the stamina needed to conclude the piece more forcefully. Careful budgeting of his time would have allowed him to prepare a stronger concluding paragraph.

Revising the first draft.   When Carl was ready to revise, he showed the first draft of his essay to several classmates during a peer review session. Listening carefully to what they said, he jotted down their most helpful comments and eventually transferred them, numbered in order of importance, to his draft. Comparing Carl's original version of his fourth paragraph (shown here) with his final version in the essay will show you how he went about revising.

Original Version of the Fourth Paragraph

A growing concern with health has also affected the way we eat, especially because the media have sent us warnings the last few years about the dangers of salt, sugar, food additives, high-fat and low-fiber diets. We have started to worry that our traditional meals may have been shortening our lives. As a result, consumers demanded healthier foods and manufacturers started taking some of the salt and sugar out of canned foods. "All-natural" became an effective selling point, leading to many preservative-free products. Restaurants, too, adapted their menus, luring customers with light meals. Because we now know about the link between overweight and a variety of health problems, including heart attacks, we are counting calories. In turn, food companies made fortunes on diet beer and diet cola. Sometimes, though, we seem a bit confused about the health issue; we drink soda that is sugar-free but loaded with chemical sweeteners. Still, we believe we are lengthening our lives through changing our diets.

On the advice of his classmates, Carl decided to omit all references to the way our concern with weight has affected our eating habits. It's true, of course, that calorie-counting has changed how we eat. But as soon as Carl started to discuss this point, he got involved in a causal chain that undercut the paragraph's unity. He ended up describing the paradoxical situation in which we find ourselves. In an attempt to eat healthy, we stay away from sugar and use instead artificial sweeteners that probably aren't very good for us. This is an interesting issue, but it detracts from the point Carl wants to make: that our concern with health has affected our eating habits in a *positive* way.

Carl's peer reviewers also pointed out that the fourth paragraph's first sentence contained too much material to be an effective topic sentence. Carl corrected the problem by breaking the overlong sentence into two short ones: "Our growing concern with health has also affected the way we eat. For the last few years, the media have warned us about the dangers of our traditional diet, high in salt and fat, low in fiber." The first of these sentences serves as a crisp topic sentence that focuses the rest of the paragraph.

Finally, Carl agreed with his classmates that the fourth paragraph lacked convincing specifics. When revising, he changed "manufacturers started taking some of the salt and sugar out of canned foods" to the more specific "Many foods, such as lunch meats, canned vegetables, and soups, were made available in low-fat, low-sodium versions." Similarly, generalizations about "light meals" and "all-natural products" gained life through the addition of concrete examples: restaurants lured "customers with salad bars, broiled fish, and steamed vegetables," and the food industry produced "everything from potato chips to ice cream—without additives and preservatives."

Carl did an equally good job revising other sections of his paper. With the exception of the weak spots already discussed, he made the changes needed to craft a well-reasoned essay, one that demonstrates his ability to analyze a complex phenomenon.

Activities: Cause-Effect

Prewriting Activities

1. Imagine you're writing two essays: One *argues* the need for high school courses in personal finance (how to budget money, balance a checkbook, and the like); the other explains a *process* for showing appreciation. Jot down ways you might use cause-effect in each essay.

2. Use mapping, collaborative brainstorming, or another prewriting technique to generate possible causes and/or effects for *one* of the topics below. Be sure to keep in mind the audience indicated in parentheses. Next, devise a thesis and decide whether your purpose would be informative, persuasive, speculative, or some combination of these. Finally, organize your raw material into a brief outline, with related causes and effects grouped in the same section.

   a. Pressure on students to do well (*high school students*)
   b. Children's access to pornography on the Internet (*parents*)

    c. Being physically fit (*those who are out of shape*)

    d. Spiraling costs of a college education (*college officials*)

Revising Activities

3. Explain how the following statements demonstrate *post hoc* thinking and confuse correlation and cause-effect.

    a. Our city now has many immigrants from Latin American countries. The crime rate in our city has increased. Latin American immigrants are the cause of the crime wave.

    b. The divorce rate has skyrocketed. More women are working outside the home than ever before. Working outside the home destroys marriages.

    c. A high percentage of people in Dixville have developed cancer. The landfill, used by XYZ Industries, has been located in Dixville for twenty years. The XYZ landfill has caused cancer in Dixville residents.

4. The following paragraph is from the first draft of an essay arguing that technological advances can diminish the quality of life. How solid is the paragraph's causal analysis? Which causes and/or effects should be eliminated? Where is the analysis simplistic? Where does the writer make absolute claims even though cause-effect relationships are no more than a possibility? Keeping these questions in mind, revise the paragraph.

> How did the banking industry respond to inflation? It simply introduced a new technology—the automated teller machine (ATM). By making money more available to the average person, the ATM gives people the cash to buy inflated goods—whether or not they can afford them. Not surprisingly, ATMs have had a number of negative consequences for the average individual. Since people know they can get cash at any time, they use their lunch hours for something other than going to the bank. How do they spend this newfound time? They go shopping, and machine-vended money means more impulse buying, even more than with a credit card. Also, because people don't need their checkbooks to withdraw money, they can't keep track of their accounts and therefore develop a casual attitude toward financial matters. It's no wonder children don't appreciate the value of money. Another problem is that people who would never dream of robbing a bank try to trick the machine into dispensing money "for free." There's no doubt that this kind of fraud contributes to the immoral climate in the country.

Stephen King

Probably the best-known living horror writer, Stephen King (1947–) is the author of more than thirty books. Before earning fame through his vastly popular books, including *Carrie* (1974), *The Shining* (1977), *Cujo* (1981), and *Tommyknockers* (1987), King worked as a high school English teacher and an industrial laundry worker. Much of King's prolific output has been adapted for the screen; movies based on King's work include *Misery* (1990), *Stand By Me* (1986), and *The Green Mile* (1999). More recent works include *Dreamcatcher* (2001); *Everything's Eventual* (2002); *From a Buick 8* (2002); Volumes V, VI, and VII in the *Dark Tower* series (published in 2003, 2004, and 2004, respectively); and *Cell* (2006). His most recent noval is *Duma Key* (2008). King's book *On Writing: A Memoir of the Craft* (2000) offers insight into the writing process and examines the role that writing has played in his own life—especially following a near-fatal accident in 1999. King lives with his wife in Bangor, Maine, and has three adult children. The following essay first appeared in *Playboy* in 1982.

For ideas about how this cause-effect essay is organized, see Figure 9.2 on page 310.

Pre-Reading Journal Entry

Several forms of entertainment, besides horror movies, are highly popular despite what many consider a low level of quality. In your journal, list as many "low-brow" forms of entertainment as you can. Possibilities include professional wrestling, aggressive video games, Internet chat rooms, and so on. Review your list, and respond to the following question in your journal: What is it about each form of entertainment that attracts such popularity—and inspires such criticism?

Why We Crave Horror Movies

I think that we're all mentally ill: those of us outside the asylums only 1 hide it a little better—and maybe not all that much better, after all. We've all known people who talk to themselves, people who sometimes squinch their faces into horrible grimaces when they believe no one is watching, people who have some hysterical fear—of snakes, the dark, the tight place, the long drop . . . and, of course, those final worms and grubs that are waiting so patiently underground.

When we pay our four or five bucks and seat ourselves at tenth-row cen- 2 ter in a theater showing a horror movie, we are daring the nightmare.

Why? Some of the reasons are simple and obvious. To show that we can, 3 that we are not afraid, that we can ride this roller coaster. Which is not to say that a really good horror movie may not surprise a scream out of us at some point, the way we may scream when the roller coaster twists through a complete 360 or plows through a lake at the bottom of the drop. And horror movies, like roller coasters, have always been the special province of the young; by the time one turns 40 or 50, one's appetite for double twists or 360-degree loops may be considerably depleted.

We also go to re-establish our feelings of essential normality; the horror movie is innately conservative, even reactionary. Freda Jackson as the horrible melting woman in *Die, Monster, Die!* confirms for us that no matter how far we may be removed from the beauty of a Robert Redford or a Diana Ross, we are still light-years from true ugliness.   4

And we go to have fun.   5

Ah, but this is where the ground starts to slope away, isn't it? Because this is a very peculiar sort of fun indeed. The fun comes from seeing others menaced—sometimes killed. One critic has suggested that if pro football has become the voyeur's version of combat, then the horror film has become the modern version of the public lynching.   6

It is true that the mythic, "fairytale" horror film intends to take away the shades of gray.... It urges us to put away our more civilized and adult penchant for analysis and to become children again, seeing things in pure blacks and whites. It may be that horror movies provide psychic relief on this level because this invitation to lapse into simplicity, irrationality and even outright madness is extended so rarely. We are told we may allow our emotions a free rein... or no rein at all.   7

If we are all insane, then sanity becomes a matter of degree. If your insanity leads you to carve up women like Jack the Ripper or the Cleveland Torso Murderer, we clap you away in the funny farm (but neither of those two amateur-night surgeons was ever caught, heh-heh-heh); if, on the other hand your insanity leads you only to talk to yourself when you're under stress or to pick your nose on the morning bus, then you are left alone to go about your business... though it is doubtful that you will ever be invited to the best parties.   8

The potential lyncher is in almost all of us (excluding saints, past and present; but then, most saints have been crazy in their own ways), and every now and then, he has to be let loose to scream and roll around in the grass. Our emotions and our fears form their own body, and we recognize that it demands its own exercise to maintain proper muscle tone. Certain of these emotional muscles are accepted—even exalted—in civilized society; they are, of course, the emotions that tend to maintain the status quo of civilization itself. Love, friendship, loyalty, kindness—these are all the emotions that we applaud, emotions that have been immortalized in the couplets of Hallmark cards....   9

When we exhibit these emotions, society showers us with positive reinforcement; we learn this even before we get out of diapers. When, as children, we hug our rotten little puke of a sister and give her a kiss, all the aunts and uncles smile and twit and cry, "Isn't he the sweetest little thing?" Such   10 coveted treats as chocolate-covered graham crackers often follow. But if we deliberately slam the rotten little puke of a sister's fingers in the door, sanctions follow—angry remonstrance from parents, aunts and uncles; instead of a chocolate-covered graham cracker, a spanking.

But anticivilization emotions don't go away, and they demand periodic exercise. We have such "sick" jokes as, "What's the difference between a truckload of bowling balls and a truckload of dead babies?" (You can't unload a truckload of bowling balls with a pitchfork...a joke, by the way, that I heard originally from a ten-year-old.) Such a joke may surprise a laugh or a grin out of us even as we recoil, a possibility that confirms the thesis: If we share a brotherhood of man, then we also share an insanity of man. None of which is intended as a defense of either the sick joke or insanity but merely as an explanation of why the best horror films, like the best fairy tales, manage to be reactionary, anarchistic, and revolutionary all at the same time. 11

The mythic horror movie, like the sick joke, has a dirty job to do. It deliberately appeals to all that is worst in us. It is morbidity unchained, our most base instincts let free, our nastiest fantasies realized...and it all happens, fittingly enough, in the dark. For those reasons, good liberals often shy away from horror films. For myself, I like to see the most aggressive of them—*Dawn of the Dead,* for instance—as lifting a trap door in the civilized forebrain and throwing a basket of raw meat to the hungry alligators swimming around in that subterranean river beneath. 12

Why bother? Because it keeps them from getting out, man. It keeps them down there and me up here. It was Lennon and McCartney who said that all you need is love, and I would agree with that. 13

As long as you keep the gators fed. 14

Questions for Close Reading

1. What is the selection's thesis? Locate the sentence(s) in which King states his main idea. If he doesn't state the thesis explicitly, express it in your own words.

2. In what ways do King's references to "Jack the Ripper" and the "Cleveland Torso Murderer" (paragraph 8) support his thesis?

3. What does King mean in paragraph 4 when he says that horror movies are "innately conservative, even reactionary"? What does he mean in paragraph 11 when he calls them "anarchistic, and revolutionary"?

4. In paragraphs 12 and 14, King refers to "alligators" and "gators." What does the alligator represent? What does King mean when he says that all the world needs is love—"[a]s long as you keep the gators fed"?

5. Refer to your dictionary as needed to define the following words used in the selection: *hysterical* (paragraph 1), *reactionary* (4), *voyeur's* (6), *lynching* (6), *penchant* (7), *immortalized* (9), *anarchistic* (11), and *morbidity* (12).

FIGURE 9.2
Essay Structure Diagram: "Why We Crave Horror Movies" by Stephen King

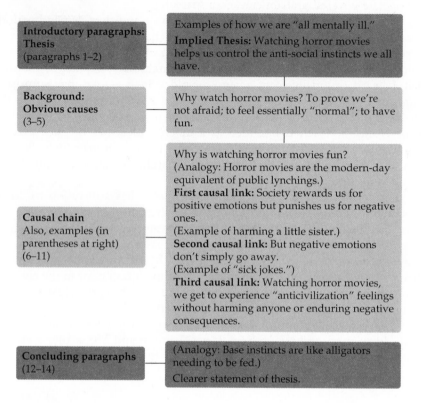

Introductory paragraphs:
Thesis
(paragraphs 1–2)

Examples of how we are "all mentally ill."
Implied Thesis: Watching horror movies helps us control the anti-social instincts we all have.

Background:
Obvious causes
(3–5)

Why watch horror movies? To prove we're not afraid; to feel essentially "normal"; to have fun.

Causal chain
Also, examples (in parentheses at right)
(6–11)

Why is watching horror movies fun?
(Analogy: Horror movies are the modern-day equivalent of public lynchings.)
First causal link: Society rewards us for positive emotions but punishes us for negative ones.
(Example of harming a little sister.)
Second causal link: But negative emotions don't simply go away.
(Example of "sick jokes.")
Third causal link: Watching horror movies, we get to experience "anticivilization" feelings without harming anyone or enduring negative consequences.

Concluding paragraphs
(12–14)

(Analogy: Base instincts are like alligators needing to be fed.)
Clearer statement of thesis.

Questions About the Writer's Craft

1. **The pattern.** Does King's causal analysis have an essentially informative, speculative, or persuasive (see pages 292–294) purpose? What makes you think so? How might King's profession as a horror writer have influenced his purpose?
2. **Other patterns.** King *compares* and *contrasts* horror movies to roller coasters (paragraph 3), public lynchings (6), and sick jokes (11–12). How do these comparisons and contrasts reinforce King's thesis about horror movies?
3. **Other patterns.** Throughout the essay, King uses several *examples* involving children. Identify these instances. How do these examples help King develop his thesis?
4. What is unusual about paragraphs 2, 5, and 14? Why do you think King might have designed these paragraphs in this way?

Writing Assignments Using Cause-Effect as a Pattern of Development

1. King argues that horror movies have "a dirty job to do": they feed the hungry monsters in our psyche. Write an essay in which you put King's thesis to the test. Briefly describe the first horror movie you ever saw; then explain its effect on you. Like King, speculate about the nature of your response—your feelings and fantasies—while watching the movie.

2. Many movie critics claim that horror movies nowadays are more violent and bloody than they used to be. Write an essay about *one* other medium of popular culture that you think has changed for the worse. You might consider action movies, televised coverage of sports, men's or women's magazines, radio talk shows, blogs, and so on. Briefly describe key differences between the medium's past and present forms. Analyze the reasons for the change, and, at the end of the essay, examine the effects of the change. For reflections on other questionable cultural practices, read Ellen Goodman's "Family Counterculture" (page 7) and Joan Didion's "Marrying Absurd" (page 448).

Writing Assignments Combining Patterns of Development

3. King advocates the horror movie precisely because "[i]t deliberately appeals to all that is worst in us." Write an essay in which you rebut King. *Argue* instead that horror movies should be avoided precisely *because* they satisfy monstrous feelings in us. To refute King, provide strong *examples* drawn from your own and other people's experience. Consider supplementing your informal research with material gathered in the library and/or on the Internet.

4. Write an essay in which you *argue,* contrary to King, that humans are by nature essentially benevolent and kind. Brainstorm with others to generate vivid *examples* in support of your thesis.

Writing Assignment Using a Journal Entry as a Starting Point

5. King believes that horror movies involve "a very peculiar sort of fun." Review your pre-reading journal entry, and select *one* other form of popular entertainment that you think provides its own strange kind of enjoyment. Like King, write an essay in which you analyze the causes of people's enjoyment of this type of entertainment. Brainstorm with others to identify convincing examples. You may, like King, endorse the phenomenon you examine—or you may condemn it. For discussion of other strange sources of people's enjoyment, read Joan Didion's "Marrying Absurd" (page 448).

Kurt Kleiner

Kurt Kleiner is a science writer for the *Economist, Nature, Science,* and other publications. Born in 1962, Kleiner grew up in Findlay, Ohio. He received bachelor's degrees in English literature and journalism from Ohio University, and a master's degree in science writing from Johns Hopkins University in Baltimore, Maryland. For many years he worked as a staff reporter, most recently for *New Scientist* magazine, before becoming a freelance journalist in 2003. Kleiner has also taught college literature and writing courses. This article appeared in *The Toronto Star* on January 14, 2007.

Pre-Reading Journal Entry

It's human nature to procrastinate; we all do it at times. Sometimes procrastination causes problems; sometimes it doesn't. What do you procrastinate about? When did putting off a task create serious problems for you? When did delaying a task make no difference at all? Use your journal to respond to these questions.

When Mañana Is Too Soon

No other anguish is quite like that of the procrastinator. He knows that the job has to get done, that putting it off just makes it harder, that the worry is worse than the work. And yet he can't...quite...get...started.   1

Procrastination seems built into human nature—the ancient Roman orator Cicero fretted about it, as did the Greek historian Thucydides.   2

Today, 95 per cent of people say that they sometimes procrastinate.   3

The real problem, though, is the 20 per cent of us who qualify as chronic procrastinators. These are people who procrastinate so routinely that their work, finances or personal relationships suffer because of it.   4

At its worst, procrastination is a form of self-destructive behaviour, like drug addiction or chronic gambling. Like them, its origins are mysterious, and its treatment difficult.   5

Now a new analysis of the psychological literature by a University of Calgary psychologist could help untangle what makes so many of us put off until tomorrow what we really should do today.   6

Piers Steel has just published a mammoth review of the scientific literature on procrastination in the journal *Psychological Bulletin,* and his conclusions are at odds with some conventional ideas.   7

"Some of them are dead wrong," Steel says.   8

His research contradicts one major theory, which is that procrastinators suffer from anxiety and so have a harder time facing a difficult task.   9

Steel looked at the literature and found that statistically there's very little correlation between anxiety and a tendency to procrastinate.   10

The same with the flattering idea that procrastinators are also perfectionists, people who care so much about doing it right that they can't bear to get started. Again, Steel found no correlation. 11

What he did find is that procrastinators are less confident that they can handle a given task. They're also more impulsive and less conscientious overall. 12

"Whether you believe you can or you believe you can't, you're right," Steel says. "Some of these old wives' tales bear out. People who believe they can are less likely to procrastinate." 13

Steel's paper is unlikely to be the final word on procrastination. But it's important because it's the best attempt so far to analyze hundreds of psychological studies that have been conducted over a period of decades. 14

Part of the problem of procrastination is defining it in the first place. We all have dozens of things we could be doing at any particular moment, and some of them have to be put off. 15

Prioritizing turns into procrastination when we know the job needs to be done, we know we'll be worse off if we don't do it, we intend to do it— and we still don't do it. It is profoundly irrational behaviour, and its very irrationality makes it tough for procrastinators and psychologists alike to understand. 16

Samuel Johnson, the prolific 18th-century writer and lexicographer, admitted to procrastinating himself, and described the remorse familiar to any procrastinator: "I could not forbear to reproach myself for having so long neglected what was unavoidably to be done, and of which every moment's idleness increased the difficulty." 17

But he also puzzled over what made people procrastinate when it was so clearly against their best interests. "The folly of allowing ourselves to delay what we know cannot be finally escaped is one of the general weaknesses," he concluded. 18

Steel thinks procrastination is probably an even bigger problem today. 19

We have more readily available distractions, like the Internet and computer games. (Steel says he's had problems with computer games himself.) And many jobs are becoming more self-structured, which means it's increasingly up to us to impose our own work goals and deadlines. 20

The harm caused by procrastination can be immense. Steel points to a study by the tax-preparation firm H&R Block that says putting off doing their taxes costs U.S. citizens an average of $400 each because of errors due to the last-minute rush. 21

Even more irrationally, 70 per cent of patients suffering from glaucoma don't get around to using their eye drops regularly, which could potentially result in blindness. 22

Fifty per cent of heart attack patients don't manage to make the lifestyle changes that could save their lives. 23

"On the one hand, it's easy to trivialize procrastination. We joke about it," says Timothy A. Pychyl, a psychologist at Carleton University who studies procrastination.   24

"But procrastination is self-defeating. It's a breakdown in volitional action. I have an intention and I'm not following through on it. You're not able to follow through on what you want to do."   25

Over the years, psychologists have come up with a lot of ideas about what makes people procrastinate. In addition to anxiety and perfectionism, some suggested that procrastinators were self-sabotaging, hostile and rebellious, or depressed.   26

But for Steel, procrastination can be explained by an insight borrowed from behavioural economics called hyperbolic discounting. This is the tendency to value near-term rewards more than long-term ones. For instance, some people will choose a payoff of $50 today over $100 tomorrow.   27

Steel combined hyperbolic discounting with a theory of motivation called expectancy theory, and came up with something he calls temporal motivational theory (TMT). It boils down to this: 28

Utility = E × V / Gamma D   29

Utility is the desirability of getting something done. E is expectancy, or confidence. V is the value of the job, and includes not only its importance but also its unpleasantness. Gamma stands for how prone a person is to delay doing things. And D means delay, or how far away the consequences of doing, or not doing, the task are.   30

The bigger the top number compared to the bottom, the less likely a task will be put off. So if you expect to do well at a job (E), and it's a pleasant thing to do (V), and you're not prone to being delayed by distractions (Gamma), and it has to be done right away (D), you're not likely to procrastinate.   31

If you expect to fail at a difficult task and you're easily distracted and it doesn't have to be done for quite awhile, you're going to procrastinate.   32

"It's a little bit unsettling that human nature can be reduced to an equation," Steel says. "But you can show that pretty much every major view of behaviour can be reduced to that."   33

Perhaps not surprisingly, other procrastination experts don't think it's quite that simple.   34

"It makes an important contribution by summing it up," says Pychyl. "It doesn't mean that he's captured the whole phenomenon. There are elements we still don't understand about these self-defeating behaviours."   35

Pychyl thinks it's still too early to rule out anxiety, perfectionism, depression or other causes that have been suggested for procrastination.   36

William J. Knaus, a psychologist and author of *Do It Now!*, a procrastination self-help book, says it's a complex behaviour that's far from being understood. But he insists procrastinators can change.   37

"It's a challenge," he says, "but it's doable. We have enough of the tools   38
now so that anyone who is serious about making strides and improvements
can do so."

Questions for Close Reading

1. What is the selection's thesis? Locate the sentence(s) in which Kleiner states his main idea. If he doesn't state his thesis explicitly, express it in your own words.
2. According to the psychologist Piers Steel, what traits are characteristic of procrastinators? How does temporal motivation theory help explain what causes procrastination?
3. Over the years, psychologists have proposed many causes of procrastination other than temporal motivation theory. What are they?
4. How does Kleiner define procrastination? How does he distinguish between procrastinating and prioritizing?
5. Refer to your dictionary as needed to define the following words used in the selection: *chronic* (paragraph 4), *mammoth* (7), *impulsive* (12), *profoundly* (16), *prolific* (17), *lexicographer* (17), *forbear* (17), *trivialize* (24), *volitional* (25), and *unsettling* (33).

Questions About the Writer's Craft

1. **The pattern.** To what extent does Kleiner focus on causes of procrastination, and to what extent on effects? How is his emphasis related to the main topic of the article, the Steel study?
2. What is the purpose of Kleiner's article? How does he accomplish this purpose?
3. **Other patterns.** What patterns of development, besides cause-effect, are used in this article? What do the other patterns contribute to the essay?
4. What do the Samuel Johnson quotations (paragraphs 17 and 18) contribute to the article? If Kleiner deleted these two paragraphs, what effect would this have on the reader's understanding of procrastination?

Writing Assignments Using Cause-Effect as a Pattern of Development

1. Choose a common human behavior other than procrastination (for example, lying, overeating, complaining, or carelessness), and write an essay in which you explain its possible causes or effects. For example, if you choose carelessness, you can write about its possible causes, such as lack of motivation, or possible effects, such as causing an accident. Use examples from your own experience to support your thesis. If you choose to write about disorganization, you can gain some insight into what's involved by reading K. C. Cole's "Entropy" (page 338).
2. Kleiner describes Steel's temporal motivation theory (TMT), and he provides an equation that can be applied to any given task to determine whether one is likely to procrastinate or not (paragraphs 28–32). The TMT equation suggests that several factors, not just one, combine to cause a person to procrastinate (or not) on

any given task. Apply Steel's equation to one or more tasks you must perform (for example, writing an essay), using general values like low, medium, and high rather than numeric values. Using the TMT model, decide how likely you are to procrastinate on each task. Then write an essay in which you analyze the causes identified by the TMT model that contribute to your procrastinating (or not procrastinating) on the task. Comment on whether you found the TMT model useful for predicting your own behavior.

Writing Assignments Combining Patterns of Development

3. Kleiner's article focuses on the causes and effects of procrastination, but he does not say much about *how* people procrastinate. Write an essay in which you *classify* the many ways in which people avoid doing what they know they should be doing. Use *examples* to support your classifications. Before you start, decide whether your purpose is to inform or to entertain, and write your essay accordingly. For some perspective on human nature, read David Brooks's "Psst! 'Human Capital'" (page 212).

4. Choose one of the psychologists mentioned in the Kleiner essay and do some Internet or library research on his work. Write an essay profiling the psychologist in which you *describe* his interests and areas of expertise and give specific *examples* of his research findings or other professional accomplishments.

Writing Assignment Using a Journal Entry as a Starting Point

5. Review your pre-reading journal entry in which you describe the consequences— and the lack of consequences—of your own procrastination. Write an essay in which you compare and contrast two instances of procrastination, one that had serious consequences for you, and one that did not. How were the instances similar? How were they different? Why did one incident have serious effects and the other did not? What conclusions do you draw from these experiences with procrastination?

Buzz Bissinger

H. G. "Buzz" Bissinger (1954–) worked as a newspaper reporter for fifteen years before moving his family from Philadelphia to Odessa, Texas, in order to write a book about high school football. In 1990 he published the best-selling *Friday Night Lights*, which was made into a movie starring Billy Bob Thornton in 2004 and into a television series in 2006. Bissinger is also the author of *A Prayer for the City* (1998), a portrait of Philadelphia, and *Three Nights in August* (2005), about Major League Baseball. Today he is a contributing editor for *Vanity Fair* and lives in Philadelphia. This essay was published in *The New York Times* on December 16, 2004.

Pre-Reading Journal Entry

Competitive sports play a large role in many high schools. What was your experience of sports in high school? Were you a high school athlete? Did you attend your school's games? How were athletes regarded in your school? How did being an athlete—or not being an athlete—affect your personal experience of high school sports? What memories do you have of your high school's athletes, teams, or coaches? Use your journal to answer these questions.

Innocents Afield

Earlier this month, the high school football season ended around the   1
country. There were the state championships and before that, the annual Thanksgiving Day games. There were the rose-colored images of innocence and valor and healthy competition, attributes that we continue to insist upon from sports in America even though such attributes have become extinct.

We are clinging to the supposed virtues of high school athletics with par-   2
ticular zeal. Everybody knows that pro sports is too far gone (take your pick of recent scandals). Everybody knows that college sports is too far gone (take your pick of recent scandals). But still there's high school sports, still the classic battle of one rival against the other in shaggy glory, what James Jones described in *From Here to Eternity*[1] as "the magnificent foolishness of youth as if the whole of life depended on this game." A half-century later, the depiction of noble sacrifice at the high school level still forms our baseline, gives us hope that something in sports is still unsullied, restores our faith in the family values fad that has overtaken the low-carb diet.

Except that high school sports in America has become an epidemic of   3
win-at-all-costs in too many places, just as corroded as college and the pros; actually more so because none of the ends can possibly justify the means when many of those involved are still too young to vote. No Super Bowl

[1]A novel published in 1951 about World War II and its aftermath (editors' note).

with television ratings through the roof. No Bowl Championship Series games with millions watching. Just millions of dollars spent by certain school districts that cannot possibly begin to explain the millions they are spending. Just booster clubs, like little Mafia families, filling in the gap between what the board of education is willing to cough up and what the athletic department claims that it needs to keep churning out those precious state championships. Just coaches in some places making close to $90,000 a year without teaching a class. Just further social stratification between the athlete and the non-athlete, those who are in and those who are out and feel humiliated and ridiculed with repercussions that can become deadly. Just steroid abuse, including a 17-year-old baseball player in a Dallas suburb who committed suicide because what of his parents believe was depression caused by stopping anabolic steroids.

Maybe I'm overselling the problem. But my point of reference is the late 1980's, when I moved to Odessa, Tex., to do research for my book. When [*Friday Night Lights*] was published in 1990, Permian High School in Odessa became a national symbol of everything that was wrong in high school sports—spending close to $70,000 on chartered jet trips to several away games, building a high school football stadium that seated nearly 20,000 and cost $5.6 million.   4

Over the past 14 years, I have had hundreds of conversations with parents about high school sports careening out of control. In virtually all of them, the reaction has been the same—approving nods of solidarity, followed by my own queasy sense that they weren't really listening to a word I said, their own private SportsCenter moment reeling in their heads for their sons and daughters. Over those 14 years, the excesses have only gotten worse.   5

As *USA Today* reported in October, millions upon millions of dollars are being spent on high school football stadiums and related buildings across the country. Texas, of course, leads the arms race with new or pending high school football stadium projects in the Dallas area alone costing close to $180 million. But in Jefferson, Ind., as part of a privately financed $8 million building project, there's a new 6,000-seat high school football stadium with an expensive video scoreboard. In Valdosta, Ga., $7.5 million was spent to renovate its football stadium, including building a museum to the glory of the Valdosta Wildcats. North Hills High, in the Pittsburgh region, spent $10 million to renovate the stadium and build a 13,000-square-foot field house.   6

The arguments for these sports centers are as familiar as they are wearying as they are transparent: the football programs not only are self-sustaining but also support other sports; these are stadiums the community wants so there's no harm, particularly when they are privately financed.   7

But no community, at least no community I would want my children to live in, can justify any of these monoliths. In an age where educational   8 resources are dwindling, how can the building of a lavish new stadium or a field house possibly be justified, much less needed? What does it say to the rest of the student body, the giant-sized majority who do not play football, except that they are inferior, a sloppy second to the football stars who shine on Friday night. How can a community brag about its ability to get financing for a multimillion-dollar football stadium when it can't conjure up the money to hire more teachers that would lead to the nirvana of smaller class sizes? If it's the desire of boosters to pour money into sports, and it usually is, then why not use these private funds for a physical education program to reduce obesity among teenagers?

It isn't simply money that has contributed to the professionalism of high   9
school sports. As a reporter for *The Chicago Tribune,* I spent a year uncovering abuses in Illinois as disturbing as anything in Texas—high school coaches recruiting eighth-grade players with glossy pitches and come-ons straight out of the major-college mold, parents getting so many calls from high school recruiters that they simply had their phones turned off, high school basketball coaches siphoning off Chicago's best players just so they wouldn't compete against them. Jump a level down into that emotional hell known as travel team—there isn't a parent of a travel team player who can't recite at least one horror story of another parent going berserk or a coach flipping out in the name of providing 10- and 11- and 12-year-olds with a little extra competition.

In October, the National Association of State Boards of Education   10
issued a report calling for greater oversight of high school athletics because of the alarming trickle-down of virtually every bad college practice. The list of concerns included steroid use, shady shoe agents, mercenary coaches, dubious recruiting tactics and extravagant gifts. Steroid abuse does exist in high schools. As many as 11 percent of the nation's youth have used them, according to a study by the Mayo Clinic. Based on other research, some of the most disturbing users are freshman high school girls, with a rate of abuse at a minimum of 7 percent. "We have a moral obligation to prevent the exploitation of high school students," the national association said.

Those are important words, but I'm afraid they are going to fall on   11
deaf ears.

Sports as an institution is every bit as powerful in this country as corpo-   12
rate America or the Catholic Church. Yet sports are still considered a sidelight, ancillary to our daily experience. It's still too easy to put on those rose-colored glasses, . . . to get wrapped up in the supposed character-building elements of it, the false narratives of heroes and come-from-behind glory fed us by newspapers and television networks and cable networks in their ceaseless search for easy emotional aphrodisiacs.

Which means that high school sports will continue to fester into shame-   13
ful overemphasis in too many places, will continue to emulate the college

sports model that is America's educational shame. Which means that by the time we completely ruin the institution of sports for our teenagers, it will be too late to do anything except appoint a national commission to try to figure out how we could have missed so many warning signs.

Questions for Close Reading

1. What is the selection's thesis? Locate the sentence(s) in which Bissinger states his main idea. If he doesn't state his thesis explicitly, express it in your own words.
2. In paragraph 2, Bissinger describes the "supposed virtues" of high school sports. What are these "supposed virtues"?
3. What is the role of money in high school sports? What is Bissinger's opinion of the role of money in high school sports?
4. In paragraph 10, Bissinger describes a way to rein in the excesses of high school sports. What solution does he present? How effective does he think it would be?
5. Refer to your dictionary as needed to define the following words used in the selection: *valor* (paragraph 1), *zeal* (2), *unsullied* (2), *social stratification* (3), *repercussions* (3), *careening* (5), *queasy* (5), *monolith* (8), *conjure* (8), *nirvana* (8), *siphoning* (9), *ancillary* (12), and *emulate* (13).

Questions About the Writer's Craft

1. **The pattern.** According to Bissinger, what has helped *cause* the recent professionalization of high school sports? What are the *effects* of this professionalization on athletes? On nonathletes? Cite the paragraphs that discuss causes and effects.
2. **Other patterns.** In paragraph 3, Bissinger *contrasts* the imaginary purchases that might be made with high school sports money with the actual purchases. What words does he use repeatedly to signal the nonexistent and the actual purchases of high school sports? How effective is this use of repetition?
3. **Other patterns.** In paragraph 5, Bissinger *argues* that the excesses of high school sports have gotten worse since he published *Friday Night Lights* in 1990. What evidence does he cite for this claim? Is the evidence convincing?
4. Bissinger concludes his essay with a prediction (paragraph 13). What is his prediction? Why is he so pessimistic about the future of high school sports?

Writing Assignments Using Cause-Effect as a Pattern of Development

1. Bissinger's essay focuses mostly on the role of money in professionalizing high school sports, but he mentions other factors as well, including recruitment practices, travel teams, and steroid abuse. Research one such factor in the library or on the Internet and write an essay about its *effect* on high school sports.
2. Bissinger's essay focuses on the negative aspects of high school sports, arguing that the worst aspects of professional and college sports have contaminated competition at the high school level. Write an essay in which you present the beneficial *effects* of high school sports on athletes, families, and communities. For example, you might discuss how playing a team sport teaches students about working with others.

Writing Assignments Combining Patterns of Development

3. *Friday Night Lights,* the movie based on Bissinger's book about high school football in Odessa, Texas, shows that the expectations of classmates, coaches, family, and community take a heavy toll on team members. Still, the film has many of the elements of the classic Hollywood underdog sports movie, in which a team battles great odds to emerge victorious. These movies—such as *Bad News Bears* (baseball), *Hoosiers* (basketball), *Remember the Titans* (football), and *Miracle* (hockey)—are all inspirational in tone. Select a sports movie that you have seen and show how this movie *exemplifies* particular values of sports in American culture. What is the message of the movie? What *causes* such movies to be so popular?

4. Bissinger contrasts James Jones's 1951 description of the nobility of high school athletics with the modern reality, which has been affected by money and fame. This contrast between an earlier, more innocent version of a present-day cultural practice underlies several of the essays in this book. For example, in "Family Counterculture" (page 7), Ellen Goodman contrasts the past influence of ministers, teachers, and societal leaders on children's development with the present influence of TV and advertising. In "Tweens: Ten Going On Sixteen" (page 163), Kay S. Hymowitz describes how today's eight- to twelve-year-olds are more like teenagers than like children. And in "Marrying Absurd" (page 448), Joan Didion describes the excesses of a Las Vegas wedding. Select a present-day cultural phenomenon, and write an essay in which you *compare* and *contrast* present-day practices with those of the past and explain how and why these practices have *affected* people's behavior. For example, you can write an essay comparing teens' social lives before and after the Internet and explain how the Internet has affected social behavior. Or you can contrast spending habits before and after credit cards became common and explain their effect on people's consumer behavior. Or you can compare modern indoor shopping malls to old-time main streets and describe the effect of malls on shopping habits.

Writing Assignment Using a Journal Entry as a Starting Point

5. Whether you were an athlete or not, sports probably had some effect on your high school experience. Review your pre-reading journal entry about high school sports. Select one of your experiences with high school sports, whether as an athlete, a spectator, or a fan, and write an essay *narrating* the experience. Was your experience good or bad, or both? How did this experience influence your overall experience of high school?

Additional Writing Topics

CAUSE-EFFECT

General Assignments

Write an essay that analyzes the causes and/or effects of one of the following topics. Determine your purpose before beginning to write: Will the essay be informative, persuasive, or speculative? As you prewrite, think rigorously about causes and effects; try to identify causal chains. Provide solid evidence for the thesis and use either chronological or emphatic order to organize your supporting points.

1. Sleep deprivation
2. Having the parents you have
3. Lack of communication in a relationship
4. Overexercising or not exercising
5. A particular TV or rock star's popularity
6. Skill or ineptitude in sports
7. A major life decision
8. Stiffer legal penalties for drunken driving
9. Changing attitudes toward protecting the environment
10. A particular national crisis
11. The mass movement of women into the workforce
12. Choosing to attend this college
13. "Back to basics" movement in schools
14. Headaches
15. An act of violence
16. A natural event: leaves turning, birds migrating, animals hibernating, an eclipse occurring
17. Text-messaging
18. Use of computers in the classroom
19. Banning disposable cans and bottles
20. A bad habit
21. A fear of _____
22. Legalizing drugs
23. Abolishing the F grade
24. Joining a particular organization
25. Owning a pet

Assignments with a Specific Purpose, Audience, and Point of View

On Campus

1. A debate about the prominence of athletics at colleges and universities is going to be broadcast on the local cable station. For this debate, prepare a speech

pointing out either the harmful or the beneficial effects of "big-time" college athletic programs.

2. Why do students "flunk out" of college? Write an article for the campus newspaper outlining the main causes of failure. Your goal is to steer students away from dangerous habits and situations that lead to poor grades or dropping out.

At Home or in the Community

3. Write a letter to the editor of your favorite newspaper analyzing the causes of the country's current "trash crisis." Be sure to mention the nationwide love affair with disposable items and the general disregard of the idea of thrift. Conclude by offering brief suggestions for how people in your community can begin to remedy this problem.

4. Write a letter to the head of your religious congregation or a civic organization that you belong to suggesting ways, such as installing solar panels, that the group can become more energy efficient. Discuss the positive impact that energy conservation can have on efforts to stop global warming.

On the Job

5. As the manager of a store or office, you've noticed that a number of employees have negative workplace habits and/or attitudes. Write a memo for your employees in which you identify these negative behaviors and show how they affect the workplace environment. Be sure to adopt a tone that will sound neither patronizing nor overly harsh.

6. Why do you think teenage suicide is on the rise? You're a respected psychologist. Write a fact sheet for parents of teenagers and for high school guidance counselors describing the factors that could make a young person desperate enough to attempt suicide. At the end, suggest what parents and counselors can do to help confused, unhappy young people.

DEFINITION

WHAT IS DEFINITION?

In Lewis Carroll's wise and whimsical tale *Through the Looking Glass,* Humpty Dumpty proclaims, "When *I* use a word . . . , it means just what I choose it to mean—neither more nor less." If the world were filled with characters like Humpty Dumpty, all of them bending words to their own purposes and accepting no challenges to their personal definitions, communication would be an exercise in frustration. You would say a word, and it would mean one thing to you but perhaps something completely different to a close friend. Without a common understanding, the two of you would talk at cross-purposes, missing each other's meanings as you blundered through a conversation.

For language to communicate, words must have accepted *definitions.* Dictionaries, the sourcebooks for accepted definitions, are compilations of current word meanings, enabling speakers of a language to understand one another. But as you might suspect, things are not as simple as they first appear. We all know that a word like *discipline* has a standard dictionary definition. We also know, though, that parents argue over what constitutes "discipline" and that controversies about the meaning of "discipline" rage within school systems year after year. Moreover, many of the wrenching moral debates of our time also boil down to questions of definition. Much of the controversy over abortion, for instance, centers on what is meant by "life" and when it "begins."

Words can, in short, be slippery. Each of us has unique experiences, attitudes, and values that influence the way we use words and the way we interpret the words of others. Lewis Carroll may have been exaggerating, but Humpty Dumpty's attitude exists—in a very real way—in all of us.

In addition to the idiosyncratic interpretations that may attach to words, some words may shift in meaning over time. The word *pedagogue,* for instance, originally meant "a teacher or leader of children." However, with time, *pedagogue* has come to mean "a dogmatic, pedantic teacher." And, of course, we invent other words (*modem, byte, e-mail*) as the need arises.

Writing a definition, then, is no simple task. Primarily, the writer tries to answer basic questions: "What does _____ mean?" and "What is the special or true nature of _____?" The word may represent an object, a concept, a type of person, a place, or a phenomenon. Potential subjects might be the "user-friendly" computer, animal rights, a model teacher, cabin fever. As you will see, there are various strategies for expanding definitions far beyond the single-word synonyms or brief phrases that dictionaries provide.

HOW DEFINITION FITS YOUR PURPOSE AND AUDIENCE

Many times, short-answer exam questions call for definitions. Consider the following examples:

> Define the term *mob psychology.*
>
> What is the difference between a metaphor and a simile?
>
> How would you explain what a religious cult is?

In such cases, a good response might involve a definition of several sentences or several paragraphs.

Other times, definition may be used in an essay organized mainly around another pattern of development. In this situation, all that's needed is a brief formal definition or a short definition given in your own words. For instance, a *process analysis* showing readers how computers have revolutionized the typical business office might start with a textbook definition of the term *artificial intelligence.* In an *argumentation-persuasion* paper urging students to support recent efforts to abolish fraternities and sororities, you could refer to the definitions of *blackballing* and *hazing* found in the university handbook. Or your personal definition of *hero* could be the starting point for a *causal analysis* that explains to readers why there are few real heroes in today's world.

But the most complex use of definition, and the one we are primarily concerned with in this chapter, involves exploring a subject through an *extended definition.* Extended definition allows you to apply a personal interpretation to a word, to make a case for a revisionist view of a commonly accepted meaning, to analyze words representing complex or controversial issues. "Pornography," "gun control," "secular humanism," and "right-to-life" would be excellent subjects for extended definition—each is multifaceted, often misunderstood, and fraught with emotional meaning. "Junk food," "anger," "leadership," "anxiety" could make interesting subjects, especially if the extended definition helped readers develop a new understanding of the word. You might, for example, define *anxiety* not as a negative state to be avoided but as a positive force that propels us to take action.

An extended definition could perhaps run several paragraphs or a few pages. Keep in mind, however, that an extended definition may require a chapter or even an entire book to develop. If this seems unlikely, remember that theologians, philosophers, and pop psychologists have devoted entire texts to such concepts as "evil" and "love."

At this point, you have a good sense of the way writers use definition to achieve their purpose and to connect with their readers. Now take a moment to look closely at the photograph at the beginning of this chapter. Imagine you're writing an essay, accompanied by the photo, for publication in your campus newspaper. Your purpose is to explain what it means to be an American in the twenty-first century. Jot down some ideas you might include in your *definition*.

SUGGESTIONS FOR USING DEFINITION IN AN ESSAY

The suggestions here and in Figure 10.1 will be helpful whether you use definition as a dominant or a supportive pattern of development.

1. Stay focused on the essay's purpose, audience, and tone.   Since your purpose for writing an extended definition shapes the entire paper, you need to keep that objective in mind when developing your definition. Suppose you decide to write an essay defining *jazz*. The essay could be purely *informative* and discuss the origins of jazz, its characteristic tonal patterns, and some of the great jazz musicians of the past. Or the essay could move beyond pure information and take on a *persuasive* edge. It might, for example, argue that jazz is the only contemporary form of music worth considering seriously.

Just as your purpose in writing will vary, so will your tone. A strictly informative definition will generally assume a detached, objective tone ("Apathy is an emotional state characterized by listlessness and indifference").

FIGURE 10.1
Development Diagram: Writing a Definition Essay

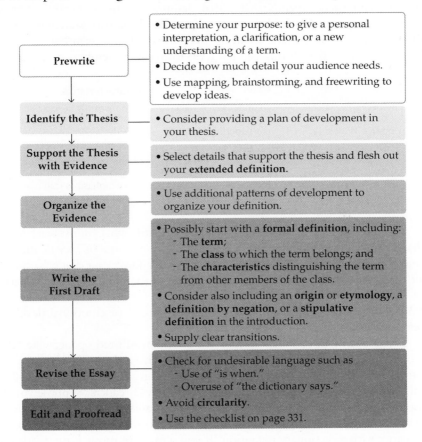

Prewrite	• Determine your purpose: to give a personal interpretation, a clarification, or a new understanding of a term. • Decide how much detail your audience needs. • Use mapping, brainstorming, and freewriting to develop ideas.
Identify the Thesis	• Consider providing a plan of development in your thesis.
Support the Thesis with Evidence	• Select details that support the thesis and flesh out your **extended definition**.
Organize the Evidence	• Use additional patterns of development to organize your definition.

Write the First Draft	• Possibly start with a **formal definition**, including:
	  - The **term**;
	  - The **class** to which the term belongs; and
	  - The **characteristics** distinguishing the term from other members of the class.
	• Consider also including an **origin** or **etymology**, a **definition by negation**, or a **stipulative definition** in the introduction.
	• Supply clear transitions.

Revise the Essay	• Check for undesirable language such as
	  - Use of "is when."
	  - Overuse of "the dictionary says."
	• Avoid **circularity**.

Edit and Proofread	• Use the checklist on page 331.

By way of contrast, a definition essay with a persuasive slant might be urgent in tone ("To combat student apathy, we must design programs that engage students in campus life"), or it might take a satiric approach ("An apathetic stance is a wise choice for any thinking student").

As you write, keep thinking about your audience as well. Not only do your readers determine what terms need to be defined (and in how much detail), but they also keep you focused on the essay's purpose and tone. For instance, you probably wouldn't write a serious, informative piece for the college newspaper about the "mystery meat" served in the campus cafeteria. Instead, you would adopt a light tone as you defined the culinary horror and might even make a persuasive pitch about improving the food prepared on campus.

2. Formulate an effective definition.   A definition essay sometimes begins with a brief *formal definition*—the dictionary's, a textbook's, or the writer's—and then expands that initial definition with supporting details. Formal definitions are traditionally worded as three-part statements that consist of the following: the *term,* the *class* to which the term belongs, and the *characteristics* that distinguish the term from other members of its class.

Term	Class	Characteristics
The peregrine falcon,	an endangered bird,	is the world's fastest flyer.
A bodice-ripper	is a paperback book	that deals with highly charged romance in exotic places and faraway times.
Back to basics	is a trend in education	that emphasizes skill mastery through rote learning.

A definition that meets these guidelines will clarify what your subject *is* and what it *is not.* These guidelines also establish the boundaries of your definition, removing unlike items from consideration in your (and your reader's) mind. For example, defining "back to basics" as a trend that emphasizes rote learning signals a certain boundary; it lets readers know that other educational trends, such as those that emphasize children's social or emotional development, will not be part of the essay's definition.

If you decide to include a formal definition, avoid tired openers like "the dictionary says" or "according to *Webster's.*" Such weak starts are just plain boring and often herald an unimaginative essay. You should also keep in mind that a strict dictionary definition may actually confuse readers. Suppose you're writing a paper on the way all of us absorb ideas and values from the media. Likening this automatic response to the process of osmosis, you decide to open the paper with a dictionary definition. If you write, "Osmosis is the tendency of a solvent to disperse through a semipermeable membrane into a more concentrated medium," readers are apt to be baffled, even hostile. Remember: The purpose of a definition is to clarify meaning, not obscure it.

You should also stay clear of ungrammatical "is when" definitions: "Blind ambition is when you want to get ahead, no matter how much other people are hurt." Instead, write "Blind ambition is wanting to get ahead, no matter how much other people are hurt." A final pitfall to avoid in writing formal definitions is *circularity,* saying the same thing twice and therefore defining nothing: "A campus tribunal is a tribunal composed of various members of the university community." Circular definitions like this often repeat the term being defined (*tribunal*) or use words having the same meaning (*campus; university community*). In this case, we learn nothing about what a campus tribunal is; the writer says only that "X is X."

3. Develop the extended definition.   You can choose from a variety of patterns when formulating an extended definition. Description, narration, process analysis, and comparison-contrast can be used—alone or in combination. Imagine that you're planning to write an extended definition of "robotics." You might develop the term by providing *examples* of the ways robots are currently being used in scientific research; by *comparing* and *contrasting* human and robot capabilities; or by *classifying* robots, starting with the most basic and moving to the most advanced or futuristic models.

Which patterns of development to use will often become apparent during the prewriting stage. Here is a list of prewriting questions as well as the pattern of development implied by each question.

Question	Pattern of Development
How does X look, taste, smell, feel, and sound?	Description
What does X do? When? Where?	Narration
What are some typical instances of X?	Exemplification
What are X's component parts? What different forms can X take?	Division-classification
How does X work?	Process analysis
What is X like or unlike?	Comparison-contrast
What leads to X? What are X's consequences?	Cause-effect

Those questions yielding the most material often suggest the effective pattern(s) for developing an extended definition.

4. Organize the material that develops the definition.   If you use a single pattern to develop the extended definition, apply the principles of organization suited to that pattern, as described in the appropriate chapter of this book. Assume that you're defining "fad" by means of *process analysis.* You might organize your paragraphs according to the steps in the process: a fad's slow start as something avant-garde or eccentric; its wildfire acceptance by the general public; the fad's demise as it becomes familiar or tiresome. If you want to define "character" by means of a single *narration,* you would probably organize paragraphs chronologically.

In a definition essay using several methods of development, you should devote separate paragraphs to each pattern. A definition of "relaxation," for instance, might start with a paragraph that *narrates* a particularly relaxing day; then it might move to a paragraph that describes several *examples* of people who find it difficult to unwind; finally, it might end with a paragraph that explains a *process* for relaxing the mind and body.

5. Write an effective introduction.   It can be helpful to provide—near the beginning of a definition essay—a brief formal definition of the term you're going to develop in the rest of the paper. Beyond this basic element, the introduction may include a number of other features. You might explain the *origin* of the term being defined: "Acid rock is a term first coined in the 1960s to describe music that was written or listened to under the influence of the drug LSD." Similarly, you could explain the *etymology,* or linguistic origin, of the key word that focuses the paper. "The term *vigilantism* is derived from the Latin word meaning 'to watch and be awake.'"

You may also use the introduction to clarify what the subject is *not.* Such *definition by negation* can be an effective strategy at the beginning of a paper, especially if readers don't share your view of the subject. In such a case, you might write something like this: "The gorilla, far from being the vicious killer of jungle movies and popular imagination, is a sedentary, gentle creature living in a closely knit family group." Such a statement provides the special focus of your essay and signals some of the misconceptions or fallacies soon to be discussed.

In addition, you may include in the introduction a *stipulative definition,* one that puts special restrictions on a term: "Strictly defined, a mall refers to a one- or two-story enclosed building containing a variety of retail shops and at least two large anchor stores. Highway-strip shopping centers or down-town centers cannot be considered true malls." When a term has multiple meanings, or when its meaning has become fuzzy through misuse, a stipula-tive definition sets the record straight right at the start, so that readers know exactly what is, and is not, being defined.

Finally, the introduction may end with a *plan of development* that indicates how the definition essay will unfold. A student who returned to school after having raised a family decided to write a paper defining the *midlife crisis* that led to her enrollment in college. After providing a brief formal definition of "midlife crisis," the student rounded off her introduc-tion with this sentence: "Such a midlife crisis starts with vague misgivings, turns into depression, and ends with a significant change in lifestyle."

REVISION STRATEGIES

Once you have a draft of the essay, you're ready to revise. The following checklist will help you and those giving you feedback apply to definition some of the revision techniques discussed on pages 60–62.

☑ DEFINITION: A REVISION/PEER REVIEW CHECKLIST

Revise Overall Meaning and Structure

❑ Is the essay's purpose informative, persuasive, or both?

❑ Is the term being defined clearly distinguished from similar terms?

❑ Where does a circular definition cloud meaning? Where are technical, nonstandard, or ambiguous terms a source of confusion?

❑ Where would a word's historical or linguistic origin clarify meaning? Where would a formal definition, stipulative definition, or definition by negation help?

❑ Which patterns of development are used to develop the definition? How do these help the essay achieve its purpose?

❑ If the essay uses only one pattern, is the essay's method of organization suited to that pattern (step-by-step for process analysis, chronological for narration, and so on)?

❑ Where could a dry formal definition be deleted without sacrificing overall clarity?

Revise Paragraph Development

❑ If the essay uses several patterns of development, where would separate paragraphs for different patterns be appropriate?

❑ Which paragraphs are flat or unconvincing? How could they be made more compelling?

Revise Sentences and Words

❑ Which sentences and words are inconsistent with the essay's tone?

❑ Where should overused phrases like "the dictionary says" and "according to *Webster's*" be replaced by more original wording?

❑ Have "is when" definitions been avoided?

STUDENT ESSAY

The following student essay was written by Laura Chen in response to this assignment:

> In "Entropy," K. C. Cole takes a scientific term from physics and gives it a broader definition and a wider application. Choose another specialized term and define it in such a way that you reveal something significant about contemporary life.

While reading Laura's paper, try to determine how well it applies the principles of definition. The annotations on Laura's paper and the commentary following it will help you look at the essay more closely.

Physics in Everyday Life
by Laura Chen

Introduction

A boulder sits on a mountainside for a thousand years. 1 The boulder will remain there forever unless an outside force intervenes. Suppose a force does affect the boulder—an earthquake, for instance. Once the boulder begins to thunder down the mountain, it will remain in motion and head in one direction only—downhill—until another force interrupts its progress. If the boulder tumbles into a gorge, it will finally come to rest as gravity anchors it to the earth once more. In both

Formal definition

cases, the boulder is exhibiting the physical principle of inertia: the tendency of matter to remain at rest or, if moving, to keep moving in one direction unless affected by an outside force.

Thesis

Inertia, an important factor in the world of physics, also plays a crucial role in the human world. Inertia affects our individual

Plan of development

lives as well as the direction taken by society as a whole.

Topic sentence

Inertia often influences our value systems and personal 2 growth. Inertia is at work, for example, when people cling to certain behaviors and views. Like the boulder firmly fixed to the mountain, most people are set in their ways. Without thinking, they vote Republican or Democratic because they have always voted that way. They regard with suspicion a couple having no children, simply because everyone else in the neighborhood has a large family. It is only when an outside

Start of a series of causes and effects

force—a jolt of some sort—occurs that people change their views. A white American couple may think little about racial discrimination, for instance, until they adopt an Asian child and must comfort her when classmates tease her because she looks different. Parents may consider promiscuous any unmarried teenage girl who has a baby until their seventeen-year-old honor student confesses that she is pregnant. Personal jolts like these force people to think, perhaps for the first time, about issues that now affect them directly.

Topic sentence

To illustrate how inertia governs our lives, it is helpful to 3 compare the world of television with real life. On TV, inertia does

Start of a series of contrasts

not exist. Television shows and commercials show people making all kinds of drastic changes. They switch brands of coffee or try a new hair color with no hesitation. In one car commercial, an ambitious young accountant abandons her career with a flourish and is seen driving off into the sunset as she heads for a small cabin by the sea to write poetry. In a soap opera, a character may progress from homemaker to hooker to nun in a single year. But in real life, inertia rules. People tend to stay where they are, to keep their jobs, to be loyal to products. A second major difference between television and real life is that, on television, everyone takes prompt and dramatic action to solve problems. The construction worker with a thudding headache is pain-free at the end of the sixty-second commercial; the police catch the murderer within an hour; the family learns to cope with their son's life-threatening drug addiction by the time the made-for-TV movie ends at eleven. But in the real world, inertia persists, so that few problems are solved neatly or quickly. Illnesses drag on, few crimes are solved, and family conflicts last for years.

Topic sentence ——→ Inertia is, most importantly, a force at work in the life of   4
our nation. Again, inertia is two-sided. It keeps us from moving and, once we move, it keeps us pointed in one direction. We find ourselves mired in a certain path, accepting the inferior, even the dangerous. We settle for toys that break, winter

Start of a series —— coats with no warmth, and rivers clogged with pollution.
of examples   Inertia also compels our nation to keep moving in one direction—despite the uncomfortable suspicion that it is the wrong direction. We are not sure if manipulating genes is a good idea, yet we continue to fund scientific projects in genetic engineering. More than sixty years ago, we were shaken when we saw the devastation caused by an atomic bomb. But we went on to develop weapons hundreds of times more destructive. Although warned that excessive television viewing may be harmful, we continue to watch hours of television each day.

Conclusion   We have learned to defy gravity, one of the basic laws of   5
physics; we fly high above the earth, even float in outer space. But most of us have not learned to defy inertia. Those special individuals who are able to act when everyone else seems paralyzed are rare. But the fact that such people do exist means that inertia is not all-powerful. If we use our reasoning ability and our creativity, we can conquer inertia, just as we have conquered gravity.

COMMENTARY

Introduction.   As the title of her essay suggests, Laura has taken a scientific term (*inertia*) from a specialized field and drawn on the term to help explain some everyday phenomena. Using the *simple-to-complex* approach to structure the introduction, she opens with a vivid *descriptive* example of inertia. This description is then followed by a *formal definition* of inertia: "the tendency of matter to remain at rest or, if moving, to keep moving in one direction unless affected by an outside force." Laura wisely begins the paper with the easy-to-understand description rather than with the more-difficult-to-grasp scientific definition. Had the order been reversed, the essay would not have gotten off to nearly as effective a start. She then ends her introductory paragraph with a *thesis*, "Inertia, an important factor in the world of physics, also plays a crucial role in the human world," and with a *plan of development*, "Inertia affects our individual lives as well as the direction taken by society as a whole."

Organization.   To support her definition of inertia and her belief that it can rule our lives, Laura generates a number of compelling examples. She organizes these examples by grouping them into three major points, each point signaled by a *topic sentence* that opens each of the essay's three supporting paragraphs (2–4).

A definite organizational strategy determines the sequence of Laura's three central points. The essay moves from the way inertia affects the individual to the way it affects the nation. The phrase "most importantly" at the beginning of the fourth paragraph shows that Laura has arranged her points emphatically, believing that inertia's impact on society is most critical.

A weak example.   When reading the fourth paragraph, you might have noticed that Laura's examples aren't sequenced as effectively as they could be. To show that we, as a nation, tend to keep moving in the same direction, Laura discusses our ongoing uneasiness about genetic engineering, nuclear arms, and excessive television viewing. The point about nuclear weapons is most significant, yet it gets lost because it's sandwiched in the middle. The paragraph would be stronger if it ended with the point about nuclear arms. Moreover, the example about excessive television viewing doesn't belong in this paragraph since, at best, it has limited bearing on the issue being discussed.

Combining patterns of development.   In addition to using numerous *examples* to illustrate her points, Laura draws on several other patterns of development to show that inertia can be a powerful force. In the second and fourth paragraphs, she uses *causal analysis* to explain how inertia can paralyze people and nations. The second paragraph indicates that only "an outside force—a jolt of some sort—" can motivate inert people to change. To support this view, Laura provides two examples of parents who experience such jolts. Similarly, in the fourth paragraph, she contends that inertia causes the persistence of specific national problems: shoddy consumer goods and environmental pollution.

Another pattern, *comparison-contrast*, is used in the third paragraph to highlight the differences between television and real life: on television, people zoom into action, but in everyday life, people tend to stay put and muddle through. The essay also contains a distinct element of *argumentation-persuasion*, since Laura clearly wants readers to accept her definition of inertia and her view that it often governs human behavior.

Conclusion.   Laura's *conclusion* rounds off the essay nicely and brings it to a satisfying close. Laura refers to another law of physics, one with which we are all familiar—gravity. By creating an *analogy* between gravity and inertia, she suggests that our ability to defy gravity should encourage us to defy inertia. The analogy enlarges the scope of the essay; it allows Laura to reach out to her readers by challenging them to action. Such a challenge is, of course, appropriate in a definition essay having a persuasive bent.

Revising the first draft.   When it was time to rework her essay, Laura began by reading her paper aloud. She noted in the margin of her draft the problems she detected, numbering them in order of importance. After reviewing her notes, she started to revise in earnest, paying special attention to her third paragraph. The first draft of that paragraph is reprinted here:

Original Version of the Third Paragraph

The ordinary actions of daily life are, in part, determined by inertia. To understand this, it is helpful to compare the world of television with real life, for, in the TV-land of ads and entertainment, inertia does not exist. For example, on television, people are often shown making all kinds of drastic changes. They switch brands of coffee or try a new hair color with no hesitation. In one car commercial, a young accountant leaves her career and sets off for a cabin by the sea to write poetry. In a soap opera, a character may progress from homemaker to hooker to nun in a single year. In contrast, inertia rules in real life. People tend to stay where they are, to keep their jobs, to be loyal to products (wives get annoyed if a husband brings home the wrong brand or color of bathroom tissue from the market). Middle-aged people wear the hairstyles or makeup that suited them in high school. A second major difference between television and real life is that, on TV, everyone takes prompt and dramatic action to solve problems. A woman finds the solution to dull clothes at the end of a commercial; the police catch the murderer within an hour; the family learns to cope with a son's disturbing lifestyle by the time the movie is over. In contrast, the law of real-life inertia means that few problems are solved neatly or quickly. Things, once started, tend to stay as they are. Few crimes are actually solved. Medical problems are not easily diagnosed. Messy wars in foreign countries seem endless. National problems are identified, but Congress does not pass legislation to solve them.

After rereading what she had written, Laura realized that her third paragraph rambled. To give it more focus, she removed the last two sentences ("Messy wars in foreign countries seem endless" and "National problems are identified, but Congress does not pass legislation....") because they referred to national affairs but were located in a section focusing on the individual. Then, she eliminated two flat, unconvincing examples: wives who get annoyed when their husbands bring home the wrong brand of bathroom tissue and middle-aged people whose hairstyles and makeup are outdated. Condensing the two disjointed sentences that originally opened the paragraph also helped tighten this section of the essay. Note how much crisper the revised sentences are: "To illustrate how inertia rules our lives, it is helpful to compare the world of television with real life. On TV, inertia does not exist."

Laura also worked to make the details and the language in the paragraph more specific and vigorous. The vague sentence "A woman finds the solution to dull clothes at the end of the commercial" is replaced by the more dramatic "The construction worker with a thudding headache is pain-free at the end of the sixty-second commercial." Similarly, Laura changed a "son's disturbing lifestyle" to a "son's life-threatening drug addiction"; "by the time the movie is over" became "by the time the made-for-TV movie ends at eleven"; and "a young accountant leaves her career and sets off for a cabin by the sea to write poetry" was changed to "an ambitious young accountant abandons her career with a flourish and is seen driving off into the sunset as she heads for a small cabin by the sea to write poetry."

After making these changes, Laura decided to round off the paragraph with a powerful summary statement highlighting how real life differs from television: "Illnesses drag on, few crimes are solved, and family conflicts last for years."

These third-paragraph revisions are similar to those that Laura made elsewhere in her first draft. Her astute changes enabled her to turn an already effective paper into an especially thoughtful analysis of human behavior.

Activities: Definition

Prewriting Activities

1. Imagine you're writing two essays: one explains the *process* for registering a complaint that gets results; the other *contrasts* the styles of two stand-up comics. Jot down ways you might use definition in each essay.

2. Select a term whose meaning varies from person to person or one for which you have a personal definition. Some possibilities include:

success	femininity	a liberal
patriotism	affirmative action	a housewife
individuality	pornography	intelligence

Brainstorm with others to identify variations in the term's meaning. Then examine your prewriting material. What thesis comes to mind? If you were writing an essay, would your purpose be informative, persuasive, or both? Finally, prepare a scratch list of the points you might cover.

Revising Activities

3. Explain why each of the following is an effective or ineffective definition. Rewrite those you consider ineffective.
   a. *Passive aggression* is when people show their aggression passively.
   b. A *terrorist* tries to terrorize people.
   c. *Being assertive* means knowing how to express your wishes and goals in a positive, noncombative way.
   d. *Pop music* refers to music that is popular.
   e. *Loyalty* is when someone stays by another person during difficult times.

4. The following introductory paragraph is from the first draft of an essay contrasting walking and running as techniques for reducing tension. Although intended to be a definition paragraph, it actually doesn't tell us anything we don't already know. It also relies on the old-hat "*Webster's* says." Rewrite the paragraph so it is more imaginative. You might use a series of anecdotes or one extended example to define *tension* and introduce the essay's thesis more gracefully.

   According to *Webster's, tension* is "mental or nervous strain, often accompanied by muscular tightness or tautness." Everyone feels tense at one time or another. It may occur when there's a deadline to meet. Or it could be caused by the stress of trying to fulfill academic, athletic, or social goals. Sometimes it comes from criticism by family, bosses, or teachers. Such tension puts wear and tear on our bodies and on our emotional well-being. Although some people run to relieve tension, research has found that walking is a more effective tension reducer.

K. C. Cole

K. C. Cole's writings about science, especially physics, have made a great deal of specialized knowledge available to the general public. A graduate of Barnard College, Cole has contributed numerous articles to such publications as *The New York Times, Long Island Newsday, The New Yorker, The Smithsonian, Discover, Esquire,* and *Ms.* Her work with the Exploratorium, a San Francisco science museum, led her to write several books on the exhibits there. In 1985, Cole published a collection of essays, *Sympathetic Vibrations: Reflections on Physics as a Way of Life.* Other books include *What Only a Mother Can Tell You About Having a Baby* (1986), *The Universe and the Teacup* (1998), *First You Build a Cloud* (1999), *The Hole in the Universe* (2000), and *Mind Over Matter* (2003). She is currently a science writer and editor at the *Los Angeles Times.* The following selection was first published as a "Hers" column in *The New York Times* in 1982.

For ideas about how this definition essay is organized, see Figure 10.2 on page 341.

Pre-Reading Journal Entry

Do you consider yourself an orderly or a disorderly person? What about those around you? What are the benefits and the drawbacks of being orderly? Of being disorderly? Use your journal to reflect on these questions.

Entropy

It was about two months ago when I realized that entropy was getting the better of me. On the same day my car broke down (again), my refrigerator conked out and I learned that I needed root-canal work in my right rear tooth. The windows in the bedroom were still leaking every time it rained and my son's baby sitter was still failing to show up every time I really needed her. My hair was turning gray and my typewriter was wearing out. The house needed paint and I needed glasses. My son's sneakers were developing holes and I was developing a deep sense of futility. 1

After all, what was the point of spending half of Saturday at the Laundromat if the clothes were dirty all over again the following Friday? 2

Disorder, alas, is the natural order of things in the universe. There is even a precise measure of the amount of disorder, called entropy. Unlike almost every other physical property (motion, gravity, energy), entropy does not work both ways. It can only increase. Once it's created it can never be destroyed. The road to disorder is a one-way street. 3

Because of its unnerving irreversibility, entropy has been called the arrow of time. We all understand this instinctively. Children's rooms, left on their own, tend to get messy, not neat. Wood rots, metal rusts, people wrinkle and flowers wither. Even mountains wear down; even the nuclei of atoms decay. 4

338

In the city we see entropy in the rundown subways and worn-out sidewalks and torn-down buildings, in the increasing disorder of our lives. We know, without asking, what is old. If we were suddenly to see the paint jump back on an old building, we would know that something was wrong. If we saw an egg unscramble itself and jump back into its shell, we would laugh in the same way we laugh at a movie run backward.

Entropy is no laughing matter, however, because with every increase in entropy energy is wasted and opportunity is lost. Water flowing down a mountainside can be made to do some useful work on its way. But once all the water is at the same level it can work no more. That is entropy. When my refrigerator was working, it kept all the cold air ordered in one part of the kitchen and warmer air in another. Once it broke down the warm and cold mixed into a lukewarm mess that allowed my butter to melt, my milk to rot and my frozen vegetables to decay.

Of course the energy is not really lost, but it has diffused and dissipated into a chaotic caldron of randomness that can do us no possible good. Entropy is chaos. It is loss of purpose.

People are often upset by the entropy they seem to see in the haphazard-ness of their own lives. Buffeted about like so many molecules in my tepid kitchen, they feel that they have lost their sense of direction, that they are wasting youth and opportunity at every turn. It is easy to see entropy in marriages, when the partners are too preoccupied to patch small things up, almost guaranteeing that they will fall apart. There is much entropy in the state of our country, in the relationships between nations—lost opportunities to stop the avalanche of disorders that seems ready to swallow us all.

Entropy is not inevitable everywhere, however. Crystals and snowflakes and galaxies are islands of incredibly ordered beauty in the midst of random events. If it was not for exceptions to entropy, the sky would be black and we would be able to see where the stars spend their days; it is only because air molecules in the atmosphere cluster in ordered groups that the sky is blue.

The most profound exception to entropy is the creation of life. A seed soaks up some soil and some carbon and some sunshine and some water and arranges it into a rose. A seed in the womb takes some oxygen and pizza and milk and transforms it into a baby.

The catch is that it takes a lot of energy to produce a baby. It also takes energy to make a tree. The road to disorder is all downhill but the road to creation takes work. Though combating entropy is possible, it also has its price. That's why it seems so hard to get ourselves together, so easy to let ourselves fall apart.

Worse, creating order in one corner of the universe always creates more disorder somewhere else. We create ordered energy from oil and coal at the price of the entropy of smog.

I recently took up playing the flute again after an absence of several months. As the uneven vibrations screeched through the house, my son covered his ears and said, "Mom, what's wrong with your flute?" Nothing was wrong with my flute, of course. It was my ability to play it that had atrophied, or entropied, as the case may be. The only way to stop that process was to practice every day, and sure enough my tone improved, though only at the price of constant work. Like anything else, abilities deteriorate when we stop applying our energies to them.

That's why entropy is depressing. It seems as if just breaking even is an   13
uphill fight. There's a good reason that this should be so. The mechanics of entropy are a matter of chance. Take any ice-cold air molecule milling around my kitchen. The chances that it will wander in the direction of my refrigerator at any point are exactly 50–50. The chances that it will wander away from my refrigerator are also 50–50. But take billions of warm and cold molecules mixed together, and the chances that all the cold ones will wander toward the refrigerator and all the warm ones will wander away from it are virtually nil.

Entropy wins not because order is impossible but because there are always   14
so many more paths toward disorder than toward order. There are so many more different ways to do a sloppy job than a good one, so many more ways to make a mess than to clean it up. The obstacles and accidents in our lives almost guarantee that constant collisions will bounce us on to random paths, get us off the track. Disorder is the path of least resistance, the easy but not the inevitable road.

Like so many others, I am distressed by the entropy I see around me   15
today. I am afraid of the randomness of international events, of the lack of common purpose in the world; I am terrified that it will lead into the ultimate entropy of nuclear war. I am upset that I could not in the city where I live send my child to a public school; that people are unemployed and inflation is out of control; that tensions between sexes and races seem to be increasing again; that relationships everywhere seem to be falling apart.

Social institutions—like atoms and stars—decay if energy is not added to   16
keep them ordered. Friendships and families and economies all fall apart unless we constantly make an effort to keep them working and well oiled. And far too few people, it seems to me, are willing to contribute consistently to those efforts.

Of course, the more complex things are, the harder it is. If there were only   17
a dozen or so air molecules in my kitchen, it would be likely—if I waited a year or so—that at some point the six coldest ones would congregate inside the freezer. But the more factors in the equation—the more players in the game— the less likely it is that their paths will coincide in an orderly way. The more pieces in the puzzle, the harder it is to put back together once order is disturbed. "Irreversibility," said a physicist, "is the price we pay for complexity."

Questions for Close Reading

1. What is the selection's thesis? Locate the sentence(s) in which Cole states her main idea. If she doesn't state the thesis explicitly, express it in your own words.
2. How does entropy differ from the other properties of the physical world? Is the image "the arrow of time" helpful in establishing this difference?

FIGURE 10.2
Essay Structure Diagram: "Entropy" by K. C. Cole

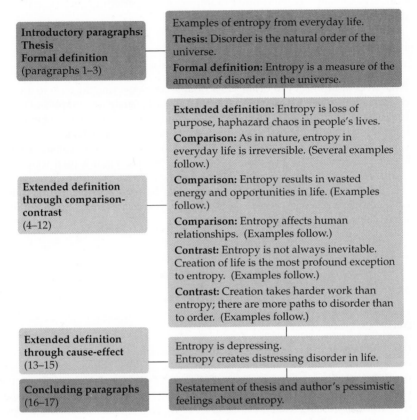

Introductory paragraphs:
Thesis
Formal definition
(paragraphs 1–3)

Examples of entropy from everyday life.
Thesis: Disorder is the natural order of the universe.
Formal definition: Entropy is a measure of the amount of disorder in the universe.

Extended definition through comparison-contrast
(4–12)

Extended definition: Entropy is loss of purpose, haphazard chaos in people's lives.
Comparison: As in nature, entropy in everyday life is irreversible. (Several examples follow.)
Comparison: Entropy results in wasted energy and opportunities in life. (Examples follow.)
Comparison: Entropy affects human relationships. (Examples follow.)
Contrast: Entropy is not always inevitable. Creation of life is the most profound exception to entropy. (Examples follow.)
Contrast: Creation takes harder work than entropy; there are more paths to disorder than to order. (Examples follow.)

Extended definition through cause-effect
(13–15)

Entropy is depressing.
Entropy creates distressing disorder in life.

Concluding paragraphs
(16–17)

Restatement of thesis and author's pessimistic feelings about entropy.

3. Why is the creation of life an exception to entropy? What is the relationship between entropy and energy?
4. Why does Cole say that entropy "is no laughing matter"? What is so depressing about the entropy she describes?
5. Refer to your dictionary as needed to define the following words used in the selection: *futility* (paragraph 1), *dissipated* (6), *buffeted* (7), *tepid* (7), and *atrophied* (12).

Questions About the Writer's Craft

1. **The pattern.** What is Cole's underlying purpose in defining the scientific term *entropy*? What gives the essay its persuasive edge?
2. What tone does Cole adopt to make reading about a scientific concept more interesting? Identify places in the essay where her tone is especially prominent.
3. Cole uses such words as *futility, loss,* and *depressing*. How do these words affect you? Why do you suppose she chose such terms? Find similar words in the essay.

4. Other patterns.   Many of Cole's sentences follow a two-part pattern involving a *contrast:* "The road to disorder is all downhill but the road to creation takes work" (paragraph 10). Find other examples of this pattern in the essay. Why do you think Cole uses it so often?

Writing Assignments Using Definition as a Pattern of Development

1. Write an essay in which you define *order* or *disorder* by applying the term to a system that you know well—for example, your school, dorm, family, or workplace. Develop your definition through any combination of writing patterns: by supplying examples, by showing contrasts, by analyzing the process underlying the system.
2. Choose, as Cole does, a technical term that you think will be unfamiliar to most readers. In a humorous or serious paper, define the term as it is used technically; then show how the term can shed light on some aspect of your life. For example, the concept in astronomy of a *supernova* could be used to explain your sudden emergence as a new star on the athletic field, in your schoolwork, or on the social scene. Here are a few suggested terms:

symbiosis	volatility	resonance
velocity	erosion	catalyst
neutralization	equilibrium	malleability

Writing Assignments Combining Patterns of Development

3. Can one person make much difference in the amount of entropy—disorder and chaos—in the world? *Argue* your position in an essay. Use *examples* of people who have tried to overcome the tendency of things to "fall apart." Make clear whether you think these people succeeded or failed in their attempts. To inform your perspective, consider reading Gerry Garibaldi's "How the Schools Shortchange Boys" (page 403) and Michael Kimmel's "A War Against Boys?" (page 410).
4. Cole claims that we humans are "buffeted about like so many molecules." Write an essay *arguing* that people either do or do not control their own fates. Support your point with a series of specific *examples*. For different perspectives on the issue, you might want to read Maya Angelou's "Sister Flowers" (page 87), Roberto Rodriguez's "The Border on Our Backs" (page 418), and Martin Luther King, Jr.'s "Where Do We Go from Here: Community or Chaos?" (page 444).

Writing Assignment Using a Journal Entry as a Starting Point

5. Write an essay arguing that disorder can be liberating *or* that it can be stifling. Review your pre-reading journal entry, and select strong, compelling examples that support your position. Aim to refute as many opposing arguments as possible. Your essay may have a serious or a humorous tone.

Natalie Angier

Natalie Angier was born in 1958 and was raised in the Bronx, New York, and in Michigan. She attended Barnard College, where she studied literature, astronomy, and physics. After working for *Discover* magazine, she became a reporter for the science section of *The New York Times* in 1990. The following year she won a Pulitzer Prize for her science reporting. In addition to reporting, Angier has written several books, including *The Beauty of the Beastly* (1995), *Natural Obsessions: Striving to Unlock the Deepest Secret of the Cancer Cell* (1999), *Woman: An Intimate Geography* (1999), and *The Canon: A Whirligig Tour of the Beautiful Basics of Science* (2008). Angier has always been interested in bridging the gap between science and the humanities. This article, about the scientific basis of cuteness, was published in *The New York Times* on January 3, 2006.

Pre-Reading Journal Entry

Some concepts—like beauty, elegance, and cuteness—are hard to explain, although people usually believe they understand what those concepts are. Take a moment to reflect in your journal on what *you* mean when you say something is "cute." What qualities come to mind? Consider the kinds of things that you would deem cute, and list as many as you can think of in your journal.

The Cute Factor

If the mere sight of Tai Shan, the roly-poly, goofily gamboling masked bandit of a panda cub now on view at the National Zoo isn't enough to make you melt, then maybe the crush of his human onlookers, the furious flashing of their cameras and the heated gasps of their mass rapture will do the trick.   1

Awww....Scientists who study the evolution of visual signaling have identified a wide and still-expanding assortment of features and behaviors that make something look cute.   2

Cute cues are those that indicate extreme youth, vulnerability, harmlessness and need, scientists say.   3

"Omigosh, look at him! He is too cute!"   4

"How adorable! I wish I could just reach in there and give him a big squeeze!"   5

"He's so fuzzy! I've never seen anything so cute in my life!"   6

A guard's sonorous voice rises above the burble. "OK, folks, five oohs and aahs per person, then it's time to let someone else step up front."   7

The 6-month-old, 25-pound Tai Shan—whose name is pronounced tie-SHON and means, for no obvious reason, "peaceful mountain"—is the first surviving giant panda cub ever born at the Smithsonian's zoo. And though the zoo's adult pandas have long been among Washington's top tourist attractions, the public debut of the baby in December has unleashed   8 an almost bestial frenzy here. Some 13,000 timed tickets to see the cub were snapped up within two hours of being released, and almost immediately began trading on eBay for up to $200 a pair.

Panda mania is not the only reason that 2005 proved an exceptionally cute year. Last summer, a movie about another black-and-white charmer, the emperor penguin, became one of the highest-grossing documentaries of all time.[1] Sales of petite, willfully cute cars like the Toyota Prius and the Mini Cooper soared, while those of noncute sport utility vehicles tanked.   9

Women's fashions opted for the cute over the sensible or glamorous, with low-slung slacks and skirts and abbreviated blouses contriving to present a customer's midriff as an adorable preschool bulge. Even the too big could be too cute. King Kong's newly reissued face has a squashed baby-doll appeal, and his passion for Naomi Watts ultimately feels like a serious case of puppy love—hopeless, heartbreaking, cute.[2]   10

Scientists who study the evolution of visual signaling have identified a wide and still expanding assortment of features and behaviors that make something look cute: bright forward-facing eyes set low on a big round face, a pair of big round ears, floppy limbs and a side-to-side, teeter-totter gait, among many others.   11

Cute cues are those that indicate extreme youth, vulnerability, harmlessness and need, scientists say, and attending to them closely makes good Darwinian sense. As a species whose youngest members are so pathetically helpless they can't lift their heads to suckle without adult supervision, human beings must be wired to respond quickly and gamely to any and all signs of infantile desire.   12

The human cuteness detector is set at such a low bar, researchers said, that it sweeps in and deems cute practically anything remotely resembling a human baby or a part thereof, and so ends up including the young of virtually every mammalian species, fuzzy-headed birds like Japanese cranes, woolly bear caterpillars, a bobbing balloon, a big round rock stacked on a smaller rock, a colon, a hyphen and a close parenthesis typed in succession.   13

The greater the number of cute cues that an animal or object happens to possess, or the more exaggerated the signals may be, the louder and more italicized are the squeals provoked.   14

Cuteness is distinct from beauty, researchers say, emphasizing rounded over sculptured, soft over refined, clumsy over quick. Beauty attracts admiration and demands a pedestal; cuteness attracts affection and demands a lap. Beauty is rare and brutal, despoiled by a single pimple. Cuteness is commonplace and generous, content on occasion to cosegregate with homeliness.   15

[1] A reference to *March of the Penguins* (2005), directed by Luc Jacquet (editors' note).
[2] A reference to the 2005 version of *King Kong*, directed by Peter Jackson and starring Naomi Watts as Ann Darrow, the oversized ape's female human ally (editors' note).

Observing that many Floridians have an enormous affection for the 16
manatee, which looks like an overfertilized potato with a sock puppet's face,
Roger L. Reep of the University of Florida said it shone by grace of contrast.
"People live hectic lives, and they may be feeling overwhelmed, but then
they watch this soft and slow-moving animal, this gentle giant, and they see
it turn on its back to get its belly scratched," said Dr. Reep, author with
Robert K. Bonde of *The Florida Manatee: Biology and Conservation.*

"That's very endearing," said Dr. Reep. "So even though a manatee is 17
3 times your size and 20 times your weight, you want to get into the water
beside it."

Even as they say a cute tooth has rational roots, scientists admit they are 18
just beginning to map its subtleties and source. New studies suggest that
cute images stimulate the same pleasure centers of the brain aroused by sex,
a good meal or psychoactive drugs like cocaine, which could explain why
everybody in the panda house wore a big grin.

At the same time, said Denis Dutton, a philosopher of art at the University 19
of Canterbury in New Zealand, the rapidity and promiscuity of the cute
response makes the impulse suspect, readily overridden by the angry sense that
one is being exploited or deceived.

"Cute cuts through all layers of meaning and says, Let's not worry about 20
complexities, just love me," said Dr. Dutton, who is writing a book about
Darwinian aesthetics. "That's where the sense of cheapness can come from,
and the feeling of being manipulated or taken for a sucker that leads many
to reject cuteness as low or shallow."

Quick and cheap make cute appealing to those who want to catch the 21
eye and please the crowd. Advertisers and product designers are forever
toying with cute cues to lend their merchandise instant appeal, mixing
and monkeying with the vocabulary of cute to keep the message fresh and
fetching.

That market-driven exercise in cultural evolution can yield bizarre if 22
endearing results, like the blatantly ugly Cabbage Patch dolls, Furbies, the
figgy face of E.T., the froggy one of Yoda. As though the original Volkswagen
Beetle wasn't considered cute enough, the updated edition was made rounder
and shinier still.

"The new Beetle looks like a smiley face," said Miles Orvell, professor of 23
American studies at Temple University in Philadelphia. "By this point its
origins in Hitler's regime, and its intended resemblance to a German helmet,
is totally forgotten."

Whatever needs pitching, cute can help. A recent study at the Veterans 24
Affairs Medical Center at the University of Michigan showed that high school
students were far more likely to believe antismoking messages accompanied
by cute cartoon characters like a penguin in a red jacket or a smirking polar
bear than when the warnings were delivered unadorned.

"It made a huge difference," said Sonia A. Duffy, the lead author of the   25
report, which was published in *The Archives of Pediatrics and Adolescent
Medicine.* "The kids expressed more confidence in the cartoons than in the
warnings themselves."

Primal and widespread though the taste for cute may be, researchers say it   26
varies in strength and significance across cultures and eras. They compare the
cute response to the love of sugar: everybody has sweetness receptors on the
tongue, but some people, and some countries, eat a lot more candy than others.

Experts point out that the cuteness craze is particularly acute in Japan,   27
where it goes by the name "kawaii" and has infiltrated the most masculine of
redoubts. Truck drivers display Hello Kitty–style figurines on their dash-
boards. The police enliven safety billboards and wanted posters with two
perky mouselike mascots, Pipo kun and Pipo chan.

Behind the kawaii phenomenon, according to Brian J. McVeigh, a schol-   28
ar of East Asian studies at the University of Arizona, is the strongly hierarchical nature of Japanese culture. "Cuteness is used to soften up the vertical
society," he said, "to soften power relations and present authority without
being threatening."

In this country, the use of cute imagery is geared less toward blurring the   29
line of command than toward celebrating America's favorite demographic:
the young. Dr. Orvell traces contemporary cute chic to the 1960's, with its
celebration of a perennial childhood, a refusal to dress in adult clothes, an
inversion of adult values, a love of bright colors and bloopy, cartoony patterns, the Lava Lamp.

Today, it's not enough for a company to use cute graphics in its adver-   30
tisements. It must have a really cute name as well. "Companies like Google
and Yahoo leave no question in your mind about the youthfulness of their
founders," said Dr. Orvell.

Madison Avenue may adapt its strategies for maximal tweaking of our   31
inherent baby radar, but babies themselves, evolutionary scientists say, did not
really evolve to be cute. Instead, most of their salient qualities stem from the
demands of human anatomy and the human brain, and became appealing to
a potential caretaker's eye only because infants wouldn't survive otherwise.

Human babies have unusually large heads because humans have unusually   32
large brains. Their heads are round because their brains continue to grow
throughout the first months of life, and the plates of the skull stay flexible and
unfused to accommodate the development. Baby eyes and ears are situated
comparatively far down the face and skull, and only later migrate upward in
proportion to the development of bones in the cheek and jaw areas.

Baby eyes are also notably forward-facing, the binocular vision a likely   33
legacy of our tree-dwelling ancestry, and all our favorite Disney characters
also sport forward-facing eyes, including the ducks and mice, species that in
reality have eyes on the sides of their heads.

The cartilage tissue in an infant's nose is comparatively soft and undeveloped, which is why most babies have button noses. Baby skin sits relatively loose on the body, rather than being taut, the better to stretch for growth spurts to come, said Paul H. Morris, an evolutionary scientist at the University of Portsmouth in England; that lax packaging accentuates the overall roundness of form.   34

Baby movements are notably clumsy, an amusing combination of jerky and delayed, because learning to coordinate the body's many bilateral sets of large and fine muscle groups requires years of practice. On starting to walk, toddlers struggle continuously to balance themselves between left foot and right, and so the toddler gait consists as much of lateral movement as of any forward momentum.   35

Researchers who study animals beloved by the public appreciate the human impulse to nurture anything even remotely babylike, though they are at times taken aback by people's efforts to identify with their preferred species....   36

The giant panda offers ... [a] case study in accidental cuteness. Although it is a member of the bear family, a highly carnivorous clan, the giant panda specializes in eating bamboo.   37

As it happens, many of the adaptations that allow it to get by on such a tough diet contribute to the panda's cute form, even in adulthood. Inside the bear's large, rounded head, said Lisa Stevens, assistant panda curator at the National Zoo, are the highly developed jaw muscles and the set of broad, grinding molars it needs to crush its way through some 40 pounds of fibrous bamboo plant a day.   38

When it sits up against a tree and starts picking apart a bamboo stalk with its distinguishing pseudo-thumb, a panda looks like nothing so much like Huckleberry Finn shucking corn. Yet the humanesque posture and paws again are adaptations to its menu. The bear must have its "hands" free and able to shred the bamboo leaves from their stalks.   39

The panda's distinctive markings further add to its appeal: the black patches around the eyes make them seem winsomely low on its face, while the black ears pop out cutely against the white fur of its temples.   40

As with the penguin's tuxedo, the panda's two-toned coat very likely serves a twofold purpose. On the one hand, it helps a feeding bear blend peacefully into the dappled backdrop of bamboo. On the other, the sharp contrast between light and dark may serve as a social signal, helping the solitary bears locate each other when the time has come to find the perfect, too-cute mate.   41

Questions for Close Reading

1. What is the selection's thesis? Locate the sentence(s) in which Angier states her main idea. If she doesn't state her thesis explicitly, express it in your own words.

2. Angier uses the scientific term *visual signaling* (paragraphs 2, 11). What is visual signaling? Give some examples from the article of the visual signaling of "cute."

3. In paragraph 13, Angier quotes researchers as saying that the "human cuteness detector is set at...a low bar." What does Angier assert is the underlying reason that people respond so strongly to cuteness?

4. In paragraph 26, Angier indicates that cute varies from culture to culture. How does the significance of cute in Japan differ from its significance in the United States? Give some examples of the differences between the two cultures.

5. Refer to your dictionary as needed to define the following words used in the selection: *gamboling* (paragraph 1), *rapture* (1), *sonorous* (7), *despoiled* (15), *cosegregate* (15), *homeliness* (15), *aesthetics* (20), *blatantly* (22), *unadorned* (24), *primal* (26), *redoubts* (27), *hierarchical* (28), *inherent* (31), *salient* (31), and *winsomely* (40).

Questions About the Writer's Craft

1. The opening of a newspaper article is called a *lead,* and its purpose is to hook the reader and set up a framework for the story. Analyze the lead of Angier's article (paragraphs 1–3). How does she try to engage your interest (the hook)? How does this lead frame the contents of the remainder of the article? How are the lead and the thesis statement related in this article?

2. The pattern. What is the tone of Angier's article? Why did she adopt this tone? Do you think her tone is appropriate given her objective of defining the term *cuteness*? Explain your answer.

3. Other patterns. In paragraph 15, Angier contrasts cuteness with beauty. What are some transitional words and phrases that help sharpen this contrast?

4. Other patterns. Paragraphs 32 through 35 contain a lengthy description of a baby's appearance. What is the purpose of this description? Is the description mostly objective or subjective? Support your answer with examples.

Writing Assignments Using Definition as a Pattern of Development

1. In paragraph 15, Angier briefly characterizes beauty as sculptured, refined, and quick. She also contrasts beauty with cuteness. Do you agree with Angier's characterization of beauty? What are some words you would use to characterize beauty? Using Angier's characterization of beauty as a starting point, write an extended definition of beauty. Your essay can be serious, lighthearted, humorous, or satiric. For a humorous treatment of beauty, read Dave Barry's "Beauty and the Beast" (page 284).

2. Angier indicates that the American view of cuteness is closely related to our celebration of youth (paragraph 29). Write an extended definition of youth in American culture. Consider actual youthfulness (children), the effort of mature adults to appear younger than they are, the efforts of young people to appear older than they are, youthful fashions, and other cultural manifestations of youth in America. For a view of changing youth culture, you might read Kay S. Hymowitz's "Tweens: Ten Going On Sixteen" (page 163).

Writing Assignments Combining
Patterns of Development

3. Angier gives examples of cuteness in movies (*March of the Penguins,* the 2005 version of *King Kong,* the characters E.T. and Yoda), product design (the VW Beetle), and advertising (an antismoking campaign aimed at teens). Select one of these examples of cuteness—or another of your own choosing—and do some research on it. For example, if you choose a character in a movie or TV show, watch the movie or show; if you choose a product, do research on it and use it if possible; and if you choose an ad campaign, collect examples of the ads. Then write an essay in which you *describe* the item, explain how it is an *example* of cuteness, and recount the *effect* it has on you.

4. Angier's article suggests that all humans respond to cuteness, although there are cultural differences in these responses. Are there other differences as well? For example, do men and women respond differently to cuteness? Teenagers and senior citizens? Parents and nonparents? Reflect on your own experiences with cuteness, and inquire into the experiences of your friends, family members, and others. Then write an essay *comparing* and *contrasting* your responses with those of someone who differs from you in gender, age, or parental status. Explain the possible *causes* and *effects* of your different responses to cuteness. For one man's take on some differences between men and women, read Dave Barry's "Beauty and the Beast" (page 284).

Writing Assignment Using a Journal
Entry as a Starting Point

5. Review the cute things you listed in your pre-reading journal. Do these things fall into categories, such as toys, cartoons, or animals? Which of them, if any, are cute according to the extended definition in Angier's article? Write an essay in which you *classify* your cute things and explain how they *exemplify* (or do not exemplify) Angier's definition of cute. If your items present different characteristics from those outlined by Angier, offer your own definition of cuteness.

Ann Hulbert

Writer Ann Hulbert was born in 1956 and attended Harvard College and Cambridge University. Her work has appeared in many publications, including *Slate, The New York Times Book Review, The New York Review of Books,* and *The New Republic.* Hulbert is the author of *The Interior Castle: The Art and Life of Jean Stafford* and *Raising America: Experts, Parents, and a Century of Advice About Children.* This article was published on March 11, 2007, in *The New York Times Magazine.*

Pre-Reading Journal Entry

One of the benefits of family life is getting to know people of other generations. What generations are represented by the people in your extended family? What generation do you belong to? What generation do your parents and your children, if any, belong to? How do the generations in your family differ? Use your journal to answer these questions.

Beyond the Pleasure Principle

It is a point of pride among baby boomers that after our kids leave home, we enjoy a continuing closeness with them that our parents rarely had with us. We certainly do keep in touch: 80 percent of 18- to 25-year-olds had talked to their parents in the past day, according to "A Portrait of Generation Next," a recent study conducted by the Pew Research Center in tandem with MacNeil/Lehrer Productions. Yet if the survey is any guide, Gen Nexters aren't getting the credit they deserve for being—as many of them told pollsters they felt they were—"unique and distinct." It is not easy carving out your niche in the shadow of parents who still can't get over what an exceptional generation they belong to. 1

So what is special about Gen Nexters? Don't count on them to capture their own quintessence. "The words and phrases they used varied widely," the Pew researchers noted, "ranging from 'lazy' to 'crazy' to 'fun.'" But if you look closely, what makes Gen Nexters *sui generis*—and perhaps more mysterious than their elders appreciate—are their views on two divisive social topics, abortion and gay marriage. On the by-now-familiar red-and-blue map of the culture wars, positions on those issues are presumed to go hand in hand: those on the right oppose both as evidence of a promiscuous society and those on the left embrace them as rights that guarantee privacy and dignity. Yet as a group, Gen Nexters seem to challenge the package deals. 2

Young Americans, it turns out, are unexpectedly conservative on abortion but notably liberal on gay marriage. Given that 18- to 25-year-olds are the least Republican generation (35 percent) and less religious than their elders (with 20 percent of them professing no religion or atheism or agnosticism), it is curious that on abortion they are slightly to the right of the general public. Roughly 3 a third of Gen Nexters endorse making abortion generally available, half support limits and 15 percent favor an outright ban. By contrast, 35 percent of 50- to 64-year-olds support readily available abortions. On gay marriage, there was not much of a generation gap in the 1980s, but now Gen Nexters stand out as more favorably disposed than the rest of the country. Almost half of them approve, compared with under a third of those over 25.

It could simply be, of course, that some young people are pro-gay   4 marriage and others are pro-life and that we can expect more of the same old polarized culture warfare ahead of us. But what if Gen Nexters, rather than being so, well, lazy, are forging their own new crossover path? When I contacted John Green, an expert on religious voters who is currently working at the Pew Forum on Religion and Public Life, he said that pollsters hadn't tackled that question. But after crunching some numbers, he suggested that there might indeed be a middle way in the making. Many individual Gen Nexters hold what seem like divergent views on homosexuality and government involvement with morality—either liberal on one while being conservative on the other or else confirmed in their views on one question while ambivalent on the other.

Oh, how these young people can confound us! All this could amount to   5 no more than what the experts call a "life-cycle effect": Gen Nexters may hold heterogeneous views now because they are exploring diverse values that may congeal in more conventional ways as they get older. But a more intriguing possibility is that it is a "cohort effect," a distinctive orientation that will stick with them. Liberals could take heart that perhaps homosexual marriage has replaced abortion as the new "equality issue" for Gen Nexters, suggested John Russonello, a Washington pollster whose firm is especially interested in social values; Gen Nexters may have grown up after the back-alley abortion era, but they haven't become complacent about sexual rights. Conservatives might take comfort from a different hypothesis that Green tried out: maybe Gen Nexters have been listening to their parents' lectures about responsibility. Don't do things that make you have an abortion, young people may have concluded, and do welcome everyone into the social bulwark of family responsibility.

Put the two perspectives together, and an ethos emerges that looks at   6 once refreshingly pragmatic and yet still idealistic. On one level, Gen Nexters sound impatient with a strident stalemate between entrenched judgments of behavior; after all, experience tells them that in the case of both abortion and gay rights, life is complicated and intransigence has only impeded useful social and political compromises. At the same time, Gen Nexters give every indication of being attentive to the moral issues at stake: they aren't willing to ignore what is troubling about abortion and what is equally troubling about intolerant exclusion. A hardheadedness, but also a high-mindedness and softheartedness, seems to be at work.

And to risk what might be truly wishful thinking, maybe there are signs   7
here that Gen Nexters are primed to do in the years ahead what their elders have
so signally failed to manage: actually think beyond their own welfare to worry
about—of all things—the next generation. For when you stop to consider it, at
the core of Gen Nexters' seemingly discordant views on these hot-button issues
could be an insistence on giving priority to children's interests. Take seriously
the lives you could be creating: the Gen Next wariness of abortion sends
that message. Don't rule out for any kid who is born the advantage of being
reared by two legally wedded parents: that is at least one way to read the
endorsement of gay marriage. However you end up sorting out the data, fun or
crazy wouldn't be how I would describe the Gen Next mix. Judged against the
boomers' own past or present, though, the outlook definitely looks unique.

Questions for Close Reading

1. What is the selection's thesis? Locate the sentence(s) in which Hulbert states her
main idea. If she doesn't state her thesis explicitly, express it in your own words.
2. What statistics about Gen Nexters are the basis for much of the extended definition in this article?
3. What is the difference between a "life-cycle effect" and a "cohort effect"? Which
type of effect does Hulbert claim her essay is about?
4. According to Hulbert, what has the elder generation—the baby boomers—failed
to do?
5. Refer to your dictionary as needed to define the following words used in the selection: *tandem* (paragraph 1), *quintessence* (2), *sui generis* (2), *promiscuous* (2),
agnosticism (3), *heterogeneous* (5), *congeal* (5), *bulwark* (5), *ethos* (6),
intransigence (6), *impeded* (6), and *discordant* (7).

Questions About the Writer's Craft

1. What is Hulbert's underlying purpose in defining the characteristics of Gen Nexters?
Is her purpose mainly informative, speculative, or persuasive? How can you tell?
2. **The pattern.**   Hulbert uses the "definition by negation" strategy throughout this
essay. Identify examples of this strategy in the article and evaluate how well it works.
3. **Other patterns.**   Hulbert also uses the compare-contrast strategy at many points
in her article. What signal devices does she use to signal when she is comparing
and contrasting?
4. What is the effect of the delayed thesis on the reader's experience of this article?
Is the delayed thesis effective? Do you think Hulbert should have stated her thesis at the beginning of the essay?

Writing Assignments Using Definition
as a Pattern of Development

1. In her essay, Hulbert presents an extended definition of Gen Nexters, Americans born
in the 1980s. Write an essay in which you define the key characteristics of another
generation. You might, for example, write an essay defining the characteristics of baby

boomers (born from 1946 through the early 1960s), Generation Xers (born from 1965 to 1980), or the as-yet-unnamed youngest generation of those under 18 (born in the 1990s or later). If you choose to define the youngest generation, be sure to give it an "official" name. Before you write, decide whether your tone will be serious or humorous. For an essay written by a member of one generation about an encounter with a member of another generation, see Joan Murray's "Someone's Mother" (page 141).

2. In her article, Hulbert mentions the current polarization of Americans—liberals versus conservatives and blue states versus red states. The meanings of these four terms can vary widely, however, often depending on the viewpoint of the writer. Write an essay in which you define what you think it means to be a liberal or a conservative, or to live in a red state or a blue state. What are the key characteristics of the term you chose? What are the values and attitudes associated with the term? Discussing these issues with friends and family might help you clarify your ideas before you write.

Writing Assignments Combining Patterns of Development

3. Go to the Pew Research Center website (http://pewresearch.org) and read *A Portrait of "Generation Next": How Young People View Their Lives, Futures, and Politics,* the 2007 report that was the occasion for the writing of Hulbert's article. Hulbert focused on Generation Next's attitudes toward abortion and gay marriage, but there are many other topics covered by this report, such as political affiliation, violence, sex, the future, technology and the Internet, body decorations, and so on. Select topic(s) that interest you and write an essay in which you characterize Gen Nexters' attitudes toward those topics. Explain what might *cause* Gen Nexters to feel as they do, and *compare and contrast* their attitudes with those of their parents.

4. In paragraph 5, Hulbert mentions the "life-cycle effect," which refers to the way people's values and behaviors change as they pass from one stage of life to the next—from adolescence to adulthood, for example. Some of these life-cycle effects are marked by ritual. For example, there are many coming-of-age rites of passage, such as graduation, bar or bat mitzvah, confirmation, the debutante's ball, the *quinceañera,* and getting a driver's license. Choose one of your own life's rites of passage and write an essay about it. Narrate what happened, describe the *process* you went through, and give *examples* of how your life changed as a result. For insight into how relationships change at different life stages, read Marion Winik's "What Are Friends For?" (page 216).

Writing Assignment Using a Journal Entry as a Starting Point

5. Review your pre-reading journal entry in which you describe the various generations represented by your relatives. Select two members of your family who come from different generations, and write an essay in which you describe them. What are their similarities and differences? What aspects of their attitudes and behaviors are generational, and what aspects are unique to them as individuals? Why is each of these people important to you? What roles do they play in your life?

Additional Writing Topics

DEFINITION

General Assignments

Use definition to develop any of the following topics. Once you fix on a limited subject, decide if the essay has an informative or a persuasive purpose. The paper might begin with the etymology of the term, a stipulative definition, or a definition by negation. You may want to use a number of writing patterns—such as description, comparison, narration, process analysis—to develop the definition. Remember, too, that the paper doesn't have to be scholarly and serious. There is no reason it can't be a lighthearted discussion of the meaning of a term.

1. Fads
2. A family fight
3. Helplessness
4. An epiphany
5. A workaholic
6. A Pollyanna
7. A con artist
8. A stingy person
9. A team player
10. A Yiddish term like *mensch, klutz,* or *chutzpah,* or a term from some other ethnic group
11. Adolescence
12. Fast food
13. A perfect day
14. Hypocrisy
15. Inner peace
16. Obsession
17. Generosity
18. Exploitation
19. Depression
20. A double bind

Assignments with a Specific Purpose, Audience, and Point of View

On Campus

1. You've been asked to write part of a pamphlet for students who come to the college health clinic. For this pamphlet, define *one* of the following conditions and its symptoms: *depression, stress, burnout, test anxiety, addiction* (to alcohol, drugs, TV, or computer games), *workaholism*. Part of the pamphlet should describe ways to cope with the condition described.

2. One of your responsibilities as a peer counselor in the student counseling center involves helping students communicate more effectively. To assist students, write a definition of some term that you think represents an essential component of a strong interpersonal relationship. You might, for example, define *respect, sharing, equality,* or *trust.* Part of the definition should employ definition by negation, a discussion of what the term is *not.*

At Home or in the Community

3. *Newsweek* magazine runs a popular column called "My Turn," consisting of readers' opinions on subjects of general interest. Write a piece for this column defining *today's college students.* Use the piece to dispel some negative stereotypes (for example, that college students are apathetic, ill-informed, self-centered, and materialistic).

4. In your apartment building, several residents have complained about their neighbors' inconsiderate and rude behavior. You're president of the Residents' Association, and it's your responsibility to address this problem at your next meeting. Prepare a talk in which you define *courtesy,* the quality you consider most essential to neighborly relations. Use specific examples of what courtesy is and isn't to illustrate your definition.

On the Job

5. You're an attorney arguing a case of sexual harassment—a charge your client has leveled against an employer. To win the case, you must present to the jury a clear definition of exactly what *sexual harassment* is and isn't. Write such a definition for your opening remarks in court.

6. A new position has opened in your company. Write a job description to be sent to employment agencies that will screen candidates. Your description should define the job's purpose, state the duties involved, and outline essential qualifications.

ARGUMENTATION-PERSUASION

WHAT IS ARGUMENTATION-PERSUASION?

"You can't possibly believe what you're saying."
"Look, I know what I'm talking about, and that's that."

Does this heated exchange sound familiar? Probably. When we hear the word *argument,* most of us think of a verbal battle propelled by stubbornness and irrational thought, with one person pitted against the other.

Argumentation in writing, though, is a different matter. Using clear thinking and logic, the writer tries to convince readers of the soundness of a particular opinion on a controversial issue. If, while trying to convince, the writer uses emotional language and dramatic appeals to readers' concerns, beliefs, and values, then the piece is called *persuasion.* Besides encouraging acceptance of an opinion, persuasion often urges readers (or another group) to commit themselves to a course of action. Assume you're writing an essay protesting the federal government's policy of offering aid to those suffering from hunger in other countries while many Americans go hungry. If your purpose is to document, coolly and objectively, the presence of hunger in the United States, you would prepare an argumentation essay. Such an essay would be filled with statistics, report findings, and expert opinion to demonstrate how widespread hunger is nationwide. If, however, your purpose is to shake up readers, even motivate them to write letters to their congressional representatives and push for a change in policy, you would write a persuasive

356

essay. In this case, your essay might contain emotional accounts of undernour-
ished children, ill-fed pregnant women, and nearly starving elderly people.

Because people respond rationally *and* emotionally to situations, argumentation and persuasion are usually *combined*. Suppose you decide to write
an article for the campus newspaper advocating a pre–Labor Day start for the
school year. Your audience includes the college administration, students, and
faculty. The article might begin by *arguing* that several schools starting the
academic year earlier were able to close for the month of January and thus
reduce heating and other maintenance expenses. Such an argument, supported by documented facts and figures, would help convince the administration. Realizing that you also have to gain student and faculty support for
your idea, you might argue further that the proposed change would mean
that students and faculty could leave for winter break with the semester
behind them—papers written, exams taken, grades calculated and recorded.
To make this part of your argument especially compelling, you could adopt
a *persuasive* strategy by using emotional appeals and positively charged
language: "Think how pleasant it would be to sleep late, spend time with
family and friends, toast the New Year—without having to worry about work
awaiting you back on campus."

When argumentation and persuasion blend in this way, emotion *supports*
rather than *replaces* logic and sound reasoning. Although some writers resort
to emotional appeals to the exclusion of rational thought, when you prepare
argumentation-persuasion essays, you should advance your position through
a balanced appeal to reason and emotion.

HOW ARGUMENTATION-PERSUASION
FITS YOUR PURPOSE AND AUDIENCE

You probably realize that argumentation, persuasion, or a combination of the
two is everywhere: an editorial urging the overhaul of an ill-managed literacy
program; a commercial for a new shampoo; a scientific report advocating
increased funding for AIDS research. Your own writing involves argumentation-
persuasion as well. When you prepare a *causal analysis, descriptive piece,
narrative,* or *definition essay,* you advance a specific point of view: MTV has
a negative influence on teens' view of sex; Cape Cod in winter is imbued with
a special kind of magic; a disillusioning experience can teach people much
about themselves; *character* can be defined as the willingness to take unpopular positions on difficult issues. Indeed, an essay organized around any of the
patterns of development described in this book may have a persuasive intent.
You might, for example, encourage readers to try out a *process* you've
explained, or to see one of the two movies you've *compared.*

Argumentation-persuasion, however, involves more than presenting a
point of view and providing evidence. Unlike other forms of writing, it

assumes controversy and addresses opposing viewpoints. Consider the following assignments, all of which require the writer to take a position on a controversial issue:

> In parts of the country, communities established for older citizens or childless couples have refused to rent to families with children. How do you feel about this situation? What do you think are the rights of the parties involved?

> Citing the fact that the highest percentage of automobile accidents involve young men, insurance companies consistently charge their highest rates to young males. Is this policy fair? Why or why not?

> Some colleges and universities have instituted a "no pass, no play" policy for athletes. Explain why this practice is or is not appropriate.

It's impossible to predict with absolute certainty what will make readers accept the view you advance or take the action you propose. But the ancient Greeks, who formulated our basic concepts of logic, isolated three factors crucial to the effectiveness of argumentation-persuasion: *logos, pathos,* and *ethos.*

Your main concern in an argumentation-persuasion essay should be with the *logos,* or soundness, of your argument: the facts, statistics, examples, and authoritative statements you gather to support your viewpoint. This supporting evidence must be unified, specific, adequate, accurate, and representative (see pages 34–38). Imagine, for instance, you want to convince people that a popular charity misappropriates the money it receives from the public. Your readers, inclined to believe in the good works of the charity, will probably dismiss your argument unless you can substantiate your claim with valid, well-documented evidence that enhances the *logos* of your position.

Sensitivity to *pathos,* or the emotional power of language, is another key consideration for writers of argumentation-persuasion essays. *Pathos* appeals to readers' needs, values, and attitudes, encouraging them to commit themselves to a viewpoint or course of action. The *pathos* of a piece derives partly from the writer's language. *Connotative* language—words with strong emotional overtones—can move readers to accept a point of view and may even spur them to act.

Advertising and propaganda generally rely on *pathos* to the exclusion of logic, using emotion to influence and manipulate. Consider the following pitches for a man's cologne and a woman's perfume. The language—and the attitudes to which it appeals—is different in each case:

> Brawn: Experience the power. Bold. Yet subtle. Clean. Masculine. The scent for the man who's in charge.

Black Lace is for you—the woman who dresses for success but who dares to be provocative, slightly naughty. Black Lace. Perfect with pearls by day and with diamonds by night.

The appeal to men plays on the impact that terms like *Brawn, bold, power,* and *in charge* may have for some males. Similarly, the charged words *Black Lace, provocative, naughty,* and *diamonds* are intended to appeal to business women who—in the advertiser's mind, at least—may be looking for ways to reconcile sensuality and professionalism. (For more on slanted language, read Ann McClintock's "Propaganda Techniques in Today's Advertising," page 204.)

Like an advertising copywriter, you must select language that reinforces your message. In a paper supporting an expanded immigration policy, you might use evocative phrases like "land of liberty," "a nation of immigrants," and "America's open-door policy." However, if you were arguing for strict immigration quotas, you might use language like "save jobs for unemployed Americans," "flood of unskilled labor," and "illegal aliens." Remember, though: Such language should support, not supplant, clear thinking.

Finally, whenever you write an argumentation-persuasion essay, you should establish your *ethos,* or credibility and integrity. You cannot expect readers to accept or act on your viewpoint unless you convince them that you know what you're talking about and that you're worth listening to. Be sure, then, to tell readers about any experiences you've had that make you knowledgeable about the issue being discussed. You will also come across as knowledgeable and trustworthy if you present a logical, reasoned argument that takes opposing views into account. And make sure that your appeals to emotion aren't excessive. Overwrought emotionalism undercuts credibility. Remember, too, that *ethos* isn't constant. A writer may have credibility on one subject but not on another: An army general might be a reliable source for information on military preparedness but not for information on federal funding of day care.

Writing an effective argumentation-persuasion essay involves an interplay of *logos, pathos,* and *ethos.* The exact balance among these factors is determined by your audience and purpose (that is, whether you want the audience simply to agree with your view or whether you also want them to take action). More than any other kind of writing, argumentation-persuasion requires that you *analyze your readers* and tailor your approach to them. You need to determine how much they know about the issue, how they feel about you and your position, what their values and attitudes are, what motivates them.

In general, most readers will fall into one of three broad categories: supportive, wavering, or hostile. Each type of audience requires a different blend of *logos, pathos,* and *ethos* in an argumentation-persuasion essay.

1. A supportive audience.   If your audience agrees with your position and trusts your credibility, you don't need a highly reasoned argument dense with facts, examples, and statistics. Although you may want to solidify support by providing additional information (*logos*), you can rely primarily on *pathos*—a strong emotional appeal—to reinforce readers' commitment to your shared viewpoint. Assume that you belong to a local fishing club and have volunteered to write an article encouraging members to support threatened fishing rights in state parks. You might begin by stating that fishing strengthens the fish population by thinning out overcrowded streams. Since your audience would certainly be familiar with this idea, you wouldn't need to devote much discussion to it. Instead, you would attempt to move them emotionally. You might evoke the camaraderie in the sport, the pleasure of a perfect cast, the beauty of the outdoors, and perhaps conclude with "If you want these enjoyments to continue, please make a generous contribution to our fund."

2. A wavering audience.   At times, readers may be open to what you have to say but may not be committed fully to your viewpoint. Or perhaps they're not as informed about the subject as they should be. In either case, you don't want to risk alienating them with a heavy-handed emotional appeal. Concentrate instead on *ethos* and *logos,* bolstering your image as a reliable source and providing the evidence needed to advance your position. If you want to convince an audience of high school seniors to take a year off to work between high school and college, you might establish your credibility by recounting the year you spent working and by showing the positive effects it had on your life (*ethos*). In addition, you could cite studies indicating that delayed entry into college is related to higher grade point averages. A year's savings, you would explain, allows students to study when they might otherwise need to hold down a job to earn money for tuition (*logos*).

3. A hostile audience.   An apathetic, skeptical, or hostile audience is obviously most difficult to convince. With such an audience, you should avoid emotional appeals because they might seem irrational, sentimental, or even comical. Instead, weigh the essay heavily in favor of logical reasoning and hard-to-dispute facts (*logos*). Assume your college administration is working to ban liquor from the student pub. You plan to submit to the campus newspaper an open letter supporting this generally unpopular effort. To sway other students, you cite the positive experiences of schools that have gone dry. Many colleges, you explain, have found their tavern revenues actually increase because all students—not just those of drinking age—can now support the pub. With the greater revenues, some schools have upgraded the food served in the pubs and have hired disc jockeys or musical groups to provide entertainment. Many schools have also seen a sharp reduction in alcohol-related vandalism. Readers may not be won over to your side, but your sound, logical argument may encourage them to be more tolerant of your viewpoint. Indeed, such increased receptivity may be all you can reasonably expect from a hostile audience. (For more help in analyzing your audience, see pages 18–19.)

At this point, you have a good sense of the way writers use argumentation-persuasion to achieve their purpose and to connect with their readers. Take a moment to look closely at the website screen shot at the beginning of this chapter. The sponsoring organization is Big Brothers, Big Sisters, a mentoring organization for young people. Imagine you're writing an article, linked to this website,  about the benefits of mentoring young people today. Jot down some ideas you might cover when *arguing* that this organization offers young people more than a place to hang out.

SUGGESTIONS FOR USING ARGUMENTATION-PERSUASION IN AN ESSAY

The suggestions here and in Figure 11.1 on page 362 will be helpful for writing an argument-persuasion essay.

1. At the beginning of the paper, identify the controversy surrounding the issue and state your position in the thesis. Your introduction should clarify the controversy about the issue. In addition, it should provide as much background information as your readers are likely to need.

The thesis of an argumentation-persuasion paper is often called the *assertion* or *proposition*. Occasionally, the proposition appears at the paper's end, but it is usually stated at the beginning. If you state the thesis right away, your audience knows where you stand and is better able to evaluate the evidence presented.

Remember: Argumentation-persuasion assumes conflicting viewpoints. Be sure your proposition focuses on a controversial issue and indicates your view. Avoid a proposition that is merely factual; what is demonstrably true allows little room for debate. To see the difference between a factual statement and an effective thesis, examine the two statements that follow:

> *Fact:* In the past decade, the nation's small farmers have suffered financial hardships.

FIGURE 11.1
Development Diagram: Writing an Argumentation-Persuasion Essay

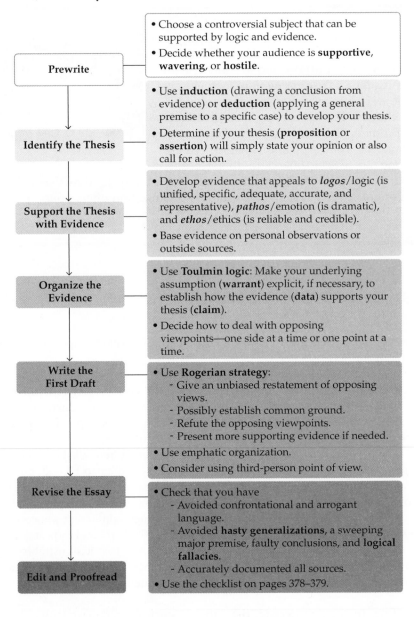

Prewrite
- Choose a controversial subject that can be supported by logic and evidence.
- Decide whether your audience is **supportive**, **wavering**, or **hostile**.

Identify the Thesis
- Use **induction** (drawing a conclusion from evidence) or **deduction** (applying a general premise to a specific case) to develop your thesis.
- Determine if your thesis (**proposition** or **assertion**) will simply state your opinion or also call for action.

Support the Thesis with Evidence
- Develop evidence that appeals to *logos*/logic (is unified, specific, adequate, accurate, and representative), *pathos*/emotion (is dramatic), and *ethos*/ethics (is reliable and credible).
- Base evidence on personal observations or outside sources.

Organize the Evidence
- Use **Toulmin logic**: Make your underlying assumption (**warrant**) explicit, if necessary, to establish how the evidence (**data**) supports your thesis (**claim**).
- Decide how to deal with opposing viewpoints—one side at a time or one point at a time.

Write the First Draft
- Use **Rogerian strategy**:
  - Give an unbiased restatement of opposing views.
  - Possibly establish common ground.
  - Refute the opposing viewpoints.
  - Present more supporting evidence if needed.
- Use emphatic organization.
- Consider using third-person point of view.

Revise the Essay
- Check that you have
  - Avoided confrontational and arrogant language.
  - Avoided **hasty generalizations**, a sweeping major premise, faulty conclusions, and **logical fallacies**.
  - Accurately documented all sources.
- Use the checklist on pages 378–379.

Edit and Proofread

Thesis: Inefficient management, rather than competition from agricultural conglomerates, is responsible for the financial plight of the nation's small farmers.

The first statement is certainly true. It would be difficult to find anyone who believes that these are easy times for small farmers. Because the statement invites little opposition, it can't serve as the focus of an argumentation-persuasion essay. The second statement, though, takes a controversial stance on a complex issue. Such a proposition is a valid starting point for a paper intended to argue and persuade. However, don't assume that such advice means that you should take a highly opinionated position in your thesis. A dogmatic, overstated proposition ("Campus security is staffed by overpaid, badge-flashing incompetents") is bound to alienate some readers.

Remember also to keep the proposition narrow and specific, so you can focus your thoughts in a purposeful way. Consider the following statements:

Broad thesis: The welfare system has been abused over the years.

Narrow thesis: Welfare payments should be denied to unmarried teenage girls who have more than one child out of wedlock.

If you tried to write a paper based on the first statement, you would face an unmanageable task—showing all the ways that welfare has been abused. Your readers would also be confused about what to expect in the paper: Will it discuss unscrupulous bureaucrats, fraudulent bookkeeping, dishonest recipients? In contrast, the revised thesis is limited and specific. It signals that the paper will propose severe restrictions on welfare payments. Such a proposal will surely have opponents and is thus appropriate for argumentation-persuasion.

The thesis in an argumentation-persuasion essay can simply state your opinion about an issue, or it can go a step further and call for some action:

Opinion: The lack of affordable day-care centers discriminates against lower-income families.

Call for action: The federal government should support the creation of more day-care centers in low-income neighborhoods.

In either case, your stand on the issue must be clear to your readers.

2. Provide readers with strong support for the thesis.   Finding evidence that relates to the readers' needs, values, and experience is a crucial part of writing an effective argumentation-persuasion essay. Readers will be responsive to evidence that is *unified, adequate, specific, accurate,* and *representative* (see pages 34–38). It might consist of personal experiences or observations. Or it could be gathered from outside sources—statistics; facts; examples; or expert authority taken from books, articles, reports, interviews, and documentaries. A paper arguing that elderly Americans are better off than they used to be might incorporate the following kinds of evidence:

- *Personal observation or experience:* A description of the writer's grandparents who are living comfortably on Social Security and pensions.
- *Statistics from a report:* A statement that the per capita after-tax income of older Americans is $335 greater than the national average.
- *Fact from a newspaper article:* The point that the majority of elderly Americans do not live in nursing homes or on the streets; rather, they have their own houses or apartments.
- *Examples from interviews:* Accounts of several elderly couples living comfortably in well-managed retirement villages in Florida.
- *Expert opinion cited in a documentary:* A statement by Dr. Marie Sanchez, a specialist in geriatrics: "An over-sixty-five American today is likely to be healthier, and have a longer life expectancy, than a fifty-year-old living only a decade ago."

As you seek outside evidence, you may—perhaps to your dismay—come across information that undercuts your argument. Resist the temptation to ignore such material; instead, use the evidence to arrive at a more balanced, perhaps somewhat qualified viewpoint. Conversely, don't blindly accept points made by sources agreeing with you. Retain a healthy skepticism, analyzing the material as rigorously as if it were advanced by the opposing side.

Also, keep in mind that outside sources aren't infallible. They may have biases that cause them to skew evidence. So be sure to evaluate your sources. If you're writing an essay supporting a woman's right to abortion, the National Abortion Rights Action League (NARAL) can supply abundant statistics, case studies, and reports. But realize that NARAL most likely won't give you the complete picture; it will probably present evidence that supports its "pro-choice" position only. To counteract such bias, you should review what those with differing opinions have to say. You should, for example, examine material published by such "pro-life" organizations as the National Right-to-Life Committee—keeping in mind, of course, that this material is also bound to present support for its viewpoint only. Remember, too, that there are more than two sides to a complex issue. To get as broad a perspective as possible, you should also track down sources that have no axe to grind—that is, sources that make a deliberate effort to examine all sides of the issue. For example, published proceedings from a debate on abortion or an in-depth article that aims to synthesize various views on abortion would broaden your understanding of this controversial subject.

Whatever sources you use, be sure to *document* (give credit to) that material. Otherwise, readers may dismiss your evidence as nothing more than your subjective opinion, or they may conclude that you have *plagiarized*—tried to pass off someone else's ideas as your own. (Documentation isn't necessary when material is commonly known or is a matter of historical or scientific record.) In brief informal papers, documentation may consist of simple citations like "Psychologist Aaron Beck believes depression is the result of distorted thoughts" or "*Newsweek* (July 27, 2009) observes that teens have embraced new technologies in their everyday lives." In longer, more formal papers, documentation is more detailed (see Appendix A, "A Guide to Using Sources"). One additional point: Because documentation lends a note of objectivity to writing, it may not be appropriate in a paper that cites sources to use the first-person point of view ("I, like many college students, agree with the government report that..."). To be on the safe side, check with your instructor to see if you should use the third-person point of view ("Many college students agree with the government report that...") instead.

3. Seek to create goodwill.   To avoid alienating readers with views different from your own, stay away from condescending expressions like "Anyone can see that..." or "It's obvious that..." Also, guard against personalizing the debate and being confrontational: "*My opponents* find the law ineffective" sounds adversarial, whereas "*Those opposed* to the law find it ineffective" or "*Opponents* of the law find it ineffective" is more evenhanded. The last two statements also focus—as they should—on the issue, not on the people involved in the debate.

Goodwill can also be established by finding a *common ground*—some points on which all sides can agree, despite their differences. Assume a township council has voted to raise property taxes. The additional revenues will be used to preserve, as parkland, a wooded area that would otherwise be sold to developers. Before introducing its tax-hike proposal, the council would do well to remind homeowners of everyone's shared goals: maintaining the town's beauty and preventing the community's overdevelopment. This reminder of the common values shared by the town council and homeowners will probably make residents more receptive to the tax hike. (For more on establishing common ground, see pages 366–367.)

4. Organize the supporting evidence.   The support for an argumentation-persuasion paper can be organized in a variety of ways. Any of the patterns of development described in this book (description, narration, definition, causal analysis, and so on) may be used—singly or in combination—to develop the essay's proposition. Imagine you're writing a paper arguing that car racing should be banned from television. Your essay might contain a *description* of a horrifying accident that was televised in graphic detail; you might devote part of the paper to a *causal analysis* showing that the broadcast of such races encourages teens to drive carelessly; you could include a *process analysis* to explain how young drivers "soup up" their cars in a dangerous attempt to imitate the racers seen on television. If your essay includes several patterns, you may need a separate paragraph for each.

When presenting evidence, arrange it so you create the strongest possible effect. In general, you should end with your most compelling point, leaving readers with dramatic evidence that underscores your proposition's validity.

5. Use Rogerian strategy to acknowledge differing viewpoints.   If your essay has a clear thesis and strong logical support, you've taken important steps toward winning readers over. However, because argumentation-persuasion focuses on controversial issues, you should also consider contrary points of view. A good argument seeks out and acknowledges conflicting viewpoints. Such a strategy strengthens your argument in several ways. It helps you antici-pate objections, alerts you to flaws in your own position, and makes you more aware of the other sides' weaknesses. Further, by acknowledging dissenting views, you come across as reasonable and thorough—qualities that may disarm readers and leave them more receptive to your argument. You may not con-vince them to surrender their views, but you can enlarge their perspectives and encourage them to think about your position.

Psychologist Carl Rogers took the idea of acknowledging contrary view-points a step further. He believed that argumentation's goal should be to *reduce conflict*, rather than to produce a "winner" and a "loser." But he recognized that people identify so strongly with their opinions that they experience any challenge to those opinions as highly threatening. Such a challenge feels like an attack on their very identity. And what's the characteristic response to such a perceived attack? People become defensive; they dig in their heels and become more adamant than ever about their position. Indeed, when confronted with solid information that calls their opinion into question, they devalue that evi-dence rather than allow themselves to be persuaded. The old maxim about the power of first impressions demonstrates this point. Experiments show that after people form a first impression of another person, they are unlikely to let future conflicting information affect that impression. If, for example, they initially per-ceive someone to be unpleasant and disagreeable, they tend to reject subsequent evidence that casts the person in a more favorable light.

For these reasons, Rogerian strategy rejects any adversarial approach and adopts, instead, a respectful, conciliatory posture that demonstrates a real understanding of opposing views and emphasizes shared interests and values. The ideal is to negotiate differences and arrive at a synthesis: a new position that both parties find at least as acceptable as their original positions. What follows are three basic Rogerian strategies to keep in mind as you write.

First, you may acknowledge the opposing viewpoint in a two-part proposition consisting of a subordinate clause followed by a main clause. The *first part of the proposition* (the subordinate clause) *acknowledges opposing opinions;* the *second part* (the main clause) *states your opinion* and implies that your view stands on more solid ground. (When using this kind of proposition, you may, but don't have to, discuss opposing opinions.) The following thesis illustrates this strategy (the opposing viewpoint is underlined once; the writer's position is underlined twice):

Although some instructors think that standardized finals restrict academic freedom, such exams are preferable to those prepared by individual professors.

Second, *in the introduction,* you may provide—separate from the proposition—a *one- or two-sentence summary of the opposing viewpoint.* Suppose you're writing an essay advocating a ten-day waiting period before an individual can purchase a handgun. Before presenting your proposition at the end of the introductory paragraph, you might include sentences like these: "Opponents of the waiting period argue that the ten-day delay is worthless without a nationwide computer network that can perform background checks. Those opposed also point out that only a percentage of states with a waiting period have seen a reduction in gun-related crime."

Third, you can take *one or two body paragraphs* near the beginning of the essay to *present in greater detail arguments raised by opposing viewpoints.* After that, you *grant* (when appropriate) the validity of some of those points ("It may be true that...," "Granted,..."). Then you go on to *present evidence* for your position ("Even so...," "Nevertheless..."). Imagine you're preparing an editorial for your student newspaper arguing that fraternities and sororities on your campus should be banned. Realizing that many students don't agree with you, you "research" the opposing viewpoint by seeking out supporters of Greek organizations and listening respectfully to the points they raise. When it comes time to write the editorial, you decide not to begin with arguments for your position; instead, you start by summarizing the points made by those supporting fraternities and sororities. You might, for example, mention their argument that Greek organizations build college spirit, contribute to worthy community causes, and provide valuable contacts for entry into the business world. Following this summary of the opposing viewpoint, you might concede that the point about the Greeks' contributions to community causes is especially valid; you could then reinforce this conciliatory stance by stressing some common ground you share—perhaps you acknowledge that you share your detractors' belief that enjoyable social activities with like-minded people are an important part of campus life. Having done all that, you would be in a good position to present arguments why you nevertheless think fraternities and sororities should be banned. Because you prepared readers to listen to your opinion, they would tend to be more receptive to your argument.

6. Refute differing viewpoints. There will be times, though, that acknowledging opposing viewpoints and presenting your own case won't be enough. Particularly when an issue is complex and when readers strongly disagree with your position, you may have to refute all or part of the *dissenting views. Refutation* means pointing out the problems with opposing viewpoints, thereby highlighting your own position's superiority. You may focus on the opposing sides' inaccurate or inadequate evidence, or you may point to their faulty logic. (Some common types of illogical thinking are discussed on pages 370–374 and 376–377.)

Let's consider how you could refute a competing position in an essay you're writing that supports sex education in public schools. Adapting the Rogerian approach to suit your purposes, you might start by acknowledging the opposing viewpoint's key argument: "Sex education should be the prerogative of parents." After granting the validity of this view in an ideal world, you might show that many parents don't provide such education. You could present statistics on the number of parents who avoid discussing sex with their children because the subject makes them uncomfortable; you could cite studies revealing that children in single-parent homes are apt to receive even less parental guidance about sex; and you could give examples of young people whose parents provided sketchy, even misleading information.

There are various ways to develop a paper's refutation section. The best method to use depends on the paper's length and the complexity of the issue. Two possible sequences are outlined here:

First Strategy	Second Strategy
• State your proposition.	• State your proposition.
• Cite opposing viewpoints and the evidence for those views.	• Cite opposing viewpoints and the evidence for those views.
• Refute opposing viewpoints by presenting counterarguments.	• Refute opposing viewpoints by presenting counterarguments.
	• Present additional evidence for your proposition.

In the first strategy, you simply refute all or part of the opposing positions' arguments. The second strategy takes the first one a step further by presenting *additional evidence* to support your proposition. In such a case, the additional evidence *must be different* from the points made in the refutation. The additional evidence may appear at the essay's end (as in the preceding outline), or it may be given near the beginning (after the proposition); it may also be divided between the beginning and end.

No matter which strategy you select, you may refute opposing views *one side at a time* or *one point at a time*. When using the one-side-at-a-time approach, you cite all the points raised by the opposing side and then present your counterargument to each point. When using the one-point-at-a-time strategy, you mention the first point made by the opposing side, refute that point, then move on to the second point and refute that, and so on. (For more on comparing and contrasting the sides of an issue, see pages 260–266.)

Throughout the essay, be sure to provide clear signals so that readers can distinguish your arguments from the other side's: "Despite the claims of those opposed to the plan, many think that..." and "Those not in agreement think that...."

7. Use induction or deduction to think logically about your argument. The line of reasoning used to develop an argument is the surest indicator of how rigorously you have thought through your position. There are two basic ways to think about a subject: *inductively* and *deductively*. Though the following discussion treats induction and deduction as separate processes, the two often overlap and complement each other.

Inductive reasoning involves examination of specific cases, facts, or examples. Based on these specifics, you then draw a conclusion or make a generalization. This is the kind of thinking scientists use when they examine evidence (the results of experiments, for example) and then draw a *conclusion:* "Smoking increases the risk of cancer." All of us use inductive reasoning in everyday life. We might think the following: "My head is aching" (evidence); "My nose is stuffy" (evidence); "I'm coming down with a cold" (conclusion). Based on the conclusion, we might go a step further and take some action: "I'll take a cold remedy."

With inductive reasoning, the conclusion reached can serve as the proposition for an argumentation essay. (Of course, the essay will most likely include elements of persuasion since strict argumentation—with no appeal to emotions—is uncommon.) If the paper advances a course of action, the proposition often mentions the action, signaling an essay with a distinctly persuasive purpose.

Let's suppose that you're writing a paper about a crime wave in the small town where you live. You might use inductive thinking to structure the essay's argument:

Several people were mugged last month while shopping in the center of town. (*evidence*)

Several homes and apartments were burglarized in the past few weeks. (*evidence*)

Several cars were stolen from people's driveways over the weekend. (*evidence*)

The police force hasn't adequately protected town residents. (*conclusion, or proposition, for an argumentation essay with probable elements of persuasion*)

The police force should take steps to upgrade its protection of town residents. (*conclusion, or proposition, for an argumentation essay with a clearly persuasive intent*)

This inductive sequence highlights a possible structure for the essay. After providing a clear statement of your proposition, you might detail recent muggings, burglaries, and car thefts. Then you could move to the opposing viewpoint: a description of the steps the police say they have taken to protect town residents. At that point, you would refute the police's claim, citing additional evidence that shows the measures taken have not been sufficient. Finally, if you wanted your essay to have a decidedly persuasive purpose, you could end by recommending specific action the police department should take to improve its protection of the community.

As in all essays, your evidence should be *specific, unified, adequate,* and *representative* (see pages 34–38). These last two characteristics are critical when you think inductively; they guarantee that your conclusion would be equally valid even if other evidence were presented. Insufficient or atypical evidence often leads to *hasty generalizations* that mar the essay's logic. For example, you might think the following: "Some elderly people are very wealthy and do not need Social Security checks" (evidence), and "Some Social Security recipients illegally collect several checks" (evidence). If you then conclude "Social Security is a waste of taxpayers' money," your conclusion is invalid and hasty because it's based on only a few atypical examples. Millions of Social Security recipients aren't wealthy and don't abuse the system. If you've failed to consider the full range of evidence, any action you propose ("The Social Security system should be disbanded") will probably be considered suspect by thoughtful readers. It's possible, of course, that Social Security should be disbanded, but the evidence leading to such a conclusion must be sufficient and representative.

When reasoning inductively, you should also be careful that the evidence you collect is both *recent* and *accurate*. No valid conclusion can result from dated or erroneous evidence. To ensure that your evidence is sound, you also need to evaluate the reliability of your sources. When a person who is legally drunk claims to have seen a flying saucer, the evidence is shaky, to say the least. But if two respected scientists, both with 20/20 vision, saw the saucer, their evidence is worth considering.

Finally, it's important to realize that there's always an element of uncertainty in inductive reasoning. The conclusion can never be more than an *inference,* involving what logicians call an *inductive leap.* There could be other explanations for the evidence cited and thus other positions to take and actions to advocate. For example, given a small town's crime wave, you might conclude not that the police force has been remiss but that residents are careless about protecting themselves and their property. In turn, you might call for a different kind of action—perhaps that the police conduct public workshops in self-defense and home security. In an inductive argument, your task is to weigh the evidence, consider alternative explanations, then choose the conclusion and course of action that seem most valid.

Unlike inductive reasoning, which starts with a specific case and moves toward a generalization or conclusion, *deductive reasoning* begins with a generalization that is then applied to a specific case. This movement from general to specific involves a three-step form of reasoning called a *syllogism*. The first part of a syllogism is called the *major premise*, a general statement about an entire group. The second part is the *minor premise*, a statement about an individual within that group. The syllogism ends with a *conclusion* about that individual.

Just as you use inductive thinking in everyday life, you use deductive thinking—often without being aware of it—to sort out your experiences. When trying to decide which car to buy, you might think as follows:

> *Major premise:* In an accident, large cars are safer than small cars.
>
> *Minor premise:* The Turbo Titan is a large car.
>
> *Conclusion:*   In an accident, the Turbo Titan will be safer than a small car.

Based on your conclusion, you might decide to take a specific action, buying the Turbo Titan rather than the smaller car you had first considered.

To create a valid syllogism and thus arrive at a sound conclusion, you need to avoid two major pitfalls of deductive reasoning. First, be sure not to start with a *hasty generalization* (see page 370) as your *major premise*. Second, don't accept as truth a *faulty conclusion*. Let's look at each problem.

Sweeping major premise.   Perhaps you're concerned about a trash-to-steam incinerator scheduled to open near your home. Your thinking about the situation might follow these lines:

> *Major premise:* Trash-to-steam incinerators have had serious problems and pose significant threats to the well-being of people living near the plants.
>
> *Minor premise:* The proposed incinerator in my neighborhood will be a trash-to-steam plant.
>
> *Conclusion:*   The proposed trash-to-steam incinerator in my neighborhood will have serious problems and pose significant threats to the well-being of people living near the plant.

Having arrived at this conclusion, you might decide to join organized protests against the opening of the incinerator. But your thinking is somewhat illogical. Your *major premise* is a *sweeping* one because it indiscriminately groups all trash-to-steam plants into a single category. It's unlikely that you're familiar with the operations of all trash-to-steam incinerators in this country and abroad; it's probably not true that *all* such plants have had serious difficulties that endangered the public. For your argument to reach a valid conclusion, the major premise must be based on repeated observations or verifiable facts. You would have a better argument, and thus reach a more valid conclusion, if you restricted or qualified the major premise, applying it to some, not all, of the group.

> *Major premise:* A number of trash-to-steam incinerators have had serious problems and posed significant threats to the well-being of people living near the plants.
>
> *Minor premise:* The proposed incinerator in my neighborhood will be a trash-to-steam plant.
>
> *Conclusion:* It's possible that the proposed trash-to-steam incinerator in my neighborhood will run into serious problems and pose significant threats to the well-being of people living near the plant.

This new conclusion, the result of more careful reasoning, would probably encourage you to learn more about trash-to-steam incinerators in general and about the proposed plant in particular. If further research still left you feeling uncomfortable about the plant, you would probably decide to join the protest. On the other hand, your research might convince you that the plant has incorporated into its design a number of safeguards that have been successful at other plants. This added information could reassure you that your original fears were unfounded. In either case, the revised deductive process would lead to a more informed conclusion and course of action.

Faulty conclusion.   Your syllogism—and thus your reasoning—would also be invalid if your *conclusion reverses the "if…then" relationship implied in the major premise*. Assume you plan to write a letter to the college newspaper urging the resignation of the student government president. Perhaps you pursue a line of reasoning that goes like this:

> *Major premise:* Students who plagiarize papers must appear before the Faculty Committee on Academic Policies and Procedures.

Minor premise:	Yesterday, Jennifer Kramer, president of the student government, appeared before the Faculty Committee on Academic Policies and Procedures.
Conclusion:	Jennifer must have plagiarized a paper.
Action:	Jennifer should resign her position as president of the student government.

Such a chain of reasoning is illogical and unfair. Here's why. *If* students plagiarize their papers and are caught, *then* they must appear before the committee. However, the converse isn't necessarily true—that *if* students appear before the committee, *then* they must have plagiarized. In other words, not *all* students appearing before the committee have been called up on plagiarism charges. For example, Jennifer could have been speaking on behalf of another student; she could have been protesting some action taken by the committee; she could have been seeking the committee's help on an article she plans to write about academic honesty. The conclusion doesn't allow for other possible explanations.

Now that you're aware of potential problems associated with deductive reasoning, let's look at the way you can use a syllogism to structure an argumentation-persuasion essay. Suppose you decide to write a paper advocating support for a projected space mission. You know that controversy surrounds the manned space program, especially since seven astronauts died in a 1986 launch and another crew of seven died in a shuttle reentry accident in 2003. Confident that these tragedies have led to more rigorous controls, you want to argue that the benefits of an upcoming mission outweigh its risks. A deductive pattern could be used to develop your argument. In fact, outlining your thinking as a syllogism might help you formulate a proposition, organize your evidence, deal with opposing viewpoints, and—if appropriate—propose a course of action:

Major premise:	Space programs in the past have led to important developments in technology, especially in medical science.
Minor premise:	The Cosmos Mission is the newest space program.
Proposition (essay might be persuasive):	The Cosmos Mission will most likely lead to important developments in technology, especially in medical science.
Proposition (essay clearly is persuasive):	Congress should continue its funding of the Cosmos Mission.

Having outlined the deductive pattern of your thinking, you might begin by stating your proposition and then discuss some new procedures developed to protect the astronauts and the rocket system's structural integrity. With that background established, you could detail the opposing claim that little of value has been produced by the space program so far. You could then move to your refutation, citing significant medical advances derived from former space missions. Finally, the paper might conclude on a persuasive note, with a plea to Congress to continue funding the latest space mission.

8. Use Toulmin logic to establish a strong connection between your evidence and your thesis.   Whether you use an essentially inductive or deductive approach, your argument depends on strong evidence. In *The Uses of Argument,* Stephen Toulmin describes a useful approach for strengthening the connection between evidence and thesis. Toulmin divides a typical argument into three parts:

- **Claim**—The thesis, proposition, or conclusion.
- **Data**—The evidence (facts, statistics, examples, observations, expert opinion) used to convince readers of the claim's validity.
- **Warrant**—The underlying assumption that justifies moving from evidence to claim.

The train engineer was under the influence of drugs when the train crashed.

(Data)

Transportation employees entrusted with the public's safety should be tested for drug use.

(Claim)

Transportation employees entrusted with the public's safety should not be allowed on the job if they use drugs.

(Warrant)

As Toulmin explains in his book, readers are more apt to consider your argument valid if they know what your warrant is. Sometimes your warrant will be so obvious that you won't need to state it explicitly; an *implicit warrant* will be sufficient. Assume you want to argue that the use of live animals to test product toxicity should be outlawed. To support your claim, you cite the following evidence: first, current animal tests are painful and usually result in the animal's death; second, human cell cultures frequently offer more reliable information on how harmful a product may be to human tissue; and third, computer simulations often can more accurately rate a substance's toxicity. Your warrant, although not explicit, is nonetheless clear: "It is wrong to continue product testing on animals when more humane and valid test methods are available."

Other times, you'll do best to make your warrant *explicit*. Suppose you plan to argue that students should be involved in deciding which faculty members are granted tenure. To develop your claim, you present some evidence. You begin by noting that, currently, only faculty members and administrators review candidates for tenure. Next, you call attention to the controversy surrounding two professors, widely known by students to be poor teachers, who were nonetheless granted tenure. Finally, you cite a decision, made several years ago, to discontinue using student evaluations as part of the tenure process; you emphasize that since that time complaints about teachers' incompetence have risen dramatically. Some readers, though, still might wonder how you got from your evidence to your claim. In this case, your argument could be made stronger by stating your warrant explicitly: "Since students are as knowledgeable as the faculty and administrators about which professors are competent, they should be involved in the tenure process."

The more widely accepted your warrant, Toulmin explains, the more likely it is that readers will accept your argument. If there's no consensus about the warrant, you'll probably need to *back it up*. For the preceding example, you might mention several reports that found students evaluate faculty fairly (most students don't, for example, use the ratings to get back at professors against whom they have a personal grudge); further, students' ratings correlate strongly with those given by administrators and other faculty.

Toulmin describes another way to increase receptivity to an argument: *qualify the claim*—that is, explain under what circumstances it might be invalid or restricted. For instance, you might grant that most students know little about their instructors' research activities, scholarly publications, or participation in professional committees. You could, then, qualify your claim this way: "Because students don't have a comprehensive view of their instructors' professional activities, they should be involved in the tenure process but play a less prominent role than faculty and administrators."

As you can see, Toulmin's approach provides strategies for strengthening an argument. So, when prewriting or revising, take a few minutes to ask yourself the questions listed on the next page.

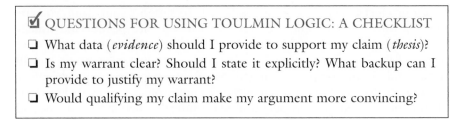

❑ What data (*evidence*) should I provide to support my claim (*thesis*)?

❑ Is my warrant clear? Should I state it explicitly? What backup can I provide to justify my warrant?

❑ Would qualifying my claim make my argument more convincing?

Your responses to these questions will help you structure a convincing and logical argument.

9. Recognize logical fallacies.   When writing an argumentation-persuasion essay, you need to recognize *logical fallacies* both in your own argument and in points raised by opposing sides. Work to eliminate such gaps in logic from your own writing and, when they appear in opposing arguments, try to expose them in your refutation. Logicians have identified many logical fallacies—including the sweeping or hasty generalization and the faulty conclusion discussed on pages 370 and 372. Other logical fallacies are described in Ann McClintock's "Propaganda Techniques in Today's Advertising" (page 204) and in the paragraphs that follow.

The *post hoc fallacy* (short for a Latin phrase meaning "after this, therefore because of this") occurs when you conclude that a cause-effect relationship exists simply because one event preceded another. Let's say you note the growing number of immigrants settling in a nearby city, observe the city's economic decline, and conclude that the immigrants' arrival caused the decline. Such a chain of thinking is faulty because it assumes a cause-effect relationship based purely on co-occurrence. Perhaps the immigrants' arrival was a factor in the economic slump, but there could also be other reasons: the lack of financial incentives to attract business to the city, restrictions on the size of the city's manufacturing facilities, citywide labor disputes that make companies leery of settling in the area. Your argument should also consider these possibilities. (For more on the *post hoc* fallacy, see page 296.)

The *non sequitur fallacy* (Latin for "it does not follow") is an even more blatant muddying of cause-effect relationships. In this case, a conclusion is drawn that has no logical connection to the evidence cited: "Millions of Americans own cars, so there is no need to fund public transportation." The faulty conclusion disregards the millions of Americans who don't own cars; it also ignores pollution and road congestion, both of which could be reduced if people had access to safe, reliable public transportation.

An *ad hominem argument* (from the Latin meaning "to the man") occurs when someone attacks a person rather than a point of view. Suppose your college plans to sponsor a physicians' symposium on the abortion controversy. You decide to write a letter to the school paper opposing the symposium. Taking swipes at two of the invited doctors who disapprove of abortion, you mention that one was recently involved in a messy divorce and that the other is alleged to have a drinking problem. By hurling personal invective, you avoid discussing the issue. Mudslinging is a poor substitute for reasoned argument.

Appeals to questionable or faulty authority also weaken an argument. Most of us have developed a healthy suspicion of phrases like *sources close to, an unidentified spokesperson states, experts claim,* and *studies show.* If these people and reports are so reliable, they should be clearly identified.

Begging the question involves failure to establish proof for a debatable point. The writer expects readers to accept as given a premise that's actually controversial. For instance, you would have trouble convincing readers that prayer should be banned from public schools if you based your argument on the premise that school prayer violates the U.S. Constitution. If the Constitution does, either explicitly or implicitly, prohibit prayer in public education, your essay must demonstrate that fact. You can't build a strong argument if you pretend there's no controversy surrounding your premise.

A *false analogy* wrongly implies that because two things share *some* characteristics, they are therefore *alike in all respects.* You might, for example, compare nicotine and marijuana. Both, you could mention, involve health risks and have addictive properties. If, however, you go on to conclude, "Driving while smoking a cigarette isn't illegal, so driving while smoking marijuana shouldn't be illegal either," you're employing a false analogy. You've overlooked a major difference between nicotine and marijuana: Marijuana impairs perception and coordination—important aspects of driving—while there's no evidence that nicotine does the same.

The *either/or fallacy* occurs when you assume that a particular viewpoint or course of action can have only one of two diametrically opposed outcomes—either totally this or totally that. Say you argue as follows: "Unless colleges continue to offer scholarships based solely on financial need, no one who is underprivileged will be able to attend college." Such a statement ignores the fact that bright, underprivileged students could receive scholarships based on their potential or their demonstrated academic excellence.

Finally, a *red herring argument* is an intentional digression from the issue—a ploy to deflect attention from the matter being discussed. Imagine that you're arguing that condoms shouldn't be dispensed to high school students. You would introduce a red herring if you began to rail against parents who fail to provide their children with any information about sex. Most people would agree that parents *should* provide such information. However, the issue being discussed is not parents' irresponsibility but the pros and cons of schools' distributing condoms to students.

REVISION STRATEGIES

Once you have a draft of the essay, you're ready to revise. The following checklist will help you and those giving you feedback apply to argumentation-persuasion some of the revision techniques discussed on pages 60–62.

☑ ARGUMENTATION-PERSUASION: A REVISION/PEER REVIEW CHECKLIST

Revise Overall Meaning and Structure

❑ What issue is being discussed? What is controversial about it?

❑ What is the essay's thesis? How does it differ from a generalization or mere statement of fact?

❑ What is the essay's purpose—to win readers over to a point of view, to spur readers to some type of action?

❑ For what audience is the essay written? What strategies are used to make readers receptive to the essay's thesis?

❑ What tone does the essay project? Is the tone likely to win readers over?

❑ If the essay's argument is essentially deductive, is the major premise sufficiently restricted? What evidence is the premise based on? Are the minor premise and conclusion valid? If not, how could these problems be corrected?

❑ Where is the essay weakened by hasty generalizations, a failure to weigh evidence honestly, or a failure to draw the most valid conclusion?

❑ Where does the essay commit any of the following logical fallacies: Concluding that a cause-effect relationship exists simply because one event preceded another? Attacking a person rather than an issue? Drawing a conclusion that isn't logically related to the evidence? Failing to establish proof for a debatable point? Relying on questionable or vaguely specified authority? Drawing a false analogy? Resorting to *either/or* thinking? Using a *red herring* argument?

Revise Paragraph Development

❑ How apparent is the link between the evidence (data) and the thesis (claim)? How could an explicit warrant clarify the connection? How would supporting the warrant or qualifying the claim strengthen the argument?

❑ Which paragraphs lack sufficient evidence (facts, examples, statistics, and expert opinion)?

❏ Which paragraphs lack unity? How could they be made more focused? In which paragraph(s) does evidence seem bland, overly general, unrepresentative, or inaccurate?

❏ Which paragraphs take opposing views into account? Are these views refuted? How? Which counterarguments are ineffective?

❏ Where do outside sources require documentation?

Revise Sentences and Words

❏ What words and phrases help readers distinguish the essay's arguments from those advanced by the opposing side?

❏ Which words carry strong emotional overtones? Is this connotative language excessive? Where does emotional language replace rather than reinforce clear thinking?

❏ Where might dogmatic language ("Anyone can see that...") and "Obviously,...") alienate readers?

STUDENT ESSAY

The following student essay was written by Mark Simmons in response to this assignment:

> In "Free-Speech Follies," Stanley Fish invites controversy with his examination of a cherished right on campuses. Select another controversial issue, one that you feel strongly about. Conduct library research to gather evidence in support of your position, and brainstorm with others to identify some points that might be raised by those who oppose your view. Then, using logic and formal, documented evidence, convince readers that your viewpoint is valid.

Your instructor may not ask you to include research in your essay. But, if you're asked—as Mark was—to research your paper and to provide *formal documentation,* you'll want to pay special attention to the way Mark credits his sources. (In *your* paper, the Works Cited list should be double-spaced—along with the rest of the paper—and placed at the end on a separate page.) You'll also find it helpful to refer to Appendix A, "A Guide to Using Sources" (page 451). If your instructor wants you to research your paper but will accept *informal documentation,* the material on pages 364–365 should come in handy.

Whether or not you include research in your paper, the annotations on Mark's essay and the comments following it will help you determine how well it applies the principles of argumentation-persuasion.

Mark Simmons

Professor Chen

English 102

17 November 2008

Compulsory National Service

Our high school history class spent several weeks studying
the events of the 1960s. The most interesting thing about that
decade was the spirit of service and social commitment among
young people. In the '60s, young people thought about issues
beyond themselves; they joined the Peace Corps, worked in
poverty-stricken Appalachian communities, and participated in
freedom marches against segregation. Most young people today,
despite their concern with careers and getting ahead, would also
like an opportunity to make a worthwhile contribution to society.

Convinced that many young adults are indeed eager for
such an opportunity, President Bill Clinton implemented in 1994 a
pilot program of voluntary national service. The following year, the
program was formalized, placed under the management of the
Corporation for National Service (CNS), and given the name
AmeriCorps. In the years 1994–2007, approximately 400,000
AmeriCorps volunteers provided varied assistance in communities
across the country ("About AmeriCorps"). Such voluntary national

service was also endorsed by President George W. Bush. Following
the devastating terrorist attacks on September 11, 2001, President
Bush urged Americans to volunteer as a way of assisting in the
nation's recovery and of demonstrating a spirit of national unity.
He issued an executive order in early 2002 establishing USA
Freedom Corps, an organization seeking to persuade Americans to
perform 4,000 hours of volunteer service over a lifetime
(Hutcheson). In general, programs such as USA Freedom Corps
and the more established AmeriCorps hold out so much promise
that it seems only natural to go one step further and make young
people's participation in these programs or some kind of national

1

2

service mandatory. By instituting a program of compulsory national service, the country could tap youth's idealistic desire to make
a difference. Such a system would yield significant benefits.

What exactly is meant by compulsory national service?
Traditionally, it has tended to mean that everyone between the
ages of seventeen and twenty-five would serve the country for two
years. These young people could choose between two major
options: military service or a public-service corps. They could serve
their time at any point within an eight-year span. The unemployed
or the uncertain could join immediately after high school; college-
bound students could complete their education before joining the
national service. Years ago, Senator Sam Nunn and Representative
Dave McCurdy gave a new twist to the definition of compulsory
national service. They proposed a plan that would require all high
school graduates applying for federal aid for college tuition to serve
either in the military or in a Citizens Corps. Anyone in the Citizens
Corps would be required to work full-time at public-service duties
for one or two years. During that time, participants would receive a
weekly stipend and, at the end, be given a voucher worth $10,000
for each year of civilian service. The voucher could then be applied
toward college credit, employment training, or a down payment on
a house (Sudo).

The traditional plan for compulsory national service and the
one proposed by Nunn and McCurdy are just two of many variations
that have been discussed over the years. While this country debates
the concept, some nations such as France have gone ahead and
accepted it enthusiastically. The idea could be workable in this country too. Unfortunately, opponents are doing all they can to prevent the
idea from taking hold. They contend, first of all, that the program
would cost too much. A great deal of money, they argue, would be
spent administering the program, paying young people's wages, and
providing housing for participants. Another argument against compulsory national service is that it would demoralize young people;

3

4

[margin annotations]

Start of two-
sentence
thesis

Definition
paragraph

Beginning of
summary of a
source's
ideas

No page
number
needed for a
one-page
source.

Topic
sentence

Beginning of
summary of
three points
made by the
opposing
viewpoint

Simmons 3

supposedly, the plan would prevent the young from moving ahead with their careers and would make them feel as though they were engaged in work that offered no personal satisfaction. A third argument is that compulsory service would lay the groundwork for a dictatorship. The picture is painted of an army of young people, controlled by the government, much like the Hitler Youth of World War II.

Topic sentence: Refutation of first point

Despite opponents' claims that compulsory national service would involve exorbitant costs, the program would not have to be that expensive to run. AmeriCorps has already provided an excellent model for achieving substantial benefits at reasonable cost. For example, a study conducted by universities in Iowa and Michigan showed that each dollar spent on AmeriCorps programs yielded $2.60 in reduced welfare costs, increased earnings, and other benefits (Garland 120). Also, the sums required for wages and housing could be reduced considerably through payments made by the towns, cities, and states using the corps's services. And the economic benefits of the program could be significant. AmeriCorps's official website gives an idea of the current scope of the program's activities. Volunteers provide crucial services including building affordable homes for families, improving health services, responding to natural disasters, and tutoring children. A compulsory national corps could also clean up litter, provide day-care services, staff libraries, immunize children, and care for the country's growing elderly population ("About AmeriCorps"; Clinton). All these projects would help solve many of the problems that plague our nation, and they would probably cost less than if they were handled by often inefficient government bureaucracies.

Parenthetical citation of a specific page of a source

Information from two sources. Sources, separated by a semicolon, are given in the order in which they appear in the Works Cited list.

Topic sentence: Refutation of second point

Also, rather than undermining the spirit of young people, as opponents contend, the program would probably boost their morale. Many young people feel enormous pressure and uncertainty; they are not sure whether they want to find a job or further their education. Compulsory national service could give these young people

5

6

Simmons 4

Attribution giving author's full name and area of expertise

Full-sentence quotation is preceded by a comma and begins with a capital letter.

Quotation with ellipsis

Parenthetical citation for source having two authors. No page given since electronic text is unpaged.

Topic sentence: Refutation of third point

much-needed breathing space. As Edward Lewis, president of St. Mary's College, says, "Many students are not ready for college at seventeen or eighteen. This kind of program responds to that need" (qtd. in Fowler). Robert Coles, psychiatrist and social activist, argues that a public service stint enriches participants' lives in yet another way. Coles points out that young people often have little sense of the job market. When they get involved in community service, though, they frequently "discover an area of interest...that launches them on a career" (93). Equally important, compulsory national service can provide an emotional boost for the young; all of them would experience the pride that comes from working hard, reaching goals, acquiring skills, and handling respon-sibilities (Wofford and Waldman). A positive mind-set would also result from the sense of community that would be created by serv-ing in the national service. All young people—rich or poor, educated or not, regardless of sex and social class—would come together and perceive not their differences but their common interests and simi-larities (Wofford and Waldman). As President Clinton proclaimed at the Year 2000 swearing-in of AmeriCorps's recruits in Philadelphia, AmeriCorps gives volunteers a chance "to tear down barriers of dis-trust and misunderstanding and old-fashioned ignorance, and build a genuine American community" (Clinton).

Finally, in contrast to what opponents claim, compulsory national service would not signal the start of a dictatorship. Although the service would be required, young people would have complete freedom to choose any two years between the ages of seventeen and twenty-five. They would also have complete free-dom to choose the branch of the military or public service corps that suits them best. And the corps would not need to be outfitted in military uniforms or to live in barrack-like camps. It could be set up like a regular job, with young people living at home as much as possible, following a nine-to-five schedule, enjoying all the personal freedoms that would ordinarily be theirs. Also, a dictatorship would

Where secondary source was quoted

Quotation is blended into the sentence (no comma and the quotation begins with a lowercased word).

Just the page number is provided because the author's name is cited in the preceding attribution.

7

no more likely emerge from compulsory national service than it has from our present military system. We would still have a series of checks and balances to prohibit the taking of power by one group or individual. We should also keep in mind that our system is different from that of fascist regimes; our long tradition of personal liberty makes improbable the seizing of absolute power by one person or faction. A related but even more important point to remember is that freedom does not mean people are guaranteed the right to pursue only their individual needs. That is mistaking selfishness for freedom. And, as everyone knows, selfishness leads only to misery. The national service would not take away freedom. On the contrary, serving in the corps would help young people grasp this larger concept of freedom, a concept that is badly need- ed to counteract the deadly "look out for number one" attitude that is spreading like a poison across the nation. "We think that there's an inherent idealism in every person, especially young people, that if we give them the right structure and opportunity, we can call it out," says John Sarvey, who trains AmeriCorps participants for work in City Year San Jose, the program he directs ("Helping").

Perhaps there will never be a time like the 1960s when so many young people were concerned with remaking the world. Still, a good many of today's young people want meaningful work. They want to feel that what they do makes a difference. A program of compulsory national service would harness this idealism and help young people realize the best in themselves. Such a program would also help resolve some of the country's most critical social problems.

Almost two decades ago, political commentator Donald Eberly expressed his belief in the power of national service. Urging the inauguration of such a program, Eberly wrote the following:

> The promise of national service can be manifested in many ways: in cleaner air and fewer forest fires; in well-cared-for infants and old folks; in a better-educated

Parenthetical citation uses abbreviated title.

Beginning of two-paragraph conclusion

Long quotation is indented one inch. Don't leave any extra space within, above, or below the quotation.

Attribution leading to a long quotation. Attribution is followed by a colon since the lead-in is a full sentence. If the lead-in isn't a full sentence, use a comma after the attribution.

8

Simmons 6

For an indented quotation, the period is placed *before* the parenthetical citation.

citizenry and better-satisfied work force; perhaps in a
more peaceful world. National service has a lot of promise.
It's a promise well worth keeping. (561)

Several years later, President Clinton took office, gave his support
to the concept, and AmeriCorps was born. This advocacy of public
service was then championed, at least in word, by President Bush.
During his administration, however, AmeriCorps was threatened
by deep budget cuts advocated by opponents of the program and
its Clintonian legacy. Fortunately, despite these measures,
Congress voted in 2003 with overwhelming bipartisan support to
save AmeriCorps and salvage a portion of its budget ("Timely
Help"). In the words of a *Philadelphia Inquirer* editorial, "The civic
yield from that investment is incalculable" ("Ill Served"). An efficient and successful program of voluntary service, AmeriCorps has
paved the way. Now seems to be the perfect time to expand the
concept and make compulsory national service a reality.

9

Simmons 7

Start list on a new page, double-spaced, no extra space after heading or between entries. Each entry begins flush left; Indent successive lines half an inch.

Works Cited

"About AmeriCorps: What Is AmeriCorps?" *AmeriCorps.*
    Corporation for National and Community Service, 3 Nov.
    2008. Web. 3 Nov. 2008.

Clinton, William J. "Remarks by the President to AmeriCorps."
    Memorial Hall, Philadelphia. 11 Oct. 2000. Transcript. *Clinton
    Presidential Materials Project.* National Archives and Records
    Administration. Web. 6 Nov. 2008. Transcript.
    <http://clinton6.nara.gov/2000/10/2000-10-11-remarks-by-
    the-president-to-americorps.html>.

For anonymous Internet material, start with title, give website (italicized) and sponsoring organization, followed by publication date. Give page numbers if available. State medium consulted ("Web") and date of access.

Transcript of a speech found online. Give URL *only* for hard-to-retrieve sources.

Coles, Robert. *The Call of Service*. Boston: Houghton Mifflin, 1993. Print.

Eberly, Donald. "What the President Should Do about National Service." *Vital Speeches of the Day*. 15 Aug. 1989: 561-63. Print.

Fowler, Margaret. "New Interest in National Youth Corps." *New York Times* 16 May 1989, natl. ed.: A25. Print.

Garland, Susan B. "A Social Program CEOs Want to Save." *Business Week* 19 June 1996: 120-21. Print.

"Helping Hands." *Online NewsHour*. Public Broadcasting Service, 19 July 2000. Web. 11 Nov. 2008. Transcript.

Hutcheson, Ron. "Bush Moves to Establish His New Volunteer Program." *Philadelphia Inquirer* 31 Jan. 2002: A2. Print.

"Ill Served." Editorial. *Philadelphia Inquirer Online*. Philly.com, 27 June 2003. Web. 8 Nov. 2008.

Sudo, Phil. "Mandatory National Service?" *Scholastic Update* 23 Feb. 1990. Print.

"Timely Help for AmeriCorps." Editorial. *New York Times*. New York Times, 17 July 2003. Web. 11 Nov. 2008.

Wofford, Harris, and Steven Waldman. "AmeriCorps the Beautiful? Habitat for Conservative Values." *Policy Review* 79 (1996): n. pag. *EBSCOhost*. Web. 11 Nov. 2008.

Book by a single author. Give medium ("Print") at the end of the citation.

Newspaper article whose text is only one page

Article from weekly magazine

Scholarly journal article, by two authors, found in a database ("EBSCOhost"). Give volume and issue numbers (if both are available) and year, followed by pages or "n. pag." if no page numbers are given in the source.

TV show transcript found online

Newspaper editorial found online

COMMENTARY

Blend of argumentation and persuasion. In his essay, Mark tackles a controversial issue. He takes the position that compulsory national service would benefit both the country as a whole and its young people in particular. Mark's essay is a good example of the way argumentation and persuasion often mix: Although the paper presents Mark's position in a logical, well-reasoned manner (argumentation), it also appeals to readers' personal values and suggests a course of action (persuasion).

Audience analysis. When planning the essay, Mark realized that his audience—his composition class—would consist largely of two kinds of readers.

Some, not sure of their views, would be inclined to agree with him if he presented his case well. Others would probably be reluctant to accept his view. Because of this mixed audience, Mark knew he couldn't depend on *pathos* (an appeal to emotion) to convince readers. Rather, his argument had to rely mainly on *logos* (reason) and *ethos* (credibility). So Mark organized his essay around a series of logical arguments—many of them backed by expert opinion—and he evoked his own authority by drawing on his knowledge of history and his "inside" knowledge of young people.

Introduction and thesis.   Mark introduces his subject by discussing an earlier decade when large numbers of young people worked for social change. Mark's references to the Peace Corps, community work, and freedom marches reinforce his image as a knowledgeable source and establish a context for his position. These historical references, combined with the comments about AmeriCorps, the program of voluntary national service, lead into the two-sentence thesis at the end of the two-paragraph introduction: "By instituting a program of compulsory national service, the country could tap youth's idealistic desire to make a difference. Such a system would yield significant benefits."

The second paragraph in the introduction also illustrates Mark's first use of outside sources. Because the assignment called for research in support of an argument, Mark went to the library and online and identified sources that helped him defend his position. If Mark's instructor had required extensive investigation of an issue, Mark would have been obligated both to dig more deeply into his subject and to use more scholarly and specialized sources. But given the instructor's requirements, Mark proceeded just as he should have: He searched out expert opinion that supported his viewpoint; he presented that evidence clearly; he documented his sources carefully.

Background paragraph and use of outside sources.   The third paragraph provides a working *definition* of compulsory national service by presenting two common interpretations of the concept. Such background information guarantees that Mark's readers will share his understanding of the essay's central concept.

Acknowledging the opposing viewpoint.   Having explained the meaning of compulsory national service, Mark is now in a good position to launch his argument. Even though he wasn't required to research the opposing viewpoint, Mark wisely decided to get together with some friends to brainstorm some issues that might be raised by the dissenting view. He acknowledges this position in the *topic sentence* of the essay's fourth paragraph: "Unfortunately, opponents are doing all they can to prevent the idea from taking hold." Next he summarizes the main points the dissenting opinion might advance: compulsory national service would be expensive, demoralizing to young people, and dangerously authoritarian. Mark uses the rest of the essay to counter these criticisms.

Refutation.   The next three paragraphs (5–7) *refute* the opposing stance and present Mark's evidence for his position. Mark structures the essay so that readers can follow his *counterargument* with ease. Each paragraph argues against one opposing point and begins with a *topic sentence* that serves as Mark's response to the dissenting view. Note the way the italicized portion of each topic sentence recalls a dissenting point cited earlier: "Despite opponents' claims that *compulsory national service would involve exorbitant costs,* the program would not have to be that expensive to run" (paragraph 5); "Also, rather than *undermining the spirit of young people,* as opponents contend, the program would probably boost their morale" (6); "Finally, in contrast to what opponents claim, *compulsory national service would not signal the start of a dictatorship"* (7). Mark also guides the reader through the various points in the refutation by using *transitions* within paragraphs: "*And* the economic benefits . . . could be significant" (5); "*Equally important,* compulsory national service could provide an emotional boost . . ." (6); "*Also,* a dictatorship would no more likely emerge . . ." (7).

Throughout the three-paragraph refutation, Mark uses outside sources to lend power to his argument. If the assignment had called for in-depth research, he would have cited facts, statistics, and case studies to develop this section of his essay. Given the nature of the assignment, though, Mark's reliance on expert opinion is perfectly acceptable.

Mark successfully incorporates material from these outside sources into his refutation. He doesn't, for example, string one quotation numbingly after another; instead he usually develops his refutation by *summarizing* expert opinion and saves *direct quotations* for points that deserve emphasis. Moreover, whenever Mark quotes or summarizes a source, he provides clear signals to indicate that the material is indeed borrowed. (If you'd like some suggestions for citing outside sources in an essay of your own, see pages 364–365 and 451–482.)

Some problems with the refutation.   Overall, Mark's three-paragraph refutation is strong, but it would have been even more effective if the paragraphs had been resequenced. As it now stands, the last paragraph in the refutation (7) seems anticlimactic. Unlike the preceding two paragraphs, which are developed through fairly extensive reference to outside sources, paragraph 7 depends entirely on Mark's personal feelings and interpretations for its support. Of course, Mark was under no obligation to provide research in all sections of the paper. Even so, the refutation would have been more persuasive if Mark had placed the final paragraph in the refutation in a less emphatic position. He could, for example, have put it first or second in the sequence, saving for last either of the other two more convincing paragraphs.

You may also have felt that there's another problem with the third paragraph in the refutation. Here, Mark seems to lose control of his counterargument. Beginning with "And, as everyone knows . . . ," Mark falls into the *logical fallacy* called *begging the question*. He shouldn't assume that everyone agrees that a selfish life inevitably brings misery. He also indulges in charged emotionalism when he refers—somewhat melodramatically—to the "deadly 'look out for number one' attitude that is spreading like a poison across the nation."

Inductive reasoning.   In part, Mark arrived at his position *inductively*, through a series of *inferences* or *inductive leaps*. He started with some personal *observations* about the nation and its young people. Then, to support those observations, he added his friends' insights as well as information gathered through research. Combined, all this material led him to the general *conclusion* that compulsory national service would be both workable and beneficial.

Combining patterns of development.   To develop his argument, Mark draws on several patterns of development. The third paragraph relies on *definition* to clarify what is meant by compulsory national service. The first paragraph of both the introduction and conclusion *compares* and *contrasts* young people of the 1960s with those of today. And, to support his position, Mark uses a kind of *causal analysis;* he both speculates on the likely consequences of compulsory national service and cites expert opinion to illustrate the validity of some of those speculations.

Conclusion.   Despite some problems in the final section of his refutation, Mark comes up with an effective two-paragraph conclusion for his essay. In the first closing paragraph, he echoes the point made in the introduction about the 1960s and restates his thesis. That done, he moves to the second paragraph of his conclusion. There, he quotes a dramatic statement from a knowledgeable source, cites efforts to undermine AmeriCorps, and ends by pointing out that AmeriCorps has earned the respect of some unlikely supporters. All that Mark does in this final paragraph lends credibility to the crisp assertion and suggested course of action at the very end of his essay.

Revising the first draft.   Given the complex nature of his argument, Mark found that he had to revise his essay several times. One way to illustrate some of the changes he made is to compare his final introduction with the original draft printed here:

Original Version of the Introduction

"There's no free lunch." "You can't get something for nothing." "You have to earn your way." In America, these sayings are not really true. In America, we gladly take but give back little. In America, we receive economic opportunity, legal protection, the right to vote, and, most of all, a personal freedom unequaled throughout the world. How do we repay our country for such gifts? In most cases, we don't. This unfair relationship must be changed. The best way to make a start is to institute a system of national compulsory service for young people. This system would be of real benefit to the country and its citizens.

When Mark met with a classmate for a peer review session, he found that his partner had a number of helpful suggestions for revising various sections of the essay. But Mark's partner focused most of her comments on the essay's introduction because she felt it needed special attention. Following his classmate's suggestion, Mark deleted the original introduction's references to Americans in general. He made this change because he wanted readers to know—from the very start of the essay—that the paper would focus not on all Americans but on American youth. To reinforce this emphasis, he also added the point about the social commitment characteristic of young people in the 1960s. This reference to an earlier period gave the discussion an important historical perspective and lent a note of authority to Mark's argument. The decision to mention the '60s also helped Mark realize that his introduction should point out more recent developments—specifically, the promise of AmeriCorps. Mark was pleased to see that adding this new material not only gave the introduction a sharper focus, but it also provided a smoother lead-in to his thesis.

These are just a few of the many changes Mark made while reworking his essay. Because he budgeted his time carefully, he was able to revise thoroughly. With the exception of some weak spots in the refutation, Mark's essay is well-reasoned and convincing.

MLA format.   Mark followed the style given in the *MLA Handbook for Writers of Research Papers* to format his paper. For more guidance on styling in-text references and Works Cited lists, see pages 470–482.

ACTIVITIES: ARGUMENTATION-PERSUASION

Prewriting Activities

1. Following are several thesis statements for argumentation-persuasion essays. For each thesis, determine whether the three audiences indicated in parentheses are apt to be supportive, wavering, or hostile. Then select *one* thesis and use group brainstorming to identify, for each audience, specific points you would make to persuade each group.

   a. Students should not graduate from college until they have passed a comprehensive exam in their majors (*college students, their parents, college officials*).

   b. Abandoned homes owned by the city should be sold to low-income residents for a nominal fee (*city officials, low-income residents, general citizens*).

c. The town should pass a law prohibiting residents who live near the reservoir from using pesticides on their lawns (*environmentalists, homeowners, members of the town council*).

d. Faculty advisors to college newspapers should have the authority to prohibit the publication of articles that reflect negatively on the school (*alumni, college officials, student journalists*).

Revising Activities

2. Following is the introduction from the first draft of an essay advocating the elimination of mandatory dress codes in public schools. Revise the paragraph, being sure to consider these questions: How effectively does the writer deal with the opposing viewpoint? Does the paragraph encourage those who might disagree with the writer to read on? Why or why not? Do you see any logical fallacies in the writer's thinking? Where? Does the writer introduce anything that veers away from the point being discussed? Where? Before revising, you may find it helpful to do some brainstorming—individually or in a group—to find ways to strengthen the paragraph.

   After reworking the paragraph, take a few minutes to consider how the rest of the essay might unfold. What persuasive strategies could be used? How could Rogerian argument win over readers? What points could be made? What action could be urged in the effort to build a convincing argument?

   In three nearby towns recently, high school administrators joined forces to take an outrageously strong stand against students' constitutional rights. Acting like fascists, they issued an edict in the form of a preposterous dress code that prohibits students from wearing expensive jewelry, designer jeans, leather jackets—anything that the administrators, in their supposed wisdom, consider ostentatious. Perhaps the next thing they'll want to do is forbid students to play rock music at school dances. What prompted the administrators' dictatorial prohibition against certain kinds of clothing? Somehow or other, they got it into their heads that having no restrictions on the way students dress creates an unhealthy environment, where students vie with each other for the flashiest attire. Students and parents alike should protest this and any other dress code. If such codes go into effect, we might as well throw out the Constitution.

Stanley Fish

Stanley Fish is best known as a scholar of the English poet John Milton and as a literary theorist. He was born in Providence, Rhode Island, in 1938. Fish has taught English at the University of California at Berkeley, Johns Hopkins University, and Duke University. From 1999 to 2004 he was dean of the College of Liberal Arts and Sciences at the University of Illinois at Chicago, and in 2005 he became a professor of humanities and law at Florida International University. His best-known work on Milton is *Surprised by Sin: The Reader in Paradise Lost* (1967). In addition to his distinguished academic career and many scholarly publications, Fish has also had a career as a public intellectual. He has written and lectured about many issues, including the politics of the university. His books on current political and cultural issues include *There's No Such Thing as Free Speech...and It's a Good Thing, Too* (1994) and *The Trouble with Principle* (1999). This article was published in *The Chronicle of Higher Education,* for which Fish writes a regular column on campus politics and academic careers, on June 13, 2003.

For ideas about how this argumentation-persuasion essay is organized, see Figure 11.2 on page 396.

Pre-Reading Journal Entry

How do you feel about freedom of speech on campus? In your journal, list several controversial issues that might be debated in a college setting. For each issue, indicate whether you feel that divergent, even inflammatory views should have an opportunity to be heard on campus—for example, in class, in the college newspaper, or in a lecture series. Reflect in your journal on why you feel as you do.

Free-Speech Follies

The modern American version of crying wolf is crying First 1 Amendment.[1] If you want to burn a cross on a black family's lawn or buy an election by contributing millions to a candidate or vilify Jerry Falwell and his mother in a scurrilous "parody," and someone or some government agency tries to stop you, just yell "First Amendment rights" and you will stand a good chance of getting to do what you want to do.

In the academy,[2] the case is even worse: Not only is the First 2 Amendment pressed into service at the drop of a hat (especially whenever anyone is disciplined for anything), it is invoked ritually when there are no First Amendment issues in sight.

---

[1]The relevant part of the First Amendment of the U.S. Constitution reads: "Congress shall make no law...abridging the freedom of speech, or of the press; or the right of the people peaceably to assemble, and to petition the Government for a redress of grievances" (editors' note).
[2]Refers to institutions of higher learning (editors' note).

Take the case of the editors of college newspapers who will always cry First   3
Amendment when something they've published turns out to be the cause of
outrage and controversy. These days the offending piece or editorial or advertisement usually involves (what is at least perceived to be) an attack on Jews. In
January of this year, the *Daily Illini,* a student newspaper at the University of
Illinois at Urbana-Champaign, printed a letter from a resident of Seattle with no
university affiliation. The letter ran under the headline "Jews Manipulate
America" and argued that because their true allegiance is to the state of Israel,
the president should "separate Jews from all government advisory positions";
otherwise, the writer warned, "the Jews might face another Holocaust."

When the predictable firestorm of outrage erupted, the newspaper's edi-   4
tor responded by declaring, first, that "we are committed to giving all people
a voice"; second, that, given this commitment, "we print the opinions of others with whom we do not agree"; third, that to do otherwise would involve
the newspaper in the dangerous acts of "silencing" and "self-censorship";
and, fourth, that "what is hate speech to one member of a society is free
speech to another."

Wrong four times.   5

I'll bet the *Daily Illini* is not committed to giving all people a voice—   6
the KKK? man-boy love? advocates of slavery? would-be Unabombers? Nor
do I believe that the editors sift through submissions looking for the ones
they disagree with and then print those. No doubt they apply some principles of selection, asking questions like, Is it relevant, or Is it timely, or Does
it get the facts right, or Does it present a coherent argument?

That is, they exercise judgment, which is quite a different thing from silenc-   7
ing or self-censorship. No one is silenced because a single outlet declines to publish him; silencing occurs when that outlet (or any other) is forbidden by the
state to publish him on pain of legal action; and that is also what censorship is.

As for self-censoring, if it is anything, it is what we all do whenever we decide   8
it would be better not to say something or cut a sentence that went just a little
bit too far or leave a manuscript in the bottom drawer because it is not yet ready.
Self-censorship, in short, is not a crime or a moral failing; it is a responsibility.

And, finally, whatever the merits of the argument by which all assertions   9
are relativised—your hate speech is my free speech—this incident has nothing to do with either hate speech or free speech and everything to do with
whether the editors are discharging or defaulting on their obligations when
they foist them off on an inapplicable doctrine, saying in effect, "The First
Amendment made us do it."

More recently, the same scenario played itself out at Santa Rosa Junior   10
College. This time it was a student who wrote the offending article. Titled
"Is Anti-Semitism Ever the Result of Jewish Behavior?" it answered the question in the affirmative, creating an uproar that included death threats, an avalanche of hate mail, and demands for just about everyone's resignation. The

faculty adviser who had approved the piece said, "The First Amendment isn't there to protect agreeable stories."

He was alluding to the old saw that the First Amendment protects   11
unpopular as well as popular speech. But what it protects unpopular speech *from* is abridgment by the government of its free expression; it does not protect unpopular speech from being rejected by a newspaper, and it confers no positive obligation to give your pages over to unpopular speech, or popular speech, or any speech.

Once again, there is no First Amendment issue here, just an issue of edi-   12
torial judgment and the consequences of exercising it. (You can print anything you like; but if the heat comes, it's yours, not the Constitution's.)

In these controversies, student editors are sometimes portrayed, or por-   13
tray themselves, as First Amendment heroes who bravely risk criticism and censure in order to uphold a cherished American value. But they are not heroes; they are merely confused and, in terms of their understanding of the doctrine they invoke, rather hapless.

Not as hapless, however, as the Harvard English department, which made   14
a collective fool of itself three times when it invited, disinvited and then reinvited poet Tom Paulin to be the Morris Gray lecturer. Again the flash point was anti-Semitism. In his poetry and in public comments, Paulin had said that Israel had no right to exist, that settlers on the West Bank "should be shot dead," and that Israeli police and military forces were the equivalent of the Nazi SS. When these and other statements came to light shortly before Paulin was to give his lecture, the department voted to rescind the invitation. When the inevitable cry of "censorship, censorship" was heard in the land, the department flip-flopped again, and a professor-spokesman declared, "This was a clear affirmation that the department stood strongly by the First Amendment."

It was of course nothing of the kind; it was a transparent effort of a bunch   15
that had already put its foot in its mouth twice to wriggle out of trouble and regain the moral high ground by striking the pose of First Amendment defender. But, in fact, the department and its members were not First Amendment defenders (a religion they converted to a little late), but serial bunglers.

What should they have done? Well, it depends on what they wanted to   16
do. If they wanted to invite this particular poet because they admired his poetry, they had a perfect right to do so. If they were aware ahead of time of Paulin's public pronouncements, they could have chosen either to say something by way of explanation or to remain silent and let the event speak for itself; either course of action would have been at once defensible and productive of risk. If they knew nothing of Paulin's anti-Israel sentiments (difficult to believe of a gang of world-class researchers) but found out about them after the fact, they might have said, "Oops, never mind" or toughed it out—again alternatives not without risk. But at each stage, whatever they did or didn't do would have had no relationship whatsoever to any First

Amendment right—Paulin had no right to be invited—or obligation—there was no obligation either to invite or disinvite him, and certainly no obligation to reinvite him, unless you count the obligations imposed on yourself by a succession of ill-thought-through decisions. Whatever the successes or failures here, they were once again failures of judgment, not doctrine.

In another case, it looked for a moment that judgment of an appropriate kind was in fact being exercised. The University of California at Berkeley houses the Emma Goldman Papers Project, and each year the director sends out a fund-raising mailer that always features quotations from Goldman's work. But this January an associate vice chancellor edited the mailer and removed two quotations that in context read as a criticism of the Bush administration's plans for a war in Iraq. He explained that the quotations were not randomly chosen and were clearly intended to make a "political point, and that is inappropriate in an official university situation."   17

The project director (who acknowledged that the quotes were selected for their contemporary relevance) objected to what she saw as an act of censorship and a particularly egregious one given Goldman's strong advocacy of free expression.   18

But no one's expression was being censored. The Goldman quotations are readily available and had they appeared in the project's literature in a setting that did not mark them as political, no concerns would have been raised. It is just, said the associate vice chancellor, that they are inappropriate in this context, and, he added, "It is not a matter of the First Amendment."   19

Right, it's a matter of whether or not there is even the appearance of the university's taking sides on a partisan issue; that is, it is an empirical matter that requires just the exercise of judgment that associate vice chancellors are paid to perform. Of course he was pilloried by members of the Berkeley faculty and others who saw First Amendment violations everywhere.   20

But there were none. Goldman still speaks freely through her words. The project director can still make her political opinions known by writing letters to the editor or to everyone in the country, even if she cannot use the vehicle of a university flier to do so. Everyone's integrity is preserved. The project goes on unimpeded, and the university goes about its proper academic business. Or so it would have been had the administration stayed firm. But it folded and countermanded the associate vice chancellor's decision.   21

At least the chancellor had sense enough to acknowledge that no one's speech had been abridged. It was just, he said, an "error in judgment." Aren't they all?   22

Are there then no free-speech issues on campuses? Sure there are; there just aren't very many. When Toni Smith, a basketball player at Manhattanville College, turned her back to the flag during the playing of the national anthem in protest against her government's policies, she was truly exercising her First Amendment rights, rights that ensure that she cannot be compelled to an affirmation she does not endorse. . . . And as she stood by her principles in the   23 face of hostility, she truly was (and is) a First Amendment hero, as the college newspaper editors, the members of the Harvard English department, and the head of the Emma Goldman Project are not. The category is a real one, and it would be good if it were occupied only by those who belong in it.

FIGURE 11.2
Essay Structure Diagram: "Free-Speech Follies" by Stanley Fish

Introductory paragraphs: Thesis (paragraphs 1–2)	Invoking the First Amendment has become a way of "crying wolf." **Thesis:** In the academy, the First Amendment is invoked often in situations that don't really concern free speech.
Opposing and supporting arguments illustrated by examples (3–22)	**Example:** Anti-Semitic letter in University of Illinois newspaper. **Opposing arguments:** (1) Editors have an obligation to give all people a voice. (2) Editors have an obligation to print views they don't agree with. (3) Not to publish is "silencing" and self-censorship. (4) Hate speech to one person is free speech to another. First Amendment protects all speech, not just agreeable speech. **Supporting arguments:** (1) Editors must use some selection criteria—for writing quality and content. (2) Exercising judgment is not the same as silencing because writers are free to publish elsewhere. (3) Self-censorship is not a crime; it's a responsibility. (4) The incident did not concern hate speech vs. free speech, but rather whether editors discharged their responsibilities. **Example:** Anti-Semitic article in a Santa Rosa Junior College newspaper. (Opposing and supporting arguments given.) **Example:** Harvard English department invites, then uninvites, then reinvites a poet who had expressed anti-Semitic views. (Opposing and supporting arguments given.) **Example:** Quotations critical of the Bush administration deleted from a University of California at Berkeley exhibit flyer. (Opposing and supporting arguments given.)
Concluding paragraph (23)	Example of a true First Amendment hero: College basketball player turning her back on the flag during the national anthem to protest government policies.

Questions for Close Reading

1. What is the selection's thesis? Locate the sentence(s) in which Fish states his main idea. If he doesn't state his thesis explicitly, express it in your own words.
2. What does Fish mean by "Self-censorship, in short, is not a crime or a moral failing; it is a responsibility" (paragraph 8)?
3. In paragraph 15, Fish refers to the Harvard English department as "serial bunglers." What does he mean by this?
4. According to Fish, why aren't the editors of student newspapers that publish inflammatory material First Amendment heroes? Who does he believe are the true First Amendment heroes?
5. Refer to your dictionary as needed to define the following words used in the selection: *vilify* (paragraph 1), *scurrilous* (1), *firestorm* (4), *coherent* (6), *abridgment* (11), *hapless* (13), *rescind* (14), *chancellor* (17), *egregious* (18), *partisan* (20), *empirical* (20), *pilloried* (20), and *countermanded* (21).

Questions About the Writer's Craft

1. **The pattern.** Fish presents the viewpoint that self-censorship is not a violation of the First Amendment. What strategies does Fish use to deal with this view and to present his own argument?
2. **Other patterns.** All the examples that Fish uses to support his argument are related to anti-Semitism. If Fish had broadened the examples to include instances of speech that defamed groups other than Jews, would the essay have been more or less effective? Support your answer.
3. Paragraph 5 is just "Wrong four times." What is the effect of this brevity?
4. Most readers of *The Chronicle of Higher Education,* where this essay was first published, are academics—administrators, faculty, and graduate students—or those with a professional interest in higher education. They are likely to know Fish by reputation, especially since he publishes a regular column. Given this, how would you assess Fish's *ethos*? How effective is his use of *logos* in this argument? How effective is his use of *pathos*?

Writing Assignments Using Argumentation-Persuasion as a Pattern of Development

1. Fish gives an example of a controversy surrounding an anti-Semitic letter to the editor published in a campus student newspaper. Since publications print letters to the editor to open up their pages to public opinion and dissent, one might argue that the criteria for printing letters to the editor should be quite broad—much broader than the criteria the publication uses for its own articles—in order to give members of the public an opportunity to air their views. Write an essay in which you *argue* that letters to the editor should (or should not) be printed with the aim of giving all readers an opportunity to state their opinions. Don't forget to acknowledge (and, if possible, to refute) opposing viewpoints.
2. Many colleges and universities have limited controversial speech to designated "free-speech zones," areas on campus where speeches, rallies, and pamphleteering

are permitted. Elsewhere free speech is subject to tight administration control. Proponents argue that universities have a right to control activities that interfere with their operation; opponents argue that free-speech zones are unconstitutional. Do some research about free-speech zones on the Internet or in the library. Write an essay *arguing* that free-speech zones are (or are not) a legitimate way to manage free-speech issues on campus. If your own campus has free-speech zones, use it as an example to support your argument. Use other colleges and universities as examples as well. Conclude your essay with a call to action.

Writing Assignments Combining Patterns of Development

3. What procedures has your college or university established so that people can file grievances if they feel they have been the targets of hate speech or have been discriminated against in some way? In an essay, describe this *process* and indicate whether you feel it is adequate and appropriate. If it isn't, explain what steps need to be taken to improve the procedures. Provide *examples* to illustrate your point of view.

4. Stereotyping isn't restricted to minorities. Most of us have felt unfairly stereotyped at some time or another, perhaps because of gender, physical or intellectual abilities, or even a hobby or interest. Write an essay *recounting* a time you were treated unfairly or cruelly because of some personal characteristic. Be sure to show how the event *affected* you. The following essays will provide insight into the potentially corrosive effect of labels and stereotypes: Audre Lorde's "The Fourth of July" (page 127) and Roberto Rodriguez's "The Border on Our Backs" (page 418).

Writing Assignment Using a Journal Entry as a Starting Point

5. Write an editorial for your college newspaper arguing that a college campus is *or* is not the place to air conflicting, even inflammatory views about *one* of the controversial issues listed in your pre-reading journal entry. Perhaps you feel that the issue warrants a public forum in one campus setting but not another. If so, explain why. To lend authority to your position, interview students who don't share your point of view. Be sure to acknowledge their position in your editorial.

Anna Quindlen

Writer Anna Quindlen was born in Philadelphia, Pennsylvania, in 1952, and now lives in New York City. While attending Barnard College, she worked as a copy girl at *The New York Times*. After graduating, Quindlen was a reporter for *The New York Post* before returning to the *Times* in 1977. At the *Times* she eventually became a regular op-ed columnist, winning the Pulitzer Prize for Commentary in 1992. In 1995 Quindlen left newspaper work and devoted herself primarily to fiction. She has written novels, nonfiction, self-help books, and children's books. Quindlen also wrote regularly for *Newsweek*, where this article appeared on June 11, 2007.

Pre-Reading Journal Entry

Getting a driver's license is an important rite of passage for young people in the United States. It's often preceded by a highly stressful process of learning to drive. Recall your own driving lessons and licensing tests. Who taught you to drive? What were the lessons like? What emotions did you experience while learning to drive and taking your driving test? If you do not know how to drive, why not? How do you feel about not having a driver's license? Use your journal to answer these questions.

Driving to the Funeral

The four years of high school grind inexorably to a close, the milestones   1
passed. The sports contests, the SATs, the exams, the elections, the dances, the proms. And too often, the funerals. It's become a sad rite of passage in many American communities, the services held for teenagers killed in auto accidents before they've even scored a tassel to hang from the rearview mirror. The hearse moves in procession followed by the late-model compact cars of young people, boys trying to control trembling lower lips and girls sobbing into one another's shoulders. The yearbook has a picture or two with a black border. A mom and dad rise from their seats on the athletic field or in the gym to accept a diploma posthumously.

It's simple and inarguable: car crashes are the No. 1 cause of death   2
among 15- to 20-year-olds in this country. What's so peculiar about that fact is that so few adults focus on it until they are planning an untimely funeral. Put it this way: if someone told you that there was one single behavior that would be most likely to lead to the premature death of your kid, wouldn't you try to do something about that? Yet parents seem to treat the right of a 16-year-old to drive as an inalienable one, something to be neither questioned nor abridged.

This makes no sense unless the argument is convenience, and often it is.   3
In a nation that developed mass-transit amnesia and traded the exurb for the small town, a licensed son or daughter relieves parents of a relentless roundelay of driving. Soccer field, Mickey Ds, mall, movies. Of course, if that's the

rationale, why not let 13-year-olds drive? Any reasonable person would respond that a 13-year-old is too young. But statistics suggest that that's true of 16-year-olds as well. The National Highway Traffic Safety Administration has found that neophyte drivers of 17 have about a third as many accidents as their counterparts only a year younger.

In 1984 a solution was devised for the problem of teenage auto accidents   4
that lulled many parents into a false sense of security. The drinking age was raised from 18 to 21. It's become gospel that this has saved thousands of lives, although no one actually knows if that's the case; fatalities fell, but the use of seat belts and airbags may have as much to do with that as penalties for alcohol use. And there has been a pronounced negative effect on college campuses, where administrators describe a forbidden-fruit climate that encourages binge drinking. The pitchers of sangria and kegs of beer that offered legal refreshment for 18-year-olds at sanctioned campus events 30 years ago have given way to a new tradition called "pre-gaming," in which dry college activities are preceded by manic alcohol consumption at frats, dorms and bars.

Given the incidence of auto-accident deaths among teenagers despite   5
the higher drinking age, you have to ask whether the powerful lobby Mothers Against Drunk Driving simply targeted the wrong D. In a survey of young drivers, only half said they had seen a peer drive after drinking. Nearly all, however, said they had witnessed speeding, which is the leading factor in fatal crashes by teenagers today. In Europe, governments are relaxed about the drinking age but tough on driving regulations and licensing provisions; in most countries, the driving age is 18.

In America some states have taken a tough-love position and bumped up   6
the requirements for young drivers: longer permit periods, restrictions or bans on night driving. Since the greatest danger to a teenage driver is another teenager in the car—the chance of having an accident doubles with two teenage passengers and skyrockets with three or more—some new rules forbid novice drivers from transporting their peers.

In theory this sounds like a good idea; in fact it's toothless. New Jersey has   7
some of the most demanding regulations for new drivers in the nation, including a provision that until they are 18 they cannot have more than one nonfamily member in the car. Yet in early January three students leaving school in Freehold Township died in a horrific accident in which the car's 17-year-old driver was violating that regulation by carrying two friends. No wonder he took the chance: between July 2004 and November 2006, only 12 provisional drivers were ticketed for carrying too many passengers. Good law, bad enforcement.

States might make it easier on themselves, on police officers and on   8
teenagers, too, if instead of chipping away at the right to drive they merely raised the legal driving age wholesale. There are dozens of statistics to back up such a change: in Massachusetts alone, one third of 16-year-old drivers have been involved in serious accidents. Lots and lots of parents will tell you

that raising the driving age is untenable, that the kids need their freedom and their mobility. Perhaps the only ones who wouldn't make a fuss are those parents who have accepted diplomas at graduation because their children were no longer alive to do so themselves, whose children traded freedom and mobility for their lives. They might think it was worth the wait.

Questions for Close Reading

1. What is the selection's thesis? Locate the sentence(s) in which Quindlen states her main idea. If she doesn't state her thesis explicitly, express it in your own words.
2. According to Quindlen, what solutions to the problem of teenage auto accidents have not worked over the last 25 years?
3. What approach to young adults' drinking and driving do European nations take?
4. According to Quindlen, what would be a more effective solution to the problem of teen auto accidents?
5. Refer to your dictionary as needed to define the following words used in the selection: *inexorably* (paragraph 1), *posthumously* (1), *inalienable* (2), *exurb* (3), *roundelay* (3), *neophyte* (3), *sanctioned* (4), *provisional* (7), and *untenable* (8).

Questions About the Writer's Craft

1. **The pattern.** What type of audience—supportive, wavering, or hostile (see pages 359–361)—does Quindlen seem to be addressing? How can you tell?
2. **The pattern.** How effective are the statistics in this essay? Use the criteria for sound evidence on pages 34–38 to evaluate Quindlen's use of statistics.
3. **Other patterns.** What other patterns does Quindlen use in this essay? Where? What purpose do these passages serve?
4. **The pattern.** What appeals to *pathos* (see pages 358–359) does Quindlen use? How effective are they?

Writing Assignments Using Argumentation-Persuasion as a Pattern of Development

1. In paragraph 4 of her essay, Quindlen claims that raising the drinking age from 18 to 21 has had an unintended negative effect on college campuses, where binge drinking has become commonplace. Many college administrators agree with her. In fact, a hundred college and university presidents launched the Amethyst Initiative in 2008, calling for "an informed and dispassionate public debate over the effects of the 21-year-old drinking age." Although the college presidents did not actually call for lowering the drinking age, they argued that the current drinking age simply drives drinking underground, where it is more tempting for students and harder to control. Do you agree with the college presidents that the current drinking age of 21 should be reexamined and possibly lowered? Or do you disagree? Do some research on the Amethyst Initiative and the drinking age issue, and then write an essay in which you argue that the current drinking age should be lowered or should remain the same. Be sure to support your position with sound evidence (see pages 32–38).

2. Quindlen supports raising the legal driving age in order to decrease teen auto accidents, indicating that the main arguments for a low legal driving age are that it "relieves parents of an endless roundelay of driving" (paragraph 3) and that "the kids need their freedom and their mobility" (paragraph 8). Are there any other reasons that might support a low legal driving age? Write an essay opposing Quindlen's argument for a higher driving age and supporting a legal driving age of 16, with or without restrictions, depending on your view. Be sure to support your argument with reasons and examples.

Writing Assignments Combining Patterns of Development

3. Provisional driver's licenses vary from state to state, but all are designed to decrease teen auto accidents by restricting driving privileges among the youngest drivers and gradually allowing them more freedom as they get older and remain accident-free. Develop your own rules for a fair and effective provisional driver's license, and write a *process analysis* essay explaining your system. Indicate what drivers are allowed to do at various ages until they are granted full driving privileges as well as the penalties you would impose for infractions and accidents, and give *examples* to illustrate the provisions. In support of your plan, explain the beneficial *effects* that your provisional license would have on teen driving.

4. Roadside memorials that mark the sites of fatal auto accidents have become commonplace, as well as controversial, in the last twenty years. Often carefully tended by family and friends of the victim for months or years, the shrines usually consist of flowers, religious symbols, and personal mementos. Some people oppose the memorials, claiming they are dangerous distractions for drivers, obstacles for road crews, or simply illegal displays of religious symbols on public property. Look at the roadside memorials in your area, or do an image search on the Internet. What do the shrines look like? What effect do these shrines have on the victim's family? on strangers? Should they be regulated? Write an essay in which you *describe* the shrines and their effects. In your essay take a position on the memorials and argue that they should be allowed, regulated, or banned. For insights into how people deal with grief and loss, you might read Gary Kamiya's "Life, Death and Spring" (page 103) or Eric G. Wilson's "The Miracle of Melancholia" (page 180).

Writing Assignment Using a Journal Entry as a Starting Point

5. Review your pre-reading journal entry in which you describe the people, events, and emotions involved in learning to drive and getting a driver's license—or in *not* learning to drive and *not* getting a driver's license. Write an essay about experiencing—or skipping—this rite of passage. You can write a process analysis essay describing how you got a license, or a cause-effect essay explaining why you didn't get a license, or an exemplification essay in which you describe your best or worst driving lessons. Since this subject has so many possibilities, you should first narrow the focus of the essay and then decide whether you are going to inform, entertain, or persuade your audience and whether your experiences lend themselves to a serious or a humorous tone.

Gerry Garibaldi

Writer and teacher Gerry Garibaldi was born in 1951, grew up in San Francisco, and attended San Francisco State University. Following college, he worked for Paramount Pictures first as a reader and eventually as a vice president of production, which involved working with writers and directors. For the next twenty-five years he worked as an executive, a freelance writer for film studios, and a journalist. Then Garibaldi changed careers, moving to Connecticut, with his wife and children, to teach high school English. This article was published in *City Journal*, an urban policy quarterly, in summer 2006.

Pre-Reading Journal Entry

Think back to your own high school days. Recall how boys and girls were treated in school and how they behaved. Did you notice any differences in the way boys and girls were treated by teachers? In the way they behaved in class? In your journal, record some of the differences between the sexes that you noted. To what extent was your own behavior as a high school student influenced by your gender?

How the Schools Shortchange Boys

In the newly feminized classroom, boys tune out.   1

Since I started teaching several years ago, after 25 years in the movie   2
business, I've come to learn firsthand that everything I'd heard about the
feminization of our schools is real—and far more pernicious to boys than I
had imagined. Christina Hoff Sommers was absolutely accurate in describing, in her 2000 bestseller, *The War Against Boys*, how feminist complaints
that girls were "losing their voice" in a male-oriented classroom have
prompted the educational establishment to turn the schools upside down to
make them more girl-friendly, to the detriment of males.

As a result, boys have become increasingly disengaged. Only 65 percent   3
earned high school diplomas in the class of 2003, compared with 72 percent
of girls, education researcher Jay Greene recently documented. Girls now so
outnumber boys on most university campuses across the country that some
schools, like Kenyon College, have even begun to practice affirmative action
for boys in admissions. And as in high school, girls are getting better grades
and graduating at a higher rate.

As Sommers understood, it is boys' aggressive and rationalist nature—   4
redefined by educators as a behavioral disorder—that's getting so many of
them in trouble in the feminized schools. Their problem: they don't want to
be girls.

Take my tenth-grade student Brandon. I noted that he was on the no-   5
pass list again, after three consecutive days in detention for being disruptive.
"Who gave it to you this time?" I asked, passing him on my way out.

403

"Waverly," he muttered into the long folding table.   6

"What for?"   7

"Just asking a question," he replied.   8

"No," I corrected him. "You said"—and here I mimicked his voice—   9
" 'Why do we have to do this crap anyway?' Right?"

Brandon recalls one of those sweet, ruby-cheeked boys you often see   10
depicted on English porcelain.

He's smart, precocious, and—according to his special-education pro-   11
file—has been "behaviorally challenged" since fifth grade. The special-ed
classification is the bane of the modern boy. To teachers, it's a yellow flag
that snaps out at you the moment you open a student's folder. More than
any other factor, it has determined Brandon's and legions of other boys'
troubled tenures as students.

Brandon's current problem began because Ms. Waverly, his social stud-   12
ies teacher, failed to answer one critical question: What was the point of the
lesson she was teaching? One of the first observations I made as a teacher was
that boys invariably ask this question, while girls seldom do. When a teacher
assigns a paper or a project, girls will obediently flip their notebooks open
and jot down the due date. Teachers love them. God loves them. Girls are
calm and pleasant. They succeed through cooperation.

Boys will pin you to the wall like a moth. They want a rational explanation   13
for everything. If unconvinced by your reasons—or if you don't bother to offer
any—they slouch contemptuously in their chairs, beat their pencils, or watch
the squirrels outside the window. Two days before the paper is due, girls are
handing in the finished product in neat vinyl folders with colorful clip-art title
pages. It isn't until the boys notice this that the alarm sounds. "Hey, you never
told us 'bout a paper! What paper?! I want to see my fucking counselor!"

A female teacher, especially if she has no male children of her own, I've   14
noticed, will tend to view boys' penchant for challenging classroom assignments as disruptive, disrespectful—rude. In my experience, notes home and
parent-teacher conferences almost always concern a boy's behavior in class,
usually centering on this kind of conflict. In today's feminized classroom,
with its "cooperative learning" and "inclusiveness," a student's demand for
assurance of a worthwhile outcome for his effort isn't met with a reasonable
explanation but is considered inimical to the educational process. Yet it's this
very trait, innate to boys and men, that helps explain male success in the hard
sciences, math, and business.

The difference between the male and female predilection for hard proof   15
shows up among the teachers, too. In my second year of teaching, I attended
a required seminar on "differentiated instruction," a teaching model that is the
current rage in the fickle world of pop education theory. The method addresses the need to teach all students in a classroom where academic abilities vary
greatly—where there is "heterogeneous grouping," to use the ed-school

jargon—meaning kids with IQs of 55 sit side by side with the gifted. The theory goes that the "least restrictive environment" is best for helping the intellectually challenged. The teacher's job is to figure out how to dice up his daily lessons to address every perceived shortcoming and disability in the classroom.

After the lecture, we broke into groups of five, with instructions to work cooperatively to come up with a model lesson plan for just such a classroom situation. My group had two men and three women. The women immediately set to work; my seasoned male cohort and I reclined sullenly in our chairs.   16

"Are the women going to do all the work?" one of the women inquired brightly after about ten minutes.   17

"This is baloney," my friend declared, yawning, as he chucked the seminar handout into a row of empty plastic juice bottles. "We wouldn't have this problem if we grouped kids by ability, like we used to."   18

The women, all dedicated teachers, understood this, too. But that wasn't the point. Treating people as equals was a social goal well worth pursuing. And we contentious boys were just too dumb to get it.   19

Female approval has a powerful effect on the male psyche. Kindness, consideration, and elevated moral purpose have nothing to do with an irreducible proof, of course. Yet we male teachers squirm when women point out our moral failings—and our boy students do, too. This is the virtue that has helped women redefine the mission of education.   20

The notion of male ethical inferiority first arises in grammar school, where women make up the overwhelming majority of teachers. It's here that the alphabet soup of supposed male dysfunctions begins. And make no mistake: while girls occasionally exhibit symptoms of male-related disorders in this world, females diagnosed with learning disabilities simply don't exist.   21

For a generation now, many well-meaning parents, worn down by their boy's failure to flourish in school, his poor self-esteem and unhappiness, his discipline problems, decide to accept administration recommendations to have him tested for disabilities. The pitch sounds reasonable: admission into special ed qualifies him for tutoring, modified lessons, extra time on tests (including the SAT), and other supposed benefits. It's all a hustle, Mom and Dad privately advise their boy. Don't worry about it. We know there's nothing wrong with you.   22

To get into special ed, however, administrators must find something wrong. In my four years of teaching, I've never seen them fail. In the first IEP (Individualized Educational Program) meeting, the boy and his parents learn the results of disability testing. When the boy hears from three smiling adults that he does indeed have a learning disability, his young face quivers like Jell-O. For him, it was never a hustle. From then on, however, his expectations of himself—and those of his teachers—plummet.   23

Special ed is the great spangled elephant in the education parade. Each   24
year, it grows larger and more lumbering, drawing more and more boys into
the procession. Since the publication of Sommers's book, it has grown tenfold.
Special ed now is the single largest budget item, outside of basic operations, in
most school districts across the country.

Special-ed boosters like to point to the success that boys enjoy after they   25
begin the program. Their grades rise, and the phone calls home cease. Anxious
parents feel reassured that progress is happening. In truth, I have rarely seen
any real improvement in a student's performance after he's become a special-
ed kid. On my first day of teaching, I received manila folders for all five of my
special-ed students—boys all—with a score of modifications that I had to make
in each day's lesson plan.

I noticed early on that my special-ed boys often sat at their desks with   26
their heads down or casually staring off into space, as if tracking motes in
their eyes, while I proceeded with my lesson. A special-ed caseworker would
arrive, take their assignments, and disappear with the boys into the resource
room. The students would return the next day with completed assignments.

"Did you do this yourself?" I'd ask, dubious.   27

They assured me that they did. I became suspicious, however, when I   28
noticed that they couldn't perform the same work on their own, away from the
resource room. A special-ed caseworker's job is to keep her charges from failing.
A failure invites scrutiny and reams of paperwork. The caseworkers do their jobs.

Brandon has been on the special-ed track since he was nine. He knows   29
his legal rights as well as his caseworkers do. And he plays them ruthlessly. In
every debate I have with him about his low performance, Brandon delicate-
ly threads his response with the very sinews that bind him. After a particularly easy midterm, I made him stay after class to explain his failure.

"An 'F'?!" I said, holding the test under his nose.   30

"You were supposed to modify that test," he countered coolly. "I only   31
had to answer nine of the 27 questions. The nine I did are all right."

His argument is like a piece of fine crystal that he rolls admiringly in his   32
hand. He demands that I appreciate the elegance of his position. I do, particularly because my own is so weak.

Yet while the process of education may be deeply absorbing to Brandon,   33
he long ago came to dismiss the content entirely. For several decades, white
Anglo-Saxon males—Brandon's ancestors—have faced withering assault
from feminism- and multiculturalism-inspired education specialists. Armed
with a spiteful moral rectitude, their goal is to sever his historical reach, to
defame, cover over, dilute…and then reconstruct.

In today's politically correct textbooks, Nikki Giovanni and Toni   34
Morrison stand shoulder-to-shoulder with Mark Twain, William Faulkner,
and Charles Dickens, even though both women are second-raters at best.
But even in their superficial aspects, the textbooks advertise publishers'

intent to pander to the prevailing PC[1] attitudes. The books feature page after page of healthy, exuberant young girls in winning portraits. Boys (white boys in particular) will more often than not be shunted to the background in photos or be absent entirely or appear sitting in wheelchairs.

The underlying message isn't lost on Brandon. His keen young mind   35
reads between the lines and perceives the folly of all that he's told to accept. Because he lacks an adult perspective, however, what he cannot grasp is the ruthlessness of the war that the education reformers have waged. Often when he provokes, it's simple boyish tit for tat.

A week ago, I dispatched Brandon to the library with directions to   36
choose a book for his novel assignment. He returned minutes later with his choice and a twinkling smile.

"I got a grreat book, Mr. Garibaldi!" he said, holding up an old, bleary,   37
clothbound item. "Can I read the first page aloud, pahlease?"

My mind buzzed like a fly, trying to discover some hint of mischief.   38

"Who's the author?"   39

"Ah, Joseph Conrad," he replied, consulting the frontispiece. "Can I?   40
Huh, huh, huh?"

"I guess so."   41

Brandon eagerly stood up before the now-alert class of mostly black and   42
Puerto Rican faces, adjusted his shoulders as if straightening a prep-school blazer, then intoned solemnly: "*The Nigger of the 'Narcissus'*"—twinkle, twinkle, twinkle. "Chapter one...."

Merry mayhem ensued. Brandon had one of his best days of the year.   43

Boys today feel isolated and outgunned, but many, like Brandon, don't lack pluck and courage. They often seem to have more of it than their parents, who writhe uncomfortably before a system steeled in the armor of "social conscience." The game, parents whisper to themselves, is to play along, to maneuver, to outdistance your rival. Brandon's struggle is an honest one: to preserve truth and his own integrity.

Boys who get a compartment on the special-ed train take the ride to its   44
end without looking out the window. They wait for the moment when they can step out and scorn the rattletrap that took them nowhere. At the end of the line, some, like Brandon, may have forged the resiliency of survival. But that's not what school is for.

———————————

[1]Short for "politically correct," usually used pejoratively (editors' note).

Questions for Close Reading

1. What is the selection's thesis? Locate the sentence(s) in which Garibaldi states his main idea. If he doesn't state his thesis explicitly, express it in your own words.
2. According to Garibaldi, how do boys and girls—and men and women—react to being given an assignment?

3. Why are so many boys tested for disabilities, according to Garibaldi?
4. How does Garibaldi's student Brandon take advantage of his special education designation?
5. Refer to your dictionary as needed to define the following words used in the selection: *pernicious* (paragraph 1), *disengaged* (2), *rationalist* (4), *precocious* (11), *bane* (11), *penchant* (14), *inimical* (14), *predilection* (15), *heterogeneous* (15), *cohort* (16), *contentious* (19), *irreducible* (20), *plummet* (23), *motes* (26), *withering* (33), *rectitude* (33), *pander* (34), *resiliency* (45).

Questions About the Writer's Craft

1. **The pattern.** What types of evidence does Garibaldi use in this essay? How effective is his evidence in supporting his argument?
2. **Other patterns.** Garibaldi uses a lot of cause-effect, comparison-contrast, and process analysis in this essay. Identify passages in which these patterns are used.
3. The first sentence in the essay is a strongly worded declaration: "In the newly feminized classroom, boys tune out." Where else does Garibaldi use such strongly worded statements? What is the effect of this style?
4. Where does Garibaldi use vulgar or offensive language? What effect, if any, does this have on his argument?

Writing Assignments Using Argumentation-Persuasion as a Pattern of Development

1. Read Michael Kimmel's "A War Against Boys?" (page 410), an essay that takes exception to Garibaldi's view of boys' education. Decide which writer presents his case more convincingly. Then write an essay arguing that the *other writer* has trouble making a strong case for his position. Consider the merits and flaws (including any logical fallacies) in the argument, plus such issues as the writer's credibility, strategies for dealing with the opposing view, and use of emotional appeals. Throughout, support your opinion with specific examples drawn from the selection. Keep in mind that you are critiquing the effectiveness of the writer's argument. It's not appropriate, then, simply to explain why you agree or disagree with the writer's position or merely to summarize what the writer says.
2. Although Garibaldi argues forcefully that boys are shortchanged by the "feminization" of education and the special education system, he does not propose any changes to improve the way boys are educated. How might public elementary, middle, and high school education be changed so that boys flourish? What activities or subjects would help boys in school? Using Garibaldi's essay as a take-off point, write an essay in which you argue for changes in education that would benefit boys.

Writing Assignments Combining Patterns of Development

3. As Garibaldi puts it, "Special ed is the great spangled elephant in the education parade." He is correct in asserting that the number of children in special education, and the amount spent to educate them, have increased dramatically in recent

years. Brainstorm with others to identify *factors* that might be contributing to this growth; then do some research on the history of special education and current trends. Focusing on several related factors, write an essay showing how these factors contribute to the problem. Possible factors include the following: increases in the number of diagnoses of learning disabilities and autism; lack of standards for determining who needs special education; assigning all low-achieving students to special education whether or not they have a disability; racism; financial incentives for school districts to increase special education enrollment. At the end of the essay, offer some recommendations about *steps* that can be taken to ensure that only children who need it are assigned to special education.

4. In paragraph 34, Garibaldi refers to "politically correct textbooks" and "PC attitudes." What does the phrase "politically correct" mean to you? What are its connotations? Write an essay in which you *define* "political correctness." Be sure to give examples to support your definition. Before you start, decide whether the purpose of your essay is to inform, persuade, or entertain, and approach your definition accordingly. You might find that Leslie Savan's "Black Talk and Pop Culture" (page 171) has interesting insights about how we use language.

Writing Assignment Using a Journal Entry as a Starting Point

5. Review your pre-reading journal entry about differences between how boys and girls were treated in high school, and how they behaved. How do your recollections compare with Garibaldi's observations? Do they support his position, or undermine it? Write an essay in which you summarize and respond to Garibaldi's argument based on your own experiences and observations of high school. Be sure to give specific examples of your points.

Michael Kimmel

Michael Kimmel is a professor of sociology at State University of New York at Stonybrook and one of the world's leading researchers in gender studies. Born in New York City in 1951, he attended Vassar College and received a master's degree from Brown University and a Ph.D. from the University of California at Berkeley. He is the author or editor of more than twenty volumes on men and masculinity, including *Manhood in America: A Cultural History* (1996) and his latest work, *Guyland: The Perilous World Where Boys Become Men* (2008). His articles appear in dozens of magazines, newspapers, and scholarly journals, and he lectures extensively. The following piece was excerpted from an article published in Fall 2006 issue of *Dissent Magazine*.

Pre-Reading Journal Entry

The phrase "boys will be boys" is often cited to explain certain types of male behavior. What kinds of actions typically fall in this category? List a few of them in your journal. Which behaviors are positive? Why? Which are negative? Why?

A War Against Boys?

Doug Anglin isn't likely to flash across the radar screen at an Ivy League admissions office. A seventeen-year-old senior at Milton High School, a suburb outside Boston, Anglin has a B-minus average and plays soccer and baseball. But he's done something that millions of other teenagers haven't: he's sued his school district for sex discrimination.

Anglin's lawsuit, brought with the aid of his father, a Boston lawyer, claims that schools routinely discriminate against males. "From the elementary level, they establish a philosophy that if you sit down, follow orders, and listen to what they say, you'll do well and get good grades," he told a journalist. "Men naturally rebel against this." He may have a point: overworked teachers might well look more kindly on classroom docility and decorum. But his proposed remedies—such as raising boys' grades retroactively—are laughable.

And though it's tempting to parse the statements of a mediocre high school senior—what's so "natural" about rebelling against blindly following orders, a military tactician might ask—Anglin's apparent admissions angle is but the latest skirmish of a much bigger battle in the culture wars. The current salvos concern boys. The "trouble with boys" has become a staple on talk-radio, the cover story in *Newsweek*, and the subject of dozens of columns in newspapers and magazines. And when the First Lady offers a helping hand to boys, you know something political is in the works. "Rescuing" boys actually translates into bashing feminism.

There is no doubt that boys are not faring well in school. From elementary schools to high schools they have lower grades, lower class rank, and fewer honors than girls. They're 50 percent more likely to repeat a grade in elementary school, one-third more likely to drop out of high school, and about six times more likely to be diagnosed with attention deficit and hyper-activity disorder (ADHD).

College statistics are similar—if the boys get there at all. Women now constitute the majority of students on college campuses, having passed men in 1982, so that in eight years women will earn 58 percent of bachelor's degrees in U.S. colleges. One expert, Tom Mortensen, warns that if current trends continue, "the graduation line in 2068 will be all females." Mortensen may be a competent higher education policy analyst, but he's a lousy statis-tician. His dire prediction is analogous to predicting forty years ago that, if the enrollment of black students at Ol' Miss was one in 1964, and, say, two hundred in 1968 and one thousand in 1976, then "if present trends contin-ue" there would be no white students on campus by 1982. Doomsayers lament that women now outnumber men in the social and behavioral sci-ences by about three to one, and that they've invaded such traditionally male bastions as engineering (where they now make up 20 percent) and biology and business (virtually par).   5

These three issues—declining numbers, declining achievement, and increasingly problematic behavior—form the empirical basis of the current debate. But its political origins are significantly older and ominously more familiar. Peeking underneath the empirical façade helps explain much of the current lineup.   6

Why now?   7

If boys are doing worse, whose fault is it? To many of the current crit-ics, it's women's fault, either as feminists, as mothers, or as both. Feminists, we read, have been so successful that the earlier "chilly classroom climate" has now become overheated to the detriment of boys. Feminist-inspired programs have enabled a whole generation of girls to enter the sciences, medicine, law, and the professions; to continue their education; to imagine careers outside the home. But in so doing, these same feminists have pathol-ogized boyhood. Elementary schools are, we read, "anti-boy"—emphasiz-ing reading and restricting the movements of young boys. They "feminize" boys, forcing active, healthy, and naturally exuberant boys to conform to a regime of obedience, "pathologizing what is simply normal for boys," as one psychologist puts it. Schools are an "inhospitable" environment for boys, writes Christina Hoff Sommers, where their natural propensities for rough-and-tumble play, competition, aggression, and rambunctious vio-lence are cast as social problems in the making. Michael Gurian argues in *The Wonder of Boys,* that, with testosterone surging through their little limbs, we demand that they sit still, raise their hands, and take naps. We're giving them the message, he says, that "boyhood is defective." By the time they get to college, they've been steeped in anti-male propaganda. "Why   8 would any self-respecting boy want to attend one of America's increasingly feminized universities?" asks George Gilder in *National Review*. The American university is now a "fluffy pink playpen of feminist studies and agitprop 'herstory,' taught amid a green goo of eco-motherism..." [author's ellipsis].

Such claims sound tinnily familiar. At the turn of the last century, cultural critics were concerned that the rise of white-collar businesses meant increasing indolence for men, whose sons were being feminized by mothers and female teachers. Then, as now, the solutions were to find arenas in which boys could simply be boys, and where men could be men as well. So fraternal lodges offered men a homo-social sanctuary, and dude ranches and sports provided a place where these sedentary men could experience what Theodore Roosevelt called the strenuous life. Boys could troop off with the Boy Scouts, designed as a fin-de-siècle "boys' liberation movement." Modern society was turning hardy, robust boys, as Boy Scouts' founder Ernest Thompson Seton put it, into "a lot of flat chested cigarette smokers with shaky nerves and doubtful vitality." Today, women teachers are once again to blame for boys' feminization. "It's the teacher's job to create a classroom environment that accommodates both male and female energy, not just mainly female energy," explains Gurian.

What's wrong with this picture? Well, for one thing, it creates a false opposition between girls and boys, assuming that educational reforms undertaken to enable girls to perform better hinder boys' educational development. But these reforms—new classroom arrangements, teacher training, increased attentiveness to individual learning styles—actually enable larger numbers of boys to get a better education. Thought the current boy advocates claim that schools used to be more "boy friendly" before all these "feminist" reforms, they obviously didn't go to school in those halcyon days, the 1950s, say, when the classroom was far more regimented, corporal punishment common, and teachers far more authoritarian; they even gave grades for "deportment." Rambunctious boys were simply not tolerated; they dropped out.

Gender stereotyping hurts both boys and girls. If there is a zero-sum game, it's not because of some putative feminization of the classroom. The net effect of the No Child Left Behind Act has been zero-sum competition, as school districts scramble to stretch inadequate funding, leaving them little choice but to cut noncurricular programs so as to ensure that curricular mandates are followed. This disadvantages "rambunctious" boys, because many of these programs are after-school athletics, gym, and recess. And cutting "unnecessary" school counselors and other remedial programs also disadvantages boys, who compose the majority of children in behavioral and remedial educational programs. The problem of inadequate school funding lies not at feminists' door, but in the halls of Congress. This is further compounded by changes in the insurance industry, which often pressure therapists to put children on medication for ADHD rather than pay for expensive therapy.

Another problem is that the frequently cited numbers are misleading. More people—that is, males and females—are going to college than ever before. In 1960, 54 percent of boys and 38 percent of girls went directly to college; today the numbers are 64 percent of boys and 70 percent of girls. It is true that the rate of increase among girls is higher than the rate of increase among boys, but the numbers are increasing for both.   12

The gender imbalance does not obtain at the nation's most elite colleges and universities, where percentages for men and women are, and have remained, similar. Of the top colleges and universities in the nation, only Stanford sports a fifty-fifty gender balance. Harvard[1] and Amherst enroll 56 percent men, Princeton and Chicago 54 percent men, Duke and Berkeley 52 percent, and Yale 51 percent. In science and engineering, the gender imbalance still tilts decidedly toward men: Cal Tech is 65 percent male and 35 percent female; MIT is 62 percent male, 38 percent female.   13

And the imbalance is not uniform across class and race. It remains the case that far more working-class women—of all races—go to college than do working-class men. Part of this is a seemingly rational individual decision: a college-educated woman still earns about the same as a high-school educated man, $35,000 to $31,000. By race, the disparities are more starkly drawn. Among middle-class, white, high school graduates going to college this year, half are male and half are female. But only 37 percent of black college students and 45 percent of Hispanic students are male. The numerical imbalance turns out to be more a problem of race and class than gender. It is what Cynthia Fuchs Epstein calls a "deceptive distinction"—a difference that appears to be about gender, but is actually about something else.   14

Why don't the critics acknowledge these race and class differences? To many who now propose to "rescue" boys, such differences are incidental because, in their eyes, all boys are the same aggressive, competitive, rambunctious little devils. They operate from a facile, and inaccurate, essentialist dichotomy between males and females. Boys must be allowed to be boys—so that they grow up to be men.   15

This facile biologism leads the critics to propose some distasteful remedies to allow these testosterone-juiced boys to express themselves. Gurian, for example, celebrates all masculine rites of passage, "like military boot camp, fraternity hazings, graduation day, and bar mitzvah" as "essential parts of every boy's life." He also suggests reviving corporal punishment, both at home and at school—but only when administered privately with cool indifference and never in the heat of adult anger. He calls it "spanking responsibly," though I suspect school boards and child welfare agencies might have another term for it.   16

[1]Harvard University now enrolls more women than men (author's note).

But what boys need turns out to be pretty much what girls need. In their   17
best-selling *Raising Cain,* Michael Thompson and Dan Kindlon describe
boys' needs: to be loved, get sex, and not be hurt. Parents are counseled
to allow boys their emotions; accept a high level of activity; speak their
language; and treat them with respect. They are to teach the many ways a boy
can be a man, use discipline to guide and build, and model manhood as emotionally attached. Aside from the obvious tautologies, what they advocate is
exactly what feminists have been advocating for girls for some time....

How does a focus on the ideology of masculinity explain what is happen-   18
ing to boys in school? Consider the parallel for girls. Carol Gilligan's work on
adolescent girls describes how these assertive, confident, and proud young
girls "lose their voices" when they hit adolescence. At that same moment,
Pollack[2] notes, boys become more confident, even beyond their abilities. You
might even say that boys find their voices, but it is the inauthentic voice of
bravado, posturing, foolish risk-taking, and gratuitous violence. He calls it
"the boy code." The boy code teaches them that they are supposed to be in
power, and so they begin to act as if they are. They "ruffle in a manly pose,"
as William Butler Yeats[3] once put it, "for all their timid heart."

In adolescence, both boys and girls get their first real dose of gender   19
inequality: girls suppress ambition, boys inflate it. Recent research on the
gender gap in school achievement bears this out. Girls are more likely to
undervalue their abilities, especially in the more traditionally "masculine"
educational arenas such as math and science. Only the most able and most
secure girls take courses in those fields. Thus, their numbers tend to be few,
and their mean test scores high. Boys, however, possessed of this false voice
of bravado (and facing strong family pressure) are likely to overvalue their
abilities, to remain in programs though they are less capable of succeeding.

This difference, and not some putative discrimination against boys, is   20
the reason that girls' mean test scores in math and science are now, on average, approaching that of boys. Too many boys remain in difficult math and
science courses longer than they should; they pull the boys' mean scores
down. By contrast, the smaller number of girls, whose abilities and self-
esteem are sufficient to enable them to "trespass" into a male domain, skew
female data upward.

A parallel process is at work in the humanities and social sciences. Girls'   21
mean test scores in English and foreign languages, for example, outpace
those of boys. But this is not the result of "reverse discrimination"; it is
because the boys bump up against the norms of masculinity. Boys regard
English as a "feminine" subject. Pioneering research by Wayne Martino in
Australia and Britain found that boys avoid English because of what it might

[2]William Pollack, author of *Real Boys* (editors' note).
[3]Yeats (1865–1939) was a major Irish poet and playwright (editors' note).

say about their (inauthentic) masculine pose. "Reading is lame, sitting down and looking at words is pathetic," commented one boy. "Most guys who like English are faggots." The traditional liberal arts curriculum, as it was before feminism, is seen as feminizing. As Catharine Stimpson[4] recently put it, "Real men don't speak French."

Boys tend to hate English and foreign languages for the same reasons   22
that girls love them. In English, they observe, there are no hard-and-fast rules, one expresses one's opinion about the topic and everyone's opinion is equally valued. "The answer can be a variety of things, you're never really wrong," observed one boy. "It's not like maths and science where there is one set answer to everything." Another boy noted:

> I find English hard. It's because there are no set rules for reading   23
> texts...[author's ellipsis]. English isn't like maths where you have
> rules on how to do things and where there are right and wrong
> answers. In English you have to write down how you feel and
> that's what I don't like.

Compare this to the comments of girls in the same study: 24

> I feel motivated to study English because...[author's ellipsis] you   25
> have freedom in English—unlike subjects such as maths and sci-
> ence—and your view isn't necessarily wrong. There is no definite
> right or wrong answer, and you have the freedom to say what you
> feel is right without it being rejected as a wrong answer.

It is not the school experience that "feminizes" boys, but rather the ideolo-   26
gy of traditional masculinity that keeps boys from wanting to succeed. "The work you do here is girls' work," one boy commented to a researcher. "It's not real work."

"Real work" involves a confrontation—not with feminist women, whose   27
sensible educational reforms have opened countless doors to women while closing off none to men—but with an anachronistic definition of masculini-ty that stresses many of its vices (anti-intellectualism, entitlement, arrogance, and aggression) but few of its virtues. When the self-appointed rescuers demand that we accept boys' "hardwiring," could they possibly have such a monochromatic and relentlessly negative view of male biology? Maybe they do. But simply shrugging our collective shoulders in resignation and saying "boys will be boys" sets the bar much too low. Boys can do better than that. They can be men.

---

[4]Stimpson, a professor of English at New York University, has written about women in culture and society (editors' note).

Perhaps the real "male bashers" are those who promise to rescue boys   28
from the clutches of feminists. Are males not also "hardwired" toward compassion, nurturing, and love? If not, would we allow males to be parents? It is
never a biological question of whether we are "hardwired" for some behavior;
it is, rather, a political question of which "hardwiring" we choose to respect
and which we choose to challenge....

Questions for Close Reading

1. What is the selection's thesis? Locate the sentence(s) in which Kimmel states his
   main idea. If he doesn't state his thesis explicitly, express it in your own words.
2. How does Kimmel interpret the statistics that show that more girls than boys go
   to college?
3. According to Kimmel, how do girls and boys change when they reach adolescence?
4. What does Kimmel mean by the phrase " 'the boy code' " (paragraph 18)?
5. Refer to your dictionary as needed to define the following words used in the selection: *docility* (paragraph 2), *parse* (3), *bastions* (5), *par* (5), *pathologized* (8),
   indolence (9), *sedentary* (9), *halcyon* (10), *deportment* (10), *rambunctious* (10),
   zero-sum (11), *putative* (11), *facile* (15), *biologism* (16), *tautologies* (17), and
   anachronistic (27).

Questions About the Writer's Craft

1. **The pattern.** What strategy does Kimmel use in the opening paragraphs of his
   essay? Is it effective?
2. **The pattern.** What is the purpose of paragraphs 4–6? Paragraphs 7–9? Where does
   Kimmel start presenting his own view of the causes of boys' difficulty in school?
3. **Other patterns.** What is the main pattern, other than argumentation-persuasion,
   that is used in this essay? Give specific examples.
4. Reread the biographical sketch of Kimmel on page 410. How does Kimmel's
   background contribute to the *ethos* of this argument? Does it influence your
   response to his claims?

Writing Assignments Using Argumentation-Persuasion
as a Pattern of Development

1. Both Garibaldi and Kimmel focus primarily on how gender inequality affects boys,
   but gender inequality affects girls as well (see Kimmel, paragraphs 19 and following). Write an essay in which you argue that gender roles and norms limit (or do
   not limit) what women can accomplish in school and in their careers.
2. Kimmel criticizes those who claim that biology, or inborn traits, are primarily
   responsible for shaping gender differences. He believes that biological differences
   may exist, but that the environment, including political and cultural forces, have
   a strong influence. Write an essay arguing your own position about the role that
   biology and environment play in determining sex-role attitudes and behaviors.
   Remember to acknowledge opposing views and to defend your own position with

examples based on your experiences and observations. Amy Sutherland's "What Shamu Taught Me About a Happy Marriage" (page 250) and Dave Barry's "Beauty and the Beast" (page 284) may give you some humorous insights on this subject.

Writing Assignments Combining Patterns of Development

3. Feminism is mentioned throughout Garibaldi's and Kimmel's essays, but neither of them defines the term. Do some research in the library and/or on the Internet about the history of feminism. Brainstorm with others—both men and women—about the topic, and write an essay in which you *define* feminism. Be sure to give *examples* of what you mean by feminism, either from your own experience or from history.

4. According to Kimmel, gender differences become more defined during adolescence, when the "boy code"—and, correspondingly, the "girl code"—begin to influence attitudes and behaviors. Look back on your own adolescence and your experiences of gender differences, and write an essay in which you *describe* the "boy code" and the "girl code" and how they affected you and your friends. *Compare and contrast* boys' and girls' attitudes and behaviors, and give *examples* to support your points.

Writing Assignment Using a Journal Entry as a Starting Point

5. In paragraph 27, Kimmel says, "Saying 'boys will be boys' sets the bar much too low. Boys can do better than that. They can be men." Kimmel clearly believes that "boys will be boys" behavior should be discouraged; yet others believe such behavior is natural and therefore acceptable. What do you think? Drawing upon your pre-reading journal entry, write an essay taking a position on this issue. Provide persuasive examples to support your viewpoint, refuting as much of the opposing argument as you can. Discussing this type of gendered behavior with others and doing some research in the library and/or on the Internet will broaden your understanding of this issue.

Roberto Rodriguez

Roberto Rodriguez was born in 1954 in Aguacalientes, Mexico, and raised in East Los Angeles. In 1972, he began his journalism career at *La Gente,* a newspaper at the University of California, Los Angeles. He has written for many publications, including *Black Issues in Higher Education, Lowrider* magazine, the *Eastside Sun* (Los Angeles), and *La Opinion,* the largest Spanish-language daily newspaper in the United States. In addition, Rodriguez's columns have been syndicated in *The Washington Post, The Los Angeles Times,* and *USA Today.* Since 1994, he and his wife, Patrisia Gonzales, have written "Column of the Americas," a blog that focuses on current issues from the perspective of indigenous peoples. Two books he wrote about police brutality were published under one title, *Justice: A Question of Race* (1997). In 2002, Rodriguez and Gonzales were named Distinguished Community Scholars at the Cesar Chavez Center at UCLA, where they are establishing the discipline of indigenous studies. The following article was posted on the "Column of the Americas" website, www.voznuestra.com/Americas, on April 17, 2006.

Pre-Reading Journal Entry

Do you think that schools should engage in discussions of immigration, ethnicity, and racism, which can be sensitive and painful topics? Why do you feel as you do? Would such discussions be appropriate at some levels of school but not at others? Take some time to explore these questions in your journal.

The Border on Our Backs

Look up the word *Mexican* or *Central American* in any U.S. political dictionary and you will find these definitions:

> 1) people who are illegal, or are treated as such, no matter how long they've been living in this country; 2) the nation's number one threat to homeland security; 3) people who do the jobs no Americans want and who threaten the American Way of Life; 4) as a result of extremist politicians, the nation's favorite scapegoats; and 5) people, who due to vicious anti-immigrant hysteria, are prone to become Democrats.

By next year, there may be two new entries: 6) Peoples who carry the border on their backs, and 7) peoples not afraid to stand up for their rights.

Who could have predicted that millions of peoples would be taking to the streets nationwide to protest draconian immigration bills that call for the building of Berlin-style walls, more *migra,*[1] massive repatriations, the

---

[1]Mexican term for "immigration police" (editors' note).

criminalization of human beings and the creation of a new anti-family apartheid-style Bracero[2] or Guest Worker program? Beyond the bills, the protests are actually about asserting the right—virtually a cry—to be treated as full human beings.

How long was this community supposed to remain in silence?   4

Perhaps it is racial/cultural fatigue.   5

Let's not pretend that this hysteria is not about race, color and dehumanization. It's not even anti-immigrant or even anti-Latino/Hispanic bigotry. It's the exploitation of a deep-seated fear and loathing of Mexicans and Central Americans by shameless politicians. Why? Because of what our color represents. Otherwise, how and why do government agents single us out at lines, borders and internal checkpoints? Otherwise, why do dragnet immigrant raids always target brown peoples? Why is all the hate and vilification directed at brown peoples and the southern border? Otherwise, why are these politicians also not bothered by the millions of Canadians, Europeans or Russians who overstay their visas? (No one should hate them either.)   6

Just what does brown represent in this country? Shall we delude ourselves like the Census Bureau and pretend that we're actually White?   7

Or should we simply stop speaking our languages, stop eating our own foods...and stop identifying with our home countries of Mexico, El Salvador, Guatemala, Peru, Colombia, etc. In other words, we're OK if we stop being who we are—if we culturally deport ourselves and conduct auto ethnic cleansing campaigns (we're also OK if we fight their illegal permanent wars).   8

And yet, there's that small matter of our red-brown skin. Just what could it possibly represent? A reminder? Memory? Might it be our thousands-of-years old Indigenous cultures—the ones that were supposedly obliterated—the ones we were supposed to reject?   9

We deny the nopal[3] no longer. We know full well we're not on foreign soil, but on Indian lands. (Were we supposed to forget that too?) So there's no going back. If anything, we are back. The whole continent, the whole earth—which our ancestors have traversed for thousands of years—is our mother. Meanwhile, we watch Congress and the president do a dance about not pardoning or not granting amnesty to those who've been remanded to live in shadows. Sinverguenzas![4] Just who precisely needs to be pardoned? Those who are exploited and who've been here forever...or those who've been complicit in our dehumanization?   10

[2]Latin American migrant worker (editors' note).
[3]Literally, "prickly pear." There is a common Mexican expression, "Pareces que tienes el nopal en la frente," which literally translated means "It appears you have a prickly pear on your forehead." Idiomatically, the meaning is "You appear to be Indian, yet you deny it" (editors' note).
[4]Mexican expression meaning "Scoundrels!" (editors' note).

Through all this, we've been baited into fighting with African Americans, American Indians, Asians, Mexican Americans, and poor and white middle class workers—because Mexicans supposedly steal their jobs and are ruining the quality of life.   11

The truth is, American Indians, African Americans and Asians should be at the head of our protests—for it is they and their struggles against dehumanization that we draw inspiration from. But in the end, it is those who allow extremists to speak in their name, who must also step forward and tell their representatives that a society divided into legal and illegal human beings is no longer acceptable.   12

Every cell in our bodies tells us this. And the unprecedented protests have created the consciousness that a two-tiered society—the definition of apartheid—is intolerable.   13

A flawed bill will pass—many bills will pass—yet some sectors of the population will continue to view and treat Mexicans/Central Americans as illegal, unwanted and subhuman.   14

But enough. Ya Basta! IKUALI![5] As is said at the rallies: Nosotros no somos ilegales ni inmigrantes. Somos de este continente.[6] We are neither illegal nor even immigrants. Tojuan Titehuaxkalo Panin Pacha Mama.[7]   15

---

[5] *Ya basta* is Spanish and *ikuali* is Nahuatl (the Aztec language) for "enough" (editors' note).
[6] Spanish for "We are neither illegal nor immigrants. We are from this continent" (editors' note).
[7] Nahuatl for "We are from this earth" (editors' note).

Questions for Close Reading

1. What is the selection's thesis? Locate the sentence(s) in which Rodriguez states his main idea. If he doesn't state his thesis explicitly, express it in your own words.
2. What is the meaning of the essay's title, "The Border on Our Backs"?
3. According to Rodriguez, how are American policies on illegal immigrants similar to apartheid?
4. According to Rodriguez, who should be the inspiration for illegal Mexican and Central American immigrants in the United States? Why?
5. Refer to your dictionary as needed to define the following words used in the selection: *scapegoats* (paragraph 1), *draconian* (3), *repatriations* (3), *apartheid* (3), *bigotry* (6), *dragnet* (6), *vilification* (6), *delude* (7), *indigenous* (9), *obliterated* (9), *traversed* (10), *amnesty* (10), *remanded* (10), and *complicit* (10).

Questions About the Writer's Craft

1. Rodriguez opens his essay with some definitions of *Mexican* and *Central American* that he claims can be found in any U.S. political dictionary. How effective is this opening? What tone does it set for the remainder of the essay?

2. **The pattern.** What evidence does Rodriguez cite to support his claim that American attitudes toward immigrants from Mexico and Central America are fundamentally racist? How effective is this evidence and the way it is presented? What is the balance between *logos* and *pathos* here?

3. Rodriguez uses many words and phrases in Spanish and Nahuatl throughout the essay without translating them. How effective is this use of language? What does it suggest about the audience for which he is writing?

4. **The pattern.** What fallacies, if any, are in this argument? Explain the nature of the fallacy or fallacies.

Writing Assignments Using Argumentation-Persuasion as a Pattern of Development

1. Rodriguez argues that the struggle of illegal immigrants is similar to the struggle of American Indians, African Americans, Mexican Americans, and other American groups who have fought against dehumanization (paragraphs 11 and 12). Do you agree? Focusing on a specific group of disadvantaged Americans, write an essay in which you support or challenge Rodriguez's argument. To ensure that your position is more than a reflexive opinion, conduct some library research on the group in question, and read Star Parker's "*Se Habla* Entitlement" (page 423), an essay that is in sharp opposition to Rodriguez's. No matter which side you take, assume that some readers are opposed to your point of view. Acknowledge and try to dismantle as many of their objections as possible. Refer, whenever it's relevant, to Parker's argument in your paper.

2. Rodriguez suggests that racial profiling at the U.S. borders unfairly targets people of color and is used by politicians to exploit whites' fears (paragraph 6). In recent years, racial profiling has been used by many law enforcement agencies to identify suspected criminals and terrorists as well as illegal immigrants, although many people dispute both the fairness and the effectiveness of the technique. Do some research on racial profiling and then write an essay arguing that racial profiling is (or is not) a fair and effective method of identifying people who are likely to be criminals. Your essay can focus on the issue of racial profiling in general, or it can focus on a particular use of racial profiling. In your essay, you should acknowledge and refute as many opposing arguments as possible.

Writing Assignments Combining Patterns of Development

3. Rodriguez believes that illegal immigrants should stand up for their right to be treated as "full human beings." Select a group that you believe is disadvantaged and should stand up for its rights. Possibilities include a specific racial, ethnic, or religious group; the disabled; the overweight; those in abusive relationships. Write an essay explaining some specific *steps* these groups could take to secure their rights. Conclude your paper by discussing the *effects* of winning such rights. What would be gained? What, if anything, would be lost? Before writing, read Audre Lorde's "The Fourth of July" (page 127), to sharpen your understanding of disadvantaged people and the struggle for human rights.

4. Rodriguez refers to Mexicans and Central Americans as threatening the American Way of Life (paragraph 1). Write an essay in which you *define* what the American Way of Life means to you. Along the way, *compare* and/or *contrast* your definition with what you think is the prevailing definition of this term. To illustrate your definition, provide *examples* and/or *stories*. Your essay can be serious, humorous, or satiric in tone.

Writing Assignment Using a Journal Entry as a Starting Point

5. Write an essay arguing that schools should or should not encourage students to discuss immigration, ethnicity, and racism. Review your pre-reading journal entry, and select a specific level of schooling to focus on before taking a position. Supplement the material in your journal by gathering the opinions, experiences, and observations of friends, family, and classmates. No matter which position you take, remember to cite opposing arguments, refuting as many of them as you can.

Star Parker

Star Parker, born in 1957, is the founder and leader of the Coalition on Urban Renewal and Education, a nonprofit organization that advocates on issues of race, poverty, education, and inner-city neighborhoods. At one time a single mother living on welfare in Los Angeles, Parker eventually returned to college for a bachelor's degree in marketing. She went on to establish an urban Christian magazine and become a strong advocate for conservative Christian political views. In 1992, her business was destroyed in the Los Angeles riots. This experience intensified her focus on faith-based and free-market approaches to solving the problems of poverty. As a social policy consultant, Parker frequently appears on national television and radio stations, including CNN, MSNBC, and Fox, and she often testifies before Congress. Parker has published three books: *Pimps, Whores, and Welfare Brats: From Welfare Cheat to Conservative Messenger* (1998), *Uncle Sam's Plantation: How Big Government Enslaves American's Poor and What We Can Do About It* (2003), and *White Ghetto: How Middle Class America Reflects Inner City Decay* (2006). This opinion piece was published on WorldNetDaily.com, an independent news website, on April 18, 2006.

Pre-Reading Journal Entry

The issue of immigration—especially questions of who should be permitted into the country and who should be permitted to stay—has recently been hotly debated both by politicians and pundits and by everyday people. What do you think would happen if U.S. immigration laws were strictly enforced and those who were here illegally were sent back to their home countries? What positive effects would there be? What negative effects would there be? What do you think would happen if all immigrants who were here illegally were allowed to stay and start the process of becoming citizens? Take some time to respond to these questions in your journal.

Se Habla[1] Entitlement

When it comes to matters of economy, I think of myself as libertarian. I   1
believe in free markets, free trade and limited government. But I must confess, our Latino neighbors are challenging my libertarian instincts regarding our immigration conundrum.

The recent pro-immigration demonstrations around the country have   2
been a major turnoff.

There is something not convincing about illegal immigrants demonstrat-   3
ing to claim they have inalienable rights to come here, be here, work here, become citizens here—and make all these claims in Spanish.

Hearing "We Shall Overcome" in Spanish just doesn't provoke my sym-   4
pathies. I don't buy that, along with life, liberty and the pursuit of happiness,

---

[1]Spanish for "is spoken" (editors' note).

our Creator endowed anyone with the right to sneak into the United States, bypass our laws and set up shop. Maybe our immigration laws do need fixing. But this is a discussion for American citizens. In English.

This could be the finest hour for the political left if we really can be convinced that illegal immigration is a right, that those here illegally are innocent victims, and that the real guilt lies with U.S. citizens who believe our laws mean something and should be enforced.   5

Draping these bogus claims in the garb of the civil-rights movement is particularly annoying.   6

The civil-rights movement was about enforcing the law, not breaking it.   7
The Civil War amendments to the Constitution were not getting the job done in what has been a long struggle in this country to treat blacks as human beings. If Americans were kidnapping Mexicans and selling them into slavery here, I might see the equivalence. But these are free people, who chose to come here and chose to do so illegally.

Just considering Mexicans, how can we understand their taking to the   8
streets of our country to demand rights and freedom when they seem to have little interest in doing this where they do have rights, which is in Mexico? There is no reason why Mexico, a country rich in beauty and natural resources, cannot be every bit as prosperous as the United States.

It's not happening because of a long history of mismanagement, corrup-   9
tion and excessive government. Although Mexico is a democracy, for some reason Mexicans seem to need to be north of the Rio Grande to get politically active and demand the benefits of a free society.

Last year the Pew Hispanic Center surveyed adults in Mexico and asked   10
them if they would come to the United States if they had the means and opportunity to do so. Forty-six percent responded yes. Almost half of Mexican adults said they'd rather live here! When asked if they would do it illegally, more than 20 percent said yes.

Yet in the contest for the Mexican presidency, the leading candidate is a   11
leftist former mayor of Mexico City who is polling in the high 30s.[2]

Maybe you can figure out why almost half of Mexican adults say they would   12
rather live in the United States, presumably because of the opportunities our free society affords, yet vote for a leftist candidate who will continue policies in Mexico that choke off any prospect for growth, prosperity and opportunity.

So forgive me for being a little suspicious of the wholesome picture   13
being painted of these folks who are pouring across our border allegedly just to be free, work and maintain traditional families.

Anyone who lives in Southern California, as I do, knows that the Latino-   14
immigrant community is far from the paragon of virtue that the forces who

---

[2]With a very narrow margin, the more conservative Felipe Calderón ultimately defeated the leftist Andrés Manuel López Obrador in the Mexican presidential election of 2006.

want to encourage open borders would have us believe. I see much of the same troubling behavior that blacks get tarred with. Much of the gang behavior in Los Angeles, unfortunately, is Latino-related. The L.A. Unified School District is over three-quarters Latino, who drop out at the same alarming 50 percent rate as inner-city blacks. Out-of-wedlock births among Hispanic women approach 50 percent.

Those who want to hoist the banner of the Statue of Liberty, Ellis Island   15 and the American tradition of immigration should remember that when immigrants were passing through Ellis Island at the early part of the last century, the federal government accounted for about 3 percent of the American economy. Today it is 25 percent.

Part of the package deal that comes with showing up in the United States   16 today is our welfare state as well as our free economy. Illegal status is really a temporary situation, anyway. Illegal immigrants' children who are born here are U.S. citizens. Significant demands are being made on our tax dollars in the way of schools, health care and government services, including law enforcement.

Yes, let's encourage freedom. But freedom is a privilege and a responsibility.   17

We have enough people already here who think it's all about entitlement.   18

Questions for Close Reading

1. What is the selection's thesis? Locate the sentence(s) in which Parker states her main idea. If she doesn't state her thesis explicitly, express it in your own words.
2. Why does Parker object to pro-immigration demonstrators adopting the strategies of the American civil rights movement?
3. In paragraph 15, Parker contrasts the size of the federal government a hundred years ago with its size now. To what does she attribute its increase?
4. Why does Parker object to the feeling of entitlement that she claims immigrants have?
5. Refer to your dictionary as needed to define the following words used in the selection: *entitlement* (title), *libertarian* (paragraph 1), *conundrum* (1), *inalienable* (3), *provoke* (4), *bogus* (6), *garb* (6), and *paragon* (14).

Questions About the Writer's Craft

1. **The pattern.** Which of the two possible strategies for organizing a refutation (see pages 368–369) does Parker use in her essay? Do you consider the points she makes in the refutation sufficiently persuasive? Explain.
2. **Other patterns.** In paragraph 14, Parker compares and contrasts the Latino and African American communities of southern California. What is the purpose of this comparison? How effective is it?
3. The second paragraph of the Declaration of Independence begins: "We hold these truths to be self-evident, that all men are created equal, that they are endowed by their Creator with certain unalienable Rights, that among these are Life, Liberty and the pursuit of Happiness." There are echoes of this sentence in paragraphs 3 and 4 of Parker's essay. What is the effect of her adopting this vocabulary?

4. Throughout the essay, Parker uses language that describes her reactions to pro-immigration demonstrations and arguments: "a major turnoff" (paragraph 2), "not convincing" (3), "doesn't provoke my sympathies" (4), "particularly annoying" (6), and "a little suspicious" (13). What do these phrases contribute to the tone of the essay? How do they help Parker communicate her argument more convincingly?

Writing Assignments Using Argumentation-Persuasion as a Pattern of Development

1. Parker, an African American, claims to have been "turned off" by the pro-immigration demonstrations that took place in spring of 2006 in an attempt to influence immigration legislation pending in Congress. She objects to the pro-immigration movement's adoption of the strategies of the American civil rights movement—the language, the demonstrations, and the songs sung in Spanish. In contrast, in "The Border on Our Backs" (page 418), Roberto Rodriguez, a Mexican American, is elated by these demonstrations, claiming that immigrants are finally asserting their human rights in the great tradition of the civil rights movement. What do you think of demonstrations in the United States by illegal immigrants? Do you sympathize with the immigrants' arguments? Do you think their demonstrations further the immigrants' cause, or set it back? Write an essay in which you argue that demonstrations by illegal immigrants are (or are not) justified and appropriate, citing at least two or three reasons for your position. Be sure to support your reasons with *examples* wherever possible.

2. Parker characterizes herself as a libertarian in matters of economics. Libertarians advocate that individuals should be free to do whatever they wish with themselves and their property, as long as they do not infringe on the liberty of others. Libertarians also believe that people are responsible for their own actions. They strongly oppose welfare programs, which they believe force taxpayers to provide aid to others. In fact, Parker's final reason for opposing illegal immigrants is that they contribute to the growth of the welfare state (paragraph 15 and 16). Write an essay supporting or opposing the libertarian position on the welfare state. Argue that government does (or does not) have the responsibility to help individuals in times of need (poor economic conditions, disability, and natural disasters, for example). Be sure to address whether the effect on individuals of such government assistance is empowering—or whether it perpetuates dependence. Use specific examples to support your position.

Writing Assignments Combining Patterns of Development

3. Imagine what your life would be like if you moved to another state or country alone or just with your immediate family. Then write an essay in which you provide *examples* showing how your life would or would not change if you moved to a strange place. Consider the language barrier, if any, in your education, your work, your friendships, and your family life. Reach some conclusions about the overall *effect* of making this move, including whether life would be easier or more difficult.

4. Choose a social program or common practice that involves the concept of entitlement. For example, among social programs you could choose affirmative action, Medicaid, Medicare, welfare, or unemployment insurance. Among common practices you might select nepotism (favoring relatives or friends when hiring), legacy admissions to colleges (admitting the children of alumni), or illegal campaign contributions. Research the program or practice on the Internet or in the library. Write an essay in which you explain the *effects* of such a program or practice on recipients. *Compare* and *contrast* the benefits and drawbacks of receiving such an entitlement. Finally, *argue* that the program or practice should be continued or abolished.

Writing Assignment Using a Journal Entry as a Starting Point

5. Review your journal entries about the possible effects of deporting illegal immigrants or allowing them to stay, also called *amnesty*. The last amnesty in the United States took place in 1986 and was granted to immigrants who could prove they had resided here for five years or more. Amnesty is always controversial. Some argue that granting amnesty rewards illegal behavior and encourages more illegal immigration. Others argue that regularizing the status of long-time illegal residents simply provides them with a path for becoming full citizens, upholding the ideals of an open and democratic society. Write an essay in which you *argue* either in favor of or against an amnesty for current illegal immigrants who have resided in the United States for at least five years. In addition to discussing the *effects* of allowing immigrants to stay that you outlined in your journal entry, do some research on the 1986 amnesty to understand its *effects*. If they are still relevant today, use them to support your point of view about amnesty.

Additional Writing Topics

ARGUMENTATION-PERSUASION

General Assignments

Using argumentation-persuasion, develop one of the topics below in an essay. After choosing a topic, think about your purpose and audience. Remember that the paper's thesis should state the issue under discussion as well as your position on the issue. As you work on developing evidence, you might want to do some outside research. Keep in mind that effective argumentation-persuasion usually means that some time should be spent acknowledging and perhaps refuting opposing points of view. Be careful not to sabotage your argument by basing your case on a logical fallacy.

1. Euthanasia
2. Hiring or college-admissions quotas
3. Giving birth control devices to teenagers
4. Prayer in the schools
5. Living at home after college
6. The drinking age
7. Spouses sharing housework equally
8. Smoking in public places
9. Big-time sports in college
10. Pornography on the Internet
11. Single parents with young children
12. Global warming
13. Legalizing marijuana
14. Political campaigns
15. Requiring college students to pass a comprehensive exam in their majors before graduating
16. Reinstating the military draft
17. Putting elderly parents in nursing homes
18. An optional pass-fail system for courses
19. The homeless
20. Nonconformity in a neighborhood: allowing a lawn to go wild, keeping many pets, painting a house an odd color, or some other atypical behavior

Assignments with a Specific Purpose, Audience, and Point of View

On Campus

1. Your college's Financial Aid Department has decided not to renew your scholarship for next year, citing a drop in your grades last semester and an unenthusiastic recommendation from one of your instructors. Write a letter to the director of financial aid arguing for the renewal of your scholarship.

2. You strongly believe that a particular policy or regulation on campus is unreasonable or unjust. Write a letter to the dean of students (or other appropriate administrator) arguing that the policy needs to be, if not completely revoked, amended in some way. Support your contention with specific examples showing how the regulation has gone wrong. End by providing constructive suggestions for how the policy problem can be solved.

At Home or in the Community

3. You and one or more family members don't agree on some aspect of your romantic life (you want to live with your boyfriend/girlfriend and they don't approve; you want to get married and they want you to wait; they simply don't like your partner). Write a letter explaining why your preference is reasonable. Try hard to win your family member(s) over to your side.

4. Assume you're a member of a racial, ethnic, religious, or social minority. You might, for example, be a Native American, an elderly person, a female executive. On a recent television show or in a TV commercial, you saw something that depicts your group in an offensive way. Write a letter (to the network or the advertiser) expressing your feelings and explaining why you feel the material should be taken off the air.

On the Job

5. As a staff writer for an online pop-culture magazine, you've been asked to nominate the "Most Memorable TV Moment of the Last 50 Years" to be featured as the magazine's lead article. Write a letter to your supervising editor in support of your nominee.

6. As a high school teacher, you support some additional restriction on students. The restriction might be "no cell phones in school," "no T-shirts," "no food in class," "no smoking on school grounds." Write an article for the school newspaper, justifying this new rule to the student body.

COMBINING THE PATTERNS

Throughout this book, you've studied the patterns of development—narration, process analysis, definition, and so on—in depth. You've seen how the patterns are used as strategies for generating, developing, and organizing ideas for essays. You've also learned that, in practice, most types of writing combine two or more patterns. The two sections that follow provide additional information about these important points. The rest of the chapter then gives you an opportunity to look more closely at the way several writers use the patterns of development in their work.

THE PATTERNS IN ACTION: DURING THE WRITING PROCESS

The patterns of development come into play throughout the composing process. In the prewriting stage, awareness of the patterns encourages you to think about your subject in fresh, new ways. Assume, for example, that you've been asked to write an essay about the way children are disciplined in school. However, you draw a blank as soon as you try to limit this general subject. To break the logjam, you could apply one or more patterns of development to your subject. *Comparison-contrast* might prompt you to write an essay investigating the differences between your parents' and your own feelings about school discipline. *Division-classification* might lead you to another paper—one that categorizes the kinds of discipline used in school. And *cause-effect* might point to still another essay—one that explores the way students react to being suspended.

Further along in the writing process—after you've identified your limited subject and your thesis—the patterns of development can help you generate your paper's evidence. Imagine that your thesis is "Teachers shouldn't discipline students publicly just to make an example of them." You're not sure, though, how to develop this thesis. Calling upon the patterns might spark some promising possibilities. *Narration* might encourage you to recount the disastrous time you were singled out and punished for the misdeeds of an entire class. Using *definition,* you might explain what is meant by an *autocratic* disciplinary style. *Argumentation-persuasion* might prompt you to advocate a new plan for disciplining students fairly and effectively.

The patterns of development also help you organize your ideas by pointing the way to an appropriate framework for a paper. Suppose you plan to write an essay for the campus newspaper about the disturbingly high incidence of shoplifting among college students; your purpose is to persuade young people not to get involved in this tempting, supposedly victimless crime. You believe that many readers will be deterred from shoplifting if you tell them about the harrowing *process* set in motion once a shoplifter is detected. With this step-by-step explanation in mind, you can now map out the essay's content: what happens when a shoplifter is detained by a salesperson, questioned by store security personnel, led to a police car, booked at the police station, and tried in a courtroom.

THE PATTERNS IN ACTION: IN AN ESSAY

Although this book devotes a separate chapter to each of the nine patterns of development, all chapters emphasize the same important point: Most writing consists of several patterns, with the dominant pattern providing the piece's organizational framework. To reinforce this point, each chapter contains a section, "How [the Pattern] Fits Your Purpose and Audience," that shows how a writer's purpose often leads to a blending of patterns. Also, the commentary following each student essay talks about the way the paper mixes patterns. Similarly, at least one of the questions in the "Questions About the Writer's Craft" section following each professional selection asks you to analyze the piece's combination of patterns. Further, the assignments in "Writing Assignments Combining Patterns of Development" encourage you to experiment with mixing patterns in your own writing. In short, all through *The Longman Reader* we emphasize that the patterns of development are far from being mechanical formulas. On the contrary: They are practical strategies that open up options in every stage of the composing process.

Now you'll have a chance to focus on the way student and professional writers combine patterns in their essays. In the pages ahead, you'll find one student essay and three professional selections, one by each of the following three writers: Virginia Woolf; Martin Luther King, Jr.; and Joan Didion. As you read each essay, ask yourself these questions:

1. What are the writer's *purpose* and *thesis?*
2. What *pattern of development dominates* the essay? How does this pattern help the writer support the essay's thesis and fulfill the essay's purpose?
3. What *other patterns appear* in the essay? How do these secondary patterns help the writer support the essay's thesis and fulfill the essay's purpose?

Your responses to these three questions will reward you with a richer understanding of the way writers work. To give you an even clearer sense of how writers mix patterns, we have annotated the student essay (Tasha Walker's "The Super-Sizing of America's Kids" below) and the first professional essay (Virginia Woolf's "The Death of the Moth" on page 438). The preceding three questions served as our guide when we prepared the annotations. By making your own annotations on these essays and then comparing them to ours, you can measure your ability to analyze writers' use of the patterns. You can further evaluate your analysis of the pieces by answering the three questions on your own and then comparing your responses to ours on pages 436–437 and 441–443.

STUDENT ESSAY

The following student essay was written by Tasha Walker in response to this assignment:

> In the essay "Tweens: Ten Going On Sixteen," Kay S. Hymowitz explores an alarming trend among children: the tendency of preteens to act much older than they are. Write an essay analyzing the causes and effects of another significant problem among young people today. Conclude your essay by offering possible solutions for the problem you've examined.

The annotations on the essay will help you look at the way Tasha uses various patterns of development to achieve her purpose and develop her thesis.

<table>
<tr><td>Introduction has narrative and descriptive elements</td><td>The Super-Sizing of America's Kids
by Tasha Walker</td><td></td></tr>
<tr><td>Examples of foods contrast with examples later in ¶</td><td>Picture this scene from the 1950s. A couple of kids wake up, get dressed, and sit down for breakfast before leaving for school. They're greeted by an array of healthy choices: a glass of orange juice, a bowl of cornflakes or oatmeal with a healthy serving of milk, perhaps a plateful of scrambled eggs and toast.</td><td>1</td></tr>
</table>

Contrast between average break- fast in the 1950s and today

Now fast-forward a few decades to the present. The situation is very different. If kids sit down for breakfast at all, they gulp down a bowl of rainbow-colored sugary bits with a dollop of milk. Or, racing out the door, they grab a syrupy jumbo cinnamon bun or a glazed, fudge-filled toaster tart.

What's the harm, you might ask, in giving kids tasty, convenient food options? After all, kids burn so much energy; they shouldn't have to worry about their diet until they're adults. Right? Wrong, says the latest information on obesity in the United States. According to several recent studies cited by the magazine *Children's Health* (October 2003), the number of overweight American kids has more than doubled in the last thirty years. As many as 22 percent of today's children are considered dangerously obese. Many are developing diet-related diabetes, a disease that used to be seen almost exclusively in adults. When California's students (grades 5 through 12) were given a basic fitness test, almost eight out of ten failed. These statistics point to a clear conclusion: There's a growing problem of childhood obesity in this country, a dire trend that must be stopped in its tracks.

Exemplification in the form of facts and statistics

Causal analysis (main pattern) begins with *effects* of problem

Statement of purpose/thesis: Need to end increasing child- hood obesity; emotional language urging action reinforces essay's *persuasive* intent

Whether they're called big-boned, chubby, husky, or plus- sized, kids are becoming heavier at younger ages and less physically fit than ever before. But why? Like most serious problems, this one has a number of causes. One factor is the massive impact of electronic entertainment on kids' lives. Kids used to go outside to play because that was more fun than sit- ting around the house. Today, kids at home have access to cable TV channels, the Internet, DVD players, and a dizzying assortment of video games, all of which diminish the lure of outdoor play.

Causal analysis shifts to several *causes* of problem

Transition signals first *cause* of problem

Another cause is the lack of parental supervision. Decades ago, most kids had an adult at home encouraging them to play outdoors. Now, a large number of American fam- ilies have two working parents or a working single parent. For most of the daylight hours, parents aren't around to make sure their kids get some exercise. Parents who can't be home may feel guilty; one way to relieve this guilt is to buy kids the game system of their dreams and a nice wide-screen TV to play it on, almost guaranteeing that kids will sit idle rather than par- ticipate in vigorous physical activity.

Transition signals second *cause* of problem

But more than any other factor, fast-food restaurants and other sources of calorie-laden junk have dramatically con- tributed to the fattening of America's kids. In *Super Size Me*, director Morgan Spurlock, dismayed by American obesity sta- tistics (particularly among children), decided to eat nothing but McDonald's fast food for a month and film the experience. To many of today's kids, normal dinnertime equals McDonald's,

Transition signals most important *cause* of problem

2

3

4

5

Domino's, Taco Bell, or Kentucky Fried Chicken. And increasingly, lunchtime at school means those foods too since a good number of schools have sold chain restaurants the right to put their food items on the lunch line. Many schools also allow candy and soft-drink vending machines on their campuses. Given the choice between an apple and a candy bar, how many kids would choose the apple?

Start of *secondary causal analysis* (*effects* of fast food on kids)

Exemplification in the form of facts and statistics

Whether for breakfast, lunch, or dinner, when fast food becomes the staple of young people's diets, it's the kids who become Whoppers. And it has become the staple for many. *Children's Health* reports that nationwide, kids get 40 percent of their meals from fast-food chains and convenience stores. And what makes the situation even worse is the increasingly huge portions sold by fast-food restaurants. In the 1950s, the standard meal at McDonald's consisted of a hamburger, two ounces of French fries, and a 12-ounce Coke. That meal provided 590 calories. But today's customers are encouraged to say "Super-size that!" For very little extra money, diners end up with a quarter-pound burger, extra-large fries, and a gigantic cup of Coke, all adding up to 1,550 calories. A whole generation of kids is growing up believing that this massive shot of fat, sugar, and sodium equals a "normal portion." Kids' perception of what's normal is also distorted by the size of the drinks sold by fast-food and convenience stores. The drinks, often sporting names like

Emotional language reinforces essay's *persuasive* intent

the "Big Gulp" or "Super Thirst Quencher," are huge in both size and popularity. Every day, the average adolescent chugs enough soda and fruit beverages to equal the sugar content of fifty chocolate-chip cookies. No wonder kids are becoming "super-sized" themselves.

Exemplification in the form of facts and statistics

End of secondary causal analysis

The fast-food franchises push youngsters to overeat in other ways too. Plunking themselves down in front of the TV to watch after-school and Saturday-morning cartoons, children see at least an hour of commercials for every five hours of programming. On Saturday mornings, nine out of ten of those TV ads are for sugary cereals, fast foods, and other

Emotional language reinforces essay's *persuasive* intent

non-nutritious junk. Watching those commercials makes the kids hungry—or at least makes them think they are. So they snack as they sit in front of the TV set. Then at mealtime, they beg for the junk food they've seen televised all day long. The result? Kids get bigger, and bigger, and bigger.

Argumentation presents several possible solutions to problem

Transitions signal several solutions

There's no overnight solution to the problem of American children's increasing weight. But there are some remedies that could be put into place easily. To begin, fast-food meals and junk-food vending machines should be banned from schools, as some states have started to do. Second, food companies should reduce serving sizes and lower the fat and sugar content of the snack items that children eat most often.

6

7

8

(Kraft Foods has recently begun to take such steps.) Third, commercials for junk food should be prohibited from being aired on TV during children's viewing time, specifically Saturday mornings. Fourth, parents and schools need to educate kids about the benefits of healthy foods and moderate portion size—and about the drawback of huge meals of junk food. Schools could, for example, mount an educational effort equivalent to the school-based anti-smoking campaign of the 1980s and 1990s. Fifth, fast-food restaurants should be required to do something like what tobacco companies have to do: clearly display health warnings on their products. If young people learned in school and at home about healthy eating, they might think twice about ordering a Double Whopper with cheese, an extra-large order of fries and a king-sized Dr. Pepper, especially if they read something like this:

- *Your meal provides 2030 calories, 860 of those calories from fat.*
- *Your recommended daily intake is 2000 calories, with no more than 600 of those calories coming from fat.*

At a glance, they could see that in one fast-food meal, they would be taking in more calories and fat than they should consume in an entire day.

Finally, parents need to curb their reliance on fast food to nourish their children. Making fast food an occasional treat rather than an everyday habit can make a significant difference. Parents may argue that they simply don't have time to cook healthy, well-balanced meals, particularly during the week. The answer may be to get the whole family involved in preparing meals ahead of time. (Younger kids, whose attitudes are still in the formative stage, love helping out in the kitchen.) Letting kids assist in preparing, packaging, and freezing their own nutritious, reasonably sized individual servings for later use can go a long way toward helping youngsters develop more healthy attitudes toward food.

Such efforts, challenging as they may be, are well worth the trouble. Why? Because overweight kids today become overweight adults tomorrow. Overweight adults are at increased risk for heart disease, diabetes, stroke, and cancer. Schools, fast-food restaurants, and the media are contributing to a public-health disaster in the making. Anything that decreases the role that super-sized junk food plays in kids' lives needs to be done, and done quickly.

Margin annotations:

More transitions signal solutions

Exemplification in the form of hypothetical situation

Transition signals last solution

Restatement of purpose/thesis; emotional language urging action reinforces essay's *persuasive* intent

9

10

The following answers to the questions on page 432 will help you analyze Tasha Walker's use of the patterns of development in her essay "The Super-Sizing of America's Kids."

1. *What are the writer's purpose and thesis?*

   Tasha's general purpose, clearly indicated in the assignment, is to explore the causes and effects of a significant problem among young people today. Tasha chooses to address the problem of increasing obesity among children. She expresses her thesis in the final sentence of paragraph 2: "There's a growing problem of childhood obesity in this country, a dire trend that must be stopped in its tracks." Over the course of her essay, Tasha marshals compelling evidence of the obesity problem, explores its causes and effects, and concludes with thoughts on how this problem might be rectified.

2. *What pattern of development dominates the essay? How does this pattern help the writer support the essay's thesis and fulfill the essay's purpose?*

   As the assignment required, Tasha uses *causal analysis* as her essay's principal pattern of development. To establish the severity of the childhood obesity problem, Tasha presents, in paragraph 2, a battery of statistics pointing to obesity's dire and pervasive *effects*. She then shifts gears in paragraph 3 to consider the *causes* of this obesity. The phrase "Like most serious problems, this one has a number of causes" announces that Tasha will discuss a series of causes. She uses various signal phrases, including "One factor" (3), "Another cause" (4), and "But more than any other factor" (5), to direct readers' attention to each factor under consideration. This clear, easy-to-follow presentation—first of effects and then of causes—allows Tasha to develop her thesis and meet her writing objectives. Along the way, several *secondary causal analyses* buttress her overarching examination of causes and effects. Consider paragraphs 5–7. There, Tasha begins by citing fast-food restaurants as the most significant cause of kids' poor eating habits; that done, she examines how the fast-food industry affects kids—how it distorts their perception of portion size and uses enticing commercials to increase their reliance on "calorie-laden junk" (5).

3. *What other patterns appear in the essay? How do these secondary patterns help the writer support the essay's thesis and fulfill the essay's purpose?*

   Although Tasha's essay is primarily a causal analysis, it contains a strong element of *argumentation-persuasion*. For one thing, Tasha's thesis takes the form of an *argument:* The "dire trend [of childhood obesity]...must be stopped in its tracks" (paragraph 2). Careful to support her argument with solid reasoning, Tasha uses facts and statistics throughout the essay. She also employs strong language to enhance the argument's *persuasiveness*. Note, for example, the way she's worded her thesis to convey a sense of urgency. Note, too, the way she forcefully restates her core argument at various points in the essay. In paragraph 3, she asserts that "kids are becoming heavier at younger ages and less physically fit than ever before," and later she argues, "No wonder kids are becoming 'super-sized' themselves" (6) and "Kids get bigger, and bigger, and bigger" (7). The essay's last sentence ("Anything that decreases the role that super-sized junk food plays in kids' lives needs to be done, and done quickly") echoes the feeling of urgency expressed in the thesis.

Tasha's essay draws upon other patterns of development as well. The introductory anecdote, *narrative* and *descriptive* in structure, *contrasts* kids' waking up to breakfast in the 1950s with what happens nowadays. Vivid contrasting *examples* ("a bowl of...oatmeal" versus a "bowl of rainbow-colored sugary bits") help Tasha establish her key point: that childhood obesity is a contemporary trend that didn't exist in the past. Tasha continues to use exemplification in the form of facts (6 and 8), statistics (2 and 7), and hypothetical situations (8 and 9). Taken together, all these patterns help Tasha make her point about the importance of reversing the dangerous trend of childhood obesity.

Now that you've seen the way one student writer brings together several patterns of development in an essay, it will be helpful to look at the way a renowned prose stylist, Virginia Woolf, does the same in her classic essay "The Death of the Moth."

Virginia Woolf

Virginia Woolf is considered one of the most innovative writers of the twentieth century. Born in 1882 in London, Woolf was educated at home by her father, Leslie Stephen, a well-known biographer, critic, and scholar. Along with her sister, Woolf became a key member of the Bloomsbury Group, a circle of writers and artists committed to the highest standards in art and literature. Woolf married a fellow Bloomsbury member, author and publisher Leonard Woolf. Together, they established Hogarth Press, which went on to publish Woolf's ground-breaking writings, including the novels *Mrs. Dalloway* (1923) and *To the Lighthouse* (1927), as well as the collection of essays *A Room of One's Own* (1920). Woolf's experimentation with point of view and her use of stream of consciousness earned her a place as a pivotal figure in English literature. Although Woolf's work met with critical acclaim and her collaboration with her husband was productive, Woolf was troubled all her life by severe depression. She committed suicide in 1941. The following selection by Woolf, "The Death of the Moth," appeared in the volume *The Death of the Moth and Other Essays* (1948).

The Death of the Moth

Description of the moth

Definition (by negation): How this moth differs from the usual kind

Part of implied purpose/thesis: Nature's energy

Description of nature's energy here contrasts with description of nature in ¶5 *(part of purpose/thesis)*

Moths that fly by day are not properly to be called moths; they do not excite that pleasant sense of dark autumn nights and ivy-blossom which the commonest yellow-underwing asleep in the shadow of the curtain never fails to rouse in us. They are hybrid creatures, neither gay like butterflies nor sombre like their own species. Nevertheless the present specimen, with his narrow hay-coloured wings, fringed with a tassel of the same colour, seemed to be content with life. It was a pleasant morning, mid-September, mild, benignant, yet with a keener breath than that of the summer months. The plough was already scoring the field opposite the window, and where the share had been, the earth was pressed flat and gleamed with moisture. Such vigour came rolling in from the fields and the down beyond that it was difficult to keep the eyes strictly turned upon the book. The rooks too were keeping one of their annual festivities; soaring round the tree tops until it looked as if a vast net with thousands of black knots in it had been cast up into the air; which, after a few moments, sank slowly down upon the trees until every

1

twig seemed to have a knot at the end of it. Then, suddenly, the net would be thrown into the air again in a wider circle this time, with the utmost clamour and vociferation, as though to be thrown into the air and settle slowly down upon the tree tops were a tremendously exciting experience.

Comparison between nature's energy and the moth's strong life force (part of purpose/thesis)

2   The same energy which inspired the rooks, the ploughmen, the horses, and even, it seemed, the lean bare-backed downs, sent the moth fluttering from side to side of his square of the window-pane. One could not help watching him. One was, indeed, conscious of a queer feeling of pity for him. The possibilities of pleasure seemed that morning so enormous and so various that to have only a moth's part in life, and a day moth's at that, appeared a hard fate, and his zest in enjoying his meagre opportunities to the full, pathetic. He flew vigorously to one corner of his compartment, and, after waiting there a second, flew across to the other. What remained for him but to fly to a third corner and then to a fourth? That was all he could do, in spite of the size of the downs, the width of the sky, the far-off smoke of houses, and the romantic voice, now and then, of a steamer out at sea. What he could do he did. Watching him, it seemed as if a fibre, very thin but pure, of the enormous energy of the world had been thrust into his frail and diminutive body. As often as he crossed the pane, I could fancy that a thread of vital light became visible. He was little or nothing but life.

Start of narrative (main pattern) about the moth's plight

Start of narrative about Woolf's reaction to the moth's plight

Description of moth's strong life force—despite its small size (these two contrasting qualities are part of purpose/thesis)

Part of purpose/thesis: The moth represents life

Narrative about Woolf's reaction continues

Restatement of part of purpose/thesis: The moth's two contrasting qualities

Restatement of part of purpose/thesis: The moth represents life

3   Yet, because he was so small, and so simple a form of the energy that was rolling in at the open window and driving its way through so many narrow and intricate corridors in my own brain and in those of other human beings, there was something marvellous as well as pathetic about him. It was as if someone had taken a tiny bead of pure life and decking it as lightly as possible with down and feathers, had set it dancing and zigzagging to show us the true nature of life. Thus displayed one could not get over the strangeness of it. One is apt to forget all about life, seeing it humped and bossed and garnished and cumbered so that it has to move with the greatest circumspection and dignity. Again, the thought of all that life might have been had he been born in any other shape caused one to view his simple activities with a kind of pity.

Narrative about the moth's plight continues; tension builds

After a time, tired by his dancing apparently, he settled 4 on the window ledge in the sun, and, the queer spectacle being at an end, I forgot about him. Then, looking up, my eye was caught by him. He was trying to resume his dancing, but seemed either so stiff or so awkward that he could only flutter to the bottom of the window-pane; and when he tried to fly across it he failed. Being intent on other matters I watched these futile attempts for a time without thinking, unconsciously waiting for him to resume his flight, as one waits for a machine, that has stopped momentarily, to start again without considering the reason of its failure. After perhaps a seventh attempt he slipped from the wooden ledge and fell, fluttering his wings, on to his back on the window sill. The helplessness of his attitude roused me. It flashed upon me that he was in difficulties; he could no longer raise himself; his legs struggled vainly. But, as I stretched out a pencil, meaning to help him to right himself, it came over me that the failure and awkwardness were the approach of death. I laid the pencil down again.

Narrative about Woolf's reaction continues

Hint of the resolution of the narrative about the moth

Narrative about Woolf's reaction continues

Description of nature's indifference here contrasts with description of nature in ¶1 (part of purpose/thesis)

The legs agitated themselves once more. I looked as if 5 for the enemy against which he struggled. I looked out of doors. What had happened there? Presumably it was midday, and work in the fields had stopped. Stillness and quiet had replaced the previous animation. The birds had taken themselves off to feed in the brooks. The horses stood still. Yet the power was there all the same, massed outside, indifferent, impersonal, not attending to anything in particular. Somehow it was opposed to the little hay-coloured moth. It was useless to try to do anything. One could only watch the extraordinary efforts made by those tiny legs against an oncoming doom which could, had it chosen, have submerged an entire city, not merely a city, but masses of human beings; nothing, I knew, had any chance against death. Nevertheless after a pause of exhaustion the legs fluttered again. It was superb, this last protest, and so frantic that he succeeded at last in righting himself. One's sympathies, of course, were all on the side of life. Also, when there was nobody to care or to know, this gigantic effort on the part of an insignificant little moth, against a power of such magnitude, to retain what no one else valued or desired to keep, moved one strangely. Again, somehow, one saw life, a pure bead. I lifted the pencil again, useless though I knew it to be. But even as I did so, the unmistakable tokens of

Restatement of part of purpose/thesis: The strength of the moth's life force— despite small size

Part of purpose/thesis: Death's inevitability

Narrative about moth continues

Narrative about Woolf's reaction continues

Restatement of part of purpose/thesis: The strength of the moth's life force— despite its size

Resolution of the *narrative* about the moth

Restatement of part of purpose/thesis: Death's inevitability

death showed themselves. The body relaxed, and instantly grew stiff. The struggle was over. The insignificant little creature now knew death. As I looked at the dead moth, this minute wayside triumph of so great a force over so mean an antagonist filled me with wonder. Just as life had been strange a few minutes before, so death was now as strange. The moth having righted himself now lay most decently and uncomplainingly composed. O yes, he seemed to say, death is stronger than I am.

The following answers to the questions on page 432 will help you analyze Virginia Woolf's use of the patterns of development in the essay "The Death of the Moth."

1. *What are the writer's purpose and thesis?*

Woolf's *purpose* is to show that the tiny moth's courageous but ultimately futile battle to cling to life embodies the struggle at the very heart of all existence. Woolf achieves her purpose by relating the story of the moth's efforts to resist death. Her *thesis* might be expressed this way: Although living creatures may make "extraordinary efforts" (paragraph 5) to hold onto life, these attempts aren't strong enough to defy death. Nothing, Woolf writes, has "any chance against death" (5).

Woolf's purpose and thesis first become apparent at the end of paragraph 2. There she shows that the moth, with his "frail and diminutive body," represents "nothing but life." Although "small...and...simple" (3), the moth is suffused with the same extraordinary energy that is evident in the natural world beyond Woolf's window. This energy, combined with the moth's tiny size, makes the creature both "marvellous" and "pathetic" (3)—two qualities that are particularly apparent during the moth's final struggles. During those moments, the moth makes a final "superb" (5) protest against death, but ultimately the "insignificant" (5) creature—like all forms of life—must cease his valiant struggle and die.

2. *What pattern of development dominates the essay? How does this pattern help the writer support the essay's thesis and fulfill the essay's purpose?*

Although the essay's first paragraph is largely descriptive, it becomes clear by paragraph 2 that the description is in service of a larger narrative about the moth's struggles. It's this narrative that dominates the essay.

At the beginning, the moth is imbued with vitality, as he flies "vigorously" (paragraph 2) and with "zest" (2) from one side of the window to the other. But narrative tension begins to build in paragraph 4. There Woolf writes that the moth tries once again to cross the windowpane, fails repeatedly, and slips "on to his back," seemingly defeated. However, even then, the moth doesn't abandon his hold on life, for—as Woolf relates in paragraph 5—he tries, despite exhaustion, to right himself.

Against all odds, he finally succeeds, but his frantic struggle to hold onto life takes its toll, and the tiny creature soon dies. This detailed story of the moth's futile battle against death is presented as an emblem of the fate of all life. Through this narrative, Woolf achieves her purpose and thesis: to convey the power of nature and the inability of living creatures—despite heroic efforts—to defy this power.

Paralleling the tale of the moth's struggle is another *narrative*: the story of Woolf's changing understanding of the event that unfolds before her. When the moth is "dancing" (3), energetic, and vital, Woolf "could not help watching him" (2) and feels a kind of wonderment at this "tiny bead of pure life" (3). Then in paragraph 4, Woolf writes that she forgets about the moth for a while until she happens to look up and see his "futile attempts" to "resume . . . dancing." For a few moments, she watches the moth's "stiff" and "awkward" efforts to fly, expecting him to demonstrate the same vitality as before. Suddenly, she understands that the moth is "in difficulties" and can no longer lift himself up. She tries to help but abandons her efforts when she realizes that the moth's labored efforts signify the "approach of death." Paragraph 5 presents the final stage of Woolf's interior narrative. She looks outside her window for an explanation of the moth's plight. But now she finds that the forces of nature—earlier so exuberant and vibrant—are, if anything, "opposed to the little hay-coloured moth." With that, her attention is once again drawn to the moth and the fluttering of his legs. Although drained, the tiny creature makes one last effort to resist death—and, improbably enough, picks himself up one more time. Struck by the sheer power of the moth's life force, Woolf is prompted, as before, to help the creature, even though she recognizes the futility. But then the "unmistakable tokens of death" appear, and the moth gives up his struggle, succumbing—as all forms of life must—to the forces of nature. With the moth lying "uncomplainingly composed," Woolf comes to accept the fact that death is stronger than life.

3. *What other patterns appear in the essay? How do these secondary patterns help the writer support the essay's thesis and fulfill the essay's purpose?*

Although the essay is predominantly a narrative, it also contains other patterns. The *descriptive* passage at the beginning of the essay includes a brief *definition by negation* in which Woolf explains how the creature she is observing differs from the usual, more colorful night moth. The rest of paragraph 1 draws upon description to evoke the sense of early autumn and nature's extraordinary energy. This description of the natural world's vibrancy and abundance, exemplified by the rooks and plowed earth, *contrasts* with Woolf's later characterization of the natural world in paragraph 5. There she writes, "Stillness and quiet . . . replaced the previous animation," and she senses not that nature fosters vitality, but that it is "indifferent, impersonal, not attending to anything in particular."

Shifting her focus in paragraph 2 from the natural world to the moth, Woolf exercises her *descriptive* powers to convey the moth's extraordinary zest as he flies across the windowpane. In this paragraph, Woolf also draws upon *comparison-contrast* to show that despite *differences* in their sizes, the tiny moth and the vast natural world embody the *same* primal energy. Woolf's considera-tion of this elemental similarity leads her to the basic *contrast* at the heart of the essay: While the moth's tiny size makes him "pathetic," his formidable life spirit makes him "marvellous." He may be small and lightweight, but he is abuzz with vitality. When contrasted to the enormous power of nature, the moth—like all forms of life—may be puny, but his impulse to defy such power inspires awe and reverence.

Martin Luther King, Jr.

More than forty years after his assassination, Martin Luther King, Jr. (1929–68), is still recognized as the towering figure in the struggle for civil rights in the United States. Born in Atlanta, Georgia, King earned doctorates from Boston University and Chicago Theological Seminary and served as pastor of a Baptist congregation in Montgomery, Alabama. Advocating a philosophy of nonviolent resistance to racial injustice, he led bus boycotts, marches, and sit-ins that brought about passage of the 1964 Civil Rights Act and the Voting Rights Act of 1965. Dr. King was awarded the Nobel Peace Prize in 1964. The following selection by King is taken from *Where Do We Go from Here: Community or Chaos?* (1967).

Where Do We Go from Here: Community or Chaos?

A final problem that mankind must solve in order to survive in the world house that we have inherited is finding an alternative to war and human destruction. Recent events have vividly reminded us that nations are not reducing but rather increasing their arsenals of weapons of mass destruction. The best brains in the highly developed nations of the world are devoted to military technology. The proliferation of nuclear weapons has not been halted, in spite of the limited-test-ban treaty.

In this day of man's highest technical achievement, in this day of dazzling discovery, of novel opportunities, loftier dignities and fuller freedoms for all, there is no excuse for the kind of blind craving for power and resources that provoked the wars of previous generations. There is no need to fight for food and land. Science has provided us with adequate means of survival and transportation, which make it possible to enjoy the fullness of this great earth. The question now is, do we have the morality and courage required to live together as brothers and not be afraid?

One of the most persistent ambiguities we face is that everybody talks about peace as a goal, but among the wielders of power peace is practically nobody's business. Many men cry "Peace! Peace!" but they refuse to do the things that make for peace.

The large power blocs talk passionately of pursuing peace while expanding defense budgets that already bulge, enlarging already awesome armies and devising ever more devastating weapons. Call the roll of those who sing the glad tidings of peace and one's ears will be surprised by the responding sounds. The heads of all the nations issue clarion calls for peace, yet they come to the peace table accompanied by bands of brigands each bearing unsheathed swords.

The stages of history are replete with the chants and choruses of the con-   5
querors of old who came killing in pursuit of peace. Alexander, Genghis Khan,
Julius Caesar, Charlemagne and Napoleon were akin in seeking a peaceful
world order, a world fashioned after their selfish conceptions of an ideal existence. Each sought a world at peace which would personify his egotistic
dreams. Even within the life span of most of us, another megalomaniac strode
across the world stage. He sent his blitzkrieg-bent legions blazing across
Europe, bringing havoc and holocaust in his wake. There is grave irony in the
fact that Hitler could come forth, following nakedly aggressive expansionist
theories, and do it all in the name of peace.

So when in this day I see the leaders of nations again talking peace while   6
preparing for war, I take fearful pause. When I see our country today intervening in what is basically a civil war, mutilating hundreds of thousands of
Vietnamese children with napalm, burning villages and rice fields at random,
painting the valleys of that small Asian country red with human blood, leaving broken bodies in countless ditches and sending home half-men, mutilat-
ed mentally and physically; when I see the unwillingness of our government
to create the atmosphere for a negotiated settlement of this awful conflict by
halting bombings in the North and agreeing unequivocally to talk with the
Vietcong—and all this in the name of pursuing the goal of peace—I tremble
for our world.[1] I do so not only from dire recall of the nightmares wreaked
in the wars of yesterday, but also from dreadful realization of today's possible nuclear destructiveness and tomorrow's even more calamitous prospects.

Before it is too late, we must narrow the gaping chasm between our   7
proclamations of peace and our lowly deeds which precipitate and perpetuate
war. We are called upon to look up from the quagmire of military programs
and defense commitments and read the warnings on history's signposts.

One day we must come to see that peace is not merely a distant goal that   8
we seek but a means by which we arrive at that goal. We must pursue peaceful ends through peaceful means. How much longer must we play at deadly
war games before we heed the plaintive pleas of the unnumbered dead and
maimed of past wars?

President John F. Kennedy said on one occasion, "Mankind must put an   9
end to war or war will put an end to mankind." Wisdom born of experience
should tell us that war is obsolete. There may have been a time when war
served as a negative good by preventing the spread and growth of an evil force,
but the destructive power of modern weapons eliminates even the possibility
that war may serve any good at all. If we assume that life is worth living and
that man has a right to survive, then we must find an alternative to war. In a

---

[1]Only after more than 58,000 Americans had been killed did the United States withdraw from
Vietnam. The war then continued until the North Vietnamese, aided by the Vietcong, took over
all of Vietnam (editors' note).

day when vehicles hurtle through outer space and guided ballistic missiles carve highways of death through the stratosphere, no nation can claim victory in war. A so-called limited war will leave little more than a calamitous legacy of human suffering, political turmoil and spiritual disillusionment. A world war will leave only smoldering ashes as mute testimony of a human race whose folly led inexorably to ultimate death. If modern man continues to flirt unhesitatingly with war, he will transform his earthly habitat into an inferno such as even the mind of Dante[2] could not imagine.

Therefore I suggest that the philosophy and strategy of nonviolence become immediately a subject for study and for serious experimentation in every field of human conflict, by no means excluding the relations between nations. It is, after all, nation-states which make war, which have produced the weapons that threaten the survival of mankind and which are both genocidal and suicidal in character.   10

We have ancient habits to deal with, vast structures of power, indescribably complicated problems to solve. But unless we abdicate our humanity altogether and succumb to fear and impotence in the presence of the weapons we have ourselves created, it is as possible and as urgent to put an end to war and violence between nations as it is to put an end to poverty and racial injustice.   11

The United Nations is a gesture in the direction of nonviolence on a world scale. There, at least, states that oppose one another have sought to do so with words instead of with weapons. But true nonviolence is more than the absence of violence. It is the persistent and determined application of peaceable power to offenses against the community—in this case the world community. As the United Nations moves ahead with the giant tasks confronting it, I would hope that it would earnestly examine the uses of nonviolent direct action.   12

I do not minimize the complexity of the problems that need to be faced in achieving disarmament and peace. But I am convinced that we shall not have the will, the courage and the insight to deal with such matters unless in this field we are prepared to undergo a mental and spiritual re-evaluation, a change of focus which will enable us to see that the things that seem most real and powerful are indeed now unreal and have come under sentence of death. We need to make a supreme effort to generate the readiness, indeed the eagerness, to enter into the new world which is now possible, "the city which hath foundation, whose Building and Maker is God."   13

It is not enough to say, "We must not wage war." It is necessary to love peace and sacrifice for it. We must concentrate not merely on the eradication of war but on the affirmation of peace. A fascinating story about Ulysses and   14

---

[2]In *The Divine Comedy* (1321), Italian poet Dante depicts the burning torments of hell endured by a lost soul before it can attain salvation (editors' note).

the Sirens[3] is preserved for us in Greek literature. The Sirens had the ability to sing so sweetly that sailors could not resist steering toward their island. Many ships were lured upon the rocks, and men forgot home, duty and honor as they flung themselves into the sea to be embraced by arms that drew them down to death. Ulysses, determined not to succumb to the Sirens, first decided to tie himself tightly to the mast of his boat and his crew stuffed their ears with wax. But finally he and his crew learned a better way to save themselves: They took on board the beautiful singer Orpheus, whose melodies were sweeter than the music of the Sirens. When Orpheus sang, who would bother to listen to the Sirens?

So we must see that peace represents a sweeter music, a cosmic melody   15 that is far superior to the discords of war. Somehow we must transform the dynamics of the world power struggle from the nuclear arms race, which no one can win, to a creative contest to harness man's genius for the purpose of making peace and prosperity a reality for all the nations of the world. In short, we must shift the arms race into a "peace race." If we have the will and determination to mount such a peace offensive, we will unlock hitherto tightly sealed doors of hope and bring new light into the dark chambers of pessimism.

---

[3]Ulysses and the Sirens, as well as Orpheus (mentioned later in the paragraph), are all figures in Greek mythology (editors' note).

Known for her taut prose style and sharp social commentary, Joan Didion (1934–) graduated from the University of California at Berkeley. Her essays have appeared in *The Saturday Evening Post, The American Scholar,* and the *National Review,* as well as in three collections: *Slouching Towards Bethlehem* (1969), *The White Album* (1979), and *After Henry* (1992). *Salvador* (1983) is a book-length essay about a 1982 visit to Central America. The coauthor of several screenplays (including *A Star Is Born* in 1976 and *Up Close and Personal* in 1996), Didion has also written novels, including *Run River* (1963), *A Book of Common Prayer* (1977), *Democracy* (1984), *The Last Thing He Wanted* (1996), and *Where I Was From* (2003), as well as *Fixed Ideas: America Since 9.11* (2003), a book of political commentary. Most recently, Didion published *The Year of Magical Thinking* (2005), a memoir. "Marrying Absurd" is from *Slouching Towards Bethlehem.*

Marrying Absurd

To be married in Las Vegas, Clark County, Nevada, a bride must swear   1
that she is eighteen or has parental permission and a bridegroom that he is twenty-one or has parental permission. Someone must put up five dollars for the license. (On Sundays and holidays, fifteen dollars. The Clark County Courthouse issues marriage licenses at any time of the day or night except between noon and one in the afternoon, between eight and nine in the evening, and between four and five in the morning.) Nothing else is required. The State of Nevada, alone among these United States, demands neither a premarital blood test nor a waiting period before or after the issuance of a marriage license. Driving in across the Mojave from Los Angeles, one sees the signs way out on the desert, looming up from that moonscape of rattlesnakes and mesquite, even before the Las Vegas lights appear like a mirage on the horizon: "GETTING MARRIED? Free License Information First Strip Exit." Perhaps the Las Vegas wedding industry achieved its peak operational efficiency between 9:00 P.M. and midnight of August 26, 1965, an otherwise unremarkable Thursday which happened to be, by Presidential order,[1] the last day on which anyone could improve his draft status merely by getting married. One hundred and seventy-one couples were pronounced man and wife in the name of Clark County and the State of Nevada that night, sixty-seven of them by a single justice of the peace, Mr. James A. Brennan. Mr. Brennan did one wedding at the Dunes and the other sixty-six in his office, and charged each couple eight dollars. One bride lent her veil to six

---

[1] Refers to a declaration made by President Lyndon Johnson regarding the draft for the Vietnam conflict (editors' note).

others. "I got it down from five to three minutes," Mr. Brennan said later of his feat. "I could've married them *en masse,* but they're people, not cattle. People expect more when they get married."

What people who get married in Las Vegas actually do expect—what, in the largest sense, their "expectations" are—strikes one as a curious and self-contradictory business. Las Vegas is the most extreme and allegorical of American settlements, bizarre and beautiful in its venality and in its devotion to immediate gratification, a place the tone of which is set by mobsters and call girls and ladies' room attendants with amyl nitrite poppers[2] in their uniform pockets. Almost everyone notes that there is no "time" in Las Vegas, no night and no day and no past and no future (no Las Vegas casino, however, has taken the obliteration of the ordinary time sense quite so far as Harold's Club in Reno, which for a while issued, at odd intervals in the day and night, mimeographed "bulletins" carrying news from the world outside); neither is there any logical sense of where one is. One is standing on a highway in the middle of a vast hostile desert looking at an eighty-foot sign which blinks "STARDUST" or "CAESAR'S PALACE." Yes, but what does that explain? This geographical implausibility reinforces the sense that what happens there has no connection with "real" life; Nevada cities like Reno and Carson City are ranch towns, Western towns, places behind which there is some historical imperative. But Las Vegas seems to exist only in the eye of the beholder. All of which makes it an extraordinarily stimulating and interesting place, but an odd one in which to want to wear a candlelight satin Priscilla of Boston wedding dress with Chantilly lace insets, tapered sleeves and a detachable modified train.

And yet the Las Vegas wedding business seems to appeal to precisely that impulse. "Sincere and Dignified Since 1954," one wedding chapel advertises. There are nineteen such wedding chapels in Las Vegas, intensely competitive, each offering better, faster, and, by implication, more sincere services than the next: Our Photos Best Anywhere, Your Wedding on A Phonograph Record, Candlelight with Your Ceremony, Honeymoon Accommodations, Free Transportation from Your Motel to Courthouse to Chapel and Return to Motel, Religious or Civil Ceremonies, Dressing Rooms, Flowers, Rings, Announcements, Witnesses Available, and Ample Parking. All of these services, like most others in Las Vegas (sauna baths, payroll-check cashing, chinchilla coats for sale or rent) are offered twenty-four hours a day, seven days a week, presumably on the premise that marriage, like craps, is a game to be played when the table seems hot.

---

[2]An illegal liquid drug, inhaled through the nose, that originally came in small capsules that would "pop" upon opening. Known for heightening sexual arousal, it also causes dizziness and sometimes a blackout (editors' note).

But what strikes one most about the Strip chapels, with their wishing wells and stained-glass paper windows and their artificial bouvardia, is that so much of their business is by no means a matter of simple convenience, of late-night liaisons between show girls and baby Crosbys. Of course there is some of that. (One night about eleven o'clock in Las Vegas I watch a bride in an orange minidress and masses of flame-colored hair stumble from a Strip chapel on the arm of her bridegroom, who looked the part of the expendable nephew in the movies like *Miami Syndicate*.[3] "I gotta get the kids," the bride whimpered. "I gotta pick up the sitter, I gotta get to the midnight show." "What you gotta get," the bridegroom said, opening the door of a Cadillac Coupe de Ville and watching her crumple on the seat, "is sober.") But Las Vegas seems to offer something other than "convenience"; it is merchandising "niceness," the facsimile of proper ritual, to children who do not know how else to find it, how to make the arrangements, how to do it "right." All day and evening long on the Strip, one sees actual wedding parties, waiting under the harsh lights at a crosswalk, standing uneasily in the parking lot of the Frontier while the photographer hired by The Little Church of the West ("Wedding Place of the Stars") certifies the occasion, takes the picture: the bride in a veil and white satin pumps, the bridegroom usually in a white dinner jacket, and even an attendant or two, a sister or a best friend in hot-pink *peau de soie,* a flirtation veil, a carnation nosegay. "When I Fall in Love It Will Be Forever," the organist plays, and then a few bars of *Lohengrin.* The mother cries; the stepfather, awkward in his role, invites the chapel hostess to join them for a drink at the Sands. The hostess declines with a professional smile; she has already transferred her interest to the group waiting outside. One bride out, another in, and again the sign goes up on the chapel door: "One moment please—Wedding."

I sat next to one such wedding party in a Strip restaurant the last time I   5
was in Las Vegas. The marriage had just taken place; the bride still wore her dress, the mother her corsage. A bored waiter poured out a few swallows of pink champagne ("on the house") for everyone but the bride, who was too young to be served. "You'll need something with more kick than that," the bride's father said with heavy jocularity to his new son-in-law; the ritual jokes about the wedding night had a certain Panglossian character, since the bride was clearly several months pregnant. Another round of pink champagne, this time not on the house, and the bride began to cry. "It was just as nice," she sobbed, "as I hoped and dreamed it would be."

---

[3]The actual title is *The Miami Story,* a 1954 film about a group of citizens destroying a crime syndicate with the help of a reformed criminal (editors' note).

A GUIDE TO USING SOURCES

Many assignments in *The Longman Reader* suggest that you might want to do some research in the library and/or on the Internet. Such research enlarges your perspective and enables you to move beyond off-the-top-of-your-head opinions to those that are firmly supported. This appendix will be useful if you do decide to draw upon outside sources when preparing a paper. The appendix explains how to (1) evaluate articles, books, and Web sources; (2) analyze and synthesize sources you find; (3) use quotation, summary, and paraphrase correctly to avoid plagiarism; (4) integrate source material into your writing; and (5) document print, Internet, and other sources.

EVALUATING SOURCE MATERIALS

The success of your essay will depend in large part on the evidence you provide (see pages 34–38 on the characteristics of evidence). Evidence from sources, whether print or electronic, needs to be evaluated for its *relevance, timeliness, seriousness of approach,* and *objectivity.*

Relevance

Titles can be misleading. To determine if a source is relevant for your paper, review it carefully. For a book, read the preface or introduction, skim the table of contents, and check the index to see whether the book is likely to contain information that's important to your topic. If the source is an influential text in the field, you may want to read the entire book for background and specific ideas. Or if a text devotes just a few pages to your topic, you might read those pages, taking notes on important information. For an article, read the abstract of the article, if there is one. If not, read the first few paragraphs and skim the rest to determine if it might be useful. As you read a source, make use of the reading checklists on pages 2–4 to get the most from the material. If a source turns out to be irrelevant, just make a note to yourself that you consulted the source and found it didn't relate to your topic.

Timeliness

To some extent, the topic and the kind of research you're doing will determine whether a work is outdated. If you're researching a historical topic such as the internment of Japanese Americans during World War II, you would most likely consult sources published in the 1940s and 1950s, as well as more up-to-date sources. In contrast, if you're investigating a recent scientific development—cloning, for example—it would make sense to restrict your search to current material. For most college research, a source older than ten years is considered outdated unless it was the first to present key concepts in a field.

Seriousness of Approach

As you review a source, ask yourself if it is suitable for your purpose and your instructor's requirements. Articles from *general* periodicals (newspapers and widely read magazines like *Time* and *Newsweek*) and *serious* publications (such as *National Geographic* and *Scientific American*) may be sufficient to provide support in a personal essay. But an in-depth research paper in your major field of study will require material from *scholarly* journals and texts (for example, *American Journal of Public Health* and *Film Quarterly*).

Objectivity

As you examine your sources for possible bias, keep in mind that a strong conclusion or opinion is *not in itself* a sign of bias. As long as a writer doesn't ignore opposing positions or distort evidence, a source can't be considered biased. A biased source presents only those facts that fit the writer's predetermined conclusions. Such a source is often marked by emotionally charged language (see page 19). Publications sponsored by special interest groups—a particular industry, religious association, advocacy group, or political party—are usually biased. Reading such materials *does* familiarize you with a specific point of view, but remember that contrary evidence has probably been ignored or skewed.

The following checklist provides some questions to ask yourself as you evaluate print sources.

☑ EVALUATING ARTICLES AND BOOKS: A CHECKLIST

❑ If the work is scholarly, is the author well-known in his or her field? Is the author affiliated with an accredited college or university? A nonscholarly author, such as a journalist, should have a reputation for objectivity and thoroughness.

❑ Is the publication reputable? If a scholarly publication is *peer-reviewed*, experts in the field have a chance to comment on the author's work before it is published. Nonscholarly publications such as newspapers and magazines should be well-established and widely respected.

❑ Is the source recently published and up-to-date? Alternatively, is it a classic in its field? In the sciences and social sciences, recent publication is particularly critical.

❑ Is the material at an appropriate level—neither too scholarly nor too general—for your purpose and audience? Make sure you can understand and digest the material for your readers.

❑ Does the information appear to be accurate, objectively presented, and complete? Statistics and other evidence should be not be distorted or manipulated to make a point.

Special care must be taken to evaluate the worth of material found on the Web. Electronic documents often seem to appear out of nowhere and can disappear without a trace. And anyone—from scholar to con artist—can create a Web page. How, then, do you know if an Internet source is credible? The following checklist provides some questions to ask when you work with online material.

☑ EVALUATING INTERNET MATERIALS: A CHECKLIST

❑ Who is the author of the material? Does the author offer his or her credentials in a résumé or biographical note? Do these credentials qualify the author to provide reliable information on the topic? Does the author provide an e-mail address so you can request more information? The less you know about an author, the more suspicious you should be about using the data.

❑ Can you verify the accuracy of the information presented? Does the author refer to studies or to other authors you can investigate? If the author doesn't cite other works or other points of view, that may suggest the document is opinionated and one-sided. In such a case, it's important to track down material addressing alternative points of view.

❏ Who's sponsoring the Web site? Check for an "About Us" link on the home page, which may tell you the site's sponsorship and goals. Many sites are established by organizations—businesses, agencies, lobby groups—as well as by individuals. If a sponsor pushes a single point of view, you should use the material with great caution. Once again, make an extra effort to locate material addressing other sides of the issue.

❏ Is the cited information up-to-date? Being on the Internet doesn't guarantee that information is current. To assess the timeliness of Internet materials, check at the top or bottom of the document for copyright date, publication date, and/or revision date. Those dates will help you determine whether the material is recent enough for your purposes.

❏ Is the information original or taken from another source? Is quoted material accurate? Some Web pages may reproduce material from other sources without identifying them. Watch out for possible plagiarism. Nonoriginal material should be accurately quoted and acknowledged on the site.

ANALYZING AND SYNTHESIZING SOURCE MATERIAL

As you read your sources and begin taking notes, you may not be able to judge immediately how helpful a source will be. At that time, you probably should take fairly detailed notes. After a while, you'll become more selective. You'll find that you are thinking more critically about the material you read, isolating information and ideas that are important to your thesis, and formulating questions about your topic.

Analyzing Source Material

To begin with, you should spend some time analyzing each source for its *central ideas, main supporting points,* and *key details.* (See Chapter 1 for tips on effective reading techniques.) As you read, keep asking yourself how the source's content meshes with your working thesis and with what you know about your subject. Does the source repeat what you already know, or does it supply new information? If a source provides detailed support for important ideas or suggests a new angle on your subject, read carefully and take full notes. If the source refers to other sources, you might decide to consult those.

Make sure you have all necessary citation information for every source you consult. (See pages 474–482 for information you will need for documenting citations.) Then, as you read relevant sources, make sure to take plenty of notes. Articles you have printed out can be highlighted and annotated with your comments. (See the checklist on page 456 for annotation techniques.) In addition, you may wish to photocopy selected book pages to annotate. However, you will also have to take handwritten or typewritten notes on some material. When you do so, make sure to put quotation marks around direct quotes. Annotating and note-taking will help you think through and respond to the source's ideas. (For help with analyzing images in your sources—for example, graphs and illustrations—see pages 5–6.)

Your notes might include any of the following: facts, statistics, anecdotal accounts, expert opinion, case studies, surveys, reports, results of experiments. When you are recording data, check that you have copied the figures accurately. Also note how and by whom the statistics were gathered, as well as where and when they were first reported.

Take down your source's interpretation of the statistics, but be sure to scrutinize the interpretation for any "spin" that distorts them. For example, if 80 percent of Americans think violent crime is our number one national problem, that doesn't mean that violent crime *is* our main problem; it simply means that 80 percent of the people polled *think* it is. And if a "majority" of people think that homelessness should be among our top national priorities, it may be that a mere 51 percent—a bare majority—feel that way. In short, make sure the statistics mean what your sources say they mean. If you have any reason to suspect distortion, it's a good idea to corroborate such figures elsewhere; tracking down the original source of a statistic is the best way to ensure that numbers are being reported fairly.

Synthesizing Source Materials

As you go along, you may come across material that challenges your working thesis and forces you to think differently about your subject. Indeed, the more you learn, the more difficult it may be to state anything conclusively. This is a sign that you're synthesizing and weighing all the evidence. In time, the confusion will lessen, and you'll emerge with a clearer understanding of your subject.

Suppose you find sources that take positions contrary to the one that you had previously considered credible. When you come across such conflicting material, you can be sure you've identified a pivotal issue within your topic. To decide which position is more valid, you need to take good notes or carefully annotate your photocopies or printed documents. Then evaluate the sources for bias. On this basis alone, you might discover serious flaws in one or several sources. Also compare the key points and supporting evidence in the sources. Where do they agree? Where do they disagree? Does one source argue against another's position, perhaps even discrediting some of the opposing view's evidence? The answers to these questions may very well cause you to question the quality, completeness, or fairness of one or more sources.

To resolve such a conflict, you can also research your subject more fully. For example, if your conflicting sources are at the general or serious level, you should probably turn to more scholarly sources. By referring to more authoritative material, you may be able to determine which of the conflicting sources is more valid.

When you attempt to resolve discrepancies among sources, be sure not to let your own bias come into play. Try not to favor one position over the other simply because it supports your working thesis. Remember, your goal is to arrive at the most well-founded position you can. In fact, researching a topic may lead you to change your original viewpoint. In this case, you shouldn't hesitate to revise your working thesis to accord with the evidence you gather.

☑ ANALYZING AND SYNTHESIZING SOURCE MATERIAL: A CHECKLIST

❏ As you read sources, note central ideas, main supporting points, and key details.

❏ Make sure to record all bibliographic information carefully, identify any quotations, and copy statistical data accurately.

❏ Annotate or take full notes on sources that deal with ideas that are important to your topic or suggest a new angle on your subject.

❏ Examine statistics and other facts for any distortions.

❏ Read carefully material that causes you to take a different view of your subject. Keep an open mind and do additional research to confirm or change your thesis.

USING QUOTATION, SUMMARY, AND PARAPHRASE WITHOUT PLAGIARIZING

Your paper should contain your own ideas stated in your own words. To support your ideas, you can introduce evidence from sources in three ways—with direct quotations, summaries, and paraphrases. Knowing how and when to use each type is an important part of the research process.

Quotation

A *quotation* reproduces, word for word, that which is stated in a source. Although quoting can demonstrate the thoroughness with which you reviewed relevant sources, don't simply use one quotation after another without any intervening commentary or analysis. To do so would mean you hadn't evaluated and synthesized your sources sufficiently. Aim for one to three quotations from each major source; more than that can create a problem in your paper. Consider using quotations in the following situations:

- If a source's ideas are unusual or controversial, include a representative quotation in your paper to show you have accurately conveyed the source's viewpoint.
- Record a quotation if a source's wording is so eloquent or convincing that it would lose its power if you restated the material in your own words.
- Use a quotation if a source's ideas reinforce your own conclusions. If the source is a respected authority, such a quotation will lend authority to your own ideas.
- In an analysis of a literary work, use quotation from the work to support your interpretations.

Remember to clearly identify quotes in your notes so that you don't confuse the quotation with your own comments when you begin drafting your paper. Record the author's statement *exactly* as it appears in the original work, right down to the punctuation. In addition, make sure to properly document the quotation. See "Documenting Sources: MLA style" on pages 470–482.

Original Passage 1

In this excerpt from *The Canon: A Whirligig Tour of the Beautiful Basics of Science*, by Natalie Angier, page 22, the author is discussing the subject of scientific reasoning.

Much of the reason for its success is founded on another fundamental of the scientific bent. Scientists accept, quite staunchly, that there is a reality capable of being understood, and understood in a way that can be shared with and agreed upon by others. We can call this "objective" reality if we like, as opposed to subjective reality, or opinion, or "whimsical set of predilections." The concept is deceptive, however, because it implies that the two are discrete entities with remarkably little in common.

Original Passage 2

The following is the entire text of Amendment I of the Constitution of the United States.

Congress shall make no law respecting an establishment of religion, or prohibiting the free exercise thereof; or abridging the freedom of speech, or of the press; or the right of the people peaceably to assemble, and to petition the Government for a redress of grievances.

Acceptable Uses of Quotation   For a paper on society's perception of important freedoms, a student writer used this quotation in its entirety:

The First Amendment of the Constitution of the United States delineates what were thought to be society's most cherished freedoms: "Congress shall make no law respecting an establishment of religion, or prohibiting the free exercise thereof; or abridging the freedom of speech, or of the press; or the right of the people peaceably to assemble, and to petition the Government for a redress of grievances."

In a paper on science education in schools, one student writer used this quotation:

In explaining scientific reasoning, Angier says, "Scientists accept, quite staunchly, that there is a reality capable of being understood, and understood in a way that can be shared with and agreed upon by others" (22).

Notice that both quotations are reproduced exactly as they appear in the source and are enclosed in quotation marks. The parenthetical reference to the page number in the second example is a necessary part of documenting the quotation. (See pages 470–474 for more on in-text references.) The first example requires no page number because quotations from well-known sources such as the Constitution and the Bible are sufficiently identified by their own numbering systems, in this case, the text's use of "First Amendment of the Constitution."

Incorrect Use of Quotation   Another student writer, attempting to provide some background on the scientific method, used the source material incorrectly.

To understand the scientific method, it is important to understand that scientists believe there is a reality capable of being understood (Angier 22).

The phrase "a reality capable of being understood," which are the source's exact words, should have quotations around it. Even though the source is identified correctly in the parenthetical reference, the lack of quotation marks actually constitutes plagiarism, the use of someone's words or ideas without proper acknowledgment (see pages 462–463).

Summary

A *summary* is a condensation of a larger work. You extract the essence of someone's ideas and restate it in your own words. The length of a summary depends on your topic and purpose, but generally a summary is *much* shorter than the item you are summarizing. For example, you may summarize the plot of a novel in a few short paragraphs, or you might summarize a reading from this book in a few sentences. You might choose to use a summary for the following reasons:

- To give a capsule presentation of the main ideas of a book or an article, use a summary.
- If the relevant information is too long to be quoted in full, use a summary.
- Use a summary to give abbreviated information about such elements such as plot, background, or history.
- To present an idea from a source without including all the supporting details, use a summary.

To summarize a source, read the material; jot down or underline the main idea, main supporting points, and key details; then restate the information in shortened form in your own words. Your summary should follow the order of information in the original. Also, be sure to treat any original wording as quotations in your summary. *A caution:* When summarizing, don't use the ellipsis to signal that you have omitted some ideas. The ellipsis is used only when quoting.

Original Passage 3

This excerpt is from *The Homeless and History* by Julian Stamp, page 8.

The key to any successful homeless policy requires a clear understanding of just who are the homeless. Since fifty percent of shelter residents have drug and alcohol addictions, programs need to provide not only a place to sleep but also comprehensive treatment for addicts and their families. Since roughly one-third of the homeless population is mentally ill, programs need to offer psychiatric care, perhaps even institutionalization, and not just housing subsidies. Since the typical head of a homeless family (a young woman with fewer than six months' working experience) usually lacks the know-how needed to maintain a job and a home, programs need to supply employment and life skills training; low-cost housing alone will not ensure the family's stability.

However, if we switch our focus from the single person to the larger economic issues, we begin to see that homelessness cannot be resolved solely at the level of individual treatment. Beginning in the 1980s and through the 1990s, the gap between the rich and the poor has widened, buying power has stagnated, industrial jobs have fled overseas, and federal funding for low-cost housing has been almost eliminated. Given these developments, homelessness begins to look like a product of history, our recent history, and only by addressing shifts in the American economy can we begin to find effective solutions for people lacking homes. Moreover, these solutions—ranging from renewed federal spending to tax laws favoring job-creating companies—will require a sustained national commitment that transcends partisan politics.

Acceptable Use of Summary   The following summary was written by a student working on a paper related to the causes of homelessness.

In his *The Homeless and History*, Stamp asserts that society must not only provide programs to help the homeless with their personal problems, it must also develop government programs to deal with the economic causes of homelessness (8).

The writer gives the gist of Stamp's argument in his own words. The parenthetical reference at the end tells the reader that the material being summarized is on page 8 of the source (see pages 463–470 for more on integrating source material into your writing).

Incorrect Use of Summary   The student who wrote the following has incorrectly summarized ideas from the Stamp passage.

Who are the homeless? According to Stamp, the homeless are people with big problems like addiction, mental illness, and poor job skills. Because they haven't been provided with proper treatment and training, the homeless haven't been able to adapt to a changing economy. So their numbers soared in the 1990s (8).

The writer was so determined to put things her way that she added her own ideas and ended up distorting Stamp's meaning. For instance, note the way she emphasizes personal problems over economic issues, making the former the cause of the latter. Stamp does just the opposite and highlights economic solutions rather than individual treatment.

Paraphrase

Unlike a summary, which condenses the original, a *paraphrase* recasts material by using roughly the same number of words and retaining the same level of detail as the original. The challenge with paraphrasing is to capture the information without using the original language of the material. Paraphrasing is useful in these situations:

- If you want to include specific details from a source but you want to avoid using a long quotation or string of quotations, paraphrase the material.
- To interpret or explain material as you include it, try using a paraphrase.
- Paraphrase to avoid injecting another person's style into your own writing.

One way to compose a paraphrase is to read the original passage and then set it aside while you draft your restatement. As you write, make sure to use appropriate synonyms and to vary the sentence structure from that of the original. Then compare the passages to make sure you have not used any of the original language, unless you have enclosed it in quotation marks.

Acceptable Use of Paraphrase   In the following example, the student writer paraphrases the second paragraph of Stamp's original, fitting the restatement into her argument.

Can we work together as a society to eliminate homelessness? One historian urges us to look at larger economic issues, claiming that the problem cannot be solved simply by the treatment of personal problems such as substance abuse. Economic conditions for the poor have worsened in the last few decades, with fewer jobs and substantially diminished federal support for low-cost housing. To find a solution to homelessness, society must deal with these economic causes. A "sustained national commitment," regardless of political ideology, to stepped-up federal spending and tax laws that promote the creation of jobs, as well as to other initiatives, is needed (Stamp 8).

Note that the paraphrase is nearly as long as the original. Apart from the single instance of original language enclosed in quotation marks, the writer has not used phrases or even sentence structures from the original. Notice also that it is easy to see where the paraphrase starts and ends: The phrase "One historian" begins the paraphrase, and the parenthetical reference ends it. Because the text does not identify the source by name, the source's name is included in the parenthetical reference.

Incorrect Use of Paraphrase   When preparing the following paraphrase, the student stayed too close to the source and borrowed much of Stamp's language word for word (underlined). Because the student did not enclose the original phrases in quotation marks, this paraphrase constitutes plagiarism, *even though* this student acknowledged Stamp in the paper. The lack of quotation marks implies that the language is the student's when, in fact, it is Stamp's.

Only by addressing changes in the American economy—from the gap between the wealthy and the poor to the loss of industrial jobs to overseas markets—can we begin to find solutions for the homeless. And these solutions, ranging from renewed federal spending to tax laws favoring job-creating companies, will not be easy to find or implement (Stamp 8).

As the following example shows, another student believed, erroneously, that if he changed a word here and omitted a word there, he'd be preparing an effective paraphrase. Note that the language is all Stamp's *except* for the underlined words, which are the student's.

Only by addressing shifts in the economy can we find solutions for the homeless. These solutions will require a sustained federal commitment that avoids partisan politics (Stamp 8).

The student in the immediately preceding example occasionally deleted a word from Stamp's original, thinking that such changes would result in a legitimate paraphrase. For example, in "Only by addressing shifts in the [American] economy can we [begin to] find [effective] solutions" the brackets show where the student has omitted Stamp's words. The student couldn't place quotation marks around these near-quotes because his wording isn't identical to that of the source. Yet the near-quotes are deceptive; the lack of quotation marks suggests that the language is the student's when actually it's substantially (but not exactly) Stamp's. Such near-quotes are also considered plagiarism, even if, when writing the paper, the student supplies a parenthetical reference citing the source.

☑ USING QUOTATION, SUMMARY, AND PARAPHRASE: A CHECKLIST

❏ For a *quotation*, give the statement *exactly* as it was originally written.

❏ Always accompany quotations with your own commentary or analysis.

❏ Don't string quotations together one after the other without intervening text.

❏ Avoid using too many quotations. One to three quotations from any major source is sufficient.

❏ For a *summary*, restate ideas from the source in your own words.

❏ Keep summaries much shorter than the original material.

❏ Make sure your summary does not distort the meaning or tone of the original.

❏ For a *paraphrase*, recast ideas with the same level of detail as the original.

❏ Make sure to use your own language in a paraphrase—finding appropriate synonyms and varying sentence structure from that of the original.

❏ Check that any original source language used in a summary or paraphrase is enclosed in quotation marks.

Avoiding Plagiarism

Plagiarism occurs when a writer borrows someone else's ideas, facts, or language but doesn't properly credit that source. Summarizing and paraphrasing, in particular, can lead to plagiarism, but improper use of quotation can also constitute plagiarism.

Copyright law and the ethics of research require that you give credit to those whose words and ideas you borrow; that is, you must represent the source's words and ideas accurately and provide full documentation (see pages 470–482). Missing or faulty documentation can constitute plagiarism and undermine your credibility. For one thing, readers may suspect that you're hiding something if you fail to identify your sources clearly. Further, readers planning follow-up research of their own will be perturbed if they have trouble locating your sources. Finally, weak documentation makes it difficult for readers to distinguish your ideas from those of your sources.

To avoid plagiarizing, you must provide proper documentation in the following situations:

- When you include a word-for-word quotation from a source.
- When you paraphrase or summarize ideas or information from a source, unless that material is commonly known and accepted (whether or not you yourself were previously aware of it) or is a matter of historical or scientific record.
- When you combine a summary or paraphrase with a quotation.

One exception to formal documentation occurs in writing for the general public. For example, you may have noticed that while the authors of this book's essays, as well as newspaper and magazine writers, identify sources they have used, these writers don't use full documentation. Academic writers, though, must provide full documentation for all borrowed information.

INTEGRATING SOURCES INTO YOUR WRITING

On the whole, your paper should be written in your own words. As you draft your paper, indicate places where you might want to add evidence from sources to support your ideas. Depending on the source and the support you need, you may choose to use quotations, paraphrases, or summaries to present this evidence, as discussed in the preceding section.

Take care to blend the evidence seamlessly into your own writing through the use of introductions (see pages 48, 53–55, 68), transitions (see pages 51–52, 69), and conclusions (see pages 48, 55–56, 70). At a minimum, each paragraph should have a topic sentence, and it may also be useful to introduce evidence with an *attribution*, a phrase that identifies the source and forms part of the documentation you will need to use (see pages 464–465).

A quotation, by itself, won't always make your case for you. In addition, you will need to interpret quotations, showing why they are significant and explaining how they support your central points. Indeed, such commentary is often precisely what's needed to blend source material gracefully into your discussion. Also, use quotations sparingly; draw upon them only when they dramatically illustrate key points you want to make or when they lend authority to your own conclusions. A string of quotations signals that you haven't sufficiently evaluated and distilled your sources.

Awkward Use of a Quotation   In the following example, note how the quotation is dropped awkwardly into the text, without any transition or commentary. (For an explanation of the parenthetical reference at the end of the quotation, see pages 470–474.)

Recent studies of parenting styles are designed to control researcher bias. "Recent studies screen out researchers whose strongly held attitudes make objectivity difficult" (Layden 10).

Effective Use of Quotation   Adding brief interpretive remarks in this example provides a transition that smoothly merges the quotation with the surrounding material:

Recent studies of parenting styles are designed to control researcher bias. The psychologist Marsha Layden, a harsh critic of earlier studies, acknowledges that nowadays most investigations "screen out researchers whose strongly held beliefs make objectivity difficult" (10).

Introducing a Source

Try to avoid such awkward constructions as these: *According to Julian Stamp, he says that...* and *In the book by Julian Stamp, he argues that...* Instead, follow these hints for writing smooth, graceful attributions.

Identifying the Source   An introduction to a source may specify the author's name, it may inform readers of an author's expertise, or it may refer to a source more generally. To call attention to an author who is prominent in the field, important to your argument, or referred to many times in your paper, you may give the author's full name and identifier at the first mention in the text. Then in subsequent mentions, you may give only the last name. Don't use personal titles such as *Mr.* or *Ms.*

Natalie Angier, a Pulitzer Prize–winning journalist who writes about science, says that.... Angier goes on to explain....

The historian Julian Stamp argues that.... As Stamp explains....

For other sources, use a more general attribution and include the source's name, along with any page numbers, in the parenthetical citation.

One writer points out...(Angier 22).

According to statistics, fifty percent...(Stamp 8).

As part of an introduction, you may mention the title of the book, article, or other source.

In *The Homeless and History*, Stamp maintains that....

According to the National Aeronautics and Space Administration (NASA),...

A recent article in *National Geographic* demonstrates that....

When the author's name is provided in the text, don't repeat the name in the parenthetical reference. (See pages 470–474 for more details on parenthetical references.)

One psychologist who is a harsh critic of earlier studies acknowledges that nowadays most investigations "screen out researchers whose strongly held beliefs make objectivity difficult" (Layden 10).

The psychologist Marsha Layden acknowledges that... (10).

Using Variety in Attributions   Don't always place attributions at the beginning of the sentence; experiment by placing them in the middle or at the end:

The key to any successful homeless policy, Stamp explains, "requires a clear understanding of just who are the homeless" (8).

Half of homeless individuals living in shelters are substance abusers, according to statistics (Stamp 8).

Try not to use a predictable subject-verb sequence (*Stamp argues that, Stamp explains that*) in all your attributions. Aim for variations like the following:

The information compiled by Stamp shows....

In Stamp's opinion,...

Stamp's study reveals that....

Rather than repeatedly using the verbs *says* or *writes* in your introductions, seek out more vigorous verbs, making sure the verbs you select are appropriate to the tone and content of the piece you're quoting. The list on page 466 offers a number of options.

Shortening or Clarifying Quotations

To make the best use of quotations, you will often need to shorten or excerpt them. It's acceptable to omit parts of quotations as long as you do not change the wording or distort the meaning of the original.

acknowledges	demonstrates	reports
adds	endorses	responds
admits	grants	reveals
argues	implies	says
asserts	insists	shows
believes	maintains	speculates
compares	notes	states
confirms	points out	suggests
contends	questions	wonders
declares	reasons	writes

Quoting a Single Word, a Phrase, or Part of a Sentence   Put double quotation marks around a quoted element you are integrating into your own sentence.

Angier says that to speak of "objective" and "subjective" realities is to imply that these are "discrete entities" (22).

Making these changes will necessitate "a sustained national commitment that transcends partisan politics," according Stamp (8).

Omitting Material in the Middle of the Original Sentence   Insert three spaced periods, called an *ellipsis* (...), in place of the deleted words. Leave a space before the first period of the ellipsis and leave a space after the third period of the ellipsis before continuing with the quoted matter.

"However, if we switch our focus...to the larger economic issues, we begin to see that homelessness cannot be resolved solely at the level of individual treatment" (Stamp 8).

Omitting Material at the End of the Original Sentence   If no parenthetical reference is needed, insert a period before the first ellipsis period and provide the closing quotation mark, as in the first example below. If a parenthetical reference is needed, use only the ellipsis and add the period after the parentheses.

The First Amendment of the Constitution of the United States lays the foundation for the doctrine of free speech: "Congress shall make no law respecting an establishment of religion, or prohibiting the free exercise thereof; or abridging the freedom of speech, or of the press...."

In discussing scientific reasoning, Angier states, "We can call this 'objective' reality if we like, as opposed to subjective reality..." (22).

Speaking of the scientific method, Angier says, "Much of the reason for its success is founded on another fundamental.... Scientists accept...that there is a reality capable of being understood...in a way that can be shared with and agreed upon by others" (22).

Omitting Material at the Start of a Quotation   No ellipses are required. Simply place the quotation marks where you begin quoting directly. Capitalize the first word if the resulting quotation forms a complete sentence.

Simply providing housing for homeless will not suffice: "Programs need to supply employment and life skills training" (Stamp 8).

Adding Material to a Quotation   If, for the sake of clarity or grammar, you need to add a word or short phrase to a quotation (for example, by changing a verb tense or replacing a vague pronoun with a noun), enclose your insertion in brackets:

Moreover, Angier discredits the concept that "the two [objective reality and subjective reality] are discrete entities with remarkably little in common" (22).

Capitalizing and Punctuating Short Quotations

The way a short quotation is used in a sentence determines whether it begins or doesn't begin with a capital letter and whether it is or isn't preceded by a comma. For the formatting and punctuation of a long (block) quotation, see pages 473–474.

Introducing a Quotation That Can Stand Alone as a Sentence   If a quotation can stand alone as a grammatical sentence, capitalize the quotation's first word. Also, precede the quotation with a comma:

Stamp observes, "Beginning in the 1980s and through the 1990s, the gap between the rich and the poor has widened..." (8).

According to Stamp, "Federal funding for low-cost housing has been almost eliminated" (8).

Using* That, Which, *or* Who *(Stated or Implied)   If you use *that, which,* or *who* to blend a quotation into the structure of your own sentence, don't capitalize the quotation's first word and don't precede it with a comma.

Stamp observes that "beginning in the 1980s and through the 1990s, the gap between the rich and the poor has widened, buying power has stagnated, industrial jobs have fled overseas, and federal funding for low-cost housing has been almost eliminated" (8).

Angier describes scientists as firmly believing there is "a reality capable of being understood" (22).

Even if, as in the first example above, the material being quoted originally started with a capital letter, you still use lowercase when incorporating the quotation into your own sentence. Note that in the second example, the word *that* is implied (before the word *there*).

Interrupting a Full-Sentence Quotation with an Attribution   Place commas on both sides of the attribution, and resume the quotation with a lowercase letter.

"The key to any successful homeless policy," Stamp comments, "requires a clear understanding of just who are the homeless" (8).

Using a Quotation with a Quoted Word or Phrase   When a source you're quoting contains a quoted word or phrase, place single quotation marks around the quoted words. (See page 473 for how to treat a source that is quoting another source.)

"We can call this 'objective' reality if we like, as opposed to subjective reality, or opinion, or 'whimsical set of predilections,'" Angier posits (22).

Punctuating with a Question Mark or Exclamation Point   If the question mark or exclamation point is part of the quotation, place it inside the quotation marks. If the mark is part of the structure of the framing sentence, as in the second example below, place it outside the quotation marks and after any parenthetical reference.

Discussing a child's epileptic attack, the psychoanalyst Erik Erikson asks, in *Childhood and Society*, "What was the psychic stimulus?" (26).

But what does Stamp see as the "key to any successful homeless policy" (8)?

Presenting Statistics

Citing statistics can be a successful strategy for supporting your ideas. Be careful, though, not to misinterpret the data or twist their significance, and remember to provide an attribution indicating the source. Also, be sure not to overwhelm readers with too many statistics; include only those that support your central points in compelling ways. Keep in mind, too, that statistics won't speak for themselves. You need to interpret them for readers, showing how the figures cited reinforce your key ideas.

Ineffective Use of Statistics   For a paper showing that Medicare reform is needed to control increasing costs, one student writer presented the following statistics.

The Centers for Medicaid and Medicare Services reports that 1992 revenues ($185 billion) exceeded spending ($120 billion). But in 1997, revenues ($204 billion) and spending ($208 billion) were almost the same. It is projected that by the year 2010, revenues will be $310 billion and spending $410 billion (Mohr 14).

The student gave one statistic after the other, without explanatory commentary or attribution. This presentation makes it hard for the reader to understand the meaning of the statistics.

Effective Use of Statistics   Instead of including so many statistics, the writer could have presented only the most telling statistics, being sure to explain their significance.

The Centers for Medicaid and Medicare Services reports that in 1992, Medicare revenues actually exceeded spending by about $65 billion. But five years later, costs had increased so much that they exceeded revenues by about $4 billion. This trend toward escalated costs is expected to continue. It's projected that by the year 2010, revenues will be only $310 billion, while spending—if not controlled—will climb to at least $410 billion (Mohr 14).

☑ INTEGRATING SOURCES INTO YOUR WRITING: A CHECKLIST

❑ Introduce an important or oft-used source by giving the author's full name and credentials at the first mention. Thereafter, refer to author by last name only. Don't use personal titles such as *Mr.* or *Ms.*

❑ Use general introductions (*One historian says...*) for less important sources.

❑ Vary the style of attributions by sometimes positioning them at the middle or end, using different verbs, or blending quotations into your own sentences.

❑ Words may be deleted from a quotation as long as the author's original meaning isn't changed. Insert an ellipsis (...) in place of the deleted words. An ellipsis is not needed when material is omitted from the start of a quotation. Use a period plus an ellipsis when the end of a sentence is deleted.

❑ Use brackets to add clarifying information to quotations.

❑ If a quotation can stand alone as a grammatical sentence, capitalize its first word and precede it with a comma. If a quotation is blended

into the structure of your own sentence, don't capitalize the quotation's first word and don't precede it with a comma. If an attribution interrupts a quotation, place commas before and after the attribution and resume the quotation with a lowercase letter.
❑ For a quotation within a quotation, use single quotation marks.
❑ Place question marks and exclamation points inside quotation marks only if they belong to the quotation.
❑ Limit statistics and explain them fully to convey essential information.

DOCUMENTING SOURCES: MLA STYLE

In Chapter 11, you learned the importance of documentation—giving credit to the print and electronic sources whose words and ideas you borrow in an essay (see page 365). That earlier discussion showed you how to document sources in informal papers. The following pages will show you how to use the documentation system of the Modern Language Association (MLA)[1] when citing sources in more formal papers.

To avoid plagiarism, you must provide documentation when you include quotations from a source or you summarize or paraphrase in your own words ideas or information from a source. However, if the information you are including is commonly known or is a matter of historical or scientific record (the date of the Gettyburg Address or the temperature at which water boils, for example), you need not document it.

The discussion here covers key features of the MLA system. For more detailed coverage, you may want to consult a recent composition handbook or the latest edition of the *MLA Handbook for Writers of Research Papers.* For a sample paper that uses MLA documentation, turn to the student essay on pages 380–386.

HOW TO DOCUMENT: MLA IN-TEXT REFERENCES

The MLA documentation system uses the *parenthetical reference,* a brief note in parentheses inserted into the text after borrowed material. The parenthetical reference doesn't provide full bibliographic information, but it presents

---

[1]MLA documentation is appropriate in papers written for humanities courses, such as your composition class. If you're writing a paper for a course in the social sciences (for example, psychology, economics, or sociology), your professor will probably expect you to use the citation format developed by the American Psychological Association (APA). For information about APA documentation, consult *The Longman Writer* or the most recent edition of the *Publication Manual of the American Psychological Association.*

enough so that readers can turn to the Works Cited list (see pages 385–386) at the end of the paper for complete information.

Whenever you quote or summarize material from an outside source, you must do two things: (1) identify the source (usually an author) and (2) specify the page(s) in your source on which the material appears. The author's name may be given either in an introduction (often called the *attribution*) or in the parentheses following the borrowed material. The page number always appears in parentheses, usually at the end of the sentence just before the period. The examples below illustrate the MLA documentation style. You may also consult pages 464–468 for additional examples of attributions and parenthetical references.

Single Source: Parentheses Only

In the following example, a complete parenthetical reference follows a summary.

Counseling and support services are not enough to solve the problem of homelessness; proposed solutions must also address the complex economic issues at the heart of homelessness (Stamp 8).

If a source is alphabetized by title in your Works Cited list, use a shortened version of the title in place of the author's name in the parenthetical reference. In the following example, the full title of the source is "Supreme Court of the United States."

The U.S. Supreme Court is fundamentally an appeals court, responsible for "cases arising under the Constitution, laws, or treaties of the United States" among others ("Supreme Court").

Complete parenthetical references follow these uses of quotation. Note the punctuation in the second example, where the comma in the quotation is part of the original sentence.

If we look beyond the problems of homelessness, to "larger economic issues," it is clear that "homelessness cannot be resolved solely at the level of the individual" (Stamp 8).

Given the fact that a significant percentage of the homeless suffer from mental illness, "programs need to offer psychiatric care…, not just housing subsidies" (Stamp 8).

Single Source: Parentheses and Attributions

The attribution should make it clear where the quotation, summary, or paraphrase begins.

Julian Stamp argues that homelessness must be addressed in terms of economics, not simply in terms of individual counseling, addiction therapy, or job training (8).

As Stamp explains, "The key to any successful homeless policy requires a clear understanding of just who are the homeless" (8).

Because half of those taking refuge in shelters have problems with drugs and alcohol, Stamp reasons that "programs need to provide not only a place to sleep but also comprehensive substance-abuse treatment" (8).

According to statistics, half of the homeless individuals living in shelters are substance abusers (Stamp 8).

In *The Homeless and History*, Stamp maintains that economic issues, rather than difficulties in people's personal lives, are at the core of the homeless problem (8).

Stamp points out that "homelessness cannot be resolved solely at the level of the individual" (8), although other experts disagree.

Note that in the immediately preceding example, the parenthetical reference follows the quotation in the middle of the sentence; placing the reference at the end of sentence would erroneously imply that idea expressed by "although other experts disagree" is Stamp's.

More Than One Source by the Same Author

When your paper includes references to more than one work by the same author, you must specify—either in the parenthetical reference or in the attribution—the particular work being cited. You do this by providing the title, as well as the author's name and the page(s). Here are examples from a paper in which two works by the psychologist Jean Piaget were used.

In *The Language and Thought of the Child*, Jean Piaget states that "discussion forms the basis for a logical point of view" (240).

Piaget considers dialogue essential to the development of logical thinking (*Language and Thought* 240).

The Child's Conception of the World shows that young children think that the name of something can never change (Piaget 81).

Young children assume that everything has only one name and that no others are possible (Piaget, *Child's Conception* 81).

Notice that when a work is named in the attribution, the full title appears; when a title is given in the parenthetic citation, though, only the first few significant words appear. (However, don't use the ellipsis to indicate that some words have been omitted from the title; the ellipsis is used only in actual quotations.) Note also that when name, title, and page number all appear in the parenthetical reference, a comma follows the author's name.

Source Within a Source

If you quote or summarize a *secondary source* (a source whose ideas come to you only through another source), you need to make this clear. The parenthetical documentation should indicate "as quoted in" with the abbreviation *qtd. in*:

According to Sherman, "Recycling has, in several communities, created unanticipated expenses" (qtd. in Pratt 3).

Sherman explains that recycling can be surprisingly costly (qtd. in Pratt 3).

If the material you're quoting includes a quotation, place single quotation marks around the secondary quotation:

Pratt believes that "recycling efforts will be successful if, as Sherman argues, 'communities launch effective public-education campaigns' " (3).

Note: Your Works Cited list should include the source you actually read (Pratt), rather than the source you refer to secondhand (Sherman).

Long (Block) Quotations

A quotation longer than four lines starts on a new line and is indented, throughout, one inch from the left margin. Since this block format indicates a quotation, quotation marks are unnecessary. Double-space the block quotation as you do the rest of your paper. Don't leave extra space above or below the quotation. Long quotations, always used sparingly, require a lead-in. A lead-in that isn't a full sentence is followed by a comma; a lead-in that is a full sentence (see below) is followed by a colon:

Stamp cites changing economic conditions as the key to a national homeless policy:

> Beginning in the 1980s and through the 1990s, the gap between the rich and the poor has widened, buying power has stagnated, industrial jobs have fled overseas, and federal funding for low-cost housing has been almost eliminated. Given these developments, homelessness begins to look like a product of history, our recent history, and only by addressing shifts in the American economy can we begin to find effective solutions for people lacking homes. (8)

Notice that the page number in parentheses appears *after* the period, not before as it would with a short quotation.

Key Points to Remember

Take a moment to look again at the preceding examples and note the points presented in the following checklist.

☑ USING MLA PARENTHETICAL REFERENCES: A CHECKLIST

❑ The parenthetical reference is usually placed immediately after the borrowed material.

❑ The parenthetical reference is placed before any internal punctuation (a comma or semicolon) as well as before any terminal punctuation (a period or question mark).

❑ If you want to call attention to a specific author, use an attribution indicating the author's name. The first time the author is referred to in an attribution, give the author's full name; afterward, give only the last name. To inform readers of an author's area of expertise, identify the author by profession (*The historian Julian Stamp argues that...*), title, or affiliation.

❑ When an author's name is provided in the attribution, the name is not repeated in the parentheses. When the author's name is provided in the parentheses, only the last name is given.

❑ If a source is cited by title rather than author, use a shortened form of the title in the parenthetical reference.

❑ The page number comes directly after the author's name. (If the source is only one page long, only the author's name is needed.) There is no punctuation between the author's name and the page number, and there is no *p.* or *page* preceding the page number.

HOW TO DOCUMENT: MLA LIST OF WORKS CITED

A documented paper ends with a list of Works Cited, which includes only those sources you actually acknowledge in the paper. Placed on its own page, the Works Cited list provides the reader with full bibliographic information about the sources cited in the parenthetical references (see pages 470–474).

By referring to the Works Cited list that appears at the end of the student essay on pages 385–386, you will notice the following:

- The list is organized alphabetically by authors' last names. Entries without an author are alphabetized by the first major word in the title (that is, not *A, An,* or *The*).
- Entries are not numbered.
- If an entry runs longer than one line, each additional line is indented half an inch. Entries are double-spaced with no extra space between entries.
- Each entry gives the medium in which the source was found, for example, "Print" for an article found in a printed newspaper or "Web" for an article found in the online version of a newspaper.

Listed here are sample Works Cited entries for the most commonly used kinds of sources. Refer to these samples when you prepare your own Works Cited list, taking special care to reproduce the punctuation and spacing exactly. If you don't spot an entry for the kind of source you need to document, consult the latest edition of the *MLA Handbook*[2] for more comprehensive examples.

CITING PRINT SOURCES—BOOKS

Titles of major works should be italicized (or underlined if your instructor prefers). Include the medium of publication (*Print*) at the end of the citation.

Book by One Author

List the author's last name followed by a comma, the first name, and a period. Then give the title (italicized or underlined),[3] followed by a period. Next, give the city of publication, followed by a colon and the shortened version of the publisher's name (for example, use *UP* for "University Press" and *Norton* for "W.W. Norton & Co."), a comma, the year of publication, and a period. End with the medium of publication (*Print*) and a period.

McDonnell, Lorraine M. *Politics, Persuasion, and Educational Testing.* Cambridge: Harvard UP, 2004. Print.

Book by Two or Three Authors

Provide all the authors' names in the order in which they appear on the title page of the book, but reverse only the first author's name.

[2]Formats given here are the latest recommendations from the Modern Language Association, published in the *MLA Handbook for Writers of Research Papers,* Seventh Edition (2009).
[3]For a review of when titles should be italicized and when they should appear in quotation marks, see page 495, the "Misuse of Italics and Underlining" section of Appendix B.

Douglas, Susan, and Meredith Michaels. *The Mommy Myth: The Idealization of Motherhood and How It Has Undermined Women.* New York: Free Press, 2004. Print.

Gunningham, Neil A., Robert Kagan, and Dorothy Thornton. *Shades of Green: Business, Regulation, and Environment.* Palo Alto: Stanford UP, 2003. Print.

Book by Four or More Authors

For a work by four or more authors, give only the first author's name followed by a comma and *et al.* (Latin for "and others"). Do not italicize "et al."

Brown, Michael K., et al. *Whitewashing Race: The Myth of a Color-Blind Society.* Berkeley: U of California P, 2003. Print.

Two or More Works by the Same Author

If you use more than one work by the same author, list each book separately. Give the author's name in the first entry only; begin the entries for other books by that author with three hyphens followed by a period. Arrange the works alphabetically by title.

McChesney, Robert W. *The Problem of the Media: U.S. Communication Politics in the 21st Century.* New York: Monthly Review, 2004. Print.

---. *Rich Media, Poor Democracy: Communication Politics in Dubious Times.* Champaign: U of Illinios P, 1999. Print.

Revised Edition

Indicate a revised edition (*Rev. ed., 2nd ed., 3rd ed., 4th ed.,* and so on) after the title.

Weiss, Thomas G., David P. Forsythe, and Roger A. Coate. *The United Nations and Changing World Politics.* 3rd ed. Boulder: Westview, 2001. Print.

Zinn, Howard. *A People's History of the United States: 1492-Present.* Rev. ed. New York: Perennial, 2003. Print.

Book with an Editor or Translator

Following the title, type *Ed.* or *Trans.* (for "Edited by" or "Translated by"), followed by the name of the editor or translator.

Douglass, Frederick. *My Bondage and My Freedom.* Ed. John David Smith. New York: Penguin, 2003. Print.

Anthology or Compilation of Works by Different Authors

List anthologies according to editors' names, followed by *ed.* or *eds.* (for "editor" or "editors").

Kasser, Tim, and Allen D. Kanner, eds. *Psychology and Consumer Culture: The Struggle for a Good Life in a Materialistic World.* Washington, DC: American Psychological Association, 2004. Print.

Section of an Anthology or Compilation

Begin this entry with the author and title of the selection (in quotation marks), followed by the title of the anthology. The editors' names are listed after the anthology title and are preceded by *Ed.* (for "Edited by"). Note that the entry gives the page numbers on which the selection appears.

Levin, Diane E., and Susan Linn. "The Commercialization of Childhood: Understanding the Problem and Finding Solutions." *Psychology and Consumer Culture: The Struggle for a Good Life in a Materialistic World.* Ed. Tim Kasser and Allen D. Kanner. Washington, DC: American Psychological Association, 2004. 212-28. Print.

Section or Chapter in a Book by One Author

Wolfson, Evan. "Is Marriage Equality a Question of Civil Rights?" *Why Marriage Matters: America, Equality, and Gay People's Right to Marry.* New York: Simon, 2004. 242-69. Print.

Reference Work

"Temperance Movements." *Columbia Encyclopedia.* 6th ed. New York: Columbia UP, 2000. Print.

Book by an Institution or Corporation

Give the name of the institution or corporation in the author position, even if the same institution is the publisher.

United Nations. Department of Economic and Social Affairs. *Human Development, Health, and Education: Dialogues at the Economic and Social Council.* New York: United Nations, 2004.

CITING PRINT SOURCES—PERIODICALS

Titles of periodicals should be italicized (or underlined if your instructor prefers). Abbreviate names of months, except for *May*, *June*, and *July*. If the article is printed on multiple, nonconsecutive pages, simply list the first page (including any section letters) followed by a plus sign (+). Include the medium of publication (*Print*) at the end of the citation.

Article in a Weekly or Biweekly Magazine

Provide the author's name (if the article is signed) and article title (in quotation marks). Then give the periodical name (italicized and with *no* period) and date of publication (day, month, year), followed by a colon and the page number(s) of the article. End with the medium of publication (*Print*).

Leo, John. "Campus Censors in Retreat." *U.S. News & World Report* 16 Feb. 2004: 64-65. Print.

Article in a Monthly or Bimonthly Magazine

Wheeler, Jacob. "Outsourcing the Public Good." *Utne* Sept.-Oct. 2004: 13-14. Print.

Article in a Daily Newspaper

Omit the initial *The* from newspaper names.

Doolin, Joseph. "Immigrants Deserve a Fair Deal." *Boston Globe* 19 Aug. 2003: A19+. Print.

Editorial, Letter to the Editor, or Reply to a Letter

List as you would any signed or unsigned article, but indicate the type of piece after the article's title.

Johnson, Paul. "Want to Prosper? Then Be Tolerant." Editorial. *Forbes* 21 June 2004: 41. Print.

"Playing Fair with Nuclear Cleanup." Editorial. *Seattle Times* 5 Oct. 2003: D2. Print.

Article in a Scholarly Journal

Most journals, like the one cited in the second example below, are paginated continuously; the first issue of each year starts with page 1, and each subsequent issue picks up where the previous one left off. Some journals do not paginate continuously; they start each new issue in a year with page 1.

Regardless of how a journal is paginated, include *both* the issue number (if available) and the volume number. After the title, give the volume number followed by a period, then the issue number, and then the year in parentheses. Use arabic, not roman, numerals, without either *volume* or *vol*. The article's page(s) appear at the end, separated from the year by a colon. Give the medium of publication (*Print*) at the end.

Chew, Cassie. "Achieving Unity through Diversity." *Black Issues in Higher Education* 21.5 (2004): 8-11. Print.

Manning, Wendy D. "Children and the Stability of Cohabiting Couples." *Journal of Marriage & Family* 66.3 (2004): 674-89. Print.

CITING SOURCES FOUND ON A WEBSITE

Citations for sources found on the Internet require much of the same information used in citations for print sources. Internet addresses (URLs) change so frequently that unless you judge that a source would be very difficult to find without one, do not give the URL in the citation. (See "Personal or Professional Website" for an example using a URL.) To cite an item from a website, supply the following information:

- Author's name
- Selection's title (in quotation marks)
- Source—generally the title of the website (italicized or underlined)
- Version or edition of the website, if relevant
- Publisher or sponsor of the website—often found at the bottom of the Web page (or *N.p.* for "no publisher")
- Publication date (or *n.d.* for "no date")
- Publication medium (*Web*)
- The date you retrieved the information (day, month, year)

Newspaper or Magazine Article

Orecklin, Michele. "Stress and the Superdad." *Time.* Time.com, 16 Aug. 2004. Web. 2 Dec. 2008.

Nachtigal, Jeff. "We Own What You Think." *Salon.com.* Salon Media Group, 18 Aug. 2004. Web. 17 Mar. 2005.

"Restoring the Wetlands." Editorial. *Los Angeles Times.* Los Angeles Times, 26 July 2008. Web. 6 Jan. 2009.

Online Reference Work

"Salem Witch Trials." *Encyclopaedia Britannica Online.* Encyclopaedia Britannica, 2008. Web. 3 Jan. 2009.

Scholarly Journal Found on the Internet

For articles accessed from a website, follow the citation format for print articles, but specify *Web* as the medium and give the date of access. If no page numbers are available, insert *n. pg.* See also the entry for "Scholarly Journal Found in an Online Database."

Njeng, Eric Sipyinyu. "Achebe, Conrad, and the Postcolonial Strain." *CLCWeb: Comparative Literature and Culture* 10.1 (2008): 1-8. Web. 12 Dec. 2008.

Qin, Desiree Baolian. "The Role of Gender in Immigrant Children's Educational Adaptation." *Current Issues in Comparative Education* 9.1 (2006): 8-19. Web. 5 Jan. 2009.

Personal or Professional Website

Because the site would otherwise be difficult to access, the first entry below contains a URL, enclosed in angle brackets and followed by a period. Note that long Web addresses should be broken up only after slashes. In the second entry below, *Uncle Tom's Cabin* is *not* italicized. It's a title that would ordinarily be italicized, but since the rest of the website title is italicized, the book title is set off in regular type.

Finney, Dee. *Native American Culture.* 23 May 2008. Web. 6 June 2008. <http://www.greatdreams.com/native.htm>.

Railton, Stephen, ed. Uncle Tom's Cabin *& American Culture: A Multi-Media Archive.* Dept. of English, U of Virginia, 2007. Web. 9 Apr. 2006.

Blog

If the blog has no title, insert "Online posting" in place of the title, without quotation marks or italics.

Waldman, Deane. "'Care' Has Deserted Managed Care." *Huffington Post.* HuffingtonPost.com, 26 June 2008. Web. 18 Nov. 2008.

Podcast

Elisabeth Arnold. "Tale of Two Alaska Villages." *NPR.org.* Natl. Public Radio, 29 July 2008. Web. 13 Dec. 2008.

CITING SOURCES FOUND THROUGH AN ONLINE DATABASE OR SCHOLARLY PROJECT

Specify the database or project, but do not include the URL or information about the library system used.

Scholarly Journal Found in an Online Database

For articles accessed through an online database, begin with the same information as for online periodicals. After the publication information (volume, issue, date, and page numbers), give the title of the database (italicized or underlined) and the medium of publication (*Web*). Complete the entry with the date you accessed the information. See also the entry "Scholarly Journal Found on the Internet."

Weiler, Angela M. "Using Technology to Take Down Plagiarism." *Community College Week* 16.16 (2004): 4-6. *EBSCOhost*. Web. 17 Oct. 2008.

Book Found in an Online Scholarly Project

When it's available, include the book's original publication information. Also include (when available) the name of the site's editor, its electronic publication date, its sponsoring organization, your date of access, and the Web address.

Franklin, Benjamin. *The Autobiography of Benjamin Franklin*. London, 1793. *Electronic Text Center*. Ed. Judy Boss. Web. 16 Jan. 2009.

CITING OTHER COMMON SOURCES

Include the medium through which you accessed the source, for example, *CD* for "compact disc" or *E-mail* for an e-mail message you received.

Television or Radio Program

"A Matter of Choice? Gay Life in America." Part 4 of 5. *Nightline*. Narr. Ted Koppel. ABC. WPVI-TV, Philadelphia, 23 May 2002. Television.

Movie, Recording, Videotape, DVD, Filmstrip, or Slide Program

Provide the author or composer of the piece (if appropriate); title (italicized or underlined); director, conductor, or performer; manufacturer or distributor; and year of release. Give the medium at the end of the citation.

Fahrenheit 911. Dir. Michael Moore. Sony, 2004. DVD.

CD-ROM or DVD-ROM

Cite the following information (when available): author, title (italicized or underlined), version, place of publication, publisher, year of publication, and medium (*CD-ROM* or *DVD-ROM*).

World Book Encyclopedia. 2006 Edition. Renton, WA: Topics Entertainment, 2006. CD-ROM.

Personal or Telephone Interview

Specify "Personal interview" for an interview you conducted in person and "Telephone interview" for an interview you conducted over the telephone.

Langdon, Paul. Personal interview. 26 Jan. 2008.

Lecture, Speech, Address, or Reading

Blacksmith, James. "Urban Design in the New Millennium." Cityscapes Lecture Series. Urban Studies Institute. Metropolitan College, Washington, DC. 18 Apr. 2005. Lecture.

Papa, Andrea. "Reforming the Nation's Tax Structure." Accounting 302. Cypress College, Astoria, NY. 3 Dec. 2004. Lecture.

E-mail Message

Start with the sender's name. Then give the title (from the subject line) in quotation marks, a description, the date of the message, and the medium (*E-mail*).

Mack, Lynn. "New Developments in Early Childhood Education." Message to the author. 30 Aug. 2006. E-mail.

AVOIDING TEN COMMON WRITING ERRORS

Many students consider grammar a nuisance. Taking the easy way out, they cross their fingers and hope they haven't made too many mistakes. They assume that their meaning will come across, even if their writing contains some errors—perhaps a misplaced comma here or a dangling modifier there. Not so. Surface errors annoy readers and may confuse them. Such errors also weaken a writer's credibility because they defy language conventions, customs that readers expect writers to honor. By mastering grammar, punctuation, and spelling conventions, students can increase their power and versatility as writers.

This concise appendix, "Avoiding Ten Common Writing Errors," will help you brush up on the most useful rules and conventions of writing. It's organized according to the broad skill areas, listed below, that give writers the most trouble. (For more extensive instruction in grammar and style, refer to the Handbook section of *The Longman Writer.*) Throughout this appendix, grammatical terminology is kept to a minimum. Although we assume that you know the major parts of speech (noun, verb, pronoun, and so on), we do, when appropriate, provide on-the-spot definitions of more technical grammatical terms.

Here are the ten common writing errors covered:

1. Fragments
2. Comma Splices and Run-ons
3. Faulty Subject-Verb Agreement

   4. Faulty Pronoun Agreement
   5. Misplaced and Dangling Modifiers
   6. Faulty Parallelism
   7. Comma Misuse
   8. Apostrophe Misuse
   9. Confusing Homonyms
   10. Misuse of Italics and Underlining

1 FRAGMENTS

A full *sentence* satisfies two conditions: (1) it has a subject and a verb, and (2) it can stand alone as a complete thought. Although a *fragment* is punctuated like a full sentence, it doesn't satisfy these two requirements.

> **NO**   Meteorologists predict a drought this summer. *In spite of heavy spring rains.*
>
> **NO**   *A victim of her own hypocrisy.* The senator lost the next election.

Some Easy Ways to Correct Fragments

A. Attach the fragment to the beginning or end of the preceding (or following) sentence, changing punctuation and capitalization as needed.

> **YES**   In spite of heavy spring rains, meteorologists predict a drought this summer.
>
> *or*
>
> Meteorologists predict a drought this summer, in spite of heavy spring rains.

B. Attach the fragment to a newly created sentence.

> **YES**   Meteorologists predict a drought this summer. *They do so* in spite of heavy spring rains.

C. Insert the fragment into the preceding (or following) sentence, adding commas as needed.

> **YES**   The senator, *a victim of her own hypocrisy,* lost the next election.

D. Supply the missing subject and/or verb, changing other words as necessary.

> **YES**   *The senator became* a victim of her own hypocrisy. *She* lost the next election.

2 COMMA SPLICES AND RUN-ONS

Consider the following faulty sentences:

> **NO**   The First Amendment cannot be taken for granted, it is the bedrock of our democracy.
>
> **NO**   The First Amendment cannot be taken for granted it is the bedrock of our democracy.

The first example is a *comma splice:* a comma used to join, or splice together, two complete thoughts, even though the comma alone is not strong enough to connect the two independent ideas. The second example is a *run-on,* or fused, sentence: two sentences run together without any punctuation indicating where the first sentence ends and the second begins.

Some Easy Ways to Correct Comma Splices and Run-ons

A. Place a period, question mark, or exclamation point at the end of the first sentence, and capitalize the first letter of the second sentence.

> **YES**   The First Amendment cannot be taken for *granted. It* is the bedrock of our democracy.

B. Use a semicolon to mark where the first sentence ends and the second begins.

> **YES**   The First Amendment cannot be taken for *granted; it* is the bedrock of our democracy.

C. Turn one of the sentences into a dependent phrase.

> **YES**   *Because* it is the bedrock of our democracy, the First Amendment cannot be taken for granted.

D. Keep or add a comma at the end of the first sentence, but follow the comma with a coordinating conjunction (*and, but, for, nor, or, so, yet*).

> **YES**   The First Amendment cannot be taken for granted, *for* it is the bedrock of our democracy.

3 FAULTY SUBJECT-VERB AGREEMENT

A verb should match its subject in number. If the subject is singular (one person, place, or thing), the verb should have a singular form. If the subject is plural (two or more persons, places, or things), the verb should have a plural form. Always determine the verb's subject and make sure that the verb agrees with it, rather than with some other word in the sentence.

> **NO**   The *documents* from the court case *was* unsealed for the first time in three decades.
>
> **YES**   The *documents* from the court case *were* unsealed for the first time in three decades.

Some Easy Ways to Correct Faulty Subject-Verb Agreement

A. When there are two or more singular subjects (joined by *and*) in a sentence, use a plural verb. (However, when the word *or* joins the subjects, use a *singular* verb.)

> **YES**   A sprawling maple *and* a lush rose bush *flank* [not *flanks*] my childhood home.

B. When the subject and verb are separated by a prepositional phrase, be sure to match the verb to its subject—not to a word in the prepositional phrase that comes between them.

> **YES**   The *quality* of student papers *has* [not *have*] been declining over the past semester.

C. When the words *either...or* or *neither...nor* connect two subjects, use the verb form (singular or plural) that agrees with the subject *closer* to the verb.

> **YES**   *Neither* the employees *nor* the store *owner was* [not *were*] aware of the theft.
>
> **YES**   *Neither* the store owner *nor* her *employees were* [not *was*] aware of the theft.

D. When using the indefinite pronouns *anybody, anyone, anything, each, either, everybody, everyone, everything, neither, nobody, none, no one, nothing, one, somebody, someone,* or *something,* use a *singular* verb.

> **YES**   *Neither* of the candidates *is* [not *are*] willing to address the issue.

When you use the indefinite pronouns *all, any, most, none,* or *some,* use a **singular** or a **plural** verb, depending on whether the pronoun refers to one thing or to a number of things.

> **YES**   The spokesperson announced that only *some* of the *report has* been confirmed.

In the preceding sentence, *some* refers to a single report and therefore takes a *singular* verb. In the following sentence, *some* refers to *multiple* reports and therefore takes a *plural* verb.

> **YES**   The spokesperson announced that only *some* of the *reports have* been confirmed.

E. When the subject of a sentence refers to a group acting as a unit, use a *singular* verb.

> **YES**   The local baseball *team is* [not *are*] boycotting the new sports stadium.

F. When words such as *here, there, how, what, when, where, which, who,* and *why* invert normal sentence order—so that the verb comes before the subject—look ahead for the subject and make sure that it and the verb agree.

> **YES**   There *is* [not *are*] a *series* of things to consider before deciding on a college major.
>
> **YES**   What *are* [not *is*] the *arguments* against energy conservation?

---

4 FAULTY PRONOUN AGREEMENT

A *pronoun* must agree in number with its *antecedent*—the noun or pronoun it replaces or refers to. If the antecedent is singular, the pronoun must be singular. If the antecedent is plural, the pronoun must be plural.

Some Easy Ways to Correct Faulty Pronoun Agreement

A. A compound subject (two or more nouns joined by *and*) requires plural pronouns.

> **YES**   Both the car *manufacturers* and the tire *company* had trouble restoring *their* reputations after losing the class-action lawsuit.

However, when the nouns are joined by *or* or *nor,* the pronoun form (singular or plural) should agree with the noun that is **closer** to the verb.

> **YES**   Neither the car manufacturers *nor* the tire *company* restored *its* reputation after losing the class-action lawsuit.
>
> **YES**   Neither the tire company *nor* the car *manufacturers* restored *their* reputations after losing the class-action lawsuit.

B. A subject that is a *collective noun* (referring to a group that acts as a unit) takes a singular pronoun.

YES   The *orchestra* showed *its* appreciation by playing a lengthy encore.

Or, if a singular pronoun sounds awkward, simply make the antecedent plural.

YES   The orchestra *members* showed *their* appreciation by playing a lengthy encore.

C. The indefinite pronouns *anybody, anyone, anything, each, either, everybody, everyone, everything, neither, nobody, no one, nothing, one, somebody, someone,* and *something* are singular and therefore take singular pronouns.

YES   *Each* of the buildings had *its* [not *their*] roof replaced.
YES   *Neither* of the executives resigned *his* [not *their*] position after the revelations.

Using the singular form with indefinite pronouns can be awkward or sexist when the pronoun encompasses both male and female. To avoid these problems, you can make the antecedent plural and use a plural pronoun.

AWK   *Anyone* who exhibits symptoms should see her or his doctor immediately.
YES   *Individuals* who exhibit symptoms should see *their* doctor immediately.

D. Within a sentence, pronouns should be in the same *person* (point of view) as their antecedents.

NO   To register to vote, *citizens* [third person] can visit the state government's website, where *you* [second person] can download the appropriate forms.
YES   To register to vote, *citizens* [third person] can visit the state government's website, where *they* [third person] can download the appropriate forms.

5 MISPLACED AND DANGLING MODIFIERS

A *modifier* is a word or group of words that describes something else. Sometimes sentences are written in such a way that modifiers are misplaced. Here is an example of a *misplaced modifier:*

NO   Television stations carried the story of the disastrous tornado *throughout the nation.* [The tornado was throughout the nation?]
YES   Television stations *throughout the nation* carried the story of the disastrous tornado.

Modifiers are commonly misused in another way. An introductory modifier must modify the subject of the sentence. If it doesn't, it may be a *dangling modifier*. Here's an example:

> **NO**   *Faded and brittle with age,* archaeologists unearthed a painted clay pot near the riverbank. [The archaeologists were faded and brittle with age?]
>
> **YES**   Archaeologists unearthed a painted clay pot, *faded and brittle with age,* near the riverbank.
> *or*
> *Faded and brittle with age,* a painted clay pot was unearthed near the riverbank by archaeologists.

An Easy Way to Correct Misplaced Modifiers

A. Place the modifier next to the word(s) it describes.

> **NO**   Passengers complained about the flight at the customer service desk, *which was turbulent and delayed.* [The customer service desk was turbulent and delayed?]
>
> **YES**   Passengers complained about the flight, *which was turbulent and delayed,* at the customer service desk.
>
> **NO**   She *nearly* ran the marathon in four hours. [Did she or didn't she run?]
> **YES**   She ran the marathon in *nearly* four hours.

Some Easy Ways to Correct Dangling Modifiers
The following dangling modifier can be corrected in one of two ways, discussed below.

> **NO**   *Leaping gracefully across the stage,* spectators were in awe of the agile dancer.

A. Rewrite the sentence by adding to the modifying phrase the word that is being described.

> **YES**   *As the agile dancer leaped* gracefully across the stage, spectators were in awe of him.

B. Rewrite the sentence so that the word being modified becomes the subject.

> **YES**   Leaping gracefully across the stage, the agile dancer awed the spectators.

6 FAULTY PARALLELISM

Items in a pair, a series, or a list should be phrased in *parallel* (matching) grammatical structures. Otherwise, *faulty parallelism* results.

> **NO**   After hiking all day, the campers were *exhausted, hungry,* and *experienced soreness.* [Of the three items in the series, the first two are adjectives, but the last is a verb plus a noun.]
>
> **YES**   After hiking all day, the campers were *exhausted, hungry,* and *sore.*

Words that follow *correlative conjunctions—either . . . or, neither . . . nor, both . . . and, not only . . . but also*—should also be parallel.

> **NO**   Every road to the airport is **either** *jammed* **or** *is closed* for repairs. [The word *either* is followed by an adjective (*jammed*), but *or* is followed by a verb and adjective (*is closed*).]
>
> **YES**   Every road to the airport is **either** *jammed* **or** *closed* for repairs.

An Easy Way to Correct Faulty Parallelism

A. Use the *same grammatical structure* for each item in a pair or series.

> **NO**   The finalists for the sales job possess *charismatic personalities, excellent references,* and *they are extensively experienced.*
>
> **YES**   The finalists for the sales job possess *charismatic personalities, excellent references,* and *extensive experience.*
>
> **NO**   We observed *that the leaves were changing color, the sun was setting earlier,* and *that the air was becoming chillier.* [The word *that* precedes the first and last clauses, but not the second. It must be inserted before the second clause or, preferably, deleted from before the last clause.]
>
> **YES**   We observed *that the leaves were changing color, the sun was setting earlier,* and *the air was becoming chillier.*
>
> **NO**   Students go to college with many goals:
>
>   1. To become more educated.
>   2. Preparing for future careers.
>   3. They also want to meet new people.
>
> **YES**   Students go to college with many goals:
>
>   1. To become more educated.
>   2. To prepare for future careers.
>   3. To meet new people.

NO	The romantic comedy that premiered last night was neither *romantic* nor *was it funny*.
YES	The romantic comedy that premiered last night was neither *romantic* nor *funny*.

7 COMMA MISUSE

The *comma* is so frequent in writing that mastering its use is essential. By dividing a sentence into its parts, commas clarify meaning.

Most Common Uses of the Comma

A. When two complete sentences are joined with a coordinating conjunction (*and, but, for, nor, or, so, yet*), a comma is placed *before* the conjunction.

YES   Many attended the political rally, *but* few demonstrated enthusiasm for the cause.

B. Introductory material, which precedes a sentence's main subject and verb, usually is followed by a comma.

YES   *Like most kids,* the children in the study were powerfully influenced by TV advertisements.

Similarly, material attached to the end of a sentence may be preceded by a comma.

YES   The children in the study were powerfully influenced by TV advertisements, *which peddled expensive toys and unhealthy snacks.*

C. When a word or phrase describes a noun but isn't crucial for identifying that noun, it is set off from the rest of the sentence with a comma.

YES   First-year film students are required to analyze *Metropolis,* a late-1920s film that exhibited important artistic innovations.

D. When words or phrases inserted into the body of a sentence can be removed without significant loss of meaning, such elements are considered *interrupters*. Interrupters should be preceded and followed by commas when they occur midsentence.

YES   Dr. Gene Nome, *a leading genetic researcher,* testified before Congress on the need for increased funding.

E. In a list of *three or more* items in a series, the items should be separated by commas.

> YES   The writing process usually entails *prewriting, drafting,* and *revising.*

F. A comma should be inserted between a short quotation and a phrase that indicates the quotation's source.

> YES   One voter commented, "This is the first candidate I've voted for enthusiastically."
> *or*
> "This is the first candidate I've voted for enthusiastically," one voter commented.
> *or*
> "This is the first candidate," one voter commented, "I've voted for enthusiastically."

G. Commas are placed between the numbers in a date and between the elements of the address with the exception that no comma precedes a ZIP code.

> YES   On November 17, 2009, the fourth graders mailed "Dear President" letters to The White House, 1600 Pennsylvania Avenue, Washington, DC 20500.

8 APOSTROPHE MISUSE

Like the comma, the *apostrophe* is a commonly used—and misused—punctuation mark.

Most Common Uses of the Apostrophe

A. In standard contractions, an apostrophe replaces any omitted letters.

> YES   can't, don't, I'm, she's, we've

B. The possessive form of most singular nouns requires adding *'s*.

> YES   Senator Ross's position is that health care is every person's right.

For *plural nouns* ending in *s,* an apostrophe only is added to show possession.

> YES   The twelve senators' position on Native Americans' rights is clear.

Plural nouns that do not end in *s* need *'s* to show possession.

> YES   Improvement in the children**'s** test scores enabled the school to rise in rank.

However, an apostrophe is *not* used to form the simple plural of a noun.

> **NO**   The central role of *radio's* in American homes has declined in recent decades.
>
> YES   The central role of *radios* in American homes has declined in recent decades.

C. Beware of confusing possessive pronouns with contractions. The possessive forms of personal pronouns do *not* include an apostrophe. Here are the correct forms:

> YES   mine, yours, his, hers, its, ours, theirs

Note that *its* (*without* an apostrophe) is the possessive form of *it*, whereas *it's* (*with* an apostrophe) means "it is" or "it has."

> YES   The factory closed *its* [not *it's*] doors last week.
>
> YES   The company president determined that *it's* [for "it is"] time to close down the factory.

Similarly, *whose* (*without* an apostrophe) is the possessive form of *who*, whereas *who's* (*with* an apostrophe) means "who is" or "who has."

> YES   The sculptor *whose* [not *who's*] work is being exhibited just arrived at the gallery.
>
> YES   The sculptor *who's* [for *who is*] exhibiting his work just arrived at the gallery.

9 CONFUSING HOMONYMS

Homonyms are words that sound alike but have different spellings and meanings. Here are some of the most troublesome.

Accept means "receive" or "agree to." **Except** means "but" or "excluding."

> YES   *Except* for your position on mandatory school uniforms, I *accept* your ideas about changing the education system.

Affect means "influence" (verb). **Effect** means "result" (noun) or "bring about" (verb).

YES   It's amazing how much a hurricane's *effects* can *affect* a region's economy.

Its means "belonging to it." **It's** means "it is" or "it has."

YES   *It's* been years since the factory produced *its* last car.

Principal means either "main" (adjective) or "the person in charge of a school (noun)." **Principle** (noun) means "a law or concept."

YES   The *principal* topic you should study for your midterm is the *principle* of gravity.

Than is a word used in comparisons. **Then** means "at that time."

YES   The insurance agent assessed the house and *then* wrote a report stating that the damage was worse *than* expected.

Their means "belonging to them." **There** refers to a place other than "here." **They're** means "they are."

YES   *They're* planning to drop off *their* donations for the food drive in the bin over *there*.

To can be part of a verb (as in *to smile* or *came to*) or a preposition meaning "toward." **Too** means "overly" (as in *too hot*) or "also." **Two** refers to the number 2.

YES   *Two* of my coworkers go outside *to* eat lunch every day; today they invited me, *too*.

Whose means "belonging to someone or something." **Who's** means "who is" or "who has."

YES   We're trying to determine *who's* going to call my aunt, *whose* son was injured in an accident.

Your means "belonging to you." **You're** means "you are."

YES   When *your* mother calls you by *your* first, middle, and last name, you know *you're* in trouble.

10 MISUSE OF ITALICS AND UNDERLINING

Computers and other printing innovations have allowed italics (*slanted type*) to replace underlining (underlined type) in printed text. The following are the most common uses of italics (or of underlining, if you're writing by hand or if your instruction prefers underlining).

A. The titles of works that are published (or, in the case of visual works, displayed) individually should be italicized. Such works, which are often lengthy, include books, magazines, journals, newspapers, websites, online databases, movies (including DVDs), TV and radio programs, musical recordings (albums, CDs, audiocassettes), plays, paintings, and sculptures.

Note: The titles of shorter works—such as poems, short stories, articles, essays, songs, and TV episodes—published as part of a magazine, anthology, or other collection are not italicized; use quotation marks for such titles.

> YES After reading Anne Sexton's poem "The Starry Night" from the collection *All My Pretty Ones,* the students went online to look at Van Gogh's painting *The Starry Night.*
>
> YES The Discovery Channel program *The Beatles: The Later Years* focused primarily on the band's albums *Sgt. Pepper's Lonely Hearts Club Band* and *Abbey Road.*

B. Foreign words not fully incorporated into mainstream English should be italicized or underlined.

> YES The labor union leaders sought a *tête-à-tête* with the company's executives in order to resolve a work strike.

C. Words that you wish to emphasize should be italicized or underlined. However, this should be done sparingly at the risk of actually *weakening* emphasis.

> YES Users of the new computer program report that they don't like it. They *love* it.

D. When a word is being referred to *as a word* or as a *defined term,* it should be italicized or underlined. Definitions of italicized terms are often put in quotation marks.

> YES When writing, avoid using a word like *conflagration* when *fire* will do.
> YES The word *conflagration* actually means "fire."

GLOSSARY

Abstract and concrete language refers to two different qualities of words. Abstract words and phrases convey concepts, qualities, emotions, and ideas that we can think and talk about but not actually see or experience directly. Examples of abstract words are *conservatism, courage, avarice, joy,* and *hatred.* Words or phrases whose meanings are directly seen or experienced by the senses are concrete terms. Examples of concrete terms are *split-level house* and *waddling penguin.*

Adequate—see *Evidence.*

Ad hominem argument—see *Logical fallacies.*

Analogy refers to an imaginative comparison between two subjects that seem to have little in common. Often a writer can make a complex idea or topic understandable by comparing it to a more familiar subject, and such an analogy can be developed over several paragraphs or even an entire essay. For example, to explain how the economic difficulties of farmers weaken an entire nation, a writer might create an analogy between failing farms and a cancer that slowly destroys a person's life.

Argumentation-persuasion tries to encourage readers to accept a writer's point of view on some controversial issue. In *argumentation,* a writer uses objective reasoning, facts, and hard evidence to demonstrate the soundness of a position. In *persuasion,* the writer uses appeals to the emotions and value systems, often in the hope of encouraging readers to take a specific action. Argumentation and persuasion are frequently used together in an essay. For example, a writer might argue for the construction of a highway through town by pointing out that the road would bring new business, create new jobs, and lighten traffic. The writer also might try to persuade readers to vote for a highway appropriations bill by appealing to their emotions, claiming that the highway would allow people to get home faster, thus giving them more time for family life and leisure activities. An essay can be organized around argumentation-persuasion, or it may contain elements of argumentation-persuasion.

Assertion refers to the *thesis* of an *argumentation-persuasion* essay. The assertion, or *proposition,* is a point of view or opinion on a controversial topic. The assertion cannot be merely a statement of a fact. "Women still experience discrimination in the job market" and "This university should devote more funds to raising the quality of the food services" are examples of assertions that could serve as theses for argumentation-persuasion essays.

Attribution is a phrase or sentence that identifies a source and helps incorporate source material into an essay.

Audience refers to a writer's intended readers. In planning the content and tone of an essay, you should identify your audience and consider its needs. How similar are the members of your audience to you in knowledge and point of view? What will they need to know for you to achieve your *purpose?* What *tone* will make them open to receiving your message? For example, if you wrote about the high cost of clothing for an economics professor, you would choose a serious, analytic tone and supply statistical evidence for your points. If you wrote about the same topic for the college newspaper, you might use a tone tinged with humor and provide helpful hints on finding bargain clothing.

Begging the question—see *Logical fallacies.*

Brainstorming is a technique used in the *prewriting* stage. It helps you discover a limited subject and also generates raw material—ideas and details—to develop that subject. In brainstorming, you allow your mind to play freely with the subject. You try to capture fleeting thoughts about it, no matter how random, minor, or tangential, and jot them down rapidly before they disappear from your mind.

Causal analysis—see *Cause-effect.*

Causal chain refers to a series of causes and effects, in which the result or effect of a cause becomes itself the cause of a further effect, and so on. For example, a person's alarm clock failing to buzz might begin a causal chain by causing the person to oversleep. Oversleeping then causes the person to miss the bus, and missing the bus causes the person to arrive late to work. Arriving late causes the person to miss an important phone call, which causes the person to lose a chance at a lucrative contract.

Cause-effect, sometimes called *causal analysis,* involves analyzing the reasons for or results of an event, action, decision, or phenomenon. Writers develop an essay through an analysis of causes whenever they attempt to answer such questions as "Why has this happened?" or "Why does this exist?" When writers explore such questions as "What would happen if a certain change occurred?" or "What will happen if a condition continues?" their essays involve a discussion of effects. Some cause-effect essays concentrate on the causes of a situation, some focus on the effects, and others present both causes and effects. Causal analysis can be an essay's central pattern, or it can be used to help support a point in an essay developed primarily through another pattern.

Characteristics—see *Formal definition.*

Chronological sequence—see *Narrative sequence* and *Organization.*

Circularity is an error in *formal definition* resulting from using variations of the to-be-defined word in the definition. For example, "A scientific hypothesis is a hypothesis made by a scientist about the results of an experiment" is circular because the unknown term is used to explain itself.

Class—see *Formal definition.*

Coherence refers to the clear connection among the various parts of an essay. As a writer, you can draw upon two key strategies to make writing coherent. You can use a clear *organizational format* (for example, a chronological, spatial, emphatic, or simple-to-complex sequence). You can also provide *appropriate signaling* or *connecting devices* (transitions, bridging sentences, repeated words, synonyms, and pronouns).

Comparison-contrast means explaining the similarities and/or differences between events, objects, people, ideas, and so on. The comparison-contrast format can be used to meet a purely factual purpose ("This is how A and B are alike or different"). But usually writers use comparison-contrast to make a judgment about the relative merits of the subjects under discussion. Sometimes a writer will concentrate solely on similarities *or* differences. For instance, when writing about married versus single life, you would probably devote most of your time to discussing the differences between these lifestyles. Other times, comparison and contrast are found together. In an essay analyzing two approaches to U.S. foreign policy, you would probably discuss the similarities *and* the differences in the goals and methods characteristic of each approach. Comparison-contrast can be the dominant pattern in an essay, or it can help support a point in an essay developed chiefly through another pattern.

Conclusion refers to the one or more paragraphs that bring an essay to an end. Effective conclusions give the reader a sense of completeness and finality. Writers often use the conclusion as a place to reaffirm the *thesis* and to express a final thought about the subject. Methods of conclusion include summarizing main points, using a quotation, predicting an outcome, and recommending an action.

Conflict creates tension in the readers of a *narration*. It is produced by the opposition of characters or other forces in a story. Conflict can occur between individuals, between a person and society or nature, or within a person. Readers wonder how a conflict will be resolved and read on to find out.

Connotative and denotative language refers to the ability of language to emphasize one or another aspect of a word's range of meaning. *Denotative language* stresses the dictionary meaning of words. *Connotative language* emphasizes the echoes of feeling that cluster around some words. For example, the terms *weep, bawl, break down,* and *sob* all denote the same thing: to cry. But they have different associations and call up different images. A writer employing the connotative resources of language would choose the term among these that suggested the appropriate image.

Controlling idea—see *Thesis.*

Deductive reasoning is a form of logical thinking in which general statements believed to be true are applied to specific situations or cases. The result of deduction is a conclusion or prediction about the specific situation. Deduction is often expressed in a three-step pattern called a *syllogism.* The first part of the syllogism is a general statement about a large class of items or situations, the *major premise.* The second part is the *minor premise,* a more limited statement about a specific item or case. The third part is the *conclusion,* drawn from the major premise, about that specific case or item. Deductive reasoning is very common in everyday thinking. For example, you might use deduction when car shopping:

In an accident, large cars are safer than small cars. (*major premise*)

The Turbo Titan is a large car. (*minor premise*)

In an accident, the Turbo Titan will be safer than a small car. (*conclusion*)

Definition explains the meaning of a word or concept. The brief formal definitions found in the dictionary can be useful if you need to clarify or restrict the meaning of a term used in an essay. In such cases, the definition is short and to the point. But you may also use an *extended definition* in an essay, taking several paragraphs, even the entire piece, to develop the meaning of a term. You may use extended definition to convey a personal slant on a well-known term, to refute a commonly held interpretation of a word, or to dissect a complex or controversial issue. Definition can be the chief method of development in an essay, or it can help support a point in an essay organized around another pattern.

Definition by negation is a method of defining a term by first explaining what the term is *not,* and then going on to explain what it is. For example, you might

begin a critical essay about television with a definition by negation: "Television, far from being a medium that dispenses only light, insubstantial fare, actually disseminates a dangerously distorted view of family life." Definition by negation can provide a stimulating introduction to an essay.

Denotative language—see *Connotative and denotative language.*

Description involves the use of vivid word pictures to express what the five senses have experienced. The subject of a descriptive essay can be a person, a place, an object, or an event. Description can be the dominant pattern in an essay, or it can be used as a supplemental method in an essay developed chiefly through another pattern.

There are two main types of description. In an *objective description,* a writer provides details about a subject without conveying the emotions the subject arouses. For example, if you were involved in a traffic accident, your insurance agent might ask you to write an objective description of the events leading up to and during the crash. But in a *subjective description,* the writer's goal is to evoke in the reader the emotions felt during the experience. For example, in a cautionary letter to a friend who has a habit of driving dangerously, you might write a subjective description of your horrifyingly close call with death during a car accident.

Development—see *Evidence.*

Dialogue is the writer's way of directly presenting the exact words spoken by characters in a *narration.* By using dialogue, writers can convey people's individuality and also add drama and immediacy to an essay.

Directional process analysis—see *Process analysis.*

Division-classification refers to a logical method for analyzing a single subject or several related subjects. Though often used together in an essay, division and classification are separate processes. *Division* involves breaking a subject or idea into its component parts. For instance, the concept "an ideal vacation" could be divided according to its destination, accommodations, or cost. *Classification* involves organizing a number of related items into categories. For example, in an essay about the overwhelming flow of paper in our everyday lives, you might classify the typical kinds of mail most people receive: personal mail, business mail, and junk mail. Division-classification can be the dominant pattern in a paper, or it may be used to support a point in an essay organized chiefly around another pattern of development.

Dominant impression refers to the purpose of a descriptive essay. While some descriptive essays have a thesis, others do not; instead, they convey a dominant impression or main point. For example, one person writing a descriptive essay about New York City might use its architectural diversity as a focal point. Another person might concentrate on the overpowering sense of hustle and speed about everyone and everything in the city. Both writers would select only those details that supported their dominant impressions.

Dramatic license refers to the writer's privilege, when writing a narrative, to alter facts or details to strengthen the support of the *thesis* or *narrative point.* For example, a writer is free to flesh out the description of an event whose specific details may be partially forgotten or to modify or omit details of a narrative that do not contribute to the meaning the writer wishes to convey.

Either-or fallacy—see *Logical fallacies.*

Emphatic sequence—see *Organization.*

Ethos refers to a writer's reliability or credibility. Such an image of trustworthiness is particularly important to readers of an *argumentation-persuasion* essay or piece. Writers establish their *ethos* by using reason and logic, by being moderate in their appeals to emotions, by avoiding a hostile tone, and by demonstrating overall knowledgeability of the subject. The most effective argumentation-persuasion involves an interplay of *ethos, logos,* and *pathos.*

Etymology refers to the history of a word or term. All English words have their origins in other, often ancient, languages. Giving a brief etymology of a word can help a writer establish the context for developing an *extended definition* of the word. For example, the word *criminal* is derived from a Latin word meaning "accusation" or "accused." Today, our word *criminal* goes beyond the concept of "accused" to mean "guilty."

Evidence lends substance, or support, to a writer's main ideas and thus helps the reader to accept the writer's viewpoint. Evidence should meet several criteria. It should be *unified, adequate, specific, accurate,* and *representative.* The bulk of an essay is devoted to supplying evidence. Supporting the thesis with solid evidence is the third stage in the writing process.

Exemplification, at the heart of all effective writing, involves using concrete specifics to support generalizations. In exemplification, writers provide examples or instances that support or clarify broader statements. You might support the thesis statement "I have a close-knit family" by using such examples as the following: "We have a regular Sunday dinner at my grandmother's house with at least ten family members present"; "My sisters and brothers visit my parents every week." Exemplification may be an essay's central pattern, or it may supplement another pattern.

Extended definition—see *Definition.*

Fallacies—see *Logical fallacies.*

False analogy—see *Logical fallacies.*

Figures of speech are imaginative comparisons between two things usually thought of as dissimilar. Some major figures of speech are *simile, metaphor,* and *personification. Similes* are comparisons that use the signal words *like* or *as:* "Superman was as powerful as a locomotive." *Metaphors,* which do not use signal words, directly equate unlike things: "The boss is a tiger when it comes to landing a contract." *Personification* attributes human characteristics to things or nonhumans: "The angry clouds unleashed their fury"; "The turtle shyly poked his head out of his shell."

First draft refers to the writer's first try at producing a basic, unpolished version of the whole essay. It is often referred to as the "rough" draft, and nothing about it is final or unchangeable. The process of writing the first draft often brings up new ideas or details. Writers sometimes break off writing the draft to *brainstorm* or *freewrite* as new ideas occur to them and then return to the draft with new inspiration. You shouldn't worry about spelling, grammar, or style in the first-draft stage; instead, you should keep focused on casting your ideas into sentence and paragraph form. Writing the first draft is the fifth stage in the writing process.

Flashback—see *Narrative sequence.*

Flashforward—see *Narrative sequence.*

Formal definition involves stating a definition in a three-part pattern of about one sentence in length. In presenting a formal definition, a writer puts the *term* in a *class* and then lists the *characteristics* that separate the term from other members of its class. For example, a formal definition of a word processor might be "A word processor (term) is an electronic machine (class) that is used to write, edit, store, and produce typewritten documents (characteristics)." Writers often use a formal definition to prepare a reader for an extended definition that follows.

Freewriting is most often used during the *prewriting* stage to help writers generate ideas about a limited topic. You write nonstop for five or ten minutes about everything your topic brings to mind, disregarding grammar, spelling, and organization. Freewriting is similar to *brainstorming*, except that the result is a rambling, detail-filled paragraph rather than a list. Freewriting can also be used to generate ideas during later stages of the writing process.

Gender-biased language gives the impression that one sex is more important, powerful, or valuable than the other. When writing, you should work to replace such sexist language with *gender-neutral* or *nonsexist* terms that convey no sexual prejudice.

First of all, try to avoid *sexist vocabulary* that demeans or excludes one of the sexes: *stud, jock, chick, fox,* and so on. Also, just as adult males should be called *men,* adult females should be referred to as *women,* not *girls.* And men shouldn't be empowered with professional and honorary titles (*President* Barak Obama) while professional women—such as congressional representatives—are assigned only personal titles (*Ms.* Gwen Moore). Here are some examples of the way you can avoid words that exclude women: Change "chairman" to *chairperson,* "layman" to *layperson,* "congressman" to *congressional representative,* "workmen" to *workers,* the "average guy" to the *average person.*

Second, be aware of the fact that indefinite singular nouns—those representing a general group of people consisting of both genders—can lead to *sexist pronoun use:* for example, "On *his* first day of school, a young child often experiences separation anxiety." This sentence appears to exclude female children from consideration, although the situation being described applies equally to them.

Third, recognize that indefinite pronouns like *anyone, each,* and *everybody* may also pave the way to sexist pronoun use. Although such pronouns often refer to a number of individuals, they're considered singular: "Everybody wants *his* favorite candidate to win." The grammatical sentence, however, is sexist because *everybody* is certainly not restricted to men. One way to avoid this type of sexist construction is to use both male and female pronouns: "Everybody wants *his* or *her* favorite candidate to win." Another approach is to use the gender-neutral pronouns *they, their,* or *themselves:* "Everybody wants *their* favorite candidate to win." Be warned, though. Some people object to using these plural pro-nouns with singular indefinite pronouns, even though the practice is common in everyday speech.

Two alternative strategies enable you to eliminate the need for *any* gender-marked singular pronouns. First, you can use nouns and pronouns that are not gender-specific. For example, you may change "A *workaholic* feels anxious when *he* isn't busy" to "*Workaholics* feel anxious when *they're* not busy." Second, you can recast the sentence to omit the singular pronoun: For instance, you may change "A *manager* usually spends part of each day settling squabbles among *his* staff" to "A manager usually spends part of each day settling *staff squabbles*" and "No *one* wants *his* taxes raised" to "No one wants *to pay more taxes.*"

Hasty generalization—see *Logical fallacies.*

Inductive reasoning is a form of logical thinking in which specific cases and facts are examined to draw a wider-ranging conclusion. The result of inductive reasoning is a generalization that is applied to situations or cases similar to the ones examined. Induction is typical of scientific investigation and of everyday thinking. For example, on the basis of specific experiences, you may have concluded that when you feel chilly in a room where everyone else is comfortable, you are likely to develop a cold and fever in the next day or two. In an *argumentation-persuasion* essay, the conclusion reached by induction would be your *assertion* or *thesis.*

Inference is the term for a conclusion based on *inductive reasoning.* Because the reasoning behind specific cases may not be simple, there is usually an element of uncertainty in an inductive conclusion. Choosing the correct explanation for specific cases means carefully weighing alternative conclusions.

Informational process analysis—see *Process analysis.*

Introduction refers to the first paragraph or several paragraphs of an essay. The introduction informs readers of the general subject of the essay, catches their attention, and presents the controlling idea or thesis. It may include an anecdote, a quotation, a surprising statistic or fact, or questions. Or you may narrow your discussion down from a broad subject to a more limited one.

Irony occurs when a writer or speaker implies (rather than states directly) a discrepancy or incongruity of some kind. *Verbal irony,* which is often tongue-in-cheek, involves a discrepancy between the literal words and what's actually meant ("I know you must be unhappy about receiving the highest grade in the course"). If the ironic comment is designed to be hurtful or insulting, it qualifies as *sarcasm* ("Congratulations! You failed the final exam"). In *situational irony,* the circumstances are themselves incongruous. For example, although their constitutional rights were violated when the federal government detained them in internment camps, Japanese-Americans nevertheless played American football, sang American songs, and saluted the American flag during their imprisonment.

Journal writing is a form of prewriting in which writers make daily entries in a private journal. Whether they focus on one topic or wander freely, journal writers jot down striking incidents, images, and ideas encountered in the course of a day. Such journal material can produce ideas for future essays.

Logical fallacies are easily committed mistakes in reasoning that writers must avoid, especially when writing *argumentation-persuasion* essays. There are many kinds of logical fallacies. Here are several:

Ad hominem argument occurs when someone attacks another person's point of view by criticizing that person, not the issue. Often called "mudslinging," *ad hominem* arguments try to invalidate a person's ideas by revealing unrelated, past or present, personal or ethical flaws. For example, to claim that a person cannot

govern the country well because it can be proven he or she has little sense of humor is to use an *ad hominem* argument.

Begging the question is a fallacy in which the writer assumes the truth of something that needs to be proven. Imagine a writer argues the following: "A law should be passed requiring dangerous pets like German shepherds and Doberman pinschers to be restrained by fences, leashes, and muzzles." Such an argument begs the question since it assumes readers will automatically accept the view that such dogs are indeed dangerous.

Either-or fallacies occur when it's argued that a complex situation can be resolved in only one of two possible ways. Here's an example: "If the administration doesn't grant striking professors more money, the college will never be able to attract outstanding teachers in years ahead." Such an argument oversimplifies matters. Excellent teachers might be attracted to a college for a variety of reasons, not just because of good salaries: the school's location, research facilities, reputation for scholarship, hardworking students, and so on.

False analogy erroneously suggests that because two things are alike in some regards, they are similar in all ways. In the process, significant differences between the two are disregarded. If you argue that just as the cure for obesity is dieting, the solution for a bloated government budget is cutting taxes and spending, you're making a false analogy. Obesity is a health threat with no positive value. However, deciding whether a budget is bloated or whether it supports necessary and worthwhile functions requires thoughtful analysis.

Hasty generalizations are unsound *inductive inferences* based on too few instances of a behavior, situation, or process. For example, it would be a hasty generalization to conclude that you're allergic to a food such as curry because you once ate it and became ill. There are several other possible explanations for your illness, and only repetitions of this experience or a lab test could prove conclusively that you're allergic to this food.

Non sequiturs are faulty conclusions about cause and effect. Here's an example: "Throughout this country's history, most physicians have been male. Women apparently have little interest in becoming doctors." The faulty conclusion accords one factor—the possible vocational preferences of women—the status of sole cause. The conclusion fails to consider pressures on women to devote themselves to homemaking and to avoid an occupation sexually stereotyped as "masculine."

Post hoc thinking results when it's presumed that one event caused another just because it occurred first. For instance, if your car broke down the day after you lent it to your brother, you would be committing the *post hoc* fallacy if you blamed him, unless you knew he did something to your car's engine.

Questionable authority, revealed by such phrases as "studies show" and "experts claim," undercuts a writer's credibility. Readers become suspicious of such vague and unsubstantial appeals to authority. Writers should demonstrate the reliability of their sources by citing them specifically.

Red herring arguments are deliberate attempts to focus attention on a peripheral matter rather than examine the merits of the issue under discussion. Imagine that a local environmental group advocates stricter controls for employees at a nearby chemical plant. The group points out that plant employees are repeatedly exposed to high levels of toxic chemicals. If you respond, "Many of the employees are illegal aliens and shouldn't be allowed to take jobs from native-born townspeople," you're throwing in a red herring. By bringing in immigration policies, you sidetrack attention from the matter at hand: the toxic level to which plant employees—illegal aliens or not—are exposed.

Logos is a major factor in creating an effective argument. It refers to the soundness of *argumentation,* as created by the use of facts, statistics, information, and commentary by authoritative sources. The most effective arguments involve an interplay among *logos, pathos,* and *ethos.*

Major premise—see *Deductive reasoning.*

Minor premise—see *Deductive reasoning.*

MLA documentation is the system developed by the Modern Language Association for citing sources in a paper. When you quote or summarize source material, you must do two things within your paper's text: (1) identify the author and (2) specify the pages on which the material appears. You may provide the author's name in a lead-in sentence or within parentheses following the borrowed material; the page number always appears in parentheses, inserted in the text after the borrowed material. The material in the parentheses is called a *parenthetical reference.* The paper ends with a *Works Cited* list, which includes only those sources actually acknowledged in the paper. Entries are organized alphabetically by authors' last names. Entries without an author are alphabetized by the first major word in the title.

Narration means recounting an event or a series of related events to make a point. Narration can be an essay's principal pattern of development, or it can be used to supplement a paper organized primarily around another pattern. For instance, to persuade readers to avoid drug use, a writer might use the narrative pattern by recounting the story of an abuser's addiction and recovery.

Narrative point refers to the meaning the writer intends to convey to a reader by telling a certain story. This narrative point might be a specific message, or it might be a feeling about the situation, people, or place of the story. This underlying meaning is achieved by presenting details that support it and eliminating any that are nonessential. For example, in an essay about friendship, a writer's point might be that friendships change when one of the friends acquires a significant partner. The writer would focus on the details of how her close friend had less time for her, changed their usual times of getting together, and confided in her less. The writer would omit judgments of the friend's choice of partner and her friend's declining grades because these details, while real for the writer, would distract the reader from the essay's narrative point.

Narrative sequence refers to the order in which a writer recounts events. When you follow the order of the events as they happened, you're using *chronological sequence*—the most basic and commonly used narrative sequence. If you interrupt this chronology to present an event that happened before the beginning of the narrative sequence, you're employing a *flashback.* If you skip ahead to an event later than the one that comes next in your narrative, you're using the *flashforward* technique.

Non sequiturs—see *Logical fallacies.*

Objective description—see *Description*.

One-side-at-a-time method refers to one of the two techniques for organizing a *comparison-contrast* essay. In using this method, a writer discusses all the points about one subject before going on to the other. For example, in an essay titled "Single or Married?" a writer might first discuss single life in terms of amount of independence, freedom of career choice, and companionship. Then the writer would, within reason, discuss married life in terms of these same three subtopics. The issues the writer discusses in each half of the essay would be identical and presented in the same order. See also *Point-by-point method*.

Organization refers to the process of arranging evidence to support a thesis in the most effective way. When organizing, a writer decides what ideas come first, next, and last. In *chronological* sequence, details are arranged according to occurrence in time. In *spatial* sequence, details appear in the order in which they occur in space. In *emphatic* order, ideas are sequenced according to importance, with the most significant, outstanding, or convincing evidence being reserved for last. In *simple-to-complex* order, easy-to-grasp material is presented before more-difficult-to-comprehend information. Organizing is the fourth stage of the writing process.

Outlining involves making a formal plan before writing a *first draft*. Writing an outline helps you determine whether your supporting evidence is logical and adequate. As you write, you can use the outline to keep yourself on track. Many writers use the indentation system of Roman numerals, letters, and arabic numbers to outline; sometimes writers use a less formal system.

Paradox refers to a statement that seems impossible, contrary to common sense, or self-contradictory, yet that can—after consideration—be seen to be plausible or true. For example, Oscar Wilde produced a paradox when he wrote "When the gods wish to punish us, they answer our prayers." The statement doesn't contradict itself because often, Wilde believes, that which we wish for turns out to be the very thing that will bring us the most pain.

Parenthetical reference—see *MLA documentation*.

Pathos refers to the emotional power of an *argumentation-persuasion* essay. By appealing to the needs, values, and attitudes of readers and by using *connotative language*, writers can increase the chances that readers will come to agree with the ideas in an essay. Although *pathos* is an important element of persuasion, such emotional appeals should reinforce rather than replace reason. The most effective argumentation-persuasion involves an interplay among *pathos, logos,* and *ethos*.

Peer review is the critical reading of another person's writing with the intention of suggesting changes. To be effective, peer review calls for readers who are objective, skilled, and tactful enough to provide useful feedback. Begin by giving your readers a clear sense of what you expect from the review. To promote specific responses, ask the reviewers targeted (preferably written) questions. Following the review, rank the problems and solutions that the reviewers identified. Then enter your own notes for revising in the margins of your draft so that you'll know exactly what changes need to be made in your draft.

Plan of development refers to a brief map of the main points to be covered in an essay. If used, the plan of development occurs as part of the *thesis* or in a sentence following the thesis. In it, the main ideas are mentioned in the order in which they'll appear in the supporting paragraphs. Longer essays and term papers usually need a plan of development to maintain unity, but shorter papers may do without one.

Point-by-point method refers to one of the two techniques for organizing a *comparison-contrast* essay. A writer using this method moves from one aspect of one subject to the same aspect of another subject before going on to the second aspect of each subject. For example, in an essay titled "Single or Married?" a writer might first discuss the amount of independence a person has when single and when married. Then, the writer might go on to discuss how much freedom of career choice a person has when single and when married. Finally, the writer might discuss, in turn, the amount of companionship available in each of the two lifestyles. See also *One-side-at-a-time method*.

Point of view refers to the perspective a writer chooses when writing about a subject. If you narrate events as you experience them, you're using the *first-person* point of view. You might say, for example, "*I* noticed jam on the child's collar and holes in her shirt." If you relate the events from a distance—as if you observed them but did not experience them personally—you're using the *third-person* point of view: "Jam splotched the child's collar, and her shirt had several holes in it." The point of view should be consistent throughout an essay.

Post hoc **thinking**—see *Logical fallacies*.

Prewriting is the first stage of the writing process. During prewriting, you jot down rough ideas about your subject without yet moving to writing a draft of your essay. Your goals at this stage are to (1) understand the boundaries of the assignment, (2) discover the limited subject you could write about, (3) generate raw material about the limited subject, and (4) organize the raw material into a very rough *scratch outline*. If you keep in mind that prewriting is "unofficial," it can be a low-pressure, even enjoyable activity.

Process analysis refers to writing that explains the steps involved in doing something or the sequence of stages in an event or behavior. There are two types of process analysis. In *directional process analysis,* readers are shown how to do something step by step. Cookbook recipes, tax form instructions, and how-to books are some typical uses of directional process analysis. In *informational process analysis,* the writer explains how something is done or occurs, without expecting the reader to attempt the process. "A Senator's Road to Political Power," "How a Bee Makes Honey," and "How a Convict Gets Paroled" would be titles of essays developed through informational process analysis. Process analysis can be the dominant mode in an essay, or it may help make a point in an essay developed chiefly through another pattern. For example, in a cause-effect essay that explores the impact of the two-career family, process analysis might be used to explain how parents arrange for day care.

Proofreading involves rereading a final draft carefully to catch any errors in spelling, grammar, punctuation, or typing that have slipped by. While such errors are minor, a significant number of them can seriously weaken the effectiveness of an essay. Proofreading is the last stage in the writing process.

Proposition—see *Assertion*.

Purpose is the reason a writer has for preparing a particular essay. Usually, writers frame their purposes in terms of the effect they wish to have on their *audience*.

They may wish to explore the personal meaning of a subject or experience, explain an idea or process, provide information, influence opinion, or entertain. Many essays combine purposes, with one purpose predominating and providing the essay's focus.

Red herring argument—see *Logical fallacies.*

Refutation is an important strategy in *argumentation-persuasion*. In refutation, writers acknowledge that there are opposing views on the subject under discussion and then go on to do one of two things. Sometimes they may admit that the opposing views are somewhat valid but assert that their own position has more merit and devote their essay to demonstrating that merit. For example, a writer might assert, "Business majors often find interesting and lucrative jobs. However, in the long run, liberal arts graduates have many more advantages in the job market because the breadth of their background helps them think better, learn faster, and communicate more effectively." This writer would concentrate on proving the advantages that liberal arts graduates have. At other times, writers may choose to argue actively against an opposing position by dismantling that view point by point. Such refutation of opposing views can strengthen the writer's own arguments.

Repeated words, synonyms, and pronouns—see *Signaling devices.*

Revision means, literally, "reseeing" a *first draft* with a fresh eye, as if the writer had not actually prepared the draft. When revising, you move from more global issues (like clarifying meaning and organization) to more specific matters (like fine-tuning sentences and word choice). While revising, you make whatever changes are necessary to increase the essay's effectiveness. You might strengthen your thesis, resequence paragraph order, or add more transitions. Such changes often make the difference between mediocre and superior writing. Revision, itself a multi-stage process, is the last stage of the writing process.

Satire is a humorous form of social criticism usually aimed at society's institutions or human behavior. Often irreverent as well as witty, satire is serious in purpose: to point out evil, injustice, and absurdity and bring about change through an increase in awareness. Satire ranges widely in tone: it may be gentle or biting; it may sarcastically describe a real situation or use fictional characters and events to spoof reality. Satire often makes use of *irony.*

Scratch outline refers to your first informal plan for an essay, done at the end of the *prewriting* stage. In making a scratch outline, you select ideas and details from your raw material for inclusion in your essay and discard the rest. You also arrange these ideas in an order that makes sense and that will help you achieve your *purpose*. A scratch outline is flexible and can be reshaped as needed.

Sensory description vividly evokes the sights, smells, tastes, sounds, and physical feelings of a scene or event. For example, if a writer carefully chooses words and images, readers can see the vibrant reds and oranges of falling leaves, taste the sourness of an underripe grapefruit, hear the growling of motorcycles as a gang sweeps through a town, smell the spicy aroma of a grandmother's homemade tomato soup, and feel the pulsing pain of a jaw after Novocain wears off. Sensory description is particularly important in writing *description* or *narration.*

Sentence variety adds interest to the style of an essay or paragraph. In creating sentence variety, writers mix different kinds of sentences and sentence patterns.

For example, you might vary the way your sentences open or intersperse short sentences with long ones, simple sentences with complex ones. Repetitive sentence patterns tend to make readers lose interest.

Signaling devices indicate the relationships among ideas in an essay. They help the reader follow the train of thought from sentence to sentence and from paragraph to paragraph. There are three types of connectives. *Transitions* are words that clarify flow of meaning. They can signal an additional or contrasting point, an enumeration of ideas, the use of an example, or other movement of ideas. *Linking sentences* summarize a point just made and then introduce a follow-up point. *Repeated words, synonyms,* and *pronouns* create a sense of flow by keeping important concepts in the mind of the reader.

Spatial sequence—see *Organization.*

Specific—see *Evidence.*

Stipulative definition is a way of restricting a term for the purposes of discussion. Many words have multiple meanings that can get in the way of clarity when a writer is creating an *extended definition.* For example, you might stipulate the following definition of *foreign car:* "While many American automobiles use parts or even whole engines made by foreign car manufacturers, for the purposes of discussion, 'foreign car' refers only to those automobiles designed and manufactured wholly by a company based in another country. By this definition, a European vehicle made in Pennsylvania is *not* a foreign car."

Subjective description—see *Description.*

Support—see *Evidence.*

Syllogism—see *Deductive reasoning.*

Term—see *Formal definition.*

Thesis is the central idea in any essay, usually expressed in a one- or two-sentence *thesis statement.* Writers accomplish two things by providing a thesis statement in an essay: They indicate the essay's limited subject and express an attitude about that subject. Also called the *controlling idea,* the thesis statement consists of a particular slant, angle, or point of view about the limited subject. Stating the thesis is the second stage of the writing process.

Tone conveys your attitude toward yourself, your purpose, your topic, and your readers. As in speaking, tone in writing may be serious, playful, sarcastic, and so on. Generally, readers detect tone more by how you say something (that is, through your sentence structure and word choice) than by what you say.

Topic sentence is the term for the sentence(s) that convey the main idea of a paragraph. Such sentences are often, but not always, found at the start of a paragraph. They provide a statement of the subject to be discussed and an indication of the writer's attitude toward that subject. Writers usually concern themselves with topic sentences during the writing of the first draft, the fifth stage of the writing process.

Transitions—see *Signaling devices.*

Unified—see *Evidence.*

Works Cited—see *MLA documentation.*

ACKNOWLEDGMENTS

INDEX

Abstracts, 452
Addison, Joseph, 1
Addition (sequence), 51
Additional writing assignments
  argumentation-persuasion,
    428–29
  cause-effect, 322–23
  comparison-contrast,
    288–89
  definition, 354–55
  description, 110–11
  division-classification,
    220–21
  exemplification, 185–86
  narration, 145–46
  process analysis, 256–57
Adequate support in an essay,
    37–38, 76, 114, 151,
    191, 226, 261, 293,
    327, 362
Ad hominem argument, 376
Adler, Mortimer, 3
  "How to Mark a Book," 3
*The Adventures of Huckleberry
    Finn* (Twain),
    114–15
Ambiguity, 150
American Academy of
    Pediatrics, 7
Analogy
  in comparison-contrast,
    260, 262
  in definition, 335
  false, 377
  in process analysis, 232–34,
    236
Anecdotes, 53
Angelou, Maya, 87
  "Sister Flowers," 87–91
Angier, Natalie, 343
  "The Cute Factor,"
    343–47
Annotating a reading,
    3, 6, 9
Announcements, 29
Anthology, 477
Apostrophe misuse, 492
Appeals to faulty or
    questionable
    authority, 377
Argumentation-persuasion,
    25, 73, 224, 431,
    434
  activities in, 390–91
  additional writing
    assignments, 428–29
  ad hominem argument, 376
  audience for, 356–61

combining patterns of
    development, 334,
    389, 397–98, 408,
    416, 421, 426
conclusions in, 371–72
connotative language
    in, 358
deductive reasoning in,
    369, 371, 373
defined, 356
development plan for, 362
documentation in, 362,
    365, 379
editing for, 362
ethos, 358–59
evidence for, 362, 365–66,
    368–69, 370
exemplification for,
    148–49
first draft for, 362
goodwill in, 365
granting validity of
    opposing view in,
    368
inductive reasoning in,
    362, 369
introduction for, 367
logical fallacies
  ad hominem argument,
    376
  appeals to faulty or
    questionable
    authority, 377
  begging the question,
    377
  either/or fallacy, 377
  false analogy, 377
  faulty conclusion, 372
  hasty generalization,
    154, 362, 370
  non sequitur fallacy,
    376
  post hoc fallacy, 376
  red herring argument,
    377
logos, 358
  in narration, 113
pathos, 358
peer review checklist for,
    378–79
premise in, 371
prewriting for, 362
proofreading for, 362
proposition in, 374
purpose and, 356–61
refutation of differing
    viewpoints in,
    368–69

revision strategies for, 362,
    378–79
Rogerian strategy in, 362,
    366–67, 368
student essay/commentary,
    379–90
suggestions for using,
    361–77
syllogism in, 371
thesis in, 361–63
Toulmin logic in, 362, 374
ways of thinking
  deductive reasoning,
    369, 371, 373
  inductive reasoning,
    362, 369
  use of syllogism, 371
Articles, evaluating, 453
Attitude. *See* Point of view
Attribution, 471–72
Audience, 18, 20, 69
  for argumentation-
    persuasion, 356–61
  cause-effect for, 291–92
  checklist for analyzing, 19
  for comparison-contrast,
    259–60
  for definition, 325
  description fitting, 72–74
  for division-classification,
    188–89
  for exemplification,
    148–50
  hostile, 360–61
  in narration, 113
  for process analysis,
    223–24
  supportive, 359–60
  tone and, 294
  wavering, 360
Authors, 475–76

Barry, Dave, 284
"Beauty and the Beast"
    (Barry), 284–86
Begging the question, 377
Bellow, Saul, 1
"Beyond the Pleasure
    Principle" (Hulbert),
    350–52
Bissinger, Buzz, 317
  "Innocents Afield," 317–20
"Black Talk and Pop Culture"
    (Savan), 171–78
Blogs, 480
"The Border on Our Backs"
    (Rodriguez),
    418–20

Brainstorming, 21, 27
  for argumentation-
    persuasion, 390
  for cause-effect, 293–94,
    305
  in comparison-contrast,
    263
  for definition, 327
  for division-classification,
    191, 202
  in exemplification, 151
  general subject, 22
  in group, 23–24, 27
  limited subject, 23
  for narration, 115
  in process analysis, 227,
    237
Bridging sentences, 70
Broad statements, 30, 52
Broad thesis, 362
Brooks, David, 212
  "Psst! 'Human Capital,'"
    212–14

Call for action, 56, 362
Carson, Rachel, 280
  "A Fable for Tomorrow,"
    280–81
Catacumba, 95
Categories, 200
Causal analysis, 73, 224,
    433–34. *See also*
    Cause-effect
  in definition, 334
  exemplification in,
    148, 158
  post hoc fallacy in, 296
  in student essay, 82
Causal chain, 295, 301–3
Cause-effect, 25, 40, 51, 430
  activities for, 305–6
  additional writing
    assignments, 322–23
  audience for, 291–92
  causal chain in, 295
  chronological order, 297
  comparison-contrast
    and, 303
  connecting strategies
    in, 304
  correlation v. causation
    in, 296
  defined, 290
  development of, 293
  editing for, 293
  emphatic order in, 297–98
  evidence for, 293, 303
  exemplification and, 303
  first draft for, 293
  immediate/remote causes
    in, 295

  introduction for, 300, 302
  language for hinting at
    complexity in, 299
  organizational pattern for,
    297
  peer review for, 299–300,
    304–5
  prewriting for, 293
  primary/secondary causes
    in, 295
  proofreading for, 293
  purpose and, 290–92,
    302–3
  revision for, 293, 299–300,
    304
  speculative approach to, 293
  student essay/commentary,
    300–305
  suggestions for using,
    292–99
  thesis for, 293
  tone for, 294
  topic sentence for, 301,
    303
CD-ROM, 482
Characteristics, 328
Checklists
  argumentation-persuasion,
    378–79
  articles/books evaluation,
    453
  audience analysis, 19
  cause-effect essay,
    299–300
  comparison-contrast essay,
    266–67
  definition essay, 331
  description, 79–80
  division-classification,
    195–96
  exemplification, 156
  for first draft, 47
  integrating sources into
    writing, 469
  Internet materials
    evaluation, 453–54
  MLA parenthetical
    references, 474
  narration, 120–21
  outlining, 43–44
  process analysis essay, 231
  quotation/summary/
    paraphrase use, 462
  reading, 2–5
  Rogerian strategy, 366–67
  source materials
    analysis/synthesis,
    456
  Toulmin logic, 376
Chronological method of
    organization, 50–51

  in cause-effect, 297
  in description, 77
  in division-classification,
    197
  in exemplification, 155
  in narration, 116–17
  in organizing essay, 41
  in process analysis, 228
  in student essay, 83
Circularity, 328
Claim, 374–75
Class, 328
Classification, 188
Close, 70
Clustering, 24
Cole, K.C., 338
  "Entropy," 338–41
Comma misuse, 491
Comma splices, 485
Common ground, 366
Comparable points, 194
Comparison-contrast, 25, 51,
    236, 430, 433
  activities for, 272–73
  additional writing
    assignments,
    288–89
  analogy in, 260, 262
  audience for, 259–60
  cause-effect and, 303
  conclusion for, 269–70
  defined, 258
  in definition, 334
  development of, 261
  editing in, 261
  evaluation using, 262
  evidence for, 261
  exemplification and, 270
  first draft for, 261
  introduction in, 267, 271
  misconceptions cleared up
    through, 262
  peer review for, 266–67
  prewriting for, 261
  proofreading in, 261
  purpose and, 259–62,
    269
  revision in, 261, 266–67,
    270–71
  selection of points in,
    263
  student essay/commentary,
    267–72
  suggestions for using,
    260–66
  thesis and, 261–63, 269
  topic sentence in, 268
  transitions in, 265
Compilations, 477
Complex concepts, 42
Concentration, 1

Conclusion to an essay,
48, 84
in argumentation-persuasion,
362, 369–74, 376,
378, 383, 389
in cause-effect, 302, 304
in comparison-contrast,
269–70
in definition, 333, 335
in description, 82–84
in division-classification,
195, 199, 202
in exemplification, 158
in narration, 122–23
in process analysis, 230,
234, 236–37
writing, 51, 55–56
Confusing homonyms, 493–94
Connecting strategies, 10, 304
Connotations, 20
Connotative language, 74, 82,
358
Contrast, 51, 68, 148, 155
"The Cute Factor" (Angier),
343–47
"Cyberschool" (Stoll), 239–43

Data, 374
"The Death of the Moth"
(Woolf), 438–41
Deductive reasoning, 369,
371, 373
Definition, 24, 25, 40,
224, 431
activities for, 336–37
additional writing
assignments, 354–55
argumentation-persuasion
in, 334
audience for, 325–26
causal analysis in, 334
characteristics in, 328
circularity in, 328
class in, 328
comparison-contrast in, 334
conclusion for, 333, 335
defined, 324
development process
for, 327
editing for, 327
etymology as basis for, 330
evidence for, 327
exemplification with, 334
first draft for, 327
introduction for, 330, 332
narration and, 329–30
by negation, 330
organization of material
for, 329
origin as basis for
introducing, 330

patterns of development
with, 334
peer review of, 331
prewriting for, 327
process analysis and, 329
proofreading for, 327
purpose for, 325–26
revision for, 327, 330–31,
335
stipulative, 330
student essay/commentary,
331–36
suggestions for using,
326–30
thesis for, 327, 332
tone for, 326
topic sentences in, 332–33
Denotations, 20
Denotative language, 74
Description, 24, 40, 432
activities for, 85–86
additional writing
assignments, 110–11
argumentation-persuasion
in, 73
around dominant
impression, 75
causal analysis in, 73
connotative language in, 74
defined, 72
denotative language in, 74
fitting to purpose and
audience, 72–74
narrative in, 73
objective/subjective,
73–74
organizational approaches
to, 77–78
process analysis in, 73
revision/peer review
checklist, 79–80
student essay/commentary,
80–85
suggestions for using,
75–79
tone in, 74
writing process for, 76
Details, 32
Diagramming, 24
Dialogue, 118–19
Didion, Joan, 448
"Marrying Absurd,"
448–50
Directional process analysis,
223, 227
Division, 188
Division-classification,
24, 430
activities in, 202–3
applying logically, 193
audience for, 188–89

categories used in, 200
chronological approach
with, 197
completeness in, 193
conclusion to, 195, 199,
202
consistency in, 193
definition of, 187
development diagram for,
192
editing in, 192
emphatic order in, 201
evidence in, 192
first draft in, 192
how not to use, 192
introduction in, 199
organization for, 194
paragraph structure for,
200
patterns of development in,
201
peer review for, 195–96
prewriting activities for,
192
principle selection in,
191–93
proofreading in, 192
purpose achieved by,
188–90, 199
revision strategies for, 192,
195–96
single principle in, 192
student essay/commentary,
196–202
suggestions for using,
191–95
thesis in, 192, 193–94,
197, 199
tone in, 200
topic sentence in, 197
Documentation, 38, 362, 365,
379. See also MLA
documentation
of print/Internet sources,
451, 453–55, 457
Dominant impression, 75, 81,
82
Dramatic facts, 54
"Driving to the Funeral"
(Quindlen),
399–401
DVDs, 481

Editorial, 478
Effect. See Cause-effect
Either/or fallacy, 377
Ellipsis, 466
E-mail, 482
Emerson, Ralph Waldo, 2
Emotional language,
434–35

Emphatic method of
    organization, 50–51,
    63, 69, 155
  in argumentation-
    persuasion, 362
  in cause-effect, 297–98
  in comparison-contrast, 270
  in description, 77
  in division-classification, 201
  in exemplification, 151,
    155, 159
  in writing process, 41
Energetic verbs, 83
English novels, 88
Entertainment, 18
"Entropy" (Cole), 338–41
Essays. See also Adequate
    support in an essay;
    Conclusion to an
    essay; Introduction to
    an essay; Organization
    in an essay
  combining patterns of
    development in,
    431–37
  how to translate journal
    entry into, 17
  revisions of, 70–71
  structure of, 57
  by students
    argumentation-
      persuasion, 379–90
    combining patterns of
      development,
      432–37
    comparison-contrast,
      267–72
    definition, 331–36
    description, 80–82
    division-classification,
      196–202
    as example of writing
      process, 66–71
    exemplification, 156–58
    narration, 121–25
    process analysis, 232–37
Ethos, 358–59
Etymology, 330
"Euromail and Amerimail"
    (Weiner), 274–77
Evaluation, of peer review, 65
Evaluation of reading
    selection, 4–6
Evidence
  for argumentation-
    persuasion, 362,
    365–66, 368–69,
    370
  for cause-effect, 293, 303
  characteristics of, 34–38
    accuracy, 37

adequacy, 36–37
documented, 38
relevance, 451–52
representative, 37–38
specific, 35–36
  for comparison-contrast,
    261
defined, 32
  for definition, 327
documentation of, 38
  in exemplification, 159
  in narration, 114
nonunifed support of, 34
organizational approach to
  chronological, 41
  emphatic, 41–42
  outline, 43–45
  simple-to-complex,
    41–42
  spatial, 41
organization of, 40–46
patterns of development to
  generate, 33
specificity of, 35–36
thesis supported through,
  32–39
where to find, 33
Examples, 51, 69
Exemplification, 24, 433–35
  accuracy in, 153
  activities in, 161–62
  additional writing
    assignments, 185–86
  for argumentation-
    persuasion, 148–49
  audience served by, 148–50
  causal analysis in, 148, 158
  cause-effect and, 303
  checklist for peer review of,
    156
  chronological approach in,
    155
  comparison-contrast and,
    270
  contrast in, 148, 155
  defined, 147
  with definition, 334
  development diagram for,
    151
  editing of, 151
  emphatic sequence in, 155
  evidence in, 159
  for explanation, 149
  first draft of, 151
  focus in, 160
  hypothetical examples in,
    153
  need for representational
    examples in, 153
  need for specificity, 154
  organization in, 154–55

paragraph development in,
    159–60
  plan of development
    in, 158
  point of view in, 155
  to prevent ambiguity, 150
  prewrite for, 151
  proofreading of, 151
  purpose served by,
    148–50
  relevancy in, 153
  revision strategies of, 151,
    155–56, 160–61
  selection of examples in,
    152–54
  spatial approach in, 155
  student essay/commentary,
    156–61
  suggestions for using,
    150–55
  thesis in, 151, 158
  tone in, 160
Expert opinion, 363–64
Explanation, 149
Extended examples, 153

"A Fable for Tomorrow"
    (Carson), 280–81
Facts, 32
Factual statements, 29–30
False analogy, 377
"Family Counterculture"
    (Goodman),
    6–9, 21
Faulty conclusion, 372
Faulty parallelism, 490
Faulty pronoun agreement,
    487
Faulty subject-verb agreement,
    485–87
Fields, W. C., 56
Figurative language, 83
Figures of speech, 5, 83–84
First draft, 14, 45–60
  for argumentation-
    persuasion, 362
  for cause-effect, 293
  for comparison-contrast,
    261
  for definition, 327
  in division-classification, 192
  for exemplification, 151,
    160
  for narration, 114
  outline into, 47
  for process analysis, 226
  sample of, 57–59
First-person plural point of
    view, 159
First-person point of view,
    119–20, 155, 227

Fish, Stanley, 392
"Free-Speech Follies"
        (Fish), 392–96
Flashback, 117
Flashforward, 117
"Flavio's Home" (Parks),
        95–101
Flow, 4, 10
Focus, 160
Format, 65
"The Fourth of July" (Lorde),
        127–31
Fragments, 484
"Free-Speech Follies" (Fish),
        392–96
Freewriting, 22–23, 27

Gallo, José, 95
Garibaldi, Gerry, 2, 403
    "How the Schools
        Shortchange Boys,"
        403–7
Generalized examples,
        153–54
General subject, 20–22
Goodman, Ellen, 6–7, 60
    "Family Counterculture,"
        6–9, 21
Goodwill, 365
Grammar, 65, 483–495
Granting validity of opposing
        view, 367
Group activities, 23
Group brainstorming,
        23–24, 27

Hasty generalization, 154,
        362, 370
Highlighting, 3
"How the Schools
        Shortchange Boys"
        (Garibaldi), 403–7
"How to Mark a Book"
        (Adler), 3
Hulbert, Ann, 350
    "Beyond the Pleasure
        Principle," 350–52
Humor, 11
Hymowitz, Kay, 163
    "Tweens: Ten Going On
        Sixteen," 163–67
Hypothetical examples, 153

Images, 5
Inductive leap, 370
Inductive reasoning, 362, 369
Inference, 370
Informal topic sentence, 78,
        83, 117
Informational process analysis,
        223, 227

"Innocents Afield" (Bissinger),
        317–20
Internet, 480
    blogs as sources on, 480
    citing sources from,
        479–80
    "Cyberschool," 239–42
    evaluating materials from,
        453–54
    online database as source
        on, 481
    online reference work,
        480
    scholarly journal found
        on, 480
Interviews, 364
Introduction to an essay,
        48, 53
    in argumentation-
        persuasion, 367
    in cause-effect, 300, 302
    in comparison-contrast,
        267, 271
    in definition, 330,
        332–33
    in division-classification, 199
    plan of development
        in, 330
    in process analysis,
        229, 232
Italics, misuse of, 495

Johnson, Marguerite, 87
Journaling, 15, 27
    essays from entries in, 17
    for narration essay, 114
    pre-reading, 16

Kamiya, Gary, 103
    "Life, Death and
        Spring," 103–8
Kimmel, Michael, 410
    "A War Against Boys?"
        410–16
King, Martin Luther, Jr., 444
    "Where Do We Go from
        Here: Community or
        Chaos?" 444–47
King, Stephen, 307
    "Why We Crave Horror
        Movies," 307–10
Kleiner, Kurt, 312
    "When Mañana Is Too
        Soon," 312–15

Lectures, 482
"Life, Death and Spring"
        (Kamiya), 103–8
Life Magazine, 95–96
Limited subject, 20–21
    brainstorming, 23

generating raw material
        for, 22
    mapping, 24
    thesis presenting, 28
Listing strategy, 16
Logic, 4, 10
Logical fallacies, 376
Logos, 358
Lorde, Audre, 127
    "The Fourth of July,"
        127–31

Madonna, 9
Main clause, 367
Main topics, 47
Mapping, 24, 27
"Marrying Absurd" (Didion),
        448–50
McClintock, Ann, 204
    "Propaganda Techniques in
        Today's Advertising,"
        204–10, 359
Meaning/significance, 115
Metaphor, 79
"The Miracle of Melancholia"
        (Wilson), 180–82
Misconceptions, 19, 262
Misplaced/dangling modifiers,
        488–89
MLA documentation,
        470–75
MLA Handbook for Writers of
        Research Papers,
        470–71
Montaigne, Michel, 13
Movies, 481
MTV, 8
Murray, Joan, 141
    "Someone's Mother,"
        141–43

NARAL. See National
        Abortion Rights
        Action League
Narration, 24, 73, 112–44,
        431, 432
    additional writing
        assignments,
        145–46
    brainstorming in, 115
    checklist for peer review,
        120–21
    chronology of, 116–17
    defined, 112
    definition and, 329–30
    dialogue for, 118–19
    editing of, 114
    evidence for, 114
    first draft for, 114
    flashback in, 117
    flashforward in, 117

Narration, *(continued)*
  identifying point of,
    114–15
  journaling for, 114
  meaning/significance
    of, 115
  narrative point in,
    115–16
  organization for, 114
  point of view in, 119
  prewrite for, 114
  prewriting for, 125
  proofreading of, 114
  revision strategies in, 114,
    120, 125–26
  student essay, 121–25
  thesis for, 114
  verb tense in, 119
  writing topics for, 145
Narrative commentary, 116
Narrative point, 115–16
Narrow thesis, 362
National Abortion Rights
    Action League
    (NARAL), 364
National Geographic, 452
Negation, 330
Newspaper, 478
Newsweek, 452
Ninja Turtles, 9
Non sequitur fallacy, 376
Nostalgia, 8

Obesity, 7
Objectivity, 452
One-side-at-a-time method,
    264–65
Online database, 481
Opinion, 362
Opposing idea, 53
Opposing points
    of view, 366
Organization in an essay
    for cause-effect, 297
    for narration, 114
    one-side-at-a-time method,
      264–65
    point-by-point method,
      264–65
Organization strategies, 83
Origin, 330
Orwell, George, 2, 133
    "Shooting an Elephant,"
      133–38
Outline, 47
Outlining, 43–44

Paragraph development,
    159–60
Paragraphs, supporting, 48

Paragraph structure, 200
Paraphrase, 456
Parental responsibility, 8
Parentheses, 471–72
Parker, Star, 423
    "*Se Habla* Entitlement,"
      423–25
Parks, Gordon, 95
    "Flavio's Home," 95–101
Past tense, 120, 227
Patterns of development,
    24, 49, 68–69,
    334, 421
  combining, 236, 334,
    389, 397–98, 408,
    416, 426
  in essays, 431–32
  in student essay,
    432–37
  in writing process,
    430–31
  defined, 40
  description, 40
  in division-classification,
    201
  generating evidence with,
    33
  for organizing evidence, 24
Peer review, 64
  for argumentation-
    persuasion, 378–79
  for cause-effect essay,
    299–300, 304–5
  for comparison-contrast
    essay, 266–67
  for definition essay, 331
  for description essay, 79–80
  for division-classification
    essay, 195–96
  evaluation/response to, 65
  for exemplification, 156
  for process analysis essay,
    231
  for revision, 62
  of thesis, 63
  in writing process, 62–65
Periodicals, 478
Personal observation, 364
Personification, 79
Persuasion, 18
Plagiarizing, 456–63
Podcasts, 480
Point-by-point method,
    264–65
Point of view, 28
  in exemplification, 155
  first-person, 119–20,
    155, 227
  first-person plural, 159
  in narration, 119

in process analysis, 227
  second person, 227
  thesis presenting, 28
  third-person, 119–20,
    155, 227
Political beliefs, 19
Pope, Alexander, 60
Post hoc fallacy, 296, 376
Poverty, 95
Prediction, 55
Premise, 371
Pre-Reading Journal
    Entry, 16
Present tense, 120, 227
Prewriting, 85
  for argumentation-
    persuasion essay, 362
  for cause-effect essay, 293
  for comparison-contrast,
    261
  for definition essay, 327
  in division-classification
    essay, 192
  for exemplification, 151
  for process analysis,
    226–27
Prewriting strategies, 15, 27
Printed material, 61
Print sources, 475
Process analysis, 24–25, 73,
    431
  activities in, 237–38
  additional writing
    assignments, 256–57
  analogy in, 232–34, 236
  audience for, 223–24
  chronological approach to,
    228
  comparison and, 236
  conclusion in, 230, 234,
    236–37
  defined, 222
  definition and, 329
  development diagram for,
    226
  directional, 223, 227
  editing in, 226
  evidence for, 226
  in exemplification, 155
  first draft in, 226
  identifying outcome
    in, 225
  informational, 223, 227
  introduction in, 232
  no commonly accepted
    sequence in, 228
  past tense in, 120, 227
  peer review for, 231
  point of view in, 227
  present tense in, 120, 227

prewriting for, 226–27
proofreading in, 226
purpose and, 223–24, 235
revisions in, 226, 230–31, 236–37
student essay/commentary, 232–37
suggestions for using, 225–30
thesis for, 225–26, 235
tone in, 229, 235
topic sentence in, 233–35
transitions in, 229, 235
Pronouns, 52, 70
Proofreading, 14, 71
for argumentation-persuasion essay, 362
for cause-effect essay, 293
in comparison-contrast, 261
in division-classification essay, 192
for essays using definition, 327
of narration, 114
in process analysis, 226
"Propaganda Techniques in Today's Advertising" (McClintock), 204–10, 359
Proper names, 65
"Psst! 'Human Capital'" (Brooks), 212–14
Pulitzer Prize, 7
Purpose, 18, 69
in argumentation-persuasion, 356–61
for cause-effect essay, 290–92, 302–3
comparison-contrast for, 259–62, 269
description fitting, 72–74
in division-classification essay, 188–90, 199
exemplification for, 148–50
in narration, 113
in process analysis, 235
process analysis as fit for, 223–24
tone and, 294

Question-and-answer format, 11
Questioning, 21, 22, 27
Questions, 54
Quindlen, Anna, 399
"Driving to the Funeral," 399–401
Quotations, 32, 54, 56, 456

capitalizing/punctuating, 467–68
long (block), 474
shortening/clarifying, 465–67

Racism, 95
Radio, 481
Rap groups, 9
Raw material, 22, 26
Readers, 19
Reading
Addison on, 1
aloud, 61, 70
Bellow on, 1
checklists for, 2–5
Emerson on, 2
Thoreau on, 6
Real-life examples, 11
Reasons, 32
Recommendation, 56
Recordings, 481
Red herring argument, 377
Redo, 59
Reference work, 477
Refutations
of common belief, 54
of differing viewpoints, 368–69
Relevance, 451–52
Religious beliefs, 19
Repeated words, 52
Repetition, 69
Research, 25, 451–82
Revision, 14, 60–62, 85
for argumentation-persuasion, 362, 378–79
for cause-effect, 293, 299–300, 304
in comparison-contrast, 261, 266–67, 270–71
for definition, 327, 330–31, 335
for description, 79–80
in division-classification essay, 192, 195–96
of essays, 70–71
of exemplification, 151, 155–56, 160–61
of narration, 114, 120, 125–26
peer review and, 62
in process analysis, 226, 230–31, 236–37
Rio de Janeiro, 95
Rodriguez, Roberto, 418
"The Border on Our Backs," 418–20

Rogerian strategy, 362, 366–67, 368
Rogers, Carl, 366
Run-on sentences, 485

Savan, Leslie, 2, 171
"Black Talk and Pop Culture," 171–78
Scholarly journal, 478–79
Scholarly project, 481
Scientific American, 452
Scratch list, 26
Scratch outline, 26
Second-person point of view, 227
"*Se Habla* Entitlement" (Parker), 423–25
Selection
deepening sense of, 3–4
evaluation of, 4–6
of examples for exemplification essay, 152–54
overview of, 1–2
of points in comparison-contrast essay, 263
Sensory description, 118
Sensory impressions, 78
Sensory language, 78, 82
Sentence outline, 44
Sentences, 81
bridging, 70
informal topic, 78
outlining using, 44
short, 11
structure of, 19, 78–79
topic, 48, 70
Sequence (addition), 51
Shipley, David, 245
"Talk About Editing," 245–47
"Shooting an Elephant" (Orwell), 133–38
Short questions, 54
Short sentences, 11
Signal devices, 51, 70, 159, 194
in description essay, 78
Simile, 79, 81, 84
Simple concepts, 42
Simple-to-complex approach, 42, 50–51
Single principle, 192
"Sister Flowers" (Angelou), 87–91
Slide program, 481
"Someone's Mother" (Murray), 141–43

Source material
  analyzing, 454–55
  documenting, 470
  integrating into writing,
    463–70
  introducing, in writing,
    464
  synthesizing, 455–56
Sources, documentation of,
    451, 453–55, 457
Southern Christian Leadership
    Conference, 87
Space, 51
Spatial approach, 50–51, 69
  to description essay, 77
  in exemplification, 155
  to organizing essay, 41
  in student essay, 81, 83
Specific details, 47, 58
  danger of too many, 77
  exemplification using, 154
Speculative approach, to cause-
    effect essay, 293
Speeches, 482
Spell checking, 65
Stamps, Arkansas, 87
Statements, 29–30
Statistics, 32, 54, 56, 364,
    468–69
Stipulative definition, 330
Stoll, Clifford, 239
  "Cyberschool," 239–43
Structure
  of essays, 57
  paragraph, 200
  of sentences, 19, 78–79
Student essays. See Essays
Stylistic devices, 5, 11
Subject, 21–24
  limited v. general, 20
  "Possible Essay
    Subjects," 16
Subordinate clause, 367
Subtopics, 47
Summary, 55, 456
Summary/Conclusion, 51
Supporting paragraphs, 48
Supporting points, 47, 50
Sutherland, Amy, 2, 250
  "What Shamu Taught Me
    About a Happy
    Marriage"
    (Sutherland), 250–53
Syllogism, 371
Synonyms, 52, 70

"Talk About Editing"
    (Shipley), 245–47
Tejada, Frank, 62–63, 66,
    69, 71
Telephone interviews, 482

Television, 481
Thesis, 14, 433
  in argumentation-
    persuasion, 361–62
  avoiding pitfalls with, 29
  broad v. narrow, 362
  for cause-effect essay, 293
  for comparison-contrast,
    261–63, 269
  for definition, 327, 332
  in division-classification
    essay, 192, 193–94,
    197, 199
  evidence supported by,
    32–39
  for exemplification,
    151, 158
  identification of, 28
  limited subject presented
    by, 28
  for narration, 114
  peer review of, 63
  point of view presented
    by, 28
  for process analysis,
    225–26, 235
  in writing process, 28–39
Third-person point of view,
    119–20, 155, 227
Thoreau, Henry David, on
    reading, 6
Time, 51
Time magazine, 452
Timeliness, 452
Title, 48, 56
Tone, 5, 11, 18, 69, 74
  audience and, 294
  for cause-effect essay, 294
  in division-classification, 200
  for essays using definition,
    326
  in exemplification, 160
  in process analysis, 229,
    235
  purpose and, 294
  shift in, 160
Topics
  main, 47
  for outline, 44
  sentences for, 48, 70
  sub, 47
Topic sentences, 48, 70
  for cause-effect essay, 301,
    303
  in comparison-contrast
    essay, 268
  for definition essay, 332–33
  in division-classification, 197
  informal, 78, 83, 117
  in process analysis, 233–35
  in student essay, 157

Toulmin, Stephen, 374
Toulmin logic, 362, 374,
    376
Transitional words, 229
Transitions, 51, 69, 235,
    265, 433
Twain, Mark, 114–15
"Tweens: Ten Going On
    Sixteen"
    (Hymowitz), 163–67

Underlining, 495
Unification, 10
The Uses of Argument
    (Toulmin), 374

Values, 19
Varied sentence patterns,
    83, 119
Verb tense, 119
  past, 120, 227
  present, 120, 227
Videotapes, 481
Vivid sensory description, 118

"A War Against Boys?"
    (Kimmel), 410–16
Warrant, 374, 375
Websites, 479, 480
Weiner, Eric, 274
  "Euromail and Amerimail,"
    274–77
"What Are Friends For?"
    (Winik), 216–18
"What Shamu Taught Me
    About a Happy
    Marriage"
    (Sutherland),
    250–53
"When Mañana Is Too Soon"
    (Kleiner), 312–15
"Where Do We Go from
    Here: Community or
    Chaos?" (King),
    444–47
Whitehead, Barbara Dafoe, 8
"Why We Crave Horror
    Movies" (King),
    307–10
Wilson, Eric G., 180
  "The Miracle of
    Melancholia,"
    180–82
Winik, Marion, 216
  "What Are Friends For?"
    216–18
Woolf, Virginia, 438
  "The Death of the Moth,"
    438–41
Word choice, 20
Writing process, 13–71